Thomas Sheridan of Smock-Alley

1719–1788

THOMAS SHERIDAN OF SMOCK-ALLEY

*recording his life as
actor and theater manager
in both Dublin and London;
and including*
A SMOCK-ALLEY CALENDAR
*for the years of his
management.*

BY ESTHER K. SHELDON

PRINCETON UNIVERSITY PRESS
PRINCETON, NEW JERSEY
1967

Publication of this book
has been aided by the
Whitney Darrow Publication
Reserve Fund of Princeton
University Press.

Printed in the United States of America
by Vail-Ballou Press, Inc., Binghamton, N.Y.

To my husband,
James F. Bechtold

Introduction

THIS BOOK is not a full-length biography of Thomas Sheridan, although at first it was planned to be. The story of Sheridan's oratorical activities during his later life has been gratefully abandoned to Professor Wallace A. Bacon, whose recently published *Elocutionary Career of Thomas Sheridan (1719–1788)* covers this part of Sheridan's life. To have included all here would have doubled the size of this volume.

Thomas Sheridan of Smock-Alley focuses on Sheridan's other interest, the theater, which filled his early years and then supported him and his oratorical projects afterward. As the title suggests, his personal life has been subordinated here to his theatrical career. This is less of an injustice to the reader and to Sheridan than it may seem. Sheridan was a public figure who lived his life publicly in his work; what he accomplished there was more important to him than any of his private activities, minimal (according to his own report) in Smock-Alley days. What life he had in Dublin with his wife and family he kept scrupulously apart from the theater and away from the public eye. Personal details beyond the usual ones found in Alicia Lefanu's biography of Mrs. Sheridan are rare to come by.

As a theatrical biography, *Thomas Sheridan of Smock-Alley* gives most emphasis to Sheridan's rise and fall as theater manager. Historians from his own time, Victor, Hitchcock, Bellamy, and others, and from our time, La Tourette Stockwell, have each told parts of this story. They have been used here but much supplemented by less familiar sources—newspapers, pamphlets, letters, and playbills. These have helped to expand our answers to various questions about the Irish theater in Sheridan's day: how the theatrical life was regarded by Dubliners; why Sheridan chose the theater as a career; how and when he became manager; what his years at Smock-Alley meant to Dublin and to the history of the theater; what really was behind the two riots of his time; what made possible the final loss of his theater. The new sources have at times upset the conclusions or shifted the emphasis of eighteenth-century historians. They have filled in the years between the riots, slighted by historians yet useful for showing the daily life of the theater. Only through following this record can one appreciate the ingenuity by which Sheridan raised his theater from ruin to an unprecedented pinnacle before his own ruin.

After the loss of his theater Sheridan supported himself by acting.

This work, much subordinated to what was now his paramount concern—his educational, oratorical project—is traced more briefly toward the end of the book. His acting career fell into the same pattern as his managerial career: it gained in prestige and popularity until it reached a peak and then fairly abruptly was cut off. Again, related questions are considered: Why did Sheridan insist on "acting on shares"? What did his contemporaries—Irish as well as English—think of his acting? What qualities made it distinctive? What roles were his best and his worst? After acting failed him, Sheridan returned briefly to his earlier career of theater management, helping Richard with Drury Lane. This interlude, about which little has been known, has been explored in the final chapter.

At the end is included a Smock-Alley Calendar for the years of Sheridan's management, giving in Part I a chronological list of entertainments with the company for each season and in Part II an alphabetical list of plays with their casts for each performance. A separate list of Sheridan's written works follows a selected bibliography of works consulted in writing this book. A table on page 2 which shows Sheridan's theatrical connections by seasons will help to keep the reader oriented. The main purpose of the whole work is to present Sheridan's theatrical life and accomplishments in as clear a light as the evidence makes possible.

Richard Sheridan's biographers, through whom Thomas Sheridan is largely known today, have decried the father because of his treatment of his son. Although Thomas' personality had its defects (and it grew more defective as time pressed and hopes kept collapsing), he was not the fool some writers have made him seem. His failures, seen in historical perspective, were not so often failures of judgment as misfortunes of circumstance. This fact has been generally overlooked by Richard's modern biographers and was not always clear to his contemporaries. Nor was Sheridan the nonentity he has become in some eyes since. To his contemporaries he was controversial; he had strong partisans and vigorous detractors; but he was not ignored. In the history of the three generations of eighteenth-century Sheridans Thomas stands in the middle so far as scope of influence goes. His father, more gifted than he, was little known outside of Ireland; his brilliant younger son became, of course, an international figure. But before Richard, Thomas Sheridan's name was familiar up and down the British Isles. Less endowed in health and talent than either his father or his son, he wrenched out a reputation by extraordinary effort and complete commitment to what he believed in. Whether this reputation deserves our regard, the reader may judge.

Inconsistencies and errors are unfortunately inevitable in a book of this size written intermittently over a long span of years. All one can hope is that they are not numerous or glaring enough to distract the reader in making this judgment. A word about the stylistic practices used in the text seems needed. The word "theater," which was spelled both "theatre" and "theater" in the eighteenth cntury, has been regularized to conform to American spelling. Within quotations, the original spellings and initial capitalizations have been kept but, unless there were reasons to the contrary, no attempt has been made to reproduce special typographical effects, such as italics, small and large capitals, et cetera. And again unless there were reasons to the contrary, dates in the cross-dating period have been regularized to accord with modern time and practice. In the footnotes, bibliographical information has generally been kept to a minimum, the bibliography at the end supplying complete data.

To all the many persons who have helped in the making of this book my gratitude goes out, but here I can thank publicly only a few. My greatest debt is to my colleague Dr. Robert H. Ball, whose encouragement and practical wisdom carried me through more than one despairing moment. Dr. and Mrs. William S. Clark of Cincinnati have been unfailingly generous in reading my manuscript and in supplying me with information on elusive facts. Mr. William R. LeFanu of London not only has given me permission to quote from his invaluable papers but has patiently and promptly answered my many questions. To the Comtesse de Renéville I am indebted for many kind favors, including her most welcome offer to let me reproduce her companion portraits of her ancestors, Thomas and Frances Sheridan. Professor Cecil Price of Swansea, Miss Sybil Rosenfeld and Mr. Ifan Kyrle Fletcher of London, Mr. Robert Walsh of Cork, Dr. Wallace A. Bacon of Evanston, and Mr. Walter A. Miller of Brooklyn have taken time to respond generously to my calls for help. My enthusiastic thanks go to the Office of Graduate Studies at Queens College for its free typing service and especially to Mrs. Florence Waldhetter for typing almost a thousand pages of my manuscript and making incredibly few mistakes. I am grateful, too, to Mrs. Virginia Hlavsa, Mrs. Ann Newton, and Miss Hilda Engelhardt for helping me with such matters as proofreading and indexing; to Mrs. Martin Tozer, for making order out of chaos in editing my manuscript; and to Mrs. William Hanle, for shepherding my manuscript through the press with efficiency and tact. Finally and hardly least is the debt I owe to Mrs. John G. Linn for her tireless and meticulous work in putting together the last, most burdensome section of all, the index.

No book of this sort could even be started without the cooperation of many libraries. To all those listed at the beginning of my Bibliography and to others, I owe thanks, but special acknowledgment must be made to individual librarians who have made my work easier and more pleasant: Dr. Richard J. Hayes and Mr. Michael Breen of the National Library of Ireland; Miss Dorothy Mason of the Folger Shakespeare Library; Mrs. Norma Balsam of the New York Public Library; Mr. Basil Hunnisett, formerly of the Bath Library; and Dr. Joseph Brewer and Miss Margaret Webb of my own library at Queens College. Here too I must specially thank certain institutions for giving me permission to quote more than once from material in their possession: the Office of Registry of Deeds, in Dublin, for citations from various eighteenth century deeds; the Library of Harvard University for excerpts from John Philip Kemble's *Manuscript Diary;* the Bodleian Library, Oxford, for passages from Dr. Thomas Sheridan's letters to Thomas Carte (MS Carte 227), which appeared in transcript in the *Lefanu MSS.* Acknowledgment for permission to cite short single passages has been made at the appropriate places within the text. Finally, I am grateful to the editor of *Theatre Survey,* who earlier published a large part of what is now Chapter IV in this book and who has given me permission to reproduce that part here; and I should add that most of my material on Sheridan's *Coriolanus* in Chapter VII has already appeared in *The Shakespeare Quarterly.*

ESTHER K. SHELDON

Queens College of the
City University of New York

CONTENTS

LIST OF ILLUSTRATIONS

Following page 196

The sketch of Smock-Alley Theater on the front of the jacket appeared in *The Gentleman's Magazine: and Historical Chronicle* for June 1789, shortly before the building was converted into a warehouse.

The map on page 310 showing a section of Dublin with Smock-Alley and Aungier-Street is taken from "A New Plan of Dublin," the title print of *Hibernia Curiosa*.

Thomas Sheridan of Smock-Alley

1719–1788

A CHRONOLOGICAL TABLE

*With the Dates of Sheridan's Acting Engagements Shown by Seasons
And with his Seasons as Manager Also Noted*

January 29, 1743	Smock-Alley debut. At Smock-Alley under Phillips through the summer	1763–1764	Crow-Street under Barry
1743–1744	Smock-Alley to January; Covent Garden under Rich, March–May	Summer 1764	Edinburgh Theater (2 or 3 nights)
1744–1745	Drury Lane with Garrick under Fleetwood. Briefly at Smock-Alley in February and during the summer of 1745	February– May, 1767	Crow-Street under Barry
		May, 1768	Crow-Street under Mossop
		Summer 1769	Haymarket under Foote
		Summer 1770	Haymarket under Foote
1745–1746	Smock-Alley, acting and co-managing with Garrick	1771–1772	Crow-Street under Dawson
1746–1754	Smock-Alley actor-manager. To *Mahomet* riot, March 1754	1772–1773	Smock-Alley under Ryder
		Summer 1773	Cork and Limerick
		1773–1774	Smock-Alley under Ryder
1754–1755	Covent Garden under Rich. To April	1775–1776	Covent Garden under Harris
1756–1758	Smock-Alley actor-manager. Crow-Street being built	June, 1776	Crow-Street under Ryder
		Summer 1776	Cork and Limerick
1760–1761	Drury Lane under Garrick	1776–1777	Crow-Street under Ryder
December 22, 1761	Covent Garden for Lying-In Hospital Benefit	March 14, 1777	Last appearance as an actor
February– March 1763	Drury Lane in Mrs. Sheridan's *Dis-. covery*	1778–1780	Drury Lane, helping Richard Sheridan with the management

CHAPTER I

Gentleman Into Player, 1719-1743

DUBLINERS who scanned the *Dublin Journal* or *Gazette* in late January 1743 would have found nothing unusual about the announcement that on January 29 at Smock-Alley [1] Theater the role of Shakespeare's Richard III would be "attempted by a Gentleman." Theatrical notices of this sort, heralding the debuts of anonymous gentlemen and even ladies, were frequent enough in the eighteenth century. But unique—and, in the light of later events, prophetic—was a postscript to this particular notice:

> As not only the Players but the Audience in general, have frequently complain'd of the ill Effects of a crowded Stage, it is to be hop'd that no Gentleman will take it ill that he is refused admittance behind the Scenes on that Night, under the above mentioned Price [half a guinea], but more particularly on this Occasion; it is to be hop'd his Complaisance will be greater, when he considers that the Confusion which a Person must necessarily be under on his first Appearance, will be greatly heighten'd by having a Number of People about him, and his Perplexity on his Exits and Entrances, (things with which he is but little acquainted) must be greatly encreas'd by having a Crowd to bustle thro'.[2]

Despite the tortuous formality of the style, few descriptions of the early eighteenth-century stage give a more personal view than this one written from the point of view of a nervous young player about to appear for the first time. Crowds of spectators gathered "behind the Scenes" (as the phrase was then for "on the stage"), milling around the actor as he spoke, blocking his movements and gestures, diverting his attention from his lines, even making it difficult for him to push through the stage doorways. These distractions

---

[1] The spelling, hyphenation, and capitalization often vary for the same street name in the eighteenth century. Capel, for example, interchanges with Caple. Smock Alley, Smock-alley, Smock-Alley appear, with perhaps a slight preference for the last. For this reason that spelling has been used throughout. (I have also seen Smoak-Alley.)

[2] *Dublin Gazette*, January 25–29, 1743. A similar notice appears in the *Dublin Journal*, January 18–22.

would vex even a seasoned actor. For a beginner they might add enough confusion to his normal panic to make the difference between success and failure. The anonymous gentleman wished to take no chances. But to banish all from the stage was more than he dared. Perhaps if the price was raised from 5/5 to half a guinea for on-stage places, the crowd there would be thinned for this special night. (Further steps might be tried later.) It was to be hoped that the gentlemen would not "take it ill."

Apparently the gentlemen were complaisant, the new actor managed his exits and entrances successfully, and in other respects did so well that a few nights later he undertook the leading part in Racine's tragedy *Mithridates*.[3] With the success of this performance he "threw off the disguise" (to quote one of his contemporaries[4]) and in a notice for a second *Richard III*,[5] revealed himself, to the few who did not already know his identity, as the late Dr. Sheridan's son, Trinity College graduate and young man about town, Thomas Sheridan.

Before he died, Thomas Sheridan led at least three lives. His theatrical life, which is the subject of this book, began professionally when he was twenty-three years old[6] with his debut as an anonymous gentleman. Later his right to the rank of gentleman was questioned by his enemies, but his claim by birth to that nebulous and shifting title would seem to have been beyond dispute. He came from a good Irish Protestant[7] family, one which commanded considerable respect

---

[3] *Dublin Journal*, January 29–February 1, 1743. This play is described in the notices as never performed before, having been taken from Racine and bearing not "the least Resemblance" to Lee's tragedy of the same name. Sheridan himself may have been the translator and adapter. Since it was advertised over a month before the *Richard III* notices appeared, he must have been preparing this play while he was learning the Richard role.

[4] Hitchcock, I, 129.

[5] *Dublin Journal*, February 12–15, 1743. "The Part of King Richard by Mr. Sheridan."

[6] Trinity College records show Sheridan as entering there on May 26, 1735, at the age of sixteen (Burtchaell and Sadleir, *Alumni Dublinenses*, p. 749). His birth date, which I have been unable to find in official records of the time, is generally agreed to have been 1719, presumably reckoned according to old style, with the year beginning in March. In January 1742/43, then, when Sheridan made his debut, he would not yet have reached his twenty-fourth birthday, which must have come somewhere between March and the end of May.

[7] The family had been Irish a long way back, and may have been Catholic until an ancestor was converted by Bishop Bedell (Sichel, I, 209). To be a

in Ireland. Pamphlets attacking him during his later troubles agreed that his background and education had been above reproach although his connection with the theater, it was argued, had automatically reduced him from the gentlemanly level. Indeed, the problem of his social position as a gentleman *and* an actor (to many a contradiction in terms) continued to plague Sheridan much of his life. Even his young son Richard, the story goes, was taunted by his schoolfellows at Harrow for being a player's son. If authentic, his oft-quoted riposte to a physician's child shows his usual spirit: " 'Tis true, my father lives by pleasing people; but yours lives by killing them." [8] Later both of Thomas Sheridan's sons reached considerable heights. Richard, though a theater manager like his father, became not only a successful playwright—in itself no social guarantee—but also an important member of parliament; Charles Francis was Secretary of War for Ireland. Richard's descendants raised the family still higher, even into the English peerage.

With the theater's possible stigma and its certain financial risk, why did young Thomas Sheridan choose it as a career? Physically he was not well suited. He was small and short, but probably not so short as Garrick, for the height of his leading lady never seems to have concerned him. His critics mention not only handicaps of stature but also of voice, which they report as inaudible when lowered and rasping when raised.[9] He was not handsome like Spranger Barry or West Digges, although his portrait shows a pleasant countenance with high forehead, dark "speaking" eyes, and a delicate mouth. He was better looking, incidentally, than his son Richard. His health was bad. A stomach disorder made him irritable and often prostrated him.[10] It could hardly have improved with the stressful career he chose.

Fifteen years after his debut Sheridan publicly tried to explain this choice: from the first, he said, he had planned to make education his profession; the stage was merely an interlude for perfecting his

Catholic in eighteenth-century Ireland was, of course, a great social, educational, and financial handicap.

[8] Fitzgerald, *Lives of the Sheridans*, 1, 69.

[9] See, for example, Boswell's *Life of Johnson*, Hill, ed., 1, 358 (Johnson's letter to B. Langton, October 18, 1760).

[10] Alicia Lefanu (pp. 269–270) reports that Sheridan suffered all his life from disorders of the head and stomach, which made him subject to bilious attacks. His wife's letters and his own writings mention the agonies he underwent during these spells.

ideas about elocution, ideas needed in his already conceived plan for reforming British education.[11] Not everybody was convinced. And indeed, if this was his true reason, he chose a roundabout, grueling means to a shadowy end, and then long forgot the end in his devotion to the means. Perhaps other forces, less consciously articulated and stemming from his earlier life, had moved him toward the stage.

As the favorite son of Dr. Thomas Sheridan, he must have been exposed to the drama as soon as he could understand language—his own and later the classical tongues. For his schoolmaster-father loved plays, and followed the English custom of school performances [12] in the commodious home in Dublin's Capel-Street, where he kept his school and his large family.[13] Thomas, who probably was born in that house, lived and studied there [14] until his early teens. The house itself was much battered by schoolboy roughhouse and neglected by both the impractical scholar and his slovenly wife. Its general state of disrepair has been immortalized in verse by Dean Jonathan Swift, who dropped in frequently at "about the hour of dining," and would retire with the Doctor to the back parlor for a plate sent in from the family dinner in the common room. Swift describes the steps to the upper hall "all torn to rags by boys and ball," the parlor door "besmear'd with chalk, and carv'd with knives," the locks that stuck, the chair that collapsed and let him down upon his "Reverend Deanship's bum," and the dilapidated fireplace where the battered nose of the bellows substituted for the missing poker.[15] Growing up in these relaxed surroundings, Thomas breathed an air which, though mainly academic, was friendly to the theater. Dr. Sheridan, as master of a classical seminary, preferred to stage classical plays in their original language; he had a Sophocles or Euripides drama performed periodically by his head class before they went to the university.[16] Important people attended and gave his productions weight: the Lord Lieutenant, Lord Carteret, who had

[11] Sheridan, *An Oration*, pp. 19–21.

[12] Lefanu, p. 12. Miss Lefanu notes that this custom was peculiar to Dr. Sheridan at that time in Dublin.

[13] Sheridan, *Life of Swift*, pp. 444, 383.

[14] In Burtchaell and Sadleir's *Alumni Dublinenses*, Thomas Sheridan's schoolmaster is listed as "his father." Sheridan's Preface to his *Complete Dictionary* refers to his early education under a master who was "the intimate friend, and chosen companion of Swift." This was obviously his father.

[15] Sheridan, *Life of Swift*, pp. 444–446.   [16] Lefanu, p. 12.

asked for a tragedy of Sophocles; [17] the Lord Lieutenant, the Duke of Dorset, who was conducted by Dean Swift to see a Terence comedy; [18] Archbishop King before whom *Hippolytus* was performed.[19] So popular did these productions become that when they occurred they threatened attendance at the professional houses. A news item of December 1731 expresses surprise that even a new play at a Dublin theater could attract a crowd against competition which included, among other things, a Sheridan performance: "Notwithstanding there was last Monday Night a Ridotto, a Latin Play acted by Dr. Sheridan's Scholars, and two or three Lodges of Free-Masons, yet the new Tragedy of Love and Ambition was play'd to a vast Audience. . . ." [20]

But not all of Dr. Sheridan's interest in the theater was classical or academic. He may once, in 1721, have been involved briefly with the Dublin stage, its actors and its playhouse; at least, he was concerned with the effect on it of a man named Stretch, master of a puppet show located near the Sheridan school on Capel-Street and extremely popular with Dubliners over many years. In parody of Stretch's puppet show Dr. Sheridan wrote a farce called *Punch Turn'd Schoolmaster,*[21] which he himself, according to Swift, "put the Players upon acting." [22] Full of puns and pedantic humor, neither the play nor the performance was a success [23] (although years later it may have encouraged young Thomas to write a more popular farce, also laced with verbal humor). Another dramatic work, Dr. Sheridan's translation of *Pastor Fido,* was not performed until after his death; [24] but it must have been made with some hope of seeing it on the Dublin stage.

[17] Sheridan, *Life of Swift,* p. 379. [18] Swift, *Correspondence,* v, 150.
[19] *Ibid.,* iii, 125. [20] *Dublin Journal,* December 14–18, 1731.
[21] Dr. Sheridan's "Prologue to the Farce of Punch turn'd School-Master" was printed by Matthew Concanen (*Miscellaneous Poems,* 1724, pp. 398–400). (See Swift, *Letters of Jonathan Swift to Charles Ford,* p. 91, n. 3.) A poem, "The Puppet-Show," perhaps mistakenly ascribed to Swift (*Poems,* Williams, ed., iii, 1102–1105), jokes about Sheridan's attempts to "refine" on Stretch.
[22] Swift, *Letters of Jonathan Swift to Charles Ford,* p. 91 (Letter of April 15, 1721). That the actors were not Dr. Sheridan's boys but professionals and adults is indicated by Swift's word "Players" and also by the references in "The Puppet-Show" (see preceding footnote) to "men" acting as puppets.
[23] Swift, *Letters of Jonathan Swift to Charles Ford,* p. 91. The poem "The Puppet-Show" disapproves of the puns and the pedantry which try to pass for humor.
[24] *Dublin Journal,* January 8–12 and 22–26, 1740.

More successful was Dr. Sheridan with his own boys in an English play not of his writing, *Julius Caesar*. He had staged it as early as 1718;[25] and in December 1732 "some of the young Gentlemen in Dr. Sheridan's School" gave it—appropriately—at Madam Violante's new theatrical "Booth," in George's-Lane, where Violante's troupe of child actors, including Peg Woffington and others less educated than Dr. Sheridan's gentlemen, had recently been doing very well. Dr. Sheridan's thirteen-year-old son Thomas played Marc Antony. He may also have spoken the prologue, whose lines, flavored with his father's characteristic humor, reassured the mammas in the audience that, despite the "dreadful Play" chosen by the Master to drive them all away, they need not fear. The thunder and lightning are merely one drum and pounded rozin, "the Blood that streams along the Floor/Is but a Bladder of Sheep's Blood—No more," and

> Tho' Hundreds fall, there's not one Mortal slain,
> And each Mamma shall have her Child again.[26]

Young Thomas, who was about to leave for Westminster School in another two months, delighted his father with his performance. "I hope that he will acquit himself upon his new Stage," Dr. Sheridan wrote to Thomas Carte of the boy's future at Westminster, "with as much honour as he did lately in the character of Marc Anthony." [27] This seems to be young Thomas Sheridan's first theatrical notice, although it may not have been his first role, considering his father's fondness for theatricals. The father's pride which prompted that gratuitous comparison in his letter to Carte must have been sensed by the son and may, in an obscure way, have been the first force to move him toward the stage, although Dr. Sheridan, if he had been alive at Thomas' professional debut, would probably have regarded it with less enthusiasm. At any rate, Thomas was introduced young to the pleasures of the drama. What other boy in eighteenth-century Dublin could, without leaving home, watch plays being rehearsed, staged, and even written; sit in the audience when they were shown; and sometimes even take a part in them?

Other advantages to being Dr. Sheridan's son were less directly

---

[25] Clark, p. 165. See *idem* for more about Dr. Sheridan's classical productions.

[26] "A Prologue to Julius Caesar As it was Acted at Madam Violante's Booth, December the 15th, 1732, by some of the young Gentlemen in Dr. Sheridan's School." Dublin, n.d.

[27] *Lefanu MSS* 227.f.47 (Dr. Sheridan to Thomas Carte, December 24, 1732).

connected with the theater. The Doctor's library must have included dramatic works; perhaps there, as well as through such school productions as *Julius Caesar*, Thomas Sheridan came to an early love of Shakespeare. From his youngest days he must have known his father's favorite pupil, Henry Brooke,[28] who become the leading Irish playwright of the mid-century and whose plays he later produced. And even though the house was filled with schoolboys, good adult company, particularly "the learned and ingenious" from among the Trinity College Fellows, flocked to Dr. Sheridan's, for "where mirth and good wine circulated so briskly, it is to be supposed there was no lack of guests." [29] Prominent among the guests was young Thomas' godfather, Swift, whose grim Irish exile was lightened by Dr. Sheridan's gaiety, fruitful invention, and warm nature.[30] For over two decades until the Doctor's death in 1738 the Sheridan and Swift households lived intimately together, not always to the domestic harmony of the Sheridan family; for Swift loathed Sheridan's wife,[31] Elizabeth McFadden Sheridan, and his influence over Dr. Sheridan may have split the couple farther apart. Otherwise Swift's interest was benign. He bespoke livings for his friend,[32] praised his

[28] Swift, *Correspondence*, III, 147. Brooke, according to Lefanu (p. 108) was Thomas Sheridan's cousin, but this relationship has been called conjectural by H. M. Scurr in *Henry Brooke* (U. of Minn. thesis, 1922).

[29] Sheridan, *Life of Swift*, pp. 370–371, 375.

[30] The long, intimate relationship between the two men had its curious aspects. Most of the time they treated each other as equals, each vying to outdo the other in the roughest sort of fooling and name-calling. But in his serious moments Swift, some twenty years older, assumed the role of Sheridan's mentor (e.g., "Let me desire you will be very regular in your accounts," *Correspondence*, v, 191, June 1735).

[31] Swift's attitude toward Mrs. Sheridan is seen in "A Portrait from the Life" (*Poems*, III, 954–955):

> Come sit by my side, while this picture I draw:
> In chatt'ring a magpie, in pride a jackdaw;
> A temper the Devil himself could not bridle,
> Impertinent mixture of busy and idle.
> As rude as a bear, no mule half so crabbed;
> She swills like a sow, and she breeds like a rabbit:
> A house-wife in bed, at table a slattern;
> For all an example, for no one a pattern.
> Now tell me, friend Thomas, Ford, Grattan, and merry Dan,
> Has this any likeness to good Madam Sheridan?

[32] See, for example, Swift's letter to Lord Carteret of April 17, 1725 (*Correspondence*, III, 234–235).

9

learning and his teaching ("the best instructor of youth in these kingdoms, or perhaps in Europe; and as great a master of the Greek and Roman languages"),[33] and worked tirelessly to promote the welfare of his school. For a time Dr. Sheridan's fortunes prospered; his seminary became the largest ever known in Ireland.[34] But because of competition from a rival academy and from other "co-operating circumstances"[35] he spent his last years in misfortune and debt; he died in middle age, a few years before the much older Swift.

Although he paid his father tribute, Thomas Sheridan, writing some half a century later his *Life of the Rev. Dr. Jonathan Swift*,[36] regarded his godfather as the most beneficent influence on his life. He tells of Swift's kindness, his gentle behavior, and the many presents and rewards which accompanied the frequent instruction he gave his godson. "I loved him from my boyish days," he concludes, "and never stood in the least awe before him, as I do not remember ever to have had a cross look, or harsh expression from him."[37] Some of the instruction given Thomas as a boy may even then have been in the art of speaking. Later, when he was well up in his teens, Swift did much to "correct" his pronunciation and give him the diction which was to attract attention in the theatrical world.

As a boy Thomas showed so much ability in his father's school that Dr. Sheridan judged him worth that highest reward of all—an English education. He sent him—though with great financial difficulty—to Westminster. Thomas was thirteen when he first crossed the Irish Sea, alone except for an acquaintance of his father's who had agreed to "undertake the trouble of him to London."[38] For a while there was the possibility that his father and the family would eventually follow and settle in England, where Dr. Sheridan hoped to retrieve his declining fortunes.[39] But these plans fell through, and Thomas,

[33] Swift, *Prose Works*, Scott, ed., xi, 161.

[34] Sheridan, *Life of Swift*, p. 374.   [35] *Ibid.*, p. 385.

[36] Published in 1784 as a volume in Sheridan's edition of Swift's works.

[37] Sheridan, *Life of Swift*, p. 386.

[38] *Lefanu MSS* 227.f.99 (Dr. Sheridan to Thomas Carte, February 23, 1733).

[39] *Ibid.*, f.287 (Dr. Sheridan to Thomas Carte, November 28, 1732). In this letter, written while he was getting his son ready to leave for London, Dr. Sheridan says: "I wish with all my soul, as well as I love my country, that I were setled [*sic*] some where near you and London. To speak the truth I would rather be a flea-catcher to a dog in England than a privy-counsellour here. I

after having attended school snugly at home, was thrust into a strange new school-world across a sea from home. There he was left pretty much on his own for two years.

The way he chose to spend his free time reveals his interests. Soon after his arrival in London Mr. Wesley, his housemaster, complained to Dr. Sheridan that his son was going out too often and spending too much money. The boy defended himself to his father skillfully:

> I layd out too much money I grant it [he wrote in July] but if I layd it out to any bad use, may I ever lose your favour. can any one think, that when I came into a city, I had no curiosity to see all their shews, to go to see their plays, &c, besides must not I make myself a friend in the beginning.[40]

So at fourteen, Thomas, alone or with some other Westminster boy, was spending several nights a week at London theaters, conveniently near the school—at Drury Lane or Goodman's Fields or the Haymarket or Covent Garden. With his diminutive frame draped in the distinctive clothes of a Westminster King's scholar, an outfit which included a long double-breasted jacket with knee breeches and a trencher cap,[41] he could hardly have remained an inconspicuous figure in the audience. Nor is it likely that his behavior made him any less conspicuous; when he had returned to Ireland, Swift found him "a little too much on the qui vive"—his sole defect, Swift adds, and one he must have learned in England.[42] But Dr. Sheridan was worried about another trait which was beginning to develop in young Thomas about this time and which was to irk many an enemy and some friends later on. "Above all," Dr. Sheridan writes to Mr. Carte, who was in charge of the Irish boy in London, "I beg you may give

---

make no doubt but you will use your endeavour to find me out some footing by which I may afterwards make my own way, when this is done a very small prospect shall incline me to breath [*sic*] in an air of Liberty."

[40] *Ibid.* (Letter from Thomas to his father, July 7. No year is given, but the contents suggest 1733, the boy's first summer in London.) Although Thomas Carte was given charge of young Sheridan and his father's friends in London entertained him (*Lefanu MSS*), this letter shows how much on his own young Thomas was.

[41] Forshall (p. 59) describes the King's scholar's dress. That the boy was small is suggested by Dr. Sheridan's reference to him about this time as "my litle son" (*Lefanu MSS* 227.f.287; Dr. Sheridan to Thomas Carte, November 28, 1732).

[42] Swift, *Correspondence*, v, 312.

him cautions against vanity. I have reason to say this from his own letters to me." [43] Thomas' early success as a King's scholar and a London boy about town may have gone somewhat to his head.

In the London theaters over the two years (1733–35) he had a great opportunity to see the noted performers of the time: Colley Cibber just before he went into semiretirement; the Irishman James Quin, so successful at Rich's Covent Garden that he moved to Fleet-wood's Drury Lane at £500 for the 1734–35 season; Denis Delane, likewise from Ireland, at the new Goodman's Fields Theater built by Giffard. He could also have watched certain promising newcomers, little suspecting that within a few years he would know some of them intimately as fellow actors he had hired for his own theater: stormy Theophilus Cibber, who in the fall of 1733 (Thomas' first in London) led the revolt to the Haymarket; gentle Henry Woodward, an engaging young comedian and pantomimist; and Charles Macklin, just come from Ireland to appear with Mrs. Clive and Mrs. Elmy at Drury Lane during 1733–34. [44] Surprisingly many Irish actors did well in London, and some of them were gentlemen, educated at Dr. Sheridan's own university, Trinity College, Dublin.

The theatrical fare for these years was less exciting, but one comedy may have had a special importance for the young outlander. *The Cornish Squire*, which, with Macklin in a main role, had a long run during the spring of 1734, was an old play, *Squire Trelooby*, slightly revised, renamed, and revived after thirty years. [45] Later, Sheridan's remembrance of this play's success, together with the fact that farcical playwriting had not been beneath his father's dignity, may have encouraged him to write a similar farce about an Irish captain in London.

Even within Westminster School itself Thomas was not entirely withdrawn from the theatrical atmosphere, for Westminster had always been partial to the drama. From Queen Elizabeth's time on, annual plays had been presented by the boys at Christmastime, a Latin play in the College (the Dormitory) and an English play in the Hall. [46] Their purpose was to make "gesture and pronunciation" familiar, in short, to make orators as well as scholars of the boys. [47] The Latin play given in the Dormitory was elaborately and expensively produced, with supper and a band. Rehearsals lasted for

[43] *Lefanu MSS* 227.f.32 (Dr. Sheridan to Thomas Carte, June 21, 1733).
[44] Genest, III; *London Stage*, Pt. 3, seasons from 1733 to 1735.
[45] *London Stage*, Pt. 3, p. 353.   [46] Forshall, p. 468.
[47] *Ibid.*; Tanner, p. 3.

weeks, and before the performance a Drury Lane dresser arrived to turn young boys into old men, unrecognizable even to their own mothers. Terence was much favored as a playwright, four of his plays being exhibited in rotation year after year against a scenic backdrop which in the early eighteenth century represented Covent Garden.[48] (Years later, Manager Sheridan planned to present a Terence play in Latin at his Smock-Alley Theater to show how many educated gentlemen he had in his company.)[49] At Westminster the parts in the Latin plays were usually taken by the boys in the upper forms, but a comedy or farce of the period was sometimes acted by the younger boys for the older ones. In 1727, a few years before Thomas Sheridan's arrival, the Town Boys of the school had performed *Julius Caesar* in the Haymarket for four days.[50] No records are available to show whether Thomas played a part in Westminster's dramatic activities, but it is probable that he did; for the scholars acted the English play in the Hall [51] (he was a scholar) and he had had earlier acting experience. In any event, his lively mind would have been curious in view of the similar performances at his father's school.

Westminster's stress on oratory, on acting, and on dramatic production affected more than Thomas Sheridan, whose later career reflects all these interests. So many boys responded to this influence that the school has been called "the nursery of many gentlemen actors." [52]

Thomas did well scholastically at Westminster. According to his godfather, Swift, he was "immediately taken notice of, upon examination: although a mere stranger, he was, by pure merit, elected a king's scholar." [53] The scholarship examination was severe and the competition keen; usually all but one or two scholars later received studentships to Christ Church, Oxford, or scholarships to Trinity College, Cambridge.[54] But when Thomas was a year and some months away from this goal, the scholar's maintenance fell somewhat short, and Dr. Sheridan "was then so poor, that," according to Swift, "he could not add fourteen pounds to enable the boy to finish the year." [55] So Thomas was forced to return to Dublin. He may not

[48] Forshall, pp. 78, 80, 471, 469.   [49] Sheridan, *An Humble Appeal*, p. 21.
[50] Forshall, p. 469.   [51] *Ibid.*, p. 468.   [52] Sichel, I, 226.
[53] Swift, *Prose Works*, XI, 162.   [54] Forshall, pp. 44ff.
[55] Swift, *Prose Works*, XI, 162. Writing these lines shortly after Dr. Sheridan's death in 1738, Swift continues, "The doctor was forced to recall him to Dublin, and had friends in our university to send him there, where he hath been

have been disappointed; two letters that remain from these years show him unhappy and in trouble.[56] Perhaps this fact as much as a shortage of fourteen borrowable pounds induced his father to recall him.

If he had gone to Oxford or Cambridge, his decision to become an actor might still never have occurred. But back in Dublin at sixteen and enrolled at Trinity College there, he was even nearer to the playhouses than in London. And playgoing was a popular recreation with most Trinitarians. From the early seventeenth century the college and the stage in Dublin had had such influence upon one another as to become "complementary institutions." [57] Trinity students formed a powerful bloc in the audiences, taking a vigorous part in various theatrical disturbances, making and ruining players, and dictating programs. In the early 1720's *The Conscious Lovers*, for example, was played at Smock-Alley by request of the "Young Men of Trinity College, Dublin." Coffey's ballad-opera, *The Beggar's Wedding*, also produced at Smock-Alley, was dedicated in 1729 to the Provost and Fellows of Trinity.[58] Nothing like this existed in the English universities. As a Trinitarian Sheridan was to do his share of playgoing, and as a lively and interested young man he must have been an active member of the audience. A later critic writing anonymously in 1754 and perhaps not from firsthand knowledge pictures Sheridan as an ignoramus because he spent his time in college "frequenting Playhouses, getting acquainted with Actors, and mixing in their Riots." [59]

Shortly after Sheridan entered Trinity in 1735, the rebuilt Smock-Alley Theater opened ("the most compleat House of that Kind in Europe") to compete with the new Aungier-Street house ("the finest

---

chosen of the foundation; and, I think, hath gotten an exhibition, and designs to stand for a fellowship." The shift to the present perfect and present tenses is significant.

[56] *Lefanu MSS.* In one letter, he had to defend himself not only against the true charges, as we have seen, of going out too often and spending too much money, but also against the false charge of stealing his house mistress's key. In the other letter, undated, he is in trouble with the great Dr. Nicoll, Master of Westminster, because he is reluctant to go into College (the Dormitory).

[57] Lawrence, "Trinity and the Theatre."

[58] *Ibid.* Lawrence dates the *Conscious Lovers* performance as 1722, but Mrs. William Clark has called my attention to a notice in the *Dublin Gazette* (January 8, 1722/23) of the first performance of the play on January 10 (1723).

[59] *Mr. Sh—n's Apology to the Town*, p. 8.

in Europe").[60] In the years that followed, young Sheridan might have seen Miss Woffington's debut as Ophelia in 1737;[61] or the Smock-Alley riot at Dr. Clancy's benefit, on January 25, 1738;[62] or James Quin playing to big houses regardless of the heat in July 1738 and again in the summer of 1741;[63] or Mrs. Furnival, in men's clothes, acting the part of Hamlet in April of that year; or Mrs. Cibber's first appearance in Ireland the next December.[64] Dublin was not London, and its smaller population, as the century was to demonstrate over and over again, could not adequately support two theaters; performances were fewer and less regular than in the British capital. But the rivalry, which inevitably edged both theaters toward financial ruin, brought times of frenzied theatrical activity much enjoyed by the town and college.

With Thomas' return to Dublin his intimacy with his godfather was renewed, and it was now that Swift particularly influenced his speech and his ideas about correct diction. Dr. Sheridan, who had given up the Dublin school, had moved his family to a house in the town of Cavan,[65] some forty miles north of Dublin, near the Sheridan country "cabbin" Quilca, which had come into the family through the wife. During the 1720's Swift, Stella, and Mrs. Dingley had spent holidays at Quilca,[66] and now in the fall of 1735 Swift, nearly seventy, arrived in Cavan to pass several months with the good Doctor. Young Thomas was there during all of this time, although his father was not, for he had been called to Dublin on business. For two or three hours each day Thomas read aloud to his godfather [67]—

[60] Kemble, *Manuscript Diary*, March 9, 1734, and November 1735. Aungier-Street Theater had opened on March 9, 1734 (*Dublin Journal*, March 9–12, 1734).

[61] *Dictionary of National Biography* (henceforth noted as *DNB*), *v.* "Woffington, Margaret."

[62] Kemble, *Manuscript Diary*, January 25, 1738.

[63] *Ibid.*, July 1738, and *Dublin Journal* for these times.

[64] *Dublin Journal*, April 4–7 and December 1–5, 1741.

[65] Swift, *Correspondence*, v, 188; Sheridan, *Life of Swift*, p. 385. Dr. Sheridan had taken over the free school in Cavan. A notice in the *Dublin Journal* (January 5–8, 1740) after his death offers for sale the lease on this "late Dwelling House" of Dr. Sheridan. The house with its three-acre park lay "upon a handsome River, in a pleasant Country, and good Neighbourhood."

[66] Swift, *Poems*, iii, 1,034. In 1725, for example, all three were at Quilca from April to October.

[67] Sheridan, *Life of Swift*, pp. 386–387.

perhaps, on pleasant days, in the large garden dotted with ponds.[68] Swift found that he much esteemed Dr. Sheridan's younger son, but it was then that he also found him turned into "an English boy" and so "a little too much on the qui vive." [69] As Thomas read, the great man, despite his impaired faculties and his uncertain temper, made instructive observations, and, we can presume, corrected the boy's pronunciation.[70] (He could not bear to hear mistakes in the speech of his friends without righting them.)[71] Swift's ideas about proper diction were conservative; his pronunciation reflected the earlier speech of Queen Anne's court. When Sheridan wrote the first complete pronouncing dictionary years later, he took as his ideal the speech of Queen Anne's court, familiar to him from other personages, such as the Earl of Chesterfield and the Duke of Dorset, as well as from Swift.[72] Not surprisingly, his dictionary entries often record older pronunciations, still current but competing with new pronunciations which were closer to the spelling, and therefore preferred by other dictionaries of the time. Sheridan's own pronunciation, like his dictionary entries, resisted these innovations based on spelling;[73] and his many years in Ireland, where changes were slower, reinforced this conservatism. As important actor, theater manager, trainer of young players, and teacher of elocution, he had a hand in keeping stage speech conservative, and so giving it, with some people, the reputation for affectation. Actually his pronunciations often represented a more natural phonetic development than the newer spelling-pronunciations.

Swift did more than affect Sheridan's pronunciation. Sometime in 1737, after Sheridan had been at Trinity for two years, a fateful conversation took place between the boy and his godfather. Swift was questioning him about what he was being taught at the college. "When I told him the Course of Reading I was put into, he asked me, Do they teach you English? No. Do they teach you how to speak? No. Then, said he, they teach you *Nothing*." [74] This conversation, remembered over the years, gave Sheridan a clue to his life,

[68] Mentioned in the notice offering the lease for sale (see footnote 65).

[69] Swift, *Correspondence*, v, 312.

[70] Sheridan, *Life of Swift*, p. 386; Sheridan, *A Complete Dictionary*, Preface.

[71] Sheridan, *A Complete Dictionary*, Preface.   [72] *Ibid*.

[73] Sheldon, Esther K., "Walker's Influence on the Pronunciation of English." Toward the end of Sheridan's life, when he was directing at Drury Lane, letters to the press comment on the pronunciation heard on stage there. (See Ch. xi.)

[74] Sheridan, *An Oration*, pp. 19–20.

providing him with inspiration, motivation, and perhaps even rationalization, as later events show.

When Dr. Sheridan died suddenly and impecuniously in 1738, Thomas was still an undergraduate and a year away from his degree. But he stayed on for his B.A.[75] and even for his M.A., which he won sometime before 1743.[76] He was preparing to enter his father's profession.[77] With his fine record as a scholar [78] and his interest in education, schoolteaching would be a logical career for him. He also had his father's reputation to build on and he had already received "some very advantageous Proposals," which gave promise of success.[79] Yet schoolmastering, whose disadvantages he knew firsthand and whose subject matter, after Swift's censure, he had begun to question, was not just what he wanted after all.

While he hesitated, he was busy in other ways. He entertained friends with dramatic readings; their enthusiastic response must have strengthened his confidence in his acting powers.[80] Even the writing he did at this time pointed toward the stage. In the hope of publish-

---

[75] The scholarship granted him in 1738 would have paid for his room, board, and part of his fees. (I am indebted to Dr. Richard Hayes, Director of The National Library of Ireland, for this information about Trinity College scholarships.)

[76] Shown by a notice advertising his father's works for publication: "Proposals for printing by Subscription, the Works of the late Rev. Thomas Sheridan, D.D. Published by Thomas Sheridan, M.A." (*Dublin Journal*, March 12–15, 1743). The fact that Burtchaell and Sadleir's *Alumni Dublinenses* ascribes only a B.A. to Sheridan has raised doubts about this higher degree, but if Sheridan had falsely assumed the M.A. in a public notice of the sort cited above, his Trinity College colleagues would hardly have given him the support and respect they invariably did. Whyte's statement in *Miscellanea Nova* (p. 61) further confirms Sheridan's M.A. from Trinity. Whyte says that it was an earned degree for which Sheridan was "regularly matriculated" and which he obtained "in due course of gradation." Since the M.A. required three years' residence, the degree could have been granted in the spring of 1742 (his B.A. had been "Vern. 1739").

[77] Sheridan, *An Oration*, p. 19.

[78] Weeks, *A Rhapsody on the Stage*. Weeks, a friend of Sheridan and a "Cotemporary in the very same Form," asserts that Thomas was "one of the best Scholars" of his time.

[79] Sheridan, *An Oration*, p. 19.

[80] In a later anonymous critical piece, *Mr. Sh—n's Apology to the Town*, Sheridan's life as a university student is recalled; he is pictured as reading fustian plays with much rant and being so encouraged by their reception that he "commenc'd Actor" (p. 8). This pamphlet is misdated 2754; internal evidence points to the Mahomet riot of 1754.

ing his father's works, he condensed them from eight volumes into four,[81] but only one piece met the public eye through his efforts. Significantly, it was the play which his father had once translated from Guarini's *Pastor Fido*. As *The Faithful Shepherd* it was performed on January 31, 1740, two years after Dr. Sheridan's death, at Smock-Alley Theater. It had been "fitted for the Stage by his Son." [82] Since Richard, the only other son still living, had no literary pretensions, Thomas must have done the tailoring on this play, probably the first of several adaptations he was to make of other dramatists' works; this may also have been his first literary effort to reach the stage. As part-author, who might be needed for interpretations and last-minute revisions, he could hardly have missed the rehearsals. In Dublin at this time even the disinterested public attended rehearsals as a pastime, ringing the players with a circle of some forty or fifty men [83] and causing as much confusion as on stage during performances. The foot-loose Sheridan must have been in this group many times, especially during the month or so when *The Faithful Shepherd* was in preparation.[84] For not only was his new literary reputation at stake; the performance was for Dr. Sheridan's family.[85] As author of a new play, Dr. Sheridan, if he had been alive, would have been entitled to a benefit, but on the third or second night, not usually on the first. With Dr. Sheridan dead, the benefit proceeds might reasonably go to his family, especially when his son was the adapter. But to have the benefit arranged for the first night (and only night, as it turned out), young Thomas must already have had connections, and perhaps a little influence, at Smock-Alley. Indeed, the whole episode shows Sheridan's closeness to the theater three years before he made his first appearance on the stage. It was to the theater he turned when he came across the translation of *Pastor Fido* in his father's writings. A theater benefit with this play would be the

---

[81] This collection is usually mentioned first in connection with Sheridan's 1744 trip to London, where he tried unsuccessfully to publish his father's works. But the *Dublin Journal* notice (see note 76 above) shows that he had tried to publish them earlier with an equal lack of success, because of lack of subscribers. The extracts, originally enough for eight volumes, had been reduced to four, the notice reports.

[82] *Dublin Journal*, January 8–12 and 22–26, 1740.

[83] Victor, *History*, 1, 94.

[84] The play is advertised as "now in Rehearsal" in the *Dublin Journal*, January 8–12, 1740. It was presented on January 31.

[85] Revealed by John Sheen's notice, p. 19.

very way to raise money for the family, semiorphaned [86] and not too well off.

One member of the family would have none of it. John Sheen, Sheridan's brother-in-law married to Anne Sheridan, washed his hands of the project in the public press:

> As it is given out that the Profit of the Play, called the Faithful Shepherd, is for the Benefit of Doctor Sheridan's Family; the Town may suppose that I have some share thereof, being married to one of his Daughters; but as I have not the least Benefit arising by the Play or the Doctor's Effects I imagine such Information, and received Opinion may be a Reflection on me, have therefore thought proper to publish this Advertisement, that no Person should think I lie under an Obligation to them on this Account. *John Sheen.*[87]

Sheen was acting in form here. When he was courting Anne (having been much encouraged by her mother), Dr. Sheridan, who despised him, described him to Swift as "a cynical thorough fop." [88] But Sheen's notice to the papers produced no permanent family break, for it was at Mrs. Sheen's house several years later that Thomas is said to have met the woman he was to marry, Frances Chamberlaine.[89]

One other episode from this time when Sheridan "was a Member of Trinity College, and therefore a Gentleman" [90] supports the pic-

---

[86] Although Lefanu (p. 17) says that she died before her husband, the mother was still living. Not only does Dr. Sheridan's will, written shortly before his death, cut off with five shillings his "unkind wife" as well as his daughter, Anne Sheridan Sheen, but a 1746 document conveying Quilca from Richard, the older son and heir, to Thomas, the younger son, mentions "Elizabeth Sheridan Widow" (MS 121.83956, Off. Reg. Deeds). She is to have certain rents therefrom for "the term of her natural life."

[87] *Dublin Journal*, January 29–February 2, 1740. The terms of his father-in-law's will (see preceding footnote) may explain Sheen's tone here.

[88] Swift, *Correspondence*, v, 154. Alicia Lefanu (p. 34) gives a totally different picture of Sheen. He was an Englishman, come over in the Viceroy's suite—"a courtier, gay, fashionable and distinguished for personal attractions." He must have been a successful man of business, for later Thomas Sheridan trusted him, rather than his older brother Richard or his other brother-in-law, John Knowles, to manage his debts for him. And again Sheen's selfishness emerged, as unpublished letters in the *Lefanu MSS* show.

[89] Lefanu, p. 29.

[90] *A Serious Enquiry into the Causes of the present Disorders* [*in the City*] [1747], p. 14.

ture of him as a powerful leader in theater audiences, but it is recorded by such a vicious enemy of his so many years after and is, withal, so unlike the later Sheridan we know that its authenticity is suspect. In it young Sheridan is represented as cheating a gentleman-actor, Mr. Este, out of the proceeds from some tickets which Sheridan sold for Este at the college; then refusing a challenge because Mr. Este was a player and not on his level; and finally, with the hisses of fellow collegians in the audience to back him up, driving Este off the stage till he should beg public pardon from him. In the course of the anecdote the student Sheridan is pictured as standing up in the audience "in a Rage," and saying that "he was amazed at his [Este's] Insolence, to put himself upon a level with any Gentleman, who, by the Place from which he spoke, was but a Vagabond and a Scoundrel." [91] Written when Sheridan was in a position similar to Este's and still claiming to be a gentleman, this anonymous account is too patly parallel to be convincing in its entirety. But if any part of it happened—and young people do many shocking things they feel shame for as adults—Sheridan surely regretted it soon after.[92]

Another witness to his early interest in the stage and also to his youthful *joie de vivre* [93] is the farce he wrote during these years before he made his debut in 1743. Sheridan's only original play, it has two titles. When it was produced anonymously as "a new Farce" at Smock-Alley Theater on February 4, 1743, a week after Sheridan's debut there, it was called *Captain O'Blunder*. During the next summer Smock-Alley advertised it as "The Brave Irishman by Mr. Sheridan," [94] who as Smock-Alley's new tragedian was too important to act in farcical afterplays but whose literary efforts would interest his

---

[91] *Ibid.*, pp. 14–15.

[92] It is perhaps significant that, when he was an actor of only four months, he played the leading role in a benefit for Mr. Este's widow (*Dublin Journal*, April 30–May 3, 1743).

[93] Alicia Lefanu (p. 377) reports that Sheridan in his youth was much attached to "conviviality and the sports of the field," but that these tastes diminished after his marriage. Even as late as 1758, though, he still had horses and hounds at Quilca, we learn from the *Lefanu MSS* ("William Sheridan Gent. Plt. vs. Thomas Sheridan Esq. Deft.").

[94] *Dublin Journal*, January 29–February 1 and July 2–5, 1743. Although performances were not always advertised, especially in the years before Sheridan took over the management, a search of theatrical notices in the Dublin papers from 1736 to 1743 unearthed no mention of the play before 1743, when it was advertised as a *new* play.

large following. *The Brave Irishman* was Sheridan's own title,[95] and it prevailed on the Smock-Alley stage and generally in the published versions.

In writing this two-act play Sheridan took the outlines of his plot from *Squire Trelooby*, a three-act translation, first produced and published in 1704, of Molière's farce *Monsieur de Porceaugnac*.[96] Others before Sheridan had used *Squire Trelooby*. In 1720 Charles Shadwell's *Plotting Lovers* had copied from it verbatim, merely changing the scene from London to Dublin and cutting extensively. In 1734, during Sheridan's Westminster days, *The Cornish Squire*, which was *Squire Trelooby* with some changes and a new title, had been a great success at Drury Lane. Young Sheridan may have known Shadwell's version; to *Squire Trelooby* he openly and ingeniously acknowledges his debt in *The Brave Irishman's* first scene. When one of the two plotters against Captain O'Blunder asks the other how he came by such fruitful schemes, Schemewell responds: "By haunting playhouses" and keeping a special eye on the farces. "Moliere's Squire Trelooby," he explains, "has furnished me with some hints which I believe I have improved." [97] How much Schemewell's young author has improved *his* source may be open to question; but his *Brave Irishman*, unlike *The Plotting Lovers* and even *Squire Trelooby*, is original in most of its plot and characterization, and in almost all of its dialogue. Those who have called it a "mere translation—and that none of the best—from Monsieur de Porceaugnac" [98] have not read Sheridan's work. It is not even an adaptation.

The many published versions of this piece, including the earliest

[95] *The Brave Irishman* appears as the only title in Sheridan's MS version of the play (*Lefanu MSS*). In the printed versions a double title sometimes occurs, usually *The Brave Irishman; or, Captain O'Blunder*, occasionally vice versa.

[96] The 1704 published version was a translation, *mutatis mutandis*, of the French work. The translator's identity has been in doubt; *The London Stage* accepts Congreve, Vanbrugh, and Walsh as the authors of the *Squire Trelooby* produced at Lincoln's Inn Fields on March 30, 1704, adding that "the edition of 1704 is a translation by another hand, but the cast [listed in this edition] presumably represents that for this night" (Pt. 3, p. 62). Thirty years later, James Ralph, in publishing *The Cornish Squire*, insisted that it was the hitherto unpublished Congreve-Vanbrugh-Walsh version with a few modifications. But this claim too has been questioned. (For further details, see John C. Hodges, "The Authorship of *Squire Trelooby*," *Review of English Studies*, IV, 1928, 404–413.)

[97] *The Brave Irishman* (*Lefanu MSS*), p. 7.

[98] Montagu Summers, ed., *Complete Works of Congreve*, III, 114.

known edition in 1754,[99] were apparently printed without Sheridan's consent.[100] They were certainly remote from the play as he wrote it; and their addition of much objectionable material must have outraged him at a time when he was trying to establish his reputation for respectability. His own version, which still exists in his handwriting,[101] is not so finished as the published versions and is, in

[99] *The Brave Irishman: or, Captain O'Blunder. A Farce. As it is acted at the Theatre-Royal in Smock-alley: with the genuine songs, Not in any other Edition. Supposed to be Written by T——s S——n, Esq; And Revised with Several Corrections and Additions by J—n P—st—n,* Dublin, 1754. The cast listed in this edition was one assembled at Smock-Alley only during the 1753–54 season. Perhaps the publication was made easier by Sheridan's withdrawal as manager early in 1754; reprisals were less likely. The name J—n P—st—n in the Huntington Library's copy of this edition has been filled out as John Preston in handwritten letters similar to those in a sidenote on the title page: "Collated & Perfect J. P.(?)K.1800" (John Philip Kemble, perhaps?). John Preston has been tentatively identified as a minor actor and author of *The Rival Father,* published in Dublin in 1754 (Hughes and Scouten, p. 224). The claim on the title page that the songs do not appear "in any other Edition" suggests that this 1754 edition was not the earliest; *Biographia Dramatica* gives "about 1748" as the date of first publication. A comparison of the 1754 Dublin edition with the 1755 Edinburgh edition shows many similarities in the two not to be found in Sheridan's manuscript or in the Larpent manuscript (see below, footnote 110); but there are also differences between these two early editions, some of which in each edition can be traced back to the manuscripts. Although the relationship of the editions and the changes made in them are irrelevant here, I hope to explore this subject further in a later article.

[100] *The Thespian Dictionary* says that it was "collected by some persons from memory, and frequently performed; but never, as Mr. Sheridan used to declare, with his consent" (v. "Sheridan, Thomas"). The great differences among the printed versions and between them and Sheridan's text in the *Lefanu MSS* indicate not only that they were collected from memory but that they were rewritten extensively by such "publishers" as J—n P—st—n. It is easy to understand why Sheridan never wanted to acknowledge the printed editions. But why did he never publish his own version? Possibly because it was too trivial, too unworthy. Even his tragedy *Coriolanus* bears no author's name on the title page. Sheridan was, on the other hand, willing enough to acknowledge his books on elocution and education.

[101] This fifty-seven-page manuscript (in the *Lefanu MSS*) seems to be Sheridan's original text; or, if not, it is a very early copy. In it a third rival, whom Sheridan added to the *Trelooby* contenders for the English girl's hand, is called "Dapper" through the first act, but through the second act Sheridan crossed this name out and substituted "Monsieur Ragout"—the name, variously spelled, which appears in later printed versions and in the Larpent MS (see footnote 110 below). He also rewrote Dapper's speeches into a French-tinged English for Act II, but did not bother to change name or dialogue in Act I. (The *dramatis*

places, duller, but O'Blunder's characterization is more consistent and the humor is rarely scatological (except where Sheridan has borrowed from his source). Yet, no matter in what version, *The Brave Irishman* had a fair success at Dublin theaters over many years. It had a few performances in England and Scotland [102] too, but its main interest is as an Irish-authored farce which had an Irishman for a hero and which appealed to Irish audiences of the mid-eighteenth century.

Sheridan's own way of winning his audiences reveals not only eighteenth-century Irish tastes but certain things about the author as a young man. English boy though he seemed to Swift, he was still Irish enough to take a poke at English snobbism toward outlanders. When the English heroine is asked by her maid how she can have such an aversion to a man "whom you never saw," she answers: "O hideous! is he not an Irishman? . . . Why I am told they are meer Beasts and have Horns in that Country." To this the maid retorts: "I believe not more than their Neighbours. But I assure you our London Citizens know to their Cost that they have an excellent Hand at Planting them come come it is time to lay aside these popular Prejudices, I have known Several of that Country, & I assure you they are the most charming, delightfull, agreable—(faith it was just out) Companions in the World." [103] In the end the blundering, true-

---

personae on the title page of the manuscript, however, shows "Ragoo" written over "Dapper.") In the whole manuscript Sheridan cut much and also made many additions and revisions, which he wrote on the blank pages opposite the emended passages. The fact that this document came down in the Lefanu family suggests that it might be the very one about which Richard, who had just left his father in Bath, wrote to him in 1772: "I packed up your Comedy by Mistake, and send the first opportunity . . ." (*Lefanu MSS*, Richard's letter of August 30, 1772). On the other hand, this version with its uncorrected Dapper-Ragout confusion and its many unincorporated changes must have needed a fair copy. (The Larpent MS, not in Sheridan's handwriting, is just that, with a few additional changes and a title that is not Sheridan's.) Since Sheridan authorized no publication, presumably a few fair copies did exist and the "Comedy" mistakenly packed by Richard might have been one of these.

[102] Under Sheridan's management at Smock-Alley it was played about forty times. In England its first performance seems to have been on January 31, 1746, at Goodman's Fields as *Captain O'Blunder or The Brave Irishman*, "wrote by Mr. Sheridan the Player" (Genest, IV, 198; *London Stage*, Pt. 3, p. 1,215). It had a few performances at provincial theaters (Rosenfeld, pp. 148, 195) and at Edinburgh, where its popularity is indicated by several Edinburgh editions which list Edinburgh players. It even was played now and then in America (see Hughes and Scouten, p. 222, n. 8).

[103] *The Brave Irishman* (*Lefanu MSS*), pp. 2–3.

blue Irish hero not only wins the English girl but outdoes his cleverer "English" rival (revealed finally as an Irishman cravenly posing as an Englishman), who is married off—this must have rejoiced the galleries—to the girl's maid. The humor throughout is more sexual than scatological, as the passage just quoted suggests.[104] The scatological was much expanded in the unauthorized editions and probably in response to eighteenth-century tastes. Young Sheridan had been willing to go along with the clysterpipe comedy of his original source, but using Irish dialect to produce *shits* from *sits* and *turd* from *third*[105] hardly appealed to him. He was more proper than his father and godfather, whose *jeux d'esprit* knew few bounds. But much of his humor is, like theirs, verbal—and fairly obvious. Captain O'Blunder raises many a horselaugh with his grammatical confusions, logical inconsistencies, and malapropisms. Even this early, Sheridan is more interested in language than in subtleties of plot or characterization.

Yet Sheridan's Captain, simply drawn as he is, not only makes more sense but is more winning than the Irish blusterer of the printed versions who just at the end turns unaccountably magnanimous, genteel, and intelligent. Sheridan conceived his Irishman as a mild, well-meaning blunderer who could be goaded to violence but whose first instinct was to please. He does not bully or swagger. And throughout the whole play his innocent mistakes, both in language and judgment, have considerable charm. But he was a temptation, probably, to actors playing him; hence the swashbuckling, loud-

[104] Sheridan bowdlerized his own version in places. He crossed out a short song to be sung by the maid on the virtues of an Irishman:

> Of all the Husbands living an Irishman's the best
>   with his fol ter rol
> Nor French nor Dutch nor English like him can stand the test
>   of your fol ter rol
> A lasting Fund of Pleasure in him alone you'll find
> Who ev'ry Day will please you & ev'ry Night be kind
>   With his fal ter rol.   (p. 36)

[105] The passage which lays the groundwork for these pronunciations appears in the Larpent MS (see note 110) but not in Sheridan's original version: "They sit down each of em on both sides me," says O'Blunder, describing the behavior of the two physicians in the madhouse scene, "and I was the Third Person, so they made me sit in the Middle. . . ." Here, although the actor may have used them on stage, the Irish substitutions are not represented in the spelling as they are in some of the printed versions which carry this passage. (The excerpt above from Larpent MS #120 is quoted by permission of the Henry E. Huntington Library.)

mouthed, fierce-tempered booby emerged as more suitable to farce and to eighteenth-century Irish audiences. This character, fresh for its time, made an early contribution to the history of that dubious type, the Stage Irishman, and influenced later creations, among them Richard Sheridan's Lucius O'Trigger.[106]

The O'Blunder role is supposed to have been written for Isaac Sparks,[107] a young Irish comedian who, as a child, had appeared in Madam Violante's Lilliputian troop [108] and who for many years must have been familiar to young Sheridan. Although he was not the first actor to be advertised in the part (Mr. Morris had this honor), Sparks did play O'Blunder often enough, under Sheridan's management, to become identified in the public mind with the character. And so popular did the character and its actor become then in Dublin that signs picturing O'Blunder as represented by Sparks hung out here and there above the streets, probably over inns and taverns. One day, so the story goes, Sparks himself happened to be walking under one of these signs when a chair-man went by. Looking first at the actor and then up at the sign, the chair-man quipped, "Oh there you are, above and below." [109] Perhaps in gratitude for the comedian's popularization of the role, Manager Sheridan regularly performed in Sparks's benefits after he had given up the practice with other actors. And the farce chosen for these benefits was usually *The Brave Irishman*.[110]

---

[106] Duggan, pp. 196–201.   [107] O'Keeffe, I, 357.   [108] Hitchcock, I, 49.

[109] O'Keeffe, I, 357. The information about Morris in the O'Blunder role comes from the *Dublin Journal*, April 9–12, 1743, in a notice of a benefit performance for Morris on April 12 at Smock-Alley Theater. He had probably appeared in the role earlier in the February 4 performance, which was for his benefit also. He is advertised for it again in July 1743, in March 1746, and as late as May 1748. Sparks's appearance in the role, apparently not till 1749–50, rejuvenated the play.

[110] When Sheridan was acting at Covent Garden in 1754–55, having given up the managership of Smock-Alley temporarily, Sparks too was in the Covent Garden company; and once, for his benefit, on March 22, 1755, he acted in *The Irishman in London*, advertised as "A farce never perform'd before" (*London Stage*, Pt. 4, p. 476). The text of this afterpiece, which exists in manuscript (Larpent MS 120), is very close to the text of Sheridan's manuscript of *The Brave Irishman*, and therefore quite unlike the printed versions of that play. Indeed, the Larpent MS provides a fair copy of the Sheridan MS with a few additional changes. My assumption has been that these few additional changes were with Sheridan's consent or perhaps even made by him, as the drastic changes in the printed versions were not. Therefore I am assuming that the productions of *The Brave Irishman* at Smock-Alley under Sheridan's management followed this

Sheridan is said to have written this only original play of his as a "mere boy" at college,[111] some have thought as early as 1736, when he would have been only seventeen. But mention of *Pamela* within the manuscript text indicates a date no earlier than 1740, though probably not later than 1741. "The admirers of Pamela will never think the worse of me for it [soliloquizes the "English" rival as he contemplates marriage with the servantmaid]. I'll have some poor Author to write a second Part of Pamela upon my Story, & crowd all the female Virtues that can be assembled into my Spouse that is to be." [112] Even without this evidence, the play would seem to be not only too linguistically knowledgeable but too socially sophisticated for a seventeen-year-old. Particularly interesting is the view of marriage expressed by the heroine's father and by her maid as they urge the heroine to accept O'Blunder. The father argues that she will have a better chance of governing a husband less intelligent than she. When the heroine asks her maid, "But Betty don't you think it is a

---

text or one like it and not the texts represented in the published editions. If Sheridan had made or even had approved of the changes appearing in the published texts and if they had been incorporated into the play which had been so popular over the years at Smock-Alley, Sparks would presumably have used some published version with Sheridan's consent and under his eye at Covent Garden. His notice that the piece had never been played before follows the not unusual practice of advertising an old and little-played piece under a new title as "never performed before." Besides, the farce had not been performed in London in any version since 1746 (*London Stage*, Pt. 3, p. 1,245) and even Sheridan's version had, as the Larpent MS shows, been changed some since then. Sparks used *The Brave Irishman* again for his benefit on May 14, 1770, at Drury Lane, this time under its regular title—but in what version, one wonders.

[111] Baker, "Captain O'Blunder." Pedicord (pp. 216–217) gives the season of the original performance as 1736–37. Both Allardyce Nicoll and W. H. Grattan Flood also assume that the farce was first produced in 1737 (February 21) anonymously (as written by a gentleman of Trinity College Dublin) at Aungier-Street Theater under the title of *The Honest Irishman; or The Cuckold in Conceit*. (Nicoll, II, 355 and 444; W. H. Grattan Flood, "Thomas Sheridan's 'Brave Irishman,' " *Review of English Studies*, II, 1926, 346–347.) Although I have not seen *The Honest Irishman* (nor, so far as I can judge, had Grattan Flood), the subtitle shows that it was probably not *The Brave Irishman*, in which there are no cuckolds.

[112] *The Brave Irishman* (*Lefanu MSS*), pp. 54–55. The last sentence, which speaks of having a sequel written to *Pamela*, is marked for excision, probably because Richardson had outdated it by publishing his own sequel in 1741. Thus the mention of *Pamela* would seem to give us a *tempus ab quo* and a *tempus ad quem* for the composition of the manuscript.

terrible Thing to marry a Man without either Understanding or good Breeding?" the answer is:

BETT.—O Lord Madam he'll make up those Defects in—Something else I warrant you. Besides don't you think it a charming thing to be free from the Tyranny of an imperious, prying, sensible Fellow. [Why Lord Madam he's the only Man in the World to make a Woman happy, for you'll enjoy in him all the Sweets of Matrimony without its Inconveniencies.]

LUC.—But don't you think that there's a great Deal of Pleasure in the Conversation of a Man of Sense?

BETT.—Not if he's a Husband I assure you Madam. There is not duller Company in the world than Man & Wife, especially if they are both people of sense. He presumes too much on his Superior Understanding, she thinks her's is at least equal to his. Their Conversation soon turns into Disputes & Wrangles. They are mighty good Company asunder but the dullest Creatures when together in the World. As for my Part I did not care if my Husband were dumb, for I assure you I think their silent Conversation is by far the best.[113]

Sheridan was a bachelor when he wrote these lines; his childhood had been spent with parents who, though unequal in "Understanding and good Breeding," had not been happy together; in a few years he himself was to marry and live happily with a woman who was quite his equal in "Understanding and good Breeding." But these passages and their cynical smartness came naturally to a twenty-one-year-old with some reputation as convivial sophisticate for all his fundamental seriousness as an M.A. scholar and a prospective schoolmaster.

During the four years after his B.A., while Sheridan was preparing to teach, Swift's remarks returned to plague him with doubts about his father's profession. Before he could begin his teaching, education needed to be reformed to include English and the art of speaking. For a young educational reformer in search of practice, rather than theory, in the art of speaking, one way was open—the stage.[114] So Sheridan reasoned then, or rationalized later. The truth was he had

[113] *Ibid.*, pp. 19, 37–38. The passage in brackets is marked for deletion. The father's scene with his daughter (Act I, sc. 4) seems to have been dropped later—possibly as too dull and preachy for farce. It is not in the Larpent MS.

[114] Sheridan, *An Oration*, pp. 20–21.

often turned to the stage before, as a relief from loneliness in London, as an outlet for his writing in *The Brave Irishman,* as a way of raising money for his family. The theater had an undeniable allure for him, which had steadily mounted over the years.

He wanted only a gentleman's reason for stepping on the boards. His long-range plans (if they existed) gave him a reason, but, he says, they were revealed to only two people besides himself.[115] To the rest of the world he would be nothing but an actor—then, in Dublin and to many Irishmen, something less than nothing. Fifteen years later when he was describing this crucial time in his life, he wrote a sentence which may reveal the real reason for his prolonged hesitation: "The miserable State in which I found the Stage, and the Meanness of the Performers at that Time, had brought the Profession itself into such a Degree of Contempt, as was sufficient to deter a young Man of any Spirit, who had gone thro' an entire Course of a liberal Education, from entering into it." [116]

He was still hesitating when events during the summer of 1742 apparently spurred him out of his indecision and into a stage career. Theatrically speaking, Dublin summers were often more exciting than winters, for then well-known London actors came to Ireland to supplement their income after the English season was over. Not every Dubliner approved, feeling that these foreign actors milked Ireland and spent elsewhere.[117] But their novelty and their superior talent attracted great houses, rare in Dublin winters—and this in spite of summer heat, ill-ventilated theaters, and the danger of infectious diseases.

The summer of 1742 brought over several London actors. Only two of them were important enough to be called by the *Dublin Journal* "celebrated": Mr. Giffard, actor-manager of Goodman's Fields, and Denis Delane, a Trinity-educated Irishman who had been much loved in Dublin since his debut there in 1728. Not "celebrated" were Miss Woffington, returning to her native city after two years in England, the dancer Signora Barbarini, and Mr. Garrick,[118] a rising young actor who had appeared for the first time eight months before at Goodman's Fields. He had made quite a sensation in London, but the *Dublin Journal* was waiting to be shown.

These visitors arrived in mid-June. Garrick performed at Smock-Alley, supported by Mrs. Furnival of the local company and by Mrs.

---

[115] *Ibid.,* p. 21. [116] *Ibid.* [117] Kemble, *Manuscript Diary,* November 1743.
[118] *Dublin Journal,* June 8–12 and 12–15, 1742. Woffington is called Miss in the press item, but Mrs. in the theatrical notices. See also p. 58, n. 3.

Woffington; Signora Barbarini danced. Delane was engaged at the rival Aungier-Street Theater, with Mrs. Cibber, who had been there through the winter, staying on to play opposite him. Advertisements indicate that these last two acted only a few nights. The main Dublin attraction that summer was Garrick. He appeared about twice weekly for two months (from June 18 to August 19), in such plays as *Richard III, Lear, Hamlet, The Orphan, Venice Preserved, Love Makes a Man,* and most frequently as Bayes in *The Rehearsal.* His interpretation of this last comic role was especially popular; years after, actors were doing Bayes à la Garrick in Dublin. He even acted in a few afterpieces—in *The Mock Doctor,* for example, and in his own farce, *The Lying Valet.* Many of these plays were presented "by the particular Desire" of people or groups in the audience. One evening the Lords Justices, rulers of Ireland in the absence of a viceroy, went to Smock-Alley to see Mr. Garrick and Mrs. Barbarini perform.[119] Although Woffington put on men's clothes and did her charming best as Sir Harry Wildair, she was too familiar to attract attention. It was Garrick who inspired a poem in the *Dublin Journal,* praising his Lear and asking how so gentle a man could play so convincingly the villainous Richard III.[120] Many a Dubliner took to his bed with what theatrical historians called "Garrick fever," an epidemic spread, it was believed, by the crowds pressing into Smock-Alley on Garrick nights.

Among these crowds was Thomas Sheridan,[121] only slightly younger than Garrick and with as much passion for the stage. He may have been one of the gentlemen who persuaded Garrick to change his benefit play from *The Fair Penitent* to *Hamlet,*[122] always one of Sheridan's favorites. He probably knew Peg Woffington from her earlier days in Dublin; his apologies sent to her in his note to Garrick the following April reveal that she was an old-enough friend to be neglected.[123] Perhaps through her he became acquainted with

---

[119] *Ibid.,* June 26–29, 1742.   [120] *Ibid.,* July 3–6, 1742.

[121] He himself in *An Humble Appeal* (p. 14) speaks of seeing Garrick on his first visit to Dublin, playing opposite Woffington.

[122] Notice in *Dublin Journal,* August 3–7, 1742: "Mr. Garrick thinks it proper to acquaint the Town, that he did not take The Fair Penitent (as was given out) for his Benefit, that Play being disapproved of by several Gentlemen and Ladies; but by particular Desire deferred it till Hamlet could be ready, which will be played on Thursday next [August 12]."

[123] Garrick, *Private Correspondence,* I, 16. Sheridan's letter to Garrick, April 21, 1743: "Pray remember my best respects to Mrs. Woffington: I should own myself unpardonable in not having wrote to her, were it in my power; but I

Garrick; but without her his interest in the theater, his authorship of an Irish farce, and his position at Trinity College could have brought the two men together. The next spring, after eight months of separation, Garrick still felt close enough to Sheridan to invite him to live with him in England. Sheridan's response shows that he recognized Garrick's genius and solid popularity with the public.[124]

This genius and popularity may have infected Sheridan with a special kind of "Garrick fever." Garrick's respectable background had not kept *him* from the stage; the social position he was winning showed old prejudices weakening; more gentlemen in the theater would strengthen the actor's status (an argument which the reformer in Sheridan would cherish). And then the nightly enthusiasm for this young actor, greater than any he had seen before! Garrick's success seems to have removed Sheridan's last scruple. Within five months, the proper time needed to persuade Manager Phillips of Smock-Alley, to learn the parts in *Richard III* and in *Mithridates* and to attend the required rehearsals, Sheridan was making his Smock-Alley debut. A gentleman who watched one of these rehearsals wrote about it in a letter to the *Journal* just before Sheridan's first appearance:

> I had the Curiosity Friday Evening to attend the Rehearsal of Richard IIId at Smock-Alley. I was pleas'd, and surprised to see a Gentleman in the Character of Richard, shew Talents superior to what I had observed in the oldest Tragedians. I am an Enemy to Puffs of all Kinds, but most of all to the [Mo]dern Way of building one Man's Fame on the Ruin of another. This Gentleman is pleased to acknowledge Garrick for [his] Master, and not to vye with him, and is prompted to app[ear] first in this Character, from a Remembrance of his Beauties.[125]

Soon Sheridan was to regard Garrick as his equal rather than his master; but Garrick's importance to him at this moment, even to the role he selected for his debut, is underlined here. The letter writer's main purpose, however, was to obviate objections being made to the

---

have been already sufficiently punished in the loss of so agreeable a companion, for, I assure you, I have a long time envied her pretty Chronon that pleasure: as soon as I have a moment to spare, I intend to do myself the honour to write to her. . . . Tommy Philips desires me to present his best respects to you and Mrs. Woffington."

[124] *Ibid.*, pp. 15–16.   [125] *Dublin Journal*, January 22–25, 1743.

young man's attempt by his friends, who were apparently urging him to try for a Trinity fellowship [126] instead of risking his honor and future in a degenerate vocation. The letter writer argues that, degenerate though it now is by the reputations of performers, the stage *can* be raised by "Persons of Genius, Character, and Education." [127]

Young Sheridan brought to his new vocation not genius but a good mind, and a better education than usual. As for his character, which had been forming over the years, he was alert and energetic, convivial, and, on the surface at least, self-confident. His self-confidence bordered at times on vanity. Like many vain people he was easily wounded and overdefensive, as his Westminster letters to his father show. Like his father, he had a sense of humor but he was basically more serious and ready to commit himself to idealistic goals. An undeniable allure may have drawn him to the stage, or a desire to master the art of speaking. Once there, his goals became clear to him and he expressed them often: he was going to raise the stage, make the actor's profession respectable, and restore the theater to its classical role as a cultural institution. He could not know then at what cost.

[126] Hitchcock, I, 129.   [127] *Dublin Journal*, January 22–25, 1743.

CHAPTER II

Theatrical Hero[1] Into Theater Manager, 1743-1745

WHEN Sheridan came to the stage, he must have known something of recent stage history in Dublin. Later he recounted it in speeches and pamphlets: how Smock-Alley Theater had prospered under Joseph Ashbury's forty-five-year monopoly and under Thomas Elrington's briefer management after Ashbury's death (in 1720); how after Elrington died (in 1732) and the Smock-Alley company had moved to the new Aungier-Street Theater, a rival group had sprung up, rebuilding the abandoned Smock-Alley house and giving Dublin a second regular company,[2] quite different from Stretch's puppets and Madam Violante's child-actors. Even though it was not London (as Swift and others complained), Dublin, when compared to other provincial capitals—Calvinistic Edinburgh, say— was becoming a city of the world.

Physically too, Dublin was growing fast during these mid-century years. In 1747 a survey showed that it measured nine and three-quarters miles around and, although still only about one-third the extent of London,[3] it was the sixth largest city in Europe for number of inhabitants, exceeded only by London, Paris, Constantinople, Moscow, and Rome.[4] Many of the buildings, houses, and streets which so delight the modern admirer of eighteenth-century elegance were being constructed during Sheridan's youth and early manhood: the beautiful Trinity College library, completed only three years before he became a Trinitarian; the Parliament House rebuilt at about the same time and regarded as "infinitely superior" to that of Westmin-

[1] An epithet for Sheridan from Weeks, *A Rhapsody on the Stage:* "Your first setting out, promised, what a Year or two performed, the Theatrical Hero" (Dedication).

[2] Sheridan, *Mr. Sheridan's Speech*, pp. 5–7 (dates have been added from Clark and Stockwell). This rival group had come from the Rainsford-Street Theater, which had offered brief competition earlier (Stockwell, p. 69). For a detailed history of these theaters, see Clark to 1720, Stockwell to the period under consideration.

[3] *Hibernia Curiosa*, p. 10.

[4] *Dublin Journal*, September 12–15, 1747.

ster;[5] the Lying-In Hospital, with its handsome gardens; and, in the residential sections to the north, neat new houses roofed with blue slate, facing one another along regular and spacious streets. At least a quarter of the city, according to one estimate of the time, had been built in the forty years between 1724 and 1764.[6]

Yet, with all of Dublin's expansion and its cosmopolitan manner, visitors were appalled by the poverty and unemployment there. Debtors' prisons were overflowing; desperate robberies for the most trifling objects brought death often to the robbed and the robber; marauding and fighting gangs roamed the streets.[7] Ireland's wealth was owned by a handful and even then was siphoned off abroad by Irish absenteeism, which in turn compounded Irish misery.[8] So, with the theatergoing public remaining small, though no longer so aristocratic, two competing companies still could not both survive. The theaters themselves were owned by "subscribers," mostly well-to-do gentlemen who had undertaken them as a public service,[9] to whom money was secondary; but they were leased and run by managers, usually actors (hence, "acting managers," where "acting" means "performing"). To these managers and their companies competition meant near starvation and the ghastly prospect of debtors' prison. When Sheridan came to the stage in 1743, just such a ruinous rivalry had been going on for eight years between Smock-Alley and Aungier-Street.

The two theaters were located not far from each other in the older part of town between the castle and the college—Smock-Alley Theater in a street by that name just off the Liffey and Aungier-Street Theater[10] a short distance across Dame-Street, Dublin's main thoroughfare. Smock-Alley's curious name went back, according to legend, to the time of a certain infamous Mother Bungy, when the district was "a sink of debauchery." Later, after a man had been

---

[5] *A Description of the City of Dublin*, p. 13; *Hibernia Curiosa*, p. 9.

[6] *Hibernia Curiosa*, pp. 10, 11.

[7] *Ibid.*, p. 14; "A Description of Dublin" lately published in the *London Chronicle*, republished in the *Dublin Journal*, June 17–20, 1758; other items in newspapers of the time.

[8] Maxwell, pp. 17–18: From a list of absentees published in 1730, the yearly value of the income spent abroad was estimated at £621,499; a similar estimate in 1769 shows an increase to £1,208,982.

[9] Hitchcock, I, 87–93.

[10] Although called Aungier-Street Theater, it was actually in Longford-Lane (Stockwell, p. 71).

murdered there, the shacks were pulled down and handsome houses put up.[11] By the 1740's the street suffered from no more serious taint than might emanate from theatergoing crowds such as these milling around the various doors:

Lords, ladys, shoe-boys, GENTLEMEN, and whores;
Dogs, horses, chairs, parsons, bullys, proctors,
Old men and widows, quacks, madmen, doctors;
Pimps, statesmen, pocket pickers, poets, fools,
Coaches and chariots, flams and chairmens poles:
All mix'd confusion, noise, tumults, curses,
Swearing, breaking shins, and picking purses.[12]

The theater aside, Smock-Alley had achieved a sort of middle-class respectability and was occupied by shops, inns, and dwellings. At the corner near Fishamble-Street Mr. Craig, the grocer, let lodgings to Smock-Alley players. Fishamble-Street, which ran at right angles, housed the celebrated Music-Hall and picturesquely named inns such as the Black Boy and the Bull's Head. Other actors and actresses stayed even nearer the theater—with Mr. Smith, the perukemaker, or at Harry of Monmouth's Head in Smock-Alley itself.[13] After Sheridan became well established as manager, in the early fifties, he began to use a large house next to the theater for an office and as a place for entertaining friends, one more spacious than the Smock-Alley greenroom and more convenient than his remote home in Dorset-Street; this annex is referred to as the Great House adjoining the theater on the Blind-Key side.[14] And sometime in 1749 Deputy Manager and Treasurer Benjamin Victor moved from lodgings in Crow-Street into a "neat little box" of a house opposite the theater.[15] Yet, for all of its respectable population and crowded theatrical activity, one walked Smock-Alley (as one walked most of Dublin) at the risk of one's limbs and even one's life. Great holes gaped in the street; in 1753, because of "the badness of the Pavement," a man fell down and broke his leg.[16] Desperate thieves lurked in the dark passageways. In one such alley a gentleman was knocked down and

[11] *The Life of Mrs. Abington*, p. 19; Chetwood, pp. 72–73.

[12] *The Gentleman*, p. 15.

[13] Notices of benefit performances often show where players lived, since tickets were to be had at their dwellings.

[14] *Dublin Journal*, January 9–13, 1753.

[15] Victor, *Original Letters*, I, 163. Victor had built the house "on an entire new plan" of his own.   [16] *Dublin Journal*, January 2–6, 1753.

robbed of his hat and wig, "the Want of proper Lights" being "a manifest Encouragement to such villainous Practices." [17]

Smock-Alley Theater, located on the north side of the street in mid-block, had been in existence since 1662. When it was rebuilt in 1735 to compete with the new Aungier-Street Theater, it had a larger auditorium than Aungier-Street, but a smaller stage.[18] Later, when both theaters were under Sheridan's control, he used the larger Aungier-Street stage for operas and spectacles, but Smock-Alley was his regular theater, "a strong, elegant, commodious, well constructed" building, which had avoided the errors of other theaters and in which the audience section was particularly good for seeing and hearing.[19] There still exists a depressing line sketch of its front façade (reproduced on the jacket), and both exterior and interior are described with much satiric license in "an Heroic Poem," composed in 1747:

> High on a hill their gothic structure rose,
> Tall as an *Alpine* mountain crown'd with snows;
> A lusty fabric whose stupendous height,
> O'ertop'd the bounded reach of human sight.
> Three various gates three various quarters fac'd,
> With golden valves, and golden portals grac'd:
> This at the north, a spacious entrance gave,
> Where the smooth *Liffy* rolls her silent wave;
> And seeks with tardy steps her native main
> Well stor'd with cats and dogs untimely slain.
> This to the east, beholds the eastern skies,
> That to the south, sees *Wicklow* mountains rise.
>
> In four divisions, form'd by art within,
> The various quarters of the world are seen:
> And first the STAGE, like *Africs* desert land,
> Where gold abounds, and APES and MONKEYS stand:
> And next, like *Europe* fam'd for Arts, the PIT

---

[17] *Ibid.*, November 16–20, 1756.

[18] Chetwood, pp. 72–73. I can find nowhere the measurements for Smock-Alley, but figures for Aungier-Street are given in the *Dublin Journal*, January 31–February 4, 1758, and are compared there with the new Crow-Street Theater just being built. (See below, Ch. ix.) Smock-Alley seems to have been between them in size. *Hibernia Curiosa* (pp. 12–13) reports Smock-Alley as smaller than Crow-Street, which was about the size of Drury Lane.

[19] Hitchcock, i, 93–94.

Where artful pimps, and artful parsons sit:
The BOXES then, *America* display,
With naked charms, and painted feathers gay;
Where ev'ry fair one deck'd in paint appears,
While gaudy Gewgaws gravitate their ears:
And then the GALL'RY *Asia's* medium hits,
Between the *Lybian* APES, and *Europe's* WITS;
While overhead, no less than GODS I trow,
Survey the world, in every act below;
And pleas'd or vex'd, their smiles or vengeance deal,
Their smiles a clap, their vengeance orange peel.
Such was the structure, such Smock-Alley stage. . . .[20]

A less colorful picture of the theater written by Sheridan himself to describe normal conditions there before his management shows only the upper gallery filled, the rest of the house almost deserted: twenty persons in the pit, no one in the boxes, one row of the middle gallery filled.[21] Half-empty houses like these had forced Manager Louis Duval to give up in 1741 to Thomas ("Harlequin") Phillips,[22] who, when Sheridan joined, was still running the company. For several years before Sheridan joined, a union of the two theaters—to save them from the disaster which threatened—had been contemplated. As early as 1739 a press item mistakenly predicted a merger for the next season, and a week after Sheridan's debut in 1743 the *Dublin Gazette* rumored that the proprietors had agreed on an immediate union.[23] Perhaps Sheridan's success, with its promise of prosperity for Smock-Alley, postponed this expedient.

For his success was immediate and spectacular. The phenomenon, frequent then, of an untrained actor without professional experience stepping into the leading part of some difficult Shakespearean play and from there leaping to fame and a future career seems strange now. Sheridan hardly ever in his life played a minor role. Stranger still seems the managerial brashness which would permit an inexperienced unknown to attempt the lead; yet Sheridan, in his early years as manager, brought out many a newcomer this way, although eventually he came to disapprove of the custom as risky and too frequently disappointing.

But his own debut was no disappointment; it turned him into a

[20] *The Gentleman*, pp. 13–14.   [21] Sheridan, *An Humble Appeal*, p. 15.
[22] Stockwell, pp. 80–81.
[23] *Dublin Journal*, March 27–31, 1739; *Dublin Gazette*, February 5–8, 1743.

leading actor overnight. For the first three months he played at Smock-Alley about once a week; then, from April on, about twice weekly. He was plagued by ill health, which forced him to postpone several performances.[24] Even so, he worked prodigiously all spring to enlarge his repertoire, adding Hamlet, Brutus, Othello, and in April trying his first comedy, as Charles in *Love Makes a Man* and Lord Townley in *The Provoked Husband*.[25] The order and proportion in this list show Sheridan's early preference for tragedy and for Shakespeare. Supporting him in the Smock-Alley company were many players who were later to serve under him: Mrs. Elmy, Mr. Beamsley, Miss Orfeur (to become Mrs. Kennedy),[26] et cetera. For a time one of the minor actors was Richard Sheridan, whose trial in the company reveals the solicitude and influence of his younger brother, the star. Richard played Cassius and at least one other role,[27] but he was not a success and in the end retired to a place in the Custom-House and to respectable living in a home of his own on Moor-Street—a "snug, cosey, friendly little man," as described by O'Keeffe, who painted his portrait.[28]

Dublin that spring is said to have gone wild over its discovery, young Thomas Sheridan. Even though it is probably not true that the veteran Quin fled Dublin, driven off by the new actor's success,[29]

[24] For example, "Mr. Sheridan being recovered from his late Indisposition, the Play of Hamlet will positively be acted at the Theatre in Smock-Alley, on Monday next" (*Dublin Journal*, February 22–26, 1743). Another such notice appears *ibid.*, June 18–21.

[25] Sheridan's *Captain O'Blunder, or the Brave Irishman* was the farce at his debut as Charles. (For dates of first appearances during 1743 see note 83.)

[26] Bellamy, I, 75. Others in the company, as shown by *Dublin Journal* notices, were Mr. Elrington (probably Ralph), Mr. Husband, Mr. Wright, Mrs. Bailey, Mr. Oates. Mrs. Elmy played Lady Townley to Sheridan's Lord Townley. At Aungier-Street were still others who were eventually to join Sheridan's company: Mrs. Furnival, Isaac Sparks, Bardin, Morris, Barrington, Layfield (probably Lewis Layfield), and Moreau, the dancer.

[27] Richard appeared as Clincher Jun. in *The Constant Couple*, a performance in which Thomas did not appear. The Cassius part was played on April 29, "the first time of his Appearance upon any Stage" (*Dublin Journal*, April 19–23, 1743).

[28] O'Keeffe, I, 123.

[29] Davies (I, 83–84) says that Quin had expectantly returned to Ireland after playing in other years to large houses there, then had left precipitously when told by the theater proprietors that all the following winter was given over to the new actor. This story is repeated in *The Life of Mr. James Quin*, 1887 edition, p. 87, and elsewhere. The arrival or departure of a celebrity like Quin

other less dramatic evidence must have persuaded Sheridan of his sudden popularity. In February his first benefit at Smock-Alley obliged an Aungier-Street player—Mr. Griffith,[30] no less—to defer *his* long-planned benefit "at the Request of several Ladies of Quality, because Mr. Sheridan's Play is that Night."[31] Plans to close Smock-Alley from mid-March to Easter were hastily revoked to keep the theater open for the new star.[32] His first appearance as Brutus produced such great satisfaction that, according to a rare *Dublin Journal* news item, "some Ladies of the first Quality" had bespoken Hamlet for the next Friday night, when the theater was usually closed; and soon after, *Julius Caesar* was repeated "by Desire."[33] Even Sheridan was surprised by his reception. In trying to explain and describe it to Theophilus Cibber less than two months after his debut, he expresses pride, but also an unexpected modesty: "I know not how it is, whether it be their Partiality to their Countryman, or whether it be owing to the powerful Interest of a Number of Friends that I have in this City, but there never was known such Encouragement, such Applause given to any Actor, or such full Houses as since I appear'd on the Stage."[34] This from a witness of Garrick's triumph the summer before! But the climax for Sheridan must have come with a letter from England, from Garrick himself, inviting this player of three months' experience to spend the summer with him at Walton and share roles with him in London the following winter.

All this fame was heady stuff to a young man whose vanity for far less cause had worried his father a decade before. No wonder,

---

would have been announced in the *Dublin Journal*, yet no mention of his name appears during the spring or summer of this year. Although possibly Quin negotiated by mail, it would seem that Smock-Alley's rival would have welcomed him for the summer at least. Both theaters were hoping to combine in the fall, but later evidence indicates that there was no firm engagement with Sheridan for the next winter, as Davies' story implies. Sheridan, in *An Humble Appeal* (p. 17), mistakenly puts Quin and Mrs. Cibber at Aungier-Street in the winter of 1742–43. A search of the advertisements shows that they were there in the winter of 1741–42, but not the next year.

[30] Griffith, at one time manager of a Dublin theater, was an important theatrical figure.

[31] *Dublin Journal*, February 15–19, 1743. Sheridan was repeating *Richard III*, his third performance of the play.

[32] *Ibid.*, March 22–26 and 26–29, 1743.

[33] *Ibid.*, March 15–19 and 26–29, 1743.

[34] *Cibber and Sheridan*, p. 38. "A true Copy of Mr. Sheridan's Letter to Mr. Cibber," March 22, 1743.

then, that Sheridan's answer declining Garrick's offers reflects a certain cockiness. His counterplan at the end has struck modern critics as a particularly offensive piece of young man's impertinence; they forget that Garrick was a young man then too, only three years older than Sheridan, and not yet the personage he later became. Sheridan, better born and better educated, felt at least the equal of Garrick socially; professionally he was on his way to rivalling him—or so Dublin thought. But he declined Garrick's offers because he felt he could not compete with him; he was only "a well-cut pebble" to Garrick the "diamond"; audiences would scorn to see a worse performer in Garrick's parts in Garrick's theater. Immature though it seems in places, his response still recognizes Garrick's superiority. His counterproposal begins charmingly with just such an acknowledgement, "if you could be brought to divide your immortality with me," and then suggests, in a half-joking way, the scheme, which though "a little extraordinary" could be advantageous to both:

> . . . we might, like Castor and Pollux, appear always in different hemispheres; (now I think on't, I don't know whether the old simile of the two buckets would not do as well, but that is beneath the dignity of a tragedian:) in plain English, what think you of dividing the kingdoms between us; to play one winter in London, and another in Dublin? I have many reasons to offer in favour of this scheme, which will not come within the compass of a letter; I shall only say, that it will make us always new in both kingdoms, and consequently always more followed; and I am satisfied that Dublin is as well able to pay one actor for the winter as London. But more of this when I have the pleasure of meeting you. . . .[35]

Garrick, for obvious reasons, was not interested.

And so Sheridan stayed in Dublin for the rest of 1743—mostly to his sorrow, for storms began to disrupt the halcyon days of early spring. At the end of April he became involved in a dispute between Duval and Phillips. Duval, who had given up the management but had stayed with the company under special provisions, now claimed in public notices that Phillips and the company had broken their contracts with him, stolen his property, and subjected him to "cruel treatment"; "neither would they suffer Mr. Sheridan, who is under their Influence, as he alledges, to play for me [in a benefit perform-

---

[35] Garrick, *Private Correspondence*, I, 15 (Letter of April 21, 1743).

ance], and therefore refused me that Service." [36] Unpleasant as this wrangle must have been for Sheridan, caught in the middle, it emphasized publicly his popularity as an actor. Not to have Sheridan for his benefit—this to Duval was the cruelest cut of all.

But Sheridan's personal difficulties, the first to disrupt his honeymoon with the Dublin public, began in July. Shortly after his debut, and at least as early as March, Aungier-Street Theater, hard-pressed by its rival's successful discovery, had approached Colley Cibber's son, Theophilus, about a "Summer Expedition" to Dublin.[37] Theophilus Cibber was a good choice. In contrast to Sheridan, he was an experienced comedian, of the slapstick sort according to contemporary descriptions.[38] (He played, less frequently and less successfully, in tragedies; it was said that his father had taught him his "old Manner of singing and quavering out . . . tragic Notes," but though the audience excused the fault in the old man, they could not forgive it in the son.)[39] Theophilus was from London, too, where he had already achieved notoriety as a theatrical hothead and a self-cuckolded husband in a scandalous lawsuit. Unfortunately, he was unattractive both in appearance and personality; [40] but since he had never acted in Ireland, he would be a novelty as well as a curiosity to Irish audiences.

Sheridan, who had quickly got wind of the Aungier-Street plan and as quickly foreseen that Cibber would threaten him in competition but complement him in supporting roles, wrote to London, asking him to join him at Smock-Alley. "I have no small cause to be afraid of so potent an Antagonist," Sheridan admitted as he drew his letter

[36] *Dublin Journal*, April 26–30, 1743. Lewis Duval, primarily a dancer who had come to Ireland with Madame Violante (Stockwell, p. 69), became a manager when Rainsford-Street Theater was built ten years before (1733). He and his company had moved to Smock-Alley after it was rebuilt. When he gave up the management to Phillips in 1741, he became entitled to one benefit play a year without charge. According to Hitchcock (II, 148), he had an annual benefit at the theater until his death at over ninety.

[37] *Cibber and Sheridan*, p. 38.   [38] Davies, I, 54.

[39] Victor, *History*, II, 163–164.

[40] Bellamy (4th edn., II, 84–85) describes him thus: "When this oddity was formed, Nature certainly was not in the best of humours. . . . To a short squat figure, was joined an enormous head, with the most frightful face I ever beheld. The latter endowment was, indeed, frequently of service to him; as, in his acting, he made ugliness to pass for grimace: besides which, he substituted pertness and assurance for wit and humour." This description does not appear in earlier editions.

to a close. This letter, written on March 22, was later published by Cibber [41] as evidence that Sheridan himself had lured him to Smock-Alley [42] before he turned against him. For Cibber did act with Sheridan after he arrived in Dublin in late April.[43] He took the lead in comedies for a month and then joined Sheridan amicably in tragedies, taking secondary roles.[44] On July 7 Sheridan first played a part for which he later became noted, that of Addison's Cato; Cibber played Syphax. A week later a second showing of *Cato* was substituted for *Macbeth*, which was to have been Sheridan's last performance of the season but which had been deferred at the request of several persons of importance.[45] If *Macbeth* had been played as his final performance, all would have been well; but *Cato* provoked an unexpected difficulty, one so insuperable that, despite the audience assembled, Sheridan did not play at all that evening.

Sheridan later explained the unexpected difficulty in a public letter to the audience he had disappointed. When he had arrived backstage at the theater that evening, everything had been in confusion: the musicians, unpaid, were refusing to perform, and Manager Phillips, according to rumor, had absconded, taking with him the robe which Sheridan as Cato was supposed to have worn. A robe, Sheridan explained in the letter, seems like a trifling thing but it was a large robe, which he needed to cover "Defects, and add Gravity and Dignity," since he felt himself particularly unfit "in his Person" for the role of Cato.[46] Faced with appearing without this robe, and suspecting that Phillips had removed it to prevent his playing, the young actor of only five months' experience seems to have gone to pieces. To shatter him further, as he continues to explain in a later *Address to the Town*, Theophilus Cibber's behavior, formerly "complaisant, or rather meanly submissive," took a sudden change for the worse; instead of trying "to appease a Person beside himself with Passion" he turned on his heel and said insolently, "D—n me if I care what you do, the Play shall not stand still for

[41] In *Cibber and Sheridan*, pp. 38–39.

[42] *Ibid.*, p. 13. Here Cibber says, "And do you not know, your particular Application since my Arrival, was one of my strongest Motives for playing in Smock-Alley. . . ."

[43] Cibber's arrival is announced in the *Dublin Journal*, April 26–30, along with Mr. and Mrs. Giffard's.

[44] Cibber played with Sheridan in such plays as *The Fair Penitent* (Lothario to Sheridan's Horatio) and *Richard III* (*Dublin Journal* notices).

[45] *Dublin Journal*, July 9–12, 1743. [46] *Cibber and Sheridan*, p. 8.

you." Thrown thus into further confusion, Sheridan rushed on stage to apologize to the audience, only to discover that he had lost his voice from the disorders he had suffered. If this had not happened, he would still have played; but how could he have acted, when he couldn't speak? At the same time Cibber followed him on stage and offered "very officiously" to read the part of Cato as he played Syphax.[47] Sheridan wanted to dismiss the audience.

Cibber, in his first public letter to Sheridan, explains that Phillips had merely returned the robes to some Dublin lady from whom he had borrowed them, that all the cast had been similarly discommoded, that Sheridan had been offered another robe (Julius Caesar's, almost new), but that he had persisted in wanting "the other uncomeatable Robe." In the end Sheridan, who had been fully dressed for his character—save for the robe—had undressed, made a broken speech to the audience (at which they showed their dissatisfaction), and had run hastily out of the house, sending back word that he would act no more. But, adds Cibber, addressing Sheridan directly, "I am informed you stay'd . . . just long enough to hear the extraordinary indulgent Reception the Audience were pleased to bestow on my proposing, with their Leave, to give them the Play. . . ."[48] The performance apparently then proceeded in this huggermugger way without Sheridan, but with, ironically, his farce *The Brave Irishman* as the afterplay.[49]

The tempest in the greenroom and on stage at Smock-Alley during the evening of July 14, 1743, did not end there. First, as often happened, Trinity College students took up the cause and in a letter to the *Dublin Journal* expressed satisfaction with Sheridan's reasons and demanded to see him righted. Another letter assured him of the college's support and hoped that his resentment would not deprive them of his genius.[50] A poem stuck up on posts about town theatened Cibber under the title "Cibber's Warning Piece." [51] Finally, a week after the original trouble, a riot between college students and "a party of ruffians" got up by Cibber to oppose them drove Cibber off the stage.[52] Since these moves were bound to be attributed to orders from Sheridan—indeed, Cibber immediately accused him of every-

---

[47] *Ibid.*, pp. 27–28, 8.   [48] *Ibid.*, pp. 11–13.

[49] *Dublin Journal*, July 9–12, 1743.

[50] *Cibber and Sheridan*, p. 6. The two letters appeared originally in the July 16–19 issue of the *Dublin Journal*.

[51] *Cibber and Sheridan*, p. 7.   [52] *Ibid.*, pp. 17–20.

thing from the Trinity College letters to the riot—another letter from the college explained that Sheridan was hardly acquainted with the authors, that he had begged them to stay away from the theater and to let Cibber play for his own benefit—something that they were still willing to let Cibber do.[53]

Actual hostilities ended on July 28, when Sheridan by "the Lords Justices Special Command" and "at the general Desire of all his Friends" performed Cato, not at Smock-Alley but at the Aungier-Street Theater in his last performance of the season.[54] Meanwhile, the paper war grew more violent and more abusive. And here Sheridan blundered even more seriously than when he lost control at the theater. In a second address to the town he tried to defend himself against charges made in Cibber's letter, forgetting that Theophilus, as the son of Colley, was not only facile with the pen, but quite at home with invective, billingsgate, and every art of offensive writing. Before the epistolary exchange was over, Sheridan had been smeared with a variety of names and charged with cheating his brother, tyrannizing at the theater, and ill-using the women there, although he was also accused of being a stranger still—as Cibber certainly was not—to the joys and pains of love.[55] After two letters apiece the writings become anonymous: most of them are even more scurrilous, and some are from other pens.

The inexperienced Sheridan must have been flabbergasted at the intense and widespread interest his impulsive moment had aroused when two collections of these writings appeared shortly after, one in Dublin and one in London.[56] The preface to the London collection made great fun of the trivial cause of the quarrel and of the "two theatrical Generals" involved—the one, a "Heroe" long known in England and not to be daunted "by the Threats of private Whispers, or publick Manifestos"; the other, a younger general, not so experi-

---

[53] *Ibid.*, p. 20.

[54] *Dublin Journal*, July 23–26, 1743; *Cibber and Sheridan*, p. 20. At Smock-Alley Cibber was scheduled to perform Pistol, but the play was deferred, perhaps because of the event at Aungier-Street.

[55] *Cibber and Sheridan*, pp. 17–19, 41–45, 50. Cibber became especially virulent after the college riot had occurred in the theater. Accusing Sheridan of being able to play only two roles well, Maskwell and Scrub, Cibber calls him "naughty-paughty Tommy," "dear Mock-Monarch," "sweet meager Sir," et cetera, and asks him where he was hiding his "calicoe Carcass" during this "noble Riot."

[56] *Cibber and Sheridan* was apparently gathered together by Cibber at a Dublin publisher's request. *The Buskin and Sock*, the London edition, has four pieces from the Dublin collection.

enced or so fierce or formidable, but well qualified for the rank from "a Disposition rather to give Orders, for the Battle, than an Inclination to hazard his person in it. . . ." Dublin's theatrical scandals frequently amused London.

Not amused was the anonymous author of a serious commendatory poem addressed to Sheridan and included as a finale to the Dublin collection *Cibber and Sheridan*. This poem, which tells how the sun reproved some foolish owls, has been traditionally ascribed to the literary daughter of the Reverend Philip Chamberlaine, Frances, who read and wrote in secret because her father disapproved of learning for women: it led, he felt, only to sentimental scribbling. Fortunately, her brothers took a hand in educating her surreptitiously, and by the time she was fifteen she was scribbling a two-volume novel (years later adapted for the Dublin stage) and, after that, two sermons.[57] She was eighteen or nineteen at the time of the Cato affair. Whether she had ever seen Sheridan act by then is doubtful, since her father disapproved of the theater too. Most of the poem expresses its ideas in general allegorical terms and could have been written any time for anybody, but one stanza refers to actual events:

> Tho' you be prais'd by half the Globe,
>   And charm its Factions dumb;
> Yet spite shall soil your newest Robe,
>   And Cato dread Tom Thumb.

Charmed himself by this tribute, Sheridan, the story goes, wanted to know his admirer. Since she was an acquaintance of his sister, Mrs. Sheen, a meeting was arranged. The two fell in love and were married—according to tradition, in 1747. Whether or not the romantic story of the matchmaking poem is true,[58] the marriage itself

---

[57] Lefanu, pp. 4–11.

[58] My hesitation to accept the story of the poem without question comes from certain errors in the traditional family account of it given by Alicia Lefanu (pp. 22–24), one which has been repeated by later historians (e.g., Fitzgerald, I, 24). She ascribes the poem to Frances but is mistaken in saying that it was written in 1747 to commend Sheridan for his part in the Kelly riot. Aside from its unassailable place in a 1743 volume, internal evidence shows that it is more appropriate to the Cato affair: *the only mention of actual events* refers to Cato's robe and not to Kelly. This one stanza out of ten is the only one omitted in Alicia Lefanu's version of the poem, otherwise corresponding closely with the poem printed in *Cibber and Sheridan*. Alicia, incidentally, has no account of the Cibber-Sheridan feud; this incident may have dropped out of family tradition

was a lifelong romance and a complete success. During their early life together Frances was so occupied with bearing children and entertaining friends that she had no time for writing and perhaps little even for the theater, although, with her active mind, she must always have been interested in her husband's work. Later, in London, she wrote again—not only a novel but two plays. Most of her literary efforts flourished while Sheridan's ventures ended in nothing; but Frances always remained his admiring, protective, intelligent supporter.

Although it may have brought him the perfect wife, Sheridan's controversy with Cibber over Cato's robe, coming when he stood so high in public esteem, was in other ways unfortunate. For, in trying to explain it, he forgot that, though people inside the company might understand and even sympathize,[59] a quarrel over such a trifling matter would appear ridiculous to the outside public. It put Sheridan in a comic light in Dublin's eyes, and Dublin in a comic light in London's eyes. To some—like Cibber, perhaps—this would

---

as unflattering to Sheridan, and the poem, minus the related and therefore meaningless stanza, may then have become transferred to the Kelly affair. Frances Chamberlaine was still very possibly the author; if so, the meeting between Frances and Thomas belongs almost four years earlier. They are supposed to have married soon after the Kelly riot in 1747. (I have found no record of their marriage, but their first child was born March 9, 1748, Register of St. Mary's Church, Dublin.) If they met in 1743 and married in 1747, the whirlwind courtship described by Alicia, and required by her mistaken dating of *The Owls*, lengthens out over several years. This is not only more in keeping with Sheridan's conservative instincts, but also more understandable in terms of his other preoccupations at the time of the riot. That he could have met, wooed, won, and married Frances in the few crowded weeks after that upsetting event (see Ch. IV) seemed incredible even for a man of Sheridan's youthful energy. A tantalizingly undated letter from Sheridan's sister Eliza to Miss Frances Chamberlaine which appears in the *Lefanu MSS* seems to support the view that Frances knew Sheridan well, before the Kelly riot.

[59] Sheridan's behavior and feelings were not unique within the theater. Eight years before, Charles Macklin had accidentally killed a fellow actor at Drury Lane in a dispute over a wig. (Cibber had been in the company when this happened.) Macklin, who was convicted of manslaughter, defended himself at his trial, saying: "The wig I then used was proper for the new play, and absolutely necessary for my character, the whole force of the poet's wit depending on the lean meagre looks of one that wanted food. This wig being so fit for my purpose, and hearing that the deceased had got it, I said to him . . . [the fatal quarrel followed]" ("An Apology for the Conduct of Mr. Charles Macklin," pp. 34–35; see also Appleton, *Charles Macklin*, pp. 29–33).

have been less important. But Sheridan was proud. (His enemies called him vain.) His pride had led to his behavior at the theater and later to his almost as childish threats to leave Ireland: his enemies, "a few Snakes in the Grass," were driving him from that fair field.[60] These enemies could hardly have been reduced by such a display of importance; but he insisted that they had all been created by his success, the public's approval of him, and, in the case of Cibber, a desire to build his own fame on the wreckage of another's.[61] Throughout his life Sheridan evoked the strongest feelings in others —of devotion or of animosity. In his coming struggles for reform an active and persisting enmity for *him* (aside from his ideas) was always an additional force to be overcome. That it often stemmed from forces within him was a fact which he could never see and one which made his task no easier.

For Sheridan himself the Cato affair so wounded his sensibilities that he often afterward felt surrounded by enemies. But it also showed him the dangers of descending to personalities [62] in paper wars. Although the need to defend his actions always drew him into such battles, he tried, after this, to keep to large issues even when his antagonists spared him nothing.

Further, the Cato affair seems to have made clear to Sheridan certain weaknesses in theatrical management which he was later to reform: the use of borrowed costumes; the custom of dismissing audiences; and the practice of reading a missing actor's part. The fact that Cato's robe had been borrowed from a Dublin lady, who had bought it at a London auction, was not unusual in 1743; clothing was sometimes lent, sometimes donated, often cast off from private wardrobes of well-to-do people.[63] Later Manager Sheridan took pride in the valuable wardrobe which he had built up for Smock-Alley Theater. Borrowed costumes, apt to be snatched away at the wrong moment, became rare.

Nor was Sheridan's impulse to dismiss the *Cato* audience unusual at the time. Irish audiences were frequently "disappointed," mainly because the house was too thin to make the performance worth while. A Cibber epistle implies that the *real* reason for Sheridan's behavior "on the fatal night" was the unexpected thinness of the audience.[64]

---

[60] *Cibber and Sheridan*, p. 10.   [61] *Ibid.*

[62] In his second letter to the public Sheridan had referred to Cibber's marital difficulties, thereby inspiring Cibber to further name-calling (*ibid.*, p. 29).

[63] Stockwell, pp. 286–290.   [64] *Cibber and Sheridan*, p. 42.

Sheridan's rather frequent deferrals had evoked suspicion earlier; and a month before, he had explained in the press that he had postponed *King Lear* because of a sudden incapacitating illness and not for the reasons spread by "malicious or designing Persons." [65] Although Sheridan's health was always uncertain, the dismissed house became uncommon within a few years, after his improvements kept the income steady enough to carry an occasional thin night.

By reading Sheridan's role while he acted his own, Cibber was doing nothing strange either, surprising as the procedure seems today. Spranger Barry later volunteered to read a part in this way; and his offer too was made to embarrass Sheridan. But in refusing Barry Sheridan pointed out that notices had led the public to expect certain players in certain parts; [66] the old unprofessional stopgap device was thus discouraged later at Smock-Alley.

In the more efficient theater run by Sheridan, the experience of Cato's robe would not be repeated.

The next fall Cibber was back in England, but this new season of 1743–44 brought Sheridan other complications and further publicity, this time on more important issues. By October the long-planned union of the theaters was effected, [67] the combined company intending to perform at Aungier-Street. Immediately Sheridan saw this move as an opportunity for himself; and when the gentlemen proprietors made him overtures of an acting spot in their united company at a good salary, [68] he countered by offering them £500 a year for the

---

[65] *Dublin Journal*, June 14–18 and 18–21, 1743.   [66] See Ch. III, p. 73.

[67] *Dublin Journal*, October 1–4, 1743: "We are informed, that the Gentlemen Proprietors of both Theatres, have finally agreed all their Affairs relating to both Houses, and are resolved to spare no Pains or Expence, to entertain the Town in the most agreeable Manner."

[68] The amount varies depending upon how it is computed and who describes it. An anonymous letter writer to the *Journal*, representing the proprietors' point of view, says that Sheridan was offered nearly £6 a week for acting only once a week, a sum never given to any but Quin and other "Birds of Prey from London." The reduction to a weekly performance was a concession to Sheridan's delicate constitution (Letter to the *Dublin Journal*, copied by J. P. Kemble in his *Manuscript Diary* for November 1743). Sheridan's reply (*Dublin Journal*, November 12–15, 1743) corrects the false impression given here by explaining that he would be getting £6 a week only up to the beginning of benefits in March; in short, the total offered by the proprietors was only £100 for the season, less than the total offered to Mrs. Furnival and Madame Chateauneuf, and about a third of that paid to Mr. Arne and Mr. Lowe. A third letter in response to this adds that Sheridan would have received £100 more from his

theater if they would let him have sole control; he promised "to give them good Security for the Payment of it." [69] Still unsatisfied by his success as Dublin's leading player, and undiscouraged by the summer's late unpleasantness, Sheridan now wanted to take on the responsibility of managing a Dublin theater. After nine months under Phillips' inept direction, he had ideas for improving it too.

The proprietors, who had less confidence in his inexperience or, perhaps, in his financial sources, rejected his plan. So Sheridan went over to help Elrington manage [70] the players who had been dropped in the merging; these new-sprung rivals of the united company had obtained from the former manager, Duval—fraudulently, says Hitchcock [71]—a lease on Smock-Alley, where they were unexpectedly arranging to open.[72] With characteristic zeal Sheridan spent time going about town to "the Houses of all Persons of Quality and Distinction (he could have Access to)," imploring support for this undertaking "as an Act of Generosity and Charity to him." His activity was dimly viewed by an opponent, who, in reporting it thus, added that no one who had refused the salary offered Sheridan could claim to be an object of charity.[73]

---

benefit, and that Mrs. Furnival averaged about 30s. for every acting night, Miss Chateauneuf about 40s. Sheridan would have been getting £10 (*Dublin Journal*, November 19–22, 1743).

[69] *Dublin Journal*, November 12–15, 1743.

[70] The anonymous letter (Kemble, *Manuscript Diary*, November 1743) reports that one or more of the former managers had "absconded." Presumably then Sheridan stepped in and joined Elrington (probably Ralph) in the direction. That Sheridan became one of the managers is suggested by remarks in *Dublin Journal* letters and announcements (see notes 75 and 79).

[71] Hitchcock, I, 137. It is unlikely that Sheridan, so upright in business matters, participated knowingly in any fraud here. Records show that the financial affairs of the two theaters were in a great snarl at this time; there may have been no fraud, just confusion and a long-standing want of funds. Furthermore, certain matters of ownership were under litigation, and therefore unsettled at the moment.

[72] *Dublin Journal*, October 25–29, 1743.

[73] The anonymous letter (Kemble, *Manuscript Diary*, November 1743). Miss Stockwell, who quotes this letter in full (pp. 83–85), feels that its author was probably Duval. In this confusing epistle first occurs the accusation that the scratched company's managers (perhaps Elrington was one) had tricked Duval into a lease. They had also managed to borrow back the "Cloaths and Scenes," sold long since for rent due the Ground Landlord. Furthermore, because they had owed their players £500, they had either run away or denied their debts. Sheridan obviously had not run away. He may, at this point, have just joined the group.

In November the "aggrieved" [74] opposition at Smock-Alley opened their season with Sheridan as Richard III, Elrington as King Henry, and "all the rest of the Parts by Persons who never appeared on this Stage." [75] Most of the scratched players had dropped out, apparently, and the new management had been forced to bring in a strolling company from the north of Ireland. From the beginning they were under attack in the press. Charges made against them by an anonymous letter writer include acting "in a House they have no Right to," "with Cloaths & Scenes that do not belong to them," "by a Lease neither good in itself, nor having paid the Conditions of it." [76] Rightfully theirs or not, the scenes were soon lost to them, seized as the property of a Mr. Norris; the "Cloaths," however, they saved by removing them "from Place to Place"; [77] yet, despite the absence of scenes and the presence of a generally inferior company, the admission price seems to have been raised, much to the outrage of another letter writer to the *Journal*.[78]

The paper fight this time was relatively genteel and brief, Sheridan, as he says, having "already experienc'd the ill Consequences" of such warfare. That he had risen above the petty bickerings of personalities and was this soon thinking of the future of the Dublin theaters is shown by his single, restrained letter to the *Dublin Journal*, in which he tells of a pamphlet he plans to publish, *The Groans of the Stage*. Here he will give his ideas about the present state of the stage, the causes for the disputes and the way of stopping them. He will also try to justify his own conduct and to show that he has entered upon a "very laborious, painful, and hazardous Undertaking, with very little Prospect of Gain, purely with an Intent to save the Stage from Ruin, and . . . to put it on a good Footing for the

[74] Hitchcock, I, 137.

[75] Advance notice in the *Dublin Journal*, October 25–29, 1743. What happened to the rest of the scratched company is not clear, since notices at this time gave the names of only principal players. The anonymous letter writer (Kemble, *Manuscript Diary*, November 1743) worries about the fate of the "poor Strollers from the North," for since the "two Kings [Sheridan and Elrington] are to divide the Profits, which I suppose is all the Money they can finger (as they did last Winter) it would have been more human in these Managers to have engaged a Set of Players out of Punch's Theatre, who would have been content with the Honour of acting with these Heroes, and never mutiny for Want of Subsistence."

[76] The anonymous letter (Kemble, *Manuscript Diary*, November 1743).

[77] *Dublin Journal*, November 5–8, 1743.

[78] *Ibid*. This letter writer speaks of the sad "Set of Players, who have the modesty to advance their Prices for such Sadness."

future." This pamphlet, lost now, would be useful in giving us Sheridan's early ideas, particularly on one thesis which he soon abandoned: that "the Stage would be entirely and for ever destroyed in this Kingdom," if "the Scheme succeeded of uniting the Houses." [79] Not long after, he was to think the exact opposite. His actual experiences in managing Smock-Alley were to teach him that two rival theaters could not survive in Dublin.

This lesson began right away. Although Sheridan and his feeble company struggled on into the winter, they were impossibly handicapped by the united theater's competition. Benefit performances started only two weeks after opening [80]—a desperate sign of the need to increase attendance through subscriptions. Sheridan's expectation that his drawing power could sustain Smock-Alley faded soon and fast.

In his single letter to the press in November Sheridan had said that to save the stage from ruin he had "neglected the fairest Opportunity that ever a young Actor had of shewing himself to Advantage in London," and had declined large proposals made to him from there.[81] By January the lure of London had brightened, as Smock-Alley affairs grew ever darker, and on January 16 Sheridan made his last appearance of the season.[82] This date marked, almost to the day, the end of Sheridan's first year in the theater—an eventful first year of serving as the principal actor, carrying on a feud with a fellow player, and managing a poverty-stricken, failing company. He had also mastered at least twelve roles in this short space of time.[83]

---

[79] *Ibid.*, November 12–15, 1743. In the November 22–26 issue appears an announcement that within a few days will be published "the Case truely and fairly stated between the Gentlemen Proprietors of both Theatres, and the pretended Managers of Smock Alley Company," exposing the fraud, trickery, et cetera of the latter, "together with authentick Letters from Mr. Sheridan, to some of the Gentlemen Proprietors, relating to the uniting their Houses; by which Letters the Publick may judge of that Gentleman's Sincerity; with Proofs of the Facts there laid down, and the Whole very proper to be bound up with Mr. Sheridan's Groans." It seems that this pamphlet has not come down to us.

[80] The first of these, *Julius Caesar*, was scheduled for November 17 (*Dublin Journal*, November 12–15, 1743).

[81] *Dublin Journal*, November 12–15, 1743.

[82] *Ibid.*, January 10–14, 1744.

[83] They were Richard III (January 29), Mithridates (February 3) (this was not Lee's play, but one "taken from Racine"), Hamlet (February 28), Brutus (March 17), Charles in *Love Makes a Man* (April 12), Othello (April 14), Lord Townley in *The Provoked Husband* (April 18), Lear (June 23), Horatio

Even before Sheridan left for England the Smock-Alley group had collapsed without him, and the united company from Aungier-Street had taken over both theaters.[84] He was probably still in Dublin and may even have been in the audience on February 15, 1744, when an event portentous to his future took place. Spranger Barry, the man who was to provoke Sheridan's theatrical downfall, made his debut with the united company in circumstances reminiscent of Sheridan's first appearance.[85] This young man, handsome, graceful, and silver-tongued, won Dublin's love as Sheridan had won its admiration the year before; he quickly became the united company's leading actor and later seems to have taken over at least its partial management.[86]

With Barry's star thus rising, perhaps it was well that Sheridan was off for England. And, as it turned out, his year abroad was precisely what his career needed. His arrival in London on March 17, 1744—just ten years after he left Westminster School—was enough of an event to be noted in the *General Advertiser:* "Mr. Sheridan, the celebrated Comedian, is arrived . . . from Dublin." [87] As a celebrated player, he was wanted by both the important London theaters. He played in Covent Garden under Rich in the spring of 1744, opening as Hamlet on March 31; during April he acted other roles he had already learned. His second appearance in *Macbeth* on May 1 was "by particular desire."

(June 27), Cato (July 7), Macbeth (December 8), and Pierre (December 22) (taken from *Dublin Journal* notices). In these notices Richard, Mithridates, Hamlet, Charles, Lear, Cato, Macbeth, and Pierre are specifically advertised as Sheridan's first appearance in each role. The others are not.

[84] During Sheridan's absence an important step in Irish theatrical history was taken, a step which, however, had no effect for some time. In October 1744, by request of "several Gentlemen and Ladies of Distinction," the pit was opened to ladies "at the same Price as the Gentlemen" (*Dublin Journal*, October 23–27, 1744)—an innovation already in practice in London and elsewhere in Ireland. But the old custom, as well as the hard benches crowded with often boisterous and drunken gentlemen, seems to have deterred ladies from the pit for years. At least through Sheridan's regime we find no mention of any but men in that section except on benefit nights, when the front part of the pit was sometimes railed off into boxes for the special use of the ladies. Even in O'Keeffe's time (1770) no female sat in the pit (1, 287).

[85] Barry's first appearance was as Othello; the play was at Smock-Alley and for his benefit (*Dublin Journal*, February 11–14, 1744).

[86] Sheridan, in *An Humble Appeal* (p. 17), speaks of the united company "with Mr. Barry at their Head."

[87] Quoted by Genest, IV, 64.

The next fall (of 1744) he was at Drury Lane under Fleetwood, driven by circumstances into acting the well-cut pebble to Garrick's diamond. He was not a regular member of the company, either here or at Covent Garden; he acted as a guest star, on shares. His first appearance at Drury Lane was on October 20, the night after Garrick's opening. From then on he played (except for a three-month gap from mid-December to March) about once a week in leading roles and usually opposite Mrs. Cibber; Garrick played several times a week and usually opposite Mrs. Woffington. In choice of roles Garrick clearly had the preference: he appeared regularly in Sheridan's favorite characters—Hamlet, Lear, Macbeth, Richard III, and, for the first time, Othello. Except for one performance each as Hamlet, Othello, and Richard III—the first two for his benefits—Sheridan had to be content with repeating Horatio, Pierre, and Tamerlane,[88] three less popular roles and not even Shakespearean. Once Garrick and Sheridan acted together, with Mrs. Cibber, in a new play, Thomson's *Tancred and Sigismunda,* with Garrick playing the title role. Many famous or soon-to-be-famous performers were in the company this season, and Sheridan had the chance of watching Delane, Havard, the Macklins, Mrs. Woffington, and Mrs. Cibber firsthand, to say nothing of his master and inspiration, Garrick. His position as a guest star in this stellar company is noteworthy.

Sheridan was given two benefits during the season, a generous number; but he found Fleetwood's careless management a trial. His *Hamlet* benefit had been arranged so hastily that he lacked time to call upon possible subscribers in accordance with eighteenth-century custom. A public announcement expressed Sheridan's regrets in his characteristic phrasing: "As his benefit was not appointed till last Friday, he humbly hopes that such Ladies and Gentlemen, as he shall omit to wait upon, will impute it rather to a want of time, than to a want of respect and knowledge of his duty." Shortly before, he had been incommoded when the "Disturbance" over Fleetwood's raised prices had closed the house and canceled two of his performances.[89] This must have been his first experience with a theatrical riot

---

[88] Sheridan's appearance as Tamerlane on November 5, 1744, seems to have been his first time in this role. The play was repeated four times during the following months (*London Stage,* Pt. 3, pp. 1,128–49).

[89] Information on Sheridan's theatrical activities in London may be found in Genest, IV, 74–75, 136–151; Winston's *Manuscript Diary;* and *London Stage,* Pt. 3, seasons of 1743–45. Notices of Sheridan's benefits show that he

from the other side of the curtain. As a player on shares he stood to lose financially each time he did not perform.

In England Sheridan became acquainted with that amazing young lady George Anne Bellamy, when she was visiting Peg Woffington in Teddington. Her account of him, undated and ambiguous in parts, seems to show that he lived in Kingston sometime during this second visit to England, perhaps in the summer of 1744. There, although not yet married, he entertained with an already famous hospitality which recalls his father's. He was this soon, George Anne shows, Garrick's competitor and a "celebrated" actor even to the English theatrical set, many of whom were originally Irish. Her memoirs throw brief light on Garrick's attitude toward him at this time. While visiting Peg's sister, she says:

> I became acquainted with Mr. Sheridan, a celebrated actor, and a competitor of the incomparable Garrick. This gentleman invited us to his apartments, which were generally crowded with Irish gentlemen from the college of Dublin. Roscius, at this time, languished to be reconciled to Mrs. Woffington, with whom he had formerly lived upon terms of intimacy. For this purpose he obtruded himself in the house of a gentleman at Kingston, of whose talents, which were great, he was jealous to a degree, though they lay *in a different line of acting*. Mr. Sheridan's hospitality was as well known as Garrick's parsimony; of which the latter condescended to avail himself. I flatter myself I shall be credited in this assertion, as I declare I have no reason to be partial to the former, as will appear in the course of the ensuing letters.[90]

Sheridan's success in London was useful if only for the impression it made on Dublin; but it destroyed the friendship between him and Garrick. Almost from the beginning a rivalry had been set up between the two by officious friends. Garrick became needlessly jealous, and a quarrel followed which was still unreconciled when Sheridan

---

was living in Bridges Street, Covent Garden, in April 1744, and in Russell Street, Covent Garden, in April 1745 (*London Stage*, Pt. 3, pp. 1,102, 1,170).

[90] Bellamy, I, 27. Bellamy's shift to "*a* gentleman" and his *house* right after her description of Sheridan and his *apartments* is confusing. Her italicized clause may or may not contain a *double-entendre*, but her observation that Garrick availed himself of Sheridan's hospitality seems to tie the Kingston gentleman and Sheridan together.

left for Dublin.[91] That Sheridan was more deeply hurt than Garrick is suggested by the lifelong coolness he felt for the man who once was his inspiration and master. The wound still smarted when he wrote the next summer, inviting Garrick to join his Smock-Alley company, but warning him to expect nothing from his friendship, for he owed him none.[92]

In Dublin, meanwhile, the united company was having a bad time. Competition from a new theater in Capel-Street was threatening; and Barry, good though he was at acting, had no talent, as later events showed, for managing a theater. Hitchcock describes the managers' arrival one evening at the theater, dinnerless: "The first shilling that came into the house they dispatched for a loin of mutton, the second for bread, the third for liquor, and so on till they had satisfied the calls of nature, when they prepared for the business of the night."[93] Later Sheridan, in his *Humble Appeal* written in 1758, reminded his readers of this grim period in 1745, when the company under Barry "did not during the whole Season play three Times to Charges, and for three successive Weeks in the height of the Season they either dismissed, or gave out no Plays."[94] Conditions such as he described are dimly reflected in the newspapers. There are notices of only two performances in the Dublin theaters for over a month from December 10, 1744, to January 17, 1745.[95] Notices for performances during November had been intermittent. The regular stage in Dublin was dwindling away, while Stretch's puppet show, its only serious rival, prospered. This unusual situation stirred public concern and called for unusual action.

The action taken by the united theater's thirty-odd[96] gentlemen proprietors "as their dernier resort [the wording is Hitchcock's], and at the request of the public"[97] was a surprise indeed. Turning to the young actor of only two years' experience, the same one who had treated them so cavalierly not long before, they approached Sheridan now with the very offer which they themselves had rejected a year ago: the management of the united theaters. Theatrical

[91] Davies, I, 84. [92] *Ibid.* [93] Hitchcock, I, 157.
[94] Sheridan, *An Humble Appeal*, p. 17.
[95] On January 17, 1745 the New Theatre opened in Capel-Street under Phillips' management for a brief time. Not much later Phillips ran off to England, taking "more Money than his own along with him" (Stockwell, pp. 86–87).
[96] Victor, a year later, speaks of thirty-six proprietors (*Original Letters*, I, 121; Letter of December 23, 1746).
[97] Hitchcock, I, 149.

tempers cool quickly if desperation or advantage—or public demand —presses. Besides, Sheridan was an energetic young man with ideas as well as ideals. His responses to them a year ago had shown that. Finally—and importantly—he was the most popular and successful Irish actor of the time, one who had been called to London, where he had made an impression on English audiences. In this century the leading actor frequently managed his theater as the acting-manager, a custom much in vogue until Richard Brinsley Sheridan, not an actor, took over Drury Lane from Garrick. Thus Thomas Sheridan, young and inexperienced as he was, was offered the position which for two years he had wanted more than anything in the world. It was a great triumph.

More than that, it put him in a position to bargain: his management was to be *on trial for a year only* "in order that he might judge what reasonable Expectation of Profit there should be on future Occasions." [98] Although he did not have, during this next year, the "sole direction and management" with "unlimited authority," which Hitchcock claims the proprietors offered him,[99] the position gave him the right to hire his company, plan its offerings, and bear the title of "manager."

Probably to discuss the proprietors' offer and perhaps to reach final terms, Sheridan left Drury Lane for three months in the winter of 1744–45 [100] and returned to Ireland. That he returned as a friend to the group he had left as a hated competitor is shown when he appeared for his own benefit with the united company on February 1, 1745.[101] His performance at Smock-Alley reactivated the Irish theater after its month and a half of dormancy, and was followed by a whole series of benefits, for Mr. Barry, Mrs. Dyer, et cetera. But he still had commitments at Drury Lane. In March he was back there, representing Siffredi in *Tancred and Sigismunda,* which Davies claims was presented under the patronage of Pitt and Lyttleton, both of whom attended rehearsals regularly.[102] By late spring he was again in Dublin,[103] acting into the summer, at a time when the theater was usually shut unless opened for visiting celebrities, like Quin and

[98] Sheridan, *An Humble Appeal*, p. 17.   [99] Hitchcock, I, 149.

[100] This explains the three months' gap in Sheridan's appearances at Drury Lane.

[101] *Dublin Journal*, January 26–29, 1745.   [102] Davies, I, 78–79.

[103] Hitchcock (I, 149) says that Sheridan returned to Dublin in May. There are later indications that Sheridan's agreement with the proprietors began on May 1 (see Ch. v), a date which allowed him to finish out his season at Drury Lane.

Garrick. His London success had not only saved him from being eclipsed by Barry; it had turned him into a visiting celebrity.

In all, Sheridan acted only four or five times [104] during the summer of 1745, twice for his own benefit. He was busy with plans for his first season as manager. The next fall some of the old company would be with him—Barry, Ralph Elrington, Mrs. Furnival, et cetera—but new talent was needed to revive Dublin's interest. A good company was always Sheridan's first concern because its drawing power was essential to other improvements. Especially now in this year of trial a good company was vital; on its success in winning back the Dublin public his future decision depended.

[104] On one of these he played Zanga in *The Revenge* for the first time (July 18).

CHAPTER III

The Garrick Winter, 1745-1746

IT is no surprise, then, to find the new Smock-Alley manager, after his three weeks of summer performances in Dublin, hurrying back to England "to raise recruits" for the next winter. This is the expression used by George Anne Bellamy, who turned out to be one of his prize recruits. Yet her engagement seemed almost accidental: Sheridan happened, one morning in London, to meet her mother on her way to ask Manager Rich of Covent Garden whether he wished to engage her daughter. Sheridan remarked that he would like Miss Bellamy to come to Dublin, and Rich, when consulted, endorsed the new idea heartily, since George Anne would have a chance not only to appear in every major role but also to "receive the instructions of so great a master." Whether or not Rich believed all that his argument asserts, Sheridan's reputation as a master had by this time reached such proportions that it could be used to persuade Mrs. Bellamy. George Anne, who had been out of town while her future was being decided, found Sheridan awaiting her at her Chelsea lodgings on her return; and she then and there concluded her agreement with him.[1]

Sheridan's engagement of George Anne Bellamy to play principal characters—indeed, as it turned out, to supplant the veteran Mrs. Furnival—is an early instance of his ability to sense potentialities in young, sometimes untried actors. George Anne had had some experience, more than she admits and over a longer period; the season before, when Sheridan was acting at Drury Lane, she had ingratiated herself enough with Quin and Rich to appear at Covent Garden in at least seven different roles,[2] and Sheridan undoubtedly had seen her there. Yet, in comparison to others he might have solicited, she was a fledgling. She fully justified his foresight, however, both in her success at Dublin and in her career afterward. O'Keeffe's description of her a little later in her life explains some but not all of her attrac-

---

[1] Bellamy, I, 61–62.

[2] *London Stage*, Pt. 3, pp. 1,744–45, shows her playing in Covent Garden as Monimia (*The Orphan*), Aspasia (*The Maid's Tragedy*), Lucia (*Cato*), Celia (*Volpone*), Blanch (*Papal Tyranny*), Arsinoe (*Mariamne*), and Anne Bullen (*Henry VIII*).

tion: "The acting of Mrs. Bellamy [3] gave me great delight: she was very beautiful, blue eyes, and very fair. . . . Garrick being a little man, and Mrs. Bellamy not very tall, he preferred her, for his heroine, to Mrs. Yates or Mrs. Pritchard." [4]

There were other, less important persons in Sheridan's bag of theatrical game, among them a "young adventurer named Lacy" [5] —*not*, as some theatrical historians have thought,[6] James Lacy, the new patentee and manager of Drury Lane—and Mrs. Elmy, Sheridan's former leading lady at Smock-Alley, an actress whose spirits off stage were livelier than on, according to Chetwood.[7] George Anne's mother, herself an old Dublin trouper,[8] "who had conditioned to attend" her daughter, was also in the group which the new man-

---

[3] Like some other unmarried women of her time, Bellamy changed her title from Miss to Mrs. Miss Peg Woffington did the same thing on November 8, 1740, when she was in her twenties (see *DNB*, *v.* "Woffington, Margaret").

[4] O'Keeffe, I, 107.   [5] Bellamy, I, 63.

[6] Hitchcock (I, 150) was among the first to mistakenly put Manager James Lacy of Drury Lane in the Smock-Alley company during the 1745-46 season; his source may have been Davies, who is less definite in his dating but quite wrong in other related facts (Davies, I, 87). Later historians, among them Gilbert (*History*, I, 79) and Knight (*David Garrick*, I, 95) have repeated the error. It is significant that none of these writers were in Dublin that season. Those who were say nothing about the Drury Lane Patentee. Victor, an admiring friend of James Lacy since 1722 (he gives a long account of him in *History*, I, 64-81), would certainly have noted the singular appearance of the new London manager as a minor player in Sheridan's troupe if he had been there. Instead, Victor says only: "When I arrived in Dublin I found my good Friend Mr. Garrick at the Theatre-Royal, with Mr. Sheridan, as Sharers and Adventurers; and Mr. Barry engaged at a Salary by the Proprietors" (*History*, I, 88-89). George Anne's description of "a young adventurer named Lacy" is hardly the one she would have used for the middle-aged, well-to-do, and powerful manager of London's most important theater and a man well known to her, since he had been Rich's assistant at Covent Garden the year before when she was a novice there. Final evidence that James Lacy was not in Ireland in 1745-46 appears in letters from Mrs. Cibber in England to Garrick in Ireland describing Lacy's activities at Drury Lane during this fall (see Garrick, *Private Correspondence*, I, 38-39, 46-47). The younger Lacy seems to have made his debut at Smock-Alley in November (*Dublin Journal* notices) but to have left before the benefit period. Victor (*History*, I, 66) and *The London Stage* (Pt. 3, p. 599) show James Lacy playing under Fielding in the Haymarket as early as 1736.

[7] Chetwood, p. 147.

[8] Mrs. Bellamy, George Anne's mother, had acted at the Aungier-Street opening in 1734 (Chetwood, p. 72), and had appeared at Smock-Alley as early as 1729 (from the unpublished notes of Mrs. William S. Clark).

ager had arranged not only to "frank" to Ireland but even to conduct personally, in what seems to have been an excess of beginner's
zeal. He got them as far as Parkgate, but there the wind proved
contrary and, after committing them to Miss Bellamy's mother, he
left them to set off directly for Holyhead. Under Mrs. Bellamy the
wayfarers continued (enlivened by Mrs. Elmy's off-stage spirits) [9]
and arrived in Dublin to appear on Smock-Alley stage early in
November.[10]

But Sheridan's "grand object," as Hitchcock puts it, was to secure
Garrick to crown his first season as Smock-Alley manager.[11] He must
have conceived of this object from the beginning, since even by July
Garrick was contemplating Smock-Alley for the fall, as letters from
Victor show.[12] Sheridan's idea of asking Garrick was a delicate point:
they had parted in anger and besides, as Hitchcock explains, his own
position and prestige in Dublin might be jeopardized by the comparison. Yet, continues Hitchcock, this man, who later was often
accused of theatrical envy, wished to bring to Dublin the only actor
of whom he had reason to be jealous.[13] One too whose transcendence
would be doubly bitter because he was no longer a friend. Even so,
Sheridan did not hesitate to sacrifice his own feelings for Smock-
Alley's advantage. Only, Garrick must be frankly apprized of the
businesslike motives prompting the new manager. The letter Sheridan wrote explaining this and offering him a position on shares struck
Garrick as "the oddest epistle I ever saw in my life." Unfortunately
lost now, it is indirectly quoted by Davies, probably from memory.
Sheridan is said to have written "that he was then sole manager of
the Irish stage, and should be very happy to see him [Garrick] in
Dublin; he would give him all advantages and encouragement
which he could in reason expect," everything "the best actor had
a right to command," everything, that is, except his friendship. As
for remuneration, he proposed to divide the profits with him after
expenses had been deducted. Garrick's friend, Colonel Wyndham,
on seeing the letter, agreed that it *was* odd but observed that it was
"surely a very honest one: I should certainly depend upon a man
that treated me with that openness and simplicity of heart." [14]

[9] Bellamy, I, 63.　　[10] *Dublin Journal* notices.　　[11] Hitchcock, I, 150.
[12] Victor, *Original Letters*, I, 106. To Wolseley, July 1745. Davies (I, 84)
implies that Garrick had intended to visit Ireland before Sheridan approached
him; but it seems unlikely that he would have made such plans without an
invitation when he knew that Sheridan felt unfriendly.
[13] Hitchcock, I, 150–151.　　[14] Davies, I, 84–85.

Although dickering with Drury Lane, Garrick had been hoping for just such a definite offer from Ireland. Both Barry and Sheridan, he knew, were to be in Dublin the coming winter—"which must," he observed, to both actors' credit, "put the wise ones of Drury-Lane into great difficulties." [15] James Lacy, the new Drury Lane patentee, had outraged his feelings in several ways, by offering him too little money and, most seriously, by accusing him of "making Interest in Ireland" while under articles to him. Although doubtless instituting no advances, Garrick had received in Litchfield a gentleman from the Smock-Alley management, possibly Sheridan himself, lingering in England to press his proposals. Sheridan's letter,[16] with its specific terms, strengthened Garrick's position. But, not surprisingly, he kept the new Smock-Alley manager suspended for weeks while he contemplated other possibilities. With the prospect of London theaters emptied by the Scottish rebellion, he could volunteer to fight for his king. (He did, and was rejected.) With Lacy so impossible, he could accept a late, unexpected offer from Rich of Covent Garden.[17] But in the end he suddenly did what he had been more and more leaning to as the season progressed: he sailed to Ireland. It was his second and his last trip. On his first, three years earlier, his arrival had been relatively unmarked; but now he was given a separate notice in the *Dublin Journal*: "Sunday morning [November 24] Mr. Garrick the celebrated Player arrived here from England." [18] The same time span had brought a more notable transfiguration to Sheridan. Three years earlier he had been only an aspiring spectator, humbly acknowledging Garrick as master, hoping to be his friend. Now he no longer wished to be Garrick's friend, but—in a sense, at least—he was Garrick's master.

The oddity of this reversal must have been in the consciousness of both when, shortly after Garrick's arrival, there arose a financial

---

[15] Garrick, *Letters*, I, 50, 54.

[16] *Ibid.*, pp. 54, 58. In a letter to his friend Draper (post October 10, 1745) Garrick mentions Sheridan's offer, at the same time reporting that Mr. Wyndham (who had been visiting him in Litchfield) had left that morning (pp. 57–58). In another letter from Litchfield (October 26, 1745) Garrick says he has had "a most civil letter" from Sheridan (*ibid.*, p. 67). This may have been a later letter from Sheridan following up the offer which Garrick and Wyndham had regarded as so odd.

[17] *Ibid.*, pp. 56–57, 68. Garrick even went so far as to draw up, with Rich, a memorandum contracting to perform for him during the coming season.

[18] *Dublin Journal*, November 23–26, 1745.

dispute, which was resolved in a strange way described by Davies. In spite of Sheridan's specific offer, Garrick had come to Ireland uncommitted, apparently hoping to better Sheridan's terms by treating with the proprietors. Even by December 1 he still had not signed a contract. What he wanted was a set sum for the season. Sheridan, who argued that the other players ought not to lose by Garrick's gain, would yield neither to the proprietors nor to Garrick on the provisions of his first proposal—that Garrick perform with him on equal shares. After a lengthy argument between the two actors Sheridan, as Davies reports it, drew out his watch and insisted upon an answer in a certain number of minutes. Garrick submitted. Hitchcock, who copies this incident from Davies almost verbatim, concludes with his own typically optimistic comment: ". . . and the affair terminated in the most amicable manner." [19] How amicable Garrick felt can be seen in his explosive letter to his friend Draper. Calling Sheridan a name that later editors declined to print, he accused him of trying to prevent his engagement (out of jealousy, he implies, although he admits at the same time that he had had the strongest solicitations from him). The final terms, he felt, were very indifferent (a third of the profits were to go to the proprietors). But he was to be joint manager with Sheridan. If the latter had not been engaged, he would have had much more, he wrote to Draper; and the gentlemen proprietors regretted not having known his plans earlier, before taking on Sheridan [20] (the preceding February, presumably). There may have been still another source for Garrick's irritation: the knowledge that morally Sheridan had the right of the whole issue.

Weeks before Garrick's arrival Sheridan had begun the 1745–46 season and he continued to assume, probably without protest from his co-manager, the main burden of the management. Garrick's few letters from this time speak only of roles he was learning or playing and of the gay time he was having in Dublin society, eating, drinking, and being rather idle, as certainly Sheridan was not. But his mere presence was enough to give the season an unprecedented brilliance, a brilliance not to be surpassed in Dublin until the twentieth century. Besides Garrick (and Miss Bellamy), there was Spranger Barry, already a member of the united company. Barry, whose physical endowment and acting abilities complemented Sheridan's, had not yet

[19] Garrick, *Letters*, i, 68–69; Davies, i, 85; Hitchcock, i, 152.
[20] Garrick, *Letters*, i, 69.

reached his full fame. Later he and Sheridan were regarded as Garrick's only serious rivals. In after years Dubliners looking back on their theatrical history remark nostalgically of the phenomenal season when Garrick, Sheridan, and Barry were playing under one roof. Even at the time, the blasé Colley Cibber, writing to Benjamin Victor in March 1746, observes that "your *Hibernian* theatre seems to be in a much better Way than the *British*" [21]—truly a miraculous accomplishment for Sheridan, when one considers the Irish theater's desperation a year earlier.

Although Garrick did not appear until December 9, the first play of the season had opened on October 30. With true showmanship Sheridan, as Hitchcock points out,[22] built up his attractions bit by bit, reserving his best for later, when audience appetites began to fail. Miss Bellamy was saved till November 11, making her first appearance in *The Orphan* with Barry and Sheridan. Sheridan's benefit on November 21, marking his first time as Sir Harry Wildair in *The Constant Couple* and performed by command of the Earl of Chesterfield, then Lord Lieutenant, was made into a highly special occasion. Prices were raised because of the extra demand for places, pit and boxes going up to a crown. When all the boxes were taken, room was provided for ladies on stage and in the pit. The stage was transformed into "an Amphitheatre, illuminated with Wax Candles, and made warm and commodious for Ladies," who graced the performance patriotically wearing Irish poplins.[23] The temporary reconstruction of the stage, whereby tiers of benches were erected around the back in a semicircle to accommodate a surplus crowd, was not unusual at benefit performances. Both Smock-Alley and Aungier-Street being available to the united company, the theater used for Sheridan's benefit and during most of the fall was Aungier-Street, with its larger stage and smaller audience accommodation. After Garrick's arrival the company moved to Smock-Alley to take care of the larger crowds. Significantly, Sheridan's May 8th performance in *The Merchant of Venice* is advertised for Aungier-Street again,[24] Garrick having left at the end of April.

[21] Victor, *History*, II, 205.   [22] Hitchcock, I, 160.

[23] *Dublin Journal*, November 16–19 and 19–23, 1745. The latter issue reports "a most numerous and polite Audience at Mr. Sheridan's Benefit," but Garrick, arriving in Dublin a few days after, wrote to Draper that Sheridan had "hurt himself as an actor among his friends" by playing Sir Harry Wildair (*Letters*, I, 69). This was not one of Sheridan's best parts.

[24] But Smock-Alley was used for other performances after Garrick's departure.

Many of Sheridan's accomplishments during this winter must have gratified him. His management of so many topflight actors, some of them unfriendly with others, most of them defensive of their prestige, was not so permanent a contribution to stage history as were some of his other achievements, but at the time it surely loomed as his most difficult task. Performances were arranged judiciously. Garrick at first starred alone in roles like Hamlet and Richard III, Sheridan's favorite parts. His success was reflected in many ways: prices were raised, new regulations were needed to take care of the crowds of people and carriages, command performances were numerous. A rare sort of news item appeared in the *Dublin Journal* for December 17–21:

> Last Night the Comedy of the Rehearsal was acted for the Benefit of Mr. Garrick, to the most polite and crowded Audience that hath been seen at any Play: His Excellency the Earl of Chesterfield, by whose Command it was performed, was present; and vast Numbers of People went away for Want of Room.

Poems to Garrick were printed almost weekly in the newspaper. Witness, for instance, this epigram, somewhat at a loss for a rime.

> Hearing that aged Crows are learn'd and wise,
>   I ask'd the antient famous one, at Warrick
> Which of all Actors best deserv'd the Prize?
>   *Roscius* it could not say—but—*Garrick—Garrick.*[25]

In January Sheridan began to accompany Garrick, sometimes featuring Garrick, sometimes himself. For example, in a notice of *The Fair Penitent*, given January 2, both actors were announced in large print, but Garrick's name appeared above Sheridan's. A later notice of the same play (to be reenacted February 7) gave Sheridan first, Garrick second, still in the same roles. A January 9th performance of *The Orphan* was advertised with Sheridan first; [26] for a February

[25] *Dublin Journal*, December 17–21, 1745. Garrick, writing to Draper (ca. December 26), exclaims "Business here is prodigious . . ." (*Letters*, I, 74).

[26] Of *The Fair Penitent* Garrick writes (*Letters*, I, 75): "I have just now played Lothario to a very good house; I never was in better spirits, and indeed Sheridan played the scene well with me." The advertisement for *The Orphan* reads as follows: "The Part of Polydore, by particular Desire, to be performed by Mr. Sheridan, being the first Time of his appearing in the Character; Chamont, Mr. Garrick; Castalio, Mr. Barry; Monimia, Miss Bellamy" (*Dublin Journal*, January 4–7, 1746).

11th performance of the same play, the order of actors was reversed in the notice to put Garrick first. Toward the end of the season Sheridan appeared alone in leading parts already acted by Garrick— as Hamlet and as Orestes in *The Distrest Mother*. The latter role, to become one of Sheridan's favorites, was advertised as played for the first time by both men that winter.[27] Contrariwise, Sheridan appeared first in *Jane Shore* (as Dumont), Garrick playing much later in the same play (as Hastings) at the request of several gentlemen and ladies who "have desired to see Mr. Garrick in a New Character." [28] In February another experiment was tried to keep the balance just and the audience interested. *King John*, not played "these many Years in this Kingdom," was presented with Garrick as the King, Sheridan as the Bastard, this being his first appearance in that role.[29] Later, according to Miss Bellamy, the roles themselves were reversed, Sheridan appearing as the King and Garrick as the Bastard.[30] The *Dublin Journal* shows that a similar alternation was used in the parts of Othello and Iago at two performances given only two days apart (February 26 and 28). To an audience familiar with the play and primarily interested in acting and interpretation of characters—as eighteenth-century audiences were—these opportunities to compare two famous performers interpreting the same part must have been exciting. For the same reason Dublin audiences were always eager to

[27] Garrick is recorded as performing Orestes first on March 6 for the benefit of Barry (*ibid.*, February 22–25, 1746). This takes no account of the amateur performance with Bellamy in Teddington, where, according to Bellamy, Garrick acted Orestes the year before (1, 27). Sheridan's first appearance in the role was March 21.

[28] *Ibid.*, April 19–22, 1746.

[29] *Ibid.*, January 21–25, 1746. *King John* had been revived successfully at Drury Lane the preceding season to compete with Covent Garden's production of *Papal Tyranny*, in which Bellamy had played Blanch. At Drury Lane Garrick had acted John for the first time (February 20, 1745); Delane had played the Bastard. Sheridan, although he was acting there, had had no part in this production (*London Stage* for 1744–45 season).

[30] Bellamy, 1, 74–75. I find no notice of this second performance, with the roles reversed, in the *Dublin Journal*, but probably not all plays were advertised there, especially in the early years of Sheridan's management. Support is given the not too trustworthy Bellamy here by her circumstantial account of a second performance, in which Sheridan played the King, Garrick the Bastard and she Constance. The only production of *King John* advertised in the *Dublin Journal* for this season shows Mrs. Furnival as Constance, Sheridan as the Bastard, and Garrick as the King (February 5). But Hitchcock lists Garrick in the Bastard (see note 32).

see their favorite performers playing a new role, and these occasions were specially advertised in the press, as "being the first time of his appearing in that character." This season, crowded as it was with managerial activities, was also an outstanding one for Sheridan in new parts added to his repertoire—at least nine, and perhaps as many as twelve.[31] To study some of these many "new Characters" Sheridan withdrew for a while to the country (probably to Quilca, at this time owned by his older brother Richard), until hastily summoned back to town to support Garrick, who had been having some thin nights at the theater. While he was away Garrick must have taken over the direction of the theater. Garrick played in only one new role, but was generous in acting a large variety of parts which he already knew; he played nineteen different characters in approximately thirty performances while he was in Dublin.[32] Barry, last year's star, usually played supporting roles. The three top actors appeared together with George Anne Bellamy in several plays besides The Orphan: in The Fair Penitent, for example, and in Tancred and Sigismunda, with which Garrick and Sheridan were familiar from their Drury Lane performances the season before. Thus the acting fare provided by Sheridan was varied and stimulating.

Less impressive were the dramatic offerings: only two "new" plays

[31] New roles for Sheridan announced as the first time of his appearing in the character: Sir Harry Wildair in The Constant Couple; Polydore in The Orphan; Bastard; Iago; Dorax in Don Sebastian; Orestes in The Distrest Mother; Dumont in Jane Shore; Comus; Shylock. Falstaff was prepared for May 14 but was not given. If the roles were reversed in King John, Sheridan probably played the King for the first time this season; and, although they are not announced as firsts, I can find no earlier performances with Sheridan as Chamont in The Orphan or as Ventidius in All for Love, revived after ten years. When a role is not listed as a "first" and yet there is no record of an earlier performance, often the play was a revived one that had not been played for many years. Therefore, the newness of the roles to many of the actors would be obvious to the reader of the advertisement.

[32] The nineteen roles advertised for Garrick were: Hamlet, Richard III, Archer, Bayes, Lothario, Macbeth, Chamont, Lear, Capt. Plume, Sir John Brute, Master Johnny (The School Boy), King John, Tancred, Othello, Iago, Orestes (advertised as first time in that role), Sir Harry Wildair, Hastings, Sharp (The Lying Valet). Probably the Bastard should be added to this list. Hitchcock, who gives a list of Garrick roles for this season, includes the Bastard (1, 161), but not the King in King John. I have added four over Hitchcock's number. In a December letter to Draper, Garrick mentions studying Jaffier and Brass, and contemplating Young Marius and Varanes (Letters, 1, 72), but none of these parts are advertised with Garrick during this season.

were advertised, *Tancred and Sigismunda* and Dryden's *Don Sebastian*, both of which had of course been produced elsewhere, although they had never been acted at Smock-Alley; and one new afterpiece, *The Anatomist*. But the presentation of all the old plays given that season was a new challenge to the new manager; Garrick's presence must have been helpful here.

On the surface at least Sheridan maintained amicable relations with and among his troupe. He came successfully through a dispute between George Anne and Garrick, in which George Anne claims to have been responsible for "the first theatrical humiliation the immortal Roscius ever met with." As she tells it, Sheridan was quite willing for her to play Constance in *King John*, according to a promise made when he first engaged her in London; but Garrick, probably for the reasons acknowledged by George Anne herself—her want of experience and her slight figure "more properly adapted to the lady's son, Prince Arthur" [33]—objected so violently that Sheridan changed his mind. Thereupon George Anne flew to her patroness, Mrs. Butler, who influenced the audience to stay away that night. As a result the house was thin and Garrick much humiliated. (At a later performance of the same play in which Bellamy acted Constance, the house was packed.) [34] This incident, if true, shows Garrick exercising his managerial authority over the strong-willed Sheridan—to his own disadvantage, it would seem.

Nor was Garrick the only colleague humiliated by George Anne that season, according to her account. [35] One evening in the green-room just before the revived performance of *All for Love*, Sheridan was shocked to see Miss Bellamy, ready to go on as Cleopatra, inappropriately dressed in plain white satin. George Anne coolly told

[33] Bellamy, I, 63, 74–75.

[34] *Ibid.*, p. 75. This is the performance of which there is no record in the *Dublin Journal* (see note 30).

[35] Bellamy, I, 81ff. This following incident is erroneously placed by Bellamy at the beginning of the next season (1746–47); *All for Love* had been revived in the fall of 1745, when Barry, whom she mentions as acting in this performance, Mrs. Furnival, and Mrs. Elmy were in the company, as they were not in 1746–47. Bellamy's memory was frequently confused. As Hitchcock says, "All the incidents related by this extraordinary lady in the memoirs of her life, are not in every respect strictly true" (I, 149). Sheridan, reading Bellamy's memoirs in 1785, called this story of Mrs. Furnival's stealing the dress a fabrication of George Anne's own brain (*Betsy Sheridan's Journal*, p. 57). Mrs. Butler, George Anne's patroness, was the wife of Col. Butler, one of the Smock-Alley proprietors. She gave loyal support to the theater.

him that she "had taken the advice [of] Ventidius [Sheridan, amusingly, was playing Ventidius, although Bellamy does not make this point] . . . and had parted with both my clothes and jewels to Antony's wife." Puzzled by this double talk, Sheridan grasped her meaning only when he went on stage and discovered Mrs. Furnival playing Octavia wearing the jewelry and the elegant gown intended for Cleopatra, a costume remodeled for George Anne from a dress worn by the Princess of Wales. Sheridan was "so confounded that it was some time before he could go on with his part." And Mrs. Butler, who had lent George Anne the jewels, threw the audience into an uproar by calling out from her box, "Good Heaven, the woman has got on my diamonds!" At the end of the act Mrs. Furnival was cried off the stage and Mrs. Elmy was called in to finish the part. Mrs. Furnival had already owed the little Bellamy a grudge "on account of my eclipsing her" with the public. George Anne's sense of triumph over her and over Garrick, Barry's attitude toward Sheridan revealed in a letter (to be shown later)—these and other hints indicate that relationships may not have been so harmonious below the surface.[36] But at least no quarrels erupted into the newspapers or the law courts.

One additional source of irritation between Garrick and Sheridan may have been the odd behavior of the Earl of Chesterfield. This patron of the arts gave unusual support as viceroy not only to the Dublin theater, but to other worthy entertainments such as musicals and oratorios. The many command performances of this 1745–46 season bespeak the frequent attendance of the earl, his countess, and other important members of the court at Smock-Alley or Aungier-Street theaters. "On such occasions," according to Miss Stockwell, "the viceroy was received in the vestibule by the patentee of the theatre dressed in regulation court attire and bearing lights in two silver candlesticks. With these, he ushered the Lord and his Lady to

---

[36] In his *Letters* Garrick's relations with Sheridan are not mentioned after his first explosion to Draper. Even there, he notes, "My brother Manager and I at present are civil, so I would not have you say anything about him—I intend to behave in such a manner, that no blame shall light upon me, but (*entre nous*) he is as shifting as Lacy. . . ." Later, around the end of December, Garrick, who had had word that Lacy might fail, was hoping to get a chance at the Drury Lane patent. Although he himself could not leave Dublin until his contract ran out in March, he was promising to send Barry over immediately to keep Drury Lane going, regardless of what it did to Smock-Alley (*Letters*, I, 69, 74).

the vice-regal box." [37] Davies tells us that Chesterfield was very gracious to Sheridan and often admitted his visits at the castle, but "he took not the least notice of Mr. Garrick; nay, when they both waited on him with candles in their hands, on the night of Mr. Garrick's benefit, he spoke very kindly to Sheridan, but did not even return the salute of the other." [38] Yet Chesterfield had requested plays with Garrick in the leading role and, as we have seen, had commanded *The Rehearsal* played at Garrick's benefit. If true, the feeble explanation reported by Davies for the cruel jilt, that "his lordship, when in Ireland, had a mind to convince the people of that kingdom, that his heart was intirely Irish," [39] would hardly have appeased Garrick.

Besides command performances and benefit performances, several other important occasions were marked in the theater that winter. The rebellion, which had threatened in the fall, finally broke out in Scotland; Dubliners showed their loyalty by elaborate celebrations of the Duke of Cumberland's birthday, including, at the theater, a prologue on the occasion by Sheridan and an epilogue by Garrick.[40] After Culloden, Sheridan, whose father had been vaguely suspected of Jacobitism, not only spoke a new prologue "on the Occasion of the glorious and happy Victory . . . over the Rebels in Scotland," [41] but also after another performance "ordered a large Bonfire before the Theatre, and a Barrel of Ale to the Populace, on Account of the Duke's Victory." [42] Sheridan enjoyed doing things on a grand scale; the publicity was desirable and, besides, his loyalty to the crown was heartfelt.

Particularly interesting, however, were the improvements which the new manager introduced during his first year. Some were trivial, as, for example, the occasional elaboration of the advertisements to give more lurid details about the play. *Richard III* might entice more people if they knew they would see "the Distresses and Death of King Henry VI; the artful Acquisition of the Crown by King Richard; the cruel Murder of King Edward V and his Brother in the Tower; the Landing of the Earl of Richmond, &c." [43] Theater no-

---

[37] Stockwell, p. 183.

[38] Davies, I, 86. Later Chesterfield was not so kind to Sheridan.   [39] *Ibid.*

[40] *Dublin Journal*, April 12–15, 1746.   [41] *Ibid.*, April 26–29, 1746.

[42] *Ibid.*, April 29–May 3, 1746.

[43] *Ibid.*, November 9–12, 1745. This elaboration had appeared occasionally in London theater advertisements, and had been used at least once before Sheridan in Dublin (see *Pue's Occurrences*, March 20–23, 1736).

tices in general became more attractive during the year, moving in the January papers from an obscure place in fine print to a prominent position with large type and indented lines. Many coming performances were featured as news items and given extra-large capitals. With another change, the omission of the comic part of *Don Sebastian*, Sheridan inspired a poem, printed in the *Dublin Journal*, "To Mr. Sheridan on his leaving out the Scenes of Ribaldry in Don Sebastian . . . ," wherein he was congratulated on his wisdom, elegance, and polished turn of mind and advised to pursue this track, since success always attends conscious virtue.[44] Amusingly, the comic part had been omitted, according to Sheridan, "on account of the great Length of the Performance," [45] but all favorable publicity was, we can be sure, welcome.

With Garrick's appearance in Dublin and the prestige it restored to the theater, Sheridan grasped the chance to press the public reforms he must have long had in mind. Some were announced as early as Garrick's opening night, on December 9, 1745. For example, to eliminate the footmen who had crowded the Great Room with flaming torches, much to the inconvenience and danger of the public, Sheridan "hoped" in a *Journal* announcement that "everyone" would "give Orders to their Servants to stand without." [46] The crowds around the outside of the theater, greatly increased by Sheridan's new attractions, created worse problems. To relieve the confusion caused by unregulated coach traffic in the narrow alley before the theater, Sheridan inaugurated a "one-way street" system, and guards were placed to prevent violations.[47] So successful was this change that the Music-Hall in Fishamble-Street published similar directions for one of its entertainments.

At Garrick's first performance Sheridan took other, more important steps: no person was to be admitted onstage "at any Time during

---

[44] *Dublin Journal,* March 11–15, 1746.

[45] *Ibid.,* February 18–22, 1746.   [46] *Ibid.,* December 3–7, 1745.

[47] *Ibid.,* December 21–24, 1745: "As there have been several Complaints made of the Difficulty of passing and repassing to and from the Theatre, on Account of the meeting of Coaches in so narrow a Place, it is hoped that all Ladies and Gentlemen will order their Coachmen to drive to the Theatre by the Passage from Essex-street and the Blind-quay, and in going from the Play to enter the Passage from Fishamble-street, which is the only Method to obviate such Inconvenience. And that this Rule may be punctually observed, Guards shall be placed at each of the above Entrances to prevent any Coaches from passing but according to the above Order."

the Performance, under 5*s.* 5*d.*" and no one was to be admitted to the servants' gallery "without a Ticket from the Book-keeper." [48] By these regulations he hoped to keep the worst offenders out of the two most troublesome sections. But the upper gallery, where for 1*s.*1*d.* sat the servants who had spent hours before the play saving unreserved seats elsewhere in the house for their masters and mistresses, continued to be so noisy that by January "the Managers" were threatening in a public notice to close the section entirely and even "never to admit the Servants into the Theatre again." [49] This prospect, which threatened the masters' convenience as well as the servants' pleasure, sobered the gallery temporarily. But Irish servants were an undisciplined lot, whom neither Garrick's golden acting nor Sheridan's direst threats could silence for long, and Smock-Alley was for years to be plagued by their misbehavior. In the end, though, Sheridan devised a way to keep the upper gallery quiet.

As for the audience on stage, Sheridan's feelings about them had been clear from the beginning. His notice at his debut had given a partial picture of the crowded inconvenience of allowing customers (sometimes more than a hundred) [50] on stage during a performance. Another excellent account by Tate Wilkinson illuminates other drawbacks. Wilkinson describes a benefit audience sitting behind the scenes "up to the clouds, with persons of a menial cast on the ground, beaux and no beaux crowding the only entrance." Three or four rows of ill-dressed lads and persons sat on stage in front. And between the audiences on stage and in the galleries there was constant shouting and quarreling amid frequent "golden showers of oranges and half-eaten pippins." [51] As if this were not enough, people could wander from the stage back into the greenroom, crowding the corridors and inter-

[48] *Ibid.*, December 3–7, 1745.

[49] *Ibid.*, January 21–25, 1746. The notice runs for some time and reads as follows: "The Disturbances in the Upper Gallery have been so frequent of late, and occasioned such Interruptions in the Performance, that there have been many Complaints made of it by all Persons who frequent the Theatre. The Managers have us'd all means in their Power to put a Stop to it but hitherto to no Purpose: They are now apprehensive that the only effectual Way to do it will be to shut up the Gallery; and therefore hope that no Gentleman or Lady will take it ill if their Servants are entirely excluded, unless they behave themselves better for the future: They shall have one Night of Trial more next Monday, and if there should be any Noise as usual then, or on any of the succeeding Nights, they are resolv'd to shut up the Passage to the Upper Gallery, and never to admit the Servants into the Theatre again."

[50] Sheridan, *An Humble Appeal*, p. 15.   [51] Wilkinson, IV, 110–114.

fering with the players there. On stage it was difficult to distinguish between actors and audience,[52] and actors were often harassed by exhibitionists and inebriates who shared the act with them. For example, both Davies and Sheridan tell of an experience of Peg Woffington, who, playing Cordelia opposite Garrick during his first visit to Dublin, found herself seated on stage, as the curtain was to be drawn, not only with the old king—asleep, with his head in her lap—but also with a "Gentleman" from the stage audience who had thrown himself down on her other side and was fondling her "with the utmost Indecency." When she resented his activities, he abused her; and later he and his gentlemen friends uttered death threats against Garrick, who though silent throughout had dared to *look* his indignation "at so brutal a Scene."[53] Sheridan, who had witnessed this incident from the audience, now hoped to prevent a recurrence by keeping stage prices at 5s. 5d. during the whole performance, instead of reducing them, as was the Dublin and London custom, after the third act. Latecomers, apt to be drunk and disorderly, would thus be discouraged from the stage.

While this may have kept stage crowds smaller and more orderly, Sheridan was not to be satisfied with such a compromise for long. He wanted to clear the stage entirely. His move to do this is usually dated from the next season; actually the big step was first taken at his debut as Shylock on May 8, 1746, soon after Garrick left. In announcing it, he astutely shifted the responsibility to the Lord Lieutenant, although it is unlikely that Chesterfield had any personal hand in it: "By Command, no Person whatever to be admitted behind the Scenes."[54] Thus the regulation which is supposed to have touched off the Kelly riot of 1747 had been tried out months before without ill effects.[55]

Garrick, whose presence in Dublin had helped Sheridan in building as well as reforming his theater, stayed in town until May 3, announcing "the last Time of his acting this Season under his present Agreement" as early as March 14,[56] but continuing on through many "last Times" until an April 26th performance of *Jane Shore*, at the close of which he spoke his farewell in *An Address to the Town*.[57] In

[52] Sheridan, *An Humble Appeal*, p. 15.

[53] See Davies, I, 331–332, and Sheridan, *An Humble Appeal*, pp. 14–15.

[54] *Dublin Journal*, May 3–6, 1746.

[55] Barry, it is true, reports a very thin house on this occasion. See the quotation from his letter to Garrick, p. 73.

[56] *Dublin Journal*, March 8–11, 1746.　　[57] *Ibid.*, April 19–22, 1746.

this charming piece he poked fun at the difference between himself on stage and off:

> The hero shrinks into his native span—
> This little sketch and miniature of man.
> "Where's Garrick?" says the beau: and as I pass,
> To mark the noted insect—takes his glass.
> Plac'd in yon box, to publish my disaster,
> "Mamma," cries miss, "who is that little master?"
> "Zounds!" says the captain, "what! is that Othello?
> Ha, ha, ha!—
> A good joke, damme—a rare hulking fellow!"

At the end he thanked Dublin for its favors and expressed his feeling that he would always be "a native by your special grace."[58] The town had given him a gay winter socially; it could have made little difference to him that in accordance with Sheridan's letter of the summer before he had not traveled in Sheridan's circles.[59] Hitchcock's comment on the final relationship of the two men may be somewhat naïve: "To Mr. Sheridan's honour, be it observed, that through the whole of the connection between him and Mr. Garrick that season, such was his strict adherence to his engagements and open unreserved behaviour, that they parted good friends, Mr. Garrick acknowledging that he [Sheridan] was the man of honour and the gentleman."[60] A letter written on June 6 to Garrick by Spranger

---

[58] This piece has come down to us under the misleading title of Henry Brooke's *Prologue to Othello* "spoken in Dublin, by Mr. Garrick" (see Alexander Chalmer's *English Poets*, XVII, 426). Supposed to have been written by Brooke to be spoken by Garrick, it starts with the line "My term expir'd with this concluding play," a line which, as Genest (X, 339) says, indicates that it was an epilogue rather than a prologue; furthermore, Garrick's concluding play in Dublin was *Jane Shore* on April 26 and not *Othello*, not acted by Garrick, according to the Calendar, after February. Added proof that this poem was written and spoken later than February—even later than April 15—lies in its last line, where it is implied that Chesterfield has left Ireland. This event did not occur until late April. Brooke may still have written the verses, but the first part (see the lines quoted in the text, for example) is the sort of thing a man would more comfortably write about himself. Garrick may have been the author.

[59] Bellamy throws light on Garrick's social life in Dublin. Sheridan is not mentioned in connection with it (I, 77–79). See also Davies, I, 88; Garrick, *Letters*, I, 72, 76.

[60] Hitchcock, I, 164.

Barry, who had finished out a month more of acting with Sheridan after Garrick's departure, could hardly have been sent to a "good friend" of Sheridan's. Barry, apologetic because he owed Garrick money, begins by explaining that through "the intrigues of Prest" he had not received a penny of his salary since Garrick left, although he had been "daily soliciting and hourly expecting [his] money from the proprietors." He continues with bitter irony:

> I know you have had an account of Sheridan's late deserved success; he played the "Merchant of Venice" to 18; the "Orphan," he contrived to put off the morning of the play, by advertising that some of the performers were ill: without the gift of prophecy, he well knew how the evening would turn out. The hero's own benefit was to have been "Harry the Fourth," advertised [as] being positively the last time of his performing in this kingdom. Mr. Watson, who was to have played the part of Poins, was fortunately taken ill; Ten pounds in the house at seven o'clock. . . .

At this point, in front of many of Sheridan's "collegiate admirers then in the green-room," Barry had offered, as had Cibber two years before, to read the part of Poins, which as it happened did not interfere with his own part. But Sheridan refused, saying that, after having advertised certain players in certain parts, he must keep his word to the public. Thereupon he dismissed the house. Barry then went on to describe the trouble that followed between the few who had paid ready money and "those who had brought in his [Sheridan's] benefit-tickets." When the doorkeepers decided not to refund a penny to either party, cuffs and blows were exchanged and the doors had to be shut in a hurry. Sheridan's action was later represented by Prest to the proprietors as a wanton dismissal of the house, which meant that Sheridan might have to pay £30 agreed upon. Barry predicted a possible lawsuit. He concludes, "To remain here next winter useless, which must be the case in our present circumstances, will be a situation most irksome to me. . . ."[61]

---

[61] Garrick, *Private Correspondence*, i, 42. I find no notice of *The Orphan* during this part of the season; *The Merchant of Venice* Sheridan had deferred from May 5 to May 8. Barry's failure, in this letter, to blame Sheridan for the difficulty about his salary supports the possibility that Sheridan had not yet become responsible for the regular payment of his troupe during this first, trial year.

Sheridan too must have been discouraged by the letdown after Garrick's departure, which had emphasized the normal decline of business in late spring. At one point he was on the verge of giving up the whole venture. A notice of a May performance as "the last Time of his performing during his Stay in this Kingdom" [62] implies not only that his position was temporary but also that he had no intention of making it permanent. Years later he looked back on the financial returns of this glorious first year without enthusiasm. Even with Garrick present, the theater was not always full, he recalls:

> . . . it is amazing to consider that Mr. Garrick, in his height of Reputation, during the November Term, in a Parliament Winter, played the fourth Night of his Performance to a Receipt of little more than forty Pounds, and that a Messenger was dispatched to Mr. Sheridan to hasten him to Town . . . for the immediate Support of the Business. That with all their Strength united they were not able to exhibit Plays oftener than two Nights in a Week, and could seldom ensure good Houses to both those Nights. And that the Receipt of the whole Season did not exceed three thousand four hundred Pounds. [63]

But this was written from a blurred memory (notices show that plays were offered as many as four and five nights weekly during February and March) and after Sheridan had done much better at Smock-Alley. It is true that the number of advertised performances totaled only about seventy for the season, half the figure which Sheridan was to achieve at his peak. Yet even seventy was a great gain over the preceding years, and £3,400 a triumph compared to the £1,200 normal for earlier seasons. [64] Garrick is said to have been pleased with the "rich harvest" [65] he took home with him as his share of the profits; Sheridan seems to have used his equal share to buy Quilca

---

[62] *Dublin Journal*, May 10–14, 1746. Several notices of this sort appear in May, and as early as April 26 this news item appears in the *Journal*: "We hear that Mr. Sheridan is engag'd to perform four Times More during his Stay in this Kingdom."

[63] Sheridan, *An Humble Appeal*, p. 18.   [64] *Ibid.*, p. 53.

[65] Bellamy, I, 77. Davies too (I, 88) reports that Garrick had "considerably added to his stock of money." Sheridan, in *An Humble Appeal*, published in 1758, recalls that twelve years ago Mr. Garrick, at the height of his reputation, asked "but four hundred Pounds of Mr. Sheridan for a Season's Playing." It will be remembered that no set salary was agreed on, since Garrick was to share the profits. This may have been what he asked in the fruitless interview with Sheridan; or it may be what Sheridan twelve years later remembered Garrick to have made that season (*An Humble Appeal*, p. 54).

from Richard in July 1746.[66] Later all the profits he could spare from his ever-growing family were turned back into improving his theater.

Welcome encouragement came in the form of two poems written on Barry and Sheridan, probably when these two actors were alone in the last month of the 1745–46 season. *A Rhapsody on the Stage*, twenty-two pages in heroic couplets by James Eyre Weeks, a friend and former classmate of the Smock-Alley manager, is even more a rhapsody on Sheridan, whose genius as an actor was established on his first appearance and whose liberal education had given him an understanding of plays, authors, history, oratory, rhetoric, and orthoëpy, among other subjects. Under him Ierne's stage will revive:

> Ev'n now the Symptoms of her Health appear,
> While our Applause by turns, two Rivals share,
> Barry, by Nature for the Stage design'd,
> In Art, and Judgment, Sherridan refin'd,
> Barry, the darling of our Ear and Eye
> And Sherridan, of Art the Prodigy,
> Never did Fruit mature in such a time,
> Nor Youth attain so speedy to its Prime.[67]

The other poem, more humorous and only eight pages long, claims to be written by a poor poet asking the freedom of the house (Weeks, he says, already has this gratuity). Although the tone wavers between seriousness and satire (the two actors are pictured nursing at Ierne's breast, Tom sucking the right breast of Apollo, Barry the left of Jupiter), most of the piece is complimentary. Sheridan's oratory as Cato, his convincing delineation of Richard, and his virtues in other roles are praised.[68] These two poems were among the first of many writings inspired by the Smock-Alley manager, some panegyric, others venomous. None, however, reached the irony—quite unintentional—to be found in the last sentence of Weeks' dedication to Sheridan: "That you may make as large Acquisitions in Fortune, as you have in Reputation; and that your Happiness may be in Proportion to your Merit, is the sincere Wish of Sir, your most obedient, humble Servant and Admirer, James Eyre Weeks."

With the last performance of the season on May 26, the year of trial ended. But Sheridan had yet to make up his mind.

[66] Ms. 121.83956 and Ms. 121.83957 (Off. Reg. Deeds); Stockwell, p. 333, n. 33.

[67] Weeks, *A Rhapsody on the Stage*, p. 10.

[68] *A Poem on Mr. Sheridan and Mr. Barry*, 1746.

CHAPTER IV

Dublin in an Uproar, 1746-1747

SHERIDAN came to no decision and the theater remained closed until late the next fall. In the meantime, Barry, who had been angling for help from Garrick back at Covent Garden, had accepted Lacy's offer of a season at Drury Lane. Some twelve other players, including the important Mrs. Furnival and Mrs. Elmy, had also left, with no one to take their place.[2] For Sheridan had made no attempt to hire replacements, his own future was so much in doubt. The proprietors had reached the point of threatening to shut the doors for the winter, even at a loss of £600 to themselves, before Sheridan agreed to try again.[3] A letter of Benjamin Victor's may give a clue to his reluctance. Victor, a former English linen merchant who joined the company that fall as deputy manager and treasurer, had been in Dublin the preceding season, had accompanied Garrick back to London, and now had returned to Ireland, where Sheridan's warm reception provided the spark for a "most agreeable friendship" between the two men.[4] Writing to an English acquaintance in December 1746, Victor explained that the theaters, owned by thirty-six nobles and gentlemen who called themselves proprietors, had for some time been under the direction of "one artful man" who served as their agent, governing all in a base and highhanded way. Although Victor does not name him, he may well be Prest, the villain of Barry's letter. His baleful presence, above the manager's place, would be enough to explain Sheridan's hesitation.[5] The theater would

---

[1] The title here is taken from the title of a collection of writings (1747) dealing with the riot (see Bibliography).

[2] Sheridan, *A State of Mr. Sheridan's Case.*   [3] *Ibid.*

[4] Victor had been in the linen trade in London. He came over to Ireland on January 20, 1746, to balance his accounts with Irish linen manufacturers. Already a good friend of Garrick's, he established a "slight acquaintance" with Sheridan that season and attended several performances. He returned to settle in Dublin in October 1746, determined apparently to connect himself with the theater. Treating with Col. Butler, one of the proprietors of the united company, Victor decided that, since Sheridan was expecting to remain in Dublin as an actor and manager, it was better to "engage with him" rather than to start an opposition "to one who was the best Actor there, and who had a natural Interest to support him" (*Original Letters*, I, 121; *History*, I, 88, 90).

[5] That Prest had influence with the proprietors and meddled to Sheridan's

76

have been closed for the winter, but Sheridan called together the board of proprietors and, supported by the whole acting company, brought articles of impeachment to displace this agent. The proprietors were thus forced to give up their man. This event, or the prospect of it, may have persuaded Sheridan to undertake the management again. Soon after the proprietors' capitulation, Sheridan "entered into articles" for the two theaters, and was given, along with Victor, the power to direct business.[6] Probably only now, rather than in his first year as Hitchcock suggests, did he start to raise salaries, arrange for punctual payments (we recall Barry's complaints of the year before), and in return demand certain obligations from his company. Hitchcock tells of regular rehearsals under Sheridan's personal guidance where scene business was planned and other details of acting worked out.[7] All this efficiency, rare in Dublin theaters in recent years, inspired the company with such confidence that punctuality became the rule and forfeits were few. The new regimen, continues Victor in his letter to his English friend, was so successful that theatrical matters in Dublin "go on in a very prosperous manner, to the amazement of every one."[8] Bellamy too reports that, though the company had opened that fall apprehensive without Garrick, they succeeded as well as when they "were aided by his powerful assistance"—all because of "the exertions of the manager, who was deservedly a great favourite with the gentlemen of the college, at which he was bred. . . ."[9]

During the summer the pit of the infrequently used Aungier-Street Theater had been floored over[10] and now could be rented for balls and ridottos to bring in needed revenue. From this time on, Aungier-

---

disadvantage is shown by Barry's letter of June 6 to Garrick, where, as we recall, Prest had "infused it into the proprietors' heads" that Sheridan had wantonly dismissed the house when he refused to allow Barry to read an extra part (see Ch. III).

[6] Victor, *Original Letters*, I, 121–122. Sheridan's articles with the proprietors must have been drawn before the date of the letter, December 23, 1746. These could not have been the long-term lease taken in March 1748. (See Ch. V, note 42.)

[7] Hitchcock, I, 156–159.   [8] Victor, *Original Letters*, I, 122.

[9] Bellamy, I, 79. The next February Sheridan himself reports that, though he had had little hope for the season, he had been agreeably surprised. He found that industry and "good and chaste Plays, decently represented, drew crowded Audiences, without the Assistance of Dances, Pantomimes, or even Farces" (*A State of Mr. Sheridan's Case*).

[10] Announced in the *Dublin Journal*, June 28–July 1, 1746.

Street except for special occasions was abandoned as a playhouse, the company moving permanently to Smock-Alley.

Sheridan could hardly have been happy with that company this fall, reduced as it was to only two players of any importance, himself and Miss Bellamy. Other means to attract audiences had to be devised—new productions and bargain rates. Sheridan's novel idea this season was a subscription series of six plays, advertised in the October 25–28 *Journal*, with tickets at the reduced fee of a guinea to cover the series and to "carry a single Person into the Boxes, or any other Part of the House, except the Stage." For three guineas one could get a ticket to all the plays of the season, except benefits, for any part of the house except the stage. As for the stage, there had been so "many Complaints last Season on Account of the Stage's being crowded" that nobody would be admitted there "under 5s, 5d." Among the six subscription plays Sheridan promised at least two revived ones. These turned out to be two by Shakespeare which, according to the notices, had never been acted "in this Kingdom": [11] *Much Ado About Nothing* (first on November 27) and *Romeo and Juliet* (first on December 15).[12] At the second performance of *Romeo and Juliet* followed by a new afterpiece, *Pyramus and Thisbe*, no person whatsoever was to be admitted behind the scenes, "as the Machinery would be much obstructed by it." [13] Here again Sheridan cleared the stage for an evening without public protest.

The two revived plays had been specially chosen because they could be carried by two strong actors in an otherwise undistinguished cast. *Romeo and Juliet*, "written by Shakespear, with Alterations," was acted nine nights [14] to great houses, "an extraordinary thing" in Dublin then; and its success there inspired its revival at both Drury Lane and Covent Garden.[15] In Dublin there was such demand for places that subscribers were urged to send "an Account of what Num-

[11] *Ibid.*, November 8–11 and December 2–6, 1746. Normally a revived play was one that had been acted in Ireland but not for some time.

[12] The revival of *Romeo and Juliet* may have been inspired by the run which Theophilus Cibber's revision of the play had had in the Haymarket two years earlier, when both Sheridan and Victor—and Bellamy too—had been in London.

[13] *Dublin Journal*, December 13–16, 1746.

[14] So says Victor, *History*, I, 93. My records show only six performances, but perhaps not all productions were advertised. On the other hand, Victor's memory or records may have been inaccurate.

[15] Again, Cibber's success two seasons earlier may have contributed to this London revival.

ber they will want" as soon as possible.[16] The crowds were due, Hitchcock says, to Miss Bellamy's playing of Juliet and to the picturesque way Sheridan represented the funeral scene.[17] Sheridan's role as Romeo was not so universally admired; nor were his alterations (for he was the reviser) entirely approved. Some years later Wilkes wrote of having seen Sheridan play Romeo, "altered by himself, in which he took Mercutio's fine speech 'O! then I see Queen Mab has been with you' very unseasonably out of his mouth, and recited it with all the melancholy solemnity of a sermon. I am sure," Wilkes perspicaciously observes, "he must have seen the impropriety of making Romeo speak a speech which was intended for the gay Mercutio to divert his own gloom: but perhaps he had no performer then in his company whom he could entrust with the speech; and things considered in this, but in no other light, his performing the part of Romeo may be pardoned." [18]

One overflow night was less profitable to the management: it occurred at a charity performance. Theater benefits for worthy persons and causes not connected with the company—families in distress, needy authors, public hospitals, et cetera—were common in Dublin, and Sheridan increased the number this year, so gaining good will from the public while he assured the house charges, at least, from the tax—usually some £40—paid by the beneficiary. The worthy object during the fall was one whose name is now lost, "a Gentleman confined in the Marshalsea of the Four-Court, For the Debt of Another Person." Efficiently managing his benefit from his prison cell, he wrote to the paper on December 12, 1746:

The Gentleman confined in the Four-court Marshalsea returns his sincere Thanks to the polite and numerous Audience that honoured him with their Company at his benefit Play last Night, but being informed that a great Number of his Friends who paid for Tickets could not get in, by their Advice and Application to Mr. Sheridan, that Gentleman has been so good to appoint Monday the 29th of this Instant, when the Beggar's Opera will be performed for the Benefit of the same unfortunate Person, at which Time the Tickets delivered out for his former Play the Orphan will be then taken.[19]

[16] *Dublin Journal*, December 6–9, 1746. [17] Hitchcock, I, 167.
[18] Wilkes, pp. 314–315.
[19] *Dublin Journal*, November 25–29 and December 9–13, 1746.

This notice records not only an overflow evening at Smock-Alley, but also the eighteenth-century custom of selling all the tickets possible (there were no reserved seats) regardless of the accommodations.[20] On the night of the performance seats were grabbed on the principle of "first come, first served" and the overflow crowds were turned away with the expectation that they could use their tickets at a later performance. After his two successful benefits it seems reasonable to hope that the magnanimous and enterprising gentleman in the Marshalsea was freed.

But for Sheridan it was not all *Romeo* and overflow crowds. Probably because of his hesitation the season had opened unusually late—on October 30. Until Christmas, plays were offered only twice, or at most three times, weekly. By mid-December the upper gallery crowds were getting out of hand again, and were throwing apples and even stones at the band during the music before the play. In a letter to the *Journal* which ran for several months, Sheridan, not prosperous enough to threaten to close the section, warned that

> . . . proper Men will be placed to mark the Offenders, who will certainly be prosecuted the next Day to the utmost Rigour of the Law; and a Reward of three Guineas will be paid by the Manager, upon the Conviction of any Offender.[21]

Most disturbing of all, though, must have been the appearance, during the fall, of competitors, Sheridan's first as manager. Apparently encouraged by his indecision about the managership, and by the possibility for a while that Smock-Alley would be closed, this rival company opened on November 1 at the City Theater (Phillips' New Theater) in Capel-Street, operating by the Lord Mayor's permis-

[20] Stockwell, p. 230.

[21] *Dublin Journal*, December 13–16, 1746. Sheridan did not close the upper gallery to all but servants in livery for six months beginning in January 1747, as some (Stockwell, p. 102; Kavanagh, p. 181) have thought. On the only two occasions when Sheridan limited the personnel of the upper gallery, it was the servants who were *excluded* by public notice (see February 11 and March 19, 1747, in Smock-Alley Calendar). The error comes from reading a Capel-Street advertisement as a Smock-Alley notice (see *Dublin Journal*, January 10–13, 1747). Nor were Smock-Alley upper gallery prices raised at this time from 6*d.* to 1*s.* (this happened at Capel-Street). At Smock-Alley, 1/1 was the advertised price for the upper gallery before January (see *ibid.*, November 8–11, 1746), as well as after, except when it was advanced to a still higher figure for special performances.

sion.[22] With rates still lower than Smock-Alley's (although Sheridan had brought his prices down somewhat [23] to compete with them) and with the promise that great care would be taken "to prevent all Irregularities" in the upper gallery,[24] the new group was in a position to draw away part of the Smock-Alley audience. Further misfortune had been caused by the failure of *Much Ado*, the play so favored by Sheridan against Victor's advice.[25] Indeed, Victor's happy report by letter of December 23 that theatrical affairs were prospering is reversed in his *History* of fourteen years later: the 1746–47 season would have been a bad one, he says there, "if a very fortunate Accident had not happened on the nineteenth of January, at the performance of *Aesop*." [26] This "fortunate Accident" later became known in Dublin history as the Kelly riot.

Eighteenth-century Dublin was prone to civil disturbances: destructive wars between rival street gangs, Trinity demonstrations and high jinks, mobs of citizens besieging government buildings in some protest or other. Not surprisingly, several Smock-Alley riots had preceded Sheridan. The small, constant, and hence intimate audiences, made up largely of men out for an evening's entertainment, felt the right to express their disapproval if occasion arose. In some of these "expressions"—perhaps in the disturbance on the night of Dr. Clancy's benefit in 1738 [27]—young Sheridan may have taken part as

[22] *Ibid.*, January 6–10, 1747. See also their petition reprinted in Lawrence, "Trinity and the Theatre."

[23] For the November 4 performance: pit 2/8½ (earlier 3/3); middle gallery 1/7½ (earlier 2/2). Boxes, stage, and lattices remained 5/5; upper gallery remained 1/1. Prices were raised back to normal for *Romeo and Juliet* and for benefit plays. For *Romeo and Juliet* upper gallery prices were advanced to 1/7½.

[24] The new City Theatre in Capel-Street advertised boxes 3/3, pit 2/2, gallery 1/1 (January 6–10, 1747). The notice includes a statement that "the greatest care will be taken to prevent all Irregularities, the Upper Gallery (which formerly had been opened for Six-pence) will be applyed solely for the Use of Servants in Livery, who shall upon the Entrance of their Master or Mistress receive a Ticket from the Box-keeper, or Pit-Office-keeper." The new company at the Capel-Street Theater included Mr. and Mrs. Mynitt, Mr. Mason, and Mr. Layfield.

[25] Victor, *History*, I, 92: ". . . from its first Appearance there, to the last Season, it [*Much Ado About Nothing*] has fully answered its Name, in regard to him as Manager."

[26] *Ibid.*, p. 93.

[27] *Dublin Journal* item copied by J. F. Kemble in his *Manuscript Diary* for January 25, 1737/38.

a theater-haunting Trinitarian. We recall later charges that he had mixed in playhouse riots when a youth.[28]

But no theatrical riot of the period inspired such pen-twirling (Victor says enough in a month's time to fill a large octavo[29]), assumed such national importance, or produced such beneficial results as the Kelly riot at Smock-Alley in January 1747. For the newspaper reader not at the play, the affair started quietly enough. The issue of the *Dublin Journal* (January 17–20, 1747) published the next day after the inciting event makes no mention of it among the current news of a new method for extracting foul air out of ships and work to be done "in the Kitchen Garden in this Month." In the following issue, appearing three days after the riot itself, no headlines screamed, no pictures called attention to the event; the first relevant item which Editor Faulkner inserts in the finest of print and in a manner so unlike modern reportorial style notifies subscribers to a hospital benefit that:

> Whereas by a Riot which happened at the Theatre-Royal on Monday the 19th Inst. and was repeated the two following Nights, whereby the Players were interrupted in their performance, and the Playhouse rendered unfit for the Entertainment of the Publick. This is to inform the Town, that the Play appointed for the Benefit of the Hospital for Incurables, is put off till further notice.[30]

In the same fine print several affidavits supporting Sheridan's part in the affair are accompanied by the manager's promise that "a whole state of the case will be published next week." And along with these notices appear three pathetic advertisements, apparently uncanceled, for coming attractions at Smock-Alley, together with Sheridan's perpetual threat to the upper gallery.

The ultimate cause of the riot has usually been ascribed to Sheridan's decision to clear the stage permanently of stage sitters, a decision which was announced in the January 13–17 issue of the *Journal* thus: "In the future no money will be taken nor no person admitted behind the Scenes except on benefit nights." He himself claimed that, for clearing the stage and thus trying to prevent the disturbances which almost nightly interrupted the entertainment of the audience,

---

[28] *Mr. Sh—n's Apology to the Town*, p. 8.   [29] Victor, *History*, 1, 109.
[30] *Dublin Journal*, January 20–24, 1747. This notice may have been placed by the hospital governors. Later notices like this bear their address.

he "was publicly insulted in the most ignominious Manner" and "afterwards us'd in private in a Way which human Nature could not bear." [31] Fourteen years later Victor too, in the *History of the Theatres*, prefaced his account of the riot with a statement that he had often urged a reform to get the audience off stage and had proposed several "Methods," all of them rejected by the manager "as too dangerous to be executed in Dublin." [32] But, in a letter to Colley Cibber written only a few months after the event, Victor emphasized an entirely different cause. [33] And, indeed, the contemporary accounts of the affair and the writings inspired by it give the impression that Sheridan's new order played a negligible part; its connection with the riot was something thought up later to rationalize irrational behavior and perhaps give Sheridan a stick to use on his enemies. Further support to this impression comes from the hitherto unnoticed fact that on the evening of the riot and probably on the evening of the inciting incident the stage was crowded with stage sitters. On the latter night Sheridan's new regulation could hardly have been enforced, since stage tickets had already been advertised; [34] and the riot occurred on a benefit night, specifically exempted from the general order.

Dublin Journal readers who felt cheated by the scanty news at the beginning of the Smock-Alley affair knew the story by heart before the end. They read it in many forms—in letters, pamphlets, affidavits, history, and biography; but the narrative of events remained remarkably the same in all. It provided Dubliners with drama when the theaters were forced to close, and it aptly followed the classical pattern they were used to in their entertainment. Barely stated, it went like this: [35]

[31] *A State of Mr. Sheridan's Case.*   [32] Victor, *History*, I, 94–95.
[33] Victor, *Original Letters*, I, 126 (to Colley Cibber, May 1747).
[34] The advertisement for the second *Aesop* performance, at which the inciting incident occurred, quotes the price for box, *stage*, and lattices as 5/5 (*Dublin Journal*, January 13–17, 1747).
[35] My summary of the inciting incident is based on [Sheridan's] *Faithful Narrative of what happen'd at the Theatre on Monday the 19th Instant.* This pamphlet, although it bears no name on the title page and refers to Sheridan in the third person, is so clearly his that it can hardly have been intended to be anonymous. Evidence of his authorship appears, for example, on page 8, where the writer concludes his account of January 19's events with the words "Having thus set forth a State of the Case, Mr. Sheridan humbly begs leave to offer a few Things to the Consideration of those Gentlemen," et cetera, et cetera. Indeed, this paper seems to be the State of the Case promised by the Smock-

The inciting incident, but not the riot itself,[36] occurred on Monday, January 19, 1747, at a second performance of *Aesop*.[37] Sheridan had revived this Vanbrugh comedy as part of his plan for fresh productions and perhaps in search for plays more suited to his "scientific talents." [38] He himself was acting old Aesop, complete with oaken stick and false nose, and the play was well under way when a young gentleman, very drunk, clambered out of the pit, over the spikes designed precisely to prevent such a happening, and onto the stage. Friends in the pit cheered him on.[39] Perhaps because the stage was already filled with audience, he crossed it unaccosted and made his way to the greenroom. There he found one of the actresses, Mrs. Dyer, who in a later affidavit described the episode genteelly enough to prove *her* respectability at least: First he "designedly" trod on her foot and then he put one of his knees between hers, she protesting, meanwhile, that he would "spoil her cloaths." His frankly stated intention has been charmingly rephrased by Mrs. Dyer: "he would do [he said] what her husband mr. Dyer, had done to her, using the obscene expression," and he followed this threat with "abusive obscene language." [40] At this point George Anne Bellamy appeared by chance in the greenroom; normally she stayed in her own dressing

---

Alley manager in the *Journal* of January 20–24. I have supplemented *A Faithful Narrative* by details from other contemporary sources: Victor's *History* and *Original Letters*; G. A. Bellamy's *Apology*; and Edmund Burke's letter to his friend Shackleton (in Samuels' edition, pp. 115ff.). Anonymous pamphlets and other writings supply the rest of the information.

[36] The *Journal* notice about the hospital benefit quoted earlier is misleading here, and later accounts often mistakenly give the riot as occurring on January 19, e.g., Samuels' account in his edition of Burke's *Early Life*, p. 115.

[37] Bellamy (I, 95) is wrong in calling this the first performance of *Aesop* (see Smock-Alley Calendar). Her narrative appears verbatim in Stockwell, pp. 94ff.

[38] *Ibid.*, p. 95.

[39] *Ibid.* Bellamy says in her second edition, "This removal received marks of disapprobation [corrected to *approbation* in the third edition] from many of the audience, who by no means approved of the new regulation, which debarred them from coming behind the scenes."

[40] Mrs. Dyer's affidavit is one of several, all supporting Sheridan, printed in the *Dublin Journal* of January 20–24, 1747. Edmund Burke, a Trinity student at this time, embroiders upon this scene, reporting to Shackleton that the young man "put his hands under their [the actresses'] petticoats." But from the way he writes he was probably not at the theater on January 19, and he was certainly not in the greenroom. His letter (of February 21) is quoted verbatim in Stockwell, pp. 96ff.

room, apprehensive of just such unrestrained behavior. The instant she saw Mrs. Dyer's straits, she interposed, "not considering the brutality of a drunken man, particularly of an illiterate Irishman when drunk." [41] Her interference momentarily distracted the young gentleman so that the two women were able to escape to a nearby dressing room,[42] where they locked themselves in; but the villain still pursued them and tried to force the door. When one of the dressers, Ann Banford, remonstrated, he struck and abused her, though she was "big with Child," [43] at the same time swearing that he would have "carnal knowledge" (Mrs. Dyer is reporting again) of one of them between the scenes. Meantime, the moment was approaching when the actresses would be needed out front.

Sheridan first heard of these backstage activities when he was onstage acting. Word was somehow conveyed to him. He retired, leaving the play at a standstill and the players staring dumbly at one another.[44] Outside the dressing room he called to the actresses to come out, but the young gentleman let forth such a "Volley of execrable Oaths, abusive Names, and obscene Expressions" [45] that they retreated again. The play would have had to close had not Sheridan, with perfect calm, ordered the young man taken into custody,[46] after warning him several times in vain. (Official guards were stationed in the theater-royal at every performance.) [47] The play could then continue.

Sheridan must have been surprised, when he next appeared on stage, to see this same young gentleman escaped from his guard and back in the pit. He must have been more surprised when an avenging orange, thrown with accuracy and the usual shower of abuse, struck his false nose with enough force to dent the iron into his forehead. The Smock-Alley manager was, as Miss Bellamy asserts, born and bred a *gentleman*, had "as much personal courage as any man breath-

---

[41] Bellamy, I, 96.

[42] Accounts disagree here. George Anne implies that she ran alone to her dressing room; Mrs. Dyer's more trustworthy affidavit states that both she and Miss Bellamy fled to Mrs. Storer's room.

[43] [Sheridan], *A Faithful Narrative*, p. 3.

[44] *An Humble Address to the Ladies*, p. 4.

[45] [Sheridan], *A Faithful Narrative*, p. 4.

[46] So *ibid.*, which would seem most reliable here. Other accounts make no mention of custody, most of them saying that Sheridan merely had the young gentleman removed from behind the scenes.

[47] Clark, p. 131. Sheridan mentions the guard in his petition to reopen.

ing," and was not one to put up with such an indignity.[48] Removing his false nose,[49] he stepped out of character, walked to the front of the stage, and began to speak.[50] What he said George Anne failed to hear because she was so distraught. But the young gentleman continued his abusive name-calling until Sheridan was provoked to respond: "I am as good a Gentleman as you are." This famous sentence, soon garbled into "I am as good a Gentleman as any in the House," [51] inflamed his enemies and, along with his punishment of the young gentleman, became the real inciting force for them, rather than any order to clear the stage.

After the curtain had dropped that evening,[52] Sheridan found himself followed back to his private room by the persistent young drunk, who now was demanding an apology. When Sheridan replied that he would apologize to no one below the royal family,[53] he recommenced his stream of abuse, calling him impudent vagabond, liar, scoundrel, rascal, before the manager's friends who were gathered there. Sheridan treated him coolly at first, but finally could take no more: he gave the man "the Usage he deserved," [54] an ample drubbing with Aesop's oaken stick which he still carried in his hand.[55] The young gentleman, who wore a military cockade and a sword, collapsed on the floor in tears, much to the delight of Sheridan's friends.[56] Vowing

---

[48] Bellamy, I, 97. George Anne is the only one who gives the vivid detail about the damage to Aesop's false nose.

[49] *A Serious Enquiry*, p. 10.

[50] Sheridan's *Faithful Narrative* omits this point, but others record it, each somewhat differently. George Anne missed what Sheridan said; Victor claims that he asked protection from the audience, which was rather thin that night (George Anne says that the house was crowded); Burke reports that Sheridan asked the young man's friends to take care of him, else he would have to be turned out of the house.

[51] Victor (*History*, I, 97–98) is the only one to include Sheridan's statement in his story at this point. Victor admits that he did not hear Sheridan speak that night, depending instead on reports from "Gentlemen of Sense and Honour" (p. 106); but the other narrators mention it elsewhere and later pamphlets and letters disputing over what Sheridan meant bear witness to its utterance.

[52] Bellamy (I, 97) says that the play was unfinished, but several other accounts imply that the play ran its course. At any rate, it is clear that no actual riot took place on this night.

[53] *A Serious Enquiry*, p. 11. This pamphlet is hostile to Sheridan.

[54] [Sheridan], *A Faithful Narrative*, p. 5.

[55] Bellamy (I, 97) gives this detail about the stick, omitted in the others. Both Burke and Victor report that the young gentleman took his beating meekly—"with Christian patience," says Burke.

[56] Bellamy, I, 97.

revenge on this usage to a gentleman, he was finally permitted to crawl away, with, ironically, a broken nose. At his coffeehouse, he incensed his club by an account of the treatment he had received, embellished by such false details as that he had been held by Sheridan's servants while Sheridan beat him.[57]

Sheridan, in writing the story of this evening later, forbore to mention the young man by name or initials; and in other writings he usually appears as "E. . . . K. . . . , Esq.," although the manager is always named or referred to contemptuously by the opposition as "the player" or "the fellow." But E.K. soon became known all over town as a Mr. E. Kelly. He was a gentleman from Galway in Connaught.

That a player should beat a gentleman, that a player should consider himself a gentleman—this more than anything else raised the riot against Sheridan, fostered by a powerful group known as the Connaught party or "the Gentlemen" in the literature that followed. This was the only cause which Victor reported to Cibber soon after the event: "From the earliest account of theatrical history, down to the present Laureat [this was Cibber] . . . I could not meet with a parallel to the case of Sheridan, which was no less than a violent dispute about the HONOUR of an actor. . . ."[58] The fear which five years before had made Sheridan hesitate to turn actor had been suddenly and dramatically realized: as actor he had lost his honor, his status as a gentleman—or so his enemies would try to persuade the public. After the heights of acclaim and power he had reached, this reversal must have been a great blow to his pride. It had to be fought with every argument he could devise.

The events just described occurred on a Monday. The next evening, passed over in all the accounts of the affair, may not have been uneventful. The *Dublin Journal* notice deferring the hospital benefit reports that the riots were repeated *two* nights following the Monday disturbance. For Tuesday a command performance, celebrating the birthday anniversary of the Prince of Wales and starring Sheridan and Miss Bellamy, had been announced. To the large audience normal for such an event would be added curiosity seekers who had heard of Monday's excitement and interested persons from both sides

[57] Victor, *History*, I, 98. Four of the men witnessing the scene in Sheridan's room filed affidavits in the *Dublin Journal* (January 20–24, 1747), swearing that the young gentleman provoked Sheridan unmitigatedly and that no person but Sheridan struck or molested him.

[58] Victor, *Original Letters*, I, 126 (May 1747).

of the dispute. But Tuesday evening's activities, if any occurred, were probably confined to interruptions of the performance and to the verbal threats which, according to Victor, were being made during this interval against all "that dared to look as if they were inclined to take the Part of Sheridan." [59]

The Wednesday [60] performance was to be a charity showing of *The Fair Penitent*, for the benefit of another poor gentleman in the Marshalsea Prison, one apparently impounded through his own efforts and not through a friend's. For this evening Sheridan had been warned by his enemies to stay off the stage; when he took their advice, Mrs. Dyer's husband going on stage to acquaint the audience with this decision, about fifty "gentlemen" rose up from the pit,[61] crying, "Out with the ladies, and down with the house." [62] With this, the actual riot commenced; and, as George Anne Bellamy put it, "It is impossible to describe to you the horrors of a riot at a Dublin theatre." [63] The rioters moved across the stage, crowded into the passages behind, broke open dressing-room doors and the wardrobe, beat up a poor "taylor," [64] thrust swords into closets and chests,[65] and "revenged themselves upon the stuffing of Falstaff, which they stabbed in many places." [66] When they entered George Anne's room, she faced them resolutely and asked them to leave, which they did after "being permitted to lift the covering of my toilette, to see whether the manager was there." [67] Unable to discover Sheridan there or anywhere at the theater,[68] a group went off to his residence, but "upon finding he had provided for their Reception, they thought proper to retire." [69]

[59] Victor, *History*, 1, 99.

[60] Wednesday, January 21. *A Faithful Narrative* takes us through Monday's events only. Victor, Bellamy, and Burke supply Wednesday's story, although they all confuse the date of it. Victor places it on Thursday, and George Anne and Burke both imply Tuesday by saying "the next night" after the *Aesop* incident. Bellamy's account in some respects confuses the night of the riot with an evening two weeks later, when the hospital benefit had to be discontinued.

[61] Victor, *History*, 1, 99.   [62] Bellamy, 1, 98.   [63] *Ibid.*

[64] Burke (Samuels, p. 116).   [65] Victor, *History*, 1, 100.

[66] Bellamy, 1, 99.   [67] *Ibid.*

[68] According to Bellamy (1, 98) Sheridan had been at the theater and had at first refused to yield to his friends' pleas to leave and go home; but finally when his life was threatened he had departed. Victor (*History*, 1, 99) says that Sheridan had never left his house that night and that he had taken "particular Care to be well guarded . . . there."

[69] Victor, *History*, 1, 100.

After this the theater was closed,[70] for repairs and for a cooling-off time.

These were the sober facts of the Kelly riot. When Dubliners got bored with the sober facts, they could turn to a mock heroic epic called *The Gentleman* and laugh at what poetic license had made of the affair. Here Kelly becomes Ergasto; Sheridan, Typhon, "monarch of the affronted STAGE." The poem opens with a description of Smock-Alley Theater on the fatal night. The stage is crowded:

> While on the shining stage, th'important beaux
> Display with like content, their tinsel'd cloaths;
> And, self-exalted, such high raptures feel,
> As turky cocks beneath expanded tail. . . .

And elsewhere too the house is busy with its usual activities before the play begins:

> And now a murmur rose of frequent claps,
> And hisses, whistlings, cat-calls, noise and raps;
> A rattling tumult spreads from end to end,
> And orange peels, like falling stars descend. . . .

The object of the assault has been changed, no doubt to Mrs. Dyer's relief. Bellamy [71] may or may not have been flattered by the description:

> Mean while upon th'illumin'd stage is seen,
> An actress fair, of soft enticing mein,
> A tempting girl, improv'd by labring art
> With ev'ry outward charm that wins the heart. . . .

The setting of the assault is changed, and the language which had referred to Mrs. Dyer's knees is appropriately elevated:

> Her young Ergast with wishful eyes surveys . . .
> And longs between her snow white arms to sin. . . .
> Then from the Pit, instinct with lust and rage,
> He springs forth lightly, sheer upon the Stage. . . .

[70] Bellamy is probably wrong in saying that the magistrates closed the theater at this time; she seems to be confusing this event with the second closing in mid-February. Burke says that Sheridan shut up his playhouse.

[71] Several of the accounts assume that George Anne was the object of Kelly's interest, and it is likely that he switched his attention to her, young and pretty as she was, after she appeared in the greenroom. Her own account has him following her alone to her dressing room (i, 96).

When burning now to raise the glorious war,
With rough assault he seiz'd the trembling fair. . . .

Sheridan's rescue mission is most delicately accomplished; he "Sets free the trembling fair, and then retires," but Ergasto and his friends are infuriated to the point of riot. Once again Sheridan comes to the rescue and brings his blow down not on Ergasto's nose but on his teeth, "His hapless teeth, that fall by fifty's out, While gore bespangles all the floor about." Ergasto's friends bear away their wounded leader, and retreat "in multitudes," leaving Sheridan the victor and the true hero of the epic.

After the riot the theater stayed closed for two and a half weeks. Sheridan tried during this time to arrange a peace, but the opposition would be satisfied with nothing less than a public apology from the manager.[72] After this, Sheridan was forced to go to law, although he offered to omit from prosecution those who applied to him and he ordered his attorney to proceed in the mildest manner against the others.[73] Seven of the Kelly party were indicted for riot.[74]

When two weeks had passed, Sheridan decided to reopen Smock-Alley on February 9 for what Victor called "the first Trial-Play after the grand Riot." [75] The support of many letter writers, pamphleteers, and a large group at the college had encouraged him to appeal to the public, now that "all Hopes of a private Accommodation [had] fail'd." [76] At first he planned not to antagonize his enemies by appearing himself; *Oroonoko* was advertised with the lead by Elrington, who assured the ladies that there would not be "the least Disturbance in the House that Night, as they [might] judge by the Disposition of the several Parts." [77] But at the last minute *Richard III* with Sheridan was boldly substituted, without explanation. Thus the Smock-Alley manager grasped the nettle and "redisposed" the parts to include himself in the "first Trial-Play."

This time—the evening of February 9—the house was well filled with Sheridan supporters, including many ladies who came to give their backing to "the Reformer of the Stage." [78] The play began.

---

[72] Sheridan, *A Full Vindication*, p. 4.

[73] Sheridan, *A State of Mr. Sheridan's Case.*

[74] *Dublin in an Uproar*, p. 2 (Letter of February 17).

[75] Victor, *History*, I, 110.   [76] Sheridan, *A Full Vindication*, p. 5.

[77] *Dublin Journal*, January 31–February 3, 1747; also February 3–7.

[78] *A Letter*, By a Freeman, p. 3. Victor also describes the events of this evening in detail, especially the composition of the audience.

Since it was Colley Cibber's adaptation of Shakespeare, Richard would not appear until the end of the first scene. On stage, Henry VI, who had heard the bad news from Tewkesbury, was conventionally bemoaning his lot before a quiet house when a messenger appeared to speak—not to him but to the audience. Sheridan, he announced, was about to make his entrance as Richard, if it was their pleasure. The generous applause which followed ended to everyone's surprise in groans, yells, and hisses from six or eight persons in boxes. All means were used to silence this unseemly clamor.[79] Meanwhile, Sheridan appeared, but was kept from beginning by calls of "a Submission, a Submission, Submission, off, off, off." [80] He came forward and said, "As I am perfectly satisfy'd that the Voice of the Publick can never be wrong, if it be their opinion that I ought to make a Submission, I am ready to do it." But his friends called out that it was no longer his quarrel, that he was not the aggressor, that he should not bow "to lawless Rage and Tyranny." [81] At this point a spectator rose up in the pit "and asserted the Rights of the Audience and the Freedom of the Stage." He deplored the fact that private quarrels were thus brought into the theater, but "since the Dispute was introduced, it must, like other Disputes, be determined by the Majority." He then asked for a show of hands of those who were for "preserving the Decency and Freedom of the Stage." His speech was heard respectfully and greeted with shouts of applause. When the vote was taken, "the Numbers were so great against the Rioters, and withal appeared so animated for Action, that the Majority [of them] suddenly went off, and left the Performance of that Night in quiet." [82] But the "Gentlemen"—one or two of their leaders having been turned out [83]—were now so incensed that they resolved renewed vengeance on Sheridan and his protectors: "He was now never to be permitted, on any Account, to perform again, and those who took his Part were doomed to Destruction." And, indeed, the citizen who spoke at the theater was assaulted on the street one night near Essex Bridge.[84] He was Dr. Charles Lucas, a noted Dublin figure and

---

[79] *A Letter,* By a Freeman, p. 3. [80] Victor, *History,* I, 113.

[81] *A Letter,* By a Freeman, p. 4.

[82] Victor, *History,* I, 113–115. A Freeman, who was, in fact, the speaker for Decency and Freedom, modestly omits the applause, saying simply that these ideas were adopted by the majority and that the play was continued with sobriety.

[83] Burke (Samuels, p. 117).

[84] Victor, *History,* I, 115–116; *A Letter of Thanks to the Barber,* p. 6.

almost certainly the author, over the signature of "a Freeman," of three pamphlets vigorously supporting Sheridan.

The fourth and final act of the Kelly drama took place two nights later, on Wednesday, February 11; but, in keeping with the usual custom of those days, it was followed by a farce and an epilogue. On this Wednesday was to be offered the annual benefit play for the Hospital for Incurables (the "poor, deformed, distempered Objects, that have long infested our Streets").[85] Deferred because of the first riot, it was being presented at the demand of the hospital governors, who had sent word to Sheridan that they would if necessary "take upon them [selves] to defend him that Night." [86] By special notice and as an added precaution, no servant was to be admitted into the upper gallery.[87] Actually, no trouble was expected, the "Gentlemen" having long promised their permission for this benefit performance,[88] and so not more than seven or eight of Sheridan's Trinity supporters appeared.[89]

The house was brilliant that evening, with over a hundred ladies seated on the stage. Except for the first few rows, preempted by "Gentlemen" who had got there first, the pit too was filled with ladies.[90] Yet when Sheridan was ushered on stage by a hospital governor, thirty armed men rose up from the front of the pit and ordered him off. A storm of clapping and hissing followed, until finally the hissing began to predominate,[91] whereupon Sheridan wisely retired to prevent further mischief.[92] After his withdrawal disputes began between the hospital governors on stage and the gentlemen in the pit (some of the governors were from the college and all the disputants were publicly known). Even the ladies took part, one of them, a "beautiful Foreigner," clapping her hands and calling for her favorite actor, Sheridan; another rising up and saying the play was not worth hearing without him.[93] For by this time the gentlemen were agreeing to the play if someone else took Sheridan's role; or they would be satisfied, they said, with any reasonable apology from the manager, even the slightest.[94] But when word of these concessions

[85] *A Letter*, By a Freeman, p. 4.   [86] Victor, *History*, I, 117.
[87] *Dublin Courant*, February 3–7, 1747.
[88] *A Letter*, By a Freeman, p. 4.
[89] Burke (Samuels, p. 117).   [90] Victor, *History*, I, 118.
[91] "Extract of a Letter from Dublin," *Gentleman's Magazine*, XVII, 123–124.
[92] Sheridan, *A Full Vindication*, p. 16.
[93] *Dublin in an Uproar*, p. 11 (The Gentlemen's Apology).
[94] *Ibid.*, pp. 6–7.

was sent to Sheridan, he was gone.[95] The dispute, meanwhile, grew warmer and menacing gestures were exchanged. One gentleman, when approached by a scholar, entrenched himself behind some ladies' hoops, crying out: "Here's an Apothecary comes with his Clyster-pipe, God demme! but I come with my Sword, by Gad!"— flourishing, meanwhile, "the pretty Bauble" over the ladies' heads.[96] Eventually someone from the pit threw an apple at a student on stage in his bachelor's gown, called him a scoundrel, and shouted that "they were all a Pack of Scoundrels." At this insult to his fellows "Away flew the Scholar like a feathered Mercury to the College (the distance half a Mile) and returned in about twenty Minutes, with about as many Youths armed for the Combat." But the rioters had left the pit, and the audience had broken up.[97] The play—*The Fair Penitent* again—was suspended.[98]

And now followed the farce. This included a council of war held all night at the college; attacks next morning by armed bands of a thousand scholars or more on the lodgings of the principal offenders; capture of at least three, a Mr. Martin, a Captain Fitzgerald, and John Brown, Esq. of the Neale;[99] public apologies made by Martin on his bare knees surrounded by a vast circle of students in the courts of the college; and, for a final memento, sufficient cold water bestowed upon the ringleaders from the college pump "as served to keep their heads perfectly cool to defend their cause against the manager," who by then had "commenced a prosecution against them."[100] Burke, who was one of the avenging Trinitarians, reports that Kelly came to the college voluntarily to avoid ill usage and made his submission meekly. In the end the city was thrown into such a fright that shopkeepers shut up their shops, several of the

[95] *Ibid.*, p. 16 (The Tradesmen's Answer).

[96] *Ibid.*, p. 11 (The Ladies' Answer).   [97] Victor, *History*, I, 119–120.

[98] So we gather from later notices in the *Journal*.

[99] Victor, *History*, I, 120–121; Burke (Samuels, p. 117); and Bellamy, I, 99–100. Victor gives no names, but Burke and Bellamy both name Martin and Fitzgerald. Burke adds Brown's name, saying that he too was obliged to make a submission at the college (see footnote 106 below). The first letter in *Dublin in an Uproar* gives "Mr. K-ll-y" as the third name, but Burke, as a Trinitarian, would seem to be more reliable here.

[100] Bellamy, I, 100. Bellamy says that the suit was commenced that same day, but it must have been instituted earlier, for it is mentioned in *A State of Mr. Sheridan's Case*, published, Sheridan says, the day he opened the house for the trial-play, February 9. (See Sheridan's *Full Vindication*, pp. 5–8, where *A State of Mr. Sheridan's Case* is reprinted.)

opposition leaders fled with "Fear and Trembling" to the Lord Chancellor, the students were confined to quarters, and the theater, since it had become a "Seat of War," was closed by order of the Lords Justices [101]—an order which applied to the rival City Theater in Capel-Street as well as to Smock-Alley. This Dublin theatrical riot was shared by all of Dublin.

The epilogue was proclaimed in the law courts. Sheridan, by this time, had been indicted by Kelly, so both sides were tried by the same jury. The three rioters (the seven had been reduced to three) [102] were charged with assault only—"a Crime," comments a Freeman, "of which no *fashionable* Gentleman is ashamed." Kelly returned Sheridan's compliment in kind, indicting him for, as a Freeman puts it, "hindering the Gentleman to ravish Actresses, abuse Actors, and for defending himself from the Outrages offered him." [103] The excitement over the trial reached such heights that wagers were taken on the outcome, most bettors feeling that no gentleman would be found guilty. To their surprise Sheridan was acquitted, with the jury not even troubling to leave the box.[104] When Kelly's trial came up, his defense attorney arose and sneeringly said that he wanted to see a curiosity. "I have often seen (continued he) a Gentleman Soldier, and a Gentleman Taylor; but I have never seen a Gentleman Player." Sheridan, who was well dressed, bowed modestly and said, "Sir, I hope you see one now." [105] On February 19 the jury found Kelly (and one of his associates) guilty. A notice in the February 17–21 *Journal* reports:

> Last Thursday Mr. Sheridan was tryed at the Court of Oyer and Terminer, for assaulting Mr. Kelly and was acquitted. At the same Time that Gentleman was tryed for assaulting Mr. Sheridan, and found guilty of three Assaults. Two other gentlemen were tryed for an Assault, and one of them acquitted and the other found guilty.[106]

[101] Victor, *History*, I, 121, 123; Burke (Samuels, p. 117).

[102] As the verdict shows. A Freeman explains that "Examinations were . . . given against the chief of the Rioters only; many being left out of the Prosecution, upon their bare Parole, to keep the Peace and give no further Disturbance" (*Second Letter*, By A. F., p. 5).

[103] *Ibid.*, pp. 5, 6.

[104] Victor describes the unusual procedure whereby an honest and able jury was selected through the good offices of Chief Justice Marlay (*History*, I, 124).

[105] *Ibid.*, p. 126.

[106] The other culprit is identified in the letter cited by the *Gentleman's Magazine* (see note 91) as Brown, "son of Brown mentioned in the Draper's

Kelly was fined the very considerable sum of £500 and on February 21 sentenced to a short imprisonment (some accounts say a month, others three months).[107] After a week in jail the young "gentleman" appealed to Sheridan, who instantly arranged to have the fine canceled and then became "Solicitor and Bail himself . . . for the Enlargement of the young Gentleman." [108]

Here ends the account of events which threw Dublin into an uproar for over six weeks. But the agitation came less from events than from the writings which appeared in unprecedented numbers [109] and

---

Letters." Perhaps Brown's son did participate in the riotous activities, but A. F[reeman]'s *Second Letter* and also "The Tradesmen's Answer" leave no doubt that the enemy leader was not the son, but the very same Brown mentioned in Swift's *Drapier's Letters*. If two Browns were involved, perhaps it was the younger one who was given the treatment by the Trinity boys, although Burke's use of the full title would seem to indicate the father.

[107] Victor (*History*, I, 127) says three months' imprisonment. Burke and the article in the *Gentleman's Magazine* say that the sentence was for one month, Burke adding that Kelly had to give security for his behavior for seven years. The writer to the *Gentleman's Magazine* reports that Brown, earlier in the article identified as the son, was fined £100 "and to give security for his good behavior for a year." Victor describes a related incident which took place in the courtroom: Lord Chief Justice Marlay "ordered his Tipstaff to whisper a Gentleman Leader he saw in Court, against whom Complaints had been laid of his bad Behaviour in Public, to meet him in his Chamber when he left the Bench; where his Lordship obliged him to give Bail for his future good Behaviour" (*History*, I, 127). This "Gentleman Leader" may have been Brown, the father (see p. 99).

[108] Victor, *History*, I, 128–129. Victor says that, when the action was first commenced, the Kelly faction talked of nothing but the hundreds of pounds that had been subscribed to help their martyred hero, but "when the Truth was obliged to appear, not one Farthing was subscribed" and Kelly was left to the mercy of his foes.

[109] For these few weeks twelve relevant items appear in Loewenberg's bibliography as contrasted with ten items for the whole twenty-year period preceding. Furthermore, these twelve are not the complete tally for the event; to be added to Loewenberg are:

A Letter of Thanks to the Barber, for his Indefatigable Pains to Suppress the Horrid and Unnatural Rebellion, Lately broke out in this City: But by His Means, now happily almost extinguished. By Mr. Francis Liberty, a Freeman and Citizen of Dublin. Dublin, 1747 (dated March 28, 1747), 15 pp.

Brutus's Letter to the Town. Printed in the Year 1747. (By William Dennis, identified as the author by Burke in a letter to Shackleton; see Samuels, p. 127.)

The Prophecies of the Book of the Prophet Lucas. (Reprinted in Samuels, p. 120.)

which kept the battle boiling even after the action had died down. Nor were these restricted to Dublin. News of the excitement traveled quickly to far-off London in a February 24th letter from Dublin to the *Gentleman's Magazine*.[110] As with the Cato affair, Londoners would be interested; but this time a reprint of a complimentary poem to the Celebrated Mr. Sheridan from the *Dublin Journal* spread Sheridan's fame in a way that must have pleased him more.

Although most of the Dublin public was on his side, Sheridan felt the need to explain and defend his actions in three pamphlets spaced over the six crowded weeks, and in several letters and notices to the newspapers. His second pamphlet, *A State of Mr. Sheridan's Case*, written to be distributed at the trial-play, stressed his improvements to the theater: his "good and chaste Plays, decently represented," his subduing the upper gallery, and his attempt to clear the stage; on this last move he now blamed the indignities he had suffered from Kelly.[111] But in his first pamphlet, *A Faithful Narrative*, written right after the inciting incident and the indignities, he nowhere mentions his order to clear the stage. Instead, after an account of Kelly's behavior and his own that evening, he argues his right to the status of gentleman, although, he insists, he never thought himself as good a gentleman as any in the house.

Sheridan's third and final pamphlet, *A Full Vindication*, dated March 4, appeared two weeks after the court verdict, but before he had appeared again on the Smock-Alley stage. Because his conduct had become the subject of conversation all over town, he felt obliged to give his side of the case, that the public might judge whether he should be kept on at the theater. In conclusion, he offered to do anything to bring peace to Dublin except give the submission the "Gentlemen" were still demanding. This he could not do against the public judgment expressed at the trial-play. All three of these writings argue convincingly. But, except for a rare flash of humor recalling *The Brave Irishman* (e.g., If the dispute is, as the oppo-

---

The Farmer's Yard (an eight-page allegorical and satirical poem). Neither Loewenberg nor this additional list includes newspaper material, which was plentiful.

[110] See note 91.

[111] If the "Gentlemen" will agree to stop disturbing the town's entertainment, Sheridan, toward the end of this pamphlet, offers to drop his prosecution and accept his financial losses (already so great as to destroy all hopes of profit for the season). Later, after the authorities had closed the theater again for over two weeks, he mentions the sum of £1,000 lost (in *A Full Vindication*, p. 18).

sition claims, "the Gentlemen's Quarrel," surely the "Gentlemen"
of the Town must have a larger body of "friends" than one "Scoundrel Actor" would have),[112] the style which Sheridan was beginning
to develop for his controversial pieces lacked appeal. Remembering,
perhaps, his too intimate outpourings in the Cato controversy, he now
wrote in the third person to create an air of objectivity and dignity.
For his enemies, though, his reference to himself as "Mr. Sheridan"
and "the Manager" must have breathed pomposity and self-regard.
On the other hand, his feelings of obligation and gratitude to the
public were often expressed in terms so lavish as to sound obsequious.
This enraged his enemies because his public loved it.

The public expressed its ideas too in pamphlets, mostly favorable
to Sheridan, and in Faulkner's *Dublin Journal* (other Dublin papers
held aloof from the controversy).[113] Faulkner had offered at the
beginning of the dispute to print essays for both sides,[114] but the
material sent to him seems to have been exclusively in Sheridan's
support. A campaign to raise funds for the mistreated Smock-Alley
manager was started early through the newspaper and some £100
were donated, mostly by ladies but £5 came from a poor clergyman
who wanted to contribute something to the "Cause of Virtue, of
Liberty, of Publick Good."[115] Numerous letters, variously signed,
defended Sheridan, who, as one anonymous writer reports, had become the universal topic of all conversation in Dublin.[116] Some

[112] *Ibid.*, p. 12.

[113] The *Dublin Courant* took only advertisements for Smock-Alley; the editor
of *Pue's Occurrences* (March 14–17) declined a letter signed by Scriblerus
Hibernicus "as I have always avoided publishing any Thing from either Side
in the late Dispute."

[114] *Dublin Journal*, January 27–31, 1747.   [115] *Ibid.*, February 3–7, 1747.

[116] The letter from which this quotation has been taken is no longer anonymous, Benjamin Victor having claimed it in his *History*, where he reprints it
in toto (I, 101–108) as "Victor's Letter to Faulkner's Journal." A comparison
of this reprint with the piece as it first appeared in the *Dublin Journal* (January
31–February 3) shows that it is not quite the verbatim copy that Victor implies,
although the changes are minor: Victor has, for example, expanded on Sheridan's
pedigree and education in his reprint; Westminster School and Sheridan's B.A.
at Trinity do not appear in the letter to the paper. The *Journal* letter, although
unsigned, concludes with a note that the name of its writer may be discovered
"by a proper Enquiry at the College." Victor, not a Trinity College man himself, had apparently allied himself with collegians interested in Sheridan's cause.
Finally, Victor's letter to the paper promises that its author will make oath that
"it was wrote and published without the Knowledge and Consent of the young
Man in whose Favour it is written."

argued his right to the title of "gentleman." A poem, written "a good while past" by a fellow scholar, was refurbished, fitted out with a new introduction on the gentleman question, and titled "On the Celebrated Mr. Sheridan." [117] A suggestion for arbitrating the quarrel envisioned a committee from both sides and perhaps composed of ladies, whose decisions would be compulsory for the two principals. For, unless something was done, people deprived of the theater would go to gaming houses and taverns, where wagers and fights would follow, to bring down whole families to ruin.[118] Letters and notices from Sheridan appeared in the *Dublin Journal*, where as late as March 6 he was still solemnly swearing that he never thought himself as good a gentleman as any in the house.[119]

Through these writings can be sensed the personalities of the other main actors in the drama. Kelly, not necessarily the illiterate that George Anne insinuates, was a Trinity College man, but younger than Sheridan. Even so, Trinity supported Sheridan, though, when he left the college, he "must have been out of the Memory of most of the present Set of young Gentlemen [at the college], and was personally known to very few of them." [120] No one, not even Kelly's friends, denied that he was quarrelsomely drunk that evening. But, from then on, he seems to have become the dupe of others, committed to them even after he was willing to quit. Sheridan said that Kelly, after the benefit fiasco, was about to agree to reciprocal apologies and a reconciliation when his party interfered.[121] After his trial and conviction he was cast off by those who had "edged" him on, his true friends proving to be those who had prosecuted him. Sheridan, "at the Peril of his Life," visited Kelly in his place of confinement and both parted in "Love and Friendship," as Sheridan went off to seek relief for the young man.[122]

Dr. Charles Lucas, a Dublin apothecary, later a physician, was regarded as, above all, a great fighter for Irish liberty.[123] A man of

---

[117] *Dublin Journal*, February 7–10, 1747. This is the poem which was reprinted in London in the *Gentleman's Magazine*, xvii, 124.

[118] *Dublin Journal*, February 14–17, 1747.

[119] *Ibid.*, March 7–10, 1747.   [120] Sheridan, *A Full Vindication*, p. 10.

[121] *Ibid.*, p. 16.   [122] *Second Letter*, By A. F., p. 12.

[123] *DNB, v.* "Lucas, Charles." Before this time Lucas had served on the city council, where he had unsuccessfully attempted reforms. His struggle with the government, which in 1749 ended in his twelve-year exile and disenfranchisement, endeared him to the Dubliners so thoroughly that, after his pardon and return, he served as their elected representative in parliament for the last ten

much public spirit and apparently a personal friend of Sheridan's,[124]
he could hardly have remained neutral in this dispute. His timely
speech at the trial-play introduced democratic methods and asserted
the rights of players and audiences. On the other hand, his writings
—the three letters to the Free Citizens of Dublin by a Freeman,
Barber, and Citizen—grew more and more hysterical, stirring up
sectional and religious antagonisms. In the end, he saw the whole
thing as a Romanist conspiracy, encouraged by a too early slackening
of Irish legal discipline, a conspiracy which aimed at "foreign Invasion, a Western Insurrection, or a Universal Massacre." [125] An
amusing parody called *The Prophecies of the Book of the Prophet
Lucas* [126] implies that a Freeman's hysteria was a calculated political
maneuver, devised when Sheridan came to him and asked:

> What shall I do, for the men of Connaught are upon me?
>
> And Lucas said unto Sheridan; fear not, neither be dismayed,
> Are there not Papists in the land of Connaught? And are not
> the Papists rebels?
>
> We will go forth into the streets, and into the market place,
> and we will say that the men of Connaught are rebels; so shall
> it be well with thee.

But most Dubliners believed in Lucas' sincerity. Like him, Anglo-
Ireland was still nervous from last year's civil war.

More interesting than any of these imputations was the mysterious
person supposed to be masterminding the anti-Sheridan activities, a
person who was never named outright but who, by hints and implication, was shown to be none other than one of the villains of the
Drapier Letters—Halfpenny Brown, John Brown of the Neale,[127]

---

years of his life. The *DNB* makes no mention of his part in the Sheridan-Kelly
controversy.

[124] *The Tickler*, No. 1, written a year later, implies that Sheridan lodged with
Lucas at one time.

[125] *Second Letter*, By A. F., p. 10.   [126] Reprinted by Samuels, p. 120.

[127] An account of John Brown or Browne of the Neale, County Mayo, is
given in Herbert Davis' edition of *The Drapier's Letters* (pp. 226–228). Brown
outraged Swift and most Irishmen by being one of four to testify that Wood's
"Copper Money was extreamly wanted in Ireland" (*ibid.*, p. 48). Swift mentions Brown's trial for rape and his conviction for perjury and subornation in an
attempt to take away the life of John Bingham, Esq. Davis quotes excerpts from
the *Dublin Journal* of 1749, showing that two years after the theatrical riots
Brown was stirring up trouble again. Having killed a man in a duel and having
been convicted of manslaughter only, in a trial at which he was "attended by a

mentioned by Burke as one of the gentlemen forced to make a submission to the Trinity College boys.[128] An "infamous old crafty Traitor and Conspirator, declared so by the unanimous Voice of the National Common Council in the Year 1723," when he was disqualified from holding office for conspiracy and perjury, he didn't dare a ballad even until the death of the Drapier. Now, some twenty-five years later, he was covering seditious falsehoods with the same solemnity as he had sworn that "stamp'd Leather was the current Coin of this Kingdom." [129] Now, "after a Trial for a Rape . . . ; after giving false Testimony in another Nation against, and to the Prejudice of the Country . . . ; after prostituting himself to the infamous Service of some vile tool of a detestable Minister," this "Parricide" was sounding "the Trumpet of Rebellion," and if his "dark, Jesuitical Schemes" succeeded, he hoped "to be made Chancellor to the Pretender." [130] If, as is unlikely, Sheridan ever doubted that his cause was right, he must have been reassured as well as stimulated to find one of Swift's old targets at the head of the enemy faction.[131]

Halfpenny Brown may well be the author of one of the anonymous attacks on Sheridan, *A Serious Enquiry into the Causes of the present disorders in the city.* . . . Far outnumbered by writings favorable to Sheridan's side, this piece and a few others [132] give the case against

---

great Number of the Nobility and Gentry," he writes to the *Journal* to deny reports that he fomented the riots and public disturbances on the night of his "acquittal," when bells were rung and bonfires built (*ibid.*, pp. 227–228). Davis' account of Brown's activities makes no mention of his part in the theatrical to-do.

[128] See notes 99 and 106.   [129] *Second Letter*, By A. F., pp. 5, 6, 9.

[130] *Dublin in an Uproar*, pp. 19, 22 (The Tradesmen's Answer).

[131] Not to mention the fact that Sheridan's father had a low opinion of this Brown. When Dr. Thomas Sheridan was corresponding with Thomas Carte, at the time that young Thomas was in Westminster, he was trying to return the favors Carte was doing for him by ferreting out some important old letters of the preceding century necessary to Carte's research. A man named Brown was in possession of them; and Dr. Sheridan writes to Carte that, if he had known what Brown it was, he could have had them long since; but he little imagined it was a gentleman "called half-peny Brown, one of our musical Society. He made many advances to me," Sheridan explains to Carte, "but I would not be acquainted with him, because of an unlucky character given him by the Drapier . . ." (*Lefanu MSS* 227.f.32).

[132] Other writings hostile to Sheridan are replies to defenses of the manager. *A Letter of Thanks to the Barber* (see note 109) answers the *Third Letter by A. F[reeman], Barber and Citizen.* Less of an attack on Sheridan than on "A. F.

the manager: he "thought to treat Gentlemen as he pleased," having had an attorney "dragged forcibly" from the house, even before the Kelly affair; [133] he failed to handle Kelly, "an unhappy Gentleman who drank too freely," with the proper tact and good humor; he so terrified his audiences that no one even dared hiss in the galleries; he set the city's inhabitants at each other's throats and filled the town with fear and confusion; and he tried to "reassume the Gentleman" after he had lost the status by turning player.

The overwhelming defense [134] of Sheridan was more spirited and

---

otherwise C— L—, Barber, Freeman and Citizen of Dublin," who was recently assaulted and given several kicks in the "A—," it sustains its irony so consistently that the modern reader is not sure until the end which side its writer is on. There one reads that gentlemen have entered into a society organized to debauch wives and daughters and to massacre every advocate for virtue. "The Gentlemen's Apology to the Ladies for their being disappointed at the Playhouse on Wednesday, the 11th of February, 1746–7," is printed in *Dublin in an Uproar* as a reply to a letter from a lady defending Sheridan and reproving the other party. "We think it greatly hard and unkind," says the *Gentlemen's Apology*, "that our standing up to require a proper Apology from an *Actor*, who had treated you so ill, should be resented by you." *The Prophecies of the Book of the Prophet Lucas* makes fun of Sheridan as well as Lucas: "Then Sheridan arose and arrayed himself in the coat which his father gave him . . . and the man was well-favored in his own eyes; and he found grace with the young men who are called Sophisters." Another satirical work, the poem "The Farmer's Yard," laughs at Kelly and Sheridan. Kelly is called a goldfinch, who courted a goose, saying he'd do to her what any gander could. Sheridan is depicted as a gander "of high Descent," who in the law court orates in a style so Ciceronian that he proves all his geese are swans.

[133] In a notice in the February 17–21 issue of the *Journal* Sheridan solemnly declares that he was not connected with the theater when the gentleman-attorney was turned out of the gallery.

[134] Writings favorable to Sheridan include *An Humble Address to the Ladies of the City of Dublin*, by a Plebeian (Dublin, 1747); the three letters by a Freeman (dated February 12, March 3, and March 26); and three of the four letters in *Dublin in an Uproar*. Two of these last three purport to be written by ladies, and the first may be Frances Chamberlaine's if it is true that she wrote an anonymous prose pamphlet defending Sheridan (Lefanu, p. 25). The third is entitled "The Tradesmen's Answer," from which I have quoted above. *Brutus's Letter to the Town*, written by Dennis after the verdict, gives a calm arraignment of Kelly's action, and supports Sheridan in an unemotional way, ending with the statement that the general voice agrees with that of the magistrate. In a more humorous style *The Gentleman*, a mock heroic epic from which lines have been quoted earlier, ridicules the behavior of the "Gentlemen." An impartial judgment of both principals is attempted in one paper, now incomplete, called *Reflections of a Gentleman in the Country on the Present Theatrical Disturbances*.

convincing. For the punishment meted out to Kelly, it was argued that Kelly struck the first blow (with an apple—or was it an orange?), that the provocation was great, and that, had Sheridan not responded as he had, he would hardly have been fit to be manager. Imagine the results otherwise! As Sheridan himself humorously points out, announcements would have to be made like this:

> Ladies and Gentlemen, Cato would wait upon you in this Scene, but a Gentleman has taken it into his Head, to entertain himself with kicking him, when the Gentleman has done he will be sure to attend you.

And,

> We hope you will excuse Monimia's Appearance this Scene, for a Gentleman is just now diverting himself with her, but she will be ready by the next Act.[135]

It has been said, another defender observes, that Kelly intended no serious harm to Miss Bellamy; he thought only to "rumple her Robes and raise the Blood into her Cheeks. And such an Honour as that, at the Hands of a Gentleman, might be deem'd a full Compensation for the coarse foul-mouth'd Ribaldry with which he persecuted her Ears." But what, it is asked, should Sheridan have done in the meantime? Come onstage and dismissed the waiting audience?[136] "Sure every one must allow that a Theatre in such a Condition . . . must be the greatest Pest that ever plagued a Metropolis."[137]

Throughout the controversy Sheridan's accomplishments as manager were granted, even by the opposing side. His enemies confessed that "By his Regulations . . . the Theatre became more entertaining and agreeable than it had been for some Years before," and that "the House has been since kept to better Order."[138] His friends stressed his improvement of the stage and his choice of moral and loyal plays. Indeed, it was this choice, said a Freeman, that gave umbrage to certain gentlemen, who then determined on the destruction of the reformed stage.[139] Furthermore, Sheridan insisted on decency behind as well as before the scenes; he cultivated good manners, harmony, and justice among the actors, said Treasurer Victor,

---

[135] [Sheridan], *A Faithful Narrative*, p. 6.
[136] *An Humble Address to the Ladies*, p. 6.
[137] [Sheridan], *A Faithful Narrative*, p. 6.
[138] *A Serious Enquiry*, pp. 6, 8.   [139] *A Letter*, By a Freeman, p. 2.

paid all his bills, and entertained the town better than ever before.[140]

During the course of the controversy three issues important to theatrical history were publicized and debated: the duty and rights of a manager, the rights of the audience, and the position of the actor.

The rights of the manager to improve his theater by making it a decent, orderly place, where the audience could enjoy the play it came to see, made the most immediate gain. After the sentence against Kelly was given, Lord Chief Justice Marlay observed that the theater was a "Place of public Resort" and that any person apprehended forcing his way behind the scenes there "should feel the utmost Severity of the Law." [141] Victor ends his account of the Kelly affair with these words: Where "before that happy Aera, every Person who was Master of a Sword, was sure to draw it on the Stage-door-keeper, if he denied him Entrance," "from that Hour, not even the first Man of Quality in the Kingdom ever asked, or attempted, to get behind the Scenes." [142] So Kelly's drunken behavior and his friends' destructive violence secured Sheridan the reform which gained him a place in stage history. It was not until some fifteen years later that Garrick, after several unsuccessful attempts to follow Sheridan's lead, was able to banish the beaux from the Drury Lane stage; [143] and this reform at Covent Garden came even later.

As for the rights of the audience, the feeling was that Sheridan's enemies, concerned only with their privileges over the actor, had ignored the rest of the house. "It is the uncontestable Right of the bulk of an Audience to be entertained in what manner and by whom they please" [144]—such was the democratic thinking which found expression during the Kelly controversy.

The issue of the actor's status, however, was the really engrossing one to the eighteenth-century public. And most of the writings revolved around the question of who was and who was not a gentleman. The view of Sheridan's enemies we have already seen. Our modern view was expressed by the republican Lucas—that a person should be esteemed a gentleman solely on the basis of his morals and

[140] Victor, *History*, I, 103.   [141] *Ibid.*, pp. 127–128.   [142] *Ibid.*, p. 129.

[143] Davies, I, 331; Wilkinson, IV, 120–123. At Drury Lane as early as 1747 Garrick, trying to abolish the custom, had advertised his intention, but the players as well as the audience objected, because they wanted their patrons on stage for their benefits. Not until about 1764 was complete reform effected (*Johnson's England*, "The Drama and the Theatre," II, 183–184).

[144] *An Humble Address to the Ladies*, p. 12.

conduct, regardless of his birth or fortune.[145] The compromise reached in the eighteenth century is best represented in Sheridan's own reasoning: By birth and education a gentleman, he had not degraded himself by any base behavior or servile employment; as a matter of fact, he was really not a player because he had taken no salary to perform, always having been a director of a theater and having had it "at his own Option to perform or not." But even if he were a player, acting ranks as an art with poetry, painting, music; famous authors, painters, and actors—Roscius, Booth, Wilks, Cibber —were gentlemen in spite of their profession and were always treated as such. The conclusion is that "tho' the Profession of an Actor, does not entitle a Man to the Name of a Gentleman, yet neither can it take it from him if he had it before"; and this can be proved both by reason and "the Custom of all polish'd Nations, who enjoy'd their Liberties." [146] The airing of this view helped to clarify and raise the social position of the eighteenth-century gentleman turned player. Afterward gentlemen like West Digges, Henry Mossop, and others whose names are now forgotten accepted Sheridan's invitation to make their debuts on the Smock-Alley stage with less hesitation because Sheridan by his affirmation—and by his behavior too—had shown that a gentleman could be an actor and still remain a gentleman.

After the theaters were closed by official order, they stayed closed for almost three weeks. At the end of February petitions to reopen were filed with the Lords Justices by both theaters. One petition was from "Thomas Sheridan . . . *Gentleman*" [italics mine]; another was signed by the employees of Smock-Alley, fifty-one in all, who had been thrown out of work for a total of over four weeks because of Kelly's inebriety.[147]

Although Smock-Alley opened again on March 3,[148] Sheridan did

---

[145] *A Letter*, By a Freeman, p. 1. Lucas' view is somewhat marred by his warning that morals can be "corrupted by conversing with Papists and Slaves."

[146] [Sheridan], *A Faithful Narrative*, p. 13.

[147] Lawrence, "Trinity and the Theatre," *Irish Times*, September 2, 1922. The petitions themselves were lost in the burning of the Public Records Office, but copies had fortunately been made by the author of this article, Mr. William J. Lawrence. The Capel-Street petitioners (R. Layfield, Michl. Mason, Wm. Mynitt) complain that, after performing peaceably since November 1, they have now been shut up through no fault of their own, but through a disturbance at a rival theater.

[148] Bellamy (I, 109) specifies no date, but says that the Lord Mayor allowed Sheridan to open his theater although he was not to perform until after his trial.

not appear. A March 6th letter from him to the *Journal* shows that, even this long after the trial, party faction and not any legal restriction was keeping him inactive. His enemies, he complains, have multiplied, and their violence is unabated.[149]

His return from exile, delayed until March 19, a month after the trial, justified the apprehensive tone of his letter. For the theatrical troubles were not quite over. The performance was to be that much postponed benefit for the Incurables and hence the stage was to be occupied, but only by "Ladies and the Gentleman Stewards . . . appointed for it." [150] Before the play Sheridan was introduced to the audience by some of the charity stewards.[151] He spoke to the spectators voluntarily, although on the advice of friends. Once more solemnly denying, one by one, all the many charges laid against him, he concluded with this near apology: "If any particular Gentlemen have taken Offence at any part of my publick Behaviour, I am extreamly sorry for it, and beg Leave to declare publickly, that I am not conscious of ever having designed to offend them in any Shape." This speech was followed by "the most general, loud, and continued Applause that was ever remembered," and *The Fair Penitent* was at last performed without interruption. But before its conclusion the Smock-Alley manager had received word from "the Gentlemen" that they were not satisfied. This incredible persistence could not have been a surprise to Sheridan, who had felt all along that his enemies

---

Actually, Sheridan's petition and *Journal* notices show that the theater did not open until two weeks after the trial.

[149] *Dublin Journal,* March 3–7, 1747. Because he asked his supporters to "drop their Pens" and join him in restoring peace, this letter, according to Samuels, the editor of Burke's early work, was regarded by Trinity students as an ignoble surrender and did much to cool their ardor for Sheridan. But Samuels' evidence consists of several passages unfavorable to Sheridan written by Burke over a year later (Samuels, p. 121) after a play of Burke's had been rejected at Smock-Alley. It is significant that six days after the Sheridan letter, Burke, in identifying his friend Dennis as the author of an article favorable to Sheridan, called Dennis' article "a good Thing, I think" (Samuels, p. 128)— approbation hardly possible if Burke had already begun to turn against Sheridan.

[150] *Dublin Journal,* March 14–17, 1747. Also, no servants were to be admitted to the upper gallery.

[151] Two sources give information on this evening's events. A long report, written by a gentleman who was present to "observe the many false Reports that have been spread upon this Occasion," appears *ibid.,* March 21–24, 1747. A *Third Letter,* by A. F., likewise reports the evening, including a few details not in the *Journal* item. "The Gentlemen," says A. F., offered the society stewards a large reward for the hospital if they would withdraw support from the play.

were still flourishing and full of ill will. At the end of the performance he advanced to the front of the stage, accompanied and advised by the stewards, and said:

> Ladies and Gentlemen, I humbly beg Leave to know what the
> Sense of this Audience is in Regard to the Apology made by me
> before the Beginning of the Play, whether it was satisfactory or
> not? The Decision of so numerous and polite an Assembly must
> be definitive to me, and I hope will be to every one else.

The response was deafening, as the entire audience rose to its feet
and cried: "No more! No more! Enough! Enough!" With this, the
theatrical feud seems finally to have come to an end. And, for the
time being, Dublin had heard the last of "the Gentlemen."

The rest of the season was uneventful. Although Capel-Street continued to run regularly, Smock-Alley did little through early April
except for a three-play subscription series, suggested by Sheridan's
friends as a way to recoup some of his losses.[152] In an interesting departure the subscribers were invited to select the plays at a dinner
meeting arranged by Sheridan.[153] Dutifully they chose three Shakespeare tragedies, *Hamlet, Othello,* and *Romeo and Juliet.* The manager continued to consolidate the gains he had won so dearly by
informing the public that "No Money will be received, nor any
Persons admitted behind the Scenes." And he took another bold step
forward when he concluded this advertisement thus: "No odd Money
will be taken during the Performances, nor any returned after the
Curtain is drawn up." [154]

In mid-April Sheridan announced that he had to go into the country till the May term "for the better Recovery of his Health." [155]
But actually, "flush'd with this happy Conquest" of his enemies, he
left for England, to shop for much needed reinforcements for his
troupe.[156] It was apparently wiser not to wait till summer; and during his month in London he made several profitable bargains,[157]
including some first-rate dancers from Drury Lane, the Mechels,
who began dancing at Smock-Alley in mid-June [158] and so enabled
Sheridan to keep the theater open later than usual. With Capel-
Street closed (its advertisements had stopped early in May), he was
hoping to make up some more of his earlier losses.

---

[152] *Dublin Journal,* March 17–21, 1747.   [153] *Ibid.,* March 24–28, 1747.
[154] *Ibid.,* March 31–April 4, 1747.   [155] *Ibid.,* April 11–14, 1747.
[156] Victor, *History,* I, 131.   [157] *Ibid.*
[158] *Dublin Journal,* June 6–9, 1747.

Smock-Alley's last performance on July 16 marked the end of a stormy year.[159] But the storm had subsided and the Smock-Alley manager stood, more fixed in his position and stronger than before. For the next seven years all his considerable energy, his unstinted time, his creativity were to be undeviatingly committed to the improvement of his theater. He regarded this mission as serious and important; looking back three years later, he was to say of his work at Smock-Alley: "No Manager before ever undertook such a Task." [160] Though colored with Sheridan's characteristic exaggeration, the statement shows his grasp of the possibilities which his more assured position offered. In the relative calm of the next seven years he began to realize some of these possibilities.

[159] In spite of the uproar, Sheridan seems to have appeared in seven new roles this season: Bevil Junior in *The Conscious Lovers*; Falstaff in *King Henry IV, Part 1*; Benedict; Romeo; Aesop; Tancred; and Ranger in *The Suspicious Husband*. Only Bevil, Falstaff, and Aesop are advertised as "firsts."

[160] [Sheridan], *State of the Case* (1750), p. 22.

CHAPTER V

Winning the Dublin Public, 1747-1749

AFTER the season of 1746-47 a calm of sorts settled over Smock-Alley affairs; and although each following season had its own problems and achievements, the events were played out against a similar backdrop—the seasonal and daily routine which Sheridan could now maintain with a regularity basic to winning the Dublin public. The seasonal routine began toward the end of September or early in October when Smock-Alley opened, after newspaper items had sufficiently whetted public interest in the improvements to the theater which Sheridan had made over the summer. "Mr. Sheridan, Manager of the Theatre Royal," reads a lead item for September 12, 1747, "is fitting it up in the most elegant and beautiful manner, by new Scenes, and very grand Decorations on the Stage, as well as other Parts of the House. . . ."[1] At first, performances were scheduled for two or three nights a week only, later in the season for more. "Agreeable to the custom of the great ones,"[2] Sheridan and usually his leading lady did not appear until several weeks after the opening. Sometimes he was not even in town for the first weeks,[3] Victor, as deputy manager, probably carrying out the prearranged and relatively commonplace schedule. November, which, along with February and May, was term time, when Dublin was most crowded and most socially inclined, was a good theatrical month. Only in November and February did the theater make enough profit to balance the deficits of other months.[4] The Christmas holidays closed the theater sometimes for a week or more, and afterward, as in the autumn, the company carried on without the top actors for a short time. The last three months, March, April, and May, were given over to that traditional theatrical bane, the actors' benefits.[5]

[1] *Dublin Journal*, September 8-12, 1747.

[2] Victor, *Original Letters*, I, 135 (Letter to Garrick, October, 1747).

[3] In the fall of 1750, for example, the theater opened on September 19. The October 6-9 *Journal* runs this press item: "Yesterday [Monday, October 8] arrived in Town, from his House in the Country, Thomas Sheridan, Esq., Manager of the Theatre-Royal." Sheridan's first appearance that season was on October 15.

[4] Sheridan, *State of the Case*, p. 12.

[5] For the beginning of actors' benefits in Ireland see Clark, p. 103. In the

During the benefit period only two nights—usually Tuesday and Saturday—were available for nonbenefit plays. For the first few seasons the theater remained closed on these nights, but toward the end Sheridan had a large-enough audience to use all spare evenings. By early June the season was usually over.[6]

Because Smock-Alley was the theater-royal, the government paid Sheridan £100[7] annually to perform plays on "Government Nights,"[8] which marked certain national anniversaries, among them the king's birthday, his coronation date, and the birthday, on November 4, of that great favorite of the Anglo-Irish, "the ever-glorious and immortal King William 3rd," whose memory was idolized in Dublin "almost to superstition."[9] On November 4, as at Drury Lane, *Tamerlane* (with Sheridan in the title role) was always the play, although for the other anniversaries comedies were invariably chosen,[10] as more suitable to the mood. These occasions were advertised as by command of the Lord Lieutenant or, if he was absent from Dublin or lacking, the Lords Justices; a prologue sometimes marked the event and the boxes were free to the ladies. "The Lords Justices gave a play to the Ladies"; thus quaintly does the *Dublin Journal* report an anniversary play ordered for the Prince of Wales' birthday.[11] Viceregal command performances for no special occasion—most advantageous to the theater's income—were more or less frequent, depending on the Lord Lieutenant's presence in Dublin and also on his interest in the theater. On "command nights" the viceregal presence filled the boxes and, consequently, all the rest of the house—with servants who had come early to hold seats for these great ones and with others who had come largely to behold these

---

early years of Sheridan's regime occasional fall benefits for players occurred, but had disappeared by 1750. Sheridan stopped taking benefits for himself in the 1747–48 season.

[6] Much of this routine parallels that at the London theaters as shown in Mac-Millan's *Drury Lane Calendar* and in *The London Stage*.

[7] Victor, *Original Letters*, I, 136.

[8] Government Nights in Dublin are described by Clark, p. 136.

[9] Maxwell (p. 72) takes this quotation from a letter written by Mrs. Delany in 1751.

[10] In 1753, for example, *The Non-Juror* was performed on June 4 in honor of the birthday of the Prince of Wales; *The Suspicious Husband* on October 22 to celebrate the anniversary of His Majesty's coronation; *The Beggar's Opera* on November 10 for His Majesty's birthday; *The Committee* on November 30 for the Princess of Wales' birthday.

[11] *Dublin Journal*, June 2–5, 1753.

great ones. Certain viceroys were much more beneficent in their support than others.

An evening's entertainment at Smock-Alley, as at Drury Lane, consisted of the play, preceded by music and followed except on rare occasions by a second short play, often a farce (straight farce, ballad farce, et cetera), sometimes a musical play (burlesque opera, ballad opera, serious masque, et cetera), occasionally a puppet show or a pantomime. Often interspersed or following was some other offering: singing, dancing, instrumental music, processions, mimicry, animated statues, tricks (such as the Escape of Harlequin into a Quart Bottle), tumbling, rope-dancing, even something called "a comical and diverting Humour Some Body and No Body . . . performed by Living Figures, some of them six Feet high." [12]

The play usually started shortly after six thirty, the time of the last music. One advertisement gives the schedule for the preliminary musical entertainment, provided primarily to pass the time for servants holding places and for other early comers: first music, five thirty; second music, six; third music, six thirty. [13] But the schedule was flexible if other matters—an assembly or a court reception—pressed; on Fridays in 1747 the curtain was drawn up at six so that the play should be finished in time "for such Ladies as please to go to the Castle." [14] Because the relationship between the theater manager and the gentry was so intimate, accommodations were easily made for these important patrons.

At Smock-Alley as at Drury Lane "the play" was usually one of the old stock comedies or tragedies, whose recurrent production seemed, strangely enough, not to bore the small and unchanging audience, although some members of it must have known *The Suspicious Husband* and *The Distrest Mother* by heart as well as the actors did. These stock plays formed about seventy-five per cent of the plays presented, the revived plays making up most of the rest. Revived plays were advertised specially as "not acted these so-many years"; they sometimes received special advance notice in the news columns of the papers. [15] After the first few seasons prices were usu-

---

[12] *Ibid.*, March 13–17, 1750. See Smock-Alley Calendar for March 22, 1750.
[13] *Ibid.*, September 27–October 1, 1748.   [14] *Ibid.*, October 10–13, 1747.
[15] For example, "The Historical Tragedy of King John is now reviving at the Theatre-Royal, and will speedily be performed, the Part of King John by Mr. Mossop, and the Part of the Bastard by Mr. Sheridan. Between the Acts there will be performed some new Choruses, in the Manner of the Antients, set to Musick by Mr. Lampe" (*ibid.*, March 13–17, 1750).

ally not raised. By far the smallest in number were the "new plays," most of which were not actually new because they had been performed in London. Also advertised as new were plays which had been revised considerably by Sheridan or someone else. On these grounds Sheridan called his version of *The Loyal Subject* new.[16] Rarest of all were the plays which had never been acted anywhere before. As at Drury Lane the time in the season for new plays was generally winter term time, February and March, before the benefits; but several made their debut in May to give a final fillip to the season. Early in his managership, in October 1747, Sheridan tried to introduce the London system of running a revived or new play on successive nights with the idea that he would have more time "to exhibit a greater Variety of new Performances."[17] But the new system did not work out, probably because the smaller playgoing public could not support a play for successive nights. Though revived and new plays were repeated two, three, or more times, their representation was scattered throughout the season and accompanied by different afterplays and entertainments.

If we are to believe the advertisements, the choice of "the play" was frequently dictated by "the Desire of several Persons of Distinction," or sometimes just "by Desire" or "by particular Desire." Probably Sheridan did receive requests from ladies and gentlemen for particular plays, and it is likely that he consulted his friends from the college and others. During his early managerial years Sheridan's collegiate admirers flocked to his greenroom. What more natural topic there than the future bill at Smock-Alley? It is significant that the notices of such request plays, very common at first, fall off in later years when Sheridan was growing away from the college and becoming more secure in his own judgment.

Although he had no luck in running one play for a continuous time, Sheridan made a great success of his various series. His chief contribution to the offerings at Smock-Alley and to the standard of taste in Dublin was his Shakespeare series, advertised enthusiastically and specially illuminated with wax candles instead of the usual tallow lights. A series, consisting at the least of six Shakespeare plays given one a week and subscribed for in advance, was presented usually twice a year, in the autumn and in the spring. So popular was this idea that

[16] *Ibid.*, February 20–23, 1748. Sheridan advertises it as having been never before acted.

[17] *Ibid.*, October 13–17, 1747.

Sheridan tried other series: in 1749–50 he planned a group of three Jonson plays,[18] but only two of them were performed. The Congreve series, started the next year, was more successful and was thereafter made a regular part of the season's offerings, usually running concurrently with a Shakespeare series.

The publicity given coming performances continued to improve. As in the past announcements were made from the stage, and bills were distributed as well as posted outside the theater. But press notices became regular and impressive. The Dubliner opening his semi-weekly *Journal* could expect to find future plays announced right after the Dublin news, usually on the second page of the four-page sheet, but sometimes even on the front page. Besides, they were set under the large, clear heading of "Theatre-Royal," rather than buried haphazardly and without distinction in the fine print of other notices. Special linear and typographical effects, usually involving Mr. Sheridan's name, caught the eye and made for easy reading. Sometimes the offerings for the whole week were given at once, and frequently a performance was advertised more than once. Details of unusual attractions—particular songs, dances, performers—appealed to the jaded playgoer. As time went on, names of the minor players were included, until sometimes a whole column or more was given over to Smock-Alley activities. The *Dublin Journal,* run by Sheridan's friend George Faulkner, was his steadiest outlet, but the *Dublin Courant, Pue's Occurrences,* and *Esdall's News-Letter* during certain seasons also carried announcements, sometimes in more detail than the *Journal.* Faulkner was always generous with theatrical news items; Sheridan's personal activities—his comings and goings, his recovery from indispositions, his charitable contributions, et cetera—were featured along with news about plays in rehearsal, plans for special series, and the arrival of theatrical notables coming to Smock-Alley from Drury Lane, Covent Garden, and other exciting places.

The annual routine of the theater, its opening and closing, the selection, timing, and advertising of productions, was only the regular part of Sheridan's occupation. Each season brought new and special problems and new and notable advances. For, until his terrible downfall in 1754, the manager of Smock-Alley, despite the gloomy diagnosis year by year of Victor, Hitchcock, and others, did improve the well-being of his theater and win more and more of the Dublin

[18] *Ibid.,* January 30–February 3, 1750.

public. So the story of these seven seasons, between riots, passed over briefly in most accounts, has its own interest.

AT THE beginning of the 1747–48 season, the first after the Kelly riot, Sheridan felt himself strong enough to lay down several significant regulations, not for sporadic evenings but for the whole year. In advertising his first play he announced that he would admit no person behind the scenes; that no odd money would be taken anywhere in the house; and that coach traffic was to follow a certain route coming and going from the theater.[19]

From this time on, Sheridan was to be firm about stage sitters; and when, occasionally, he relaxed his ban for unusual events such as benefits with overflow crowds, the special boxes "formed" on stage were *for ladies only;* no gentleman, he announced, would "on any Account be admitted behind the Scenes." [20] Nor would he relax this rule even to let men use the stage as a passageway to their seats. When, in 1753, he opened the slips (over the lattices), hitherto closed, he opened them to women only. "As there is no Passage to them but by the Stage," he explained in the *Journal* advertisement, "Men will not be admitted there on any Account." [21] By 1749 he could discontinue his notices banning stage sitters, so complete had been his victory there. Although after he left Dublin there were occasional lapses,[22] Sheridan's continued firmness during his time, and his success in this battle encouraged other managers and led to the final elimination of the pernicious custom.

About a month after the theater opened in the fall of 1747 Sheridan made permanent his regulation against odd money, at the same time widening the scope of his decree: "No odd Money for the future will ever be received in the Theatre, nor any Money returned after the Curtain is drawn up." [23] With this announcement he hoped

[19] *Ibid.*, September 22–26, 1747.

[20] *Ibid.*, November 24–28, 1747. A Bellamy benefit and a benefit for Mlle. Mechel in the fall of 1747 had seats on stage for ladies.

[21] *Ibid.*, September 22–25, 1753. The slips, also called pigeonholes, were above the lattices and level with the upper gallery (O'Keeffe, 1, 287). The lattices, called greenboxes by Londoners (Wilkinson, 1, 7), were on a line with the middle gallery.

[22] Stockwell, p. 336, n. 54.

[23] *Dublin Journal*, October 24–27, 1747. The announcement was repeated at the beginning of each season until 1750–51, but not after that, so thoroughly

to wipe out another pernicious custom which allowed latecomers to enter at a reduced price and permitted earlygoers to claim a refund of part of their entrance fee.[24] Full admission prices during this period were normally 5/5 for the boxes and lattices; 3/3 for the pit; 2/2 for the middle gallery; and 1/1 for the upper gallery.[25] In order to collect the full price Smock-Alley managers, even before Sheridan, had published occasional notices: "No odd Money to be taken." [26] The preceding spring, right after the Kelly riot, Sheridan had begun his fight against reduced prices and refunds. At first he refused to return money after the curtain had been drawn up at some performances; then he declined to accept odd money from latecomers during some performances. But his notices were sporadic until the last few nights of the 1746–47 season, when he announced in every advertisement that no odd money would be taken. It is interesting that this first regular notice refused to *accept* money rather than make refunds after the performance had begun; latecomers, often drunk and noisy, were more of a nuisance than earlygoers. To eliminate these and so improve his house Sheridan was willing to sacrifice the financial profit from odd money—not inconsiderable if Dublin theaters were like London theaters.[27] For Dublin

---

had the practice been eliminated. Burke, who criticized more than he complimented Sheridan, liked the reform which Sheridan had established in refusing to admit for odd money "a Set of Wild Fellows who generally come flustered from Taverns, to the Disturbance of the more orderly Part of the Audience" (Samuels, pp. 299–300).

[24] Dublin theaters followed the practice of London theaters, beginning reduced prices and refunds (called in London "half price") after the third act of the main play (O'Keeffe, I, 286–287). So far as I can determine, the phrase "odd money" applied, in Dublin, only to reduced prices for latecomers.

[25] Prices had gone back up to normal this season after Capel-Street failed to reopen. Occasionally prices were raised for unusual occasions, for special benefits, for the Shakespeare subscription series, et cetera. For example, the pit seats for the hospital benefit and for the special subscription series after the riot were raised to 5/5, the gallery seats to 2/8½ (*Dublin Journal*, March 10–14, 1747). For Sheridan's benefit on July 13, 1747, only upper gallery seats were raised— to 1/7½. Sometimes other benefits charged 2/2 for both galleries. Stockwell (p. 230) lists lattices as 4/4, but I find that when they are mentioned in the advertisements they are 5/5. It is interesting that Smock-Alley prices in the mid-eighteenth century under Sheridan are about the same as those postulated for the end of the seventeenth century by Clark (p. 108), although salaries had risen enormously.

[26] Stockwell, p. 232.   [27] Pedicord, pp. 38–39.

theatergoers too the new ruling must have been a financial hardship. Not only were there the same reasons as in London for coming late—late dinners, late work, et cetera—but the more limited offerings of only one theater would make some people wish to avoid a familiar main play and come simply for the entertainments or the farce. This new regulation was, then, more of a hardship to more people, probably, than Sheridan's rule against stage sitters. But, perhaps because of his complete victory over the Kelly faction, no outbreaks occurred as they did in London when, over fifteen years later, the English managers tried to follow Sheridan's example and eliminate "half-price." [28] For in this improvement, as in clearing the stage, Sheridan antedated the London theaters by a number of years. O'Keeffe shows what an advantage this gave the Dublin stage. "In my day," he recalls, "there was no half-price at a theatre in Ireland; so that a noisy fellow, for paying his sixpence after the third act, as in the London theatres, could not drive a new comedy for ever from the stage by a hiss, (for a single hiss may do that;) neither could a critic come into the pit, or a man of fashion into the boxes, for his eighteen-pence, or half-crown, and censure the fourth and fifth act of a play, ignorant of the previous parts which led to the dénouement." [29]

Almost as much of a problem for Sheridan was the abuse of "silver tickets," [30] tokens which entitled the holder to a free seat at any time. The number of such permanent free-riders—members of the viceregal court, theater proprietors, their relatives and descendants, et cetera—had reached the disturbing total of ninety-two by 1747, when Victor wrote to Garrick to find out what the London practice was in this matter. He asked because he and Sheridan were forming an "application to the Lord Lieutenant, to redress [this] insupportable grievance. . . ." [31] Although the Dublin theater royal

---

[28] Fitzgerald, *A New History of the English Stage*, ii, 187ff. In 1763 Garrick had a two-day riot on his hands when he tried to abolish half price (Pedicord, p. 29).

[29] O'Keeffe, i, 286–287.

[30] Regular tickets, those used for benefits, for example, were cardboard or paper, we gather from a notice published by Victor in May 1747: "N.B. The Card Tickets delivered out for this Benefit which was to have been performed on the 23d of January last, will not be taken the above Night, there being a new Set of Paper Tickets printed on this Occasion" (*Dublin Journal*, May 16–19, 1747).

[31] Victor, *Original Letters*, i, 135 (Letter of October 1747).

was officially allotted its £100 a year for the governor and his court, this sum could soon be outweighed if each silver-ticket holder used his privilege regularly. The "redress" which the Smock-Alley application requested was probably not granted, for a month later Sheridan was trying to improve the situation himself by systematizing the methods of admitting his permanent "guests," some of whom had long since lost their tokens, others of whom were using cards and written orders, illegal according to the terms of the original agreement. To these Sheridan served notice that no person would be admitted unless he deposited his silver ticket in the doorkeeper's hand, that no cards or written orders would be accepted, and that those who had lost their tokens would need to have new ones made forthwith.[32] With all these new regulations, which his critics regarded as officious, Sheridan hoped to make his theater an orderly and well-run place, attractive to the Dublin public primarily for the good entertainment he could then provide.

The great stumbling block to the realization of this hope continued to be the upper gallery.[33] Sheridan's long struggle with the rowdies here, which started in his first year as manager, had been less successful than his other reforms. His periodic threats to close the section, to punish the guilty (who were being warned before the Kelly riot that "proper Men" were stationed there to mark them) had not availed, although in the Kelly disturbance itself the upper gallery, it seems, took little part, the riot having been limited to "Gentlemen."

Now, in the autumn of 1747, Sheridan thought of a new approach for quieting this unruly section of his house: he would woo the gallery with good entertainment. Believing that part of the ferment there stemmed from boredom with inferior preliminary music, he hired the best band he could find, hoping, he said, to please the town in general, but especially the gallery audience, who, having come early for seats, ought to welcome some first-rate music to make the time pass less heavily. The galleries did welcome the band to make the time pass—but not quite as Sheridan had hoped. When several musicians had been injured and their instruments damaged (in one night to the sum of £10), Sheridan, feeling less anger than "great Surprise" that the "best Pieces performed by the best Hands" were so unappreciated, had to warn his audience that they could

---

[32] *Dublin Journal*, November 17–21, 1747.

[33] Although the notices sometimes speak of galleries, most of the disturbance seems to have come from the upper gallery.

expect "worse Hands" or no music at all, if such behavior continued.[34] This notice, milder than that of the preceding season, appeared several times in November; but the soft approach had little effect. In early February, just a year after the Kelly riot, an English visitor who called himself Brittanicus remarked to the *Dublin Journal* that in the pit and boxes of the Dublin theater he never saw "genteeler Behaviour" (although Irish gentlemen, unlike English playgoers, did boorishly wear their hats during the performance), but he was appalled by the Dublin gallery, "the Part of the House that most wants Regulation." In London, he said, they have learned how to deal with the offender:

> for upon any Disturbance there, they Cry thro' the whole House *Throw him over—Throw him over*. Every One in the Gallery contributes to shove the Disturber forward, and the People in the Pit very politely make Room for the Reception of their new Guest. And this Discipline having been more than Once put into Practice, has struck such a Panick thro' the Heroes of the upper Regions, that the sturdiest of 'em All upon hearing those Words, is, immediately frighten'd into a proper Behaviour.[35]

The best kind of audience reform, Brittanicus felt, occurred when the members reformed one another. Despite this sound English advice, the Smock-Alley gallery continued to be a problem for several years more.

Goaded partly perhaps by the gallery, Sheridan was about to give up Smock-Alley and its management at one point in this season. Near the end of January 1748 he announced plans to leave soon for London and, in mid-February, he was asking all persons who had demands on him to send their accounts to Mr. Victor.[36] A few days after his first announcement, a public notice, hidden away in the fine print of *Dublin Journal* advertisements, came from the theater proprietors:

> To be let for any Term of Years from the 1st Day of May next, The Theatre-Royal in Smock-Alley and the Theatre-Royal in Aungier-Street with all the Cloaths, Scenes, Machines, etc. thereunto belonging.

[34] *Dublin Journal*, November 21–24, 1747, and following issues.
[35] *Ibid.*, January 30–February 2, 1748.
[36] *Ibid.*, January 19–23 and February 13–16, 1748.

Bidders were asked to submit their proposals to the proprietors.[37]

Additional reasons may have been behind Sheridan's sudden intention. His health had not been good; he did no acting from mid-December to mid-January, and performances had fallen off during this time.[38] George Anne Bellamy reports that receipts had begun to decline over last season's and tells of passes given her to paper the house. She blames Sheridan's misjudgment in attempting characters inappropriate to him such as Antony (instead of his usual role of Ventidius) in *All for Love* and Sir Charles Easy in *The Careless Husband*.[39] Burke writes Shackleton in a letter of February 2, 1748: "Sheridan is to lose his house, which we count a judgement on his arrogance and ignorance."[40] By this time Burke had thoroughly turned against Sheridan—because of that play of his which Sheridan had rejected earlier this winter?[41]—and had launched an attack on him in his new weekly, *The Reformer*. The attack, indeed, may have been designed to influence the proprietors.

Whether Sheridan was to "lose" his house (Burke was hardly writing from firsthand knowledge) or whether he was giving it up of his own accord, the main reason for the January notices in the *Dublin Journal* was probably that Sheridan and the proprietors were undecided about a lease for the future.[42] That Sheridan had had over-

[37] *Ibid.*, January 23–26, 1748. Proposals for the theaters at Waterford and Cork were solicited in this same notice. Except for Samuels, who notes the proprietors' advertisement only (p. 164), both this notice and Sheridan's announcement have been overlooked by writers about the period.

[38] Notices were sporadic in early December and entirely missing from December 16 to 30, a longer period than the usual week's intermission for the holidays. The first half of January was almost as barren. The January 9th *Journal* reports that "Mr. Sheridan being perfectly recovered from his late Indisposition intends shortly to appear in the Character of Anthony in All for Love." But he did not appear until January 18.

[39] Bellamy, I, 111–113.

[40] Burke (Samuels, pp. 163–164). This is the only contemporary reference I have found to this whole shadowy affair.

[41] Samuels speaks of a comedy which Burke may have written for Sheridan, one which was not accepted. In October and November of 1747 it was in Victor's hands. Burke expected it to be produced after Christmas (Samuels, pp. 113–114).

[42] It has been generally assumed, I think mistakenly, that Sheridan took his twenty-one-year lease on the theater in March of 1747 (the year before). If this was so, either Sheridan or the proprietors were now breaking that lease after just a year. And if such an untoward rupture threatened, why is there no mention of it in the press, no account of it in Victor or Bellamy, both on the scene

tures from Covent Garden to act during the spring is revealed in Hiffernan's *Tickler,* which names the six different roles he will play there and the money he will make (£50 sterling for each performance), at the same time that it sneers at "the late advertisement of the young hero's indispensible necessity of going to *London, where, doubtless, he is greatly wanted."* [43]

Before he left, Sheridan became so much the center of public interest that this season rivals the last in the amount of print devoted to him. Not all of it is derogatory. As early as mid-December his friend James Eyre Weeks published a poem, "To Mr. Sheridan. On his being appointed Director of the Irish Theatre," in which he expects that now Hibernia's stage will vie with the British and asks

---

and much involved, no memory of it left for Hitchcock, who came later? If, on the other hand, Sheridan's short-term lease had run out, and the question of renewal was pending for a while with one side or the other undecided, the absence of excitement and the fading of memory would be more understandable. The evidence on the dating of the lease is not perfectly clear, with the lease itself no longer in existence. But reference to it occurs in two later deeds, Sheridan to Victor, 1754 (169/346/114101, Off. Reg. Deeds) and Victor to Sowdon, 1755 (174/248/116009), where it is described as having been "dated on or about the Nineteenth Day of March, One Thousand Seven Hundred and Forty Seven." March 19 before 1751 falls within the period of cross-dating; the actual date then was March 19, 1748, unless the persons writing the later deeds after the fixing of the calendar adjusted the year—an unlikely possibility in view of the circumstances and the wording of the passage quoted just above. One other reference to the lease occurs in a petition to parliament by Sheridan (1758) in which, looking back on his history as manager, he says, ". . . your Petitioner in the Year 1747, took a Lease of the united Theatres of Aungier-Street and Smock-Alley, from the Proprietors of the said Theatres." But again Sheridan may not have allowed for the change in the calendar, and, besides, his dating of past events was frequently vague and inaccurate. Other evidence supports the probability that a lease's renewal rather than rupture was pending in 1748 and that the problem was resolved that year by the new contract: The date mentioned in the proprietors' January advertisement, May 1, suggests the expiration of a lease; it could well have been on May 1, 1745, that Sheridan first took over the management (Hitchcock says he returned to Dublin from England in May 1745). Sheridan himself says he first took the theater on trial for a year (this would mean until May 1, 1746). The Irish writer to the *Gentleman's Magazine* at the time of the Kelly riot describes Sheridan as having taken a lease on the Dublin theaters for *two* years, which would put the expiration date at May 1, 1748. (See also note 58.)

[43] *Tickler,* February 18, 1748, i, 3; March 11, 1748, iv, 23. In the latter we read, ". . . he is to perform six nights in Covent-garden Theatre for 50 l. sterl. each; the parts are as follow: In Tragedy, Orestes, Tancrede, Marc-Antony; in Comedy, Ranger, Archer, Captain Plume."

the public to strike a medal for "so bright a Date. The Irish Theatre resumes its State." [44] More disinterested was the praise from Brittanicus, who was surprised to find Smock-Alley "perhaps one of the best regulated Theatres that either is, or ever was, in Europe," and especially noteworthy for the decorum on stage. [45] By mid-February a letter to the *Journal* reports that Sheridan has again become the sole subject of our present writers, and thus their chief source of income—all much to the alarm of the manager's friends who fear an insufferable increase in his already sufficient vanity. [46] By this time Burke's *Reformer* and Hiffernan's *Tickler* were devoting many of their weekly issues to attacks on the theater and its manager.

Burke—he was about twenty years old when he launched *The Reformer* from Trinity College—made his onslaught less personal than Hiffernan, although the rejected author in him may emerge occasionally in statements like this: "The Poverty of this Kingdom can be no Excuse for not encouraging Men of Genius, one tenth of what is expended on Fidlers, Singers, Dancers, and Players would be able to sustain the whole Circle of Arts and Sciences." His chief protests were against the quality of the entertainment: the badly chosen plays; the players who changed whole speeches and even the plot; the attention and money spent on extra trimmings. But Burke admitted that the audience was largely to blame, entranced as it was with the dancing and the scene paintings:

> I have seen what they call a polite Assembly, sit in Rapture a full half hour at the Gestures of a foreign Dancer, and after reward him with the loudest Applauses, while an endeavouring Native who has racked his Lungs in their Service met with Inattention, or had his Words drowned in their Clamours.

Burke was hard to please. He ridiculed Sheridan's great foible of being "too nice in the Choice of his Dullness," serving up learning with his buffoonery and calling the dance of the statues introduced into *All for Love* a "Pyrrick Dance" when not one in five hundred knew it as anything but a common country dance. The manager would have done better, Burke decides, to order M—l (M. Mechel, the dancer) "to clap his Posteriors in Cleopatra's lap." (Cleopatra,

---

[44] *Dublin Journal*, December 15–19, 1747. I can find no other mention of this appointment, nor do I know whether the title meant anything more than manager.

[45] *Ibid.*, January 30–February 2, 1748.

[46] *Ibid.*, February 16–20, 1748.

incidentally, was George Anne Bellamy.) And yet Restoration and eighteenth-century comedy was distasteful to the young critic, who also disapproved of kissing, at least on stage. Sheridan's personal appearance and acting are derided briefly—the effeminate carriage, the squeaky voice which "fribilizes" even the most masculine characters, and Sheridan's manner of dying on stage, one which will "afford you the double Delight of a Hero and Harlequin." [47] *The Reformer* ran from January 28 to April 21. Sheridan, away for the last half of this time, made no response. In May Burke, writing to Shackleton, describes Sheridan as "a pitiful fellow who was never able to defend himself." [48]

Dr. Paul Hiffernan was Sheridan's archfoe during this time and for some years after. Just Sheridan's age, Hiffernan had recently returned from France, where as a Roman Catholic he had gone to be educated, at first for the priesthood and then, after meetings with Rousseau and other advanced thinkers, in medicine. Back in Dublin, he gained entrance through his wit to high society and was encouraged in a life of indolence and dissipation. What living he earned, he earned by his pen. He may, as Samuels suggests, have written for the "Gentlemen" after the Kelly riot; [49] his sympathies would certainly have been with them. His measure is suggested by the fact that he calls Burke a Sheridan partisan and is in turn characterized by Burke as "sometimes *too severe*," though a man of "good Sense." [50] His *Tickler* began in February and consisted largely of outrageous attacks on Faulkner, Lucas, and Sheridan, whom he nicknames "the arbitrary Lewis [King Louis] of the Stage." Like Burke, Hiffernan disapproves of the dullness and especially the obscenity of Sheridan's offerings. Nowadays, he says, the custom in the audience is for gentlemen, "at every smutty allusion, to look the ladies triumphantly out of countenance, who timidly skulk behind their fans." No beauty himself, he ridicules Sheridan's indifferent stature, his aspect inexpressive of dignity or passion, his "native sneer exclusive of all tender scenes," his "puppet-like strut." Like *The Reformer, The Tickler* jeers at Sheridan's acting, especially his method of dying, for which,

---

[47] See Burke's *Reformer*, Nos. 1–4 (Samuels, pp. 297–308) and No. 8 (Samuels, pp. 318–320). The word *fribilizes* is taken from Fribble, an effeminate dandy in Garrick's popular *Miss in her Teens*.

[48] Samuels, pp. 121–122.

[49] *Ibid.*, p. 119. For short biographies of Hiffernan see Baker's *Biographia Dramatica; European Magazine*, xxv, 110, 179; Madden, i, 320ff.; *DNB*.

[50] *Reformer*, Nos. 5, 6 (Samuels, pp. 309, 312).

according to Hiffernan, he has been so injudiciously applauded by would-be critics: he dies in a series of starts and flounces possible only to one in perfect health (obviously an allusion to Sheridan's frequent "indispositions").

Even more cutting must have been the attacks on Sheridan's literary style, for, as the future author of English grammars, dictionaries, and plans for English language teaching in the schools, Sheridan would have been hypersensitive there. Hiffernan takes apart several passages of Sheridan's prose, italicizing constructions which he dislikes, such as the tautology in "*all the whole* house shall be *entirely* illuminated.*" Both Burke and Hiffernan express apprehension over Sheridan's revisions of older plays. Hiffernan speaks of *The Loyal Subject*, on which Sheridan has exhibited his "*inoculation*." [51] Burke hopes that Sheridan's revision of this play will be better than "his late modest Attempts on Shakespear." [52]

Sheridan paid little or no public attention to these barbs; he knew Hiffernan too well, says Davies, to fear his criticism and he thoroughly despised Hiffernan's attacks on his acting.[53] Besides, he was too busy. In the same January *Journal* in which he had announced his intention of leaving soon, he had projected a crowded series of plays to be given before his departure. These were gratifyingly successful. Performances rose from almost none to the surprising average of four a week, with Sheridan himself taking the lead in many. A Shakespeare series of six was included; *The Careless Husband* was revived, with Sheridan playing Sir Charles Easy for the first time; Woodward's new pantomime was elaborately staged; and *The Loyal Subject*, "now first altered and adapted to the Stage by Mr. Sheridan," [54] was produced. That all this activity brought happy results is inadvertently revealed by Hiffernan, who, writing on February 18, speaks of the "crowded audiences this winter," attracted by

[51] See Hiffernan's *Tickler*, I–III, VI, and also *The Tickler Tickled.*

[52] *Reformer*, No. 2 (Samuels, p. 302). Probably a reference to *Romeo and Juliet.*

[53] Davies, I, 248.

[54] *Dublin Journal*, February 16–20, 1748. See also *ibid*, February 20–23, where it is called "a new Play never before exhibited." Baker (*Biographia Dramatica*, II, 207), implying that the alterations were not extensive, says Sheridan thought it worthwhile to revive this only fair play and reprint it "with a few alterations of his own." S. A. Tannenbaum ("Beaumont and Fletcher," *Elizabethan Bibliographies No. 3*) lists under *The Loyal Subject* as item 267 "[Altered] Mrs. [*sic*] Sheridan ad'r—Ln. 1750."

Sheridan's many artifices, such as "parsimoniously dealing out Shake-spear by the half-dozen, and illuminating him with wax-lights (which predilection to a favorite saint has a distant cast of Popery)." [55] Sheridan could hardly have taken this last thrust seriously, but some attack on his use of foreign and Catholic performers seems to have provoked him to a rare response: he is supposed to have declared that "if he thought himself indebted to the Mechels' dancing for any part of the extraordinary receipts of this winter" (another side light on his financial success), he would refund the money or give it to charity because the Mechels were Papists and subjects of the French king. [56]

Sheridan's last performance was in *Hamlet* on March 4. But he did not leave for England immediately, as he had planned; and indeed *The Tickler* reports him as uncertain "whether he shall or no." [57] The reason would seem to have been that an agreement on the Smock-Alley lease was being reached, with Sheridan's success during the last few weeks perhaps playing a part in the decisions. For "on or about the Nineteenth Day of March" he leased the two theaters and their appurtenances for twenty-one years from May 1 at a yearly rental of £200 Sterling. [58] When Sheridan went to England at the end of March, he went as Smock-Alley manager with this twenty-one-year lease in his possession. He did not perform at Covent Garden, a fact of which *The Tickler* makes much; [59] instead, he spent his time providing for the next season in Dublin. In May he returned to Ireland, still very much the manager of Smock-Alley,

---

[55] *Tickler*, I, 3. This remark takes on added humor when we remember that Hiffernan had been a Catholic.

[56] *Ibid.*, II, 12. So reported by Hiffernan, who makes fun of him for saying so.

[57] *Ibid.*, v, 29.

[58] Ms 169/346/114101 and MS 174/248/116009, Off. Reg. Deeds, Dublin. These are the 1754 deed from Sheridan to Victor and the 1755 deed from Victor to Sowdon, which describe the earlier lease. The date given for beginning the terms, May 1, supports the argument outlined in note 42 above. Also significant is the fact that Sheridan did not leave for London until March 22, after the day of signing the lease (March 19). The £200 annual rental was, incidentally, over and above the ground rent and taxes.

[59] *Tickler*, VII, 54. "Mr. Sh-r-d-n arrived [back in Dublin] last Sunday from London, and is to perform the part of Hamlet to night, which, we hear, he was not ask'd to play in London, or any other part;—but the inhabitants there are poor tasteless wretches—and we Dublinians compose the most polite, and judicious audience in Europe. I am sure the manager told us so from the stage before Christmass."

and from then on until 1754 there is no talk of his losing the theater or of giving up his position. If Burke and Hiffernan had hoped to drive him from his management by their criticism, they had failed. Some of this criticism Sheridan was to answer in the next few years, not by words, but by improving the quality of his programs—and doing it so tactfully that he won ever larger numbers of the Dublin public. He himself had, for some time, preferred Shakespeare to Vanbrugh, tragedy to tumbling.

Part of the financial success of the 1747–48 season—and in the end it was a success [60]—must be laid to Sheridan's company, particularly to his two principal players, Henry Woodward, new from Covent Garden,[61] and George Anne Bellamy, now in her third season at Smock-Alley. These two, according to Bellamy, were no strangers, George Anne having earlier (at Covent Garden) refused Woodward's proposal of marriage. At first somewhat embarrassed at finding his scornful lady here in Dublin, Woodward soon became reconciled and indeed pleased to have a "tolerable actress" performing with him. All this is according to George Anne herself.[62] But, whatever their relationship then (and it was to be very intimate toward the end of Woodward's life), Woodward, a most gentle and winning person, became a great favorite in Dublin that year. On his arrival he was hailed by the *Dublin Journal* as "not only the best Harlequin, but one of the best Comedians of the Age." [63] Because Sheridan shaped his entertainment by the particular talents in his troupe, comedy and pantomime predominated during this season, when he himself was the only male actor suitable for tragic leads. Here lies one of the reasons for offerings so offensive to Burke and Hiffernan. Three comedies new to Dublin were produced that season, all starring Woodward: Crowne's *Sir Courtly Nice; The Little French Lawyer*, "written by Beaumont and Fletcher"; [64] and Moore's *Foundling*.

---

[60] Victor, *History*, I, 131. Victor calls the season a "gainful" one to the manager "and indeed to the whole Company."

[61] *Dublin Journal*, September 12–15, 1747.

[62] Bellamy, I, 112. The Bellamy-Woodward "alliance," as Oulton calls it, was formed long after this time in London and lasted ten years (Oulton, I, 53).

[63] *Dublin Journal*, September 12–15, 1747. Both Bellamy and Victor report Woodward's popularity, Victor in the *History* and in a letter to Garrick (October 1747); Bellamy in the *Apology*, where she says that Woodward's Lord Foppington was, as usual, justly admired (I, 112).

[64] So advertised in the *Dublin Journal*, October 17–20, 1747, and see also *The London Stage*, Pt. 4, p. 142. The *Drury Lane Calendar* (p. 272) lists the

For the afterpiece, pantomimes vied with farces, and most of the pantomimes were either entirely new or new to Smock-Alley. Sheridan had expected much financial gain from them, some of which had been composed by Woodward; but, according to Hitchcock, they added little to the season's receipts.[65] On the other hand, the not-new farce *Miss in her Teens* was revivified by Woodward's acting of Captain Flash and by his changing roles, toward the end of the season, to Fribble, performing it "alamode Garrick." Here an announcement in the press from Woodward to the town is interesting for what it shows of his character: Lest it be supposed from his playing Fribble that he feels "he can be equally right in all Characters," he wishes to explain that several ladies and gentlemen wanted to see a picture drawn from the original actor in that character.[66] It was in this very art of mimicry that Woodward made his greatest triumph of the season and at a time when Sheridan was away in London, during the spring, when theatrical business normally fell off. The beginning of this particular success was touched off in early March by the arrival of Samuel Foote, the celebrated mimic, who spent three weeks in Dublin treating the nobility and gentry to chocolate in the London manner.[67] Burke, in his *Reformer* of March 17, says that Foote came to supplant Sheridan "by exhibiting Entertainments still more monstrous and incoherent." According to him, Foote refused Sheridan's offer of his house and his cooperation, and took,

---

version revived at Drury Lane on October 7, 1749, as altered from Fletcher and Massinger (?) by an unknown alterer. In his productions of *Sir Courtly Nice* and *The Little French Lawyer* Sheridan preceded Garrick by several years. *The Foundling* at Smock-Alley followed Drury Lane by two months.

[65] Hitchcock, I, 193. Although much touted and freshly dressed and painted, a new pantomime by Woodward, *Fairy Friendship*, played the second night to not more than £20, and was not a success even after later "Alterations" (*Dublin Journal*, February 2–6 and 23–27, 1748; Victor, *History*, I, 132–135). Victor thinks that this same pantomime ran successfully later at Drury Lane as *Queen Mab*. Dubliners, he felt, had too much good sense to like pantomimes.

[66] *Dublin Journal*, April 26–30 and April 30–May 3, 1748. *Miss in her Teens* was revived on October 8, 1747, when Woodward played the Captain.

[67] Bellamy (I, 111) mentions Foote's arrival and his *tea*, an exhibition "which consisted of mimickry, wherein he imitated or *took off* the voice and manner of most of the performers in England and Ireland. I never could find out [Bellamy adds] what analogy there was between tea and the talent of mimickry." What George Anne apparently hadn't heard was that Foote had invented this device of summoning his friends to take tea (or chocolate) with him in April 1747 as a means of circumventing the English Licensing Act.

instead, a little theater of his own (it was Capel-Street), drawing away Sheridan's best and most constant auditors.[68] But his activity seems to have redounded to Smock-Alley's eventual advantage, for Woodward quickly swung into action and began treating "his Brother Atall [Foote] with a Dish of his own Chocolate" [69]—with such success, according to Miss Bellamy, that Foote was driven from Ireland "precipitately." [70]

But, fortunately for Woodward, this was not the end. A local person calling himself "Foote the Second" and "Young Atall" [71] invited old Atwou'd (note the pun on Woodward) to a new Chocolate, "in which three celebrated Originals of this City will be taken off in a picturesque Manner. . . ." Some of the "taking off" seems to have started in this notice, which concludes:

> Absolutely the last Time of performing in this Kingdom. The Whole House will not be illuminated with Wax, nor will there be any Tickets given gratis to swell the Pitt.[72]

[68] *Reformer*, No. 8 (Samuels, p. 319). Foote's chocolate is announced in the March 1–5 issue of the *Dublin Journal*, his first appearance scheduled for noon, March 7.

[69] In a *Dublin Journal* notice (March 8–12 issue) for a March 14th performance. Woodward answered Foote, then, in just a week. Bellamy says that Foote had attacked Woodward first. Atall is the name of a protean character in Cibber's *Double Gallant*; Woodward had played the role earlier in the Smock-Alley season.

[70] Bellamy, I, 112.

[71] Notices (*Dublin Journal*, April 5–9 and 16–19, 1748) indicate that this local person was John Pilkington and that his gag writer was his mother, Letitia Pilkington, Swift's old favorite who had turned out so badly. Not only must Letitia have been familiar to Sheridan through his parents and godfather, but a Master Pilkington—probably John—played Tom Thumb on Aungier-Street stage during Sheridan's first spring at Smock-Alley. Later, in revenge for Sheridan's arresting her son for having forged (as a joke, Letitia implies!) two orders to his theater one night, she wrote a vicious satirical poem about him (*Memoirs*, pp. 438–439). Tracing in it his evil heritage, she reviles his mother as sordid and greedy (this à la Swift), his father as "lavishing all upon a whore"; he himself is a "beggars brat" and a "scoundrel thief," whose "very looks presage a halter."

[72] *Dublin Journal*, March 22–26, 1748. Sheridan's notices inspired others to satire. When the New Theatre in Capel-Street was opened briefly the preceding December "by an artificial Company of Comedians," their play, *The Sorceress*, was advertised "with all the Sinkings, Flyings, and Decoration . . . interspersed with several diverting Interludes of Dancing, too tedious to insert" (*ibid.*, December 29–January 2, 1748).

Woodward's Chocolate (and Coffee) became so popular that he repeated it frequently (see the Smock-Alley Calendar for this year), often by request and at benefit performances. George Anne reports that he was paid an extra ten guineas a night by fellow actors at whose benefits he performed this piece.[73] His financial gains, whereby he cleared £300 from the manager, 60 guineas from Foote's Chocolate, and £120 apiece from two of his benefits, aroused an anonymous critic to sneer that a harlequin could get more money in Ireland than anybody with real genius—all because "Tommy now is King." [74] Press publicity like this and Woodward's own popularity brought him an unusual number of benefits—three in one season. After Sheridan returned from London in May, all Chocolate ceased. Mimicry, which may even have involved him, would hardly have suited his revivified ideals for Smock-Alley Theater. The following autumn Woodward was at Drury Lane.

George Anne Bellamy was Sheridan's other principal player during this season. Her popularity continued unabated,[75] but her autobiography, written years later, pictures her as growing more and more discontent, partly for personal reasons, but partly because Smock-Alley receipts were falling off—this must have been during that mid-season slump—and she was regretting that she had declined Garrick's invitation to Drury Lane. To fill the house Sheridan, she says, gave her some passes to distribute to her young lady friends; later Victor tried to charge her account with £75 for these. Not only did George Anne refuse to pay, but, after a dispute with Sheridan, she refused to play. Changes had to be made in the schedule,[76] and,

---

[73] Bellamy, I, 112.

[74] *A Letter to Mr. W—DW—RD, Comedian*, signed T. S. This piece was certainly not written by Sheridan or in 1747, as Loewenberg thinks; the phrase I have quoted, "Tommy now is King," is enough to disprove Sheridan's authorship, even if the whole tone were not entirely uncharacteristic of him. Loewenberg errs too about the date, which must have been 1748, since Foote's performances in Dublin did not begin till March of that year. This piece could well have been written by one of the Pilkingtons. Another undated piece, entered by Loewenberg as [?1758], belongs to this season (1747–48): *Punch's Petition to Mr. S—n, to be admitted into the Theatre Royal*. This is signed by Punchinello, who, since all his harlequins have been drawn into Sheridan's company, asks to be taken on at Smock-Alley and offers to play second to Woodward (mention of whom dates the piece).

[75] Her fall benefit occasioned such an extra demand for seats that boxes had to be formed on stage (*Dublin Journal*, November 24–28, 1747).

[76] As shown by *Dublin Journal* notices (February 13–16, 1748).

with his own departure threatening about this time, Sheridan must have found her fractiousness almost unbearable. Victor, trying to patch things up, offered to pay her whole account (she goes on to report) if she would "enter into a fresh engagement," an offer hardly possible without Sheridan's consent. "The illiberal treatment" she had had from the manager, however, would have deterred her from another Smock-Alley season even if she had not decided to depart for other reasons.[77] She played a month or so more, and then at the end of March, a few days after Sheridan's departure, left Smock-Alley without a leading actress. Some years later, meeting Sheridan in London, she says: "I was not upon the best terms with that gentleman for more reasons than one. In the first place, I could not forgive his making me pay for the orders I had issued during my being with him in Ireland."[78]

The only other performers to receive constant billing throughout this season, aside from Sheridan himself, were the Mechels. When he had good dancers in his troupe—like the Mechels now, and others in several later seasons—Sheridan introduced dancing not only between the plays but often between the acts and sometimes into the play itself. As we have seen, Burke speaks of the "Pyrrhic Dance" interjected into *All for Love*; this seems to have been the same piece which Bellamy calls a dance of the gladiators, introduced to make the play "as pleasing as possible" and to counteract the unfortunate effect of Sheridan as Antony.[79] Some indication of the importance now attached to dancing lies in the space and emphasis given it in the notices; fairly often, as a glance at the calendar shows, the names of the dances are included, while the names of all but the main actors in the plays are omitted. Mademoiselle Mechel's benefit precedes Woodward's. In thus stressing the dance Sheridan, Burke implies, was only giving the public what it wanted.

Sheridan tried to please the public by other devices. He dressed his cast of the revived *Careless Husband* entirely in "the Manufactures of OUR OWN COUNTRY,"[80] "which [Bellamy says] he judiciously thought, would increase at once his popularity and receipts."[81] Considerable publicity, at any rate, resulted and Sheridan tried the idea at least once more that season.[82] Other favorable publicity came from

---

[77] Bellamy, I, 113.   [78] *Ibid.*, p. 271.   [79] *Ibid.*, pp. 111–112.

[80] *Dublin Journal*, January 30–February 2, 1748. For the whole advertisement see Smock-Alley Calendar for February 9.

[81] Bellamy, I, 113.

[82] In *The Provoked Husband* on February 27 (see Smock-Alley Calendar).

his frequent charities, both personal and theatrical. He gave large sums from his own pocket, lent his musicians for benefit performances elsewhere at his own expense, used the proceeds from his own benefit for charity. These activities were often reported as the lead item under "Dublin" in the *Journal*, and, besides, they satisfied his own generous impulses. At Smock-Alley, benefit performances were given to persons in distress, *The Merry Wives of Windsor* playing for one "in deep Distress" under the aegis of Charles Lucas.[83]

With the performances themselves Sheridan took special pains in his effort to win larger audiences. News items in the *Journal* indicate that new entertainments were "in Practice" (i.e., in rehearsal) for some time before they were performed; [84] and Sheridan's insistence that his company act smoothly is reflected in this unique postscript to the notice of a second showing of the farce *A Duke and No Duke:* "Care shall be taken to have it more perfectly performed than it was last Time." [85]

Sheridan arrived back in Dublin on May 8,[86] performed a few times at Smock-Alley, and closed the theater at the end of May. The 1747–48 season, like the preceding one, had had a bad mid-year slump. But this time, when no fortunate accident like the Kelly riot occurred to save him, he had expanded his efforts and, with the help of his company, had saved himself, even turning a winter of despair into a profitable year. The season's end had left him with several other comforting achievements. Personally he had weathered the most violent criticism, without involving himself in retaliation; he had added seven new roles [87] to his repertoire, while he was also much occupied with managerial problems. In the interests of building a more attractive theater he had successfully introduced new permanent regulations; he had tried a Shakespeare series with such happy results that he could follow it with a second; best of all, he had secured from the proprietors a warrant of confidence and sufficient time to gain Dublin's confidence and make Smock-Alley into the theater of his dreams.

[83] This very successful performance, on May 4, yielded the surprising sum of £110, 10s, 7d (*Dublin Journal*, May 7–10).

[84] For example, see *ibid.*, November 3–7, 1747.

[85] *Ibid.*, January 26–30, 1748. [86] *Ibid.*, May 7–10, 1748.

[87] Archer in *The Stratagem*; Antony in *All for Love*; Varanes in *Theodosius*; Sir Charles Easy in *The Careless Husband*; Archas in *The Loyal Subject*. All these are advertised as "firsts" for Sheridan. Apparently new roles, although not listed as such, were Jaques, and Captain Plume in *The Recruiting Officer*.

PART OF SHERIDAN'S REGAINED ENTHUSIASM AND DETERMINATION WAS
spent during the summer of 1748 on an elaborate remodeling of
Smock-Alley's interior—the only one of note in this seven-year period,
although almost every summer after this minor improvements were
made.[88] A new passage was constructed to the upper gallery to relieve
the crowding caused when both galleries had to use the same stair-
way. A new passage was also constructed through the boxroom to the
lattices. The back part of the middle gallery was made "much more
warm and commodious for hearing." And the orchestra was greatly
enlarged to accommodate "the extraordinary Number of Hands" [89]
engaged for the season.

The new passages must have been of special help in emptying the
theater; the modifications in the middle gallery, perhaps including
partitions to keep out drafts and keep in sound, were also improvements for the comfort of the public. More surprising, in view of
Sheridan's difficulties the season before with the musically illiterate
galleries, would seem to have been the extra space for an enlarged
band. Victor, who disapproved of Sheridan's extravagances this season
in hiring too many performers at too high salaries, particularly resented the members of "the Musical Tribe" with their two-year
contracts. These "woeful Bargains" [90] included Signor Pasquali, formerly first violin at the opera in London, who was to lead the band
and direct the musical entertainments at Smock-Alley; Mr. Lampe,
the celebrated composer and harpsichordist from Covent Garden;
twenty-two instrumentalists; and at least five principal singers.[91] As
owner of this costly equipment—the *Dublin Journal* calls Pasquali's
group "the best Band of Instrumental Performers ever heard in this
Kingdom" [92]—Sheridan laced his evenings with musical productions,

[88] Almost every summer minor construction was reported at the theater. In
1751 the galleries were made still more spacious and commodious (*Dublin
Journal*, August 27–31, 1751). In 1752 alterations and improvements were
made (*ibid.*, September 30–October 3, n.s. 1752). In 1756, on his return from
two years in England, Sheridan made a drastic change in the upper gallery.

[89] *Ibid.*, September 24–27, 1748. The orchestra, note, was no longer in the
music box over the stage but now down in the pit (music pit) in front of the
stage.

[90] Victor, *History*, I, 143.

[91] The band consisted of ten violins, a harpsichord, two double basses, a
tenor (?), a violoncello, two hautboys, two bassoons, two French horns, and a
trumpet (*Dublin Journal*, September 24–27, 1748). The principal singers were
Mr. Sullivan, Mrs. Storer, Mrs. Lampe, Mrs. Mozeen, Mr. Howard.

[92] *Ibid.*, November 29–December 3, 1748.

sometimes even replacing the afterpiece with music.[93] As a performer Pasquali became more prominent than Lampe (although Mrs. Lampe's singing kept the name before the public); but over their years at Smock-Alley both men presented a very large number of original compositions, which are emphatically noted in Sheridan's advertisements. During this first season Dublin enjoyed three new masques with music by Pasquali and two burlesque operas with music by Lampe—these in addition to scores of minor pieces.[94] Contemporary critics of Sheridan's entertainments fail to mention his encouragement to this one of the arts—no small contribution from a man who himself had little use for music.

Besides, there were the singers. Some of these could be used in straight acting parts,[95] but generally they were saved for the masques, operettas, et cetera; and they also sang within plays, between the play and the afterpiece, after the afterpiece: they sang cantatas, ballads, duets, solos, even a new serenata with words by Theophilus Cibber.[96] The importance attached to these pieces can be gathered by the fact that titles of songs to be sung (like the names of dances in the previous season) are sometimes included in the theatrical advertisements. Were people enticed to Smock-Alley to hear "Elin-a-Roon" [97] sung by Mrs. Storer? It would almost seem so.

During this 1748–49 season the extra entertainment was almost exclusively musical. Perhaps stung by Burke's and Hiffernan's criti-

[93] See Smock-Alley Calendar for 1750–51.

[94] See *ibid.* for 1748–49. It is indicative that last year's Pyrrhic Dance, introduced into *All for Love*, was replaced by a short new masque written by Henry Brooke with music by Pasquali. The three 1748–49 masques by Pasquali, which were used as afterpieces, were premiered in Dublin; Lampe's burlesque operas had been given earlier in London.

[95] For example, Mrs. Mozeen and Mrs. Storer. The latter had been acting and singing in the company at least since Sheridan's first year at Smock-Alley; she was extremely popular in Dublin as a singer. Even dancers occasionally attempted dramatic roles "by particular Desire" (e.g., Mlle. Granier as Miss Biddy, March 28, 1751, and Miss Baker as Juliet, March 29, 1751).

[96] *Dublin Journal*, February 20–24, 1750. Apparently songs between acts were not specially chosen to fit the play. A performance for Mr. Sullivan's benefit of *The Merchant of Venice*, which included many songs within the acts (Sullivan often played Lorenzo "with Songs in Character") was advertised with various songs and singers between the acts. Later the projected *Merchant of Venice* was replaced by *The Careless Husband*, but all the interact singing was kept unchanged (*Dublin Journal*, February 27–March 3 and March 10–13, 1750).

[97] This title, like others, varies widely in its spelling in different notices.

cism, but more certainly influenced by Dublin's rising enthusiasm for music, Sheridan had eliminated the harlequins and dancers of the previous year; now there were only the members of the cast to perform an occasional country dance after such plays as *The Suspicious Husband* and *The Beggar's Opera*. The next season dancers were to return and for a few years share the stage with the musicians, whom they eventually nearly replaced; but for the time being Pasquali's band and the Smock-Alley singers held sway. From the beginning the position of Pasquali himself was important and rose even higher; his benefits were as numerous and as well-advertised and attended as those of the top actors. He seems soon to have become a personal favorite of Sheridan. When the new masque, *The Temple of Peace*, was staged in February 1749, the music was, not unexpectedly, by Pasquali; but the "Machinery," heralded long in advance as "the finest" ever exhibited here, was conceived and executed by an artist from England, eventually revealed as Pasquali Junior, brother to Signor Pasquali.[98] In years to come Sheridan used Pasquali as his deputy in missions that provoked critics to call him Sheridan's foreign minion and other less flattering terms.

From the beginning Sheridan had to devise ways to make these Smock-Alley musicians more financially productive. Soon after their arrival they played at a concert of the Charitable Musick Society around the corner in Fishamble-Street,[99] and this opportunity recurred off and on. The following year an agreement was worked out whereby regular weekly concerts were to be given for the Fishamble-Street musical society by the Smock-Alley band. This arrangement, though profitable, brought complications for Sheridan and sparked one of the most unpleasant controversies of his career.

In the meantime, a less explosive solution for the problem of the band was the Grand Festino, a new kind of entertainment which utilized the unused Aungier-Street Theater as well. This playhouse had remained closed during the preceding season (1747–48) except for an occasional ball. Now, in September 1748, the "large Room"

[98] *Dublin Journal*, December 27–31, 1748 and February 7–11, 1749.
[99] *Ibid.*, October 22–25, 1748. Victor (*History*, I, 143ff.) claims that it was he who, seeing Sheridan's distress *after a season* with his "musical Tribe," thought of how to save him by letting out his musicians and singers to the musical society. Hitchcock (I, 200) mentions this move but credits it to Sheridan's judicious contrivance. At any rate, the appearance of Sheridan's musicians before the musical society occurred only a month after their arrival and not a season later.

there was fitted up most elegantly for a reception to honor His Majesty's birthday. The entertainment, which included a birthday ode set to music by Lampe, was dubbed a "Grand Festino," done in Italian style.[100] This festino was a great success, and Aungier-Street festinos, consisting of music, refreshments, and dancing, and managed monthly by Victor, became so much the rage this year in Dublin that a rival series of "Grand Festinatas" started up at the Music-Hall in Crow-Street, in hopes of attracting Victor's customers by more easily attained liquid refreshment. The Crow-Street notice that "Wine and Glasses, &c. will be delivered by proper Attendants as often as called for" counters Victor's announcement that "there will not be any Bottles or Glasses delivered from the Side-Boards on any Account."[101] The Aungier-Street festinos, under Victor and Sheridan, were respectable social events.[102] They kept the band busy too.

The rest of the freight with which Sheridan (in Victor's metaphor)[103] had overloaded his vessel this season, consisted of players. Woodward had been replaced by Charles Macklin, a more versatile actor but a much more temperamental personality. To prevent the embarrassments of the last season when Smock-Alley had had only one leading actress, Sheridan had engaged several women to succeed Miss Bellamy—especially Mrs. Vincent and Mrs. Bland from Covent Garden. These gave Sheridan little trouble and indeed Mrs. Bland served him loyally for four seasons.[104] With Macklin came his wife, Ann, who played minor roles. Sheridan's two-year contract provided the two of them the very generous salary of £800 a year.[105]

An Irishman returning from London successes, Macklin was greeted enthusiastically by Dublin theatergoers. Not surprisingly, for his first performance he played Shylock, giving the role the new serious interpretation that had won him fame in London. A poem,

[100] *Dublin Journal*, September 24–27 and October 22–25, 1748. The word *festino* is first recorded by the OED for 1741. Apparently festinos had already been popular in London.

[101] *Ibid.*, January 21–24 and April 11–15, 1749.

[102] Festinos were given the following fall too at both Aungier-Street and Crow-Street, the latter advertising them then as Venetian Balls (*ibid.*, October 31–November 4, 1749).

[103] Victor, *History*, I, 136.

[104] Mrs. Bland had been mainly a singer before she came to Smock-Alley (*Thespian Dictionary*, v. "Bland"). She stayed with Sheridan until 1752. She later became Mrs. Hamilton (see Hitchcock, I, 196).

[105] Cooke, *Macklin*, p. 77; Appleton, p. 87.

published in the press the following year, describes the effect of his acting in this part:

> When in the frantic Jew we see him rage,
> We then no longer view him on a Stage . . .
> When from his Eyes the Jewish Vengeance darts
> Ev'n Nature at her own Performance starts! [106]

Usually, however, he played comedy roles, while Sheridan appeared in the tragedies, although sometimes they acted together, both in comedies and in tragedies.[107] Particularly excellent as a comedian, Macklin had a flair for originality and (says Chetwood, writing at about this time) always added something fresh to any part.[108] His literary talents were also profitable to Sheridan, who used as an after-piece Macklin's farce *A Will and No Will*, which had been "performed with universal Applause" in Drury Lane.[109] Mrs. Macklin, who knew "the Power of her own Talents," played such minor roles as Emilia and Mrs. Peachum. She was noted for the propriety of her dress.[110]

During this year Sheridan enlarged his acting troupe by discovering Miss Danvers. This "young Lady . . . who never yet appeared on any Stage" first played anonymously as Indiana in *The Conscious Lovers* on February 3, 1749.[111] Some time later she appeared again under the pseudonym of Danvers and from then on she remained one of Smock-Alley's steady players, usually in secondary roles, for many seasons. In using an assumed name (Victor says it was "out of Respect to a Family of Distinction in Dublin"),[112] she showed that, while gentlemen like Sheridan could risk their family's reputation on the stage, ladies might still hesitate. And understandably so. When in 1753–54 Miss Danvers left "to try her powers for capital characters" in Edinburgh, Victor anxiously pulled strings to get her under the

---

[106] *Dublin Journal*, September 30–October 3, 1749.

[107] For example, *The Suspicious Husband* (Ranger by Sheridan, Strictland by Macklin) and *Hamlet*, where Macklin played the gravedigger, or *Othello*, where he played Iago. This season Macklin played Bayes in *The Rehearsal* for the first time.

[108] Chetwood, p. 188.

[109] *Dublin Journal*, December 3–6, 1748. This farce was a translation from the French. Its first performance was for Macklin's benefit; it had sporadic production thereafter.

[110] Chetwood, p. 190.   [111] *Dublin Journal*, January 21–24, 1749.

[112] Victor, *History*, I, 142, footnote.

protection of some highborn lady. "I would, by no means," he explains, "have a recommendation to any gentleman. . . . Gentlemen are inclined to think lightly of actresses, and often with too much reason." [113]

Though trouble with Macklin simmered underneath and was to erupt the next year, Sheridan's relations with his company were, on the surface, unruffled this season. But to some Dubliners his very presence gave offense. An anonymous satirical piece in the form of a "Letter to the Admirers of Mr. S—N," which appeared sometime during this season, brings the grievances of his enemies down to date, at the same time that it shows, inadvertently, how much progress he had made in winning the Dublin public at large. Among his other offenses Sheridan, "notwithstanding his known aversion to drawing a sword," had overcome two powerful parties (a reference to the "Gentlemen" and perhaps to Hiffernan and Burke?); he had held the affections of Dublin for two years by banishing all rival merit, even actresses (a reference to Miss Bellamy, doubtless); he had relieved the worst plays and worst actors by the dullest of harlequins (Woodward) and dancers (the Mechels) the previous winter, fiddlers (Pasquali, Lampe, et cetera) and singers (Mrs. Storer, Mr. Sullivan, et cetera) this winter—next winter probably tumblers "and so on until he has reform'd the stage of all wit and just action to make room for *tumbling, fiddling, capering, juggling, rope-dancing,* and *festinism.*" The details and the style of the personal attack which follows suggest Hiffernan's fine Irish hand:

> Shall I add to all this, how naturally qualified he is for a tragic hero? whether we observe the languishing deadness of his eyes, his cadaverous complexion, his person, the burlesque of majesty and antidote of love, or his face, capable of no passion but one which he expresses by a constant and indeed very significant sneer. Or what, I believe works more with you [the admirers of

[113] Victor, *Original Letters*, I, 213. (Undated letter to Mrs. Irwin, but Dibden, p. 74, shows Danvers playing in Edinburgh in February 1754.) From the beginning the agreeable Miss Danvers (often "Miss W—" in Victor's letters) seems to have had a special attraction for Victor, married, middle-aged, and, by his own testimony, paunchy (*Original Letters*, I, 155); Colley Cibber twits him for the minute accounts he sends of her (*History*, II, 208). The first Mrs. Victor died in 1757. It is no surprise, then, when Hitchcock informs us that Victor married Miss Danvers, although he errs in dating the marriage and her retirement about a year after her debut (I, 197); her debut occurred in 1749 and she was still playing in 1758.

Sheridan], the manner of adorning this excellent person? the index ring, which he so critically displays on his little finger, the jantiness of his motions, or his cloaths in which you doubt whether to prefer the fashionableness of the cut, or the richness of the lace? These, indeed, are powerful charms, and by which he has won your hearts so surprisingly, that some have attributed it to witchcraft.

In conclusion the letter reports that Sheridan recently spoke from the stage about certain "machinations against him from the remains of a certain faction, the known enemies of his person and government." These frequent alarms of his are designed to arouse the public's affection by fear of losing him; his reward to them for all the insults and suffering he puts upon them is to call them from his own mouth "the politest audience in Europe."

The machinations hinted at so mysteriously by Sheridan from the Smock-Alley stage may well have been the plan of a group of gentlemen, led by Hiffernan, to open the Capel-Street Theater again and to produce plays in rivalry with Smock-Alley. This plan, announced in the *Dublin Courant*, was calculated to improve upon Sheridan's practices: new plays and Irish writers were to be encouraged, and, between Irish plays, there were to be exhibited none "but the most moral of the English." Novel provisions were planned to encourage native writers: authors were to have all the profits, and their plays were to run as long as house expenses were defrayed; promising playwrights were to be given benefits to allow them to perfect their work; anonymous authors were to receive their "Emoluments" by "whatever Channel they please." [114] In May 1749, earlier than had been expected, this company of gentlemen, "By Permission of the Right Honourable the Lord Mayor," ran two performances of a new comedy, *The Election*, written by an Irish author "little known in this City." [115] The cast, unfortunately, was not named in the *Dublin Courant* notices. No notice of this company, its proposals or its performances appears in Faulkner's *Dublin Journal*—a fact which gives some support to later claims that Sheridan manipulated the press; on the other hand, Hiffernan and Editor Faulkner were no friends, as issues of *The Tickler* show.[116] On June 3 a Sheridan supporter,

[114] *Dublin Courant*, February 28–March 4, 1749.

[115] *Ibid.*, April 29–May 2 and May 20–23, 1749.

[116] See *Tickler*, II, 13, where Faulkner appears as "the lying Chronologer" and "Face of Brass."

writing under the pseudonym of Frank Somebody for *The Censor*, sharply criticized the magistrate who had promised to support *"one free and well regulated theatre"* and then had licensed another theater and encouraged a set of nameless actors to present performances in which "personal, perhaps, undeserved Invective should be attempted." The reference must have been to the Hiffernan group at the Capel-Street Theater; the renegade magistrate must have been the Lord Mayor.

Another threat to Sheridan's monopoly this season added to his anxiety, although in the end it aborted sooner than the Capel-Street plan. In April the last "Grand Festinata" was advertised for Crow-Street Music-Hall, because the proprietors, at the urging of several eminent persons, had decided to turn the place into a theater, "fitted up in as elegant a Taste as any thing of the Kind in this Kingdom."[117] For some reason this project too fell through and Crow-Street remained unconverted until years later when, under Barry's direction, it became the site for a new theater, one which finally broke Sheridan as well as his monopoly.

During these anxious months in the spring Sheridan held his peace, at least in the public press, and chose other ways to compete for the good will of his company and the public. At the end of May he set aside a benefit performance, the proceeds of which were to establish a fund for "decayed, distrest, and superannuated Players."[118] Annual benefits and small weekly deductions from the company's salaries (to which all had "chearfully agreed") were to support the fund in the future. So sensible was this idea that a letter writer to the *Journal* signing himself Theatricus wonders why it was never initiated before. People hitherto deterred from an acting career by fear of the many accidents which could disable a player—a disorder of the lungs, the loss of an eye, a limb, or a few teeth—would now be encouraged to take up the profession; and good actors, at present imported and exported annually, would be eager to settle in Ireland, putting the Irish theater (so concludes Theatricus) on a more permanent and respectable basis.[119] How regularly the annual benefit was performed is not clear, but in 1751 we find advertised *The Suspicious Husband*, to be

[117] *Dublin Journal*, April 11–15, 1749.

[118] *Ibid.*, May 16–20, 1749. It was not until 1758 that Garrick started something similar in his benefits for distressed actors who formerly belonged to the theaters.

[119] *Ibid.*, May 20–23, 1749.

given for a "Fund begun for the Support of maimed, reduced, and superannuated Players."[120] Proof of the importance of this latter performance to Sheridan is given by the almost unique note attached: tickets were to be obtained at Mr. Sheridan's house "in Dorset Street, the upper end of Bolton Street." This was Sheridan's home, a place which he tried to keep quite separate from the theater. Of all Sheridan's many theatrical reforms this first step toward social security for his actors—one, incidentally, which has been hitherto overlooked—shows his imaginative concern for those working with him.

To win public approval he provided more genuinely new productions than usual—two main plays and three new afterpieces. Furthermore, both main plays were by Irishmen. Irish playwrights had not been encouraged for years in Ireland, not since early in Ashbury's regime.[121] Yet patriotic Dubliners were eager for them, as Burke, Hiffernan, and the new Capel-Street proposals imply. Now to answer this demand Sheridan risked two Irish-born plays in one season (he was a successful Irish playwright of sorts himself). Neither play used native material. One, written by Henry Brooke, popular Irish political writer, former pupil of Dr. Sheridan's and lifelong friend of Manager Sheridan's, was an allegorical ballad-opera called *Jack the Giant Queller*.[122] Its first performance, with Mrs. Lampe as Jack and with a new prologue spoken by Macklin and a new comic overture by Sign. Pasquali, met with "universal Applause"; the announcement of its next performance was greeted "with the loudest Claps of Approbation"; and its songs ran quickly into a second edition.[123] But the Lords Justices, under what Brooke later called "some Misapprehensions,"[124]

[120] *Ibid.*, April 30–May 4, 1751.   [121] Clark, p. 175, and passim.

[122] Henry Brooke had composed several other plays before this and in 1750 was to do *The Earl of Essex*, his most popular piece at Smock-Alley. His works, filled with a strong spirit of liberty, were, Baker's *Biographia Dramatica* says, often suspect, but those who knew him were convinced of his loyalty to "the present happy succession." During 1745, as the Farmer, he wrote pamphlets supporting the government; later, when Lucas was being persecuted, he became his spokesman in attacking the government (Madden, II, 374).

[123] *Dublin Journal*, March 25–28, 1749.

[124] *Ibid.*, February 26–March 1, 1757. This was when it was revived eight years later by Sheridan. In his letter to the *Journal* at that time Brooke avows that his meaning was always intended to be general, and that "the Author would not write, nor the Manager represent, what could justly give Cause of public or private Offense." The play ran five nights in 1757 without incident. And Victor (*History*, I, 197) tells of an earlier revival during his interregnum (1754–56) by government permission—one which aroused little interest, politically or theatrically.

suspected local applications in its ridicule of bad governors, lord mayors, and aldermen, and they banned its second performance.[125] Despite the considerable financial loss Sheridan promptly and without protest withdrew the play from the boards. Like the public, the authorities had to be won to his side.

The other new Irish-born play, Darcy's remotely located *Orphan of Venice*, though inoffensive to the Lords Justices and reported as winning "more universal Applause than any new Piece that ever was exhibited on this Stage," [126] was not the success expected from this enthusiasm. Even though its second performance, which had been deferred once rather significantly "at the Request of the Author," evoked an equally favorable audience response and a request that the play be printed, this performance seems to have been its last.[127] Thus Sheridan's experiences with new plays by Irishmen did not encourage him to further trials in that direction. Indeed, this was the only season of his career in which he produced as many as two really new main plays. Sheridan had more luck with the season's new afterpieces. These were the three new masques with music by Pasquali, all elaborately staged. One of them did what the Irish-born plays did not—it celebrated the Dubliners' native land. *The Triumphs of Hibernia*, written for the November 4th command performance, had six other performances and turned out to be a triumph for Pasquali. A very special masque, *The Temple of Peace*, to commemorate "the present happy Peace established over Europe," must have rivaled a similar commemoratory masque at Drury Lane in new scenes, machines, habits, decorations, and especially in "a grand view of the Temple of Peace." [128] The third new musical entertainment, *Apollo and Daphne*, with music by Pasquali ingeniously introduced comic scenes from *Trick Upon Trick*, particularly the skeleton scene and that famous escape of Harlequin into a quart bottle. No wonder Pasquali became a favorite of Sheridan's.

[125] According to Hitchcock (I, 197), it was vetoed the morning following its first performance. This was not the first play of Brooke's to run into trouble with the authorities. Some ten years earlier his tragedy *Gustavus Vasa* had been banned before production at Drury Lane (Baker, *v.* "Brooke").

[126] *Dublin Journal*, March 11–14, 1749.

[127] *Ibid.*, March 14–18 and April 11–15, 1749. A benefit planned for the author apparently did not materialize. A poem to Darcy by Philo-Dramaticum, which appears in the May 23–27 issue, salutes him as "the Orpheus of our Age."

[128] *Ibid.*, February 14–18, 1749. This was the masque for which Pasquali, Jr., designed the machinery and scenes.

The year 1748–49 was the first uninterrupted season under Sheridan's continuous and permanent direction at Smock-Alley. Victor's prognosis made in mid-November 1748 in a letter to Colley Cibber glows with hopes for the year: "I make no Doubt but the surprising Success of this Theatre has reached you in London; the Auxiliaries we got from thence prove of eminent Service, and the Profits of this Winter promise, already, to be much greater than were ever yet known in this Kingdom." [129] It is surprising, then, to find him, in his *History* written years later, quite gloomy about this season, chiefly because the musicians' salaries totaled nearly £1,400 and were, Victor figured, "a dead Loss to the Manager." [130] A gross gain, at least, seems indicated by the fifteen more performances over the previous year's. There is no evidence that attendance fell off; during March Victor writes to Cibber: "We have great houses." [131]

Because this season is the first uninterrupted one for Sheridan after Garrick started managing Drury Lane (in September 1747), a comparison of the season's offerings of the two managers is profitable. In the production of new plays neither man made much of a contribution to theatrical history. Like Sheridan, Garrick brought out two new main plays and three new afterplays (or perhaps only two). In total number of performances the Smock-Alley Calendar shows 111 performances as compared with 175 at Drury Lane. [132] But, despite the fewer performances, Smock-Alley offered more variety in its principal plays—54 different main plays as compared with 44 at Drury Lane. Both Smock-Alley figures are to be explained by the smaller size of the theatergoing public in Dublin. Credit must be given to Sheridan's energy and foresight in meeting the problem of the small audience by providing an attractive variety. In this respect his task was more difficult than Garrick's.

During this season there was cross-fertilization between the two theaters, as might be expected. Actors coming from London to Dublin, and vice versa, brought suggestions and successful roles with them. Sheridan often advertised plays as having been performed to universal applause in London. [133] Garrick, of course, did not describe plays as

[129] Victor, *History*, II, 212.   [130] *Ibid.*, I, 137.

[131] Victor, *Original Letters*, I, 150. The letter is dated 1748 (in accordance with O. S.), but references to Macklin and the revival of Cibber's *Refusal* show clearly that it was written in March 1749.

[132] My sources for information about Drury Lane are MacMillan's *Drury Lane Calendar* and *The London Stage*.

[133] For example, *A Will and No Will* (*Dublin Journal*, December 3–6, 1748).

having been first shown at Smock-Alley, but the surprising truth is that Sheridan preceded him over and over again. During this season, for example, two Shakespearean plays never before acted at Drury Lane had smashing successes there. Both of these, *Romeo and Juliet* and *Much Ado About Nothing*,[134] had been presented earlier at Smock-Alley, Sheridan thus leading the way for Shakespeare-loving Garrick. Sometimes Smock-Alley preceded Drury Lane by only a month or so: *The London Merchant*,[135] for example, was revived at Smock-Alley in April, at Drury Lane in May, of 1749. But many other plays showing in Dublin during the 1748–49 season were not presented by Garrick until several years later.[136] Garrick, more creative as an actor and writer, seems often to have followed Sheridan as a theater manager, largely, as has been suggested, because necessity did not press, as it did in Dublin.

Variety was essential in Dublin, and Sheridan, as Smock-Alley advertisements show, let hardly a week go by without some excitingly different production. Perhaps it was a revived play, such as *The Mistake* or *The Refusal;* or it may have been an old play with some new variation rung upon it, like *Theodosius* with the original songs set to music by Lampe. Two of the most important and successful productions of the year were the Shakespeare-Dryden-Davenant *Tempest*, with the Purcell music, sinkings, flyings, and "an extra-ordinary Piece of Machinery representing the rising Sun," [137] and *Oroonoko*, with a scene never exhibited at Smock-Alley before "wherein Mrs. Lampe and Mrs. Storer will sing the two original Songs, new set to Musick by Mr. Lampe, in the Habits of American Slaves; and a Foreigner, lately arrived, will perform a Piece of Musick on a new invented In-

[134] Sheridan had, we must remember, at least a season's advantage over Garrick, having been sole manager, at the beginning of this 1748–49 season, two years to Garrick's one. (The year before that both men were co-managers in Dublin.) For example, these two Shakespearean plays had been revived by Sheridan before Garrick became Drury Lane manager (as early as fall 1746). The next season, 1747–48, Smock-Alley saw *Much Ado About Nothing* once and *Romeo and Juliet* several times. Incidentally, in Garrick's first production of *Romeo and Juliet*, the following year, Woodward played Mercutio, a role he probably filled the year before at Smock-Alley (full cast is not given).

[135] As in London, this play is often advertised as *George Barnwell*.

[136] For example, Dryden's *Spanish Fryar* and *All for Love*, Vanbrugh's *Mistake*, Southerne's *Oroonoko*, Steele's *Tender Husband*, Congreve's *Way of the World* and *Old Batchelor*, Addison's *Cato* and *Drummer*, Farquhar's *Twin Rivals*, Fletcher's *Rule a Wife*, Lee's *Theodosius*. Some of these had, of course, been played earlier at Covent Garden.

[137] *Dublin Journal*, January 17–21, 1749.

strument, never heard in this Kingdom." [138] If there was nothing else to draw the crowds, there was always some principal actor in a role new to him.[139]

While a part of Sheridan's reputation and success as Smock-Alley manager can be laid to his clearing the stage and running an orderly theater, much more must be attributed to the variety of his programs; for, though people might stay away from disorderly performances, an orderly stage in itself, without interest or variation, would hardly be enough to attract them. This fact has been obscured to moderns, who, reading over the Smock-Alley offerings, are apt to be more impressed by their repetition and monotony. Only a comparison with concurrent programs in London and a study of each evening's total entertainment show how Sheridan won his great popularity with the Dublin public. Particularly this last season, relatively placid if not financially all he had hoped, had given him a chance to approach his own high standards and so begin winning a reputation with the Dublin public.

---

[138] *Ibid.*, February 7–11, 1749. The weird instrument is later revealed as a cymballo (*ibid.*, March 28–April 1, 1749).

[139] Sheridan added five new roles to his repertory during this year: Heartwell in *The Old Batchelor*; Maskwell in *The Double Dealer*; Oroonoko; and a role in Darcy's *Orphan of Venice*. Sheridan also appeared for the first time (although not listed so) as King Henry in *King Henry V*, revived after five years.

CHAPTER VI

King Tom, 1749-1751

THE SEASON of 1749–50 was full of unpleasant overtones for Sheridan personally, starting with the inauspicious death of the Smock-Alley prompter, whom Victor describes as a normally "well-behaved, sensible" man: [1]

> Last Thursday Morning, Mr. Harrington, Prompter to the Theatre Royal, being delirious and in a high Fever, in the Absence of his Nurse-keeper, threw himself out of his Lodging Window, and was killed by the Fall.[2]

Harrington's madness, tragic death, and particularly his occupation as prompter inspired a satiric attack, early the next spring, on all enemies of liberty, of justice, and of Charles Lucas, in a pamphlet titled *A Full and True Account of the Woefull and Wonderfull Apparition of Hurloe Harrington.* These enemies of Lucas, according to the author, a "Parson Fitz-Henery," are being prompted by Harrington's mad ghost. Some time ago Manager Sheridan hired a sane, well-behaved, and modest Harrington through friends in London (he had served at Covent Garden). But, because a theater prompter has the actors' lives and fortunes at his disposal, Harrington soon began taking over all the powers of the manager—except for command of the cobblers, the porters, and the women, the last of whom the manager insisted upon keeping under his sole direction. Then our prompter went to London to hire actors, tumblers, and fiddlers. When he brought back only Irish strollers already rejected in London, the Dublin company threatened him so horribly that he fell into a fever and eventually threw himself out a window. Since then his ghost has returned, first to the theater, where he began prompting everybody to do things wrong, then to the castle, and finally to all public institutions. Nights, though, he still spends at the playhouse, where he prompts musicians to play "Italiano piano" to Irish ears; a promising young army officer (probably West Digges) to turn actor; and the manager himself "to attempt Characters quite out of the Reach of his Genius and natural Disposition; nay, to expose himself in attempting Comedy, when the

---

[1] Victor, *Original Letters,* I, 143.
[2] *Dublin Journal,* September 12–16, 1749.

Bent of his whole Body and Soul is to Tragedy, at least, on our Stage."

This exposition is doubly interesting. It suggests the power of the prompter in the eighteenth-century theater: Victor reveals that Harrington *had* gone to London the year before "with commissions for the next season"; [3] and within the theater, says Parson Fitz-Henery, no one would think of disputing with him about "the painting the Scenes, or providing new Actors, Guards, and other Attendants for the Theatre." Fitz-Henery's account also reflects the political storm which had broken over Charles Lucas and, peripherally, over Sheridan. Lucas, Sheridan's loyal friend and main supporter in the Kelly affair, had been fighting for his political life during the preceding summer. His troubles with the authorities, who feared him as too radical, filled the press then. In January he was to be "disfranchised from his Freedom of the City" and in February declared an enemy of his country, as a preliminary to his long exile. Some of the anonymous letters and pamphlets written during the summer in his support were apparently attributed to Sheridan, for whom Lucas had written letters and pamphlets two years before. But Sheridan, arguing that the theater manager was busy enough without engaging in "Matters out of his Sphere," publicly disavowed his authorship of these pieces in a notice which ran for some ten issues in the *Journal*. "Whilst I have the Honour to be in that Office," he says of his position as manager, "the faithful Discharge of my Duty shall be the sole Object of my Ambition, nor have I Leisure or Inclination to attend to any Thing else." [4] Sheridan's desertion of Lucas implied in the word "Inclination" can be somewhat explained by his steadfast determination to keep the peace he had enjoyed since the Kelly riot. But another reason may be found in his private political leanings, to be revealed more openly before and during the theatrical riots of 1754. Sheridan was a Tory, who took the side of the Court party. Lucas was a democrat, in trouble with the authorities for his subversive activities.

Almost from the beginning of this season there were complications too in connection with the Smock-Alley musicians. During the last year the band and the singers, it will be recalled, had been occasionally lent out for various charities and benefits. Now a regular agreement [5] was worked out between the Fishamble-Street Charitable Musick Society and Sheridan's musicians, whereby concerts, conducted by Pasquali,

[3] Victor, *Original Letters*, I, 143.

[4] *Dublin Journal*, September 12–16, 1749.

[5] Announced *ibid.*, September 19–23, 1749.

were to be given every Tuesday during the 1749–50 season. (On Tuesdays Smock-Alley was normally closed.) Announcement of this arrangement seems to have stirred up a quarrel over Sheridan's discrimination against "native established musicians"; [6] but Sheridan stayed on the side lines in this minor skirmish, and Pasquali's group functioned as planned on Tuesday nights, played many Saturday nights at Aungier-Street affairs, and spent the rest of the week at Smock-Alley, keeping themselves fairly well occupied. Other charities used the band occasionally, for example the Charitable Infirmary on the Inn's Quay.[7] These outside activities may have given Dr. Mosse the idea of engaging Sheridan's musicians for his charity, an idea which stirred Sheridan to some tactless behavior and involved him in his most unpleasant public wrangle so far.

Dr. Bartholomew Mosse, an eminent and philanthropic Dublin physician who was raising funds to build a new lying-in hospital [8] by concerts given in the New Garden, found himself in a most embarrassing position at twelve noon on March 8, 1750. He had advertised the opening of the New Garden for that time with a "grand Band of Vocal and Instrumental Musick," which was to be continued every fair day until the end of April and from then on every fair evening during the season.[9] But, when the usual "polite and numerous" audience had assembled, there was no entertainment. Sheridan had not allowed his band to perform. Because of the clamor which followed, Sheridan felt impelled to defend himself, with notices in the papers, affidavits, and states of the case. Briefly, the difficulty was this: Dr. Mosse had engaged Sheridan's musicians for a long-term arrangement without consulting Sheridan himself. The negotiations had been carried on through intermediaries: a Mr. Storace, band director at the New Garden, acting for Dr. Mosse; and Pasquali, acting for Sheridan. Early in January Storace approached certain Smock-Alley musicians [10] and had word back from Pasquali that Sheridan would

[6] *Ibid.*, October 3–7 and 10–14, 1749. These native musicians, according to the musical society, had in the past asked such fees that little charitable money was left. Now Sheridan was to have the subscriptions, but the "6*d*. halfpenny fund"—about £100—was to go to charity; also, Sheridan was to perform *The Messiah* for the annual benefit (usually costing £50 to £60).

[7] *Ibid.*, January 9–13, 1750.

[8] The foundation of the hospital at the New Garden, Great Britain-Street, was laid in the summer of 1751.

[9] [Sheridan], *State of the Case*, p. 3.

[10] Seven of these musicians were bound in articles to Sheridan "in the penal Sum of 300 l. sterl. not to perform in any publick Place whatsoever, before the

agree to let them perform at the Garden, but only at such times as he "had no Occasion for them." [11] Pasquali apparently also reassured his musicians that they might engage with Mosse, that it was not necessary to put Sheridan's leave in writing, and that Smock-Alley rehearsals could be arranged so as not to interfere with the noon-to-three p.m. performances at the New Garden.[12] When, however, Dr. Mosse's advertisement appeared, promising musical entertainment in the *evenings* after April 28, Sheridan informed Pasquali that he would not release the band until he had seen Mosse and received assurances from him that he would not interfere with the theatrical business.[13] This demand was not made until the morning of Mosse's scheduled performance, although Pasquali, without Sheridan's authority to speak, had pressed Mosse to see Sheridan the day before.[14] But Mosse refused flatly to speak to Sheridan or to permit anybody else to (he said later that he had cooperated with Sheridan once before and that it had cost him above £50 sterling).[15] Storace, however, and another musician, according to their affidavits, did go to Sheridan, who refused to confirm their application and threatened to put the articles in force against anyone who performed.[16] So it happened that the usual polite and numerous audience at the New Garden was disappointed in its entertainment that day. Sheridan kept his musicians rehearsing for a production of *King Arthur* from twelve to three on the eighth of March.[17]

Once more the press was full of defenses and explanations. The poor confused musicians published signed certificates supporting Sheridan's arguments one week and Mosse's arguments the next week: Sheridan's account of their contract with him was correct, and, furthermore, Mosse knew all about it; Mosse's story of Storace's activities and Pasquali's assurances was accurate, and, furthermore, Sheri-

---

first Day of June next, without Leave first had in Writing from Mr. Sheridan." Four others, though not bound thus to Sheridan, testified that they felt themselves obliged to play for him for the season (*Dublin Journal*, March 6–10, 1750).

[11] [Sheridan], *State of the Case*, p. 5.

[12] *Dublin Journal*, March 10–13, 1750.

[13] [Sheridan], *State of the Case*, pp. 9–10.

[14] *Dublin Journal*, March 10–13, 1750.

[15] *Ibid.*, March 6–10 and 10–13, 1750. The performance referred to was of *Judas Maccabeus*, which had been conducted by Pasquali on February 21 at the Music Hall in Fishamble-Street (*ibid.*, January 16–20).

[16] *Ibid.*, March 10–13, 1750.

[17] *The Man of Honour, but not of his Word*, p. 13.

dan knew all about them. But one musician, a John Kemplin, who
had signed the certificate supporting Sheridan, refused to confirm
the Mosse account, because, as he said, "he looked on the Band of
Musicians . . . as the Slaves of the said Sheridan, and that they
ought to be subject to him as such." [18] Before the affair was over,
even Faulkner, the *Dublin Journal* publisher, was defending himself
in print against rumors that he had refused advertisements for Dr.
Mosse.[19] On April 10 Sheridan's long-promised *State of the Case*,
deferred by "the Quantity of Business . . . on his Hands" and by
unforeseen accidents, was published by Faulkner and included "some
Remarks upon the present State of the Stage." [20] This pamphlet in
turn provoked anonymous responses: *To the Publick* and *The Man
of Honour, but not of his Word*, both of which could have been
written by Dr. Mosse. After this the affair died down, leaving Sheridan with a few more enemies to be concerned about.

This time again Sheridan seems to have had the literal right of it,
but his judgment at the crucial moment was hasty and ill-advised.
What disturbed him most was that Mosse was advertising evening
performances—with the theater's band, presumably [21]—for May,
when the theater would still be open. Sheridan's request to see Mosse
personally for further assurances, made as it was through Pasquali,
must have sounded like an ultimatum. But Mosse was surely at fault
in refusing to speak to Sheridan on the subject. On the other hand,
Sheridan's decision to prevent the band's appearance at the New Garden seems unnecessarily highhanded, since it penalized not only
Mosse and the musicians, but also an innocent audience which had
turned out to support a worthy charity. Some less drastic way of
settling with Mosse, one less damaging to Sheridan's own reputation,
must have been possible.

Relevant to Sheridan's behavior, however, is his state of mind, as
shown by his written defense, *A State of the Case*. In this pamphlet

[18] See *Dublin Journal*, March 6–10 and 10–13, 1750.

[19] *Ibid.*, March 24–27, 1750. He also denies the rumor that Mosse himself
sent the musicians' affidavits to be inserted in the paper.

[20] *Ibid.*, March 20–24 and March 31–April 3, 1750.

[21] Although the author of *The Man of Honour* (p. 10) asks Sheridan how
he knew *his* band was to be used at the New Garden in May ("What, was there
no Music in Dublin, but Your Band!"), Mosse admitted in his early statement
to the press that Storace had approached the Smock-Alley musicians for "every
fair Morning from March 5th to the 28th of April" and for "the Evening the
remaining Part of the Summer" (*Dublin Journal*, March 10–13, 1750).

the last ten pages are taken up with near hysterical complaints that he who had done so much for the public should have to take time so often to defend himself, innocent as he invariably was. Why, it is often asked, has the manager so many enemies? The reasons are as varied as their numbers are vast. Some resent his rules for the "well Government of the Stage"; others still harbor a grudge, having been part of that large and formidable body raised against him several years ago; still others, managers of concerts, assemblies, et cetera, having been refused music when it interfered with the theater, feel ill will toward the manager, although he tried to conciliate them by rendering all reasonable assistance. "If it be objected that no Manager before ever had so many [enemies], the Answer is very easy, that no Manager before ever undertook such a Task." In his private capacity, Sheridan rejoices, not many have more friends. And the public voice is much in his favor.[22] Although through this period Sheridan generally refrained from replying to attacks and even illustrated to O'Keeffe his indifference to them,[23] Sheridan's obsession with his "enemies" bespeaks a mind not untouched by the many unpleasant things said about him.

Interesting light is shed by this same pamphlet on certain problems of theater managership in Dublin at this time. Sheridan argued that if May were cut off by Mosse's engagement with the band, the three months of actors' benefits would have to commence in February and thus would take from the theater itself the most profitable month of the season. Sheridan's expansion of the company, desirable as it was, made it necessary not only for him to have the income from the most profitable periods but also to perform more frequently than before. On Saturday nights the theater had formerly remained closed out of

---

[22] [Sheridan], *State of the Case*, pp. 15, 19–23.

[23] O'Keeffe, I, 358–359. O'Keeffe tells of an incident in which a gentleman, much agitated, called on the Smock-Alley manager to apologize for the "irreparable injuries" he had done to Sheridan's professional reputation by writing him down in a popular publication. " 'I am sure I must have hurt your mind exceedingly,' he said. 'Hurt my mind!' Sheridan exclaimed. 'This is the first knowledge I ever had of the circumstance; and, as to injuring my professional reputation—here! bring the box-book,' (calling out the door to the box-keeper), 'There, Sir, look, I play this night; and, as you see, every box is taken by persons of the first rank and consequence in Dublin; therefore, pray comfort yourself, as to having hurt either my mind, or my reputation.' " O'Keeffe dates this incident "about the year, 1750," and says it was told him by Sheridan himself when O'Keeffe had "the happiness of his company, much to the profit of my own mind, in the years 1775 and 1776."

regard for the assemblies; but during the past season, if Sheridan had not reversed the custom and opened on Saturdays, he would have lost £1,000. These Saturday performances, Sheridan asserts, created other enemies.[24]

The newly introduced Saturday-night performances were given usually at Aungier-Street, which during the last season and for two months of this had been open for festinos, but which in November was remodeled again: "The Form of the Great Room will be altered . . . in order to have Dramatick Operas exhibited there." [25] After its opening in February Sheridan's players, especially his singers, went over to give *Comus* or *King Arthur* on Saturday evenings, and sometimes on Tuesdays, when Smock-Alley was closed.

When Aungier-Street was reopened, the *Dublin Journal* notice reported the event with this N.B.: "The Upper Gallery is intirely removed." [26] Taken literally, this would mean a major structural innovation like that accomplished some years later at Drury Lane when Garrick remodeled his stage to eliminate stage sitters. But the fact that three years later Sheridan again advertised upper gallery seats at Aungier-Street (and without notice of any major reconstruction there) [27] suggests that now he merely closed that section or combined it with the middle gallery.

The reason is not far to seek. At this very time Sheridan was having more than his usual trouble with the upper gallery at Smock-Alley. Early in the fall of 1749 "evil minded Persons" there had once more been throwing "Stones and other Things at the Band of Musick, during the Time of Performance, to the great Disturbance of the Audience, and Peril to the Musicians." For the discovery of any such offender Victor, as treasurer, had offered a reward of ten guineas.[28] But the violence went from bad to worse, and two months later Sheridan had to step in with his old threat to close the section, hoping, vainly, that the offenders were "not so much his Enemies, as to do him so great an Injury, to answer no good Purpose to themselves, and, at the same Time, be the Means of depriving a Number of Persons of a rational Entertainment." [29] Instead of closing the Smock-Alley gallery, however, Sheridan tried a plan less injurious to

[24] [Sheridan], *State of the Case*, pp. 12, 20–21.

[25] *Dublin Journal*, October 31–November 4, 1749.

[26] *Ibid.*, February 3–6, 1750. [27] *Ibid.*, February 13–17, 1753.

[28] *Ibid.*, October 3–7, 1749.

[29] *Ibid.*, January 9–13, 1750. The notice runs to about the 20th.

himself: he doubled the price of the seats there on January 17, and then on January 27 he revoked the rise with a warning that "the same Cause continued will produce the same Effect" again. His notice concludes:

> It will therefore be incumbent on all such as wish to have the Gallery kept open on the usual Terms, if the same Behaviour be continued, to use their utmost Endeavours to detect those Persons, who clandestinely are in Effect injuring them, by robbing them of a Right which they might otherwise possess, and depriving them of an Entertainment which they might otherwise enjoy. N.B. No Money or Tickets paid into the upper Gallery will be returned.[30]

It is no surprise, then, when Aungier-Street opened a month later, that it was advertised as without an upper gallery.

The postscript in Sheridan's notice was aimed at eliminating another disruptive custom. Earlier, in his fight against odd money, Sheridan had refused to admit latecomers at reduced prices or to return any part of the admission fee after the curtain had gone up. But idle people could still come, sit with friends, contribute to the uproar until the play began, and then leave. These people Sheridan had begun discouraging in the fall of 1748 by the following regulation: "No Persons will be admitted into the Pit or Galleries without Tickets, which are to be sold at the Offices." [31] For a time after this, people apparently could still circumvent Sheridan's purpose by buying a ticket and then getting their money back if they left before the curtain. This new regulation that "no Money or Tickets paid into the upper Gallery" would be returned kept some of the troublemakers out and plugged up another loophole.

About this time Sheridan ran into another problem connected with admissions. The crowds in Smock-Alley before the doors opened were always barely manageable; but if, as happened once in January, the doorkeepers were late, even the gentlemen, who had come early for good places in the pit, got out of hand. On this particular occasion some found a way in through "a private Passage," while the better behaved waited outside and lost their chances for seats. Sheridan in a public notice apologized for the treatment these met with and assured them that he had "punished the Door-keepers, whose neglect of coming in proper Time was the Occasion of it, in a most exemplary

---

[30] *Ibid.*, January 23–27, 1750. [31] *Ibid.*, September 27–October 1, 1748.

Manner." [32] In trying to keep his theater orderly, Sheridan found it easier to discipline his employees than his audience.

The Smock-Alley company this year grew in size and stature although Sheridan lost the Macklins in March in what must have been an especially disagreeable explosion, one which, if Victor is right, had been building up for a year and a half, or almost from the beginning of their two-year contract. Victor reports that Macklin had not been in Dublin a month before he was calling Sheridan "manager-mad." [33] But Macklin, according to his own biographer, Cooke, was over-ambitious, unconciliatory, and suspicious in his dealings with Sheridan. [34] As a comedian he resented Sheridan's emphasis on tragedy; and he was particularly offended by Sheridan's practice of printing his own name, on advertisements and bills, in larger type than Macklin's—a custom which Sheridan had followed for years with all his fellow actors. In any event, Macklin's resentment reached the point where he began to measure the print, so determined was he not to yield "a hair's breadth to the manager!" Sheridan gave in on this matter, Victor says, and the *Dublin Journal* advertisements amusingly reflect his concession: [35] the Macklins and Sheridan share the same typographical effects for a while. But Macklin, obsessed by what he called "marketable fame," continued to abuse Sheridan in the greenroom, his temper doubtless unimproved by the addition of a rival comedian—none other than Theophilus Cibber—in the fall of 1749, at a time when Sheridan was the only tragic actor of any importance. Matters came to a head sometime in March 1750, when Macklin went on stage one night after the play and announced a

---

[32] *Ibid.*, January 9–13, 1750.

[33] Victor, *Original Letters*, I, 160. This was in a letter to Garrick, who had asked him about the quarrel.

[34] Cooke, *Macklin*, pp. 195–197. Macklin's quarrelsome disposition had before this caused breaks with Fleetwood and Garrick and was later to lead to conflict with Barry and Woodward, a lawsuit with Mossop and trouble with Reddish (see Parry's and Appleton's biographies of Macklin). Molloy records a story of Macklin's violence with a well-meaning prompter (I, 239).

[35] After November 15, 1748, the type changes, Sheridan, Pasquali, and the two Macklins sharing the same largest print. Before that, only Sheridan and Pasquali were so distinguished, the two Macklins appearing in the smaller capitals allotted to the other members of the cast. Later not only was Macklin's name printed in larger type but it was sometimes shifted to last position in the listing of the cast, the position normally occupied by the name of the leading actress. For the peculiar effect of this, see Smock-Alley Calendar, Pt. II, *Oroonoko*, October 27, 1749.

comedy for his wife's benefit without first settling the play or the date with Sheridan. Harassed at this very time by his much publicized dispute with Dr. Mosse, Sheridan found Macklin's breach of theatrical etiquette unforgivable, and he discharged both husband and wife.[36] The Smock-Alley Calendar shows how sudden (and inconvenient) this action must have been; hasty substitutions had to be made in plays or roles, and Mrs. Macklin's benefit with *Twelfth Night* had to be withdrawn entirely.[37] Dismissed from Smock-Alley, Macklin "filed a bill in Chancery against his manager," claiming that Sheridan had discharged him in mid-season without notice or cause and had withheld money (£800) due him according to agreement.[38] But rather than stay in Dublin with nothing to do, he was forced to take the £300 which Sheridan had paid into court.[39] Both Macklins then left for Chester and, the following season, for Covent Garden.

But if Sheridan made an enemy in Macklin, he regained a friend in Theophilus Cibber, their quarrel over Cato's robe now conveniently forgotten. After Macklin left, Cibber became the principal comedian and stayed at Smock-Alley for three peaceful years. The elaborate advertisements for his benefits reflect his ingenious turn of mind.[40]

Most notable for this year's company, however, was Sheridan's discovery of two new talents, which so strengthened his troupe that the season almost rivaled the Garrick-Barry-Sheridan winter of 1745. Many times during his career as manager Sheridan was accused of tolerating no rivalry in his own field of tragedy. His engagement of Cibber rather than of a tragic player may have supported the suspicions of other people besides Macklin on this subject. But from England Cibber had brought with him a young gentleman "who never yet appeared upon any Stage," [41] yet who was immediately en-

[36] Victor, *Original Letters*, I, 160–161. Victor's letter to Garrick, in which much of this gossip appears, is undated but it must have been written after March 1750.

[37] For example, Sullivan's benefit play for March 14 (*The Merchant of Venice* with Macklin) was changed to *The Careless Husband* with Cibber and Sheridan. *The Alchymist* on March 8 seems to have been Macklin's last performance. Possibly Macklin's benefit on March 5 was the occasion of his speech to the audience on his wife's behalf. It is significant that Mrs. Macklin's benefit had once before inspired her husband to curious behavior (see Genest, IV, 244–245).

[38] Parry, pp. 105–106; Appleton, p. 91.

[39] Molloy, I, 240; Parry, p. 106; Appleton, p. 91.

[40] See Smock-Alley Calendar, for example, for March 12, 1750.

[41] *Dublin Journal*, November 4–7, 1749.

gaged to perform at Smock-Alley. He had come at Cibber's urging
to try his fortune "under the auspices of so liberal a manager." [42] He
played his first role as Jaffier in *Venice Preserved* on November 29.
And the next night another untried unknown—this time an Irishman
—appeared as Zanga in *The Revenge*.[43] From then on, Sheridan had
two first-rate competitors in his company—West Digges from England and Henry Mossop the Irishman. There is no evidence from
the advertisements that he held these two down in order to preserve
his own fame. Within two weeks Mossop played Othello and Digges
Lear, both favorite Sheridan roles, and after that, plays with these
actors "by Desire" frequently replaced others, sometimes plays that
had been scheduled with Sheridan.[44] Mossop, Digges, and Sheridan
played together sometimes—in *Julius Caesar,* for example. During
the season both newcomers enlarged their repertory, taking over
other Sheridan roles, Hamlet (Digges), Macbeth (Mossop), et cetera. That both men became immediately popular is clear from several
poems appearing in the press during December 1749—two to Digges
and two to Mossop, who is flatteringly compared to Sheridan in one.[45]
The equal balance of favor shown the two in these poems seems to
have been carefully maintained by the manager, in distribution of
parts, in advertising, in timing of benefits, and so on. In this delicate
situation Sheridan—for some time, at least—was more successful than
usual. It is significant that both Digges and Mossop were well-
educated gentlemen from good families. Digges's background was
excellent, his breeding "Chesterfieldian"; [46] it will be remembered
that young Boswell in planning his personality wished to achieve
"Mr. Addison's character in sentiment, mixed with a little of the

[42] Hitchcock, I, 204. Hitchcock (*ibid.,* p. 205) gives the wrong date for
Digges's opening.

[43] *Dublin Journal,* November 21–25, 1749. It is interesting that, contrary
to usual custom, neither actor appeared anonymously.

[44] For example, *The Careless Husband* with Sheridan (December 16) was
replaced by *King Lear* with Digges; Mossop's *Othello* substitutes for *Much
Ado About Nothing* on December 19.

[45] See *Dublin Journal* issues from December 9 to 19, 1749. The poem to
Mossop, signed "F. R.," declares, "We now a Sheridan, in Mossop find, / To
every Act of Nature, like inclin'd." Another poem to Mossop, signed "J. M.,"
also manages to compliment Sheridan. Victor writes to C. Cibber in December
1749 that he is much impressed with Digges as Jaffier, but as Lothario, although
he supported the role "with the necessary accomplishments," he did not appear
so advantageously because of "the superior strength of Mr. Sheridan, in Horatio"
(*Original Letters,* I, 151–152).

[46] Hitchcock, I, 204.

gaiety of Sir Richard Steele and the manners of Mr. Digges." [47]
Mossop was the son of a clergyman and had been liberally educated
at Sheridan's university, Trinity College.[48] The fact that such men
now felt it possible to make an honorable career in the theater was
due largely to Sheridan's victory in the Kelly dispute and to the
sobriety and decorum which he had instituted on both sides of the
curtain at Smock-Alley. Mossop gained his start through Sheridan,
after having been rejected by Garrick and Rich.[49] By improving the
position of actors, Sheridan could attract men like Digges and Mossop; by recognizing their possibilities and hiring them, he could further improve the position of actors.

Although Sheridan's company was more brilliant this season, the
record of performances seems somewhat less exciting than for the
preceding year. Or perhaps the advertisements merely reflect fewer
attempts at originality. The main plays new to Smock-Alley were not
new plays except for *The Earl of Essex*, written by Henry Brooke
"upon the Plan of the old one." For a special attraction the characters were "new dress'd, *in the Habits of the Times* [italics mine]." [50]
Notices that plays were "new dressed" are frequent; indeed, Sheridan's constant efforts to keep his productions inviting raised the
worth of the Smock-Alley wardrobe from £200 when he took over to
£4,000 when he left.[51] But, despite these announcements and such
tag-lines as "with Habits, Scenes and Decorations proper to the
Play," we know that normally there was little attempt at historical
accuracy in costuming. Both Barrington and O'Keeffe describe the
anachronisms here in a most amusing way: Sheridan as Cato in a
bright armor under a "fine laced scarlet cloak," topped by a "white,
bushy" wig like Dr. Johnson's, surmounted by a helmet; [52] Sheridan
as Macbeth in a scarlet-and-gold English uniform.[53] Sheridan's learning and his respect for the past would have inclined him to prefer
historical accuracy. But the price was high. At times he tried mixing
modern and ancient dress, outfitting his casts of *Richard III* and
Henry VIII in modern clothes but himself in period, and so,
O'Keeffe says, looking like a "Merry-Andrew" among his perform-

---

[47] Boswell, *London Journal*, p. 62.   [48] Hitchcock, I, 206; *DNB*.
[49] Hitchcock, I, 206–208.
[50] *Dublin Journal*, April 17–21, 1750. Brooke adapted from Ralph, who
adapted from Banks (Sichel, I, 244). Victor (*History*, I, 146) reports that
Brooke "made no Alteration but in the last Act."
[51] *Mr. Sheridan's Speech*, 1772, p. 11.   [52] Barrington, II, 201.
[53] O'Keeffe, II, 111.

ers.[54] With *The Earl of Essex* Sheridan seems to have taken the next step and dressed his whole cast "in the Habits of the Times." Wilkes commends Sheridan for "his cloaths elegant and in character." [55]

Of the three plays written by Irishmen and premiered during Sheridan's management at Smock-Alley, *The Earl of Essex* was the only one to have much success in spite of a rather inauspicious beginning late in the spring of 1750. With Sheridan in the role of Essex— a favorite of his—it soon became part of the regular repertory at Smock-Alley and eventually was the one play from this time which crossed the Irish Sea to London, taken by Sheridan himself to Drury Lane, where it made a good showing as his vehicle in 1761 and without him saw a few performances almost annually for a decade or more thereafter.[56] For his "new" plays of the season Sheridan was satisfied to follow Garrick; [57] and his record of new roles for himself seems to have dropped to three.[58]

But the season's performances are outstanding in one way—their emphasis on Shakespeare. Sheridan's special contribution to his favorite playwright, his Shakespeare series, had been growing in popularity since 1747. Almost every season of his management saw at least two such series and sometimes three. Advance notices placed prominently in the newspapers and headed "SHAKESPEAR" alerted Dubliners that a series of six (or eight or nine) plays would be given at the rate of one or two a week; titles were named; readers were assured that Mr. Sheridan would act the leading roles; and ladies were advised to send their commands to the boxkeeper as soon as possible "to prevent Disappointments."

The idea of such a series in Dublin was not Sheridan's. The fall before his debut Aungier-Street Manager Swan had tried a Shake-

---

[54] *Ibid.*   [55] Wilkes, *General View of the Stage*, p. 313.

[56] According to the *Drury Lane Calendar* (p. 238), the Brooke play may have been revised by Garrick for Drury Lane.

[57] In opening Shirley's *Edward the Black Prince*, Smock-Alley was a month behind Drury Lane. Likewise *The Alchymist*, "never acted in this Kingdom," had been one of Garrick's best plays for three seasons. Of the two "new" afterpieces, *The Chaplet* is advertised as "as it was performed at the Theatre Royal in Drury Lane for forty Nights with Universal Applause"; *Mock Pamela* was not presented at Drury Lane, although it was given in Richmond in 1750 (see Nicoll, III, 402).

[58] Essex, the Black Prince, and the King in *2 Henry IV*. I can find no record of an earlier performance in this last role, although it is not advertised as his first appearance in that character. The play is a revived one (first time in seven years).

speare series on the model of the London practice,[59] but without success apparently. Perhaps for this reason, when Sheridan offered his first series in 1747, he offered it cautiously, planning to give it only if the boxes were taken for each play. The importance he gave to the occasion is shown by his press announcement that the plays would be performed with the "utmost Regularity" and that nothing would be wanting to the "Elegance of the Entertainment," even to the use of wax candles, instead of tallow, throughout the whole house.[60] The response was heartening enough for a second series a month later. By the following season (1748–49) the "extraordinary Demand . . . from Numbers of Persons who could not get Room in the Theatre" for the first series,[61] was so great that a new series was immediately planned and the number of plays raised from six to eight. As early as this, Sheridan had made his Shakespeare series the event of his theatrical season.

This took considerable doing, for the plays which were given series after series varied little. *Hamlet, Richard III, Romeo and Juliet, Othello, Macbeth, The Merchant of Venice* were the staples, with *Julius Caesar, Much Ado About Nothing, As You Like It,* and some six or seven others providing only occasional variation. Nor was there much variety in the principal actor, except once or twice when other actors—Mossop, Digges, Macklin—were given a chance or when the series included *The Merry Wives of Windsor,* in which Sheridan never acted. Then the principal role of Falstaff was usually played by Isaac Sparks. Sheridan's acting in the Shakespeare series, even in the most familiar roles, continued to be the great attraction. In the last year of his management, after he had played Richard III it would seem almost to nausea, the play was performed with such applause that the Duke and Duchess of Bedford, hearing of its success apparently, commanded it for the next Saturday "as they never saw Mr. Sheridan in that Character." And this, the *Dublin Journal* is "sorry to add," was to be "the last Time of his acting it" for the season.[62] Once, to spark interest in the series, Sheridan allowed the ladies to determine the *order* of the plays (though not the plays themselves) by the demand they made for places. The results, announced in the newspapers, show a preference for tragedy and for Sheridan's favorite vehicles.[63]

---

[59] *Dublin Journal,* November 13–16, 1742.
[60] *Ibid.,* November 3–7, 1747.　　[61] *Ibid.,* December 31–January 3, 1749.
[62] *Ibid.,* February 28–March 4, 1758.
[63] *Ibid.,* October 29–November 2, 1751.

Sheridan's organization of Shakespeare into a series, which had the advantage of keeping the dramatist's name prominent and of giving the manager some indication of his house, did not mean that there was no Shakespeare at other times. The same plays recur abundantly throughout the season, and others like *The Tempest*, never included in the series, were played. In these extra-series productions other principal actors were given more opportunities to take leads; and often actors chose and acted in Shakespeare plays for their benefits, encouraged, we can be sure, by Sheridan. Thus the total of Shakespearean plays during Sheridan's early years increased spectacularly.

The 1749–50 season represents the peak of Sheridan's efforts in bringing Shakespeare to Dublin. In 1747–48, when Burke was criticizing Smock-Alley offerings and audiences, advertised Shakespearean performances had numbered only 20. The next season (1748–49) the figure had risen to 29—the beginning of Sheridan's quiet response to Burke and Hiffernan. Now, in 1749–50, an unprecedented 44 performances out of 143 were of Shakespeare's plays. This year's percentage, about one third of the plays performed, seems to have exceeded the London percentage for the five-year period of 1746–50,[64] and gives some measure of Sheridan's achievement. In the variety of the plays too the 1749–50 season is unusual. The year before, with only about two thirds as many plays given throughout the season as at Drury Lane, Sheridan had produced thirteen different Shakespeare plays to Garrick's eleven. This 1749–50 season he raised the number to fourteen and put three of Shakespeare's tragedies—*Othello*, *Julius Caesar*, and *Lear*—among his six most frequent plays.

Assisting him in passing this miracle were Macklin, whose Iago was almost as famous as his Shylock, and Sheridan's two new discoveries, Digges and Mossop. The popularity of these two, who brought fresh talent to Shakespearean tragic roles, attracted great crowds to plays not normally among the most popular. Digges did six performances of Lear; Mossop, four of Othello. And with Sheridan as Brutus, Mossop as Cassius, and Digges as Anthony, *Julius Caesar* became a new and irresistible experience.

On the staging of these productions Sheridan lavished money, energy, and imagination—the last sometimes so excessively as to provoke outbursts from his critics. Burke decried the burlesque of

---

[64] Hogan (1, 459) for the five years 1746–50 estimates Shakespearean performances at 483 out of 1,814.

the witches scene in *Macbeth*, which featured brooms, buffooneries, and jigs [65] (Irish, presumably). The witches' parts were often performed by men; and sometimes as many as ten dancing and singing witches romped over the stage. The advertisements for this great tragedy make strange reading now: "Macbeth . . . with all the Songs, Dances, Sinkings, and Decorations proper to the Play." [66] *Hamlet* was interrupted between the fourth and fifth acts by "The Country Revels," given by Italian dancers whom Sheridan happened to have in his troupe.[67] The singing and dancing introduced into both tragedy and comedy depended upon the talent in the company at the time. In the 1749–50 season he had an especially wide range of extra entertainers, who now included not only the familiar musicians and singers but two leading dancers, Mons. Granier and Mlle. Vandersluys, both new this season from Covent Garden. Since Dublin audiences were especially taken with processions, processions were provided with every possible Shakespeare play. The funeral procession in *Romeo and Juliet* was especially admired and frequently improved with solemn dirges; advertisements for *Henry VIII* stressed Anne Bullen's coronation ceremony as well as "the Ceremony of the Champion in Westminster-hall." [68] Admirer of Aristotle though he was, Sheridan did not overlook the chance for spectacle.

This pardonable emphasis on the lurid, underlined in the public notices (e.g., "Containing, The Death of the Duke of Buckingham; the Fall and Death of Cardinal Wolsey; the Divorce and Death of Queen Catherine"),[69] attracted the uninitiated to Smock-Alley. Once there, they stayed to have Shakespeare's other virtues impressed on them, spelled out in a special tribute which sometimes accompanied an important performance of some tragedy. This might be a recitation of "Milton's Epitaph to the Memory of Shakespear" by West Digges, "representing the Shade of Shakespear as figured on his Monument erected in Westminster abbey." [70] Or it might be "a Eulogim on Shakespear, the Stage and the Admirers of both," [71] spoken by the actor Robert Montgomery, a gentleman, scholar, and poet, who undoubtedly had written the eulogism himself. Through

---

[65] Burke, *Reformer*, No. 3 (Samuels, p. 303).
[66] *Dublin Journal*, December 31–January 4, 1746.
[67] *Ibid.*, March 8–12, 1757.   [68] *Ibid.*, April 4–8, 1758.
[69] *Ibid.*, May 9–12, 1752.   [70] *Ibid.*, March 27–31, 1750.
[71] *Ibid.*, March 27–31, 1753.

such encomia Dublin audiences were made to feel their debt to the greatest poet of them all.

Not all of the poet's works were presented by Sheridan, nor were those that were presented always pure Shakespeare. In the eleven seasons of Sheridan's management, a total of 18 plays—a little more than half of the corpus—was distributed over approximately 295 performances. Most played were three tragedies, *Hamlet* (some 35 times); *Romeo and Juliet* (about 30 times); *Richard III* (about 29 times). Least played was 2 *Henry IV* (with only one performance). Among those not played at all were, surprisingly, such now familiar comedies as *Midsummer Night's Dream*, *The Taming of the Shrew*, *Twelfth Night*, and *All's Well That Ends Well*. Two of these, Dubliners saw extracts from in shortened versions played as afterpieces. *Pyramus and Thisbe*, a musical afterpiece, ran a few times, enlivened with music by Lampe.[72] *A Cure for a Scold*, a ballad opera taken from *The Taming of the Shrew*, was revived briefly but had less success in Dublin than another version, Garrick's *Catherine and Petruchio*. Still another afterpiece, *Florizel and Perdita*, gave Dubliners a taste of *A Winter's Tale*. Dryden's *All for Love* took the place of the more difficult-to-stage *Antony and Cleopatra*. In general, the Shakespeare which Sheridan popularized in Dublin was that which did best at Drury Lane too. But *Twelfth Night*, given by Garrick in his first season's management, was never produced by Sheridan. Planned once for Mrs. Macklin's benefit (she had played in the Drury Lane performance earlier), it was canceled when her husband whisked her off after his quarrel with Sheridan. One Shakespeare play which Garrick seems never to have staged or played in, *Julius Caesar*, owes much of its popularity during this period to Sheridan. And in reviving Shakespeare plays that had not been acted for some time, Sheridan often set the pace for Garrick.

As at Drury Lane, the Shakespeare produced at Smock-Alley was not always as Shakespeare wrote it. *The Tempest*, which had a great vogue in Dublin, especially during stormy winters, was proudly announced as having been revised by Dryden and Davenant. Not announced as such, but clear from other evidence, was Cibber's *Richard III*; and the *Lear* was in Tate's version. Other Shakespeare plays

[72] Before the Lampe version a performance which was to have included "a celebrated Cantata, The Words by Dean Swift, The Musick by the late Dr. Sheridan" was advertised for May 14, 1746, but canceled when the whole evening was canceled.

are advertised "with Additions and Alterations," the additions probably consisting of the processions, dances, and songs, rather than actual interpolations; the alterations, probably slight changes often made by Sheridan himself to adapt the play to his stage or company. To Sheridan's credit is his early revival of *King John* (in 1745-46) rather than Cibber's popular *Papal Tyranny,* a revival encouraged by Garrick's presence in the company and probably inspired by Garrick's performance the year before when Sheridan was acting at Drury Lane. To Sheridan too the eighteenth-century theater owed the restoration of a scene to *Hamlet* (Act IV, Scene iv), one which, as Davies says, had been "for a long time disused." [73]

Freighted as the 1749-50 season was with Shakespeare (Sheridan never again achieved forty-four performances a year, though he kept the figure well up in the twenties from then on), it was still the kind of season that delighted Victor most—a financial success. He calls it "the most profitable Season to the Manager; the Sum total was encreased two thousand Pounds beyond any of the preceding Years." [74] Sheridan had accomplished the unbelievable in eighteenth-century Dublin, a Shakespeare revival,[75] without any loss—indeed, with a gain—in his audience and his treasury.

Also during this season Sheridan met and scotched the last threat to his monopoly until his return in 1756. For a time during the winter the Capel-Street Theater had again raised this threat by re-opening with a company which may or may not have been the Hiffernan group of the year before. Their nature and activities are obscure; no announcements appear in the *Dublin Journal* because, one critic claims, Sheridan had given a mandate not to advertise any play there. But remarks by this same critic in his *Play-House Journal* [76] and a few notices in the *Courant* indicate performances of some old plays and Hiffernan's new comedy, *The Self-Enamour'd,* which ran six nights in February and March. Prices were lower than at Smock-

---

[73] Davies, *Dramatic Miscellanies,* III, 120-121. See G. W. Stone, "Garrick's Alteration of *Hamlet,*" *PMLA,* XLIX (1934), 910, where the Fortinbras-Hamlet scene with the Hamlet soliloquy is reported as having been missing since the Restoration.

[74] Victor, *History,* I, 148.

[75] During the 1670's the Dublin theater had an extensive Shakespeare repertoire, as Clark shows (p. 73).

[76] *The Play-House Journal,* No. 1 (Thursday, January 18, 1750). This may have been its only issue. Miss Stockwell (p. 109) quotes three paragraphs from this piece.

Alley; [77] and, with Smock-Alley in mind, the prologue spoken at the beginning of their season lamented the decay of the stage when Otway and Shakespeare had to stoop for aid from Madam Vandersluys and foreign fiddlers. Most of the players were people who had been (or were to be) connected with Smock-Alley; [78] they had expected to be joined, says the *Play-House Journal*, by "two auxiliary princes from England" but "the French King, of Smock Alley" bribed them to come over to him "in modest violation of any sign'd contract." (Were the two princes Cibber and Digges?) By spring the Capel-Street Theater was closed again, Sheridan having crushed the rivalry by more ways than one. Most of the Capel-Street group turn up soon as members of the Smock-Alley company; furthermore, Sheridan himself took a lease around this time on the Capel-Street Theater for twenty-one years, and closed it down except for rare exhibitions. [79]

Fragmentary glimpses such as these show that Sheridan's struggle to keep a monopoly, although it did not erupt into public notice until after his return in 1756, was being carried on intermittently and under the surface until 1750. From then on until 1754, he ruled without threat of rivalry and became, in fact, what his enemies dreaded most—"Monarch of the Stage." And whereas in 1744, as head of a second company, he had favored financial competition between rival theaters, these years free from that extra harassment were to make him feel that the Dublin stage flourished best when there was only one theater for the limited public to support.

WITH THE Dublin public won—not by the monopoly but by Sheridan's own vigorous efforts—the season of 1750–51 was marred only by the unexpected departure of Mossop, who left in mid-March and

[77] For *The Recruiting Officer*, boxes 3/3; pit 2/3; first gallery 1/7; upper gallery 1/1. Prices for *The Self-Enamoured* were slightly higher: boxes 4/4; pit 2/8½; first gallery 1/7½; upper gallery 1/1. "No Spectator on what account soever will be admitted behind the Scenes; and no Ticket will be returned at the Pit Door after the Play begins" (*Dublin Courant*, February 17–20, 1750).

[78] For example, Giffard, Layfield, Mr. and Miss Mason, Heaphy, Morgan, Pitt, Mrs. Butler, Mrs. Rowley. (Listed in *The Play-House Journal*, p. 2).

[79] *Mr. Sheridan's Speech*, 1772, p. 11. On December 4, 1753, Mr. Powell the Fire-Eater was scheduled to perform there (*Dublin Journal*, November 27–December 1, 1753). Since he had come from London to perform at the Theater-Royal (see *ibid.*, November 17–20), possibly Sheridan, if he had the Capel-Street Theater in lease at this time, arranged to open it for him.

so suddenly that several benefits and plays in which he was to act had to be replaced. Both Victor [80] and Hitchcock say that he left after a quarrel with Sheridan, but they fail to record the cause or the date. If Hitchcock's story of the contretemps over Mossop's costume as Richard III is true, it must belong to this time, although Hitchcock dates it over a year earlier and speaks of a friendly settlement. For Mossop never played Richard III until March 13, 1751—the day of his last performance at Smock-Alley under Sheridan. Hitchcock says that, as Richard, Mossop "unaccountably dressed . . . in white satin puckered." Sheridan's observation that it gave "a most coxcombly appearance" reached Mossop, and the next morning in the manager's room Mossop spoke to Sheridan emphatically: *"Mr. She-ri-dan,* I hear you said I dressed Richard like a *Cox-comb:* that is an *af-front;* you wear a sword, pull it out of the *scab-bard;* I'll draw mine, and thrust it into your *bo-dy."* Sheridan, according to Hitchcock, is supposed merely to have smiled at this furious onslaught and, by timely explanations, to have brought the affair to a peaceful conclusion.[81] But, since Mossop's first Richard was his last performance under Sheridan, it seems likely that Hitchcock's story, if it has a basis in fact, was wrong in its conclusion. In any event, Mossop's temper, unstable at best, could not have been improved by the fact that Digges's benefit performance had preceded his this spring and had been so successful that five rows in the pit had had to be railed in as extra boxes for the ladies, whereas only four rows had accommodated them at Mossop's benefit.[82] There is other evidence that, after the year and a half of rivalry between the two men, Digges was pulling ahead. But the novelty of both, according to Victor, had begun to wane by this time.[83]

Because of this and to support Cibber, Sheridan had brought over

[80] Victor, *History,* 1, 149. Victor says, "Mr. Mossop went off for London before the Season was closed, on some Dispute with the Manager."

[81] Hitchcock, 1, 215. Hitchcock's account of Mossop contains several errors. He says that Mossop performed Zanga three successive nights at his first onset in the fall of 1749. Notices in the press contradict this, *The Revenge* playing on November 30 and December 7 only. Then for his fourth appearance Hitchcock says that Mossop chose Richard III and it was after this performance that the contretemps with its happy ending occurred. But, according to *Dublin Journal* notices, in the one performance of Richard after Mossop's debut in the 1749–50 season Sheridan played Richard. Over a year later Mossop is announced as playing Richard for "the first time."

[82] See Smock-Alley Calendar, March 11 and 13, 1751. When Mossop left he went to London and Drury Lane.

[83] Victor, *History,* 1, 149. The preceding season Victor had compared these

this season from Drury Lane the comedian Thomas King, a promising young actor [84] who over thirty years later (Sheridan would have been surprised to foresee) was to assist Richard Sheridan, as yet unborn, in the management of Drury Lane. King was good at mimicry and noted as "a great wit" and joker. According to O'Keeffe, he kept the company in lively spirits—sometimes too lively to suit Sheridan, who on tragedy nights preferred his actors properly serious.[85] King's benefit shows his interest in mimicry; he interspersed his part in *The Rehearsal* with Chocolate and did other imitations of Foote.[86] Like Digges, King stayed with Sheridan until the end of 1754; and he was with him again after he returned in 1756.

Of the two discoveries Sheridan made this season—Robertson and Montgomery—Montgomery added the more strength to the company, although his career never reached the success of Mossop's or Digges's, cut off as it was by a lengthy illness and then death. His obituary recalls that he was not only a celebrated Irish player but a scholar, a poet, and a "*Gentleman* of exceeding good Character." [87]

To reinforce his women, Sheridan hired Miss Cole, who like King was from Drury Lane. From the preceding season he had, among others, Miss Danvers and his leading actress, Mrs. Bland, who was kept so very busy that when her benefit came round on March 8, 1751, she had no leisure to "wait on the Ladies in Person, her Time being wholly taken up in the Business of the Theatre." [88] Her popularity as well as her activity was at its peak this season. A poem in the *Dublin Journal* celebrates her efforts and her assiduity:

> But of real Perfection no Mortal e'er tired,
> Bland is seen every Night, every Night is admired.[89]

---

two actors of five months' standing in a letter to Garrick (*Original Letters*, I, 157). Mossop had at first seemed a "wild, awkward youth" given to imitating Quin; but he was improving, as Digges, more promising at the onset, was not. Mossop had been much supported by the college and the town "to the mortification of Digges, who seems to be a great way beyond him, *at present*, in merit." Victor's expectation that Mossop would surpass Digges in the end seems not to have been realized, for the 1750–51 season anyhow; support for Mossop was apparently falling off.

[84] Victor, *History*, I, 149.

[85] O'Keeffe, *Recollections*, I, 360. O'Keeffe's story that King used to open the greenroom door, pop in a joke, and then leave the tragedians untragedized and in a roar of laughter, to the manager's indignation, is retold in Stockwell (p. 107).

[86] See Smock-Alley Calendar, March 20, 1751.

[87] *Dublin Journal*, April 17–21, 1753.   [88] *Ibid.*, March 2–5, 1751.

[89] *Ibid.*, January 15–19, 1751. Mrs. Delany reports having been well enter-

But this season's company was most distinguished by its extra entertainers: its dancers, its equilibrists, and its fireworks' operator. Last season's music, after the affair with Mosse, was to give way to dancing. With the opening of the theater in September, the arrival of Miss Baker, a celebrated dancer from Drury Lane, was announced and two famous dancers were awaited from Paris.[90] When these arrived—a Mons. Billioni, first dancer and ballet master to Count Saxe, and a Mlle. Pajot from the Royal Opera House in Paris[91]— they raised the number of capital dancers to five.[92] Except for a rare song and an occasional violin solo by Pasquali (the Lampes[93] and Mrs. Storer had left), the extra entertainment was provided by these five, supported by other less noted dancers. For some time during the spring the dancers even replaced the afterpiece. Some indication of the importance Sheridan gave them is to be gathered from the place of their benefits in the Smock-Alley Calendar.[94]

The performer of the year, however, was the equilibrist, Mahomet Caratta, rarely mentioned without the epithet "celebrated." His coming is announced in early November: "Last Sunday arrived in the Packet Boat from Holyhead, the celebrated Turk, known all over Europe for his extraordinary Performances on the Slack Rope. He is to exhibit on Tuesdays and Saturdays, at the Opera House in Aungier-Street." [95] With his "apprentice," Giovanni Baptista Perghen,[96] who did tricks on the tightrope, he entranced Dublin for

---

tained at a performance of *Macbeth* (November 9, 1750). "Sheridan acted Macbeth very well, the other parts very tolerably done. Lady Macbeth by Mrs. Bland—a very handsome clever woman, acts with spirit, but wants judgment" (Delany, II, 615).

[90] *Dublin Journal*, September 15–18 and 11–15, 1750.

[91] Their arrival is announced in the *Dublin Journal*, November 24–27, 1750. As is to be expected, their names are spelled in a variety of ways, e.g., Billiony and Pachos.

[92] Mons. Granier was still in the company; Mlle. Granier replaced Mlle. Vandersluys.

[93] The following summer Lampe's death at forty-eight in Edinburgh on July 25, 1751, is reported in the *Dublin Journal*. He was buried in Edinburgh.

[94] Benefits were normally scheduled according to the importance of the performer, with the leading performers first, the least important toward the end of the period. Second benefits for a few of the most important actors were given after the first round was over.

[95] *Dublin Journal*, November 3–6, 1750.

[96] There still exists in Sheridan's handwriting a "check" made out to this assistant of the celebrated Turk: "Be pleased to pay to Mr. Giovanni Baptista Perghen or order the Sum of twenty-five Pounds Irish Money which place to

nearly three months (from mid-November till February) by balancing almost everything—from nineteen glasses on his chin to himself on the wire, blindfolded with a sack over his head. He stood upside down on the slack rope; and to the particular suspense of the audience he wheeled a child in a wheelbarrow. Most of his performances were on the larger stage of Aungier-Street on evenings when there was no play at Smock-Alley. In December, according to a notice in the *Journal*, he went through his whole course of equilibres in six nights, because his stay was to be short; [97] but he was still performing in January, even moving into Smock-Alley to complete the offerings there. [98] After numerous notices of his positively last appearance, he finally departed for Cork, Limerick, and Kilkenny, [99] only to return to Dublin and Smock-Alley in late March for some more last performances. So pervading was his influence that at the end of May the comedian Messink, for his own benefit, advertises performances on the wire after the manner of the celebrated Mahomet Caratta, "being his first Attempt of that Kind in Publick." [100] He survived to give another on the last night of the season.

This last performance of the year was climaxed by a new dance featuring Billioni and Pajot, and by fireworks exploded by Signior Gillio "from the Theatre Royal in London." Gillio had taken over at Smock-Alley soon after Caratta finally left. [101] When the Smock-

---

the Account of/Your humble Servant/Thomas Sheridan," (quoted by permission of the Harvard College Library). Sheridan's order is dated March 30, 1751; the check is endorsed to John Hincks in Chester on April 6, 1751.

[97] *Dublin Journal*, December 8–11, 1750.

[98] See Smock-Alley Calendar for January 1751.

[99] *Dublin Journal*, March 9–12, 1751. Even in January Sheridan was promising Caratta's departure: "We hear that Mr. Sheridan intends to appear in the Character of the Earl of Essex on Monday se'nnight the 4th of February, being the first Time of his performing since the Holydays. We can assure the Publick that the celebrated Mahomet Caratta will not perform any longer in this city than the ensuing week, and that his Departure is absolutely fixed for Monday se'nnight" (*ibid.*, January 22–26, 1751). Although the last sentence was written to lure the public to the equilibrist's final performances, its somehow apologetic tone suggests Sheridan's true attitude.

[100] Smock-Alley Calendar, May 21, 1751.

[101] His first notice for Smock-Alley calls it the second time of his showing in this kingdom (Smock-Alley Calendar, April 27, 1751). Gillio continued his fireworks during the summer at Marlborough Green, after the theater closed. A touching note to the press (*Dublin Journal*, August 13–17, 1751) says that because Gillio was unfamiliar with the language he could not pay his respects before his benefit.

Alley stage proved too small for his best efforts, the company moved over to Aungier-Street for "Fireworks of a more magnificent Kind than any hitherto performed, as the Largeness of the Stage will admit of it." [102]

Equilibrists and fireworks may have fascinated the town this season, but they were not to Sheridan's taste. The important accomplishment for him must have been the increase in the number of performances and the opening of more new plays than in any previous season. Starting with only two and three performances a week in 1746–47, Sheridan was able to make this announcement by October 1750: "There will be performed for the future, at the Theatre-Royal, four Plays each Week, on Mondays, Wednesdays, Thursdays, Fridays, besides occasional Plays other Nights." [103] With the occasional plays on other nights (often at Aungier-Street), Sheridan actually achieved a five-night week regularly, and frequently (especially from mid-November to Christmas and during the spring benefits) a six-night week. In all, despite a two-week closing in April because of Prince Frederick's death, Sheridan raised the number of performances to 157 for this year, some fourteen over the number of the preceding season, which was itself a record.

In the number of new plays this season sets another record—six main plays and three afterpieces. Two, at most three, new main plays a year were normal both at Smock-Alley and Drury Lane during this period. As usual, most of the new plays in this season of 1750–51 were "new" to Smock-Alley rather than performed for the first time. But even in three of these Sheridan led the way for Garrick. Edmund Smith's *Phaedra and Hippolitus* and Nicholas Rowe's *Lady Jane Grey* were not produced by Garrick until the following year, Mossop, then at Drury Lane, having apparently reported favorably on them. (He played the lead in both there, and, curiously, was supported by George Anne Bellamy.) *The Chances*, by Fletcher, altered by Buckingham, did not show under Garrick until two seasons later.

Sheridan followed Garrick in Aaron Hill's *Merope*, which he opened late in the season (May 11) and in Whitehead's *Roman Father*, to become one of his favorites. Happily, an Englishman who had seen the Drury Lane performance was at Smock-Alley for the opening of *The Roman Father* and writes his reaction in a rare letter

[102] Smock-Alley Calendar, May 18, 1751.
[103] *Dublin Journal*, October 13–16, 1750.

to the *Dublin Journal*. Surprised to have seen so much justice done
this noble tragedy, he found it as well performed at Smock-Alley as
at Drury Lane. Yet he wonders at the different response of the
audience: the glorious sentiments of patriotism had been clapped
vigorously in London, but in Dublin "though the Actor received the
Applause due to his Merit . . . the poor Author was entirely neglected, and some of his most masterly Strokes passed unheeded by."
The letter writer himself tried to lead applause for them but was
not supported, indeed was eyed as singular. In conclusion, he hopes
that all patriots will be at the play next Thursday to have the pleasure
of hearing such sentiments and sharing the joy which comes from
knowing that such sentiments "produce proper Fruits in the Hearts
of their Fellow-hearers." [104] But not all Irishmen were so wildly
enthusiastic about their government, as their behavior three years
later (almost to the day) would show. Then a Smock-Alley audience
was to respond to some patriotic sentiments for a reason unimagined
by this loyal Englishman—and in a manner unforeseen by the loyal
Sheridan himself.

The only play advertised as "never acted before" was *Don Sebastian*, altered from Dryden not by Sheridan this time, but by
someone else employed to bring it into bounds.[105] Five years earlier
Sheridan's curtailment of this overlong play had had only one night.
This later revision was not much better received, with three performances. Very successful, however, was a new afterpiece, Garrick's
Lethe, which became as popular in Dublin as in London.

Sheridan, who hardly ever performed in afterpieces, took no part
in *Lethe*; but, since he acted the leads in most new main plays, he
added more than the usual number of new roles to his repertoire
this season—perhaps as many as seven.[106] All this was made less of

[104] *Ibid.*, February 23–26, 1751. The letter writer must have had in mind
such passages as "All private Duties are subordinate/To what we owe the
Public . . ."; "Yet still superior must that Heroe prove/Whose first, best Passion is his Country's Love."

[105] A letter to *ibid.*, March 12–16, 1751, signed "J. K.," tells about the
revision. It is not clear that J. K. is the reviser, but cuts, additions, and a change
in the catastrophe are mentioned.

[106] Theseus in *Phaedra and Hippolitus*; the Roman Father; Eumenes in
Merope; Pembroke in *Lady Jane Grey*; Dorax in the new version of *Don
Sebastian*; and the surprisingly minor role of Trusty in the revived *Funeral*.
He also acted Ventidius in *All for Love* for the first time in six years. And
apparently the part of Strictland in *The Suspicious Husband* was new to him,
although not so advertised.

a burden by the fact that he himself did not start the season until almost a month after the theater opened, and he took an unusually long rest after Christmas [107]—more possible than hitherto because of the support from Mossop and Digges. In addition, he began the practice of not acting in his players' benefits, which were exceptionally numerous this season, occupying four nights a week from early March to the end of May. This new policy must have relieved company tensions as well as Sheridan's acting burden; but this year, for the second benefits taken by a few top players in May, he relaxed his new policy. Although in the future he almost undeviatingly abstained from players' benefits, he was always generous toward charitable performances and he made it a habit to appear for *one* of his actors—Isaac Sparks, the Captain O'Blunder of his *Brave Irishman.*

Although the Shakespeare series fell off, the usual spring series having been abandoned perhaps because of the two weeks of mourning or perhaps from a Shakespeare surfeit the year before, this season rivaled the 1748–49 one for the variety and interest of its offerings. Writing in December 1750 to Sir William Wolseley, Victor exclaims: "The entertainments of Dublin were never in so high a tide as now. We have the famous Turk from London, who exhibits at Aungier-street Theatre, on Tuesday and Saturdays; and we have four plays a week, at Smock-alley Theatre, from all which I have received six hundred pounds a week, for many weeks past—great doings for Dublin!" [108] If the average of £100 a night suggested by Victor's letter was maintained through the 157 performances of the season (and the steady playing would seem to show a steady demand), this was hardly a losing season financially, in spite of the mourning period in April and the numerous benefits.

"Great doings for Dublin!" Although Victor's later *History* lacks enthusiasm for this season,[109] the spontaneity of his on-the-spot re-

---

[107] His first performance in the fall was October 15; after Christmas, February 6.

[108] Victor, *Original Letters*, I, 164.

[109] Victor, *History*, I, 149. Here Victor reports from memory not only that Digges and Mossop had lost their novelty, but that Mrs. Bland was unable to support all the characters, and, even worse, that Mossop had left for London before the end of the season. "This therefore," he concludes, "may be supposed (if compared with the last) to be a losing Winter." Victor seems to have in mind the stature of the company rather than the financial record of the year; and his vague "may be supposed" implies a backward guess rather than a factual remembrance.

action conveys the excitement Sheridan had aroused in his public. This, more than great financial success, was important to him. His rivals and critics having at last subsided, he was now giving himself totally to his task, withdrawing, he later claims, so far from all other interests that he became "almost a Stranger in the City of his Birth." [110] His reward, he points out, was the riot of 1754 and the destruction of all his work. But in the meantime as "Monarch of the Stage" he was to enjoy several peacefully productive seasons notable for the variety of their performances and the brilliance of their casts.

[110] Sheridan, *An Humble Appeal*, p. 23.

CHAPTER VII

Calm Before Storm, 1751-1753

THE SEASON of 1751–52 became one of Smock-Alley's most brilliant for several reasons. A new Lord Lieutenant, the Duke of Dorset, returned (he had been Irish viceroy before) to replace the socially moribund Harrington, whose recall to England Dubliners celebrated with bonfires.[1] Sheridan must have done a bit of celebrating too, for the chronically ailing Harrington had given the theater minimal support, commanding—with few exceptions— only the performances required of the theater-royal, those for royal anniversaries. Victor, early in Harrington's five-year viceroyalty, complained of this neglect in a letter to Colley Cibber: "Our present *Lord Lieutenant* remains in the utmost Obscurity; he has been at no one Place of Entertainment since he came."[2] But Dorset, his lady, and his son, Lord George Sackville, in their support of the theater and other arts, were to bring back the glories of the Chesterfieldian era some six years earlier. Indeed, although Chesterfield was more noted for his patronage, Dorset was probably more loyal in fact. In mid-October the viceregal couple made their first appearance at the theater, which was illuminated with wax and packed with nobility and gentry for the occasion. They were greeted with "uncommon Testimonies of Joy" and treated to a special prologue on the event spoken by Sheridan himself, and apparently written by him. The gist of this piece was that Dorset had come to dispel night:

> His Presence here fresh Vigour shall inspire
> New warm the Poet's Lay, new rouze the Actor's fire.

The stage, in turn, would offer him relief from his weightier cares; and even our youth (here we see Sheridan's hand) would profit as they saw the hero on the stage materialized in the person of the Duke.[3]

Dorset may have been pleased with this effort but *The Nettle* was not. This little sheet in its only issue, dated October 24, shows what Sheridan critics had been reduced to by 1751—attacks not on

[1] O'Mahony, p. 156.
[2] Victor, *History*, II, 214 (Letter of November 17, 1748).
[3] *Dublin Journal*, October 15–19, 1751.

Sheridan's offerings, company, acting, or person, but on his poetic abilities. Sheridan was no Alexander Pope. To demonstrate this, *The Nettle* dissects the prologue, "spoken and said to have been written by the Manager," line by line, because "nothing serves to instruct young Geniuses in the poetic way so much as the unfolding the mechanism of any *original* work to them, and shewing whence the auxiliary images are drawn." For example, commenting on the first line of the couplet quoted above, *The Nettle* has this to say about "fresh vigour": "Heaven grant it, for it is much wanted." But particularly wonderful to *The Nettle* is the Alexandrine which follows (in the second line above), "wonderful for the down-hill familiarity of the images." For, "Be it known to you, O Reader we are now in the profoundity of the Kitchen. 'New warm the poet's lay' excites the necessary idea of a sauce-pan, to *new-warm* soup, milk, or any substance in a cool, phlegmatic, and vapid state, such as the poets lay, is commonly served in, to us from *Smock-Alley* stage. 'New rouze the actor's fire.' Admonished by this expression who does not find his fingers impatient to seize the recreant poker, and with its fire-proof point rouze the dormant coals from their inactive lethargy. . . ." Recited in a hobbling, abject manner, this travesty of Pope, says *The Nettle*, would have been bad enough if it had been allowed to pass into deserved obscurity unnoticed; but its publication (in the *Dublin Journal*, regularly exported to England) was unpardonable. "What must they think in *London* when they read such a prologue. . . ."

One amusing passage in *The Nettle* describes an important moment in a Smock-Alley evening. The prologue begins with Dorset metaphorically dispelling the Harrington pall: "Our tedious night/ At length is broke by a meridian light." But the image itself, *The Nettle* japes, is borrowed from "the heaving up of the lamps on the stage . . . which affords great joy to those benighted in the galleries from three to seven in the evening." This blazing spectacle regularly brings a response from the audience recorded by *The Nettle* in two lines of its own, which, the author says, could be added to the prologue without hurt: ". . . our *Gallerians* view the rising lamps/ Hailing them with an universal—O." Relief at last from boredom, restlessness—and semidarkness! The word "benighted" in the quotation above is to be taken literally.

From mid-October 1751 on, the Lord Lieutenant not only commanded the usual anniversary plays, but he and the duchess ordered a play almost weekly. How much part those who "commanded" plays took in the selection of them is problematical. Some viceroys, among them Dorset, seem to have used their right of choice more than others; Victor, as deputy manager, waited on the Duke of Dorset every Friday morning to receive his commands for the next week.[4] For other, less interested Lord Lieutenants the manager may have planned the program and been grateful for the chance to advertise that it was by command. The viceregal presence must have had a sobering effect on the upper gallery, for in these later years, when command performances are numerous, we hear nothing about that section. On the other hand, it is unlikely that the duke and duchess would have attended so frequently if the house had been the "bear-baiting" arena it was before Sheridan's time. Thus the benefits were probably reciprocal.

Some idea of the splendor with which the Dorsets surrounded themselves can be imagined from the description of a grand and superb ball attended by the viceregal couple, the nobility, and the gentry, and given at Aungier-Street Theater in March of this year. As on the earlier occasions of festinos and ridottos, the pit must have been floored over; and the room, illuminated by twelve hundred large wax candles, was decorated lavishly with "Orange Groves, Myrtles, Bays, Jessamins, Trees in Blossom and full grown, Fruits of all Sorts," to say nothing of statues, rocks, grottoes, caverns, and cascades with perfumed water. Above, the ceiling was painted with the moon and stars to imitate night but there was also a representation of the morning with the rising sun. Instrumental and vocal bands provided music from different parts of the house. After an elegant supper, the ball was opened.[5] There had been a viceregal command performance of *The Distrest Mother* earlier that night at Smock-Alley, with Sheridan playing the leading role. With both his theaters utilized in one evening, and with himself probably an important figure at both functions, this must have been as gratifying a night for Sheridan as for the ducal couple.

The other leading player in *The Distrest Mother* that evening was Mrs. Peg Woffington, and she even more than the viceroy added luster to the 1751–52 season. When she came to Dublin a few months

[4] Victor, *History*, I, 203.

[5] *Dublin Journal*, March 3–7, 1752. The month before, on February 15, Mrs. Delany wrote, "On Thursday morning we went to see the ball-room, that is the great play-house converted into a ball-room." Lord Belford, her stepson-in-law, was "chief manager and contriver" (*Autobiography*, III, 88).

earlier after disagreements with Quin and Rich,[6] it was not at Sheridan's invitation. And strangely enough, according to Victor, though she intended to stay in Dublin the next winter, Sheridan had "no thoughts of making her any overtures."[7] He had other plans and other prospects for the season: a new dancer, Mr. McNeil from Drury Lane, to replace Mons. Granier; Italian singers and operas[8] (these did not materialize); and a large variety of new players. The new players included Mr. and Mrs. Davies (Davies later was to introduce Boswell to Johnson and to become Garrick's editor and biographer); Mr. and Mrs. Kennedy (Mrs. Kennedy, as Miss Orfeur, had been with Sheridan before); Tottenham Heaphy, who made his first attempt on Smock-Alley stage in October and who was to become important in Dublin theatrical affairs; and Mrs. Lee, who with Mrs. Bland was to play the leading female roles, beginning with Juliet to Digges's Romeo.[9] Again according to Victor, Sheridan was not easily persuaded to believe Mrs. Woffington superior to Mrs. Bland, but, pushed by friends, his "good genius" prevailed and he hired Woffington for the one season only, at £400. The "Happy Consequences of that Engagement," Victor elsewhere remarks, "are recent in the Knowledge of everyone who frequented the Theatre of that Time."[10]

Whether Victor is right or not in his observation and memory of Sheridan's attitude, one thing is clear. From the moment he hired her, Sheridan behaved as though he had secured a great prize. Her first performances received special notice by extra large advertisements and type[11] (all this before she had appeared at all). Her first

---

[6] The *Dublin Journal* (August 13–17, 1751) reports that on August 15 "the celebrated Mrs. Woffington arrived here from England." Speaking of her departure from Covent Garden, Bellamy (1, 171) says that "she took dudgeon, and set off for Dublin; where her beauty alone would insure her success." With Drury Lane closed to her, Garrick, "her quondam admirer," choosing rather to appear with Mrs. Pritchard (Bellamy, 1, 124) and with Covent Garden now unavailable, it was natural for her to go back to her home city, where she had first acted as a child, where her mother still lived, and where she had made an earlier triumph when she returned with Garrick in the summer of 1742. Sheridan had known her from this time, if not before. (See Ch. 1.)

[7] Victor, *Original Letters*, 1, 174.   [8] *Ibid.*, p. 185.

[9] See Smock-Alley Calendar, October 7 for Heaphy's debut; September 30 for Mrs. Lee's.

[10] Victor, *Original Letters*, 1, 185; *History*, 1, 151.

[11] Particularly for *The Distrest Mother* (see *Dublin Journal*, October 1–5, 1751).

role was as Lady Townley in *The Provoked Husband* (Sheridan played Lord Townley); two nights later she appeared as Andromache to Sheridan's Orestes in *The Distrest Mother*. In less than a week the *Dublin Journal* was reporting that Mrs. Woffington's performances continued to draw "the most crowded Audiences hitherto known." [12]

Sheridan's engagement of Peg was even luckier than it seemed on the surface, for Mrs. Lee did not work out as expected. From the beginning, Woffington took over the leading female parts and appeared almost nightly. Mrs. Bland continued to play, in secondary parts or on rare nights when Mrs. Woffington did not. One wonders how Mrs. Bland took her decline from public favor, especially how she felt when after being advertised for the leading role, now rare for her, in a viceregal command performance of *Richard III*, she was replaced "by Desire" by Mrs. Woffington, who had never played the part before. [13] The four players—Sheridan, Digges, Woffington, and Bland—appeared together frequently. With these four actors at the top the Smock-Alley company was stronger than it had been for some time.

To say that Peg Woffington was a success in Dublin is a pale understatement; she was a sensation. The fever which she, and the theater too, generated this season reechoes in the press. She is praised effusively for many talents: for her elegant deportment, her unaffected ease and vivacity in comedy, her majestic pathos in tragedy; for her beauty, her eyes, her goddesslike form; for her skill in making every character her own. She is hailed for her portrayal of Constance in *King John*, of Andromache and Hermione in *The Distrest Mother*, of Lady Townley, of Coriolanus' mother. [14] Especially noteworthy in view of Sheridan's interests is mention of Woffington's distinct, articulate pronunciation, observed by one correspondent who describes her as a "compleat . . . Mistress" of "Oratory or Declamation." [15] These encomia appear in all forms: in press items, in letters, in poems. One verse writer sings in Latin about the worth of "Woffingtonia," who herself could hardly have been expected to appreciate his effort; fortunately an English translation of the piece was provided in a later issue, which perhaps indicates that the interest

---

[12] *Ibid.*, October 8–12, 1751.   [13] This was on February 13, 1752.

[14] *Dublin Journal*, October 8–12; October 19–22; November 30–December 3, 1751; February 29–March 3, 1752.

[15] *Ibid.*, February 29–March 3, 1752.

in Peg was felt to be general and not confined to the educated classes.[16]

The other actors of the company were overshadowed, although Sheridan received his usual share of tributes. One of these is amusing if Victor was right in his picture of a reluctant Sheridan, engaging Woffington only through pressure from friends. As an afterthought in a fulsome poem to the actress, Sheridan was thanked for the reformations he had brought to the stage after the dark ages of the Goths and Vandals:

> For this we owe you much, but more is due,
> We owe our darling WOFFINGTON to you.[17]

During this first season at Smock-Alley her two benefits [18] were gala affairs, both commanded by the Duke and Duchess of Dorset, and, even more unusual, both supported by Sheridan, who otherwise was tightening his custom of not acting for his players. At the first benefit she spoke a special epilogue; and the demand for places was so great that the *whole* pit was "laid open to the Boxes for the Convenience of the Ladies." [19] Not all the actors, we gather from *Dublin Journal* notices, were so successful in getting together an audience for their special performances. But Woffington herself had the reputation of being most generous in giving her time and talents to the benefits of others. During this year, for example, she is advertised as playing in twenty-two benefits out of a total of twenty-six.[20]

Both Hitchcock and Victor report Woffington's contribution to Smock-Alley in terms of cold cash. In this 1751-52 season she played the lead in *The Non-Juror*, *The Provoked Husband*, *The Constant Couple*, and *The Distrest Mother* and kept them going for ten nights apiece. The receipts of these forty nights were "upwards of £4,000"—"an instance never known at that time, or perhaps since, on the Irish Stage, to four old stock plays, as in the dramatic phrase they are denominated." [21]

Mrs. Lee, it will be recalled, had not worked out as Sheridan had hoped. Her first appearance, as Juliet, took place just a week before

[16] *Ibid.*, December 31–January 4 and January 11–14, 1752.

[17] *Ibid.*, October 19–22, 1751.

[18] See Smock-Alley Calendar, March 9 and April 20, 1752.

[19] *Dublin Journal*, February 29–March 3, 1752.

[20] Not, as Hitchcock reports, twenty-four out of twenty-six (1, 221).

[21] *Ibid.*, p. 220. See also Victor (*History*, 1, 151), who is especially surprised that these four did so well when "the Manager acted no Part" in two of them.

Mrs. Woffington's. But she failed to please,[22] and, even more than Mrs. Bland, fell into obscurity and minor roles. We can judge her status by the fact that her benefit, as originally planned, was to be shared with the very subordinate Mrs. Rowley. But from this ignominy she was saved when her husband, John Lee, made arrangements to come to Dublin from Drury Lane, where he was finishing out a stormy contract with Garrick.[23] Her benefit was deferred until his arrival in May and together they acted *Romeo and Juliet*, advertised as "With Alterations, as performed at the Theatres in England." [24] Hitchcock's rare sneer that Mrs. Lee "chose to treat the town with an exhibition of her own Juliet" [25] tells something of the company's reaction to Mrs. Lee and her ideas. After the benefit, which was Lee's only appearance at Smock-Alley for the time being, he and his wife left for Edinburgh, where he was to manage a new theater. But Sheridan had not seen the last of them. Five years later a public quarrel with Lee, back again in Dublin with his wife, added to Sheridan's troubles when he was fighting for his managerial life.[26] And even after that their careers crossed occasionally.

When the theater opened in the autumn of this season, the galleries had been made "more Spacious and Commodious" than before.[27] The changes there, which had occupied part of the summer and which seem to have been the most elaborate in three years, came none too soon to accommodate the growing crowds. Even so, the demand for gallery seats at Victor's benefit (March 20) and again at Sparks's benefit (April 15) was so extraordinary that both men seized the chance to double upper gallery prices, at the suggestion of their "Friends." [28]

This was not an outstanding year for new plays, either at Smock-Alley or at Drury Lane. At Smock-Alley three plays acted elsewhere first but never there were produced: *Zara*, by Voltaire and Hill, not produced by Garrick until 1754; *The Rover*, by Mrs. Aphra Behn;

[22] *A Letter from Mr. Lee to Mr. Sheridan*, 1757, quotes a letter from Sheridan to Lee in which Sheridan indicates that Mrs. Lee had not been well received in Dublin during this 1751–52 season (pp. 3–5).

[23] *DNB*, *v.* "Lee, John." The Rowley-Mrs. Lee benefit had been scheduled for April 22.

[24] Lee's arrival is announced in the *Dublin Journal*, May 2–5, 1752; the *Romeo and Juliet* notice appears in the May 9–12 issue.

[25] Hitchcock, I, 221. [26] See below, Ch. IX.

[27] *Dublin Journal*, August 27–31, 1751.

[28] See Smock-Alley Calendar for those dates.

and Southerne's *Fatal Marriage,* altered by Garrick and produced by him two years earlier.[29] The only really new play given at Smock-Alley was *Coriolanus.* Three years before, in the late spring of 1749, Sheridan had planned to stage Thomson's version of the Coriolanus tragedy and had in fact brought the piece almost to production, deferring it once and then postponing it till next season "because of an Indisposition of a principal Player."[30] But the next season nothing was heard of the play, which had been a failure at Covent Garden. Now, in February of 1752, Sheridan announced a new tragedy never before performed called *Coriolanus* and taken partly from Shakespeare and partly from Thomson.[31] Sheridan himself had been the surgeon who had grafted the two versions together. Although we know from press reports and contemporaries' comments that Sheridan altered, less extensively, a number of other plays, this combination of two very different works into one play is the only one of his revisions to come down to us. It was first published in 1755.[32]

The play ran five nights at Smock-Alley during the spring of 1752 and was revived successfully in later seasons, doing well even at Covent Garden when Sheridan was there to play in it in 1755. As the basis for John Philip Kemble's version, which restores more of Shakespeare but keeps some of Sheridan's excisions and additions, it had an influence well down into the nineteenth century. Sheridan always staged it with a most elaborate spectacle, representing on stage a Roman ovation and employing, at some performances, as many as 118 persons.[33] An eighteenth-century reaction to its opening night in Dublin, recorded in a letter to the *Journal,* expresses surprised enthusiasm. The writer admits that after reading the advertised descriptions of the work he had had his doubts (as who wouldn't?), but he was delighted to find that the play had "its own

[29] Of the three new afterplays apiece for each theater, Woodward's *Harlequin Ranger* was the only one produced by both. *The Constant Captives* and *A Lass to be Let* were new at Smock-Alley; both were pantomimes, the first very popular.

[30] *Dublin Journal,* May 23-27, 1749.   [31] *Ibid.,* February 1-4, 1752.

[32] [Thomas Sheridan], *Coriolanus: or, the Roman Matron. A Tragedy Taken from Shakespear and Thomson. As it is Acted at the Theatre-Royal in Covent-Garden: To which is added, the Order of the Ovation,* London: A Millar, 1755.

[33] For a fuller analysis of how Sheridan combined the two plays, how he staged the ovation, and what significance the work has for the eighteenth and nineteenth century, see my article "Sheridan's *Coriolanus:* An Eighteenth-Century Compromise," *Shakespeare Quarterly,* XIV (Spring), 1963.

intrinsick Merit" and was "intitled to the greatest Applause." The "very Striking" character of Coriolanus was "incomparably well performed" by Sheridan. The letter ends in a climax of praise for the achievement of that inimitable actress Mrs. Woffington,[34] who played the part of Coriolanus' heroic mother.

February was a particularly busy month for Sheridan, with the production and acting of *Coriolanus* and "first appearances" in three new Congreve roles,[35] all three within ten days. The Congreve series of five plays, which Sheridan offered for the first time this year, was more of a success than his Jonson series of two years earlier (when three Jonson plays had been planned but only two given).[36] Experimenting in another way, he ran this first Congreve series concurrently with a Shakespeare series, and provided his audience with a pleasant alternation. The Congreve went so well that as the series came to an end four of the original five plays were announced for a rerun the following week.[37] One of these, *The Mourning Bride,* had not been acted at Smock-Alley for eight years.[38]

Partly because of the excitement stimulated by Mrs. Woffington, this season saw a few welcome theatrical reviews in the press, written in the form of unsolicited letters by anonymous playgoers. One gentleman who saw *The Mourning Bride,* a play generally thought inferior, had not been more agreeably entertained all winter: the ending of the play had often been criticized as labored, but this never could have been gathered from the Smock-Alley representation; it was hard to decide who had the greater merit, Osmyn (played by Sheridan) or Almeria (a first for Woffington) at the tomb of Anselmo. Sheridan had never appeared to more advantage; he played with heroic ardor; his horror and rage were gloriously performed and he did surprisingly well as a lover. All in all, *The Mourning Bride* was a noble entertainment which the town should see again![39] (It did, a few days later by command of the Duke and Duchess of Dorset.)

[34] *Dublin Journal,* February 29–March 3, 1752.

[35] Valentine, Osmyn, and Fondlewife. His other new roles for the season were Coriolanus; Osman in *Zara;* Sir John Brute in *The Provoked Wife;* Dorimant in *The Man of Mode;* and apparently Leon in *Rule A Wife.*

[36] See Smock-Alley Calendar, February 15 and March 8, 1750.

[37] *Dublin Journal,* February 11–15, 1752.

[38] There were three other important revivals this year—Cibber's *Non-Juror* and Etherege's *Man of Mode,* neither of which appeared at Drury Lane until 1753, and *Henry VIII,* in which Drury Lane preceded Smock-Alley by a month. *The Non-Juror* became particularly popular in Dublin.

[39] *Dublin Journal,* March 10–14, 1752.

In another letter Sheridan does not have to share the glory with Peg; the role was Hamlet, Sheridan's favorite and best. Never was a single part so well written, "never was any so well performed." At his first entrance, Sheridan appeared with "such solemnity of Woe" that he drew the audience's earnest attention. In "O that this too too solid Flesh," he was so affected that he seemed to be the one he performed. In the scene with Ophelia, "he was Great," with the players "admirable," but with the queen "beyond all Imitation." Perhaps never were words so emphatically spoken as "O there be Players." The whole part was performed almost without a fault; several gentlemen present who had visited most European theaters "never were so pleased with any Performance whatsoever." [40] These embryo reviewers of eighteenth-century Dublin are more unrestrained and panegyric than their full-grown, more jaded descendants.

Never was Sheridan in such high esteem as this season. For two years now, nothing had occurred to disrupt his relations with the public. Critics of his person, his behavior, his theatrical offerings had subsided; the Mosse affair had been forgotten. This happy position Sheridan undertook to consolidate by two public-spirited benefit performances. The first, given on December 13, in conjunction with a worthy charitable group, the Society for the Relief of Clergymen's Widows and Children, [41] was apparently a success. The other, a public benefaction initiated by Sheridan and certainly important to him out of sentiment, brought him only annoyance and disappointment.

In the 1750's commemorative monuments to dead heroes had a great vogue in Dublin; in 1751 and 1752 collections were afoot for a monument to Thomas Prior, patriot, and to the virtuoso musician Sign. Castrucci, whose funeral in Dublin in that year attracted such

---

[40] *Ibid.*, November 23–26, 1751. The letter is signed "A.B." The following winter the praises continue. Sheridan is saluted—rather unusually—for his comedy. A letter writer saw his "inimitable Performance" as Archer and is inspired to a poem "To Thomas Sheridan Esq." In this are commended his grace, ease, gentility, passion, and particularly his voice: "Tho' manly, clear; tho' Steddy, yet not dull; Soft, without weakness; without Hoarseness, full." The total effect is electric:

> "Won by thy Air, how ev'ry Bosom thrills!
> We view the Eye, that fires! the Smile, that kills!
> But when thou speaks't, how female Breasts rebound!
> The Angel Choir have taught their Songs, the Sound."

A similarly fulsome tribute to the inimitable Woffington follows (*Dublin Journal*, November 21–25, 1752).

[41] See Smock-Alley Calendar, Pt. 1, 1751–52, footnote 3.

a crowd that a St. Mary's beadle was crushed to death.[42] The thought of monuments to such as these when the greatest Irishman of them all had none must have galled Sheridan. So Dubliners picking up the *Journal* of January 21-25 read in a news item, the first under Dublin news, that Thomas Sheridan, Esq., Manager of the Theater Royal, was planning a benefit play to raise funds toward a monument for "that glorious Patriot and great Genius, the late Jonathan Swift." This example, it was hoped, would set other lovers of Ireland to raising more money for this purpose. Faulkner, Swift's printer, was accepting private contributions and already had received over £60. Later issues carry notices of further contributions. And Mrs. Delany reports to her friend Mrs. Dewes, along with her judgment that Sheridan is a just actor but rather *a dull one*, "he is going to give a play gratis to raise a sum of money to erect a monument to Swift; he has many of the Dean of St. Patrick's letters, that show he was a *most friendly and generous man.*"[43]

The benefit play, *The Conscious Lovers,* with the very best the company could offer—Sheridan, Digges, King, and Woffington—was scheduled for March 23; and the *Journal* announced that most of the ladies, who had bought a great number of tickets, had agreed not to wear hoops that night, with the result that the boxes would hold more than double and those sitting elsewhere would fit into the pit and other parts with more "Ease and Satisfaction."[44] The evening began with a Prologue on the occasion spoken by Sheridan and probably written by him (a copy in what may be his handwriting still exists). Sheridan's Prologue to Dorset the season before had been a namby-pamby piece; now his more worthy subject and his love for it inspired him. The result was not great poetry; indeed, there are feeble verses and confused passages. But some rousing eighteenth-century lines begin the tribute:

> When public Gratitude erects the Bust,
> Where public Worth has dignified the Dust;
> When Nations strive the Patriots Fame to save,
> It speaks them worthy of the Good he gave.

The whole concludes with lines equally forceful:

> Dullness be dumb, Detraction drop thy Quill,
> A people lov'd, a People love him still.[45]

[42] Maxwell, p. 104.   [43] Delany, iii, 80.
[44] *Dublin Journal*, March 14-17, 1752.
[45] From British Museum MS Collection, Egerton Add.26036.

These vigorously expressed thoughts, spoken in Sheridan's clear, emphatic way to a house already enthusiastic, must have evoked considerable applause. A news item after the play indicates "a very full Audience." [46]

A month later, however, a letter to Faulkner signed "Hibernicus" sounds a warning note. The undertaking, the first of its kind attempted here, is no less than Swift deserved, but the success of it depends upon the conduct of its undertakers. Hibernicus fears "lest the Management of a few, may bring a Reflection upon the Nation." He proposes a meeting of all subscribers and would-be subscribers for the selection of trustees to handle the money. [47] Nothing more is heard on the subject for almost a year and then Sheridan apparently took Hibernicus' advice. All persons subscribing to Swift's monument are asked to meet at the Great House adjoining the theater to choose trustees to carry on "that laudable Undertaking." [48] From that time on, Swift's monument once more drops out of the news, although we read the next April of a most elegant marble structure being finished to the memory of Thomas Prior, patriot. [49] The following season Thomas Sheridan left Dublin.

In 1758 when Sheridan, back as Smock-Alley manager but now more interested in education, was trying to get financial as well as spiritual backing for his new academy, one of his anonymous critics remembered Sheridan's earlier fund-raising and asked an embarrassing though somewhat confused question: What happened to the money collected for the monument to Shakespeare? [50] The confusion was understandable; Sheridan had done much to keep Shakespeare's name before the public. But, Swift or Shakespeare, the question was one that needed answering. A letter to the *Dublin Journal*, written not by Sheridan but by a friend, gives this explanation: Sheridan *had* contributed the receipts of the play (£101), and he *had* arranged the meeting to select trustees. But the shocking truth was that only three people showed up, among them George Faulkner. After waiting nearly three hours, these three felt that it was unwise to push the design further at that time. Sheridan agreed to give another benefit play for the monument the next season; but the next season Sheridan had had to leave the country. He has not, however, lost sight of the monument, the letter avers. "He stands indebted in the Theatrical

[46] *Dublin Journal*, March 21–24, 1752.   [47] *Ibid.*, April 25–28, 1752.
[48] *Ibid.*, January 9–13, 1753.   [49] *Ibid.*, April 17–21, 1753.
[50] *The Case of the Stage in Ireland*, p. 28.

Books for the Receipt of that Night"; he will pay the money in an hour to any group taking up the cause. If no group materializes, he must be allowed to pursue his present course, as the largest contributor; those who saw the play received full value for their money. In a final affidavit the facts of this explanation are sworn to by Faulkner,[51] who, incidentally, as collector of the outright donations, would seem to have owed more of an explanation than Sheridan. The conclusion to the whole unfortunate story comes in the form of a quip, made by another anonymous critic at Sheridan's expense: the money is on the books of the theater, we are told—as safe as in the Bank of England! [52]

Thus Sheridan's plan for improving the city and honoring Swift's memory was to come to nothing but embarrassment, although in 1752 he could not know this. The idea was part of Sheridan's attitude toward his work: the theater was to be his means for public improvement. At the end of the season, at the performance honoring the new Prince of Wales' birthday, the prologue spoken (and printed in the *Journal* because it was so well received) reflects another side of this same thought. The great virtue of acting is that it *teaches* people; mainly it teaches people their blessings and shows to whom they owe them.[53] Whether Sheridan wrote this prologue or not, he approved the role it gave to his profession.

THE SEASON of 1752–53, the most uneventful of Sheridan's regime, opened at a later date than usual (October 16). The loss of the eleven days in September when the calendar changed to new style was partly responsible, but alterations and improvements in the theater and perhaps the late arrival of Sowdon from Drury Lane caused extra deferrals.[54] The Dorsets were not in Dublin this season; command performances fell back to the minimum and were by order of the Lords Justices. Much of last year's excitement had faded, although Sheridan had brought over a flock of new players, most of them from Drury Lane. Despite the continued popularity of Mrs. Woffington, he added more leading women than men; he had lost

[51] *Dublin Journal*, February 4–7, 1758.

[52] Shea, *A Full Vindication*, p. 21.   [53] *Dublin Journal*, May 23–26, 1752.

[54] The plan first was to open October 9, then on October 14, finally on October 16 (*ibid.*, September 30–October 3, 1752, n.s., and following issues. All dates given from now on are in New Style.) I find no announcement of Sowdon's arrival in Ireland, but his first performance, scheduled for October 14, a date the theater was to have opened, had to be postponed to October 18.

Mrs. Bland at last and Mrs. Lee. Miss Danvers too had dropped out for the time being.[55] To replace these, he hired three actresses, only one of whom made any stir in the Dublin papers and that by an extra-theatrical event. A press item which records it explains why her appearance on the stage was delayed until late in November:

> Last Wednesday Morning Mrs. Ward, who is engaged to perform this Season, at the Theatre Royal in Smock-Alley, was safely delivered of a Daughter, and is in a fair Way of Recovery.[56]

Mrs. Ward's pregnancies achieved considerable publicity, it seems. George Anne Bellamy tells in her memoirs how, when she first met her at Cowley, Rich's country home, Mrs. Ward was pregnant. Bellamy says of her that she had "one of the most beautiful faces I ever beheld," but her figure was vulgar, her shoulders large and stooped.[57] Among the men Sheridan still had Digges and King, but Cibber had left. In his place Sheridan hired not a comedian but a predominantly tragic actor, John Sowdon from Drury Lane. Sowdon had accepted the invitation, according to Victor, with the hope of becoming joint manager with Sheridan.[58] His first appearance was in a favorite Sheridan role, Othello. At the end of May, John Dexter, having finished out his Drury Lane contract, appeared at Smock-Alley in two roles and stayed on for the following season.

One other addition to the acting troupe must be specially mentioned: George Stayley, whose playing contributed little (he took small roles after his first appearance on October 19), but whose later writings touch often on Dublin theatrical matters. In his *Life and Opinions of an Actor* he tells how, when he joined the Smock-Alley company in 1752 as a minor actor, he wanted to render himself useful and, "contrary to general custom, laboured and studied the Man-

---

[55] The Davies left too—for Drury Lane.

[56] *Dublin Journal*, October 24–28, 1752. The other two actresses were Miss Falkner, who became Mrs. Donaldson, from Covent Garden, and Mrs. Green, who, like Mrs. Ward, was from Drury Lane. Hitchcock calls Mrs. Green "an excellent comic actress" (I, 224). She enlivened many an afterplay, as the Smock-Alley Calendar shows.

[57] Bellamy, I, 123.

[58] Victor, *Original Letters*, I, 232. John Sowdon came of a good family, being brother to "Thomas Otway of Castle Otway, Esq." (*Dublin Journal*, June 5–9, 1753). He came to Smock-Alley from Drury Lane and earlier Covent Garden, where he had made his debut probably on December 4, 1747 (Genest, IV, 247–248).

ager's interest, more than mine own advancement." Perhaps because of this and because he had more of a flair for writing than for acting, he was made poet laureate of the company in 1753: he wrote state prologues for nothing, he says—and spoke them for the same price.[59] But, in spite of his seeming bitterness here, he later became a Sheridan partisan and indeed attributes his dismissal by Mossop from Smock-Alley in 1760 to his "particular Benevolence, on all Occasions expressed, for a late worthy Manager,—even so far as to wish to see him once more re-established in the Theatre." Such talk, he feels (and with some reason), may have lost him Mossop's heart. But, he continues, "if I were to repeat it again now, I do not think I should wish Harm to any-body; for Mr. *Sheridan* and the *Irish* Stage never did better than when he was a Manager." [60] Stayley's play, *The Rival Theatres*, 1759, satirizes the destructive rivalry between Crow-Street and Smock-Alley predicted by Sheridan before he left Dublin in 1758.

This year Sheridan featured singing more than he had for some time. His two chief dancers, Mr. McNeil and Miss Baker, were still with him (having been joined by a Mr. Pitt), but he needed more variation: Mr. Sullivan and Miss Falkner, who became Mrs. Donaldson, were engaged primarily to sing, and the extra entertainment often consisted of both dancing and singing.

Sickness and death plagued the company throughout this season. Digges was ill intermittently during February, the all-important term time, and finally was forced to drop out entirely most of March. His benefit on March 26 featured him in the leading role, but he had to apologize for not waiting on his friends in "a personal Application." By April 2 he was well enough to perform Hamlet in Robert Montgomery's benefit, Montgomery himself being too weak to do more than attempt the Prologue, "a Eulogim on Shakespear, the Stage and the Admirers of both." [61] In April, Montgomery, who had been discovered by Sheridan three years before and whose first year had been so notable as to provide him with two benefit performances, died after a long indisposition.[62]

Montgomery's death was the second in the company that year. Earlier, in February, Sheridan lost loyal John Beamsley, a minor actor, who had been with him from the beginning. His death, appar-

[59] Stayley, *Life and Opinions*, p. 24.
[60] Stayley, *Reference to the Public*, p. 7.
[61] See Smock-Alley Calendar, March 26 and April 2, 1753.
[62] *Dublin Journal*, April 17–21, 1753.

ently quite sudden, came at the time that Digges was incapacitated, and must have caused Sheridan more grief and harassment. The *Dublin Journal* calls Beamsley "a very honest Man," who from the small size of his income left a widow and several young children unprovided for.[63] We read therefore with relief that a benefit assembly for the Beamsley family, by desire of some ladies of quality, was to be held at the Music-Hall in Fishamble-Street; [64] and a share in a benefit play seems to have been arranged for the widow by Sheridan.[65]

Sheridan's generous salaries to his top people have been recorded, and deplored, by Victor. Mrs. Woffington, who had joined the company at £400 the preceding season, was lavishly rewarded for her success by an increase, this next year, to double that amount, £800,[66] to which must be added the income from two benefits (over £200 more). Even Sheridan's normal contracts of £300 and £400 a season for his principal players were regarded as high by Treasurer Victor. Cibber, one recalls, described Sheridan to Digges as a "liberal" manager—a fine tribute from a onetime enemy, whether he was thinking in terms of acting opportunities or of money. Sheridan's instincts were to pay employees well; the salaries he set up later for his professors in the Hibernian Academy were reported as fantastic.[67]

But Smock-Alley income was still too small to permit more than a modest wage, probably well under £100 a year, to the minor players (benefit money would be additional). Twenty years later, in 1771, Snagg, a minor player of the Dublin company, received a guinea and a half a week, exclusive of benefits. On this sum he could save money, so reasonable was living then, but he was a single man at the time.[68] Beamsley, with a family, would feel pinched and, dying unexpectedly, would leave his family poor. But for the past seven years of his life employment had been steady, at least; before Sheridan, playing had often been uncertain and actors often destitute. If Sheridan's salaries to his minor players were small, at least they were paid. A

---

[63] *Ibid.*, February 20–24, 1753.   [64] *Ibid.*, March 20–24, 1753.

[65] For a May 24 performance of *Ulysses* with Sheridan and Woffington: "Tickets delivered out by the Widow Beamsley, Mr. Pit, Mr. Costello, Mr. Maurice, and Tickets delivered out by Mr. Hamilton for Jane Shore, and all other Tickets for the above Play will be taken this Night" (*ibid.*, May 19–22, 1753).

[66] Victor, *History*, I, 152.   [67] Sichel, I, 242.

[68] Snagg, *Recollections of Occurrences*, p. 76; see also introduction, p. xiii. Sheridan's pension fund seems to have been planned—at first, anyhow—for incapacitated players only and not for bereaved families. Even for incapacitated players, it would hardly have been adequate enough yet.

glance at the company rolls shows that many actors remained with him year after year: Beamsley, Sparks, Mr. and Mrs. Mynitt, and others. Even principal actors, among whom there would naturally be more turnover, stayed two, three, and sometimes more seasons. This fact and the loyalty of his minor players speak well for Sheridan's management.

Much evidence shows that Sheridan continued to improve the conditions and position of his actors. In enforcing a new regularity he exercised considerable strictness over his company's professional activities and possibly even over their private lives. Burke's grudging compliment that under Sheridan actors had to know their parts and be more regular in their exits and entrances gives some idea of what Irish acting had been like before Sheridan.[69] Much has been made of Sheridan's custom of marching his company, two by two, on Sundays to St. John's church, where he had "purchased a Pew . . . for the Accommodation of the Actors and Actresses under his Care." But no one has noticed that the source for this story is a bitter satire on Sheridan and therefore not entirely reliable as a true report.[70] On the other hand, his company was, in general, quite "respectable." Bellamy and Woffington, it is true, were in the old tradition—and perhaps this accounts for Sheridan's initial reluctance to engage the latter—but no scandal attaches to the others, and one is impressed with the large number of married couples: the Macklins, the Mynitts, the Dyers, the Storers, the Greens, the Kennedys, some even with children handy to play children's roles. Master Mynitt appears regularly and shares in his parents' benefits; and later we note his successor, a boy with an equally engaging name, Master Pye, whose mother played minor roles. Of further help in improving the reputation of the actor was, as we have seen, the "gentlemanly" origin of many of Sheridan's stars, for example, Mossop, Digges, Montgomery. Throughout this period, in spite of jibes from Hiffernan, Burke, and other Sheridan enemies, the evidence grows, in letters and verses to the paper, that Sheridan's company had the enthusiasm and even the respect of much of the Irish public.

This increased status was extended to the minor players too. As time went on, Sheridan expanded the details of the notices so that even the less important actors saw their names in public print and knew the pleasures of fame. The number of benefits was extended to

[69] Burke, *Reformer* 2 (Samuels, p. 299).
[70] Shea, *A Full Vindication*, pp. 21–22.

include these same less important people. Although not all of them could sell a houseful of tickets, and sometimes benefits had to be combined or canceled, at least each had his opportunity.

During this season of 1752–53 the shining attraction was still Peg Woffington, dimmed hardly at all. One of her most popular roles the year before had been Sir Harry Wildair in *The Constant Couple*, a play commanded by the Dorsets and performed repeatedly throughout the season. This year Peg had considerable success in another male role, which she played by desire and for the first time—Lothario in *The Fair Penitent*,[71] a part usually acted by Digges. Although not quite the success of *The Constant Couple*, *The Fair Penitent* with its new and charming Lothario had several performances during the spring. Dublin audiences especially enjoyed seeing women actors "in Boy's Cloaths" or "in Breeches." A special note of these occasions was taken in the advertisements.[72]

During Woffington's three years as Sheridan's leading lady the two worked together without friction, even amicably. The place he arranged for her in his Beefsteake Club may have seemed socially expedient at the time (although how terribly inexpedient he later learned), but the part he played in her religious conversion could have been possible only between close friends. Indeed, Dublin gossips suspected the worst when, during Christmas week of 1752, Sheridan and Woffington took off together on a public journey to Quilca, the site of the Sheridan country home, leaving Mrs. Sheridan behind, possessed—again according to Dublin gossip—by "raging Fits of Jealousy." The truth was that Sheridan was conducting Peg to a place less embarrassingly public than Dublin for her recantation. Although a sound churchman himself, Sheridan probably had little to do with the actual change in Peg's religion (the will of an old admirer offering her a yearly income if she would convert seems to have accomplished that), but he knew "a worthy clergyman" near Quilca who would officiate. Mrs. Sheridan had been privy all along to the plan and, besides, was a lady of "such distinguished good Sense" as to be "at all Times, fully satisfied with the Conduct of her Husband." Well she might be, for he was a model of respectability. Indeed, he had found it impossible, Alicia Lefanu reports, to introduce to his wife this woman whose "moral character was such as to exclude her

[71] First played on January 29, 1753.
[72] On March 22, for example, Mrs. Ward appeared as Fribble, "being the first Time of her appearing in Boy's Cloaths" (*Dublin Journal*, March 17–20, 1753).

from the society of her own sex." Moreover, by this time, Victor hints, Woffington had lost much of her physical attractiveness; both Sheridan and he felt that she "had captivating Charms as a jovial, witty Bottle-Companion, but very few remaining as a mere Female." As a "bottle-companion," she officiated in the Beefsteake Club, formed this same season (1752–53) with herself as the only woman member because, says Alicia Lefanu, Sheridan, unable to introduce her to his wife, wished in some way to pay tribute to her genius.[73] Another sign of his appreciation was, as we have seen, his custom of playing in her benefits against his established policy.

Sheridan's offerings this years were less impressive than in some former seasons. The new sensation was an equilibrist from Covent Garden named Maddox. Maddox performed for a while at Smock-Alley, and then Sheridan opened Aungier-Street, reported early in December as "now preparing" for the equilibrist;[74] and *Comus* was revived to accompany the equilibres. But Sheridan's customers needed reassurance about the condition of the disused Aungier-Street Theater. The day of the opening the audience was notified that "the whole House is compleatly well aired, as there have been several Stoves kept constantly burning there for more than a Fortnight past." On the larger stage of this comfortably warm and well-aired house Maddox performed Thursdays and Saturdays.[75] So successful were his performances that he evoked a complimentary poem, printed in the *Journal* and hailing him as "amazing Creature!"[76] Like Mahomet Caratta, he ended up "by Desire" in a succession of nights at Smock-Alley and was given a benefit. And, as with Caratta, Sheridan kept

[73] Victor, *History*, I, 154–156; Lefanu, p. 53. See especially W. J. Lawrence, "Peg Woffington's Recantation and its Sequel," *Dublin Magazine*, N.S. xiv (July–Sept. 1939), 25–33. As for Woffington's physical attractiveness at this period, it must be remembered that she was nearly forty and considerably older than Sheridan. But on stage apparently she was timeless. The praises in the newspapers rarely fail to mention her beauty, and Bellamy's comment that this alone would ensure her success in Ireland comes from one who was otherwise disposed to judge her harshly.

[74] *Dublin Journal*, November 28–December 2, 1752.

[75] *Ibid.*, February 3–6 and 13–17, 1753. In the latter notice we read: "The Passage to the Upper Gallery is opened to Longford-street Side, and the Gallery rendered very commodious," an announcement which implies that the Aungier-Street upper gallery had never been "intirely removed," as Sheridan had reported three years before. (See Ch. vi.)

[76] *Ibid.*, January 2–6, 1753. This appeared even before Maddox moved to Aungier-Street.

promising his early departure.[77] Before he left, Maddox accomplished the feat of balancing a straw and playing a violin at the same time; and when Maddox was not balancing and fiddling, a ten-year-old boy-organist was playing a concerto at the Aungier-Street production of *Comus*.[78] The quality of Sheridan's instrumental offerings this year was not, one suspects, what it was in the time of Pasquali and Lampe.

The "new" plays this year, those "never acted here before," numbered two main plays and one afterpiece,[79] Sheridan's lowest showing so far. In presenting John Hughes' *Siege of Damascus* for the first time in Dublin Sheridan anticipated Garrick by six years. Rowe's *Ulysses*, the other main play, never became a part of Garrick's repertoire. For both of these plays Sheridan learned the leading roles. The only other roles which he seems to have mastered this season were Wolsey in *King Henry VIII* and Hastings in *Jane Shore*. The latter play had long been a Sheridan favorite, but he had played Dumont, with Digges as Hastings; Digges's indisposition may have had something to do with this change. A Congreve series seems to have met with less success than in the preceding season; it ran sporadically from December to March and was not repeated.

All through his time as manager the problem of admission had concerned Sheridan. As Miss Stockwell shows, the practice of reserving specific seats was not introduced until long after his day.[80] Ordinarily, as in the local movie house today, people bought, at the door, the mere right to enter and to find what seats they could, a hazard which could be somewhat obviated by coming hours early oneself or by sending a servant to hold a place. An *advance* sale of tickets allowing these same privileges was introduced through the benefits, the

---

[77] *Ibid.*, March 3–6, 1753: "By desire, Mr. Maddox will perform the few remaining Nights at Smock-alley." March 10–13 issue reports that Mr. Maddox's engagement expired last Saturday, but that "upon his Application to the Manager since that Time," he was given *Love's Last Shift* as his benefit on March 24.

[78] See Smock-Alley Calendar, February 17, 1753, for example.

[79] The afterpiece was Mrs. Cibber's *Oracle*, which had debuted at Covent Garden the preceding season and which now opened at Smock-Alley the day before it was first given at Drury Lane (where it was performed by children). In Dublin it was (by Desire) the afterpiece for Mrs. Green's benefit; she and King played the leads. The only revived play of interest this year was *The Pilgrim* by Fletcher, altered by Vanbrugh and revived two years earlier at Drury Lane.

[80] Stockwell, pp. 243ff.

particular beneficiary peddling space in the theater to his friends and patrons. But either way people could arrive at the theater and find it full; for, in the case of the benefits, more tickets were often sold than the house could absorb. Then apologies had to be made to the people who were "disappointed" because of the "overflow" crowds, and the tickets had to be "taken up" at later performances.[81] To spare ladies this disappointment in his growingly popular Shakespeare series, Sheridan had early introduced a special arrangement, which he describes as the custom in London theaters: [82]

> There will be a Book opened by Mr. Neil, Boxkeeper . . . to whom such Ladies as are desirous to secure Places at any of the above Plays, are requested to send their Commands as soon as possible, as he is under a Necessity of always letting the Boxes in the Order of sending.[83]

By these means a lady could be sure of getting into the theater and even into a particular box; but apparently she still could not reserve a particular seat, if the following notice means what it seems to mean, i.e., that a servant was needed to hold the seat desired:

> It is requested that the Ladies who have engaged Places in the Boxes will send their Servants at Half an Hour after four, to prevent Confusion.[84]

The box book kept by Mr. Neil served another purpose; through it Sheridan could partly foretell the demand. His early Shakespeare series had been offered only on the provision that the boxes were taken for each play. Later the number of requests for places was used to determine the order of the plays.[85] An amusing side light to this advance arrangement is that Mr. Neil became one of the most popular members of Sheridan's company. His annual benefit always provoked an extraordinary demand for tickets, the boxes had to be laid open to the pit to accommodate the many ladies springing to his support, and his evenings became gala affairs.[86]

---

[81] For example, "As there were a Number of Persons who had Tickets of Mr. Mossop's that were obliged to go from the Theatre last Night, the play of the Distrest Mother is again to be performed this Night for his Benefit" (*Dublin Journal*, March 6–10, 1750).

[82] *Ibid.*, January 23–27, 1750.   [83] *Ibid.*, December 31–January 3, 1749.

[84] *Ibid.*, November 21–25, 1749.   [85] *Ibid.*, October 22–26, 1751.

[86] See Smock-Alley Calendar, April 4, 1753, for example.

Most interesting is the evidence that in 1752–53 Sheridan extended the advance sale of tickets to all parts of the house, not just the boxes, for an ordinary performance, not a benefit or series. After the usual notice of the play *The Suspicious Husband* for January 5, 1753, this N.B. follows:

> All Persons who want to purchase Tickets for any Part of the Theatre, before the Doors are open, may have them at Mr. Esdall's, Bookseller, on the Blind-quay, and no where else.[87]

Since early playbills for the fall of 1753 show a similar notice, the practice was continued for a while and may have become permanent. Either way, it represented a move in a wise direction.

Financially, the 1752–53 season was not a bad one, even though Woffington's salary rose by an extra £400. "If my Memory does not greatly fail me," says Victor (thereby revealing that his conclusions about the financial success or failure of these years depended on his memory and not on any records he had preserved), "the Profit at closing the Account did not fall more than 300 Pounds, short of the first Season" [88]—meaning the preceding very profitable year, Woffington's first season. Writing to Lucas in April 1753, Victor reports, with considerable satiric exaggeration, that Sheridan was transforming his little inheritance at Quilca into "a *palace* in miniature," buying eight hundred acres of bog and stone around it, "all of which by theatrical art, and Smock Alley chemistry, is to be transformed into fine arable land, to be an establishment for his younger children." [89] The October before this, Sheridan had apparently expanded Smock-Alley's territory by leasing an adjacent house or part of it, where meetings could be held and other theatrical business more comfortably accommodated.[90] The efforts Sheridan had put into the theater were beginning to pay off financially, in a small way.

In many ways Sheridan's situation seemed enviable at the end of the 1752–53 season, the last full year between riots. His theater might

---

[87] *Dublin Journal*, December 26–30, 1752.   [88] Victor, *History*, I, 152.
[89] Victor, *Original Letters*, I, 199.
[90] The deed of 1754 between Victor and Sheridan, in addition to referring to the two theaters, their buildings, wardrobe, scenes, et cetera, mentions a room and passage leading thereto to hold the wardrobe. This room, "among other premisses," was leased to Sheridan on October 1, 1752, for twenty-three years. (MS 169/356/114101. Off. Reg. Deeds, Dub.) Subscribers to the Swift Monument were asked to convene at the Great House adjoining the theater, and the Beefsteake Club held meetings there.

not quite have been responsible for all the improvements that lyrical Hibernicus, writing in 1754 to defend Sheridan, claimed: the growth of Dublin, the construction of many elegant homes for persons of quality, the great concourse of people attracted principally by the enhanced "State of the Stage." [91] Even Hitchcock, not speaking from firsthand knowledge, is to be suspected of exaggeration when he says that Smock-Alley was crowded nightly with all levels of people, especially with "the first characters of the kingdom" and that its exhibitions might have graced "a Greek or Roman stage." [92] But, as our history has shown so far, the Dublin theater had greatly prospered under Sheridan. The number of annual performances had more than doubled: from some seventy during Sheridan's first season (with Garrick and Barry) to about 162 in 1751–52,[93] only a score fewer than Drury Lane's for this time.[94] The population of Dublin, though growing, had made no such spectacular increase over the seven years. Sheridan himself had enlarged his audiences by ways that we have seen—by improving his theaters, his productions, his company, and by giving himself totally to his work.

Increased performances meant an increase in income. Sheridan's *Humble Appeal*, 1758, a pamphlet which denies charges of his extravagance at the same time that it shows his improvements to the theater, reports his first season as having grossed £3,400, £400 of which went to Garrick. In less than four years, Sheridan says, the annual income—and this seems to have been a gross figure exclusive of benefits—rose to over £9,000.[95] If this £9,000 applies to the fourth season after Sheridan took command, 1749–50, when approximately 110 nonbenefit performances were played, we can estimate that the theater averaged between £80 and £90 a night. This tallies with what contemporaries suggest when they say that £110 represented an unusually successful evening (Lucas collected that much for his charity showing, and Woffington's £4,000 for forty nights comes slightly

[91] *Dublin Journal*, February 19–23, 1754. He continues, "This Concourse of Company and those Number of Buildings [have been brought about] since the Theatre has been under the Conduct of the present Manager."

[92] Hitchcock, I, 227.

[93] Because of the late opening in 1752–53, the number for that year, the last of our period, drops slightly, so that I have used the figures from the preceding year, which represented the peak.

[94] Pedicord, p. 15.

[95] Sheridan, *An Humble Appeal*, p. 21. Lefanu's statistics are even rougher; she says (pp. 28–29) that from 1743 to 1758 the sums (benefits excluded) increased from £2,000 to £10,000 a year.

lower).[96] Pedicord gives Drury Lane's average daily receipts for this year as £134,[97] higher than even the best Smock-Alley could do. The more commodious theater and the larger theatergoing public gave Garrick the advantage.

But if Smock-Alley's gross income continued to improve, expenses were high and going higher. Sheridan speaks of the incumbrances when he took over the management: £400 yearly for annuities to people who had given up their interests to accomplish the Smock-Alley and Aungier-Street merger; £200 rent to the proprietors; and, of course, taxes and ground rent for the two houses.[98] Top actors drew generous salaries. In 1749–50 we know of the Macklins' £400; Pasquali received £300.[99] By 1749–50 the company had grown; some thirty-five people took benefits, and, although this number includes dancers and singers, it does not take in the musical band of twenty or more performers, the lowliest of whom received twenty shillings a week, the better ones reaching thirty to forty.[100] When we add Sheridan's other employees—the painters, machinists, doorkeepers, wardrobe mistresses, dressers, prompters, scene shifters, et cetera—the total roster may not come to the 140 given by Colley Cibber for a London house,[101] but by 1750 it well exceeds the fifty-one who signed the Smock-Alley petition in 1747. If Smock-Alley employees totaled eighty and averaged £90 a year apiece in income (exclusive of benefits) there would have been little over £1,000 left for improving the theater, its wardrobe and scenery, staging new plays, paying for new music, and so on. Yet Sheridan reports that under his aegis the value of the wardrobe alone increased from £200 to £4,000.[102] When we see such figures as these, we believe Sheridan's claims that he personally made nothing out of Smock-Alley. Writing in 1758, he asserts that he never took more than five guineas a week for himself (this would come to less than £300 annually, while he was giving Woffington £800); and sometimes he reduced his income to three guineas

---

[96] See above, p. 175. Recall also Victor's glee at £600 a week for six evenings. Several years later, in 1757, £150 "was a great house indeed" at Dublin, according to Tate Wilkinson (IV, 123). Isaac Sparks's benefit on April 11, 1753, which brought in over £165, provoked comment in the press (see the Smock-Alley Calendar for that date).

[97] Pedicord, p. 15.   [98] *Mr. Sheridan's Speech*, 1772, pp. 10–11.

[99] *Ibid.*, p. 11.   [100] *Ibid.*

[101] Cibber's description of the duties of a manager, quoted in *The Life of Mr. James Quin*, 1766, pp. 57–58.

[102] *Mr. Sheridan's Speech*, 1772, p. 12.

a week.[103] His property in Quilca was not the palace represented by his enemies but a modest thatched cabin on which he had spent only some £400.[104] We conclude too that the way Smock-Alley prospered was through Sheridan's plowing back all surplus into his venture. As the income rose, the extra money was spent on higher salaries to attract better stars, on new sets, new costumes, new and lavish productions, all to attract larger houses and so more money to spend on improvements. As far as we can judge, Sheridan did not raise entrance fees during all this time, except for an occasional special performance.

Sheridan's detractors railed against his "extravagance," and even Victor now and then protested. But Sheridan's extravagance this time was good business. His theater was thriving, and not simply because it was a monopoly. In the end causes other than extravagance brought about its ruin. And Sheridan paid in full for his only extravagance— the generous sacrifice of his own wages to bring about the improvement of the Dublin stage.

[103] Sheridan, *An Humble Appeal*, p. 27.   [104] *Ibid.*, p. 28.

CHAPTER VIII

Cry Havoc Again, 1753-1754

THE SEASON of 1753-54, which was to become the most disastrous in Sheridan's career, promised well. In mid-September the Duke of Dorset returned to Dublin with his son and his duchess, the latter marking her arrival in an outfit of striped Irish poplin. In mid-October their first appearance at the theater after a year's absence was the occasion for a command performance and a special prologue, spoken by Peg Woffington as the Tragic Muse and complimenting Dorset and Dublin on their patronage of the arts.[1] From this time on, command performances in almost weekly succession began again. The Congreve and the Shakespeare series picked up; new plays and revivals[2] were projected in larger numbers and with more enthusiasm; and Sheridan appeared in more new parts.[3]

Many signs indicate the high place and well-being of Sheridan's theater. At a tremendous castle ball in November the celebrated Smock-Alley scene painter, Joseph Tudor, prepared the paintings and decorations; Benjamin Victor, later to be named the official poet laureate of Ireland, wrote the ode for the occasion.[4] And the Smock-Alley manager, who as a friend of the viceroy was frequently invited to the duke's private dinners and parties,[5] must certainly have been an important figure at this celebration.

Because of the still-growing theatrical audience Sheridan this season opened the slips, the section above the lattices, which had been closed since the Kelly riot. As we have noted, he restricted their occupancy to women since there was no passage to them except by the stage and he would not admit men there on any account. The slips

[1] *Dublin Journal*, September 18–22 and October 16–20, 1753.

[2] During this season Sheridan anticipated Garrick by two years with Mrs. Centlivre's *Wonder* on January 14; by nine years with *Mahomet*, taken from Voltaire by Miller and Hoadly; by two years with Cibber's *Lady's Last Stake*.

[3] Oedipus; Celadon and Palamede in Dryden's *Comical Lovers*; Lord George Brilliant in *Lady's Last Stake*; Zaphna in *Mahomet*; Heartly in *The Non-Juror*.

[4] The ball, on November 12, was reported in the *Dublin Journal*, November 10–13, 1753. Earlier the *Journal* had announced that there would be no play at the theater that night because of the ball at the castle (November 3–6). Victor became official Poet Laureate in 1755 (see his *History*, 1, 203, and the date of Dorset's recall from Ireland, *DNB*).

[5] Lefanu, p. 69.

sold at middle gallery prices, 2/2,[6] and so brought in a little extra revenue.

Sheridan's own high position and influence are inadvertently revealed in another way—in a satiric poem which recalls earlier attacks on the manager. Printed sometime in the fall of 1753 for its author, B—t B—n, *The Stage: or Coronation of King Tom* pictures full houses attracted just by new scenery, new dresses, and waxen tapers; fustian actors met by the plaudits of a thousand hands; and Dublin engrossed in theatrical gossip:

> 'Tis now the talk what Players wafted o'er,
> Forsake their own for a more tasteless shore.
> With what new singers does their chief engage,
> If Stuart still or Baker holds the stage?
> And now the bills set up, appoint the day;
> It is his fifth and a most tragick play.[7]

Over all rules Irish Tom, "A Prince as absolute in his domain/As Lewis once, or greater Charlemain. . . . A realm so rich in pleasures of the fool/What head so fit as S—s to rule?" Though Sheridan is crowned king by Dullness, he can console himself with the knowledge that Victor, shipped off to Ireland by a jealous Cibber, is an even worse fool:

> V—r whose dullness does all sots surpass,
> A blund'ring stiff incorigible ass. . . .
> Nor must you Tom! however large your share,
> Thy weak stupidity with his compare;
> V—r has parts to other fools unknown
> And in his art of sinking yields to none.

This stale imitation of the *Dunciad*, and of earlier Smock-Alley satires themselves imitated from the *Dunciad*, must have amused rather than annoyed the Smock-Alley manager.

From London sometime in 1753 came a sober estimate of Sheridan and his work. *The Present State of the Stage in Great Britain and Ireland* devotes eight of its fifty-five pages to Dublin. Here "Mr. Sherridan" is introduced to the reader as the manager who has done what nobody in England can do: he has cleared the stage. No longer are his exits and entrances "jammed up with an immoveable Country

---

[6] *Dublin Journal*, September 22–25, 1753.

[7] "It is his fifth and a most tragick play"—a sneer at Sheridan's subscription series and his advertisements of them.

Sheridan as Theater Manager, resting his elbow on a Shakespeare folio

Frances Chamberlaine Sheridan, ". . . a most agreeable companion to an intellectual man."—BOSWELL

Reproduced by permission of the Comtesse de Renéville

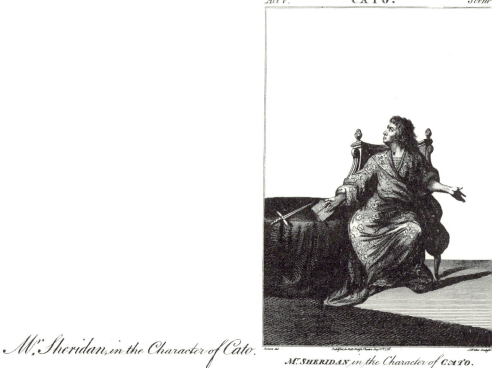

Act V. **CATO.** *Scene*

Robert del. *Publish'd for Bell's British Theatre Aug.r 7.th 1776* *A.Walker Sculp.t*

M.r SHERIDAN in the Character of CATO.
Eternity! thou pleasing dreadful Thought

M.r Sheridan, in the Character of Cato.

My Bane and Antidote, are both before me.
Act V. Scene 1.

Sheridan as Cato, without and with the Robe
(See the Cato's Robe Controversy in Chapter II.)

Publish'd for Bells British Theatre June 7th 1776.   Reading Sc.

M.ʳ SHERIDAN *in the Character of* OEDIPUS.
What mean these exclamations on my Name?

Act 2ᵈ   JULIUS CÆSAR   Scene 1ˢᵗ

Roberts ad vivum del   Publish'd for Bells Edition of Shakespeare Jan 9 1776   White fc.

M.ʳ SHERIDAN *in the Character of* **BRUTUS**
——— *"It must be by his Death:*

Sheridan as Actor. "He went through Oedipus happily," and as for his Brutus, "the orations . . . were never better spoken."—WILKES

Sheridan as Lexicographer, Orator, and Educational Reformer
(This portrait appeared as the frontispiece of his dictionary.)

Squire" or with a fop made of lace and punctilio. Sheridan's theater through his care and judgment presents an "Oeconomy, Elegance, and Decency unexpected." No man "understands the Business of the Stage better" than Sheridan; "he is an Excellent Scholar, an exceedingly good Commentator on his Author, and very judicious in his Delivery." [8] In the remarks which follow, Sheridan the actor receives almost as high praise as Sheridan the manager.

But Sheridan was not entirely without annoyances. Something had happened between him and Victor, who records a mutual coldness which had been growing steadily worse for some time and which had now reached a point where the two men were barely speaking. [9] If Alicia Lefanu is to be credited, Sheridan had also made an enemy of Digges, his principal actor. Their dispute arose over a stage call which Sheridan accused Digges of ignoring and which Digges insisted had not been made. When Sheridan took the word of the caller (who, he said, had never told him a lie) rather than of the "gentleman" Digges, Digges was said to have boasted afterward to Mrs. Ward in the greenroom that he would "be revenged on Sheridan for doubting my word." Miss Lefanu implies that this incident could account for Digges's later contribution to Sheridan's downfall. Her account is very circumstantial, with direct quotations, for example, but her purpose throughout is to extenuate Sheridan. [10]

Furthermore, according to Victor, the sentiments of the general public were being roused against Sheridan, because of his political activities in the Beefsteake Club, [11] a group which he himself had founded about 1752. [12] That it was established originally, as Victor says, with "no Party Intention" but merely to help the manager decide on future exhibitions and to support him in other ways seems probable in view of Sheridan's apolitical years in the past. [13] But his

---

[8] *The Present State of the Stage in Great Britain and Ireland*, pp. 50–51.

[9] Victor, *History*, I, 161. Could the rift have been caused or widened by Sheridan's treatment of Miss Danvers, whose name does not appear after the 1751–52 season? (She is back in the company by 1756, after an interlude in Edinburgh.) Or could the arrival of Sowdon with his prospects of becoming joint manager with Sheridan have disappointed certain hopes in Victor?

[10] Lefanu, p. 59. This incident is not given in any other of the early accounts. Miss Lefanu cites as her source for all anecdotes her mother, Sheridan's daughter. Although actually she leans heavily on Victor for many, this incident is not from him.

[11] Victor, *History*, I, 153–154; 157–160.   [12] Gilbert, II, 87.

[13] Victor (*History*, I, 153–158) says that clubs attached to theaters were an almost universal custom at the time, the members usually being the principal

inclinations, as revealed earlier in the Lucas affair, lay with the court; he was a friend of the Duke of Dorset; and, unavoidably, the group of thirty or forty which gathered each week for dinner at Sheridan's expense and in his quarters next to the theater [14] included the son of the Lord Lieutenant, Lord George Sackville; [15] Lord Delawar, "a man of large fortune, great rank, and many temptations"; [16] Sir John Whiteford, commander of the Dragoon guards; Lord Lucan; the Provost of Trinity College, Dr. Andrews, a "fine, jolly, fresh looking man, very fond of the theatre" [17]; and other persons of that first quality and distinction which Sheridan so admired. The political position of Peg Woffington, president of the club and the only female present at its meetings, is emphasized in the various accounts: her patron was the viceroy,[18] and, according to Watkins, she was a favorite at the castle, engaged in intrigue and secretly in the viceroy's employ.[19] So, though an actress sat at the head of the table and the host had no party intentions, "politics was the favourite dish, for which Thomas Sheridan . . . had his old house pulled over his ears —'Mahomet' for that!" [20]

All the commentators, perhaps following Victor, connect this second riotous destruction of Sheridan's house with his support of the Beefsteake Club, Victor describing how the toasts given there became the talk of the town,[21] Alicia Lefanu insisting that Sheridan was accused "most falsely and injuriously" by the ill-humored *"uninitiated,"* jealous at the distinction bestowed by the club on Peg Woffington.[22] But the riot itself was certainly inspired by something larger than Sheridan or Sheridan's activities.

---

performers, authors, "and other Geniuses." But Sheridan's club was unusual in being made up of *non*theatrical people. Both Sheridan and Victor felt that these people could be more useful to the theater.

[14] Victor (*ibid.*, p. 153) tells us that Sheridan paid for the dinners; Hitchcock (I, 223) describes the quarters: "A very large apartment in the manager's house, adjoining the theatre, was dedicated to this convivial meeting, where every thing was furnished in the most plenteous and elegant stile at his expence." This was not the Sheridan residence, but the house or part of a house Sheridan had recently leased (see Ch. VII). Victor (*ibid.*, pp. 217–218) mentions this apartment ("contiguous to the Theatre") when describing events in the fall of 1758.

[15] O'Keeffe, I, 31. Sackville was later Lord George Germaine. O'Keeffe calls him the "soul of the party."

[16] Molloy, II, 7.   [17] O'Keeffe, I, 31.   [18] Molloy, II, 2.
[19] Watkins, I, 53.   [20] O'Keeffe, I, 31.   [21] Victor, *History*, I, 159.
[22] Lefanu, p. 54.

For several months Ireland had been in great discontent, split into the Court Party and the Country Party over a clause in a money bill implying that the king had the power of consent over surplus Irish moneys. Those Irish who supported the king and the court were accused of betraying their country for bribes of gold or preferment. Pamphlets poured from the presses and so inflamed the people of Dublin with "the most outrageous spirit of party" that by January 1754 public entertainment had begun to fall off, and the great Woffington herself was playing to empty boxes.[23] Even worse, every possible occasion was seized on as significant to the dispute. Victor tells us that, while it was only in rehearsal, the tragedy *Mahomet*, selected long before by Sheridan to be one of the season's revived plays, was discovered by the Country Party to contain lines pleasingly relevant to the present situation.[24]

This play opened on the very day the papers carried the inflammatory news that the king had prorogued the Irish parliament.[25] Small wonder that the audience, predominantly Country Party (especially in the pit),[26] responded clamorously to Digges as Alcanor, defender of the city and of the people's liberty, rather than to Sheridan or Woffington in the leading roles of Zaphna and Palmira.[27] Almost at the very beginning of the first act applause and cries for an encore greeted a speech by Alcanor in which the "Powers divine"

[23] Victor, *Original Letters*, I, 217.

[24] Victor, *History*, I, 160. Hitchcock stresses that the play had been cast the season before but laid aside as too late and as interfering with the benefits (I, 228). Sheridan, in his *Vindication*, also says that the play had been "delivered out" toward the end of the preceding year for representation, but audiences were then too thin to hazard a new play (p. 6). An eight-page pamphlet, *A Grand Debate between Court and Country*, points out that almost every line had application to the present situation in Ireland (p. 6). But Victor says that nearly any tragedy of the type popular then could have been seen as relevant (*History*, I, 161).

[25] The proclamation, issued by Lord Lieutenant Dorset, appeared in the *Dublin Journal*, January 29–February 2, 1754: "Whereas his Majesty hath signified unto Us his Royal Pleasure, that the Parliament of this Kingdom be prorogued, We do therefore Publish and Declare, that the said Parliament be, and accordingly the said Parliament is hereby prorogued unto Tuesday the 2d Day of April next. . . ."

[26] Hitchcock, I, 229.

[27] Victor (*History*, I, 162–174) is a chief source for the account which follows. Hitchcock and Lefanu lean heavily on Victor without acknowledgement. Sheridan himself supplies some of the details in his *Vindication*. Pamphlets and newspaper material round out the picture.

were called on to mark and bring to account "those vipers" who, entrusted with the protection of the people, "shall for a Grasp of Oar [Ore]/Or paltry Office, sell 'em to the Foe!" [28] Digges, taken by surprise perhaps by the earliness of the audience's reaction, paused shortly and then repeated the speech, again to loud applause. Throughout the rest of the evening the other players received scant attention, but Alcanor's lines were frequently clapped.[29] The performance concluded without incident.

Some little publicity followed this occurrence, a relatively modest part of all the political activity at the time. Readers of the next issue of the *Dublin Journal* were provided with *An approved Receipt to make an English Tragedy in the present Taste:* "Take the Words *Liberty, Patriot, Country, Tyranny, Oppression, High-Priest, Priestcraft, Bribery, Corruption, Pensions, Placemen;* of each an equal quantity. Take out of the Dictionary as many Words as will make up two thousand Lines of English Verse, but take Care that at least one of those above-recited Words be in each Line. Divide these into five equal Parts; between each Part let there be a Chorus of Groans in the Upper Gallery.—Your Tragedy will do, depend on't." [30] Readers of the *Dublin Spy* found a summary of the *Mahomet* plot and a commentary on the performance—from the Country point of view. The *Spy* had remarked "several diabolical hisses" coming from the "tongue of two clergymen" at the time of the encore—proof of how "infamous is a Courtier's heart." [31] *A Grand Debate between Court and Country* may also have appeared during this interim and was designed to let the reader into "the Nature of this Quarrel between the Politest Audience in the World, and a Saucy Impudent Manager of a Theatre." [32] Two letters, signed "Theatricus" and "Hibernicus" and printed in the *Dublin Journal*, protest party madness in a theater and praise Sheridan's indefatigable work in raising the Irish stage from the lowest ebb to its present glorious position as "the only free

[28] *Mahomet, The Imposter* [by Voltaire, trans. by James Miller and John Hoadly], 1744, p. 2.

[29] *A Grand Debate between Court and Country* quotes three other such passages, all from Act 1 (pp. 7–8).

[30] *Dublin Journal*, February 2–5, 1754. This item refers to the upper gallery, rather than the pit mentioned by Hitchcock, as the source of the trouble. The night of the riot Sheridan was more concerned about the upper gallery than about the pit.

[31] Quoted by Stockwell, pp. 111–112.

[32] P. 7. This pamphlet, not recorded in Loewenberg, could have been written after the riot.

Stage now in the World, or that perhaps has been since the flourishing State of Athens." It is Hibernicus who points out that Dublin owes everything to Sheridan: its recent growth, the decline in absenteeism (rich young gentlemen stay home in Ireland now), the increase in trade and industry—everything.[33] An unfriendly reply by Libertus to these two letters assumes right away that they both were written by Sheridan, and indeed familiar echoes of Sheridan's phrases and rhetoric ring through them, although in the Kelly affair he had made a point of not writing anonymously. Libertus ridicules the claim that Smock-Alley is the only *free* stage in the world, although it is true that at no other theater are more *free* tickets given to support shoddy entertainers and poor plays, many of them obscene. Through a mistake which must have galled Sheridan Libertus asserts that the year before Sheridan became manager all plays were better performed than ever since and at that time Garrick, Barry, Sheridan, and Bellamy acted together in the same play.[34] This assemblage of actors was possible only in 1745 during Sheridan's first year in charge of the theater.

At any rate, the argument might well have petered out had Sheridan not made the fatal mistake of his career—he revived *Mahomet* a second time; no one can say why. Later, in his *Vindication*, Sheridan himself gave several inadequate reasons: His friends had advised that he had spent too much time and money preparing the play to lose the advantage of another performance; also, that since it was not a party play, not performing it would imply that Sheridan thought it was; also, that not more than twenty persons in the former audience had stamped the name of party on it. Furthermore, it had been requested by many and unless performed would have been "insisted on." [35] Unfortunately, Sheridan himself had invited these requests by advertising, a fortnight after the first *Mahomet*, that to give "the greatest Variety of Plays," he would repeat none but those "particularly bespoke." Ladies were asked to "send their Commands to the Box Keeper" so that the manager could learn which plays were most in demand.[36] What an opportunity for the Country Party! And no wonder *Mahomet* had been bespoken by many! From his misjudgment here and elsewhere we must conclude that Sheridan simply had

[33] Theatricus' letter appears in the *Dublin Journal*, February 9–12, 1754; Hibernicus' letter in the February 19–23 issue.

[34] Libertus, *Remarks on Two Letters Signed Theatricus and Hibernicus.*

[35] Sheridan, *A Vindication*, pp. 11–12.

[36] *Dublin Journal*, February 12–16, 1754.

not gaged the forces involved in the larger struggle, insulated as he was by his theater and his Beefsteake Club. His idea that only about twenty persons had been active at the first revival shows how he minimized the event; his failure to grasp the significance of the "many requests" for the play's repetition shows how blind he was to the future.

At the same time anyone reading more of the story than Victor's account and those accounts based on him must feel that Victor has exaggerated the political significance of Sheridan at this time. For, despite Victor, Sheridan seems less the carefully selected target of a revenge-thirsty group than an unlucky and almost accidental victim in a greater issue. It is certainly clear that, when he ordered a second performance of *Mahomet*, Sheridan could hardly have believed that his enemies were awaiting this chance for revenge, although, looking back on the events of that evening, he and Victor claimed that they were doing just that.

The second *Mahomet* performance was planned for Saturday, March 2. But first, on Friday morning, occurred the famous meeting of the cast in the greenroom, assembled, at Sheridan's request, for instruction on the proper behavior of an actor—a step later given by Alicia Lefanu as another reason why Sheridan felt that the play could safely go on.[37] Sheridan read to his actors from a paper in his hand; what he read is reproduced in his *Vindication* "from some Heads" which he had written down.[38] He talked of the duties of an actor in the face of party spirit. An actor, he said, had an obligation to the character he represented; to step out of the character in order to please part of the public by emphasizing or repeating a passage could rightly be regarded as an incendiary act. Sheridan claimed that he himself in his public capacity had been careful to preserve "a strict Neutrality." The earlier repetition of the *Mahomet* passage was an innovation "never known before in the Theatre" and might set a dangerous precedent. For example, a performance might never get through the first act because every speech was encored; a player might incur great ill will for obliging one side and disobliging another. Some time ago, when the audience could call the music, the musicians, who could play only one request at a time, became the physical target of the dissatisfied party, so much so that they finally

[37] Lefanu, p. 55.

[38] Sheridan, *A Vindication*, pp. 3–9. Hitchcock quotes this speech *in toto*; Victor summarizes briefly; Miss Lefanu quotes two paragraphs (pp. 55–56).

had to play behind the scenes until the custom died down. But actors cannot act behind the scenes.

> In short [Sheridan concludes] this is a Blow struck at the very Vitals of the Stage, calculated to destroy all Taste in the Audience, and Spirit in the Performers; to breed perpetual Feuds, and Divisions amongst the Spectators, and entail perpetual Slavery upon the Actors. I hope you have all too great a Sense of Liberty, and have the Good of the Society too much at Heart, to encourage so fatal an Encroachment upon your Rights; and in that Hope I shall leave you entirely free, to act as you think proper, wishing that your Conduct may rather be the Result of a manly Sense of Freedom, than Obedience to an Order. In all new Cases, indeed, I would rather persuade than direct, convince than command.[39]

At the close, Digges, who had felt himself the target of Sheridan's remarks, asked for more exact guidance if requests for an encore arose again the next night. Sheridan told him that he would give him no directions but leave him to do as he thought proper. Digges persisted, "Sir, If I should comply with the Demand of the Audience, and repeat the Speech, as I did before, am I to incur your Censure for doing it?" To this Sheridan ambiguously replied, "Not at all; I leave you to act in that Matter as you think proper." [40] Ever-loyal Alicia Lefanu, the only one to defend Sheridan's confused and confusing behavior at this period, finds his lecture in the greenroom an instance of his "spirit of order and system," and of his desire to impress upon his company "a sense of moral responsibility, and of their duties" to the public. At the same time she says of Sheridan's ambiguous response to Digges: "Nothing could be more moderate or conciliatory than this answer, the meaning of which was apparent." Its obvious meaning, Lefanu implies as she continues, was that, though Sheridan could not authorize repetition of a speech, at the same time, "as Mr. Sheridan was no courtier, he assumed it as an incontrovertible position, that, should the audience take the responsibility into their own hands, by insisting on the repetition of their favourite speech, the actor, as the servant of the public, was bound to obey them." [41] If Lefanu is right, Sheridan openly occupied two flatly contradictory positions that morning and it is no wonder that Digges was baffled

---

[39] Quoted by Hitchcock, I, 239.   [40] Victor, *History*, I, 166.
[41] Lefanu, p. 58.

then as well as on the following night, when the performance began.

Even as the curtain rose and Digges made his appearance on stage, he was greeted with an uncommon round of applause, a token of what he was to expect. Yet a few moments later when the encore came, as come it did after the critical speech, Digges seemed confounded.[42] Finally, stepping out of character, he said to the audience that, much as he would like to comply with their request, he had "Private Reasons" for asking to be excused, because "his Compliance would be greatly injurious to him."[43] At this statement the audience began calling for Sheridan.

Outside of Shakespearean dramatic tragedy, it is not always easy to put one's finger on the turning point of a man's life. Especially when we look back over what we call real life, the changes seem so gradual that the moment might be here or here or here, and is probably nowhere. But Sheridan's career resembled the Shakespearean drama he admired so much—except that the denouement to come was more protracted and the conclusion less dramatic. When the audience began its call, Sheridan faced his life's climax. This was the fateful moment of decision.

Victor remembered the words of that decision. "They have no Right to call upon me"—Sheridan spoke them with agitation—"I'll not obey their Call."[44] Digges had withdrawn.[45] The curtain was lowered at the manager's order; the prompter, sent out to give the audience a choice of its money back or a quiet house for the rest of the play, could not make himself heard. Sheridan's friends, backstage, begged him to appear.[46] Instead, he went to his room, changed his clothes, and took a chair home in much perturbation of mind. He was vowing even then that, since he could no longer support the stage upon a footing which the world had approved of for many years, he would give up his career as manager.

At home, affairs were not in a much better state. Mrs. Sheridan, alarmed by exaggerated reports before her husband's arrival, endured such mental agony that the child she was carrying at the time (she was near her fifth confinement) was affected and died in con-

---

[42] Hitchcock, I, 242.   [43] Victor, *History*, I, 167.   [44] *Ibid.*, p. 168.

[45] Heaphy, playing Pharon, was also on stage with Digges and must have left with him.

[46] Hitchcock (I, 245) tells of the attempts of one friend in particular, Mr. Adderley, to persuade Sheridan to face the audience. He even would undertake that the pit should offer him no insult. When Sheridan refused his mediation, he too went home.

vulsions three months after birth. So Alicia Lefanu reports, adding as another bit of family tradition that Mrs. Sheridan neither then nor later revealed that evening's shock to her husband. It is significant of Sheridan's political views that the blighted child when born was christened Sackville, after the viceroy, who stood godfather to the infant.[47]

Back in Smock-Alley, the house was still in an uproar; nor was it in the least pacified by Mrs. Woffington's appearance on stage or by Digges's belated explanation that he had been given free will by the manager, who had "laid him under no Injunction not to repeat the Speech." [48] Sheridan's presence was still demanded and the audience waited for over an hour while messengers were sent to his house in Dorset Street to try to persuade him to return. But no arguments could prevail, and after an hour the audience began to renew its call, whether because it had received word of Sheridan's refusal Victor does not say. When two persons "of Gravity and Condition" rose in the pit and went off over the boxes, this was the signal to fall to. Ironically, in view of the Country Party's attitude toward the court, a young fellow stood up and called, "God bless his Majesty King George, with three Huzzas!" And with three huzzas the demolition of the house began: the audience section was all to pieces in a few minutes, the "finely painted" curtain and the scenes slashed, the wardrobe attacked, but defended. A fire set in the boxroom by a grate of burning coals was luckily extinguished [49] by six servants belonging to the theater, who in the end drove out the mob and fired out of the windows upon the crowd. But the riot lasted from eight o'clock until two.[50]

Victor tells of his vain attempts to get help—from the Lord Lieutenant at the castle, who passed the request to the ill Lord Mayor, who passed the request to the high sheriffs. Victor could find no magistrate till one o'clock, the implication being that all had designedly made themselves "unavailable." From this Victor concludes that Sheridan now had the public against him, while in the Kelly riot "all the Advantages were on his Side." [51]

[47] Lefanu, pp. 67–68.   [48] Victor, *History*, I, 169.
[49] *Ibid.*, pp. 170–172.   [50] Sheridan, *A Vindication*, pp. 10–11.
[51] Victor, *History*, I, 172–174. Later on in his *History* (pp. 195–199), Victor gives an account of *Mahomet* after the riot. The next season, after Sheridan had left and when Victor and Sowdon were managing Smock-Alley, voices were raised for another showing of *Mahomet*. With trepidation it was produced, and performed—to a house less than half full (£60). *The* speech was encored and

Later, in defending his refusal to face the audience, Sheridan said he had felt that the house was hostile to him, not so much the gentlemen in the pit as the crowd in the galleries. Stones and bottles had been seen there. Although Sheridan—we recall Bellamy's words—"possessed as much personal courage as any man breathing," [52] his memories of the Kelly riot were fresh; at that time his judicious withdrawal had not only saved him from physical injury but had paid well in other ways. And besides, when the audience called for him, Sheridan conjectured that he was being summoned for no other reason but to give Digges an order "to repeat that Speech." This he knew he could not do, especially after his advice to the players. [53] It is useless to speculate on what would have happened had Sheridan gone on stage that night, either to comply with the audience's demands or to reason them away. All we know is that from this moment Sheridan's life was a falling action. As in a good drama, there were to be many periods of hope. He was to return to Dublin as manager again; his acting career was to have its triumphs; and his educational ventures right up to the end of his life seemed on the point of bringing him success and fortune. But he never again reached the same peak of secure achievement. He was thirty-five when the turning point came.

In the next issue after the riot the *Dublin Journal* ran a notice, dated from the theater-royal and probably written by Sheridan, asking the public to suspend judgment of the whole disastrous affair until they saw a narrative to be published soon and to be "supported by the most authentick Persons." [54] But the next Saturday, March 9, Sheridan had to make this sad announcement:

Mr. Sheridan, lately Manager of the Theatre Royal, thinks it necessary to acquaint the Publick, that he has entirely quitted the Stage, and will no more be concerned in the Direction of it. He has lent the House to the Performers during their Benefits, without any Emolument to himself. He hoped to have been able before this Time to have laid before the Publick, a full

---

repeated, after which the audience sank into an apathy. A second demand produced a second performance, with so poor an audience that the house had to be dismissed. Party feeling had died away, "and so this famous Affair quietly ended."

[52] Bellamy, I, 97.

[53] Sheridan, *A Vindication*, pp. 12–13; 16–17. One wonders whether Alicia Lefanu ever saw this work of Sheridan's.

[54] *Dublin Journal*, March 2–5, 1754.

Vindication of his Conduct, but a new domestick Concern has so far affected him for some Days past, that it was impossible for him to give that Attention to the Subject which is required. He hopes, however, to have it published on Thursday next; and, in the mean Time, earnestly intreats of all candid, and impartial Persons, that they will not give Ear to the many Stories and Falshoods [*sic*] which are industriously propagated to his Prejudice. He makes no Doubt of convincing all, (who are to be convinced) that he has done Nothing but what he ought to have done; and could not have acted otherwise consistent with the Character of a good Citizen, or a good Manager.[55]

It is challenging to speculate on the "domestic Concern" affecting the late manager. A "Mr. Sheridan's child," doubtless the Sackville described by Alicia Lefanu as living only three months, was buried on May 3, 1754.[56] Perhaps it was born during this dreadful week; clearly it lived an even shorter time than Alicia allots to it. This was an unhappy time for all the Sheridans.[57]

Sheridan's *Vindication* was, however, published on March 15, about two weeks after the riot.[58] In it Sheridan reconstructs the speech which he made to the actors before the play, describes some of the riot, explains why he repeated the play and why he did not appear upon the call of the audience, traces his earlier struggles with the theater, and concludes with four affidavits (two from repairmen) testifying to brickbats, glass bottles, stones, and oranges on stage after the riot. This pamphlet, Sheridan says, was "written in great Grief of Heart and Uneasiness of Mind." If he was wrong in what he did, his punishment has surely been too severe—the loss of eight years of incessant labor and sums of money up to £9,000. Now he must give it all up and start again, "except that his Constitution, formerly a good one, is greatly impaired and broken." This apologia

[55] *Ibid.*, March 5–9, 1754.

[56] Parish Register, St. Mary's Church, Dublin.

[57] Other troubles, especially in the Chamberlaine family, brought grief. The death "after a lingering Illness" of a Mrs. Anne "Chamberlain," relict of the late Rev. Dr. Philip "Chamberlain" is announced in the *Dublin Journal* of April 2–6. (Is Alicia Lefanu wrong in saying that Frances Chamberlaine Sheridan's mother died soon after Frances was born [p. 4], or did the father remarry?) In July a favorite brother of Mrs. Sheridan, the Rev. Walter Chamberlaine, died too "after a tedious Indisposition" (*ibid.*, July 2–6, 1754).

[58] *Dublin Journal* notice, March 9–12, 1754. It was published by Faulkner, price 3*d*.

touched at least one heart. In a letter to the *Journal*, a person signing himself T.C.D. (Trinity College Dublin?) writes to say that he had been among those prejudiced against the manager, having exclaimed loudly at his behavior on the fatal night. But now he has been won over by the "Truth, good Sense, and honest Concern" breathing through the *Vindication*. Since, judged from their "public Principles," the majority of the audience that night were honorable gentlemen who would scorn oppression and cruelty, let Sheridan appear on stage; his offense was undesigned, his punishment has already been too severe. He will be received with mercy by a public who remembers the delight he has given them and the regularity of his conduct.[59]

But Sheridan was not ready to take this chance. When the theater reopened on March 18 after two weeks of temporary repairs, he was not in the company. The actors' benefits followed and the season ran into May. Sheridan, resolved that his company should not share his misfortune, had given them the use of the theater "not only without any emolument, but at a certain loss each night to himself." [60] Even this generosity was besmirched by his enemies and another notice had to be given to the paper. This notice, signed by three leading actors, King, Sparks, and Dexter, denied reports that Sheridan was profiting by the receipt of £40 from each actor's benefit, and certified, from examination of the actual expenses, that a night's performance cost £42.14.5 without allowance for wear and tear on the wardrobe, scenes, et cetera, which Sheridan had freely lent to the company. Thus every benefit meant a loss to Sheridan of over £2 at the very least.[61] In the meantime, advertisements, running for a month in the *Dublin Journal* (from March 9 to April 6) reinforce Sheridan's intention:

> To be let, from the First Day of September, next, or the Interest to be sold, of a Lease of the two Theatres, in Aungier Street and Smock Alley, together with a large Wardrobe, and some Scenes belonging to Aungier Street, and some that escaped the Wreck in Smock Alley.[62]

[59] *Dublin Journal*, March 16–19, 1754.   [60] Hitchcock, I, 250.

[61] *Dublin Journal*, March 12–16, 1754.

[62] John Knowles, Sheridan's brother-in-law connected with the financial side of the theater, was to receive proposals; any coming from England had to be postpaid.

But it was not until early April that Sheridan irrevocably made up his mind. He had been waiting till then to learn the reaction to his *Vindication*. Although he had found it approved, and had heard no reasonable objection to it, he was surprised at the still warm resentment against him. Upon looking farther, he discovered that "infinite Pains had been taken to inflame the Minds of the People"; hence baseless accusations had gained wide belief, and vilest falsehoods had been spread under strict injunctions of secrecy. As the object of this whispering campaign, how could he meet with a good reception or be restored to public favor, regarded as he was with hate and contempt? With these sentiments, expressed in a pathetic *Address to the Public*,[63] Sheridan took leave of his theater, resolved, Victor says, "to set his Foot there no more." [64] Since the advertisements for leasing the theaters end just before this time, it is probable that Sheridan had worked out his agreement with Victor and Sowdon, to whom he sublet the houses for two years at the sum of £5 for every acting night; the two also agreed to lend Sheridan £2,000 upon a mortgage of the wardrobe, then valued at £4,000.[65] This business was not finally completed until June 1.[66]

The resentment which Sheridan sensed in Dublin weeks after the riot, had been kept warm not only by the whispering campaign but also by the writings which, although not so numerous as after the Kelly riot, were now more inimical to him. *Mr. Sh—n's Apology to the Town . . . written by himself* is, despite its title, a vicious attack on the manager, as is *The Play-House Prorogued*, which also pretends to be in his favor.[67] The former blames Sheridan's arrogance on the town, which has spoiled him by comparing him to Roscius and Shakespeare and by supporting him in his mistreatment of all rival actors such as Cibber, Barry, Dyer, and Mossop. Incidentally, the improvement in the actor's lot accomplished through these years is

[63] *Dublin Journal*, April 6–9, 1754.   [64] Victor, *History*, I, 175.

[65] *Ibid.*, pp. 180–181. The deed, dated May 30, 1754, is between Victor and Sheridan only (it was registered August 15). On May 31 Victor declared in a deed poll that half the sum paid by him to Sheridan had belonged to Sowdon (see Stockwell, p. 382). In January 1755 a second deed, made by Victor, assigned one half interest in Smock-Alley and Aungier-Street to John Sowdon. Sowdon, it will be remembered, had come to Dublin in the hopes of assuming joint managership with Sheridan.

[66] Victor, *Original Letters*, I, 232 (Letter to Dorset, September, 1754).

[67] This title had special significance since parliament had been prorogued not too long before.

shown when the anonymous author has Sheridan say, We players are no longer the same scoundrels we were; we "are now Company for the best Lords in the Land," have "Access to Great Men's Chambers," are the center of all conversation and the superiors of the poets we recite. In conclusion, Sheridan is made to cry: If you drive me from Dublin where shall I go? Where shall I have a college at my beck to "vindicate my Fopperies," where will the ladies fight for my cause "with so much Acrimony," et cetera, et cetera? *The Play-House Prorogued* directs itself more toward Sheridan's political activity, satirically defending the actions of both the manager and Peg Woffington, "best friends to the M—y for some years past."

Much more diverting is another anonymous tract, *Rules of Accommodation . . . to establish a right Understanding between the Town and the Manager of Smock Alley Theatre*,[68] which pretends to be the result of a meeting of blockheads to consider what shall be done if the manager should leave Smock-Alley. A committee is formed to prevent "so great and national a Calamity" and the rest of the piece consists of nine resolutions drawn up by this committee. In one of them the duty of a manager is defined as the obligation to domineer; to be fastidious and petulant to underlings, compliant and submissive to superiors; to mangle and castrate good plays, and so on. In another, it is declared unlawful to dispute the honor or virtue of an actor or actress, regardless of their infamy; they are to be entertained with highest respect and two or more are to sit with "a certain great Council" of state. The last resolution gives a final view of the cataclysm to be expected by Sheridan's departure: the exodus of our nobility, the decay of trade, the death of the arts, and the collapse of our constitution. A postscript of twenty-four toasts "to be drank by the Gentlemen assembled for the re-establishing of the Smock Alley Theatre" includes: "1. The Royal Family, not forgetting the Manager of Smock-Alley Theatre. 2. Confusion to the Kings, and all Mr. S—n's Enemies. 3. May Arts and Science never gain Footing in this Kingdom. . . . 8. The Scribblers of Ireland for ever! and the noble Earl or Earls who support them. . . . 10. The College in its present Situation. (And as the toasts presumably begin to take more and more effect) . . . 11. A groan for Shakespear. 12. Confusion to the Memory of Ben Johnson. 13. To the glorious and immortal Memory of Cibber and Farquhar. . . . 16. Licentiousness for ever! . . . 18.

---

[68] This item (eight pages) is not in Loewenberg.

No bounds to Scurrility. . . . 20. Loyalty and Drunkenness," et cetera, et cetera.

These *Rules of Accommodation* are clearly a satire on a meeting which did occur and which shows the concern of Dubliners—not all of it hostile to Sheridan—for the Irish theater. Shortly after the riot, a group of gentlemen got together to consider the deplorable situation of the stage and its possible destruction, which to them would be a national calamity.[69] Another larger meeting was planned and advertised, to which were invited all people who regarded the stage as important to the city and the nation. Particularly *citizens* were urged to attend, because noblemen and independent gentlemen could go to other countries for diversions, but those who by profession must remain in Ireland must get their diversions "here or nowhere." That this meeting was held and that it was friendly to Sheridan we gather from the satire in *Rules of Accommodation*. Otherwise, we hear nothing more of this group or their activities. Almost two months later, after Sheridan had made his decision, a letter written by a stranger to the manager and addressed "to Such as Esteem Theatrical Entertainments" speaks out for Sheridan. Readers are reminded of his industry and good taste and of his success as a result. They are asked to contrast the contempt for and infamy of the stage before him, the "unbecoming Lives of the Actors," the ignorance and dishonesty of earlier managers. Shall one error efface all the gain made under Sheridan? Moderates on all sides think he has suffered more than he deserves. "Justice bids Resentment cease, and Honour calls for Reparation." [70]

It was too late. What reparations were offered, Sheridan refused. Without his knowledge the Earl of Shelburne and other friends had applied to the Lord Lieutenant, intending to request for Sheridan indemnities up to £1,000 for the destruction of his theater and also an annual pension of £300.[71] Forestalling the offer, Sheridan told the Duke of Dorset that he wouldn't take a shilling. He wouldn't even let the duke subscribe heavily to four plays which were to have been performed to supply new scenes for those destroyed.[72] In giving

---

[69] This meeting is reported in the *Dublin Journal*, March 16–19, 1754, and the future meeting is advertised in the March 19–23 issue.

[70] *Ibid.*, May 4–7, 1754.   [71] Sheridan, *An Humble Appeal*, pp. 30–31.

[72] There is mention of six subscription plays to repair damages and procure new scenery in the *Journal* of April 6–9, 1754. Apparently the plan lagged, for the time for subscribing had to be extended and then the number of plays had

these details four years later in his *Humble Appeal to the Public,* Sheridan explains that he had refused because he believed in a free stage. Alicia Lefanu gives other reasons: Sheridan felt that by accepting he would have merely confirmed his enemies' allegations. By refusing, he hoped that someday the public would see his conduct in its true light and provide him with another opportunity "by means of the theatre, to raise a fortune for his family." [73] Probably all of these motives had a place in Sheridan's refusal.

His relations with the theater severed, Sheridan retired to the country (to Quilca undoubtedly), where he spent the summer peacefully and productively writing on "his academical project," [74] which was to replace the theater as his preoccupation and by which he hoped to save his falling fortunes. On September 15 he embarked for Holyhead, leaving his wife and family in Ireland [75] until he could be more certain of the future. It would be two years before he would return to Dublin again.

With Victor and Sowdon running Smock-Alley, Dublin theatrical affairs, as might have been expected, began almost immediately to decline. For the financial falling-off, Victor gives the reason that no theater manager can prosper without being a capital actor himself or being connected with one who was. [76] Sowdon apparently qualified on neither score. The kind of salaries Manager Victor had to pay Barry (£800) and Barry's protégé, Miss Nossiter (£500) [77] had made Treasurer Victor writhe a few years before. To get full value from his actors Victor wrote into their contracts various niggling provisions which in the end brought grief and loss on him. [78] In his dealings with his company he lacked Sheridan's generosity and breadth of spirit. In his productions he lacked Sheridan's imagina-

---

to be reduced to four, with only one of these at advanced prices. Sheridan, although he did not act in the plays and had withdrawn from the managership, may have had something to do with arranging the series.

[73] Lefanu, p. 71.   [74] Victor, *Original Letters,* I, 233.

[75] When he did settle down in London, Mrs. Sheridan joined him with their oldest child, Charles Francis, leaving the two younger children, Richard and Alicia, in Dublin in the care of relatives (Lefanu, p. 74). In London the Sheridan family lived in lodgings, "next door to the Cross Keys, in Henrietta Street, Covent Garden" (given as the address where subscriptions for Sheridan's lectures were to be taken. *Public Advertiser,* February 13, 1756). Henrietta Street is also his address in the correspondence with Lee written in August of 1756.

[76] Victor, *History,* I, 187.   [77] *Ibid.,* p. 186.

[78] *Ibid.,* pp. 188, 191–192.

tion, so much so that he himself in his *History* could recall just three "remarkable Anecdotes," two of which were unsuccessful revivals of *Mahomet* and *Jack the Giant Queller*. Only one new play was memorable enough to be mentioned for the two seasons.

Even in the first year of Sheridan's absence, an anonymous pamphlet, entitled *A Letter to Messieurs Victor and Sowdon*, revealed the deterioration that had set in in the audience. Because the same plays were being repeated too often, attendance had fallen off: "Dublin has never afforded above three different Audiences to most dramatic Entertainments. Nothing but Variety or Novelty can draw the Fair Ones from dear Cribbage and their Admirers from still dearer Claret and Politicks." [79] Still worse, for those who could be drawn, the curtain was not rising at the time promised, a laxity which encouraged late arrival, more after-dinner claret, and then inevitable disorders at the theater. The behavior of the rabble in the upper gallery, obstreperous as it had been at times before, worsened under the inadequate Victor. Their insolence and obscenity had become a scandal, exclaimed the anonymous pamphleteer, which "revives the Charge of Barbarism against us." [80] and keeps many persons of distinction away from the play.[81] The word "revives" suggests what Sheridan's firmness, efficiency, and superior entertainment had accomplished during his regime.

Victor did not, however, cut himself off from Sheridan. Their friendship restored, a regular correspondence [82] kept Sheridan informed of the unrewarding activities of the new managers; and Victor in return received advice and even actual assistance from London, although some of Sheridan's friends were hoping for Smock-Alley's decline in his absence. Not only did Sheridan manage to get Barry for Victor's first season; [83] when Barry left to return to Covent Garden, he secured Mossop for the second season.[84] But though Victor consulted Sheridan on every step, the 1755–56 season—with Mossop ill during most of it—was even worse than the one before.[85] When finally Victor's management drew to a close, he summed them

---

[79] *A Letter to Messieurs Victor and Sowdon*, pp. 12–13.   [80] *Ibid.*, p. 9.

[81] Sheridan, probably using Victor's records, reports that even Victor's leading actor, Barry, after the first month played only two nights to full houses up to the commencement of the benefits in the 1754–55 season under Victor (*An Humble Appeal*, p. 57).

[82] Victor, *History*, I, 208.   [83] Sheridan, *An Humble Appeal*, p. 37.

[84] *Ibid.*   [85] Victor, *History*, I, 192.

up as two years "full of Cares, Anxieties, and Dangers"; and he commented thus on "the envied Office of Managers of a Theatre Royal":

> An honest Man so circumstanced, can stand no other Chance than that of losing his good Name. The many bad, envious, discontented Spirits that infest a Theatre, vent all their Malice against the Manager they cannot impose on, and must hate the Man who only treats them as they deserve.[86]

[86] *Ibid.*, pp. 206–207.

CHAPTER IX

A Plague on Both
Your Dublin Houses, 1754-1758

IN THE meantime, Sheridan was having an uneasy two years in England. When he had said that he was entirely quitting the stage, he had spoken too rashly. Debts, a wife, three children,[1] and only embryo plans for improving English education were to drive him back where—at least consciously—he no longer wanted to be. By October of the first year he was acting on shares in Covent Garden under Rich, with whom he had negotiated a hasty agreement designed to put Barry out of the company and into Victor's arms. At least this is the explanation given by Sheridan, in his *Humble Appeal*, for Barry's much-needed appearance in Dublin.[2]

With Sheridan at Covent Garden were Peg Woffington and George Anne Bellamy among so many other former Smock-Alley[3] figures that Sheridan's awareness of his loss must have been heightened. Peg Woffington had had no proposals from Victor—somewhat to her chagrin, for she had wanted to stay in Ireland.[4] But her presence at Covent Garden acting opposite Sheridan meant a better chance to use two plays from the Smock-Alley repertoire which would be new to London: *Phaedra and Hippolitus* ("short-lived" at Covent Garden, according to Bellamy)[5] and Sheridan's own version of *Coriolanus*, which did well in competition with Shakespeare's *Coriolanus*, revived by Garrick at the same time. Just one really new play, Moncrief's *Appius* (with Sheridan as Virginius, his only new role) was all that Rich could manage to produce this year.[6] The season came to

[1] Their last child, Betsy, was not born until 1758 (in London). This made four children who survived.

[2] Sheridan, *An Humble Appeal*, p. 37. Bellamy gives another reason for Barry's departure from Covent Garden. He had left, she says, when Rich refused to comply with his exorbitant demands "relative to the engagement of Miss Nossiter," then under his protection (I, 271). Victor *had* complied reluctantly, to the tune of £500 for this actress of only moderate ability.

[3] For example, Cibber, Sparks, Dyer, Mrs. Green, Mrs. Vincent, Mrs. Hamilton (formerly Mrs. Bland). See *London Stage* (Pt. 4) for 1754–55 season.

[4] Victor, *Original Letters*, I, 232.   [5] Bellamy, I, 273.

[6] *London Stage* (Pt. 4, 1754–55 season). Several new musical mainpieces were produced.

an end early for Sheridan—on April 7. He took no benefit night, possibly as part of his original financial agreement.

Although Sheridan acted with his usual force, some spark must have been lacking; the critics viewed his appearances as Covent Garden's principal tragic actor and occasional comedian without enthusiasm. He had followed the popular Barry and he was competing with Garrick, who played to packed houses every night at Drury Lane.[7] The rumor spread around Dublin by his enemies that Sheridan frequently acted to empty benches may have had a basis in fact.[8] In Dublin, according to Wilkinson, no performer, not even "the Garrick," would have been as "universally crowned with laurel" as Sheridan; but Rich was not happy enough about Sheridan's London record this season to renew his contract, especially with Barry returning for the next season. Nor did Sheridan, according to Wilkinson, offer his services for the next year. Aside from the discomfort of his new subordinate position, he could hardly have been contented under the slapdash Rich, whose season commenced "with some . . . stock comedies, very ill acted indeed, and as dingily dressed." [9] Later he came to regard this disappointment with Rich as a blessing in disguise, for it left him free to work on his educational writings.[10]

Sheridan's first achievement in this new field was *British Education*. Published late in December 1755,[11] this 536-page book must have occupied most of his time from the end of his Covent Garden contract until its publication. Here he poured out, in a form and style showing his haste, a variety of ideas which his theatrical experience must have been shaping for some time. Basic among them was his discovery that the ability to speak English well could be taught by

[7] Watkins, I, 58. [8] Shea, *A Full Vindication*, p. 7.

[9] Wilkinson, IV, 206, 218, 204.

[10] Sheridan, *An Humble Appeal*, Appendix, p. 38.

[11] First notice of publication in the *Public Advertiser*, December 22, 1755: *British Education; or the Source of the Disorders of Great Britain laid open; being an Essay towards proving that the Immorality, Ignorance, and False Taste which so generally prevail are the natural and necessary Consequence of the present defective system of Education with an Attempt to show that a Revival of the Art of Speaking, and the Study of our Language might contribute, in a great Measure, to the Cure of those Evils . . . by Thomas Sheridan, A. M.* Preliminary notices show that the book was finished by mid-November. Sheridan claimed that the whole thing was begun and finished in the last summer (1755) but it probably had a first drafting when he was writing on education at Quilca in the summer of 1754.

rules and principles, without interfering with established educational institutions and without costing much. Two months later he tried to organize "by Subscription" a series of twelve lectures in which his plan for improving spoken English would be revealed.[12] But, although in later years he was to have considerable success in lectures on the subject, this series seems not to have materialized, perhaps because he was premature in assessing public interest.

By January, however, Smock-Alley Manager Sowdon, now sick of his bargain, had begun advertising for sale his share of the Dublin theaters' mortgage.[13] Sheridan, at the same time, was getting word from Ireland that the party spirit of two years ago had abated and that Dubliners now regretted their oversevere treatment of him.[14] When *British Education* emerged triumphantly from Faulkner's press early in February, Ireland was made to feel even more sensible of her loss by a letter to the *Journal* praising this book and recommending it to every Irishman of taste and learning.[15] With Sheridan's stock thus rising and with many of his friends now ready to help in his restoration, Sowdon probably hoped that the former manager would buy up his share.[16] And Sheridan himself must have had this possibility in mind when he set sail for Ireland late in April 1756,[17] after the collapse of his lecture plan. A job—even in the theater—was imperative after a year's unemployment which had produced nothing more lucrative than his book and a lecture plan not yet ripe. If he returned to Smock-Alley, he would not give up this plan; indeed, he would leave the theater—in good hands[18]—as soon as he could get his educational project underway; and Dublin was an even better place than London to launch it. It was more needed there.[19]

[12] *Public Advertiser*, February 13, 1756.

[13] Victor, *Original Letters*, I, 259–260 (Letter to James Donaldson, February, 1756).

[14] Victor, *History*, I, 207–208.

[15] *Dublin Journal*, March 23–27, 1756. Notice of the impending publication of the Dublin edition appeared *ibid.*, January 31–February 3.

[16] Victor, *Original Letters*, I, 260.

[17] *Dublin Journal*, May 1–4, 1756, announces his arrival on May 1.

[18] Indications that, although now Sheridan was thinking of Smock-Alley as only a stopgap, he still had the theater's interests at heart appear in a letter to John Lee, written in August 1756, and quoted in *A Letter from Mr. Lee to Mr. Sheridan* (p. 3).

[19] Sheridan, *An Humble Appeal*, Appendix, pp. 39–40.

BY THE END OF MAY, SHERIDAN HAD APPARENTLY DECIDED TO RETURN permanently; he had accepted the post of "Deputy Master of the Revels and Masques of this Kingdom" from Robert Wood, the patentee.[20] Money—£1,000—was forthcoming somehow to buy back Sowdon's share of the mortgage.[21] An agreement was worked out whereby Victor returned gladly to his former station of deputy manager and treasurer.[22] By July Sheridan was sole manager of Smock-Alley Theater again.[23] By August he was back in London,[24] winding up his affairs there and organizing his company for the next season. Much as he wanted to leave the stage, his sense of respon-

[20] *Dublin Journal*, May 25–29, 1756. (Wood's first name is erroneously given as Thomas in this notice.) For the origin and history of the office of the Master of the Irish Revels, see Clark, pp. 71, 156, 169, et cetera, and his Appendix A, pp. 179–193. Miss Stockwell (p. 26) says that apparently around 1720 the precedent was established whereby the manager of the theater automatically took over the post of Deputy Master of the Revels and actually conducted the business of the Office of the Master, since the latter had become a sinecure (with a fee of £300 a year). If so, then the announcement of his appointment to the post notified Dublin that Sheridan was returning as theater manager. The only time I have noted his using the title is in his 1758 *Humble Appeal*, "By Thomas Sheridan, Deputy Master of the Revels, and Manager of the Theatre-Royal." In this very work Sheridan tells that when, after the *Mahomet* riot, the viceroy asked what he could do for him, he declined all offers, requesting only the position of Master of the Revels. But the post was occupied then and, when it became vacant, a new viceroy was in the castle and Sheridan was in England. So Robert Wood was appointed, on January 29, 1756, just a few months before Sheridan's return. He held the office until 1771 (Stockwell, p. 309).

[21] Victor (*History*, I, 208) gives the figure £1,000 and reports that Sheridan borrowed it from a "Gentleman in London," to whom Sowdon's moiety of the mortgage was transferred and who, Sheridan told Victor, was to be concerned with him in the profits. Victor's statement here is very circumstantial except for the name of the lender. On the other hand, mortgages upon the two Dublin theaters held in trust for Mrs. Clotilda Tickell, show that Thomas Tickell's widow advanced money in 1756 to help Sheridan in his theatrical ventures (Tickell, p. 175). This same source shows that Sheridan on February 20, 1758, mortgaged Quilca to borrow £1,000 from Robert Wood of London (Robert Wood was the name of the Master of the Irish Revels). Perhaps this latter mortgage (of 1758) was what Victor remembered.

[22] The terms of this interesting agreement are given in full by Victor (*History*, I, 209–214) but misdated July 15, 1755, for 1756.

[23] The *Dublin Journal*, June 29–July 3, 1756, publishes a notice of a benefit performance for a child singer, concluding, "Mr. Sheridan has generously given the Theatre and the Company's Performance on that Occasion."

[24] Letters to John Lee in Edinburgh are dated from London in August. They are quoted in *A Letter from Mr. Lee to Mr. Sheridan*, 1757.

sibility—and his concern for his old theater—would allow no slackening in his renewed task.

Sheridan's return in October 1756 was briefly triumphant: he crossed the Irish sea in the viceregal yacht *The Dorset*,[25] a vessel reserved for persons of the highest quality. But the triumph was very brief. For, although all the commentators—Victor, Hitchcock, Lefanu —insist that by this time a repentant public now regarded him "as a much injured man" [26] and wanted him back, his first appearance at Smock-Alley—and indeed his troubles through the next two years— show that there was still strong feeling against him.

It was to be a hard and discouraging season in other ways too. Smock-Alley had now to be built up again. Performances had to be restored to that punctuality for which Sheridan was noted; full houses had to be rewon by the variety and novelty which had marked his former programs. Much physical improvement was needed too. Immediately upon his return Sheridan set to work with his usual vigor to refurbish the stage, repair the theater, freshen up the wardrobe, and have new sets made by Mr. Lewis, the scene painter.[27]

Even before he returned he had met the problem of what to do with the upper gallery, probably through instructions to Victor. Early in October, with the opening of the theater still two weeks away, the *Dublin Journal* informed the public that as several ladies had applied "to have some Part of the Theatre allotted to them where they might see and hear well, without being at the constant Trouble of Dressing for the Boxes," and as there were objections to the slips, the middle gallery, and the pit, "no Part of the House remained which could effectually answer the End but the Upper Gallery." That part had therefore been formed into boxes, where the admission price was to be raised from 1/1 to an English half crown.[28] With this crafty maneuver Sheridan ousted the ruffians in a body; and onus for the move was borne by the ladies rather than by the manager, who could not afford the ill will it might arouse. Thus a long-cherished aim of Sheridan's was realized: the upper gallery now became the quietest place in the house.[29] The only trouble was

[25] Announced in the *Dublin Journal*, October 16–19, 1756. Mrs. Sheridan was with him. This was, so far as I know, Sheridan's first trip in this style.

[26] Hitchcock, I, 270.   [27] *Ibid.*, p. 273; Victor, *History*, I, 214–215.

[28] *Dublin Journal*, October 2–5, 1756.

[29] A final show of ruffianly resistance was cleared out about a month later when servants were barred from keeping places in these upper boxes (*ibid.*, November 2–6, 1756).

that it proved to be a mistake financially. The section grew popular with the ladies, then naturally with the gentlemen, so that the higher-priced pit was "much thinned." [30]

Indeed, all of Sheridan's diligence and attention would be required, Mrs. Sheridan wrote to Samuel Richardson in late November, to get through the season with any profit, so unfavorable did things look by then: a most depopulated town (it was an off-winter for parliament), able to support only a small audience, though a "constant genteel" one, Mrs. Sheridan hastened to add. [31] In this same letter is also described, in muted terms, Mr. Sheridan's first appearance that fall on Smock-Alley stage. [32]

The theater opened on October 18 with King and without Sheridan, who, as usual, was waiting until somewhat later in the season to make his appearance. After an uneventful first act, the audience— or some few in the audience—began to shout for an apology from the manager. (Victor reports that even before this opening evening rumors linking *Sheridan* and *Apology* had been spread around the town.) Dexter, then on stage, retired to consult Victor, who sent him on again to say that Sheridan was in his apartment next to the theater and ill with a cold. But by this time the audience wanted a promise from the manager that he would apologize. Eventually Victor and Dexter went next door to Sheridan, who, though much upset, bowed to Victor's urging and agreed to make the audience an apology at his first appearance. When Dexter returned with this news, the performance proceeded without further disturbance.

In spite of his shocked surprise, Sheridan may have expected trouble at his return and perhaps even worse trouble than this. [33] From London, at the end of August, he had written to John Lee, whom he had just engaged as his principal performer: "It is a Matter of more Consequence to me than I can now represent to you, that you should be in Dublin before the Opening of the Campaign. . . . The least Delay might disconcert my Plan in such a Manner that it couldn't easily be remedied. When we meet you will be fully convinced of the Cause of my urging this on you with so much

[30] Sheridan, *An Humble Appeal*, p. 40.

[31] Richardson, *Correspondence*, IV, 145–150 (Letter of November 20, 1756).

[32] My account of this first appearance is drawn also from Victor, *History*, I, 215–221; Hitchcock, I, 275–279; Lefanu, p. 75.

[33] Sheridan says (*An Humble Appeal*, p. 39) rumors in London before his return that he would never be permitted to appear on stage kept good performers from signing with him.

Importunity." [34] From these dark hints, never really explained, Lee later concluded that Sheridan wanted his foremost player on hand to take over in case of trouble.[35]

To pay for the chance to rebuild Smock-Alley stage Sheridan was first to be made to crawl before those who had brought it down. He was a proud man; his feelings, as he saw the injustice of this, can be imagined. But so important was the work to him and so desperate his position, that crawl he would—and properly. Even the advertisement announcing his apology for October 25 is touching:

> NB. Before the Play begins Mr. Sheridan intends to make an humble Tender of his Duty to the publick. He is sorry that his present weak State, occasioned by his Indisposition, will not suffer him to perform on the same Night; but he chose not to defer it longer, that he might take the first Opportunity of shewing to the Publick his Readiness to pay an implicit Obedience to their Commands.[36]

Despite the poor play, *The Suspicious Husband*, chosen at Victor's canny suggestion to capitalize on Sheridan's unavoidable mortification, this notice packed the house with over a thousand people.[37] As the curtain rose, Sheridan advanced with paper in hand and spoke modestly and briefly, denying that he had ever "intended to give public offence." [38] Tears, says the ordinarily matter-of-fact Victor, streamed from the eyes of some of the men in the audience and the speech was accepted with the loudest acclamations, so continually reiterated that Sheridan returned to the audience as he was withdrawing and "with broken, fault'ring, Accents" spoke: "Your Goodness to me at this important Crisis has so deeply affected me, that I want Powers to express myself; my future Actions shall shew my Gratitude." [39]

Mrs. Sheridan's account to Samuel Richardson is, interestingly, the least indignant at Sheridan's abasement. In a protective, wifely fashion she omits mention of the demands made on him for an apology, saying only that her husband "thought it most prudent, be-

---

[34] Quoted in *A Letter from Mr. Lee to Mr. Sheridan*, p. 10.

[35] *Ibid.*, pp. 13–16.   [36] *Dublin Journal*, October 19–23, 1756.

[37] Victor, *History*, I, 219–220. Victor recommended that some comedy be given that didn't normally "bring Charges." He also recommended that the apology be pompous—"to make them pay for it."

[38] Richardson, *Correspondence*, IV, 147 (Mrs. Sheridan's letter of November 20, 1756).

[39] Victor, *History*, I, 221.

fore he again launched out into a troubled sea, to conciliate the minds of the few remaining malecontents." She thinks almost everybody left in town was there that night, and Sheridan was scarcely permitted to finish what he had to say, so prompt and enthusiastic was the applause. From the results she finds verified that wise saying, "A word spoken in season, how good is it." [40] Victor, who had urged Sheridan to make the speech, feeling that it would act "like the Reconciliation of Lovers after a Quarrel," does observe that "in Sense and Reason" those persons (all known) who had destroyed the scenes at the *Mahomet* riot owed Sheridan the apology and more.[41] Alicia Lefanu is purposefully vague in her comment, saying merely, "It being thought necessary to address the audience with a few words of apology and explanation . . . Mr. Sheridan complied with this requisition." [42] But Hitchcock is outraged by the whole affair. A spectacle which perhaps "was never presented to the public before or since," it represented the shameful triumph of despotism over right and reason. Posterity "must blush at the degeneracy of the times, which could reduce a man of Mr. Sheridan's abilities and sentiments to the humiliating situation of apologizing to the destroyers of his property, for their ruining his fortune and demolishing the labours of so many years!" [43]

After this compliance Sheridan was allowed to provide Dublin with entertainment, an increasingly difficult task because the town was poor as well as thin. This winter was a time of great scarcity and suffering. Shortages caused by the renewed war with France were aggravated by a very destructive hurricane in the fall, other dreadful storms, and extreme cold, more extreme even than the remarkable frost of 1739. From early autumn into April the papers are full of calamity. Coal became scarce and expensive; heating the theater must have been a problem. The very severe weather forced the Sheridans back to their cramped town quarters [44] from suburban

---

[40] Richardson, *Correspondence*, IV, 147.   [41] Victor, *History*, I, 219, 216.
[42] Lefanu, p. 75.   [43] Hitchcock, I, 277–279.
[44] Mrs. Sheridan had moved her family to Glasnevin in November to improve the health of her two younger children, Richard and Alicia, whom she had found ailing on her return from London, and also to give Sheridan a chance to be more "master of his time, such a portion of it . . . as he is not unavoidably obliged to pass in Dublin" (Richardson, *Correspondence*, IV, 148–149). The town quarters may not have been the Dorset-Street house, but Sheridan's apartments adjoining the theater; that the family used these rooms is suggested several years later when Mrs. Sheridan wrote to Sam Whyte that if he needed extra beds he could use those from the Blind Quay (Whyte, p. 92).

Glasnevin, where the bitter air had threatened Mrs. Sheridan with a return of her "rheumatism in the head." [45] Sheridan, she reported to Samuel Richardson in February, had had a heavy cold for over three weeks, with no time to nurse it.[46]

With his audiences small and growing smaller, Sheridan tried his old devices for luring a fuller house. Two Italian dancers from the opera house in London arrived in October, probably having been engaged by Sheridan during the summer. A dreadful mistake in the press announcing the arrival of five *French* dancers had to be hastily corrected to two less inimical Italians, the "Figure Dancers employed under them" all being "Natives of this Country or England." [47] (Sheridan had been in England the year before when the Chinese Festival riot at Drury Lane had expressed London's disapproval of French dancers hired by Garrick from an enemy country.) Besides dancers, spectacles were stressed. When *Coriolanus* was revived in January, the Roman ovation conceived by Sheridan some years before was so elaborate that preparations for it caused one postponement and shut the theater entirely the night before it finally was staged. Then, because it occurred at the beginning of the play, Sheridan deferred the curtain by desire to seven o'clock: [48] no one would want to miss the ovation. Even more publicity was given to a production of *The Tempest* which opened "with a Scene of a Ship at Sea in a Storm, and a Representation of a Shipwreck." [49] At this very time in January, news of gales and shipwrecks filled the papers; Sheridan's idea that Dubliners would feel a horrid fascination in seeing them reproduced on Smock-Alley stage was justified, for the play ran four nights that month and seven nights during the season. The spectacles this year were more impressive than the plays. In January Sheridan planned to revive old plays on Saturday nights,[50] taking advantage of a gracious concession made by several Dublin ladies who had "entered into a Resolution not to have any Drums on

[45] Richardson, *Correspondence*, IV, 154, 148.

[46] *Ibid.*, pp. 153–154 (Letter of February 8, 1757). In this letter Mrs. Sheridan writes about dreadful weather and the high cost of living.

[47] *Dublin Journal*, November 6–9, 1756. [48] *Ibid.*, February 5–8, 1757.

[49] *Ibid.*, January 11–15, 1757. For a March 11 performance of *The Tempest* we note: "By Desire, the Curtain will not be drawn up till seven o'clock, on Account of the Shipwreck beginning the Play" (*ibid.*, March 5–8, 1757). Incidentally, Hitchcock (I, 280) says that Sheridan was "excellent" as Prospero, but his name does not appear in any of the notices.

[50] *Dublin Journal*, January 22–25, 1757.

Mondays or Saturdays for the Encouragement of the Theatre Royal." [51] Ladies, as Sheridan always said, were his strongest supporters, a fact which his enemies wondered and railed at. This was the first time, though, that they had had to forego their private assemblies "for the Encouragement of the Theatre Royal."

Victor attributes the season's small houses to the lack of a "capital Female Actress." [52] Although Sheridan had many women in his company—Miss and Mrs. Kennedy, Miss Danvers, Mrs. Wilder, et cetera—and discovered the Misses Phillips [53] in the fall, not one of these touched Woffington or Bellamy in drawing power, or even Mrs. Fitzhenry, now at Covent Garden after two successful years under Victor and Sowdon. His new men were Wilder, popular but limited, and John Lee, former stage manager in Edinburgh. These two could not have been more different. Wilder, bred to the business of painting, was attractive, easygoing, much esteemed by his employers as a dependable trouper; [54] Lee was a man "of extreme and aggressive vanity and of a quarrelsome disposition." He had left Edinburgh under a cloud, his theater having been seized by creditors and he himself having spent time in prison. [55] At about the time of his departure he seems to have started a suit (reported in the *Dublin Journal*) against Lord Elibank, his former supporter and benefactor. [56]

Like his wife a few years earlier, Lee was a failure this season at Smock-Alley, and a source of great embarrassment to Sheridan. The story goes back to the summer before Sheridan's return, when he was in London organizing his company for the season. The Edinburgh manager had impressed Pasquali, Sheridan's old bandmaster now Master of Music in the Scottish capital. [57] Sheridan, who said later he had never seen Lee act, commissioned Pasquali to make him offers, which were afterward elaborated in a series of letters from Sheridan to Lee. This correspondence, published by Lee at the end of the season, reveals that from the beginning the situation called for much tact on Sheridan's part. He wanted to engage Lee, but not Mrs. Lee. The letter in which he explained this to Lee shows Sheridan's writing at its best:

[51] *Ibid.*, January 18–22, 1757.   [52] Victor, *History*, I, 222.
[53] Genest, x, 408 and *Dublin Journal* notices.
[54] *Thespian Dictionary*, v. "Wilder (James)."
[55] *DNB*, v. "Lee, John."   [56] *Dublin Journal*, October 2–5, 1756.
[57] *Remarks on Mr. Lee's Letter*, p. 3. Pasquali, incidentally, died in Edinburgh the next year (announcement in the *Dublin Journal*, October 29–November 1, 1757). Lampe had died in the same city just a few years before.

As you seem to like Candour in Dealings, it will not offend you if I speak my Mind frankly on this Occasion: Mrs. Lee was with me in Dublin during a Season; there was no one whose private Conduct I more esteemed; but I know in what Estimation she was held by the Town in her public Capacity, and consequently what Rank she must be placed in; this it is highly probable, from a very allowable Partiality, you would think inferior to her Merit, and hence might arise a Source of perpetual Discontent, to avoid which, were we to engage, I should think it a fundamental Article that Mrs. Lee should not play at all.[58]

Lee's "very candid and equitable" response in which he asked for no more for his wife "than her Merit palpably entitles her to" in the opinion of the Dublin manager, and suggested that "the Town's Acceptation . . . determine her Fate," so impressed Sheridan that it not only removed his former objection but persuaded him "to give her every fair Opportunity of standing or falling by her own Merit, as it shall be rated by the Town." He ended by raising his offer £100 to make a total of £400 salary for their joint performance.

Lee would never have come to Dublin at this price, he later said, if Sheridan had not opened another prospect: the future managership of Smock-Alley Theater. "I have been long weary of the Stage," Sheridan wrote on August 12, 1756, "and as I have a much more important Point in View, am determin'd to quit it as soon as possible." At that time, he told Lee, he knew "no theatrical Person whom I would so readily chuse for a Successor." In another letter he said that it would be Lee's own fault if he did not come hereafter to have a share in the profits.

There was, it soon turned out, another person whom Sheridan would as readily "chuse for a Successor"—Spranger Barry, just entering upon a second season at Covent Garden. Apparently about the time of Lee's engagement Sheridan learned that Barry, with some friends' help, had it in mind to build a new theater in Dublin. Such a catastrophe, which Sheridan knew would ruin Barry as well as himself, had to be averted. One way would be to engage Barry that season at Smock-Alley and promise to give him the stage after a year or two, by which time Sheridan hoped to be in a position to give it up. Such an offer was made in London before Sheridan's return,

---

[58] Sheridan's first letter to Lee in *A Letter from Mr. Lee to Mr. Sheridan*, p. 3. The other excerpts which follow are from other letters quoted in this same pamphlet.

Sheridan at the same time pointing out to Barry the dangers of his other project. On Barry's promise to consider it, the offer was left in abeyance.[59]

When Sheridan returned to Smock-Alley after his two-year exile, it was with this sword hanging over his managership, and with the ill-omened Lee as his "foremost player." He should have known better, an Irish commentator said afterward, than to take the recommendation of an Italian fiddler in Scotland.[60] Lee acted first as Lear. On the second night of his appearance (as Archer), he was almost hissed off the stage, and a representative of the audience was sent to Sheridan to ask that Lee not appear again in principal characters; in the opinion of many, he was so far from equipped to be head of a theater that "he was but indifferently qualified to be set at the Tail." Sheridan out of "Delicacy and Tenderness . . . could not bear to have him degraded." [61] Yet Lee's unpopularity and Sheridan's hope that the idolized Barry would accept his offer must have colored the manager's behavior. For Lee claims that as soon as Sheridan found Dublin amenable to his apology and Lee unnecessary as a stopgap, he grew cool toward his foremost player, said nothing more about the managership, and tried to persecute him out of his agreement. "Your Conduct then thus nicely plann'd," Lee wrote later in his published pamphlet, "I was received with all the dignify'd Plausibility that constitutes your Character; mixed and foreign Conversation pass'd an Evening or two with strain'd Civilities, then Shyness spoke your Fraud: In short a total Breach of every Article ensued." One specific persecution mentioned by Lee was fixing his benefit "in a singular and most injurious Manner." [62] As the season progressed, the calen-

[59] Sheridan, *An Humble Appeal*, p. 38. If my conjectures are right, the offer must have been made after August, the time of Sheridan's letters to Lee. It will be remembered that Sheridan (perhaps occupied with this new problem) did not return to Dublin until mid-October.

[60] *Remarks on Mr. Lee's Letter*, p. 3.   [61] *Ibid.*, p. 4.

[62] *A Letter from Mr. Lee to Mr. Sheridan*, pp. 13–16. Just what this particular persecution involved is perhaps suggested by the *Journal* notices. The summer before, when the terms of Lee's engagement were being worked out, one of the points made in a letter from Lee to Sheridan was that as first player he should receive the first benefit. When benefit time came round in March, Lee was originally scheduled for the first night; but it was, unprecedentedly, a Tuesday night, on which Smock-Alley was normally closed. (This might have increased Lee's difficulty in selling tickets.) Then, when Signora Bugiani's benefit was suddenly slipped in on the Monday before his, Lee no longer had the first night. Possibly these slights are what Lee was complaining of.

dar shows that Lee was used less and less (perhaps in compliance to public demand) until in the end he dwindled to roles in the after-piece, King and Dexter sharing the leads with Sheridan in the main plays. (Mrs. Lee played only a few times.) Lee explained his un-popularity by saying that followers of other players resented him, a stranger, in their favorites' parts.[63] But he was quickly reminded that he was no better received in the new tragedy *Douglas,* where he played an unfamiliar role; and that Wilder, also new that season and a stranger to Dublin, had become the support of Smock-Alley Theater.[64]

In June, when his contract ran out, Lee aired his grievance by publishing, with commentary, the correspondence which had pre-ceded his engagement. His failure to mention, as another breach of etiquette, Sheridan's offer to Barry seems to show that this was Dublin's best-kept secret, although Victor's trip to Barry in London in April 1757 should have tipped Lee off. Probably long before this, Sheridan had decided that, Barry or no Barry, Lee was not the man to succeed him. If Barry raised a rival theater, Lee could hardly have competed. If Barry came with Sheridan, there would be no place for Lee. Lee, then, was not encouraged to hope. Perhaps Sheri-dan should have been more candid with him, as he had been earlier on the subject of Mrs. Lee. But probably no amount of candor or tact could have soothed that "extreme and aggressive vanity," un-avoidably crushed by the situation itself.

Lee's publication aroused no response from Sheridan, but two anonymous pamphlets followed, one (*Remarks on Mr. Lee's Letter*) defending Sheridan on the whole, the other making fun of both sides in *A Letter from Tom the First, King of Ireland, to John the Second, King of Scotland, with the King of Scotland's Answer Thereto.* In this latter piece King Tom describes to Cousin John how he keeps the Dublin public in line: through "Shew and Pomp"; money spent on Regalia, Shipwrecks, and Burials; and by supporting a set of "turgid, unintelligible Poets" whose writings he "corrects" if they grow too clear.

Shipwrecks (in *The Tempest*) and burials (in *Romeo and Juliet*) could go only so far. Late in the season, on May 12, a "new" play supporting a poet was produced. John Home's *Douglas,* recom-mended for Drury Lane by Lord Bute, had been rejected by Gar-

---

[63] According to *Remarks on Mr. Lee's Letter,* p. 5.

[64] *Ibid.,* p. 6. This pamphlet is our source for Dublin's attitude toward Lee.

rick the year before as dull and improbable.[65] Yet with Barry in the leading part it had succeeded at Covent Garden; and when Sheridan received the printed copy of the play from London, he thought he had the perfect tragedy. Its first night in Dublin was "crammed," says Samuel Whyte; its second night (Whyte errs in reporting it as its third) was to be for the Scottish author's benefit, an "unprecedented act of liberality" from Sheridan, who was treating Home as though the play had been originally brought out at Smock-Alley. This night, however, "fell miserably short of Expences," [66] perhaps because Sheridan was unequipped (as Hitchcock says) to play the blooming young Norval [67] and Lee, we recall, was no success in the secondary role of old Norval. Whyte gives another reason for its failure; word had gone round that the author was a dissenting clergyman "with an ecclesiastical anathema [from the presbytery] against him." [68] After the disappointment of the benefit, whatever its cause, Sheridan, still eager to do something for Home, took the advice of two friends who had suggested a piece of gold in the form of a medal. The medal, engraved with laurel, bore an inscription which Whyte remembers thus:

Thomas Sheridan, Manager of the Theatre Royal, Smock-alley, Dublin, presents this small token of his gratitude to the Author of Douglas, for his having enriched the Stage with a Perfect Tragedy.[69]

Some years later, in an Oxford coffeehouse, Dr. Samuel Johnson called over to Sheridan, "Mr. Sheridan, Mr. Sheridan, how came

[65] Garrick, *Some Unpublished Correspondence*, pp. 108–112.

[66] Whyte, pp. 45–46.

[67] Hitchcock, 1, 282. Young Norval seems to have been Sheridan's only new role this season. And my records show no new roles for the next season (1757–58).

[68] Whyte, p. 46. When *Douglas* was produced in Edinburgh (after Garrick's rejection but before its production at Covent Garden), the presbytery ejected Home from the pulpit for having written a play (Garrick, *Some Unpublished Correspondence*, p. 107). Whyte says that in Dublin a faction was raised against the play, which was "considered as a profanation of the clerical character" (Whyte, p. 46).

[69] *Ibid.*, pp. 46–47. Whyte was commissioned by Sheridan to take the medal to London, where it was put in the hands of Lord Bute, who got it to the author. Whyte tells how on the road near London he was set upon by highwaymen, but preserved "the well-meant offering" at the sacrifice of his purse and the peril of his life. This must have been sometime before Sheridan himself went to London in the summer of 1758.

you to give a gold medal to Home, for writing that foolish play?"
This question, he explained later, was "wanton and insolent" and
meant to be so. For a "medal has no value but as a stamp of merit."
And what right had Sheridan to give a stamp of merit? If he had
wanted to make such an award, he should have asked a university
to choose the recipient.[70] Actually, as Whyte reports, the award did
have intrinsic value, the gold in the medal amounting to about
twenty guineas; the medal itself had been a second thought, Sheridan at first having planned a letter accompanied by "a handsome
piece of plate"; but plate, he had soon realized, would have been
superfluous to the young unmarried author. As Whyte says, Sheridan
had meant only good; [71] for his pains, Boswell gave him the reputation for tasteless arrogance that still pursues his memory.

The season dwindled off in early June, by all comments a poor
one. Yet, while the record of performances did not reach his highest
past score of 162, Sheridan had advertised about 130 performances
this season, almost twice as many as during the Garrick winter of
1745–46. Even so, it could not have been a comfortable year for the
Smock-Alley manager, in suspense all winter long over Barry's
answer. This answer, when it finally came in April or early May via
Victor in London was *No*. Barry claimed that he had gone too far
in his plans to give them up then.[72] On May 14 he took a lease on
the old Crow-Street Music-Hall to be razed for his new Crow-Street
Theater.[73] In early July Victor returned—uncomfortably, one can
imagine—on the same ship with Barry and his new associate,
Macklin.[74] The two men were in Dublin all summer until September 9, leasing additional land for their new building and raising
mortgages.[75] Sheridan's feelings as he contemplated these develop-

[70] Boswell, *Life of Johnson* (Hill, ed.), II, 320 (A.D. 1775, Friday, March
24). When most of London was acclaiming *Douglas*, Johnson was saying that
there were not "ten good lines in the whole play" (Garrick, *Some Unpublished
Correspondence*, pp. 112–113).

[71] Whyte, p. 47.

[72] Victor, *History*, I, 223–224. In *An Humble Appeal* (p. 45), Sheridan says
that Barry's lease on the Crow-Street Music-Hall wasn't signed till a long time
after he had been approached by Victor. Victor went to England in April and
Barry signed the lease in mid-May.

[73] Stockwell, p. 121. Actually the Crow-Street Theater was in Cecilia-Street
near Crow-Street (Stephenson, P. J., *Dublin Theatre Notes*, MS read before the
Old Dublin Society now in possession of Pearse Street Library, Dublin).

[74] *Dublin Journal*, July 5–9, 1757.

[75] Notice of their departure *ibid.*, September 6–10, 1757.

ments can be easily imagined. For some time he had been thoroughly sick of the stage, its ingratitude, its uncertainties, its internal bickerings, its exposure to never-ending attacks from outside. Now Barry's blindness, the unfavorable reply through Victor, the growing certainty of a rival theater—these new threats must have seemed beyond bearing. With what a sense of urgency must he have turned to his educational plan, in abeyance during the pressing months of the past season! If he were ever to escape the theater, this had to be the way, and the time had to be soon. Yet, even with the possibility of his own escape, his concern over the future of the Dublin theater remained. As it turned out, progress on Crow-Street's construction was to be slow, and the theater was not to open until October 1758. Sheridan had, therefore, almost a year and a half to launch his academical project and to try to circumvent, by some means, the theatrical rivalry which would ruin one or both of the theaters. He also had to carry on his main job—that of running Smock-Alley.

THE SEASON of 1757–58 was one of incredible activity. Sheridan spent most of the summer at Quilca, "immersed in turf-bogs" and probably writing on his elocution lectures, since by December he was compiling "another" course.[76] But frequent trips to Dublin must have been required by another extensive and costly redecoration going on at Smock-Alley under Lewis, who was redoing the sounding board, ceiling, lattices, et cetera, "in a new Taste."[77] When the theater opened on October 6, it was not for a performance, but for a reception of distinguished Dubliners "to see the new Scenes, fine Paintings, Decorations, Silver Branches [for candles], &c.," which all allowed to be superior to any ever seen in Ireland or even in England,[78] and which, if the worst came, should outdo anything Crow-Street could offer.[79] A visitor to Dublin, attending the season's first performance a few nights later, was struck by the beautiful and unusual decorations, the wax lights, the regularity and decorum on stage, and in general "the decent and polite Behaviour of the Audience." One trace of barbarism, however, remained—a strange custom

---

[76] Richardson, *Correspondence*, IV, 164 (Letter of July 24, 1757); p. 165 (Letter of December 18, 1757).

[77] *Dublin Journal*, August 16–20, 1757.   [78] *Ibid.*, October 4–8, 1757.

[79] At about the time these elegant decorations were put on view, Sheridan received a new distinction: he was appointed "Deputy Master of his Majesty's Band of Music" in Ireland (*ibid.*, October 4–8, 1757). The Smock-Alley reception may have been partly in celebration of this honor.

he had heard about incredulously in London: Dubliners stood on the pit benches between the acts—apparently to see the boxes better. If Sheridan could have adopted this Englishman's waggish suggestion and limited the practice to men under five feet,[80] much wear and tear on his pit benches would have been saved.

Shortly before this opening, the arrival of the Duke of Bedford as the new viceroy—it was to be a parliament year—had reactivated the city, slowly recovering, with the help of a good harvest, from its terrible winter. A round of social activities and celebrations began.[81] And, not surprisingly, Smock-Alley improved during this season.[82] The duke was an enthusiastic playgoer. He and his duchess were on hand at the season's first performance (October 10); they commanded many nights, and once at least asked for a special repetition of *Richard III* because they had missed Sheridan in the leading role a few nights before and had never seen him in that character.[83]

Foote's reappearance from mid-November to Christmas (he had acted at Smock-Alley a few nights the preceding spring) [84] was a grand success. His benefit on December 21 brought a full house by three o'clock; "half Guineas and Guineas [were being] offered for Places in any Part of the House. The uncommon Success this Gentleman hath met with," adds the *Journal*, "is more than ever was known in Ireland." [85] He played no new roles, but he did give his

[80] *Ibid.*, October 25–29, 1757.

[81] The duke and his wife were noted for their hospitality, opening the castle to people of all ranks (O'Mahony, pp. 161–162). For a description of the lavish celebrations on November 4 and the king's birthday, see *Dublin Journal*, November 1–5, 8–12, 1757.

[82] In November Victor reports the audiences as middling, having been cut into by the warm parliamentary debates at that time (*Original Letters*, I, 277–278. Letter to Garrick); but the next April Sheridan, reviewing the season, says, "The Play-House was hardly ever more frequented." The 1757–58 receipts, he continues, were likely to exceed Barry's (under Victor in 1754–55) by nearly £2,000 (*An Humble Appeal*, pp. 64–65).

[83] *Dublin Journal*, February 28–March 4, 1758.

[84] At that time Foote had appeared a few times in May, Sheridan having "embraced" the offer of his services. His appeal then, with the nobility and viceroy absent, may not have been so great as had been hoped, since his new *Englishman returned from Paris* seems to have been given only one performance during his stay; and *The Author* and *The Knights*, with Foote playing in both, were advertised only twice each.

[85] *Dublin Journal*, December 20–24, 1757. While in Ireland this time, Foote was enthusiastically entertained by the nobility and the viceroy. His last appearance was on December 26 in *The Double Dealer*.

always popular "Tea." One performance of his farce *The Author*
provoked an amusing newspaper notice, probably written by Sheridan,
still smarting from the *Mahomet* riot:

> As there were some Things said in the Farce of the Author last
> Friday Night, which might be considered as Party Strokes; lest
> any Blame should be imputed to the Writer of that Piece, it is
> thought necessary to acquaint the Publick, that those Passages
> were ignorantly and impudently put in by the Person who
> played the Part of the Poet. On which Account, the Manager,
> after the Entertainment was over, reprimanded him very se-
> verely in Presence of the Company, and that very Night put the
> highest Mulct upon him which Theatrical Usage will permit.[86]

Many years before, Burke had complained of Irish actors ad-libbing
in their parts to attract applause;[87] Sheridan, who would hate this
practice on all grounds, was still trying to stamp it out.

While Foote was at Smock-Alley, two young actors made their
first stage appearance. One of these, Thomas Ryder, was later to
become a Dublin theater manager and, along with other troubles, to
bring a suit on himself for pirating and producing under another
title a play enthralling London—*The Duenna* by Richard Brinsley
Sheridan.[88] The other beginner (he was only eighteen) was Tate
Wilkinson, whose memoirs of the season provide us with lively
reading. He had come to Dublin with Foote, who had promised to
fix him "on genteel terms with Mr. Sheridan."[89] After an illness
which lasted almost until Christmas and then a dinner party at which
Sheridan was "all politeness," Wilkinson appeared first as a "pupil"
in Foote's tea, giving imitations of Luke Sparks (not Isaac), Barry,
Mrs. Woffington, and even, unexpectedly to his master's pained
surprise, of Foote himself.[90] So promising was this debut that he was

---

[86] *Ibid.*, November 19–22, 1757.

[87] Burke, *Reformer*, No. 3 (Samuels, p. 303).

[88] *Thespian Dictionary*, v. "Ryder (Thomas)."

[89] Wilkinson, I, 148. Although Wilkinson, during May of the season before,
had gone on stage twice unsuccessfully at Covent Garden, the *Dublin Journal*
(December 3–6, 1757) advertises his Smock-Alley performances as first on any
stage—perhaps because he wanted to forget the Covent Garden disaster. Also, he
had acted just the summer before in a "wooden booth at Maidstone" (*ibid.*, pp.
123, 133). And in the early fall of 1757 he had had walk-on parts at Drury
Lane, but Garrick had released him to go to Dublin with Foote.

[90] *Ibid.*, pp. 159, 169–175.

promptly engaged by Sheridan at three guineas a week until the end of February. When Foote left, Wilkinson took over his comic roles, often doing them "after the Manner of the Original" and he even attempted serious parts—Othello, Hastings, and so on.[91] His benefit, late in February, aroused such a demand that part of the pit was railed into boxes.[92] Wilkinson's cruelly amusing account of what happened when he and Sheridan were planning this benefit has probably been retouched and has often been retold, but it is worth summarizing here. After some discussion between the two men in which Wilkinson saw deep plots for self-aggrandizement in Sheridan's attempts to save the young actor money, and after the benefit had been settled for a Saturday (a bad night), Sheridan suggested that it would be better for Wilkinson to "take off" performers in the present Smock-Alley company rather than other actors whom Dubliners perhaps had not seen. Wilkinson demurred, saying that he had not had time to study them nor did he wish to offend those who could help him in his benefit. As Sheridan persisted, Wilkinson asked if he could use Sheridan's name and say that he "did not do it" of his own accord. This request displeased Sheridan, who felt that the mimicry should come before the audience as Wilkinson's spontaneous and voluntary act; after that, the audience's demands would be so enthusiastic that no performer, angry as he might be, could prevent it. For, Sheridan observed, the more it vexed the players, the greater relish it would give the audience—an observation which Wilkinson had found only too true. At this point Wilkinson conceived his famous idea, which he broached in these terms:

My good Mr. Sheridan, I have hit upon the very thing to establish myself as a favourite with you, and the town. . . . My dear Sir, a thought has just entered my pate, which I think will draw money, and be of infinite service to myself.—What is it! What is it! says Sheridan, with the utmost eagerness.—Why, Sir, says I, your rank in the theatre, and a gentleman so well known in Dublin, on and off the stage, must naturally occasion any striking imitation of yourself, to have a wonderful effect. I have paid great attention to your whole mode of acting, not only since I have been in Dublin; but two years before, when you played the whole season at Covent-Garden theatre; and do actually think,

---

[91] *Ibid.*, January 3–7, 1758. See also the Smock-Alley Calendar.
[92] *Dublin Journal*, February 14–18, 1758.

I can do a great deal on your stage with you *alone*, without interfering with any other actor's manner whatever.

As Wilkinson describes Sheridan's reaction, Hogarth could never
have caught his look of astonishment; he turned white and red, his
lips shook, but he couldn't speak. Snatching a candle from the table,
he showed Wilkinson the door and then finally found words: "he
never was so insulted. What! to be taken off by a buffoon upon his
own stage! etc. etc." Politely desiring Wilkinson to walk downstairs,
he lighted him only to the first landing (the meeting may have occurred in Sheridan's quarters next to the theater). From there he let
him stumble his way out, while he turned back upstairs, "grumbling
and squeaking to himself." Wilkinson claims that, from this moment
on, Sheridan neither spoke to him nor permitted him to play "my
own night excepted." [93] This night, incidentally, included no mimicry.

This episode is a favorite among those who have presented Richard Sheridan's father in a few revealing scenes. Perhaps they did not
know that, months before this Sheridan interview in which Wilkinson's famous idea occurred to him so spontaneously, Garrick and
Foote had laughed themselves ill over Wilkinson's imitations of
Barry, Sparks, Woffington, and *Sheridan;* [94] that Garrick would
never permit anyone to take him off on Drury Lane stage; and that
Samuel Johnson once threatened to cane Foote if he "mimicked"
him. [95] As for Sheridan, Wilkinson's proposal came at a time when
he was trying to establish himself as an educator in the public eye;
buffoonish ridicule on his own stage by his own employee would have
shattered this image. Not that his behavior with Wilkinson can be
completely extenuated, but mimics bring out the worst in others, even
in good men. Wilkinson himself was hardly without malice in proposing the take-off or in printing the story years later.

As for the rest of the Smock-Alley company this season, it remained much the same, except for a desirable strengthening of the
female side by Mrs. Fitzhenry. Victor tells of his excited discovery
of this actress several years before, when she was Mrs. Gregory. [96]
He had sent her to Covent Garden for her training and then, when
he was Dublin manager in 1754, had engaged her at Smock-Alley.
Now she was back again under Sheridan, the two of them, Victor
says, making an excellent pair. [97]

[93] The episode summarized here appears in Wilkinson, 1, 184–189.
[94] *Ibid.*, p. 148.   [95] Cooke, *Foote*, 1, 66.
[96] Victor, *History*, 1, 184–186.   [97] *Ibid.*, p. 233.

Another woman, who was not in the company but wanted to be, gave Sheridan much trouble this season. The Irish manager's reputation for recognizing and encouraging ability for some years had been attracting would-be players from as far away as London. Mrs. Beauclerk, a lady with no theatrical experience, had come to Dublin the preceding May in the hopes of appearing on the stage there. But by this time in his managerial career Sheridan, "on Account of repeated and continual Disappointments," [98] was offering no terms to performers he had not seen in three or four characters on the stage. Finally, after calling on Mrs. Beauclerk twice at her lodgings to hear her read (as a preliminary test, apparently) and each time being disappointed because she had a cold and could not, Sheridan turned the matter over to Victor, who made arrangements for her to appear during November. The terms of the arrangement are interesting: Mrs. Beauclerk was to perform the same play twice at weekly intervals without salary, and then to treat for terms. If none were agreed upon, her third appearance, a week later, was to be for her benefit, she to pay forty guineas for the house. Mrs. Beauclerk's first performance, as Andromache in *The Distrest Mother*, acted, Victor says,[99] to a dissatisfied, half-filled house, was such a disaster that Sheridan refused to permit her a second performance of that play. So she played Zara in *The Mourning Bride*, with applause and approval, she claims, though dressed in rags and insufficiently rehearsed. Sheridan, who had discouraged her from the beginning, offered her no contract. But in February she was permitted her benefit, all through which, she asserts, the manager practiced endless chicanery. To have her revenge, she published *Mrs. Beauclerk's Letters*. Here she accused Sheridan of countless inhumanities to his players and railed on in such a sordid and incoherent way that the details merit no more than a short footnote.[100]

[98] From a letter written by Sheridan on April 16, 1757, and quoted by Mrs. Beauclerk in *Mrs. Beauclerk's Letters*, February 27, 1758.

[99] In Victor's letter reprinted *ibid.*, p. 20.

[100] The facts which have been given are from letters reprinted *ibid.*. Her accusations against Sheridan include turning Mrs. Hopkins out to starve just after she had "lain in"; ill-using Mr. Mossop; holding back £300 to £400 on Mrs. Woffington; forcing Macklin to go to law to get his salary; breaking agreements with Wilkinson, Lee, et cetera. As for his treatment of her, he overcharged her for her benefit (forty guineas instead of the usual £40), refused to change the inconvenient night, and then failed to open the doors until four forty-five, all the while he was sitting in his window gleefully watching her subscribers go away rather than stand outside in the cold and rain!

As in the preceding season, dancers provided the extra entertainment,[101] supported in January by an equilibrist, supposedly a Laplander with the impossible name of Ulan Smolenzco Czernznigorf.[102] In the number of "new" plays and special series this season recalls Sheridan's earlier efforts: two Shakespeare series, three main plays,[103] and several afterpieces. Sheridan himself learned no new roles this year and his number of performances declined, not much but enough so that in January he issued a public apology for his absence from the stage during the preceding weeks.[104] His popularity in old roles was still unshaken, as a table of statistics given in his *Humble Appeal* shows. The income from twenty-one nights of his acting during this winter averaged £77, a figure which may not seem large compared to later statistics for Dublin theaters and Drury Lane, but which Sheridan uses to contrast with the £69 average made by the fresh and popular Barry under Victor in 1755, with two new actresses to assist him.[105]

Running Smock-Alley Theater at such a pitch all fall would have kept any ordinary man fully occupied, but Sheridan had, as we know, two more important concerns which claimed his chief energies: starting his educational venture, and saving the Dublin stage from the ruin theatrical rivalry would surely bring. These two projects kept not only Sheridan but Dublin in a fever all season. The uproar caused by the Kelly riot dies into a murmur in comparison; its excitement was over in a few weeks and its battle easily won. This time the activity lasted for months, all kinds of important people became involved, and the fight itself was the hardest and most crucial of Sheridan's career.

Because this book is a theatrical biography only, Sheridan's educational plan is not relevant here, except where in a strange way it touches the theater. But to Sheridan it had become paramount. Early

[101] Signor Tioli and Signora Ricci from Italy replaced the two Italian dancers of the year before, although in April Signor Maranesi returned with a new partner Signora Provencale (*Dublin Journal*, April 11–15, 1758).

[102] *Ibid.*, December 31–January 3, 1758.

[103] Most successful of these was Dryden's *Amphitryon*, with all exceptionable passages cleared (the press notice does not say whether by Hawkesworth, whose version had run eleven nights the year before at Drury Lane, or by someone like Sheridan). *The Gamester*, "never acted here," ran only two nights, with the roles never specified in the press notice. *Isabella*, Garrick's version of *The Fatal Marriage*, was given for Dexter's benefit.

[104] *Dublin Journal*, January 28–31, 1758.

[105] Sheridan, *An Humble Appeal*, Appendix, pp. 44–45.

in the fall a demand, perhaps planted by friends, had come for him to explain how Ireland could be saved by a new kind of education.[106] He responded, during the winter, in two well-attended orations at the Music-Hall in Fishamble-Street. At the first, on December 6, "the Hibernian Society for the Improvement of Education" was formed to promote Sheridan's ideas. This group, even Sheridan's enemies had to admit, was most impressive; and indeed the list of subscribers, well over two hundred and including "Lords, both Spiritual and Temporal, Privy-Counsellors, Members of Parliament, Doctors of Divinity, Fellows of the College, and Gentlemen of Fortune," [107] reads like a *Who's Who* of Ireland in the mid-eighteenth century. Nor were most of these merely lay figures; frequent meetings were held and a very active committee formed, which convened almost weekly at Mr. Sheridan's quarters next to the theater. For them Sheridan prepared many long reports, developing his ideas down to the last penny. By late spring the society had completed plans to open the Hibernian Academy, a public school to prepare youths for the university in a new style; terms of admission were set; some of the staff was engaged; parents and guardians were notified; and during the next summer Sheridan was sent by the society to London "to execute an important Commission" for their opening on October 1. (Apparently he was to hire additional instructors.) The curriculum of the Hibernian Academy incorporated Sheridan's new ideas: the English language and oratory were stressed; [108] a variety of courses was to be offered to suit the interests and vocational aims of a variety of students; diet, sports, and recreation were to receive attention; and no corporal punishment was to be permitted. In other words, Sheridan's educational ideas were advanced—too advanced for some tastes.

[106] In case this sounds like more of Sheridan's grandiose language, the reader should hear briefly his argument: Ireland's great source of misery is absenteeism; the number of youths being sent to England for their education has increased (over a hundred are now at Westminster and Eton, where recently there were fewer than ten); these boys will be anglicized and estranged from Ireland, with the resulting decay of all noble improvements here. The important reason for all this is the want of reputable schools in Ireland. In the October 22–25, 1757, *Journal*, an anonymous paragraph had stressed the need for an educational academy in Ireland, where oratory, arts, and sciences would be learned, "to save the Nation from impending Ruin."

[107] *Dublin Journal*, January 14–17, 1758.

[108] Latin and Greek were not to be minimized, but were to be strengthened by this knowledge of English.

Although Sheridan's first oration at the Music-Hall was enthusiastically received,[109] he made one bad mistake in it: he suggested that a proper theater might supply helps to the right kind of educational institution. The theater bandmaster might, for example, be its music instructor; the scene designer, its drawing master; the actors, its models of eloquence.[110] These ideas, Sheridan implied, grew out of an earlier plan to open a small academy for training young people with stage talent. Later Sheridan saw that the theater could become "an admirable Assistant to the School of Oratory," [111] which he now hoped to incorporate into the educational background of all young gentlemen.

It can be imagined what Sheridan's critics made of this tentative proposal. Writing seriously, they protested that young gentlemen would be seduced and debauched by the "ladies" of the theater, or at least led into idleness and folly by the men; that the stage was the worst school of oratory extant, its pompous diction and ridiculous delivery justly known by the name of "theatrical"; that younger sons of honorable families would be encouraged to become players; and that oldest sons and heirs might be drawn to *marry* actresses "to the heart-breaking disappointment of their parents, the disgrace of their families, and the total ruin of themselves." [112] Writing humorously, they joked that Sheridan's plan would improve the eloquence of the young blood visiting a brothel. Now his speech is inarticulate: "Damn my Eyes, you are a fine Piece, come Buss me Slut, Dam me, we'll Pig together to Night." After instruction by our great orator, the young Academic will breathe out in "moving and persuasive Accents":

> Thou Nature's whole Perfection in one Piece,
> Thou yeilding [*sic*] Softness, Down of all my Care,
> O let me fly into thy twining Arms!
> And riot in the Soft luxurious Fold,
> 'Till, lost in Extacy, I dye in Joys,
> Greater, than any I can guess hereafter.

[109] At this meeting a motion was unanimously passed that Mr. Sheridan should be desired to print his Oration (*Dublin Journal*, December 6–10, 1757). This was speedily done. Sheridan's second Oration (reported *ibid.*, January 24–28, 1758) "took up almost two Hours," was heard with profound attention, and received uncommon applause.

[110] Sheridan, *An Oration*, pp. 23–24.   [111] *Ibid.*, p. 24.

[112] *The Case of the Stage in Ireland*, pp. 18–20.

Sheridan himself, rumor has it, will teach the dancing by delineating figures on the floor with chalk. In music, solos and sonatas on the broomstick will be featured; and Signor Gillwayboni, who imitates an organ with his voice, will instruct in church music. In architecture, scholars will study the structure of the city Tholsel and of Quilca.[113]

From the handle it supplied his enemies and from the failure of his supporters to develop this side of his plan, it is clear that Sheridan had overrated the social standing of the theater and that his attempt to combine the projected academy and the stage was a grave mistake. For, despite his well-behaved houses, his gentlemanly and ladylike players with their pew in St. John's Church, the old feeling against the theater still survived. Smock-Alley stage, much as it needed to be saved from Crow-Street threats, could not be saved this way. Other ways, Sheridan soon learned, had to be tried.

The proprietors of Smock-Alley and Aungier-Street took the first step. At several meetings held in November they had drawn up a petition to be submitted to the Irish parliament at its winter session.[114] They reminded parliament that their two theaters were combined in response to public demand because two theaters could not operate profitably in Dublin; and that the united theaters were still encumbered with debt, the proprietors even now making no profit. In conclusion, they asked parliament to confine "all Dramatic Representations" to the united theaters.[115] Victor accurately foresaw the result. Since some of the owners were old members of parliament and all were men of property, he predicted that Crow-Street would "get a little sweating at least" but that the petition would come to nothing in the end.[116]

[113] Shea, *A Full Vindication*, pp. 13–16.

[114] Two meetings of the proprietors are advertised in the *Journal*, November 8–12 and 22–26, 1757. Victor summarizes their petition to Garrick in December (*Original Letters*, I, 282). Another meeting was held on April 3, 1758, "to consider of some Affairs in which their Interests are nearly concerned" (*Dublin Journal*, March 21–25). Perhaps they heard Sheridan's petition and proposal at this last meeting.

[115] The proprietors' petition, which is undated, is headed thus: "To the Honourable the Knights, Citizens and Burgesses, in Parliament assembled: The humble Petition of John Putland, Esquire, and Thomas Desbrisay On Behalf of Themselves and the other Proprietors of the united Theatres of Aungier-Street and Smock-Alley, in the City of Dublin."

[116] Victor, *Original Letters*, I, 276. As early as November 1757 Victor reports to Garrick that now that Barry's theater is being organized the proprietors are planning to meet and propose to lay the state of their case before parliament, offering reasons against an increase of theaters.

In January Sheridan took over the fight, burdened though he was by the management of the theater and many duties to the even more important Hibernian Society. After this season he had "no Intention," he announced, "of continuing any longer in the same Situation," but he could not be indifferent to the future of the stage and, before quitting it, he wanted to prevent the ruin with which it was threatened.[117] The week after he made this announcement, carpenters began to roof over the new theater in Crow-Street. Measurements given in the newspaper compare the new building to Aungier-Street,[118] Smock-Alley figures being unavailable. These measurements show that the new Crow-Street *stage* was almost as deep as the whole of the Aungier-Street house. When we remember that Aungier-Street stage was larger than Smock-Alley's, we echo the *Dublin Journal*'s question about this huge Crow-Street stage: "What proportion then must it bear to that in Smock-Alley?" In addition, it was formed to admit machinery never attempted in Dublin, whereby twenty different views of scenes could be shifted in less than a minute by one man.[119] Structurally at least, Crow-Street would be a formidable rival.

Sheridan's side of the case is presented mainly by himself, although this time he had many supporters, even according to his enemies, who grant that "the Friends of Mr. Sheridan . . . are undoubtedly in the Majority." [120] The several anonymous letters which appear in the *Journal* are favorable to the Smock-Alley manager. One of these, written by Romanus, defends Sheridan against charges that he hired a man to play on a broomstick (this was during Victor and Sowdon's regime) and that he had rejected Mrs. Fitzhenry

---

[117] *Dublin Journal*, January 28–31, 1758.

[118] *Ibid.*, January 31–February 4, 1758. The figures are as follows:

		Aungier-Street
Crow-Street length in clear	131'	94'
breadth	50'9"	46'
stage breadth	36'6"	29'
stage depth	90'	54'
(to which may be added 45')		
pit depth	26'	26'
(to which may be added 9')		

The new house was exactly the same height as Covent Garden.

[119] Sheridan was quick to point out that no play required such fast shifting; the machinery would be used only for certain kinds of pantomime (*An Humble Appeal*, pp. 57–58).

[120] *The Case of the Stage in Ireland*, p. 5.

when she first attempted the stage (denied by Mrs. Fitzhenry herself).[121]

When the proprietors drew up their petition for the winter term, Sheridan at first planned to offer one too. But perhaps waiting to see what success the proprietors would have, he saved his till the spring term,[122] submitting it sometime in April after parliament had taken no action on the proprietors' request. Sheridan's petition is short, rather ordinary and unpersuasive. Parliament is told that the new Crow-Street Theater would be the ruin of the Irish stage as well as of Sheridan himself, whose past efforts surely have deserved a better reward; the legislature is reminded that it has the power to limit the number of theaters, as the English parliament recently did. But Sheridan does not repeat the proprietors' request for a monopoly; he prays only for "such Relief . . . as to your great Wisdom shall seem meet." [123]

The bombshell—the relief he was hoping for—was planted in a proposal expressed in *The Case of Thomas Sheridan* . . . and apparently designed to accompany the petition. Here Sheridan doesn't ask for a monopoly; he asks parliament to buy his lease and theatrical property. "Is not this a homestroke in policy?" Victor exclaims, after describing the proposal in a letter to Garrick.[124] Sheridan's plan is, as usual, complex and specific. Parliament would turn over its purchase to the Dublin Society (this was not the Hibernian Society, but

[121] *Dublin Journal*, January 31–February 4, 1758. Another letter from Romanus had preceded this one (see *ibid.*, January 21–24). In February an anonymous letter defends Sheridan against the base libel that he defrauded the public of money collected for a Swift monument (*ibid.*, February 4–7, 1758).

[122] Victor, writing to Garrick in December, describes its contents and also some accompanying proposals of Sheridan's (*Original Letters*, I, 283). A Barry supporter suggests that Sheridan postponed submitting his petition because the arguments against monopoly in the anonymous forty-eight-page pamphlet *The Case of the Stage in Ireland*, published soon after Sheridan's first oration in December and sent to all members of parliament, had made such an impression that he wanted to wait till its effects had worn off (*An Answer In Behalf of Spranger Barry*, p. 1). But, if he had thought this, Sheridan was the sort to have taken immediate steps to counteract the impression.

[123] "To the Honourable the Knights, Citizens and Burgesses, in Parliament assembled: The humble Petition of Thomas Sheridan, Manager and Lessee of the united Theatres of Aungier-Street and Smock-Alley." (This item is misdated 1756 in Loewenberg.)

[124] Victor, *Original Letters*, I, 284.

an older group formed to promote improvements of all kinds).[125]
The Dublin Society would rent out the theater to Sheridan for £3
every playing night.[126] Another pound for each playing night would
be laid aside for the upkeep of the theater. And four plays each year
would be performed absolutely free for four public charities. If this
proposal were to be accepted, Sheridan would be able to realize some
long concerted plans, among them that of making the Dublin theater
a pleasing school of manners and instruction to youth. Victor concludes his comments to Garrick on this proposal thus: "This may be
called another sweater! Here is really some invention—but, perhaps,
you will say, a little too chimerical." [127] Yet Victor, reading the paper
a month earlier, might have learned that parliament had addressed
the king to grant, among other large sums, £2,000 to Dr. Mosse for
his "Care and Inspection" of the Lying-In Hospital; £1,000 to build
galleries in St. Mark's Church; £4,000 to Bottle and Glass Manufacture; £300 to Robert Randall, papermaker; £500 to two men for
gold and silver lace manufacture; £2,000 to build the parish church
of St. Thomas; £5,000 for nurseries.[128] To Sheridan, the theater was
as important and as useful as any of Ireland's manufactures, and
perhaps even as necessary as galleries in St. Mark's Church, although
he was a religious man.

Victor had noticed that, by Sheridan's proposal, "almost the whole
body of the people become interested to support" his theater, and
frequenters of Crow-Street would "be looked on as enemies to their
country." [129] A Barry representative too, in *An Answer In Behalf of
Spranger Barry* (p. 3), points out that if parliament grants Sheridan's
request, the ruined Barry, who has laid out several thousand pounds
on his almost finished building, would be thrown into jail, where he
would die of disappointment and despair. Such an outcome would
hardly appeal to Sheridan, who was, no matter what his enemies said,

[125] The Dublin Society was founded in 1731 to foster improvements in hus-
bandry, manufactures, the arts, et cetera. Premiums were given to persons responsible for new inventions and outstanding achievements. In 1746 the society
was, by the king's letter, granted an allowance of £500 per year. It was chartered
in 1750; in 1758 an art academy was established in its building (Gilbert, II,
281ff.)

[126] The income of £3 every playing night would be used by the society for
the encouragement of the arts or other worthy projects, Sheridan points out.

[127] Victor, *Original Letters*, I, 284.

[128] *Dublin Journal*, November 12–15, 1757.

[129] Victor, *Original Letters*, I, 283–284.

a generous and decent man. His next step, then, was to extend his plan to save Crow-Street and Barry. In his *Humble Appeal,* a ninety-page pamphlet published in April,[130] Sheridan includes "A Proposal Offered to the Consideration of the Subscribers to the Theatre in Crow-Street." Assuming that parliament accepts his earlier plan for subsidizing Smock-Alley, Sheridan suggests that all work on Crow-Street be stopped temporarily, that Smock-Alley be opened to Barry next winter at a superior salary or "let to him at a Reasonable Rent," and that the subscribers and Sheridan then apply to parliament for a fund to establish "one good Company of Actors in Dublin." Sheridan will make over his £9,000 investment to the public for £4,000 (this was probably the amount which parliament was to be asked to pay for Sheridan's lease and properties); the Crow-Street subscribers will ask parliament for £2,000 to finish their house. There, on the grander stage, tragedies will be played; comedies will be confined to Smock-Alley. But *one* company will play both houses. All this will cost parliament only £6,000, a sum which couldn't be laid out better to the Benefit of the Nation and of the City.[131] By this plan all the Dublin theaters would be saved and brought together as a national stage.

Unlike the earlier controversies, which had *followed* some event (a riot, for example), the battle this time was being fought over future possibilities and it had an urgent seriousness lacking in the earlier skirmishes. Pamphlets on both sides are longer and weightier,

---

[130] *An Humble Appeal* also contains an historical survey of Sheridan's experiences as manager. Details which Sheridan gives of Smock-Alley's financial condition at various times, of salaries paid to players, of reforms effected, and of the two famous riots have been incorporated at appropriate places in the preceding chapters. In the rest of the paper Sheridan refutes lies told about him and argues against a new theater. He has *not* been extravagant; he has *not* been jealous of eminent actors, and so on. In answer to those who pity Barry, Sheridan points out that Barry left Ireland and now wants to return to reap Sheridan's harvest. As for the suffering of Barry's family, Sheridan has twice as many children, all young. "Nor will he yield to Mr. Barry in parental Tenderness" (p. 73). The forty-six-page appendix includes passages from Colley Cibber and Chetwood on the evil effects of rival theaters; a reprint of Sheridan's *Vindication* first published in 1754; "Extracts from a Letter written by Mr. Sheridan, to a Gentleman of Consequence in this Country, at a time when he had no Expectation of returning to Ireland"; and a table of statistics showing Sheridan's average intake as compared to Barry's, designed to reveal, apparently, the relative popularity of the two men.

[131] Sheridan, *An Humble Appeal,* pp. 88–91.

a few running from fifty to ninety pages. This time Sheridan could be attacked on two flanks, and his educational ideas drew as much fire as his theatrical plans. Some critics covered both, especially his suggestion that the theater be used by the academy. Those who concentrate on the theatrical issue revive the old criticisms of Sheridan—his use of cheap spectaculars, his mangling of good plays, his mistreatment of actors, and so on. The misconception that he had nothing to do with the success of the Garrick winter is repeated.[132] Thus, as his defenders note,[133] the technique of the bold lie is freely used. For another obviously absurd example: Sheridan himself planned the *Mahomet* riot "to enhance his own merit with a party that disclaimed him." [134] New arguments focus on Sheridan's attempts to keep a monopoly. Competition, his critics claim, will revive a dying interest in the stage and encourage fresh efforts in the complacent Sheridan as well as in his competitors; it will give Dublin a new and magnificent theater with all the latest equipment; and, best of all, it will take the Smock-Alley manager down a peg. Attacking the proprietors' petition and Sheridan's proposals, one Barry supporter points out that the very proprietors who are petitioning for a monopoly originally built or rebuilt two theaters to compete against each other; so why should they complain of others for following their example? Finally, if, as Sheridan claims, his theatrical contributions have been made at a financial loss, how could he have offered Barry a share in the *profits* or how can he now offer to run the theater for the Dublin Society at a *profit* for them or for himself? The present encumbrances on Smock-Alley can be explained, according to the critics, by Sheridan's personal extravagance. And, as for Sheridan's assertion that he is the first to establish a regular theater, Dubliners have only to recall "Ashberry" and Thomas Elrington.[135]

Not all of the writing is serious.[136] Swiftian irony [137] and light parody relieve the heavy artillery. *The Humble Petition of Thomas*

---

[132] *An Answer In Behalf of Spranger Barry*, p. 1.

[133] *Dublin Journal*, January 31–February 4, 1758.

[134] *The Case of the Stage in Ireland*, pp. 44–45.

[135] *An Answer In Behalf of Spranger Barry*, pp. 1–2.

[136] Additional changes and additions to be made in Loewenberg's bibliography of the writings at this time (pp. 21–22) are:

[Sheridan, Thomas]: *The Case of Thomas Sheridan, Lessee and Manager* . . . should be dated 1758 rather than 1750.

An Answer In Behalf of Spranger Barry was written not by Barry but by a person "who transacts his Affairs in this Kingdom." It was issued in April 1758 (not in 1756).

Punch, Esq. informs parliament that the petitioner, who has lost his whole fortune and impaired his constitution in his puppet show, is anxious to make a present of the same to the D.bl.n S.c..ty for £1,500, which will then give same back to him with an act prohibiting all other puppet shows. If the proposal (which is developed in comic detail) is not complied with, "The Stage is in Danger! The Stage is in Danger! oh! The Stage is in Danger! and, of Consequence, the Church, the State, the Academy are in Danger! and your Petitioner is in such Danger, that he knows not of *any other Power* that can relieve him." [138]

The satiric piece which must have pained Sheridan most, considering his happy marriage and his efforts to protect Mrs. Sheridan from theatrical involvements, was an eight-page poem called "The Curtain Lecture . . . A Dialogue between a Stage-Director and his Wife." In it, Sheridan is pictured as saying to his wife, "I'd rather be hissed than lye by your side," and his wife, who in reality seems never to have reproached her husband, is pictured as berating him for abandoning his true friends, "the people," in hopes of a pension from the castle; for afterward skulking to London, where he provoked such hissing, scorn, and derision as had never been known before; for putting himself on a level with Garrick:

You'd with Garrick compare, with Garrick be seen!
Compare me as well with Sheba's famed queen,
For beauty and knowledge . .

The Case of the Stage in Ireland is an attack on Sheridan, his management of the theater, and his educational ideas.

Shea, P.: *A Full Vindication of Thomas Sheridan* is an ironic piece pretending to defend Sheridan against *The Case of the Stage*, but actually continuing the attack.

An Enquiry into the Plan and Pretensions of Mr. Sheridan is concerned with Sheridan's educational plan and not with the theater.

The Curtain Lecture: or, The Manager Run Mad. A Dialogue between a Stage Manager & his Wife, London, 1758.

[137] Shea's *A Full Vindication of Thomas Sheridan*, for example.

[138] "To the Honourable the K—s, C—s and B—s assembled. The Humble Petition of Thomas Punch, Esq: Principal Performer and Sole Manager of the Still-Life-Theatre in Caple-Street." (This item is misdated 1756 in Loewenberg; it must have followed Sheridan's petition, and belongs therefore in 1758.) Punch's list of the wardrobe of his theater amusingly includes: 1 Banner, inscribed *Io Triumphe!* 1 ditto, inscribed *Io Sheridan!*, 1 triumphal Chariot, one long-concerted Scheme, An excellent Peal of Thunder, Adam and Eve, the Fig-Leaf wanting.

245

and for—of all things—not being a gentleman like Manager Rich:

> He [Rich] wants not true feelings:—a gentleman too.
> Would Tommy, with truth, I could say so of you!

If the poet had been Sheridan's best friend, he could not have touched his sensitive spots more unerringly. But this was not all. His book "that's cry'd up so fine" (*British Education*, no doubt)—the wife claims that she wrote half of it, the best half; and the rest was stolen from his daddy's papers and from Swift. When the manager speaks again, the reader is brought back to Sheridan's present project, which unquestionably provoked this whole scurrilous piece:

> I will have the Theatre tack'd to my plan,
> I will have it tack'd:—forbid it who can!

In the end Knowles, Sheridan's brother-in-law employed with the theater's finances, enters to report the failure of Sheridan's petition and to ask for a recommendation to Barry. As the poem closes, Sheridan runs mad.

Sheridan's answer to all such attacks and all arguments is simple. Dublin, as history shows, cannot support two theaters; it can barely support one, with performers' salaries double and sometimes triple what they were. Even in vastly more populous London, an increase in theaters has been prevented by law and still that city cannot "keep up two in credit": when one rises, the other declines, and today one London theater subsists "entirely upon the Strength of Pantomime."

> Is it not well known, that Mr. Garrick, with all his Merit, all his Popularity, all his Skill as a Manager (and never Man shewed more) notwithstanding he takes care always to secure the best Actors, and to exhibit the greatest Variety of Plays, and the best adapted to the Taste of the Times, yet, without the Assistance of those same living Puppet shews, would not long be able to keep open his Doors with any Profit to himself.[139]

Sheridan's *Humble Appeal*, embodying these points amid a mass of other material, went quickly into a second edition. Pamphlets from both sides were reprinted in London, where many people were interested in this greatest battle of Sheridan's career.

In writing of this controversy which divided most of Dublin, Hitchcock observes that each side "had an appearance of reason." [140]

---

[139] Sheridan, *An Humble Appeal*, pp. 54–55.   [140] Hitchcock, I, 295.

But it should be noted that Sheridan alone attempted to work out a compromise, one by which Crow-Street would profit along with Smock-Alley. Whether his proposal was sound is another question. One is tempted to ask: if the government does subsidize the theater, what happens to Sheridan's much vaunted Free Stage? Was the Dublin Society trusteeship devised by him because it could be counted on to keep hands off? But, right or wrong in his solution, Sheridan was quite right in his contention that Dublin then could not support two theaters, as Victor, Barry, Woodward, Mossop, and others found to their ruin.

Sheridan's petition was presented to parliament in April 1758. Writing to Samuel Richardson in March, Sheridan reported that, although important men in London were supporting Crow-Street and were sending letters to powerful people in Ireland, he had the Lord Primate on his side and possibly the speaker of the Irish House of Commons. He was writing to ask Richardson's influence in persuading the latter.[141] That Richardson did try is clear from a letter of Mrs. Sheridan's, thanking him for his help, which did her husband honor although "it did not gain the full intent of it." [142]

Parliament's rejection of Sheridan's petition and proposal was no surprise to Victor, aware that "many of the leading Members . . . were Subscribers to the new Building in Crow-Street, and many more were Well-wishers to it." [143] But Sheridan, in *An Humble Address*, written on May 6, ascribed his failure to the lateness of his application. Far from discouraged, he intended to appeal again at the next session. Meantime, Dubliners were asked to show their support of him by subscribing to a series, paying what price they thought proper (this was a novel idea!) and selecting the plays by majority decision. Well-filled houses would encourage him to fight on. The *Dublin Journal*, reporting the meeting of subscribers, says that "in less than an Hour there was near 200 Guineas subscribed upon this Occasion." [144]

During much of the season and even as late as May, Sheridan had expected to give up the stage, hoping no doubt to head the new Hibernian Academy. By early June, however, it had become clear to

[141] Richardson, IV, 167–174 (Letter of March 16, 1758).

[142] *Ibid.*, pp. 174–175 (Letter of April 11, 1758).

[143] Victor, *History*, I, 236.

[144] *Dublin Journal*, May 16–20, 1758. The four subscription plays, given the last week of May, apparently met with success, in spite of "the Thinness of the Town, and the uncommon Heat of the Weather" (*ibid.*, June 6–10, 1758).

him that, if this institution were to prosper, he should hold no prominent position in it: an announcement at that time informed the public that he would continue to manage the theater next season. His educational undertaking, he added, would not interfere, since only part of his scheme would materialize and his job would be merely general inspection.[145] Much as he must have hated the idea of returning to face thin houses and a triumphant rival, Sheridan could not yet give up the stage.

The Smock-Alley company had to be strengthened if Crow-Street was opening with the people's idol, Barry, and with the almost equally popular Woodward replacing Macklin as Barry's partner.[146] An earlier blunder of Sheridan's had lost him his two best actors, King and Dexter, to Barry for the next fall.[147] To recoup this loss Victor was quickly dispatched to London to hire Mrs. Ward, Theophilus Cibber, and, more crucially, Digges, the only performer Sheridan felt could stand up to Barry.[148] He himself went over soon after for the Hibernian Society and to engage other performers for Smock-Alley (especially, by request, a company of singers for operas and burlettas). When Victor returned to Dublin, Sheridan stayed in England; Victor was to manage the company until January 1759, when Sheridan's appearance would be the more welcome with the novelty of Barry at Crow-Street somewhat worn off.[149]

Crow-Street opened on October 23, only moderately successful the first few nights without Barry. Smock-Alley's first night, the evening before, had been dismal (£12 in receipts); and a series of disasters followed which were climaxed by the loss of Theophilus Cibber and Maddox, the equilibrist, in a shipwreck off the Scottish coast.[150] To

[145] *Ibid.*, June 6–10, 1758. In speaking of the part of his educational scheme which had not yet materialized, Sheridan may have been referring to the postgraduate course which he had projected for students just out of the university.

[146] The actual contract of partnership between Barry and Woodward was not drawn until July (Stockwell, p. 342), but it seems likely that the change in command was known in Dublin earlier than this. The reason for Macklin's withdrawal may have been a quarrel with Barry (Kirkman, I, 391) or the fatal illness of his wife (Cooke, pp. 220–221) or a combination of both (Appleton, pp. 113–114).

[147] Victor, *History*, I, 237. They had defected when Sheridan, upset at Mrs. Fitzhenry's hesitation over his offer of a next year's contract with a £100 raise, had refused for a time to sign contracts with anyone.

[148] Hitchcock, I, 306.

[149] Victor, *Original Letters*, I, 288 (Letter to Dorset, February 1759).

[150] Victor, *History*, I, 248–251.

Victor this was the beginning of the end. Recalling that he had persuaded Cibber into the fatal engagement, he was much affected; [151] and Sheridan, remembering Cato's robe, must have been heartsick. Then sometime in November Victor had word that Sheridan, detained in London by his oratorical scheme, probably would not come over in January.[152] This news drove the hitherto "neuter" [153] Mrs. Fitzhenry over into Crow-Street's already attractive company, which now included Barry, Woodward, King, Dexter, Sowdon, and a new discovery from York, Mrs. Dancer.[154] Against this array Digges and Mrs. Ward at Smock-Alley could hardly prevail. By February Sheridan had decided to sell all his Irish property and "return no more." [155] Another, lesser disappointment finished Victor's last hope: Macklin and his daughter, who were to come in March, failed him because of illness.[156]

At about this same time Sheridan sent Victor orders to "dissolve the Company from acting any longer on his Account," but if the actors wished to, they could continue to use the theater on their own account.[157] The company accepted this offer, publishing their intention in a "pompous" [158] advertisement on May 2, wherein they declared themselves "unexpectedly deserted and abandoned," the victims of "Irregularity and Confusion" and a "Variety of Disappointments." [159] Less censorious was Victor. By Sheridan's decision, he says, "no Man was more hurt than I . . . nor had more seeming Reason to resent it; but when I was informed of the true Cause, I lamented, that a Man of his Abilities should meet with such hard Fate." [160]

The "true Cause," we must conclude, was Sheridan's fear of his

---

[151] *Ibid.*, pp. 250–252. Also lost was "the Man who played on the twelve Bells fastened to his Head, Hands, and Feet." The pantomime machinery was saved because it came another way; and the pantomime carpenter because he missed the boat.

[152] *Ibid.*, pp. 254–255.   [153] The word is Hitchcock's (1, 310).

[154] Mrs. Dancer became Mrs. Barry and then Mrs. Crawford.

[155] Victor, *Original Letters*, 1, 290. As early as November 11, 1758, Mrs. Sheridan, writing to Whyte from London, had said, "I doubt Mr. Sheridan, without a much better prospect than the present, will hardly be induced to take the burthen again upon his shoulders; for my own part I think we have had a sufficient proof how far Dublin is to be depended upon; I speak in general, for I am sure we have some very worthy friends there" (Whyte, p. 92).

[156] Victor, *History*, 1, 265–266.   [157] *Ibid.*, pp. 266–267.

[158] The word is Victor's (*ibid.*, p. 269).   [159] *Ibid.*, p. 268.

[160] *Ibid.*, p. 265.

Irish creditors.[161] The manager who had generously lent his theater for the benefit of many an insolvent debtor was in danger now of the Dublin Marshalsea himself. Whyte estimates that at this time Sheridan's obligations amounted to about £7,000, of which the £5,687 named as exclusive of mortgages on Quilca must have been theatrical debts. (Sheridan's Dublin printer, for example, is mentioned as a particularly obdurate creditor.) [162] This sum was large; but with several undisturbed seasons to reap the harvest which Sheridan felt he had sown at Smock-Alley, the obligation might have been discharged. Crow-Street finished that possibility.

Sheridan's career as Dublin theater manager ended in 1758. The eleven years of his control had brought the Irish stage many benefits, the more striking of which have been noted by himself and by later writers. Perhaps because he had a schoolmaster for a father, he was determined to run a disciplined house. His well-known, pioneer reforms, such as clearing the stage, eliminating odd money, and turning his upper gallery into boxes for ladies were all to this end. Most, but not all, Dubliners were grateful for the quiet which permitted them to hear and enjoy the better programs now being devised by their tireless manager. His improvements here and in the acting increased performances from two and three a week to five and sometimes six; the Dublin theater became a source of almost nightly entertainment, as it had never been before, and achieved a steadiness that raised it, for the first time, to a level with the London theaters. It became a national institution under Sheridan.

As such, it elevated the standard of taste in Dublin—not spectacularly (for tastes change gradually), but considerably. Shakespeare, as we have seen, began to dominate Smock-Alley's stage; tragedies on noble themes grew as frequent as farces. Tightwire performers and fire-eaters were still needed and Sheridan knew better than to

[161] This is also indicated by something else in Victor (*History*, 1, 265): ". . . that he [Sheridan] was prevented, by the unhappy Situation of his Affairs, from coming to serve himself as well as his Company, must be called his *Misfortune*, and not his *Fault*." At one time, when Victor first learned that Sheridan would not return and was planning to sell his Irish property, he thought, mistakenly, that the proceeds would clear Sheridan's debts (*Original Letters*, 1, 290). By a £2,000 mortgage to Robert Patrick of Dublin, drawn in February 1758, Sheridan had given Quilca as security, having borrowed £1,000 from Robert Wood of London. Patrick was apparently acting as trustee for Wood at this time. John Sheen already held a mortgage on Quilca from 1752 (Tickell, 175; MS 192/127543 Off. Reg. Deeds, Dub.).

[162] Whyte, p. 80.

throw them out, as Burke had advised, but, once attracted by Mahomet Caratta, the audience listened to *Othello*. Victor stressed the need for novelty in Dublin companies; new actors, he said, kept Irish interest awake.[163] Sheridan's forte was providing variety in *program*, within the limits of an eighteenth-century repertory theater.

Not that he neglected his company. Perhaps his now least-known but most creative contributions were in this area. His gift for discovering theatrical talent and encouraging it was famous in his own day. An example of his lifelong interest in helping less experienced actors is given by a young comedian with the stage name of Wilks (later under his real name, Thomas Snagg, he was to write *Recollections of Occurrences*). In 1772 Sheridan and Wilks were both playing in Ryder's company in Dublin, Wilks in his late twenties, Sheridan in his mid-fifties. From Sheridan, says Wilks, "I received every friendly acknowledgment for my services in his pieces and likewise several instructions in particular characters that he had remembered in the acting of great performers. He pointed out strokes in Sir Henry Wildair practised by Mrs. Woffington, stage effects in the Fops of Colley and Theophilus Cibber and communicated his own great judgment and long usage of the stage." [164] This same interest had inspired Sheridan earlier with the idea of establishing a school for acting to be attached to his theater and to train young players with ability. For aged and incapacitated actors he conceived a theatrical fund in an attempt to bring security to lives then tragically insecure, as any eighteenth-century *biographia dramatica* will show. And always he worked to raise the status of the profession. As a university-bred gentleman, the first to manage a Dublin theater, Sheridan brought prestige to the Irish actor and encouraged other gentlemen and even ladies to "attempt the Stage," until he could say that "during the space of a few Years there were more Gentlemen, who were such both by Birth and a liberal Education, upon his Stage, than all the Theatres in England had produced, from the Time of Booth, Wilks, and Cibber to that; as also a greater Number of Actresses, whose Characters were entirely free from Stain." [165] Thus a giant step was made in the player's slow, difficult progress from vagabond to knight. Sheridan sometimes overestimated this progress; and sometimes he undercut it by arguing that his own status had been saved because he had never accepted a salary. But that the profession

---

[163] Victor, *History*, I, 232.   [164] Snagg (Wilks), p. 83.
[165] Sheridan, *An Humble Appeal*, p. 21.

rose under his rule is clear from his enemies, who resented the social place and even political power held by Smock-Alley actors. The idea that a man no longer lost rank by turning player began to be accepted outside the theater; and from this gain all actors—upper class or lower, major or minor—profited. For the public's contempt was no longer universal and automatic; a new feeling of worth could reach down to the lowest member of the company.

This gain was strengthened by Sheridan's insistence on acting as an art, one good enough to rank with literature, music, painting, and by his scholarly knowledge of theatrical history. The latter inspired him and gave him an aim beyond the routine achievement of a well-run business, an aim which sustained his great expense of energy, otherwise so ill-rewarded. And for those who listened to him or read his writings, Sheridan's scholarly knowledge added perspective. His audiences were often ridiculed by his critics for their blind enslavement to him: he had only to call them the most enlightened public since Greece or Rome and they supinely accepted his orders and his offerings. Actually, they seem to have caught his purpose; they saw themselves as helping to raise the kingdom's cultural level. And, besides, they had never been better or more consistently entertained. Dubliners who, before Sheridan, had shunned the theater began to come and add their respectability; troublemakers were discouraged; and finally Sheridan did have a public he could boast about.

As for the acting, Sheridan was the only Dublin manager up to his time to have been a first-rate actor too, one ranked near the top by London critics. From the beginning he demanded that his players give as much to their acting as he did; he would not tolerate careless, half-learned performances; he fined irregularity, tardiness—and ad-libbing. Improved acting not only meant better, more attentive audiences; it meant more respect for the actor. Smock-Alley's reputation as a disciplined training ground for young players spread abroad. Where, in the past, Irish beginners had looked toward London, now new actors came from England to learn under Sheridan. And experienced actors were drawn to Dublin by another inducement—money. In the end, all but a few of the mid-century's great players appeared at Sheridan's Smock-Alley: Garrick, Barry, Macklin, Woodward, Digges, Mossop, King, T. Cibber, Foote, Woffington, Bellamy, Ward, Green. Some of these had made their start there. Only a few of London's important actors declined: Mrs. Cibber, for example, who dreaded the crossing, and Mrs. Clive, Garrick's leading lady during these years. It was not easy to lure snugly placed Londoners across the unpredictable Irish Sea for a strange and often uncomfortable Dublin winter. For no longer were London actors permitted to use Smock-Alley as a summer stopgap. Sheridan had done away with that harmful practice almost from the first when he saw how Dubliners shunned local winter performers after a summer of superior importations. He closed Smock-Alley during summers, and imported foreign talent for the regular winter season. The high salaries he used as bait not only brought talent good enough to raise a provincial stage to a national theater, but coming at a time when money had begun to challenge birth as the measure of importance, they helped the actor up another step of the social ladder. A fellow who couldn't count on his dinner until a few admission fees had been collected was only a mouthful away from a vagabond; but a man making £800 a year—why, some *gentlemen* couldn't be sure of that much!

Sheridan's misfortune as a manager was that he himself could never be sure of that much. Unlike Ashbury or Garrick, he did not—could not—make money. He was not interested in money. Ashbury, by letting the Smock-Alley building run down and by being satisfied with fewer and cheaper productions, had wrung a satisfactory living out of his monopoly. But Sheridan could not be content with this businesslike point of view. Instead, he spent his proceeds and energy on, as he would say, "raising the Dublin stage," not letting it stand still or fall back. Some gains were temporary, since cyclic regressions were inevitable. But others were permanent. In almost all ways he set a higher standard than before. He made Irishmen see that the Dublin theater could rival London theaters, perhaps even surpass them. This new idea—that Ireland could support a great theater of her own—faded at times in the centuries to come; it never died. Sheridan would have been pleased, but not surprised, at the Abbey Theater.

Why, then, with all his improvements to the Dublin stage, did Dublin let him go? Why was he not more supported in his struggle against the rival theater? This was the question Sheridan asked, forgetting that his friends were busy with what they, and he, felt a more important project—his Hibernian Academy. His enemies were busy too, writing their attacks and distributing their "states of the case" among MP's. To the few neutral people left, the arguments for a new theater must have seemed plausible. They had forgotten what had happened to the rival houses fifteen years ago; competition would be exciting for them and stimulating for the rivals; Barry was popular; Crow-Street, on its way to completion, would be an ornament; and if one theater had entertained them well, two might be even better. The arguments for a theatrical monopoly, on the other hand, seemed academic: Sheridan, who might have deserved their support, was quitting the stage; and his plan for one Dublin company under Barry might be realized in the natural course of events without the new complication and expense of nationalization. Sheridan and the Smock-Alley proprietors would lose money, of course; but this consideration alone seldom rouses others to action. The academical project would, it was to be hoped, repay him better. The neutrals saw nothing to fight for. By the time Sheridan had decided to remain as Smock-Alley manager, the fight was over. Crow-Street had been built and Barry's company was almost organized. Sheridan had lost.

CHAPTER X

The Reluctant Actor, 1758-1777

ALTHOUGH some have supposed that Sheridan's stage career almost ended when he abandoned Smock-Alley's management and although Sheridan himself would have liked nothing better, his connection with the stage lasted for twenty-two years more. During this time he acted, for whole seasons or parts of seasons, both in Ireland and England (and even one summer in Scotland), for fifteen out of the twenty-two years.[1] For the last two of the twenty-two (from 1778–80) he turned manager again, this time at Drury Lane, where his son Richard was a patentee. The truth was that he could not afford to give up the theater. His nontheatrical projects, though they frequently held out the hope of making his fortune and sometimes even brought in a profit, were not lucrative enough. Yet for most of his remaining life they occupied his chief attention.

Sheridan's great hope, which he never lost from the 1750's on, was to direct an academy where he could realize his educational reforms. The Hibernian Academy's failure in Dublin after a few years, far from discouraging him, proved only that proper direction was lacking. Afterward he came near to establishing an academy in Edinburgh; in Bath and in London he made heroic efforts; and in the last years of his life the possibility grew of his having charge not of a mere academy but of a whole reformed system of national education in Ireland. This larger purpose and the regard it inspired in many lent dignity to other activities designed to keep his ideas before the public and his family fed.

One of these activities put him on the speaking platform and as much in the public eye as when he was on the stage. At first it took the form of public lectures on the importance of elocution. Then, to illustrate the results of elocutionary training, Sheridan devised something lighter called Attic Entertainments, readings of prose and poetry. Although training in English elocution, with its stress on the spoken word over the written word and on English as well as the

---

[1] These figures are reckoned by calendar years, not seasons. For two of these years Sheridan was exiled in Blois, France, where, of course, he did no acting. (For specific dates and activities see the chronological table at the front of this book.)

classical tongues, was only one of his educational aims, its effect was publicly demonstrable and could even be made entertaining. To enliven the appeal still more he eventually added a singer or two and an instrumentalist. His Attic Entertainments never quite reached the dramatic level, but they kept moving in that direction guided by his old theater manager's instincts. In the 1780's he reverted briefly to lectures on language and elocution, called now Rhetorical Prelections and attended by such theatrical notables as Mrs. Siddons, Henderson, and Macklin (who may have come to sneer). Finally he returned to English Readings, but this time with Henderson, who had served as his leading tragedian at Drury Lane. Even here he introduced a short talk on the proper cultivation of speech.[2] In all of these courses, though the emphasis shifted sometimes to entertainment, his basically serious purpose raised him far above the scores of orators, debaters, and lecturers flooding the newspapers with notices, often in imitation of him.

Also adding to his prestige and giving wider influence to his ideas were the books and pamphlets he wrote over these years, beginning with *British Education*. Invited to speak at both Cambridge and Oxford during his first winter back in London, he published in 1759 *A Discourse Delivered in the Theatre at Oxford, in the Senate-House in Cambridge, and at Spring-Garden in London. By Thomas Sheridan, M. A. Being Introductory to his Course of Lectures on Elocution and the English Language*. Both universities had regarded his plans as important enough to merit the reward and encouragement of the honorary M. A.[3] In 1762 he brought out his elocution lectures in book form under the title *A Course of Lectures on Elocution*. Earlier this same year he had published a prospectus, dedicated to Lord Bute, for producing an English dictionary and a rhetorical grammar "upon a Plan entirely new," and was encouraged in this work by a government pension of £200 yearly.[4] By 1769 his ideas on education had

---

[2] See, for example, the *Public Advertiser*, March 4, 1785.

[3] "We hear from Oxford, that on Tuesday last, in Congregation, Mr. Sheridan was admitted to the Degree of Master of Arts" (Jackson's *Oxford Journal*, Saturday, December 2, 1758). "On Friday last Mr. Sheridan, Master of Arts, was admitted ad eundem in this University; and on Tuesday he delivered in the Senate House, a preparatory Discourse . . . which met with general Approbation" (*Cambridge Journal*, March 24, 1759).

[4] The pension was announced in the *Annual Register's* "Chronicle" for October 1762 (p. 107). Mrs. Sheridan refers to it in a letter to Whyte, adding that it came "without solicitation, which makes it the more valuable" (Whyte,

become more specific and more advanced; *A Plan of Education* followed. Six years later (1775), at a period when he was in the theater more than on the platform, he wrote the two-volume *Art of Reading*, devoted to both prose and poetry. Five years after this (1780), his *General Dictionary of the English Language*, with rhetorical grammar prefixed, finally appeared; the first complete pronouncing dictionary in English, it is still regarded as a landmark in the history of our language. All these works were produced while he was active in the theater; after 1780 he turned his whole attention to lectures, public readings, educational plans, and publications, including a 544-page volume totally divorced from all his other interests and surely a labor of love, *The Life of Swift.*[5]

To increase his income until his academy should materialize and to demonstrate how his methods could improve speech, Sheridan turned, at times, to private tutoring. At least two of his pupils, men with illustrious names, profited from his instruction—Grenville, recovering from a painful boyhood stutter to become an "animated" parliamentary speaker,[6] and Wedderburn, acquiring so "elegant, classical and correct a pronunciation" that not a single word revealed his origin "on the other side of the Tweed." [7] But tutoring was a long way from directing an academy; and its monetary rewards were meager.

It is ironic that the theater, which in the past had often cruelly rejected Sheridan's efforts and which at last he no longer wanted, now became his main source of support. Indeed, so precarious was his

---

p. 111, Letter of November 29, 1762). Many today, who know nothing more of Sheridan, remember Johnson's cutting remark on this event.

[5] A manuscript letter from Sheridan to his booksellers, dated "Windsor Castle August 4th" (1762—from a reference to the sale of his lectures) reveals that he had the idea for this biography almost twenty years earlier and started work on it. He asks for copies of Ld. Orrery on Swift, Hawkesworth's edition of Swift, Hume's *History of England* (the volume containing the reign of King William and Queen Anne), *The Tale of a Tub*, and with these "a gr. of a hundred of your best writing pens and six quire of large writing paper" (quoted from MS. 968, f. 111 by permission of the National Library of Scotland.)

[6] Angelo, ii, 417; *DNB, v.* "Grenville, George." (Grenville became Marquis of Buckingham.)

[7] *London Chronicle*, August 16–19, 1788. (Wedderburn became Lord Loughborough.) Not everyone agreed that Sheridan did improve his pupils. One critic, in the *Public Advertiser*, August 21, 1788, reports that before instruction his students could read very tolerably, but afterward they were almost unintelligible from an overapplication of "scientific grace."

educational project financially and so chimeric were its prospects that twice during the twenty-two years he tried briefly to abandon it and return to Dublin stage management; and he did take over a managing job at Drury Lane under his son Richard, although then he was busy too with his nontheatrical plans. But generally it was not as manager that the theater welcomed him back and supported him. It was as actor. And again ironically, acting, which at first had had such allure for Sheridan that he almost lost his reputation for it, now held little attraction and less importance for him. "I don't value acting," he told Boswell in 1763, adding that he wouldn't want to be remembered for it, even if he were acknowledged to be the greatest actor that ever lived. "I would have it erased," he insisted, "out of the anecdotes of my life."[8] Boswell felt (and a theatrical biographer must hope he was right) that Sheridan was exaggerating here. But because the theater after 1758 did come second with him, we may justly curtail, if not "erase," his record as an actor by abandoning the year-by-year narrative followed up till now and selecting instead only characteristic experiences or those especially important to theater history. These include Sheridan's later relations with Garrick, his further attempts to gain a monopoly over the Dublin stage, his venture into provincial playing and the Irish attitude toward provincial players, and—most interesting to theater historians—his fairly steady performance of acting on shares.[9]

To act only on shares was necessary to Sheridan's prestige. His position as a scholar and a gentleman was more secure so long as he took no salary to act, became, in other words, no man's hireling. When he acted on shares, he paid the expenses of the theater for each night he appeared and then divided that night's profits with the manager according to an agreed-upon percentage. The expenses of different theaters at different times varied, sometimes running as low as £20, sometimes as high as £80. The profits varied even more. Perhaps for this reason most performers preferred a salary. During Sheridan's entire management at Smock-Alley, only Garrick, and possibly Foote, acted on shares, and after Garrick arrived in Dublin, we recall that he tried (in vain) to change this arrangement to get a "stipulated sum"—a salary—for the season. All other actors, no matter how "celebrated"—Macklin, Cibber, Barry, Digges, Woffington

---

[8] Boswell, *London Journal*, p. 136 (January 12, 1763).

[9] Both Whyte (p. 63) and Lefanu make much of the fact that Sheridan "never performed any where as an articled actor" (Lefanu, p. 357).

—were hired for the season and subject to Sheridan's bidding. By acting on shares Sheridan not only made more money, especially in Ireland where he was still much admired, but he also kept his independence. He selected his own plays and sometimes "got them up," arranging for the cast and the total production. One summer, for example, when he appeared at the Haymarket Theater, its manager Foote wrote to his friend Wilkinson: "I have this summer entertained the veteran Sheridan, who is dwindled into a mere Cock-and-Bottle Chelsea pensioner. He has enlisted some new recruits unfit for service, and such as might be expected to issue from his discipline." [10] Foote was, as usual, contemptuous (although he had invited Sheridan back for a second summer). But Irish managers were eager to get him. Even on shares he was more profitable to them than another actor on a salary; his presence frequently saved an otherwise-hopeless season.

Of special interest is Sheridan's experience of acting on shares at Drury Lane under Garrick's management. He had been in England for two years without appearing on any stage. The first year, 1758–59, he spent in London, settled with his wife and his older son, Charles Francis,[11] in his former locale near Covent Garden,[12] working on his elocution plans and giving the lectures in Oxford, Cambridge, and London.[13] The following fall, September 1759, he moved to Windsor with his wife, all four of his children,[14] and three servants. Here he began work on his grammar and finished a second course of elocu-

[10] Cooke, *Foote*, I, 96.

[11] At this time (1758) Anne Elizabeth, called Betsy, was born. The other two children, Richard and Alicia, with their nurse, had been left in Ireland again, under the supervision of relatives. There they attended Samuel Whyte's Grammar School in Dublin's Grafton-Street, an institution recently set up with Sheridan's advice and with the warm support of Whyte's "cousin," Mrs. Sheridan (Lefanu, pp. 82–85; Whyte, p. 95, letter from Mrs. Sheridan, March 29, 1759).

[12] There is disagreement about the exact street. Lefanu (p. 85) mentions Henrietta-Street, but Whyte, who visited there, says, "Bedford-street opposite Henrietta-street" (p. 49).

[13] His London lectures on elocution and the English language ran daily for four days at the end of February 1759, and were so successful that they were repeated at the end of April. His discourse given at the universities was published this spring (*Public Advertiser*, February 9, 19; April 19; June 26, 1759).

[14] Richard and Alicia had arrived from Dublin shortly before September 12, 1759 (Whyte, p. 96). Victor mentions the four children and the three servants at Windsor (*Original Letters*, I, 305–306). Victor was now living in London, his home until his death in 1778.

tion lectures, but not in time to give them in London as he had intended. Not much money was coming in, now that all resources from Ireland had been cut off;[15] and, as Victor remarks without further comment, Windsor was "a dear place for provisions."[16] By the following June (1760), through Victor's intercession, Sheridan had reached an agreement with Garrick "to be together on shares, on those nights he performs."[17] "The acquisition of such an actor as Mr. Sheridan," comments Davies, "must have been desirable to the managers of either of the London theatres. It was, perhaps, the mutual interest of Mr. Garrick and Mr. Sheridan to come to a reasonable agreement: this was soon effected, notwithstanding a coldness had subsisted between them for some time."[18] Perhaps the tribute to Garrick's acting in Sheridan's *British Education*—where the Drury Lane manager had been called "inimitable in the representation of such comic characters as he has an opportunity of observing" and "of equal perfection in such parts of tragic characters as can be taken from life"[19]—had warmed the feeling between the two men and facilitated the agreement. Sheridan, it was decided, was to act a stipulated number of nights and receive a one-quarter share of the profits after £80 a night for expenses had been deducted[20]—a much less favorable rate, incidentally, than Sheridan had offered Garrick fifteen years before at Smock-Alley.

An undated announcement, composed by Sheridan and appearing among Garrick's correspondence as "Mr. Sheridan's plan for acting with the managers of Drury-Lane," may have opened the way for this arrangement. In it he offers his services, part-time and on shares; as further inducement he is ready with two plays never performed in England, nor published, but played successfully in Dublin, and with a number of revived plays not acted for some time at Drury Lane. He indicates that he will suit his appearances to Garrick, appearing or not appearing in Garrick's parts "at the choice of Mr. Garrick"; he will expand or contract the number of his appearances as occasion requires. Sheridan's eagerness to conciliate Garrick and to adapt himself to Garrick's wishes shows through the stiffly formal phrasing with its third-person references, so useful for preserving dignity: "He [Mr. Sheridan] neither expects nor desires that any part

[15] Whyte, pp. 99, 96 (in letters from Mrs. Sheridan, March 21, 1760, and September 12, 1759).

[16] Victor, *Original Letters*, I, 305.   [17] *Ibid.*   [18] Davies, I, 291–292.

[19] Sheridan, *British Education*, pp. 371–372.   [20] Davies, I, 292.

of the general views and interests of the theatre should give way to his particular views or interests." [21]

This same determination persisted throughout the 1760–61 season at Drury Lane. Sheridan's behavior in the *King John* episode shows to advantage when compared with Garrick's, as even Davies, usually a Garrick partisan, grants. *King John,* one of the few plays to feature both Garrick and Sheridan, was produced in mid-December. Fifteen years before, at Smock-Alley, the two actors had played amicably together in this tragedy, perhaps even exchanging the roles of the King and the Bastard. Now, in planning the Drury Lane production, Garrick at first chose the role of the King; Sheridan was to act the Bastard. Later, whether because Garrick felt the Bastard a more desirable role or because he felt King John more suitable to Sheridan ("a heavy declamatory part, not at all in my way," quotes Alicia Lefanu,[22] "I am sure you could make a great deal more of it"), he wanted to exchange roles. Reluctantly, but in keeping with his new plan of appeasement, Sheridan agreed. The ironic turn came when Sheridan's King proved to be a greater success than Garrick's Bastard. Davies, a member of the company this season, tells how Garrick in spite of "all his spirit and art" could not achieve the proper exuberance and romantic excess for the Bastard, while Sheridan, with the deep tones of his voice and the vehemence of his action, represented strikingly the turbulent and gloomy passions of the King; and his scene with Hubert in the third act moved not only Davies [23] but more important critics. At a command performance, ordered for the third night (December 23),[24] Sheridan "uncommonly" pleased the new king, George III,[25] regarded as quite an authority on King

[21] Garrick, *Private Correspondence,* II, 350. Since no clear proof of its date appears in its contents, this announcement may belong to the 1754–56 interlude when Sheridan was in England, except that *then* from the beginning, he claimed, he had plans to replace Barry at Covent Garden (see Ch. IX). His mention of two plays in the announcement would seem to provide a clue but yields only complexities. Brooke's *Earl of Essex,* not published until the winter of 1760–61, may have been one of the two; I have not identified the other.

[22] Lefanu, p. 102. Alicia's source for this quotation is not given, but if, as is likely, it was a remark passed down in the family for some sixty years, it is hardly verbatim.

[23] Davies, I, 300–301.   [24] *London Stage,* Pt. 4, pp. 831, 833.

[25] Although Sheridan's pension, bestowed less than two years later, was for his educational work rather than his acting, His Majesty doubtless recalled his pleasure with *King John,* when he approved Sheridan's pension among the first (*Thespian Dictionary,* v. "Sheridan, Thomas").

John and on acting. News of this royal preference reached Garrick, "who had been so accustomed to applause, and who of all men living most sensibly felt the neglect of it," so much so at this time that he is supposed to have canceled all future performances, although boxes had been sold for several evenings in advance; and, adds Davies, he "would never more permit the play to be acted." [26] Garrick, it would seem, had forgotten earlier honors bestowed on him that season when the king had commanded a performance in which he played Richard III, a role up to then played by the equally sensitive Sheridan three times without any command.[27] *King John* was, *The London Stage* shows, abandoned after December 23; but it was given once more on April 2, 1761, for Mrs. Yates's benefit, with Sheridan as the King and Garrick as the Bastard.[28]

Sheridan was successful this season in London, much more so than he had been five years earlier under Rich at Covent Garden. Johnson, writing to Bennett Langton on October 28, says that Sheridan, then playing Cato, had played Richard twice and had more of an audience the second night than the first.[29] He will make, Johnson believes, "a good figure on the whole," although his faults are many, the result both of "natural deficience" and of "laborious affectation." [30] Davies, speaking from firsthand observation, says that Garrick found Sheridan's presence a great advantage to him. "Little difference in the bulk of audiences was to be perceived when they acted separately, the part of Hamlet, or of Richard, or any other capital character. The manager himself owned that, except Barry, he had never found so able an assistant. . . . But," continues Davies, "Garrick's ruling passion was the love of fame; and his uneasiness, arising from the success of Sheridan, began every day to be more and more visible. However, he seemed for a time to suspend his jealousy, and promote every scheme proposed by Sheridan for their mutual profit." [31]

One of these schemes was the production of *The Earl of Essex*, perhaps one of the two plays which Sheridan described in his application. It had been successfully staged at Smock-Alley for years, and now for the first time it was brought to Drury Lane by Sheridan,

---

[26] Davies, I, 301.   [27] *London Stage*, Pt. 4, pp. 820–825.
[28] *Ibid.*, p. 853.
[29] Boswell, *Life of Samuel Johnson* (ed. Hill), I, 358 (October 18, 1760). Sheridan played Cato on October 18 and 21.
[30] *Ibid.*   [31] Davies, I, 293.

who had made "some judicious alterations" in it.[32] He played Essex and was "unexceptionably just almost to a degree of excellence" in several passages. One moment particularly brought applause from the usual critical audience: when ready to burst out with rage and resentment at the queen in Act III, Sheridan suppressed the anger and lowered his voice instead, to produce an especially tense and dramatic effect. And when he was led off to execution, "his tears were accompanied with manly sorrow" without the blubbering into which some actors were "incautiously betrayed." [33] This description by Davies is valuably firsthand; he acted Cecil in the play.[34]

Mrs. Sheridan, writing to Samuel Whyte in Dublin on February 26, 1761, just after the *Essex* run, reports that her husband "stands here in high reputation, with a prospect of being every day more and more esteemed." She may have had partly in mind the second course of elocutionary lectures which Sheridan was then preparing to give and publish, but mainly she was thinking of his theatrical success; for, she continues, "the late King's death, which shut up the Theatres for a time, together with the necessity the Managers were under of bringing on the stage five new pieces (Farces and Comedies) has prevented him appearing so often as it was expected; this, however, tho' it has a little curtailed his profit, has been no hindrance to his reputation, which stands very high in all the parts he has been seen in." [35] An actor on shares would suffer (as a salaried player would not) from an unexpected closing of the theater and from the competition of five new plays. As Mrs. Sheridan was writing, George Colman's new comedy, *The Jealous Wife*, which had opened two weeks earlier to "greater Applause than anything since the Suspicious Husband," was on its way to a twenty-night run (*Essex* had done nine nights). Garrick played the leading role.[36]

---

[32] *Ibid.,* p. 295. MacMillan, without mentioning Sheridan, says there is evidence that Garrick extensively revised if not rewrote the play for Drury Lane (p. 238). It ran for nine performances between January 3 and February 24, 1761 (*London Stage*, Pt. 4, pp. 835–845).

[33] Davies, I, 295–296. Davies, in writing of this year, tells of the *Essex* production as a sign of cooperation and follows it by his account of the *John* episode, which he makes appear the end of the union. But actually *John*, produced December 17, preceded *Essex*.

[34] *London Stage*, Pt. 4, p. 835.   [35] Whyte, p. 102.

[36] MacMillan, *Drury Lane Calendar*, pp. 81–84. The quotation about *The Jealous Wife* (*ibid.,* p. 81) is taken from Cross's Diary. See also *The London Stage*, Pt. 4, pp. 843–870.

Sheridan concluded his part in the 1760–61 season with *Othello* on April 30. He had played thirty-four times, in ten of his favorite roles, and had carried the tragedies much more than had Garrick. The two had joined forces in at least one other play besides *King John—The Fair Penitent*, where Sheridan had played Horatio and Garrick Lothario [37] as in the old Smock-Alley days of 1745–46. Successful as he had been this year, his arrangement with Garrick was not renewed for the following season. The royal opinion about King John, Davies observes, "contributed to dissolve the union between these rival actors: it was impossible they could longer continue in one theatre." Meetings to reconcile disagreements and end animosities were vain; "one could not bear an equal, nor the other a superior." [38] Garrick's jealousy here as revealed by his admirer Davies makes the jealousy ascribed to Sheridan by his Irish enemies pale in comparison. But the rivalry between these two onetime friends, although it bred ill feeling on occasions, may well have been exaggerated by contemporary reporters searching for the sensational. Garrick was to befriend Sheridan soon again; and Sheridan, who frequently attacked Garrick's acting and interpretation, responded unequivocally to Boswell's remark that the world thought Garrick a good tragic actor: "So do I, Sir; I think him the best I ever saw." [39]

This had been the judgment too of critic Charles Churchill some months before, although when Sheridan read it in Churchill's *Rosciad* his reaction may have been more mixed. During much of Sheridan's season at Drury Lane Churchill regularly sat in the front row of the pit for a better view of the players.[40] His satire, published in March of this season and destined to become the most popular poem since *The Dunciad*,[41] weighed the qualifications of contemporary actors to ascend the throne of Roscius. Churchill finds Sheridan "a doubtful name,/ As yet unsettled in the rank of Fame." Some concede him every merit; others, not one. *The Rosciad* steers a "middle course." Sheridan's conceptions are "natural and great," his feelings strong, his words forceful. But nature has been niggardly: his facial expression is fixed and glaring; his voice, deep and shrill by fits; his

[37] Davies, I, 296; Enthofen Collection Playbill for December 6, 1760; *London Stage*, Pt. 4, 825.

[38] Davies, I, 302.

[39] Boswell, *London Journal*, p. 136 (January 12, 1763).

[40] Davies, I, 306.

[41] Brown, *Charles Churchill*, p. 38. The poem went through eight editions before Churchill's death three years later.

actions, overactive. Yet with all these defects "his glories rise." The scene between King John and Hubert, which Davies admired so much, is singled out for high praise. And in general *The Rosciad's* judgment of him should have pleased more than hurt Sheridan, particularly when he considered the savagery with which his fellow actors were attacked. On the ascending scale to Roscius' chair he is ranked *next to the top*, just below Garrick and above Quin. Mossop and Barry had been dismissed before Quin, Mossop because of his ridiculous practice of emphasizing unimportant syllables, and Barry for being not only too light-voiced, but also derivative and over-studied. Unlike Samuel Johnson, who saw "laborious affectation" com-pounding Sheridan's natural deficiencies, Churchill concludes:

> Where he falls short, 'tis Nature's fault alone;
> Where he succeeds, the Merit's all his own.[42]

Yet Sheridan's satisfaction, diluted by the vivid account of his natural handicaps, must have been thinned still more by the picture of Gar-rick, which follows directly. Here we have the great genius who overrides all defects and seeming departures from nature to produce an effect both thrilling and natural. Garrick succeeds to the chair of Roscius.

A year and a half later (in 1763), Sheridan was to have one more experience—his last—of performing on Drury Lane stage and with Garrick. The occasion was unexpected. For almost two years he had been away from the theater, lecturing and publishing. Then his wife wrote a comedy.

Mrs. Sheridan's *Discovery* had been planned and almost finished during the summer of 1762, when she and the rest of the family were living again at that "unsociable place," Windsor.[43] The year before that she had surprised her world and, according to family legend, her husband by publishing an anonymous novel called *The Memoirs of Miss Sidney Bidulph*. Sheridan, the story goes, had known only that his wife was working on something "from which she expected benefit to her family"; [44] Mrs. Sheridan, with her usual self-effacement, had dropped her manuscript into a small trunk be-side her chair whenever her husband happened into the room where

[42] Churchill, *The Rosciad*, lines 663–702.

[43] In a letter of November 29, 1762, Mrs. Sheridan tells Whyte of writing *The Discovery* (Whyte, pp. 110–111). She had called Windsor "unsociable" in a December 2, 1759 letter (Whyte, p. 98).

[44] Lefanu, p. 109.

she was writing.[45] The success of this novel, modeled as it was on the works of "her master" and friend Samuel Richardson,[46] had been gratifying; it had run into a new edition within three months,[47] and it was republished often thereafter, O'Keeffe reporting that it was "more read and admired in Ireland" than any novel he ever heard of.[48]

It is probable that Sheridan knew about her next venture, her comedy, and, from his theatrical experience, was able to help her with it.[49] Back in town the next autumn, she showed it to some people there, and Garrick, who had got wind of it, "was pressing to see it."[50] By the end of November it was in rehearsal at Drury Lane, with Garrick playing the second character, Sir Anthony Branville, and Sheridan the first, Lord Medway, a man "of a graver cast, and a great deal of variety, and which requires a considerable actor to perform." Sheridan would not have appeared at all this season, Mrs. Sheridan continues to explain in a letter to Sam Whyte, "if my play could have been got up well without him, as he has been far from being well these two months past."[51] In this production both Garrick and Sheridan, coming together again after a cool parting, cooperated amicably. Garrick, especially, leaned over backward, offering Sheridan not only the main role but "the advantage of two nights profits, besides those of two more for the author."[52] The press notice for the first performance advertised a new overture, new music between the acts, the characters new dressed, and both a prologue and an epilogue.[53] Mrs. Sheridan's name was not mentioned; it was only with its publication that the play was announced even as "written by the Editor of Miss Sidney Bidulph."[54] About a month after its opening a new feature was added for several performances: after the play Sheridan recited "by particular Desire" Dryden's "Ode on the Power

---

[45] *Ibid.*   [46] *Ibid.*, p. 108. It was dedicated to Richardson.

[47] *Public Advertiser*, July 13, 1761.   [48] O'Keeffe, 1, 86.

[49] The speech indicated for her comic character Sir Anthony Branville shows pronunciations which Sheridan considered affectations: Chris-*ti*-an (Sheridan wanted Chris-chun); extra-or-dinary (Sheridan wanted an assimilation of the *a* before the *o*); pre-sum-*ed*; fa-mi-liar (Sheridan wanted elision and unstressed vowel). See Sheridan's *Dictionary* and Mrs. Sheridan's *Discovery*.

[50] Whyte, p. 111 (Mrs. Sheridan's letter of November 29, 1762). Mrs. Sheridan herself read the play to Garrick.

[51] *Ibid.*, pp. 111–112.   [52] Davies, 1, 302.

[53] *Public Advertiser*, February 3, 1763.   [54] *Ibid.*, February 10, 1763.

of Music," [55] a piece which had become very popular in his elocution lectures.

Two firsthand reports of the play's opening night, on February 3, give two opposite reactions. Boswell, up temporarily from his sickbed and dressed against the cold in "two pair of stockings, two shirts, and a greatcoat," [56] was in no mood to enjoy the production for another reason too: the Sheridans, at one time his close friends, had mortally offended him just before this by rejecting the prologue which he had written for this very play at Mrs. Sheridan's solicitation. Sheridan had disliked it, preferring one by his wife.[57] Now, sitting in the pit as the curtain rose, Boswell and his lively companions kept up a "clever enough chat" while the prologue was spoken, although he admits to feeling "a little pain." The play itself "acted heavily," but was "allowed to jog through" because he felt he could not join in the "damnation" which his friend Dempster proposed. Goldsmith, sitting behind Boswell, said "many smart acrimonious things." [58] A month earlier Boswell had spent an evening at the Sheridans' home, listening to the two of them read *The Discovery* alternately to a pleasant gathering of friends. He had "liked it much and was well entertained." That was when he was expecting to write the prologue.[59]

O'Keeffe thoroughly enjoyed the opening performance of *The Discovery*. Garrick's "great laugh-exciting point was speaking the most impassioned speeches with a calm voice and placid face." His dress was fantastical, and his acting made such an impression on young O'Keeffe that years later he could call to mind "his first coming on, at the near entrance at the right hand." Sheridan, as Lord Medway, was dressed in a full suit of crimson velvet. The play, O'Keeffe concludes, "gave great delight, and the success was perfect." [60] Others recalled Garrick's uncharacteristic acting and unusual interpretation in this play—his unwonted woodenness and his "immoveable Face." [61] Davies felt that he "either did not, or would not, understand the idea of the author," but adds that he pleased the public in the part,[62]

---

[55] *Ibid.*, March 9, 1763, and following issues.

[56] Boswell, *London Journal*, p. 176 (February 3, 1763).

[57] *Ibid.*, pp. 150–152 (January 18, 1763).   [58] *Ibid.*, pp. 176–178.

[59] *Ibid.*, p. 113 (n. 5).   [60] O'Keeffe, I, 86.   [61] Victor, *History*, III, 49.

[62] Davies, I, 303. The year Garrick left the stage, Davies adds, a command performance called for *The Discovery* with Garrick as Sir Anthony.

so much so that Sheridan in the major role made little impression by contrast.

Despite the disapproval of Boswell and his friends the play ran for a highly satisfactory total of seventeen nights. Sheridan acted on sixteen of these; and the run included a command performance (which must have delighted the Sheridans) and not two but three benefits for the author.[63] Also highly gratifying to the Sheridans must have been the rivalry between the two Dublin theaters to be the first to produce *The Discovery* in Ireland. At victorious Smock-Alley Mossop's production, got up in two days, proved a less satisfactory performance, although Baddeley as Sir Anthony Branville was acclaimed. Barry, at Crow-Street, gave his actors more time and even went so far as to have a new scene or two painted for the play.[64] It is unlikely that Mrs. Sheridan made any money from these Dublin performances, but they kept the family name before the Irish public in a desirable way and might even have made a few more Dubliners regret the loss of the talented Sheridans (although Mrs. Sheridan was the last person to indulge in petty or spiteful feelings).

Sheridan's appearance in *The Discovery* was to end his acting on Drury Lane stage, and also his connection with Drury Lane Theater until he returned fifteen years later, after Garrick's retirement, to help his son Richard Sheridan with the management. Before this arrangement with Richard he had one other acting season in London—in 1775–76 at Covent Garden—and for two summers (1769 and 1770) he appeared at Foote's theater in the Haymarket.

BUT HIS great successes were not in London; they were in Dublin, where he returned again and again, often in response to a desperate manager who regarded Sheridan as the one way to save his theater from the ruinous competition of a rival. Often the desperate manager was a former enemy of Sheridan's. Barry, who had ruined him

[63] But Sheridan seems to have had neither of the two benefits promised, according to Davies, by Garrick (MacMillan, *Drury Lane Calendar*, 1762–63; *London Stage*, Pt. 4, pp. 976–991). Genest says, probably mistakenly, that the sixteenth night was for Sheridan's benefit (v, 21). A last performance on April 26 was given without Sheridan, Love replacing him as Lord Medway.

[64] From an unidentified magazine giving "Theatrical Intelligence" in the New York Public Library Theatre Collection. The date line is Dublin, March 29. On March 14, at Mossop's benefit, the farce *Sir Anthony in Love* had been taken from Mrs. Sheridan's *Discovery*. Whatever merit it might have had was due to the original piece (*ibid.*).

four years earlier, was forced to ask him back for the 1763–64 season at Crow-Street; and Sheridan, himself desperate for money, was forced to accept. In 1767, after his two-year exile in France and the tragically unexpected death of his wife there, Sheridan again responded to Barry's plea to save Crow-Street,[65] but this time with less success. After Barry gave up the next season, Sheridan signed with Mossop for three nights in May 1768; Mossop, who had left Sheridan's Smock-Alley in a huff many years before, now had—for the moment—a monopoly over the Dublin theater; but he apparently felt it desirable to have Sheridan appear, although, according to reports, he refused to act with him.[66]

In all three of these Dublin engagements Sheridan's main concern was elsewhere. Each time he was working to get a course of lectures started or intending to give a course after he completed his theatrical commitments or—at last in 1767–68—actually giving lectures on the art of reading and an Attic Evening with instrumental performers for the first time in Dublin.[67] His three acting nights at Mossop's theater came at the end of this busy winter of lecturing.

Yet, for all these efforts on the lecture platform, Sheridan was more successful on the Dublin stage, where his popularity was always remarkably high. During his first month with Barry, on his first return (in 1763) after his ruin, he had three command performances [68]—the only actor to have any; and throughout the rest of the season commands for his appearance were flatteringly frequent. That season, acting on shares, Sheridan earned about £863 (Woffington's top salary during Sheridan's monopoly had been £800). Incidentally, the range of profits on individual nights had been enormous: a January production of *The Provoked Wife* (this had been by command)

---

[65] In 1766 Sheridan was able to return to Dublin because of an Irish parliamentary act for the relief of insolvent debtors, passed in June 1766, while he was still in Blois. With much pains and some risk to himself, Samuel Whyte, who was one of his creditors, succeeded in getting the absent Sheridan's name included under the provisions of the bill—all without Sheridan's knowledge (Whyte, pp. 27–28; 32ff; 82–83).

[66] *Ibid.*, p. 87.   [67] From *Dublin Journal* notices for the season.

[68] As Hamlet, on November 11, 1763; as Richard III on November 17; and as Shore on November 26 (from *Dublin Journal* notices). Supporting him were Mrs. Fitzhenry, who had had a hand in his 1758 ruin, and Mrs. Dancer, who became Mrs. Barry. On his first appearance Lady Northumberland, wife of the viceroy, paid him a singular compliment; she "stood up in her box, upon which all the ladies present followed her example, and welcomed Mr. Sheridan by the very unusual and marked tribute of personal applause" (Lefanu, pp. 244–245).

had brought him fourteen shillings; his most profitable evening had been his own benefit performance as Hamlet, which had netted him £94.[69]

Although Sheridan appeared on the Dublin stage during eight out of the fourteen seasons from 1763–77, the most interesting period is from 1771–73, a time which may be explored in more detail as both typical of Sheridan's experiences as a Dublin star actor and historically interesting because of several unusual events.

Sheridan came to Dublin in the fall of 1771 from Bath, where, the season before, he had been tutoring and giving his oratorical readings. The opportunity to return to Ireland had seemed more promising for several reasons; and, leaving his now adult children in Bath, he went back in October to appear at Crow-Street Theater with William Dawson. The winter before, Dawson had started up a competition with Mossop, renting Stretch's little theater in Capel-Street which "had for many years been shut up, and appropriated to other uses." [70] He flourished so surprisingly there that Mossop had been forced to relinquish to him Crow-Street, with its title of Theatre-Royal. By spring 1771 Mossop had had to give up entirely, leaving Smock-Alley under the management of his friend Thomas Ryder.[71] In the fall of 1771 Macklin came over to Dublin to help Dawson manage Crow-Sreet, and it was here under his old antagonist Macklin that Sheridan had engaged with Dawson to perform in November

[69] Whyte, p. 78. Sheridan, debt-ridden from 1758, had been enabled to return to Ireland in 1763 by a Letter of License from a majority of his creditors. Through this arrangement half of his total earnings for the season—£431 —was due on his debts, but by strict economy he had been able to increase this amount to £643. For himself he had reserved only £112 to cover food, lodging, a servant, and necessary costumes; the remaining £107 he had sent to Mrs. Sheridan, whose second comedy, *The Dupe*, had failed miserably at Drury Lane in December—a great disappointment to both. Despite Sheridan's obvious efforts, his economy, and his plan to start his Course of Lectures in May, a number of his creditors arranged for his arrest at the end of his Crow-Street engagement and forced him to flee to England and eventually to France. Whyte blames "his quondam printer" whom Watkins and others assume to be Faulkner, but, aside from other indications against this (see under "Sheridan, Thomas" in the *Thespian Dictionary*, the story of how Faulkner canceled Sheridan's debts at about this time), Faulkner had been selling tickets to Sheridan's coming lectures. For the name of another printer who was connected with Smock-Alley and who may be the true villain, see Smock-Alley Calendar, Pt. 1, April 21, 1749. Sheridan's debt at this time is estimated as "upwards of 7,000*l*" (Whyte, pp. 79–80).

[70] Hitchcock, ii, 170; O'Keeffe, i, 165–167.   [71] Stockwell, pp. 135–137.

and December for six nights, playing Cato, Hamlet, Richard III, and Lear.[72]

This kind of short-term contract was customary for Sheridan. Usually at the end of it a notice that this was the last night of Sheridan's performing brought overflow crowds; and then the contract was renewed, sometimes with the announcement of a subscription series. As Garrick had found in the 1745–46 season at Smock-Alley, it was advantageous to stay on in response to popular demand.

Sheridan arrived late in October to find many of the Crow-Street performers familiar to him, some happily, others not so happily. Macklin was his costar among the men, Mrs. Lee his leading lady. With neither had he last parted on good terms; Macklin, ever since Sheridan discharged him from Smock-Alley some twenty years earlier, had missed no opportunity to deride him publicly, and Mrs. Lee had probably not forgiven him for his treatment of her and her husband fifteen years before. More pleasant must have been the sight of Tottenham Heaphy and "O'Blunder" Sparks. New to him was Heaphy's son-in-law, a young actor named Keeffe, or O'Keeffe, a future writer of recollections in which the Dublin stage and Sheridan would be much admired.

At the rival Smock-Alley, which Macklin vainly expected to collapse to his and Dawson's benefit,[73] a Mr. and Mrs. Jackson sustained Manager Ryder, playing both in comedy and tragedy; Walker's *Hibernian Magazine* for this year reports Smock-Alley as "greatly on the decline." [74] Sheridan found much to criticize in both. After acting three nights at Crow-Street, from November 25 to December 4, he wrote to his son Richard at Bath that the Dublin stage was in a most deplorable condition, two wretched theaters driving each other into starvation by their opposition. "I chose the least bad of them," he continued; "and, wretched as they are, it has had no effect on my nights, numbers having been turned away every time I played, and the receipts have been larger than when I had Barry, his wife, and Mrs. FitzHenry to play with me." Sheridan adds that he doesn't expect this prosperity to last long, since with such miserable material he could hardly "get up" enough plays. He plans "to

---

[72] Announcement in *Dublin Journal,* November 21–23, 1771, and following issues.

[73] Stockwell, p. 138, who quotes from Macklin's letter to his daughter given in Kirkman's *Memoirs of Macklin,* ii, 396.

[74] Walker's *Hibernian Magazine,* December 1771.

have done the week after next, and apply vigorously to the material point" which had brought him to Dublin. All ranks and parties, he finds, are eager to advance his scheme, which he thinks will be carried in parliament unopposed.[75]

The success which Sheridan reported of himself to Richard was unquestionable and typical; and the deplorable state of the Dublin stage was likewise familiar news all through this and the preceding decade. As Sheridan had predicted and as he shows here, two miserable theaters were almost always opposing and starving each other. If one, at great cost, succeeded and forced the other to close, it held its monopoly briefly; another rival would rent a vacant theater and start up undeterred. And then the same cycle, so ruinous to those involved, would repeat itself.

With Barry, Brown, Woodward, Mossop, and himself all thus obviously ruined, Sheridan must have felt that the lesson he had preached in 1758 had at last been sufficiently demonstrated to the Dublin public. The "material point" which, as he reminds Richard, had brought him over to Ireland seems to have been this time not educational but theatrical. During this season, in contrast to earlier ones, his name appears nowhere in any elocutionary or educational plans. He seems, for the time, to have given these up and to have returned to Dublin expressly to accomplish something with the stage. "I am perpetually asked," Richard writes to his father from Bath, "when Mr. Sheridan is to have his patent for the theatre, which all the Irish here take for granted, and I often receive a great deal of information from them on the subject . . . the folks here regret you, as one that is to be fixed in another kingdom." And the children are often asked, Richard adds, whether they have not had the letter calling them over.[76]

What Sheridan planned to do first was to arouse the public, by now "heartily tired" of theatrical rivalry,[77] into accepting the idea of a theatrical monopoly. His *Humble Appeal to the Public*, a ninety-one-page pamphlet first published in 1758 when he was fighting Barry and the new Crow-Street building, was brought out sometime before the new year (in a revised edition dated 1771) and retitled *An Appeal to the Public, containing an account of the rise, progress, and establishment of the first regular theatre in Dublin, with the causes of its decline and ruin.* About thirty pages of now outdated

---

[75] Quoted in Moore, I, 59–60 (Letter of December 7, 1771). The earlier period mentioned was 1763–64 at Crow-Street.

[76] Moore, I, 61 (Letter of February 29 [1772]).   [77] Hitchcock, II, 213.

material were eliminated. But the main section of the earlier pamphlet contrasting the theater before and after Sheridan came to manage Smock-Alley was kept, with its emphasis on his contributions to the stage and its arguments against two theaters in Dublin.

It must have been no surprise, then, to anyone when Mr. Sheridan was invited to address a meeting at the request "of several persons of distinction" to consider what should be done to save the stage. His speech, published on February 25, 1772, as *Mr. Sheridan's Speech Addressed to a Number of Gentlemen with a View of considering the best Means to establish one good Theatre in this City*, made the main point that now "no actor of consequence, or person of property," would dare undertake even a united theater, so great was the financial burden, and so clear had been the lesson pointed by the ruin of recent managers. He himself would never think of it, without assurances that the same thing might not happen again. Reiterating his argument that in London and even in smaller provincial cities acts of parliament limited the number of theaters, Sheridan concluded that the situation could be saved *only by an act of legislation*. The people who had called the meeting, he added, wanted to form a society for the establishment of a good stage in Dublin; they hoped to choose a committee, raise a petition, and address parliament. His plan for the best theater "in the British dominions," which he promised to present to the committee, was not revealed, but it probably included some kind of government subsidy.[78]

Almost before Sheridan had pronounced these words, the old controversy had started up again. Dublin newspapers immediately printed the opposition's plea to all enemies of monopoly and oppression, asking them to suspend judgment for a few days, when a candid account would persuade them of the dangers to come if "the Bill, now framing, relative to the Stage, meet with the smallest Encouragement from Parliament."[79]

Nevertheless, a society was formed to pursue Sheridan's suggestions; several meetings were held[80] and a petition materialized. Parchment copies were distributed in coffeehouses, clubs, et cetera,

---

[78] Sheridan, *Mr. Sheridan's Speech*, pp. 1, 14, 16, 21.

[79] *Dublin Journal*, February 27–29, 1772. This "candid account" was probably the pamphlet published under the title *An Appeal to the Public Against Mr. Sheridan's Reviv'd Scheme for a Monopoly of the Stage*. The first few words here reproduce those in Sheridan's title for an obvious purpose.

[80] The March 3–5 *Dublin Journal* announces that a meeting of the Stage Society is to be held at Mr. Bardin's Hotel in College-Green, March 8 at twelve o'clock.

where society members were to solicit signatures.[81] At the same time another petition to parliament was being prepared in the Crow-Street Theater by Crow-Street subscribers called together there to stop "an Invasion against their Right and their Property, by the intended Monopoly." This petition, unanimously agreed to, sought especially to defend the property of "Spranger Barry, Esq. against the Invasion intended by Thomas Sheridan, Player." [82] The invidious contrast between *Esquire* and *Player* could hardly have been approved by Barry, still nominally the Crow-Street owner but now in England and "incapable from infirmities" [83] largely induced, it would seem, by his Crow-Street experiences. A few months before this, James Wilder, who had had such acclaim under Sheridan's management in the old days, had been imploring public support at his Smock-Alley benefit to save his "all," about to be attached by the sheriff because he had rashly underwritten a theatrical debt of Mossop's.[84] Mossop himself had been arrested for debt in England, "on the very Eve of his Return" to Ireland.[85]

While Crow-Street subscribers were meeting to defeat "Thomas Sheridan, Player," Sheridan was increasing his successes at their theater. He had renewed his engagement [86] (despite his plans to quit in December). In February The Theatrical Chronicle in Walker's *Hibernian Magazine* congratulated Dawson for having engaged Sheridan, "from whom the town has received much pleasure." We have seen, The Chronicle continues, some of Shakespeare's fullest plays most elegantly dressed; although Sheridan could have used a capital actress, Mrs. Lee is one of the "best second-rate" performers; and—greatest improvement of all—one actor did not have to play several parts in one play! [87] This season, for the first time, the notices make much of Sheridan's reappearance in popular old roles.[88] One great night, given for Dawson's benefit, starred Sheridan as Othello and Macklin as Iago,[89] their only production of *Othello* this season

---

[81] *Ibid.*, February 27–29, 1772.   [82] *Ibid.*, March 5–7 and 7–10, 1772.

[83] From Macklin's letter to his daughter, quoted by Stockwell, p. 138 (see footnote 73 above).

[84] *Dublin Journal*, December 14–17, 1771.

[85] *Ibid.*, November 7–9 and 14–16, 1771.

[86] Announced *ibid.*, January 11–14, 1772. He planned to appear in a Shakespeare series of six plays, with wax illumination as in the old days.

[87] Walker's *Hibernian Magazine*, February 1772.

[88] *Dublin Journal*, January 28–30 and April 11–14, 1772.

[89] Advertised for February 5 *ibid.*, January 18–21, 1772.

and the only time these two actors played together. No wonder crowds were turned away!

An occasion that must have touched as well as flattered Sheridan was the performance of *Cato* by the children of Samuel Whyte's grammar school [90]—a performance which The Theatrical Chronicle calls beyond conception: "To begin with Cato, (Master Whyte), he appeared so close a copy of Sheridan, that I, and almost every person present, supposed he had been instructed by that actor," but he had never had a lesson from that gentleman nor seen him in the part more than once or twice. "Is it too much to suppose," The Chronicle asks, "that the child follows nature, and that in this character Sheridan and nature are one and the same?" Headmaster Samuel Whyte, Sheridan's lifelong disciple and admirer, may have assisted nature here.[91]

This winter in Ireland was the worst in the memory of anyone living; never had there been such distress, with prices and taxes soaring and trade and manufactures dwindling.[92] Against these conditions Sheridan's success on Crow-Street stage was even more notable. It was not, unfortunately, paralleled in parliament. Here the hard times may have had more effect, making theatrical distress and theatrical improvement seem unimportant. But to Sheridan and his future they were hardly unimportant. Although pressing reasons required his presence in Bath, he stayed on in Dublin even after his Shakespeare series ended in March. The crucial petition was to come up in the May term and perhaps his influence would be useful to counteract the growing opposition to it. While he was waiting, he played six more times at Crow-Street, either for some fellow actor's benefit or "by particular Desire." [93] But in parliament the May term came and went without action on the theatrical question. On June 1 [94]

[90] On December 24, 1771, in Capel-Street Theater (*ibid.*, December 26–28, 1771).

[91] So successful was the performance that the children repeated the tragedy by popular demand in Crow-Street Theater, where Sheridan himself was acting. Dawson and his company were reported as giving them every assistance (*Hibernian Magazine*, January 1772).

[92] See *Dublin Journal* items: December 11–14, 1771; January 9–11 and March 10–14, 1772.

[93] *Dublin Journal* notices up to his last performance on May 22. Since he was no longer manager, he had given up his practice of not appearing in actor's benefits.

[94] *Hibernian Journal*, June 3–5, 1772: "The Le Despencer Packet-Boat sailed for Holyhead, with Thomas Sheridan, Esq."

Sheridan, beaten once more by circumstance and public indifference, sailed for England and Bath to deal at last with Richard's elopement with Elizabeth Linley.

This event had occurred in March, when Sheridan was at his busiest in Dublin both with his Shakespeare series and his petition. At another time he might have hurried back, but now the future of his children as well as himself must have seemed to depend upon his presence in Ireland. He had kept in touch with his family as best he could, writing to his other son, Charles Francis, in mid-May that he had just heard "of Dick's safe return from France with Mr. and Miss L[inley] and was well enough reconciled to the part he [Richard] had taken in the affair." Charles, writing this to his uncle Chamberlaine, wonders how his father will take the more recent news of Dick's duel with Mathews,[95] fought on May 4 in the Castle Tavern in London, where Henrietta and Bedford Streets join,[96] almost on the same spot where the Sheridan family had lived for years before Mrs. Sheridan's death.

Sheridan had left the Dubliners all agog over Richard. They had known of the Linleys for some time, and, as recently as May 24, Crow-Street, subtly taking advantage of Dublin's interest, two days after Sheridan's last performance there had advertised *The Royal Merchant* with "Music composed by Mr. Lindley of Bath." [97] Elizabeth Linley's name had been spread everywhere by Foote's comedy brought out in London just a year earlier. Dubliners knew the "Plan of *The Maid of Bath*" a month after the play's London debut through an article in Walker's *Hibernian Magazine*.[98] During the summer after Sheridan left, letters from Bath in Dublin newspapers kept people informed of the latest developments. News of Dick's second duel was written off to Dublin the same day it happened: "Young Sheridan and Captain Mathews of this Town, who lately had a Rencounter in a Tavern in London upon Account of the Maid of Bath, Miss Linley, have had another this Morning upon Kingsdown, about four Miles hence." [99] Richard's wounds were reported;

---

[95] Quoted in Rae, I, 186.   [96] Sichel, I, 364–365.

[97] *Dublin Journal*, May 19–24, 1772.

[98] *Hibernian Magazine*, July 1771. The play itself, *The Maid of Bath*, seems not to have been performed in Dublin until more than two years later on November 19, 1773, with Foote, who was acting at the time at Ryder's Smock-Alley with Sheridan. Advertised as never performed here (*Dublin Journal*, November 11–13, 1773), the performance must have been quite unpleasant for the Maid's new father-in-law.

[99] *Dublin Journal*, July 9–11, 1772.

by July 16 he was not expected to recover; by July 20 he was declared out of danger.[100] In the meantime, Dubliners were reassured that "nothing criminal passed between Mr. Sheridan and the Maid of Bath, in their late Tour to France: that Mr. Sheridan (the young Gentleman said to be killed in a Duel with Captain Mathews) at every Place they put up, requested the Land-lady's Company, and took Care to have Miss Linley constantly provided with a Female Bedfellow." [101] Richard had not been in Ireland since he was eight years old, but his father's reputation for respectability had been maintained against the stiffest opposition from people who would now be saying that Richard's elopement was what might be expected from a player's son. When Richard married Elizabeth Linley the next year in violation of his promise to his father, Thomas Sheridan practically disowned him. Although he himself had once used Elizabeth Linley as his principal singer in his Attic Entertainments, Sheridan's disappointment at his son's alliance with the somewhat less than respectable Linley family [102] can be understood best in the light of his past.

After a feverish summer involving Richard's duel and wounds, the recent appointment of Charles as secretary to the British envoy in Sweden,[103] and many changes of plans for the two girls, Sheridan returned to Dublin in the autumn of 1772, having permanently given up his house in Bath and having decided to take his daughters to Ireland with him.[104]

[100] *Ibid.*, July 9–11 and July 14–16, 1772. *Hibernian Journal*, July 13–15 and 17–20, 1772.

[101] *Dublin Journal*, July 11–14, 1772.

[102] Miss Linley sang in the Attic Entertainments at Bath in November 1770. The *Bath Chronicle*, November 22, 1770, advertises for Simpson's Concert Room "First Attic Entertainment, consisting of Reading and Singing: The Reading Part by Mr. Sheridan; Singing by Miss Linley." Biographers of Richard have sneered at Thomas Sheridan, player, for objecting to Richard's marriage to a singer. But romantic perspective has blurred their vision to the social differences between the two families: between the literary, well-bred Mrs. Sheridan and the vulgar Mrs. Linley; between the protected Sheridan girls and the Linley sisters, who were public performers, and so on. Such distinctions, mattering less today, would mean much to Thomas Sheridan; but particularly the notoriety which inspired Foote's comedy, and then resulted from it, would have been the stumbling block.

[103] *DNB*, *v.* "Sheridan, Charles Francis."

[104] *Dublin Journal*, September 29–October 1, 1772: "Thomas Sheridan, Esq; and his two Daughters . . . arrived [September 29] in the Bessborough Packet from Holyhead." In the same issue, "[George] Grenville, Esq; and his

But he did not return to Dawson's Crow-Street. Dawson had re-garded Sheridan's parliamentary efforts as a threat to himself and his theater-royal; [105] so Sheridan threw his weight to Ryder of Smock-Alley, stepping out on the stage of his old theater [106] for the first time in fifteen years. The effect on the theater was as usual. Described by Sheridan the year before as the worse off of the two, it began to improve, while Dawson's Crow-Street went into a decline. Smock-Alley's gross for the season was £15,402—more than Sheridan ever took in as manager; and the costs (£30 a night) were lower. [107] Sheridan performances yielded him £1,365 [108]—more by £500 than he had made with Barry nine years before. But while figures of Sheridan's income on various visits to Dublin provide interesting statistics, more impressive of his continued appeal is this fact: his presence revived a dying Dublin theater; his departure sank a flourishing one.

THE FOLLOWING summer (1773) is noteworthy because of Sheridan's unprecedented expedition to Cork and Limerick to act on the pro-vincial stages there. This move must have been made with mis-givings. For the first time he was to perform in "country theaters" (Dublin and Edinburgh, where he had acted briefly in the summer of 1764, were capital cities)—a step down which might expose him to the sneering label of "itinerant actor." The respectable place barely won for the eighteenth-century gentleman-actor could be endangered if he wandered into the smaller towns. Years later Alicia Lefanu felt obliged to defend her grandfather's reputation here by stressing the respect with which he was treated everywhere on this journey, being entertained by the leading persons of the county and even invited to join the Trinity College dining club in Cork. Her concluding remark is especially interesting: "Those who reflect upon the little prejudices entertained by the aristocracy of the provinces far more than of the

---

Brother . . . arrived [September 28] on the Hillsborough Packet from Holy-head."

[105] Dawson, in apologizing for his early benefit (November), complains that he has had "uncommon Disappointments" from performers engaged and from schemes to ruin his company and the property of Mr. Barry (*ibid.*, November 26–28, 1772).

[106] On November 9. He played "by particular Desire" his favorite role, Hamlet (*ibid.*, November 3–5, 1772).

[107] Snagg, p. 83.

[108] *Ibid.* Faulkner gives the figure as over £1,400 (Garrick, *Private Corre-spondence*, I, 580).

capital, against common theatrical performers, will at once perceive, by this distinguished compliment, that Mr. Sheridan was held in quite a different light." [109]

The theater-royal in Cork, which had been built in 1760 by Crow-Street's manager, Spranger Barry, was, like the Limerick playhouse, designed to be a summer theater for the Dublin company; and the Cork house had proved profitable, often making up the winter's losses. [110] For some time now its management had been under Heaphy, who had persuaded Sheridan to make this summer trip. [111] Sheridan may have been more easily swayed because for the first time, with his educational and oratorical plans abandoned, he had nothing else to do.

Corkonians showed their appreciation of Sheridan's decision by giving him an appropriate welcome. His arrival was announced as the first news item in the *Hibernian Chronicle*. [112] When Corkonians were "to be favoured with Mr. Sheridan's Appearance . . . in *Hamlet*," the *Chronicle* reprinted the "celebrated Soliloquy on Death" as it was directed to be pronounced in a book some would know, *The Art of Speaking*. The first three lines of "To be or not to be . . ." were to be spoken with anxiety, the fourth with courage and deep thoughtfulness, and so on. [113] Corkonians who had prepared themselves for the performance by practicing these lines would be most eager to watch Sheridan's interpretation. But some saw him only intermittently. After the play a letter from "A Frequenter of the Pit" complains that the Macaroni headdresses of the ladies, with their high hair and hats cocked up behind, had so much intercepted the view that "we got but few peeps at Mr. Sheridan." [114] Cork ladies, unlike Dublin ladies, apparently sat in the pit. And, since women of these days did not remove their hats in the theater, they were now urged to leave their hats at home when they meant to go into the pit.

After nine acting nights in Cork Sheridan went on to Limerick,

[109] Lefanu, p. 353.   [110] Flynn, *Random Recollections*, p. 7.
[111] Lefanu, p. 355.   [112] *Hibernian Chronicle*, June 7, 1773.
[113] *Ibid.*, June 10, 1773. For most Irishmen *The Art of Speaking* (1762, ascribed to James Burgh, who ran an academy at Stoke-Newington) must have meant Samuel Whyte's edition of this work, published in Dublin in 1763. With a quotation from Sheridan's *Lectures on Elocution* on the title page and with evidence of his influence on many other pages, *The Art of Speaking* was an appropriate book to call to Corkonians' attention.
[114] *Hibernian Chronicle*, June 14, 1773.

touring the Killarney lakes along the way with his two daughters, who had come along for the jaunt.[115] In Limerick he rejoined Heaphy and the company. Heaphy, knowing "that it was against Mr. Sheridan's general rule to perform in country theatres," had not mentioned Limerick when he engaged Sheridan for Cork, but he had cajoled him later by insisting that ruin would follow if he had Sheridan at one and not the other city.[116]

But the Limerick engagement was not so rewarding. Although the theater there had been built more recently, in 1770, under Heaphy's auspices, it was far from impressive. A carriagemaker had the front of it as a workshop and showroom; and for some time box-ticket holders had to pass through Mr. Gubbins' kitchen to get to their seats.[117] Yet a news item in the *Limerick Chronicle* reports that *Cato* was performed to a very crowded audience, and never were "so many lovely Eyes dissolved in tears." [118] Limerick theatergoers got their money's worth: a performance of *Julius Caesar* included a grand procession of lictors, trophies, et cetera, and was accompanied by an occasional interlude called *The Debating Society*, also by the farce of *The Apprentice*, singing and dancing, "Bucks Have at Ye All" recited by Mr. Lewis, and a paraphrase on Shakespeare's Seven Ages given by Mr. Keeffe.[119] Although "the whole of the money taken in Limerick that season was £548.7.6," [120] Sheridan had had a profitable summer, adding more than £700 [121] to the £1,365 he had reaped during the winter at Smock-Alley. An income of almost £2,100 for acting a year in Ireland must have set the record up to that time.

ONE MORE of Sheridan's acting seasons is historically important: the winter at Covent Garden in 1775–76 with Harris. When he had returned to Dublin from Limerick, he had continued at Ryder's Smock-Alley for the less successful year of 1773–74. Illness had kept him generally incapacitated until mid-January and he had played only through early March. Back in England by the next year, he did no acting for the first season since his return from Blois. He published, instead, his two-volume *Lectures on the Art of Reading*.[122]

---

[115] Lefanu, p. 354.   [116] *Ibid.*, pp. 355–356.   [117] Lenihan, p. 364.
[118] *Limerick Chronicle*, August 9, 1773.   [119] *Ibid.*, August 12, 1773.
[120] Snagg, p. 93.
[121] Garrick, *Private Correspondence*, 1, 580 (Letter of George Faulkner).
[122] See *Public Advertiser* notices, February and May 1775. Part the First, on the art of reading prose, seems to have been issued on February 15; the Second Part, on the art of reading verse, on May 10 in another volume.

The next autumn his appearance in *Cato* on October 21, 1775, marked his first appearance at Covent Garden in fourteen years.[123] Richard, writing to Mr. Linley, remarks with surprise, "My father was astonishingly well received on Saturday night in Cato." [124] After this, Sheridan played more regularly than he had for several years— on an average of almost once a week until his benefit on March 5, 1776. His son's play *The Duenna,* which ran seventy-five nights on the same stage, may have reduced the number of his performances and therefore his profits, although he could not have failed to be gratified by the competition it gave Drury Lane. Garrick's frenzy is reflected in the changes he tried to draw the crowds from Covent Garden. His most popular roles were offered—Abel Drugger, Hamlet, Archer. The peak of the rivalry came when, on January 20, Garrick revived Mrs. Sheridan's *Discovery* to compete with *The Duenna,* he himself playing his old role of Sir Anthony Branville. This amused the London public, who called the rivalry between *The Duenna* and Garrick "the Old Woman against the Old Man"; but Sheridan was so disgusted by Garrick's lack of taste that he forbade his daughters to see the Drury Lane production of their mother's play.[125] At one time during this season of 1775–76 London playgoers could hardly avoid the Sheridans, go where they would: if to Drury Lane, they encountered the wife's comedy; if to Covent Garden, they saw the father or listened to the son's beguiling words. What other family of the time could claim such a display?

Sheridan turned out to be the leading actor at Covent Garden this winter, although Barry, who was also there, might have been intended to outrank him. During October and November he and Barry appeared together as an old team in several plays; but after this Barry was indisposed for some months [126] and Sheridan took over the main tragic roles, including King John—the part that had caused the

---

[123] Although his appearance is advertised as his first at Covent Garden for sixteen years, I have given the fourteen-year figure because he appeared there once in 1761 at a benefit performance in December (see *London Stage,* Pt. 4, pp. 1,921 and 909).

[124] Moore, I, 165. (He adds, "I think it will not be many days before we are reconciled.")

[125] Lefanu, p. 224.

[126] Barry and Sheridan appeared together in *Venice Preserved, Tamerlane,* and *The Fair Penitent;* Barry seems not to have acted from about mid-November to mid-January. An announcement on a December 19 playbill says, "Mr. Barry still continues indisposed" (British Museum Playbills).

rift with Garrick years ago. For his benefit, on March 5, he performed in his first comedy of the season, *The Double Dealer*, "carefully revised and corrected by expunging the exceptionable passages."[127] The alterations here were probably his. *The Thespian Dictionary*, reviewing Sheridan's career as an actor, rather underestimates this year's activities when it says that in 1776 he acted "several nights" at Covent Garden.[128]

This same work mistakenly puts a period to Sheridan's acting at this point by stating, "After this he never performed again as an actor." By June 15, after his strenuous Covent Garden engagement, he had made the exhausting trip to Ireland and was acting in Crow-Street, now also under Ryder's management. During that same summer (of 1776) he repeated his Cork-Limerick expedition, but not so agreeably. The following season (1776–77) he performed twenty-two nights at Crow-Street from November to March, with his drawing power still remarkable, as Whyte's statistics show,[129] although financially this season did not quite reach his peak winter with Ryder four years before.

Sheridan was fifty-seven years old. For the first time there are references to a decline in his dramatic powers, particularly from The Dramatic Censor, who as regular theatrical critic for *Freeman's Journal* represents an innovation in Dublin newspapers. Full of praise for Sheridan's propriety and elegant dress, The Censor has only one fault to find with many Sheridan performances: he was "too old for the character" of Essex; he was "not quite young enough for Lady Touchwood's gallant"; he made everyone present wish "Hamlet a few years younger."[130] Sheridan had for some time given up such youthful parts as Romeo. After four months of The Censor's criticism, he not surprisingly appeared as *Old* Norval in *Douglas* for the first time.[131] This was, appropriately, his last new role in what turned out to be his last year of acting. The final theatrical performance of his life, on March 14, 1777, was aptly constituted, pointing backward with his most successful role of Hamlet and ahead to his activities of the 1780's with a recitation "by Desire" of a work which his readings

---

[127] *London Stage*, Pt. 4, p. 1,957.

[128] *Thespian Dictionary*, v. "Sheridan, Thomas."   [129] Whyte, pp. 64–65.

[130] *Freeman's Journal*, November 30–December 3 and December 7–10, 1776. Earlier that season a pseudonymous letter to *Freeman's Journal* had questioned Sheridan's powers to represent Zanga, "to the satisfaction of a Dublin audience" (November 14–16, 1776).

[131] Revived on March 10 (*ibid.*, March 1–4, 1777).

had helped to repopularize—"Dryden's Celebrated Ode on the Power of Music." [132]

For all that Sheridan did not value acting in 1763, he gave it up unwillingly in 1777. Perhaps the continued public acclaim he received, despite the increasingly unfavorable critical judgments, had somewhat changed his mind. In any event, his acting must have sustained his morale as well as his pocketbook over the long years of disappointment which marked the falling action of his life after the 1754 turning point.

[132] Whyte, p. 66.

CHAPTER XI

Clear the Exits Once Again, 1777-1788

ALTHOUGH Sheridan was to act no more, his connection with the theater was not at an end. For two years he went back to the work he had not done for two decades—superintending, or at least partially superintending, a theater. It was another stopgap occupation, but one which he apparently valued more than acting. Even before Richard (with Linley and Ford) finally took over the Drury Lane patent in June 1776, his father had offered his services to him on Richard's own terms.[1] In January of that year, while Thomas Sheridan was at Covent Garden under Harris, and Garrick was trying to countervail the success of *The Duenna* with *The Discovery*, Richard was planning the future when he should succeed Garrick, about to retire at the end of the season. The "astonishingly" good reception of his father at Covent Garden and his own success as author of *The Rivals* and now *The Duenna* at the same theater must have done much to increase mutual respect and so to bring about the long-deferred reconciliation. That January (1776) Richard wrote to Linley: "My father purposes to be with us but one year; and that only to give me what advantage he can from his experience. He certainly must be paid for his trouble, and so certainly must you." [2] According to Richard's plan, the two irreconcilable fathers-in-law were both to be working for him—not to mention his mother-in-law, Mrs. Linley, who as wardrobe mistress would be referring to Thomas Sheridan as "old Surly Boots." [3]

In the final arrangement Thomas Sheridan stayed longer and took over more than he had originally "purposed"—to free Richard for other things.[4] But agreement on this arrangement was not reached for over two years, perhaps because Mr. Linley raised objections. The first season after Garrick's retirement (1776–77) Sheridan had

[1] Moore, I, 187 (Letter from Richard to Linley, January 4, 1776).

[2] *Ibid.*, p. 189 (Letter of January 31, 1776).

[3] Rae, II, 2. Mrs. Linley's daughter Mary was still referring to Thomas Sheridan as "Old Surly Boots" in a 1784 letter to her sister, Mrs. Richard Sheridan (*Betsy Sheridan's Journal*, p. 15).

[4] One of these seems to have been the management of the opera house at Sadler's Wells, taken over from King (King's letter in Garrick, *Private Correspondence*, II, 120).

been in Ireland acting at Crow-Street. And the next season (1777–78), although he was "at liberty" and although Richard had negotiated Henderson out of a Bath theater contract and onto the Drury Lane stage,[5] his father still did not join them. Letters from Ireland written by the dramatist Robert Jephson and his friend Tighe to Garrick that summer of 1777 had urged Garrick to push the elder Sheridan's claims. These two, who were later to speak in far less respectful terms about Sheridan, pointed out to Garrick the "present dearth of theatrical merit," Sheridan's need for a situation, and the scandal that such a man, whose powers Garrick well knew, should be useless. "Though I am by no means his indiscriminate admirer, like some of my countrymen," says Jephson, "yet for his own sake, and for the public, I heartily wish to hear of his being established to his satisfaction at Drury-lane." "I hope that you, who must be powerful," writes Tighe, "will, upon every good account, secure a place for Sheridan." [6]

But it was not until September 1778, a year after these pleas and a year after his last season at Crow-Street, that Thomas Sheridan came to Drury Lane. The delay was Richard's. This his father indicates in a letter written long after and in much bitterness to his other son, Charles Francis: with the retirement of Garrick "whose jealousy had long shut the London theatres" against him, an opportunity, Sheridan thought, had been made for him as manager and actor which "might soon have retrieved my affairs. . . . But here a son of mine steps into possession, whose first step was to exclude me wholly from having any share in it. Afterwards when by extreme ill conduct, they [the Drury Lane patentees] were threatened with ruin, he agreed to put the management into my hands upon condition that I should not appear as a performer, and in this he got his brother to join him with such earnestness, that merely to gratify him I acquiesced." [7] Sheridan has exaggerated here the widespread influence of

[5] *Public Advertiser*, September 23, 1777. He is supposed to have given Manager Palmer the Bath rights to *The School for Scandal* in exchange (Macqueen-Pope, p. 199).

[6] Garrick, *Private Correspondence*, II, 252 (Letter of August 7, 1777); *ibid.*, II, 262 (Letter of August 23, 1777).

[7] Quoted in Rae, II, 4 (Letter of April 15, 1783). Sheridan's eagerness to continue his acting may have been fanned by the success of his old enemy Macklin the year before at Covent Garden. Among Macklin's favorable reviews Sheridan may have read the one in the *Public Advertiser*, September 30, 1777: "It is highly pleasing . . . to behold a Veteran of Mr. Macklin's Abilities still in such full Possession of his Powers, and without any Marks of Age about him,

Garrick's jealousy; Drury Lane under Garrick may have been shut to him, but Covent Garden had been open and he had served as its principal actor the whole of Garrick's last season in the theater. As for the injunction against his acting, he was almost sixty when he went to Drury Lane. Many of his contemporaries—Mossop, Barry, Woodward, Foote,[8] et cetera—had died; Garrick and others were retired. The connivance of his sons (and Charles Francis, we see, was involved in this) was surely to keep him from overextending himself physically and with the public.

For his services Sheridan accepted £600 a season—£100 more than Richard paid his father-in-law to look after the music, but a sharp decline from Thomas' earnings as actor in Dublin. Yet Richard must have felt the amount generous, for when he resumed total management after his father left he paid himself only £500. Personal money problems of this sort as well as the larger financial straits of the theater must have caused uneasiness between father and son. Later Sheridan is supposed to have complained of not having been regularly paid; but that he got his money by the end of each season is recorded in the Drury Lane account books, e.g., "to Mr. Thos. Sheridan in full for this Season this £5 compleating the £600." [9]

Sheridan's addition to the Drury Lane management pleased the *Morning Chronicle* for several reasons:

> It is much for the benefit of the young performers now of Drury Lane, as well as for the advantage of such adventurers as may in future offer to try their talents on that stage that Mr. Sheridan, senior, is invested with the management behind the curtain. Mr. Sheridan, the father, is not less polite, or less a man of ability, than his son, but he is at the same time one of the most punctual persons in existence. In every sense of the words, he is a man of business, and God knows such a man was much wanted at Old Drury. Since Mr. Garrick left the direction, the performers have been like ships without a pilot.[10]

---

except his Aspect." Sheridan must have felt that he could do at least as well as Macklin.

[8] Foote had died suddenly the season before, inspiring this Footism: "How quick poor Foote has from the Stage been hurl'd!/ Death took him off, who took off the world." George Colman had succeeded to the management of the Haymarket (*Public Advertiser*, October 31, 1777).

[9] *Journal Drury Lane Theatre*, May 27, 1780. See also June 5, 1779. (The quotation is by permission of the Folger Shakespeare Library.)

[10] *Morning Chronicle*, September 25, 1778.

The Drury Lane company had deteriorated thus, under the relaxed discipline of Richard Sheridan, himself undisciplined. Another reason for a professional and experienced manager is suggested a short time later by the *Chronicle:* to assign the parts judiciously.[11] Richard had had neither acting nor managerial experience. As an experienced professional, his father set out energetically to reform defects, to impose restrictions, to assign parts judiciously. His innovations were frequently resented by his actors and even the patentees gave him little support.[12]

There were many other sources of irritation to a man of Thomas Sheridan's temperament and past successes. The offerings went from bad to worse during the two years, through whose fault is not clear. Thomas, as the *Chronicle* announced, had the management "behind the curtain." The public considered Richard the man in charge of the theater and letters addressed to him in the press complain of everything from his use of a foreign scene designer (de Loutherbourg) to his injustice to other comic writers.[13] The father's influence seems reflected in an early announcement of the first season (1778–79), greeted approvingly by the *Morning Chronicle*, that foreign dancers and foreign scene decorators [14] would be replaced by esteemed old plays and by new works to encourage living dramatists. But most of the new productions, except for Richard's *Camp*, which did remarkably well during 1778–79, were dismal. Fielding's posthumous comedy, *The Fathers*, criticized as wanting proper revision, new scenes, and "friendly attention" from the manager,[15] was followed a few weeks later by a farcical afterpiece devised by the "Drury-Lane managers" out of Vanbrugh's full-length comedy *Aesop*. Though it gave Henderson a chance to recite "The Town Mouse and the Country Mouse," this play was so bad that it was hissed off the stage. The managers, in defending it, said that they had not taken *"great care"* with it.[16] Jephson, who was writing to Garrick about his own play

[11] *Ibid.*, December 1, 1778.   [12] Watkins, I, 108, 165.

[13] *Morning Chronicle*, November 20 and November 11, 1778.

[14] *Ibid.*, October 2, 1778. De Loutherbourg remained on the monthly pay list all season, however (*Journal Drury Lane Theatre*, 1778–79).

[15] *Morning Post*, December 1, 1778; *Morning Chronicle*, December 1, 1778. Financially *The Fathers* proved discouraging too. It opened to £210, but declined in its nine-night run to a low of £96 (*Journal Drury Lane Theatre*, 1778–79).

[16] *Morning Chronicle*, December 21, 1778; *Morning Post*, December 24, 1778.

then in production at Drury Lane, assumes that the *Esop* (as he spells it) was Thomas Sheridan's responsibility. "I suppose the fate of his Esop has chagrined him; but it will not make him a grain less confident." [17]

Jephson, the Irish poet, dramatist, and recently elected member of the Irish parliament,[18] who had importuned Garrick earlier on Thomas Sheridan's behalf, had written a new tragedy, *The Law of Lombardy* (his earlier *Braganza* had been successful at Drury Lane in 1775). This new play was almost finished as early as August 1777,[19] but it was not performed until February 1779. The latter part of the time Jephson wrote frequently to Garrick from Dublin to complain about "Mr. Sheridan, Senior," who seems to have had considerable authority over this production, at least. Jephson's fears for his play, which Sheridan wanted to cut and condense, and his concern about the choice of actors drove him into a frenzy of hatred for the man whose appointment to Drury Lane he had wanted a year or so ago. His cry to Garrick now runs as follows:

> Mr. Sheridan tells me that my play, like every other he has ever known, must undergo some retrenchments, and if I trust the amputation knife to him, he promises to use it very tenderly. This is a part of the business, which though in appearance I was obliged to permit, yet, between you and me, I think him of all men the least qualified for it. . . . I have no objections to necessary omissions, and to cutting off in the representation all superfluous poetry which does not promote the spirit of the action, but, let me entreat you will not suffer them to make additions of their own, or to substitute their words for mine, but particularly have an eye to our friend Sheridan. If you do not choose to appear to give your opinion directly upon these points, you may prevent his doing much injury through the medium of his son. There is no person except yourself to whom I would wish to trust this delicate matter. . . .[20]

After complaints about the casting, he exclaims:

> For Heaven's sake, have an eye to what they are doing! The town has such a prejudice against Sheridan, and he has such an

---

[17] Garrick, *Private Correspondence*, I, 502 (Letter of December 27, 1778, misdated 1772).

[18] *DNB*, v. "Jephson, Robert."

[19] Garrick, *Private Correspondence*, II, 261.

[20] *Ibid.*, I, 589 (Letter of December 10, 1778, misdated 1773).

inordinate partiality for himself, that I receive with some mistrust all the strong assurances he sends me. I am convinced he believes the world has been in a mistake above thirty years, in thinking you the greatest genius the stage ever saw, and that the *judicious few* give him the preference in their private opinion.[21]

Sheridan may have been unaware of Jephson's growing animosity and of his attempts at manipulation behind the scenes. "I have received a very kind and satisfactory letter from Mr. Sheridan senior," Jephson begins one of the letters quoted from above, "in which he tells me how much he admires 'The Law of Lombardy,' that he should on account of its own merit have brought it out with all possible *éclat*, and that his knowing me to be the author will not slacken his diligence." [22] Jephson, at Garrick's suggestion, had been playing a two-faced role: "As you advised me, I lately wrote to Sheridan senior in the most flattering style to which I could shape my pen." [23] But he was not too secure about Garrick; in one letter he begs him not to "communicate this letter to any person, for fear it should come to the ears of S——." Again he says, "It is unnecessary to beg you will not disclose my opinion of his vanity and folly, at least till our affairs are entirely out of his hands." [24] Jephson's friend Tighe, who had no play at stake, is less discreet. Speaking of Sheridan, he tells Garrick, "Both Jephson and I have written to old *Bubble-and-squeak*." [25] Garrick's well-known vanity would be indirectly fed by these sneering allusions to his old rival. In recommending that Jephson flatter Sheridan, did he not recognize that Jephson's letters to *him* were subtle in their appeal to his ego?

Garrick, however, was in no position to do much for Jephson at this crucial time; for he and Thomas Sheridan had had another (and their last) falling-out. It had happened at a rehearsal of that ill-omened play *Mahomet* sometime before its presentation on November 11, 1778, when Mr. Bannister, Jr., was to be introduced for the first time as Zaphna. Garrick, who had now been retired for more than two years, had attended Bannister's rehearsal and apparently had offered advice about the part, which he once played and which (he wrote Richard later) "your father never saw." Richard had urged his presence; and it is not impossible, judging from the way

[21] *Ibid.*, p. 502 (Letter of December 27, 1778, misdated 1772).
[22] *Ibid.*, p. 588.
[23] *Ibid.*, p. 500 (Letter of November 30, 1778, misdated 1772).
[24] *Ibid.*, pp. 589, 500.   [25] *Ibid.*, II, 322 (Letter of November 29, 1778).

Jephson and Tighe were importuning Garrick, that young Bannister may have asked him to be there. But what both Richard and Garrick had forgotten was that the elder Sheridan had also played Zaphna (indeed, was playing it at the time of the Dublin riot twenty-four years before) and would certainly feel that he needed none of Garrick's help. A message from Thomas Sheridan, brought to Garrick by Bannister, had apparently told Garrick as much, and that same night the following note was written to Richard:

> Dear Sir, You must oblige me with the sight of Fielding's play, or it will be impossible for me to write an epilogue, which I suppose you intend for Miss Younge. Pray assure your father that I meant not to interfere in his department: I imagined (foolishly indeed) my attending Bannister's rehearsal of the part I once played, and which your father never saw, might have assisted the cause, without giving the least offence. I love my ease too well to be thought an interloper, and I should not have been impertinent enough to have attended any rehearsal, had not you, Sir, in a very particular manner desired me. However, upon no consideration will I ever interfere again in this business, nor be liable to receive such another message as was brought me this evening by young Bannister.
>
> You must not imagine that I write this in a pet:—let me assure you, upon my honour, that I am in perfect peace with you all, and wish you from my heart all that yours can wish.[26]

Garrick's reasonable tone here is much to be admired; it is unfortunate that the incident was bruited all over both kingdoms and blown up into a "case." The following January, two months after the event, Thomas Wilks (né Snagg) wrote to Garrick from Dublin, "It was reported at our coffee-houses last week, that old Sheridan had behaved in a very unpolite manner to you at the theatre; but the story is told here in so many different ways, that I should wish to know *the truth of it.*"[27] Before this, other Dubliners—Jephson and Tighe, for example—had heard of the quarrel. Jephson, as usual, is worried about the effect on his play: "I am unable to express my astonishment at the absurdity and impertinence of Mr. Sheridan senior's conduct to you. He was, is, and always will be the most superlative of coxcombs: I do not wonder at his son's concern. It may have very serious consequences to the gentleman himself hereafter; and in the

[26] *Ibid.,* p. 357. [27] *Ibid.,* p. 332 (Letter of January 14, 1779).

mean time my play and the public will suffer if you continue determined not to interfere about it." He concludes, "Our friend Tighe will, I am certain, be shocked beyond measure when he hears of his monstrous presumption." [28] In a later letter Jephson reports to Garrick that Sheridan, in writing to him, "slurs over the transaction between you and himself in regard to the rehearsal of 'Mahomet,' and from his own manner of mentioning it, I shall be convinced of his absurdity. He tells me, however, what I hope is true, that you are now upon easy terms." [29] Easy or not, the relationship was terminated soon after by Garrick's death on January 20, 1779. Although Richard, as a patentee of Drury Lane, was a chief mourner at the funeral, Thomas is said not to have attended—from spite, some have implied. As a manager he certainly had a hand in the production of Richard's monody on Garrick's death, presented at Drury Lane. The poem, accompanied in places by music, was recited by Mrs. Yates in a setting which represented a grove of bays and cypresses, complete with a funeral pyre and bas-reliefs.

Sheridan had been right about Jephson's *Law of Lombardy;* but he had not cut it enough, apparently. The *Morning Chronicle*'s reviewer calls it tedious and weighty, and much too long. Although the dresses were "superb," its production suffered from inferior minor performers, and even Henderson failed to please.[30] At that, it did much better [31] than the farce *Jehu,* which opened at the seventh performance of the Jephson tragedy and which was interrupted by such disapprobation that the curtain had to be dropped in the middle of the second act.[32] The late spring brought a more acceptable new play, Miss Richardson's posthumous *Double Deception,* which did its "authoress" honor, but on which the managers bestowed little trouble, not giving it a single new scene or costume.[33] On the other hand, a new farce, Mrs. Cowley's *Who's the Dupe?* which couldn't have been better exhibited, brought a different kind of criticism: it was produced at the wrong time of year. During the period when new plays were usually introduced, nothing exciting had happened. Now, between the benefits and the hot weather, this

[28] *Ibid.,* I, 499–500.   [29] *Ibid.,* p. 589.
[30] *Morning Chronicle,* February 9, 1779.
[31] It did somewhat better financially than *The Fathers.* The author's three benefits netted about £100 (*Journal Drury Lane Theatre,* 1778–79).
[32] *Morning Post,* February 22, 1779; *Enthofen Collection,* February 20, 1779.
[33] *Morning Post,* April 29, 1779.

"provokingly laughable" farce was "calculated to give the public a sweating in the dog-days." It was hoped that the managers would end this topsy-turvy plan begun last season and arrange the schedule more conveniently in the future.[34]

That the season's new plays had been unimpressive is not so surprising. Good plays were rare at this time and Thomas Sheridan had never had much luck or ability in discovering them. But that productions were careless, mountings poor, actors improperly or ill dressed, performers inadequate, new plays ill-timed—these are strange inadequacies to come from the former Smock-Alley manager. An occasional favorable comment praising the beauty of the costumes or the perfection of the production shows that he had not so much lost his touch as that facilities (including money) were lacking and that the company, as well as its morale, was poor. Henderson, the only important actor, had to be overused; [35] some felt that his reputation had been built up so high earlier that he had never quite recovered.[36] But Sheridan's old ability to get the best out of his actors seems also to have failed. Indeed, a poem printed two months after he came to Drury Lane suggests that his influence may have depressed them, although his name is not mentioned in the piece and in the two years that had intervened without Garrick the company's *esprit* had deteriorated badly. Entitled "On the visible Alteration in the Players of Drury Lane, since Mr. Garrick resigned the Management," it reads:

> O Drury, how fallen! by Yates now bereft
> What lifeless, insipid successors are left!
> Younge's present instructor, who lately has taught her
> He made her as flat and as dead as ditchwater.
> Ev'n Henderson's Richard, so pleasing before,
> Which charm'd us at Coleman's, now charms us no more.
> By dull declamation they're languid and dead
> For nature and passions with Garrick are fled.[37]

To add to Sheridan's discomfort, the audience, which at Smock-Alley he had finally tamed, grew out of hand in the spring. The two-shilling gallery took to throwing bottles, the one-shilling gallery a lighted serpent, and even in the boxes there was fighting (with spurs on). Again the managers were blamed for not providing the

---

[34] *Ibid.*, April 12 and 24, 1779.
[35] *Morning Chronicle*, September 23, 1778.   [36] *Ibid.*, February 9, 1779.
[37] *Ibid.*, December 31, 1778.

proper peace officers.[38] Other complaints poured in to the papers. The bad taste of certain notices offended: the bottom of the bill which announced Drury Lane's closing for Garrick's death should not have borne, in red letters, "Tomorrow the School for Scandal." [39] Other viewers were disturbed by anachronisms: the scene of Charing-Cross with Charles I on horseback should not have been introduced into 2 *Henry IV;* Alcanor's bier in *Mahomet* should have been decorated with Egyptian solar symbols rather than with moons.[40] A republican felt that it was wrong to have moved an *after*piece to *before* the play to accommodate the West-End gentry.[41] The ears of some listeners were irked by Miss Younge's artificial delivery.[42] The eyes of another spectator were offended by the *breeches* on female actors, most of whom—be it noted—had been corrupted by the hardening waters of Shannon or the Liffey! [43]

But Sheridan's most uncomfortable moment of all must have come with the totaling of the yearly accounts. Bad as had been the year before, when Richard was muddling along alone (but with the invaluable help, it must be remembered, of his new *School for Scandal*), this present season's gross income was some £4,000 lower. In spite of a peak evening of £287 and the continued appeal of Richard's *Camp* and *School for Scandal,* the many discouraging nights had included one with an intake of only £55.[44] How much to blame was Thomas Sheridan for such a falling-off? Was it caused by the eight months of heavy exhibitions which had tired the public? (So thought one critic, who included under this explanation the decline of Covent Garden too.) [45] Or was it due, as the *Morning Chronicle* suggests, to the hard times, which were much against the theater? [46] Two years before, opening night in September had brought £270; in September of this season, when Sheridan had barely taken over, the same night brought only £226.[47] Even benefit performances often failed to make the £105 house charge, to the theater's further loss.[48] At the most worthy benefit for the Theatrical Fund [49]—a cause dear

[38] *Ibid.,* April 26, 1779.   [39] *Ibid.,* January 22, 1779.
[40] *Ibid.,* October 1 and November 14, 1778.   [41] *Ibid.,* October 1, 1778.
[42] *Ibid.,* April 12, 1779.   [43] *Morning Post,* May 14, 1779.
[44] *Journal Drury Lane Theatre,* 1778–79. (See January 11 and May 27.)
[45] *Morning Chronicle,* May 11, 1779.   [46] *Ibid.,* September 21, 1779.
[47] *Drury Lane Nightly Accounts,* 1776–79.
[48] *Journal Drury Lane Theatre,* 1778–79.
[49] This was the fund for destitute or incapacitated actors. After Garrick's death an item in the *Morning Chronicle,* January 25, 1779, reports the general surprise that Garrick had left nothing to this fund.

to Sheridan, who had started the idea in Dublin many years before—Drury Lane Theater was only about a quarter full. Commenting on this very thin audience, a correspondent who is interested in words that come to reverse their meanings but who is not fortunate enough to own the dictionary "lately advertised by Mr. Sheridan, sen." thinks its author should be informed of the true meaning of *benefit* in the theatric sense. Is it gain or loss? he asks.[50]

This is one of the few times during the 1778–79 season that Thomas Sheridan's name appears in the press. The next season, his second, was full of publicity for him, mostly unpleasant. But at first the comments were friendly and concerned with a subject closer to him then, as author of the soon-to-be published pronouncing dictionary, than even the management of Drury Lane. A correspondent wonders "from whence" Drury Lane performers get their novel pronounciation *handkercher* for "handkerchief." The *Morning Post* can't say "from whence," but it can say "from whom": *handkercher* is a correction of a barbarous pronunciation by one of "the best English grammarians now existing—Mr. Sheridan, sen. who has at present, the superintendence of the Drury Lane stage."[51] Other letters on the two pronunciations appear, and then other pronunciations are criticised, one writer particularly protesting the stage (and pulpit) pronunciations *nachure, forchune, pitchure, opporchunity, joinchure, creachure, Urshula, ashume, preshume,* and *tortchure.*[52] In many such words, as his dictionary shows, Sheridan preferred these older assimilations to the newer pronunciations based on spelling—*naityure, fortyoon,* et cetera. In the painful year to come, Sheridan must have warmly remembered the *Morning Post*'s description of him with its absolutely right emphasis: one of the best English grammarians now existing, who has, at present, the superintendence of the Drury Lane stage.

The unfavorable publicity broke in November, but its origins went back over a year. Then an arrangement had been worked out between Drury Lane (probably by Richard) and Covent Garden (still under Harris) to permit borrowing of each other's performers when necessary.[53] Though it was called "the theatrical union" by its critics

---

[50] *Ibid.*, May 26, 1779. Sheridan's dictionary, which, except for the grammatical introduction, he had completed in Blois fifteen years earlier (Whyte, p. 34), was not published until 1780.

[51] *Morning Post*, October 21, 1779.

[52] *Morning Chronicle*, October 27, 1779.

[53] An illustration of this reciprocal agreement can be found in a Drury Lane

and though some of the actors resented it as a monopoly,[54] it was not
a true monopoly (as Thomas Sheridan would conceive one), since
there was no pooling of income and only an occasional exchange of
performers; and both theaters competed for the public's attendance,
neither very successfully, but Drury Lane more successfully in the
first season than Covent Garden. The next fall, of 1779, Covent
Garden had the advantage, having lured over Miss Younge and
Henderson, the latter by topping Drury Lane's offer of twelve
guineas a week.[55] The "theatrical monopoly" did not even eliminate
competition in hiring performers. And, although criticism of the
"coalition" had been frequent in the beginning, it had died down
until the publication of *The Theatrical Monopoly* in the second
autumn, September 1779.[56] This anonymous pamphlet, written possibly by a disappointed playwright, was dedicated to the hero of the
"anti-Monopolists," George Colman, who as manager of the Haymarket summer theater was not involved in the coalition although
he had the advantage of both companies and no competition in the
summer. *The Theatrical Monopoly* protests the policy which elimi-
nates "emulation" among actors and between theaters and which resulted in the dismissal of twelve minor players from Drury Lane.
Although Richard Sheridan and Harris are the main subjects of
attack, Thomas, as the father of monopoly and present manager of
Drury Lane, gets his share. He is called the "living Monopolist"
and theatrical Machiavel. His history is recalled: his dictatorial behavior as manager of Smock-Alley and his vain attempts to secure a
monopoly in Dublin from the Irish parliament. There he "played
the Orator with almost as much success, as when he made his pro-
prosals for an Universal Academy; and with the same effect: for the
folly of committing the money of the Theatre or the education of
their children to a Bankrupt Player, was evident *even* to Irish-

---

press notice of November 12, 1778: "Mrs. Abington, being taken ill, Mrs. Mat-
tocks (from the Theatre Royal, Covent Garden) has kindly undertaken to perform the part of Lady Teazle this Evening" (*Enthofen Collection*).

[54] As early as October 1778 the Robin Hood Society was debating whether
the agreement between Covent Garden and Drury Lane to employ each other's
performers would promote the interest of the drama (*Morning Chronicle*, October 20, 1778; see also October 4 and November 20).

[55] *Ibid.*, October 9 and 29, 1779. This paper thought the salary of twelve
guineas a week very high. But it was lower than Sheridan's income, which
in turn was less than half what he made acting in Dublin earlier.

[56] Publication announced *ibid.*, September 18, 1779.

men." [57] Now he has succeeded in London where he failed there, the "giddy Vanity of his Son" and the ignorance of Mr. Harris having played into the hands of "this universal Projector." And recently he has extended his scheme of "universal theatric monopoly" to Ireland in a coalition which is to take place under "one Heaphy." His activities have produced the greatest "Revolution in the Mimic World" and have done greater injury to genius and literature "than they can ever receive from his Labours as a Compiler of Dictionaries," [58] et cetera, et cetera. The pamphlet urges Colman to appeal to parliament for a third theater, because of the alarming coalition between the other two. Ironically, Colman, at about this time, was joining with Sheridan's recent enemy, Robert Jephson, to try to get from the Irish parliament the exclusive right to one theater in Dublin [59]—in other words, a theatrical monopoly more monopolistic than any in London.

It was this move of Colman's, and Sheridan's reaction to it, that brought Sheridan back into the limelight of the London press and kept him there during mid-winter. By some chance, a letter of his to a Dublin gentleman found its way back to London and into the newspapers there: after thanking his correspondent for telling him of Colman's plans, he wonders what pretensions Colman, who has never set foot in Ireland, has over "a man whose services and sufferings may entitle him to such a recompence." Some years ago he tried to get parliament to establish one theater in Dublin, but dropped the idea because of opposition. Asked whether he would take the management now if his former plan could be realized, he unhesitatingly answers yes. Because he still wants to revive the stage and serve his native land, he would relinquish his place at the head of Drury Lane to spend the rest of his life in Ireland. As this has been his first object in life, he finds it cruel that a stranger to Ireland should be preferred merely on recommendations from England.[60] This letter brought many comments. One correspondent believed (or pretended to believe) it fictitious, something invented by Colman's friends, and to be resented: Mr. Sheridan was a grave character, "and ought not to be sported with." [61] A correspondent from Ireland addresses Sheridan: he can't imagine why Dublin doesn't recall him, consider-

[57] *The Theatrical Monopoly*, p. 29.   [58] *Ibid.*, pp. 29–30.
[59] Stockwell, pp. 146–147.
[60] *Morning Chronicle* and *Morning Post*, November 17, 1779.
[61] *Morning Chronicle*, November 18, 1779.

ing the variety he's given London as *head* of Drury Lane and the *crowded* houses his vigorous efforts have produced.[62] Another by-stander remarks that Colman's presumption in wanting to set foot in Ireland is equal only "to that of an Irishman's coming to London to teach the natives of this island the true pronunciation of their language." [63]

A week later, word came to London gossips that Mr. Sheridan senior had been informed by official letter that the Lord Lieutenant would exert influence to get him any theater patent granted by the government.[64] Mr. Sheridan had indeed received such a letter, written by the viceroy's private secretary, Mr. Tighe, whose hand must have withered as he addressed these hopeful words to "old Bubble-and-squeak." In the meantime, Colman had arrived in Dublin, but had become totally discouraged in his canvass of the situation.[65] His judgment thus supported what Sheridan had said eight years before—that even a monopoly would not be enough. Sheridan himself, though, was now reported as memorializing the castle; and Robert Jephson was still trying for the patent.[66] "The Castle for Jephson, the few for old Sheridan, and the many for Colman . . ." but Colman was no longer a candidate [67] and the next rumor had it that Sheridan and Jephson were to share the patent which, with claims on the theater, was to cost £1,100 a year! [68] But again the opposition was so strong and the conditions so unpromising—to both principals, probably—that the plan failed.

By the end of 1779 the coalition between Drury Lane and Covent Garden had fallen through. Its dissolution was announced on December 27, with the postscript that each theater was now bent on "showing themselves noun substantives." [69] It was fortunate that Sheridan's new dictionary, long delayed in appearing, was published in February, for he had little to be pleased with at Drury Lane during the 1779–80 season. The new play *Zoraida* was too much like the burlesqued tragedy in *The Critic* to be well received; [70] and, besides,

---

[62] *Ibid.*, November 20, 1779.   [63] *Ibid.*, November 22, 1779.

[64] *Ibid.*, November 27, 1779. The letter, dated November 12, 1779, still exists among the *Lefanu MSS.* Robert Jephson was also to be recommended along with Sheridan.

[65] *Morning Post*, December 5, 1779.

[66] *Ibid.* There were two letters from Dublin in this issue.

[67] *Morning Chronicle*, December 6, 1779.   [68] *Ibid.*, December 12, 1779.

[69] *Ibid.*, December 27, 1779.

[70] *Morning Post*, December 14, 1779. The tragedy *Zoraida* was by Hodgson.

the public had been bored with tragic drama for some time.[71] (After new scenes had been substituted for the old pantomime scene first used, the play did better.) [72] And although *The Critic* had saved the autumn, its appearance had been delayed for so long that the father's pleasure must have been spoiled in his exasperation with his son. On opening night two gentlemen gazing at the bill outside Drury Lane wondered why the spelling was *Critic* and not *Critick*. A passing prompter's boy explained, "Lord, sir, that was owing to a joke of my Master's who meant to intimate by his short spelling, that the Piece was not *finished* when the bills were printed." [73] In the author's party that night was the Duchess of Devonshire, who led "the claps all the evening," and no expense had been spared in the production, more dressing having been used than on all the tragedies in the last three years; but the managers were still censured for putting on, along with *The Critic*, the dullest play in the repertory—*Hamlet*, as altered by Garrick.[74] At the end of the 1779–80 season the Covent Garden manager was applauded for "his diligence and attention in his public department"; a new Drury Lane afterpiece, *The Miniature Picture,* was criticized as far from well performed.[75]

But another afterpiece, Woodward's old pantomime *Fortunatus* revived, had, along with *The Critic*, done its best to save the season. Either one of these, given after almost any main play, brought in upward of £150 a night for some time; without one of these in the bill the receipts dropped shockingly—to as low as £40 at one performance.[76] In the end, however, the stale diet of old repertory drama [77] resorted to after the failure of the two new main plays could not be permanently relieved by two afterpieces, themselves growing stale. The gross for this season dropped almost £3,000 more,[78] making a decline of some £7,000 during the two years while Thomas Sheridan was at Drury Lane.

---

[71] *Morning Chronicle*, December 15, 1779.   [72] *Ibid.*, January 5, 1780.

[73] *Ibid.*, October 30, 1779. *The Critic* opened this evening.

[74] *Ibid.*, November 1, 1779.

[75] *Ibid.*, May 3 and 26, 1780. *The Miniature Picture* was a dramatic piece in three acts by Lady Craven.

[76] This was a performance of *The Rivals* and *The Genii (Journal Drury Lane Theatre,* 1779–80; see especially May 17).

[77] There were many more new plays and revivals at Covent Garden all season than at Drury Lane.

[78] *Journal Drury Lane Theatre,* 1779–80.

This was the end of his engagement. Just what his jurisdiction had been never becomes clear; perhaps it was never clear to him. He was "invested with the management behind the curtain"; he had the "superintendence of the Drury Lane Stage"; he was "at the head of the Drury-Lane Theatre." But he was, in the public eye, not the manager. The manager was Richard Brinsley Sheridan, alone or with his two copatentees. This was an unsatisfactory arrangement in other ways. Sheridan's position was, technically, lower than his son's—a situation doubtless aggravated by memories of their former estrangement. Nor were they temperamentally suited for such a relationship. Richard's ignorance about theatrical management and especially his dilatoriness must have infuriated his experienced and punctual father. At the beginning of the 1779–80 season the *Morning Chronicle* reports that, for the first time in the history of the theater, Drury Lane was to open in two days without the name of the play being announced, a fact which showed "great irresolution in the theatrical cabinet." [79] No wonder opening night, with *Hamlet* and *Comus*, brought in only £173, some £50 less than a year before and £100 less than in 1776. [80] On a Saturday night in March there was no play announced for Monday—another "very unusual circumstance." [81] Richard's inability to complete the plays he was writing was a byword. In money matters he was casual and imprecise; his father had always prided himself on his prompt payments to his company.

But the arrangement must have been equally uncomfortable to Richard. His father had never in his life taken orders, and was not amenable to suggestions. The contretemps with Garrick over Bannister shows Thomas Sheridan defensive of his position, Richard the harassed man in the middle. He must often have been harassed thus when the inevitable disagreements arose within the company. [82] For

[79] *Morning Chronicle*, September 17, 1779. Richard was supposed to write a prelude for this evening, one intended to "mow down all who would not acknowledge that Drury Lane Theatre was better managed now than it had ever been," but his idea turned into a farce against critics (*ibid.*, September 20, 1779). The farce was not finished until the end of October.

[80] *Journal Drury Lane Theatre*, 1779–80; *Drury Lane Nightly Accounts*, 1776–79.

[81] *Morning Chronicle*, March 6, 1780.

[82] One such disagreement found its way into the press. When the managers of Drury Lane, in the fall of 1779, ordered their performers to stay out of the first seats in the boxes if others were present, the actors were reported as being "in high dudgeon," claiming that they were individuals with rights off stage (*ibid.*, October 29, 1779). An earlier letter writer to the press had complained

the inferior entertainment Thomas Sheridan was at least partly to blame. Much of the old fare was probably selected by him. But the choice of the new plays, which were, on the whole, failures, seems to have been largely Richard's responsibility. Tighe, for example, writes to Garrick of *The Law of Lombardy:* "Manager Sheridan, i.e. Scandal Sheridan, has promised to produce the play whenever the author [Jephson] pleases."[83] The poor productions, with inappropriate dresses and old scenes, show a lack of money and of interest. (Thomas Sheridan was working on the grammar prefixed to his dictionary and then seeing the whole through the press. Richard, on the other hand, was beginning to be occupied by politics, a time-consuming interest.) Yet for the inferior entertainment at Drury Lane Richard bore the criticism in unfavorable reviews and letters to the press. He, in turn, would be apt to blame his father. So Thomas Sheridan's superintendence of Drury Lane, which should have come as a crowning fulfillment to him, was full of theatrical grief.

It is not surprising, then, that when Thomas left Drury Lane the two Sheridans had fallen out again, the father as usual feeling the more hurt. Yet four years later, when King was engaged as manager, Thomas Sheridan had been expecting to reassume the position, having "not declined" proposals advanced by Mr. Siddons. No final offer was made, however, and Sheridan, low in funds, health, and spirits, felt again that he had been "materially injured by Dick." Betsy, who was now living with her father, and as anxious as Richard for a reconciliation between the two of them, thought that advances from Richard "would have come with a better grace [if] accompanied by some solid [i.e., material] offer of friendship."[84] After two years more of bitterness, Sheridan, softened by age and ill health, and encouraged by rumors of assistance from Dick and from Ireland,[85] made up the quarrel and took much of the blame for the

---

that the best box seats at Drury Lane were taken by the company—free, he presumed (*Morning Post*, October 16, 1779). Afterward another letter congratulated Richard for moving the players from the front seats, but suggested that perhaps the order should not apply to the principals, who had had a liberal education and were used to associating with gentlemen (*ibid.*, October 29, 1779). Here Richard is assumed to have been the prime mover, and he may have been.

[83] Garrick, *Private Correspondence*, ii, 311 (Letter of September 16, 1778).
[84] *Betsy Sheridan's Journal*, p. 27.
[85] *Ibid.*, p. 78: "Dick talks stoutly of assisting my Father—God send he may not again dissappoint [*sic*] him" (Letter of 21–23 January, 1786). Betsy sent

rift on himself—even for "the Theatrical business which so severely hurt him." Now he did not wonder at Richard's conduct, "when he reflected that tho' it was done with a view to serve him and the other Patentees, yet still he [Thomas] so thwarted Dick's schemes and wishes that he was not surprised he opposed him." [86] But Sheridan's two-year visit to Dublin shortly afterward separated father and son and revived the coolness, although they met again in London "on civil terms" [87] and were completely reconciled at Sheridan's death.[88] Thomas' will, however, drawn in his own hand on June 2, 1785, and never altered, bears witness to his earlier feeling: it leaves everything (less than £600 at his death, although the sale of his books continued to bring in something) to his two daughters.[89]

Sheridan's departure from Drury Lane at the age of sixty-one ended his connection with the theater. He returned to his lecturing and to his public readings (these latter with great success, especially after Henderson joined him early in 1785); he wrote and published his *Life of Swift;* and he continued active in pushing educational reform. His educational proposals appeared again in *A Short Address,* a sixteen-page pamphlet published in 1783, and were used by Thomas Orde, the Irish viceroy's secretary, in formulating a parliamentary bill to remodel Irish education entirely and to introduce a National Educational System. Sheridan went to Dublin in 1786, apparently expecting "to assist the plan of public schools, meditated by Mr. Orde." [90] Also by way of assistance, he published "A View of the State of School Education in Ireland," "A Short Sketch of a Plan for the Improvement of Education in this Country," and *Elements of English,*[91] a little book to be used in schools for teaching young children to read by a new method. Orde's illness and the viceroy's sudden death cut short the Secretary's proposals and Sheridan's prospects of having the direction of the whole plan, as Orde had intended when it materialized.[92] Thus, until the very end (he was to die the next year), the hope of retrieving his fortunes and achiev-

---

Richard "a list of the Names my Father has already received" in the expectation that he would add to them (pp. 79–81). This was in connection with Sheridan's educational plans for Ireland.

[86] *Ibid.,* pp. 93, 97.   [87] *Ibid.,* pp. 103, 107.   [88] *Ibid.,* pp. 116–117.

[89] Thomas Sheridan's Will (Probate Registry, Somerset House, London).

[90] *Freeman's Journal,* April 5–7, 1787.

[91] This work is not usually listed in Thomas Sheridan bibliography. Two rare copies exist in the University of Edinburgh Library.

[92] Sheridan, "A Short Sketch," p. 2.

ing a permanently respectable position was raised high and then cut down.

Meanwhile, there were some who missed him in the theater. A newspaper item from this time regrets that Sheridan is not, like Macklin, continuing occasionally "his exertions on the Stage." His readings have been useful and entertaining, but "surely do not engross him wholly." With his help as Brutus and with Mrs. Siddons, what a cast could be assembled for *Julius Caesar*, for example, including Kemble as Marc Antony, Palmer as Cassius, Henderson as Casca—"O si sic omnia!"[93] In Ireland his theatrical accomplishments were remembered nostalgically. When the monopoly patent was again being pushed in the Irish parliament in 1786—at last, successfully—Lord Earlsfort, in arguing for the bill, remarked that "there had been almost one uninterrupted series of ruin and distress, occasioned in this City by theatrical oppositions" except for the time when Mr. Sheridan had control of the Irish stage.[94] But, beyond standing as a symbol of proper stage management, Sheridan played no part in this final struggle. He was busy with Mr. Orde and with educational prospects that would bring more satisfying results with less financial investment. So the man who won the Dublin theatrical monopoly for which Sheridan thirty years earlier had petitioned parliament was Richard Daly. But Daly lacked the abilities which Sheridan had had thirty years before, he did little to improve the stage beyond remodeling Crow-Street, and his monopoly lasted only a few years. While Sheridan was still alive, Smock-Alley Theater was shut permanently; and not long after his death it was converted into a great warehouse.[95]

When Sheridan died at Margate [96] in August 1788, appraisals of his achievements appeared in the London and Dublin papers. Few

[93] British Museum Clippings. Item dated 1785.

[94] Reported in the *Morning Chronicle*, April 11, 1786.

[95] Stockwell, pp. 156ff. The monopoly patent was for fourteen years (Stockwell, p. 160), but by 1792 there had sprung up amateur competitors whose success in effect canceled the monopoly.

[96] *Betsy Sheridan's Journal* tells how she and her father, now quite ill, had left Dublin with the idea of going to Lisbon for her father's health. In London Sheridan's doctor discouraged the voyage, recommending, instead, Margate as a place where he himself planned to spend part of the summer (pp. 102–105). Sheridan is reported as having died of a dropsy (*Public Advertiser*, August 18, 1788). Betsy's letters show that his last illness was a culmination of the disorder which had plagued him all his life—a digestive affliction of some sort.

people then were in a position to foresee how much a part of the next century his ideas about oratory and elocution would be,[97] how much a part of modern times his ideas about education would be. His work in the theater was more adequately recognized, although his acting divided his judges into two camps—those who felt that it showed too much good sense to be relished by more than "the judicious few" and those who observed that his reputation had declined as he grew more stiff and as the easy style started by Garrick spread.[98]

Sheridan's abilities as an actor had always been controversial. Everybody agreed, however, that he *understood* the plays and their writers. "No performer ever conceived his author better, or marked him more correctly," says Francis Gentleman,[99] himself an actor who had come out under Sheridan and had played in many a performance with him. Sheridan's knowledge of his characters, his "judgment" (to use the eighteenth-century term), is praised repeatedly. He himself stressed the importance of *studying character*, because "people of different characters [as he told Boswell] feel and express their feelings very differently." Garrick, he thought, in playing Henry IV should not have whined piteously to his crown-stealing son; rather, considering the king's past manner and his fears for England's future, he should have upbraided Harry with "bitter sarcasm and bold figures." "And then," Sheridan observed, "what a beautiful variety is there, when, upon young Harry's contrition, he falls on his neck and melts into parental tenderness."[100] To his own portrayal of Hamlet Sheridan apparently brought a fresh interpretation—the one which he expounded to Boswell [101] and which anticipated the Romantic view of that character as a contemplative, delicate, irresolute young man; Davies notes that his playing, "in several situations of Hamlet's character," was original and different from all other actors'.[102] His insight into this role merged well with qualities in his own personality—a certain seriousness and complexity—to pro-

---

[97] At least one person, however, was aware of their importance. The obituary in the *Public Advertiser*, August 21, 1788, concludes: "Of his Oratory, it will be recorded as forming an aera in the history of his country."

[98] *Ibid.*, August 21 and 22, 1788.

[99] [Gentleman], II, 486. Francis Gentleman published anonymously under the title "The Dramatic Censor."

[100] Boswell, *London Journal*, pp. 135–136.   [101] *Ibid.*, pp. 234–235.

[102] Davies, *Dramatic Miscellany*, III, 115.

duce a Hamlet which fascinated his public right up to the end of his acting career.

Hamlet was conceded to be Sheridan's masterpiece; "it is a character," says Wilkes, "into the spirit of which he enters." [103] In entering thus, Sheridan must have felt that he had achieved "propriety of theatrical action," for not only did an actor have to understand his roles, he had—Sheridan felt—to "forget himself and the audience entirely, and be quite the real character." He himself was so much so, he claimed, that he "remembered nothing at all but the character." [104]

Yet, much as Sheridan understood and "became" the character, certain kinds of roles he failed to convey to his auditors. He failed in portraying sophisticatedly casual parts, such as Lord Townley, Dorimant, Sir Charles Easy. He did no better with Falstaff, lacking in his portrayal "that festivity, that joy, which nature must have given an Actor who fills up this character. . . ." Nor could he project what he felt when he wandered into "the walks of tenderness," as Wilkes quaintly expresses it, and tried to be a Romeo, an Anthony, or a Varanes. He was "sometimes happy in conveying horror and terror"; [105] he was good in Macbeth, King John, and Richard.

Most of the characters in which, according to the critics, Sheridan was at his best—Hamlet, Brutus, Cato, Coriolanus, Jaques—were not only serious personalities; they were also men gifted with superior intellect. Though he lacked it himself, this endowment seemed to inspire the actor in Sheridan more than did other human qualities like passion, humor, worldliness. The parallel which Gentleman's *Dramatic Censor* draws between Sheridan and Jaques is revealing here: Sheridan "looks the part . . . and speaks it with the same degree of emphatic, descriptive feeling with which the author wrote." [106] This and other remarks like it show not only that Sheridan responded to the intellectual in his roles but also that he responded intellectually rather than with his whole self, despite his feeling that he was "quite the real character." And here Garrick's wider range of reaction made him a more varied and more popular actor, although he may have lacked some of Sheridan's thoughtful understanding.

This same understanding, the critics imply, extended to the lines Sheridan spoke. And, impelled by the teacher within him, he would

[103] Wilkes (Derrick), p. 316.   [104] Boswell, *London Journal,* p. 109.
[105] Wilkes (Derrick), pp. 314–317.   [106] [Gentleman], I, 476.

want his audience too to understand the lines and not merely be carried away by the rhythms or by emotional acting. "All the powers of acting are nothing," he told Boswell, "without propriety of speech" —a virtue rare in the theater of 1762, when on Drury Lane stage there were "not three lines in a play spoke well." [107] By speaking well, Sheridan meant, primarily, conveying ideas smoothly and clearly, although he never underestimated the importance of fancy or passion and, indeed, devoted pages to these two subjects in his *Lectures on Elocution*.[108] "Propriety of speech" was what made him notable in soliloquies, orations and in speaking what had weight in it: Brutus' orations; Henry V's, Hamlet's, Iago's soliloquies; Hamlet's speeches in the Closet Scene.[109] Sometimes, the critics felt, he did little more than convey meaning and, especially as he got older, defects in his voice countervailed this virtue of propriety, in the view of Francis Gentleman: "If it was possible for spectators to be pleased with meaning alone, uttered through very ungracious, inadequate organs, Mr. Sheridan [as Othello] might stand high in public estimation." [110] At his best, his delivery evoked high praise from this same critic: "[As Horatio in *The Fair Penitent*] he broke with chaste judgment the lines into good sense, without violating just harmony." [111]

Sheridan's concern with meaning first, his careful enunciation to convey the meaning, his excellence in orations and soliloquies have, erroneously, connected him with the declamatory school of acting, and even with the mouthing and ranting of some of his predecessors. But he loathed nothing so much as artificiality and theatrical declamation, which he called still the chief vice of the stage, though not so prevalent now as a few decades before.[112] The emphasis in all his works is on *naturalness* of speech: "The finest artificial tones in the world, and the most musical cadences, can never stand in the place, or answer the ends, of such as are natural, or appear so by being always used in discourse." [113] Even with gesture the only advice he

---

[107] Boswell, *London Journal*, pp. 57–58.

[108] Sheridan, *Lectures on Elocution*, pp. ix–xii; 99–111; 121–124; 132–134.

[109] Wilkes (Derrick), pp. 314–317; [Gentleman], I, 56, 152; II, 363.

[110] [Gentleman], I, 152.   [111] *Ibid.*, I, 272.

[112] Sheridan, *Lectures on Elocution*, pp. 4, 53–54.

[113] *Ibid.*, pp. 4–5. Proper and, at first, slow articulation is necessary to prevent unintelligible utterance, but the greatest fault in public speaking and in theatrical pronunciation is to give equal weight to all syllables through a mistaken idea "that words are rendered more distinct to a large assembly, by dwelling longer

urges is to be natural. Since the chief defect today is "an artificial manner" which comes of trying to affect the style of another, a return to natural looks and gestures is itself revolutionary.[114]

References to acting and to the theater are surprisingly infrequent in Sheridan's elocutionary works; nor is he much concerned there with acting or with stage speech. The languages of the bar, the senate, the pulpit—these he discusses and hopes to improve. As for the stage, to read his books one would hardly think that he had stepped before the footlights. But his many years there had made him, of course, an excellent public speaker, able to convince any audience of the desirability of elocutionary training. Although, unfortunately, their enthusiasm faded before Sheridan had any material rewards, the influence of his ideas, somewhat garbled, on nineteenth-century education was to be inestimable.

To his contemporaries looking back on his life, Sheridan's greatest achievements were as theater manager in Dublin: there he was the reformer of the Irish stage, the patron of rising merit, the corrector of theatrical taste. He laid the foundation of all the advantages the Irish theater had since received.[115] To his own age, then, the profession which he had entered with the most apprehension had brought the fullest benefits. To him too it had brought the one time in his life when his efforts had had their fullest realization. And after it had ruined him, it had supported him when other ventures failed. All his life it was that capricious mistress to whom he had given his first, most spirited love—thrilling, cruel, benign, hateful, but inescapable.

Sheridan's burial at Margate, a strange place so far from Dublin, where he had gone in search of health and died after a fortnight, was

---

upon the syllables" (p. 54). The only rule, Sheridan feels, is to lay the accent on the same syllable in public speaking as in private discourse and *on no other* (pp. 55–56). We speak well, he says, in private conversation, but, because we are taught, mistakenly, to read differently from the way we speak, an artificial manner has replaced the natural one in all recitals and readings (p. 4). Sheridan's dictionary shows his strong feelings about this distortion.

[114] *Ibid.*, pp. 120–123.

[115] *Public Advertiser*, August 22, 1788, "The Character of Mr. Sheridan." The writer of this letter seems to be referring to Sheridan's efforts for a theatrical fund when he also says that "by dividing the profits amongst the Company," Sheridan planned to interest the actors in the theater's success and to make their situation happier and more honorable. This writer too felt that Sheridan's educational thinking had produced beneficial effects in Ireland and would have results in England later.

the result of a special provision in his will, drawn three years before. There he had directed that his body be buried in the parish where he "should happen to die" and "in as private and cheap a manner as may be." [116] In contrast to Garrick's great final show, Sheridan's exit was on an almost bare stage, with only Richard, Richard's brother-in-law Tickell, and a few others attending. For his last appearance Sheridan had insisted on the conditions he had required for his Smock-Alley debut forty-five years earlier—a clear Stage with no Crowds around to perplex his Exit.

---

[116] Thomas Sheridan's Will (quoted by permission of the Record Keeper, Probate Registry, Somerset House, London).

Smock-Alley Calendar

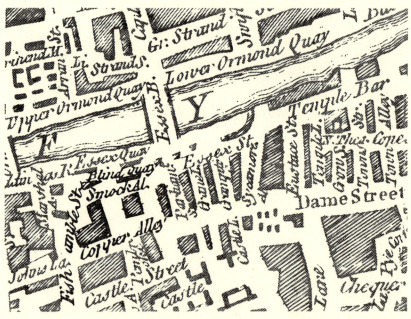

A section of Dublin showing Smock-Alley and Aungier-Street from "A New Plan of Dublin," the title print of *Hibernia Curiosa*. (Reproduced by courtesy of the Map Division, New York Public Library.)

PART I

A Chronological Listing of Performances Given Under Sheridan's Management 1745-March 2, 1754; 1756-1758

FAULKNER's *Dublin Journal* has been the main source for the information assembled in this Smock-Alley Calendar. It has been supplemented by the *Dublin Courant, Pue's Occurrences, Esdall's News-Letter,* and *Williamson's Universal Advertizer,*[1] whenever these papers were available and carried theatrical notices. The few playbills which survive from this period have also been consulted.

Performances have been listed by theatrical seasons, not by calendar years. The company recorded for each season includes all people listed in the advertisements or bills as performers (except those performing only once or twice, usually by request). The records become more complete in later years, when Sheridan began to give fuller casts in the daily advertisements. Information about roles and their players will be found in Part II of the Calendar under the title of the play.

The total number of performances for each season, as well as the number of benefits and of command performances, has been given with the understanding that all figures are approximate, since some evenings may not have been advertised and others may have been canceled. Although the performers' names in the company lists have been alphabetized for easy reference, the order of benefit takers has been preserved, since benefits were assigned roughly by rank, with those of the most important players coming earliest. Sometimes benefits failed to materialize, sometimes they were oversold, and in both cases the tickets were taken on another evening. When the names of several minor players are grouped together in a notice that their benefit tickets will be taken on a certain night, we can conclude that none of these people could sell enough tickets to support a benefit alone.

As manager of the theater-royal, Sheridan was paid by the government for giving, at certain times each season, performances to cele-

---

[1] For information from *Williamson's Universal Advertizer* I am indebted to Mrs. William S. Clark.

brate certain royal anniversaries. There were usually seven of these: for His Majesty's coronation (normally October 11, n.s. October 22); for His Majesty's birthday (normally October 30, n.s. November 10); for the birthday of the late King William III (normally November 4); for the Princess of Wales' birthday (normally November 19, n.s. November 30); the Prince of Wales' birthday (normally January 20 up to his death in 1751, May 24 for the new prince, n.s. June 4); and sporadically for the birthday of the Duke of Cumberland (April 15). Anniversary performances were generally advertised as by the viceroy's command, or, when he was absent, as by command of the Lords Justices, sometimes with boxes free to the ladies. In the following calendar the free boxes have been noted, but the repetitive headlines announcing the anniversary of "His Sacred Majesty's Birth Day," the birthday of "King William III, of Glorious Memory," et cetera, have been replaced after the first season by the notation "Anniversary performance."

Entertainments of music or dancing (sometimes of both) were part of most bills, and the performers were usually named in the notices. In the listing below, these entertainments have been more briefly noted, and only specially featured titles of songs, dances, or musical pieces have been given. The performers, if they are not named, can be assumed to have been one or more of the singers, dancers, or musicians listed in the company for the season. The second play, or afterpiece, was sometimes not specified, appearing only as "a Farce." Sometimes even this was omitted, the main play alone being advertised; but that other entertainment was included we know from the note occasionally appended: "With Entertainments as expressed in the Bills." No attempt has been made to preserve certain special typographical devices (such as names in capital letters), which appear in the advertisements. Titles and names have been regularized.

ABBREVIATIONS AND SYMBOLS

*—Never acted before

†—Never acted here

A.S.—Performance given at Aungier-Street Theater

Wax—Wax candles replace the usual tallow

Anniversary performance—See explanation above

By viceregal command—Used here when both the viceroy and his lady commanded a performance. When only the viceroy commanded, the entry indicates that fact.

The Company: ACTORS: Bardin, Barry, Beamsley, Dyer, Francis Elrington, Ralph Elrington, Garrick, Lacy, Layfield, Morgan, Morris, Sheridan, Vanderbank, Watson. ACTRESSES: Miss Bellamy, Miss Davis, Mrs. Elmy, Mrs. Furnival, Miss Jones (beginning March 17), Mrs. Walter. DANCERS: Moreau, Master Kelly. SINGERS: Mrs. Storer, Sullivan. EQUILIBRIST: Guitar.

Number of Performances: About 70.

Number of Command Performances: About 20.

Number of Benefit Performances: About 31. Sheridan (2), Barry (2), Mrs. Storer (2), Garrick (3), Ralph Elrington, Mrs. Furnival, Miss Bellamy (2), Francis Elrington, Bardin (2), Vanderbank, Neil (boxkeeper), Dr. Clancy (author), Moreau, Morris, Mrs. Elmy, Husband (former actor), an author, Watson, Sullivan, Beamsley and Connor, Guitar, Parsons, Jo. Elrington, a gentleman in confinement.

OCTOBER

W. 30
(A.S.)   *The Constant Couple.* "Being the Anniversary of His Sacred Majesty's Birth Day."

NOVEMBER

M. 4
(A.S.)   *Tamerlane.* Prologue, and singing by Mrs. Storer. "Anniversary of the Birth-Day of the Late King William III, of Glorious Memory."

Th. 7
(A.S.)   *Hamlet.*

M. 11
(A.S.)   *The Orphan.*

Th. 14
(A.S.)   *Richard III.* Dancing and singing.

M. 18
(A.S.)   *Othello.* By command of the Lord Lieutenant.

Tu. 19
(A.S.)   *The Conscious Lovers.* By command of the Lord Lieutenant. "Being the Anniversary of the Princess of Wales's Birth-Day."

Th. 21
(A.S.)   *The Constant Couple.* Entertainments. By viceregal command. "On Account of an extraordinary Demand for Places, Pit and Boxes are laid together at a Crown each. The Stage will be formed into an Amphitheatre, illuminated with Wax Candles, and made warm and commodious for Ladies." [1] Benefit of Sheridan.

[1] In the next issue of the *Dublin Journal* (November 16–19): "As the Boxes are all taken, such Ladies as intend to bespeak Places on the Stage, or in the Pit,

M. 25   *Julius Caesar.* Singing and dancing. "Particularly a Dialogue
(A.S.)   call'd Colin and Phoebe by Mr. Dyer and Mrs. Storer."

Th. 28   *All for Love* (not acted in this Kingdom these ten years). Sing-
(A.S.)   ing and dancing. By command of the Lord Lieutenant.

DECEMBER

M. 2   *The Spanish Fryar.* Farce. Singing and dancing. By viceregal
(A.S.)   command. Benefit of Barry.

W. 4   *The Provoked Husband* (at the Desire of Several Ladies of Qual-
(A.S.)   ity). *The Virgin Unmasked.* Singing and dancing. Benefit of
  Mrs. Storer.

Th. 5   *All for Love.* By Permission of the Right Hon. the Lord Mayor.[2]

M. 9   *Hamlet.* Singing and dancing.

Th. 12   *Richard III.* Singing. By command of the Lord Lieutenant.

M. 16   *The Stratagem.* Singing and dancing. "Also a Hornpipe by Master Kelly."

F. 20   *The Rehearsal.* "Being the last Time of Acting before the Holydays." Probably by command of the Lord Lieutenant.[3] Benefit of
  Garrick.

M. 30   *The Rehearsal* (being particularly desired).

JANUARY

Th. 2   *The Fair Penitent.* Singing.

Tu. 7   *Macbeth,* as written originally by Shakespeare. "With all the
  Songs, Dances, Sinkings, and Decorations proper to the Play."
  Command of the Lord Lieutenant.

Th. 9   *The Orphan.* "This Play was advertised last Saturday to be by
  Command of his Excellency the Lord Lieutenant by Mistake."

M. 13   *King Lear.* Singing and dancing.

Th. 16   *The Recruiting Officer.* Singing and dancing.

---

shall be waited on by Mr. Neil, the Boxkeeper, upon leaving a Memorandum at
the Bar of the Merchants Coffee-House, where Tickets may be had, or at Lucas's
Coffee-House."

[2] The company moved to Smock-Alley with this performance; its opening was
by the mayor's permission.

[3] A *Dublin Journal* news item speaks of this benefit performance for Garrick
as having been by command of the Lord Lieutenant, although it is not so advertised. (*Dublin Journal,* December 17–21: "Last Night the Comedy of the
Rehearsal was acted for the Benefit of Mr. Garrick, to the most polite and
crowded Audience that hath been seen at any Play: His Excellency the Earl of
Chesterfield, by whose Command it was performed, was present; and vast Numbers of People went away for Want of Room.")

M. 20   *The Committee*. By command of the Lord Lieutenant. "Anniversary of the Birth Day of his Royal Highness the Prince of Wales."

W. 22   *The Orphan* (by particular Desire).

F. 24   *The Stratagem* (by particular Desire).

M. 27   *The Provoked Wife. The School Boy*. Benefit of Garrick.

W. 29   *The Stratagem*. Singing and dancing.

F. 31   *King Lear* (by particular Desire).

FEBRUARY

M. 3   *The Distrest Mother*. Singing and dancing. Benefit of Ralph Elrington.

W. 5   *King John,* as written originally by Shakespeare.

Th. 6   *The Funeral*. Singing. By viceregal command. Benefit of Mrs. Furnival.

F. 7   *The Fair Penitent* (by particular Desire).[4]

M. 10   *Theodosius. The Devil to Pay*. By command of the Lord Lieutenant. Benefit of Miss Bellamy.

Tu. 11   *The Orphan.*

Th. 13   *All for Love,* with Songs by Mrs. Storer. Farce. Singing and dancing. By viceregal command. For "the Entertainment of the Right Hon. the Lord Chancellor, and the Chancellor of the Exchequer, the Right Hon. and Hon. the Judges, and the rest of the Hon. Society of the King's-Inns." Benefit of Fran. Elrington.

F. 14   *The Fair Penitent* (by particular Desire).

M. 17   [The First Part of] *King Henry IV,* with the Humours of Sir John Falstaff. *The Anatomist*. Singing and dancing. By command of the Lord Lieutenant. Benefit of Bardin.

W. 19   *Tancred and Sigismunda.*

M. 24   *Oroonoko*. Singing and dancing. "With several Solo's on the Violin between the Acts to be performed by Master Woder." By command of the Lord Lieutenant. Benefit of Vanderbank.

Tu. 25   *Love Makes a Man* (by Desire of several Ladies of Quality). Farce. Singing and dancing. Benefit of Neil, Boxkeeper.

W. 26   *Othello*. Singing and dancing.

Th. 27   *The Fair Penitent*. By command of the Lord Lieutenant. Benefit of Dr. Clancy.[5]

F. 28   *Othello.*

---

[4] This may not have been given, since Barry, scheduled to play Altamont, was apparently ill around this time. His first performance as Altamont was on February 14.

[5] Undoubtedly Michael Clancy, a writer of tragedies (*Herman, Prince of Corea*), who was ill at this time.

MARCH

W. 5   *Love for Love* (not acted these two years). Farce and entertainments. Benefit of Monsieur Moreau.

Th. 6   *The Distrest Mother*. Singing. Benefit of Barry.

M. 10   *Don Sebastian*. "The Comic Part of the Play, on Account of the great Length of the Performance, is by particular Desire omitted." *The Brave Irishman*. Singing by Sullivan.[6] By viceregal command. "Boxes are formed on the Stage, which will be illuminated with Wax Candles. Three Rows of the Pit are rail'd in for the Accommodation of Ladies where Servants will be admitted to keep Places." Benefit of Sheridan.

Th. 13 *Hamlet* (by Desire of several Ladies of Quality). *The Dragon of Wantley*. Benefit of Morris.

F. 14   *King Lear. The Brave Irishman.*

M. 17   *The Provoked Husband. The Dragon of Wantley.* By command of the Lord Lieutenant. Benefit of Mrs. Elmy.

W. 19   *The Constant Couple* (by Desire of several Persons of Quality). Benefit of Husband.

F. 21   *The Distrest Mother* (by particular Desire). A Pantomime Entertainment not exhibited these three Years.

APRIL

Th. 3   *Hamlet.* By viceregal command. Benefit of an Author.[7]

M. 7   *Jane Shore.* Entertainments. Benefit of Miss Bellamy.

M. 14   *The Provoked Wife.*

Tu. 15 *The Distrest Mother.* "A Prologue on the Occasion spoken by Mr. Sheridan, and an Epilogue by Mr. Garrick, written by the Farmer." [8] By viceregal command. "Being the Birth Day of his Royal Highness the Duke of Cumberland."

Th. 17 *Julius Caesar* (by Particular Desire of several Persons of Quality). *The Vintner Tricked.* Singing and dancing. Benefit of Watson.[9]

[6] Up to this time Mrs. Storer had been the singer. Sullivan had arrived in Dublin in January according to Garrick, who reports him "as gay and sensible as usual" (*Letters*, I, 75).

[7] An N.B. in the notice reads: "This Play is not for the Benefit of Mr. Brooke; but for another Gentleman who has wrote for the Stage."

[8] This epilogue appears in Alexander Chalmer's *English Poets*, XVII, 427. The Farmer was Henry Brooke, Irish author of *Gustavus Vasa*, et cetera. About this time (during the Rebellion), he was writing the Farmer's Letters in imitation of the Drapier's Letters (Baker, v. "Brooke"). See also Garrick's *Letters*, I, 75.

[9] A performance of *King Richard* with Garrick is also advertised for this date, probably by mistake.

M. 21   *Cato.*

Tu. 22   *Comus* (by particular Desire of several Persons of Quality).
"Written by Milton, and set to Musick by Mr. Arne. With all
the Grand Chorussus [*sic*], Machinery, and Decorations. . . .
N.B. The House to be illuminated with Wax Lights, and convenient Boxes for the Ladies on the Stage." Benefit of Sullivan.

W. 23   *King Lear.* Singing and dancing.

F. 25   *The Beggar's Opera* (not acted here these two years). Benefit of
Mrs. Storer.

S. 26   *Jane Shore. The Lying Valet* (by Desire). After the farce, An
Address to the Town, by Mr. Garrick. Benefit of Garrick.[10]

M. 28   *The Revenge* (by Desire of several Ladies of Quality). *The Contrivances.* Singing and dancing. Benefit of Beamsley and Connor.[11]

Tu. 29   *The Miser.* Singing. "After the Play Mr. Guitar will perform
several surprizing Feats of Activity. 1. The Somersets on the Ca-
chets. 2. The Leap over three Tables raised one above the other,
and a Chair above the uppermost. 3. A Leap over twelve Men's
Heads, and a Boy in the Middle. 4. A Leap through a Hogshead,
ten Foot from the Ground, with a Flambeau in each Hand. 5. A
Spring over a Man's Head on Horseback. 7. The surprizing
Spring of the double Fountain." Benefit of Monsieur Guitar
(equilibrist).

W. 30   [First Part of] *King Henry IV. The Devil to Pay.* Singing and
dancing. "A New Prologue on Occasion of the glorious and happy
Victory lately obtained by his Highness William Duke of Cumberland over the Rebels in Scotland, to be spoke by Mr. Sheridan." Benefit of Parsons.

MAY

Th. 8   *The Merchant of Venice* (by particular Desire). *The Necro-
(A.S.)   mancer,* or *Harlequin Dr. Faustus.* Singing. "By Command, no
Person whatever to be admitted behind the Scenes." [12]

F. 9   *Cato* (by Desire of several Persons of Quality). Singing and dancing. Benefit of J. Elrington.

[10] "As several Gentlemen and Ladies have desired to see Mr. Garrick in a
New Character, the Play of Macbeth is altered to Jane Shore" (*Dublin Journal,*
April 19–22, 1746). For Garrick's "Address to the Town," see Ch. III.

[11] After this performance a bonfire before the theater and a barrel of ale for
the public celebrated the duke's late victory (*Dublin Journal,* April 29–May 3,
1746).

[12] This performance had had to be postponed from the preceding Monday
"because the Machinery of the Entertainment of Dr. Faustus could not be got
ready by that Time" (*Dublin Journal,* April 29–May 3, 1746).

S. 10   *The Careless Husband.* Benefit of Bardin.

M. 26   *Oroonoko. The Hussar.* Benefit of a Gentleman in Confinement.

JUNE

M. 2   *Venice Preserved. The Virgin Unmasked.* By command of the Lords Justices. For the benefit of "distressed Widows, Orphans, &c. to the Number of fifty Families of the Officers and Soldiers Defenders of Londonderry and Inniskillen, at the Time of the late glorious and happy Revolution, set on Foot at the Recommendation of his Excellency the Earl of Chesterfield." [13]

1746–1747

The Company: ACTORS: Bardin, Beamsley, Dyer, Jo. Elrington, Ralph Elrington, Gemea, Giffard (beginning June 22), Layfield, MacLean (MacLelan?), Sheridan, Storer, Vanderbank, Watson. ACTRESSES: Miss Bellamy, Mrs. Dyer, Mrs. Gemea, Mrs. Giffard (beginning June 22), Miss Jones, Mrs. Walter. DANCERS: Mons. and Mlle. Mechel (beginning June 15). SINGERS: Miss Pocklington, Mrs. Storer.

Number of Performances: About 58.

Number of Command Performances: About 6.

Number of Benefit Performances: About 25. Sheridan (2), Bellamy (3), Mrs. Storer (2), gentleman in the Marshalsea (2), Bardin, family in great distress, another gentleman in the Marshalsea, family in distress, Ralph Elrington, Duval (former manager), Hospital for Incurables, Layfield, Senr., Neil (boxkeeper), Mr. and Mrs. Dyer, Dugere (limner), Victor (treasurer), Miss Jones and Jo. Elrington, Husband (former actor), widow of the late Francis Elrington, Watson and Beamsley.

OCTOBER

Th. 30   *Love for Love.* With a new Prologue. Anniversary performance by command of the Lords Justices. "Boxes open for the Ladies."

NOVEMBER

Tu. 4   *Tamerlane.* "With a new Prologue on the Occasion written by the Farmer,[1] to be spoke by Mr. Sheridan." Anniversary performance by command of the Lords Justices. "As there were many Complaints last Season on Account of the Stage's being

---

[13] Because of Barry's illness arising from his "Misfortune of being overturned in a Coach" (*Dublin Journal,* May 17–20, 1746), this performance had had to be deferred several times.

[1] For the identity of the Farmer, see footnote 8, p. 316.

crowded, no Person for the future will be admitted behind the Scenes under 5s.5d."

M. 10   *The Conscious Lovers* (First Subscription Play). Singing between the acts by Mrs. Storer.[2]

Th. 13   *Jane Shore* (Second Subscription Play). Singing.[3]

M. 17   *The Revenge* (Third Subscription Play). Singing.

W. 19   *The Conscious Lovers.* Singing. Anniversary performance by command of the Lords Justices.

Th. 20   *Hamlet* (Fourth Subscription Play).

M. 24   [First Part of] *King Henry IV.* Entertainments. Benefit of Sheridan.

Th. 27   †*Much Ado About Nothing* (Fifth Subscription Night). Singing.

DECEMBER

M. 1   *The Merchant of Venice.* Entertainments. Singing by Mrs. Storer: Act. II. Ellin a Roon. Act III. Behold the Sweet Flowers, &c. Act IV. A new Song called A well-a-day. *Damon and Phillida.* Benefit of Miss Bellamy.

Th. 4   *Richard III* (by particular Desire of some Ladies of Quality). Singing.

M. 8   *Much Ado About Nothing.*[4] †*The Lover's Opera.* Benefit of Mrs. Storer.

Th. 11   *The Orphan.* Farce. Singing. Benefit of a Gentleman confined in the Marshalsea of the Four-Court, for the Debt of Another Person.

M. 15   †*Romeo and Juliet* (Sixth and Last Subscription Play). "Written by Shakespear, with Alterations. . . . As the Play is a revived one, and as the Manager has been at a great deal of Expence in Decorations for it, the Prices according to the Custom of all Theatres will be encreased the above Night."

W. 17   *The Constant Couple.* Farce and entertainments. Benefit of Bardin.[5]

[2] "The Curtain both on that and all the succeeding Nights will certainly be drawn up precisely at Half an Hour after six; so that it is hoped the Ladies will come early to the Boxes" (*Dublin Journal*, November 1–4, 1746). "The Ladies are desired to send their Servants to keep Places at four o'Clock in order to prevent Mistakes" (*ibid.*, November 4–8).

[3] "The Subscribers are requested to send an Account to the Theatre of the Number of Places they want the Day before the Play, to prevent Confusion" (*Dublin Journal*, November 4–8, 1746).

[4] "Tickets delivered out for The Fair Penitent will be taken the above Night" (*Dublin Journal*, November 29–December 2, 1746). *The Fair Penitent* had originally been scheduled for this date.

[5] "N.B. Mr. Bardin not having it in his Power, from the Shortness of the Time, to pay his Respects personally to his Friends, takes this Method of doing

F. 19   *Romeo and Juliet.* †*Pyramus and Thisbe.* "The Words are to be found in Shakespear's Midsummer's Night's Dream. The Musick by Mr. Lampe. . . . No Person whatsoever will be admitted behind the Scenes, as the Machinery would be much obstructed by it."

M. 29   *The Beggar's Opera.* Benefit of the Gentleman in the Marshalsea.[6]

JANUARY

F. 2   *Jane Shore. Damon and Phillida.* Benefit of a Family in Great Distress.

M. 5   *First Part of King Henry IV* (by Desire of several Ladies and Gentlemen who were not present at the last Representation).

Th. 8   *Romeo and Juliet.*

M. 12   *Cato* (First Subscription Play). *Damon and Phillida.* Singing.

Th. 15   *Aesop,* not acted for many Years in this Kingdom (Second Subscription Play). Singing. "As this is a revived play the prices are raised."

M. 19   *Aesop.* "N.B. For the future no money will be taken nor no person admitted behind the Scenes except on benefit night."

Tu. 20   *The Provoked Husband.* Anniversary performance by command of the Lords Justices. "The Boxes will be free to the Ladies as usual."

W. 21   *The Fair Penitent.* Singing and entertainments. For the Enlargement of a young Gentleman confined in the Marshalsea of the Four-courts.

         (The theater was closed by the Kelly riot.)

FEBRUARY

M. 9   *Richard III.* Entertainments and singing. "No money will be taken, nor no person whatsoever [admitted] behind the scenes. No money will be returned after [the curtain is drawn] up." [7]

W. 11   *The Fair Penitent.*[8] "N.B. No Servants will be admitted into the Upper Gallery." Benefit of Hospital for Incurables. (This

---

it, and humbly hopes they will favour him with their Company the above Night" (*Dublin Journal,* December 13–16, 1747).

[6] This second benefit for the Marshalsea gentleman was to take care of the overflow crowds at his first benefit on December 11.

[7] The print is obscure here, but the intent of the notice is clear. This was the trial-play, at which *Richard III* with Sheridan replaced *Oroonoko* with Elrington (see Ch. iv).

[8] "By particular desire of several persons of distinction, the play of Much Ado About Nothing was changed to the Fair Penitent . . ." (*Dublin Journal,* February 7–10, 1747).

performance was suspended and all Dublin theaters were closed by order of the Lords Justices.)

MARCH

Tu. 3   *The Constant Couple*. Singing.

Th. 5   *The Conscious Lovers*. Benefit of family in distress.

M. 9   *The Orphan* (at the particular Desire of several Persons of Quality). †*Miss in her Teens*. Benefit of Miss Bellamy.

Tu. 10   *Oroonoko*. *Damon and Phillida*. Benefit of Ralph Elrington.

Th. 12   *The Provoked Husband* (at the particular Desire of several Ladies of Quality). "With a new Farce as will be expressed in the bills." Benefit of Duval.

M. 16   *Rule a Wife and Have a Wife*. *Chrononhotonthologos*. Benefit of Mrs. Storer.

Th. 19   *The Fair Penitent*. Singing. By command of the Lords Justices. "N.B. No Servants will be admitted into the Upper Gal[lery]. No Persons to be admitted on the Stage but Ladies, and the Gentlemen Stewards who are appointed for it." Benefit of Hospital for Incurables.

M. 23   *The Beggar's Opera*. *Miss in her Teens*. Benefit of Layfield, Senr.

M. 30   *Cato*. *Miss in her Teens*. "No money to be returned after the Curtain is drawn up."

APRIL

F. 3   *The Conscious Lovers* (Desire of several Ladies of Quality). *Miss in her Teens*. "N.B. The Boxes will be laid open to the Pit for the Convenience of the Ladies." Benefit of Neil, Box-keeper.

M. 6   *Hamlet* (First Subscription Night). *Miss in her Teens*. "No Money will be received, nor any Persons admitted behind the Scenes. No odd Money will be taken up during the Performance, nor any returned after the Curtain is drawn up."

W. 8   *Othello* (Second Subscription Night). *Miss in her Teens*.

F. 10   *Romeo and Juliet* (Third Subscription Night).

M. 27   *The Careless Husband*. *Miss in her Teens*. Benefit of Mr. and Mrs. Dyer.

Th. 30   *The Royal Merchant*. "With the whole Order and Procession of the Coronation of King Clause. All the Characters, Lord Chancellor, Lord Chamberlain, Dukes, Privy-Councellors, Knights of the Garter, Knights of the Bath, &c. In the exactest Manner. With several historical Passages; particularly the Tryal of the three Boors before the Lord Chief Justice Higgen, and Attorney-General Prigg. The Christening of Prince Hubert;

the Fall of Wolfort, and the Restoration of Earl Florex, &c."
Singing by Miss Pocklington. *Miss in her Teens.*

MAY

M. 4   *The Revenge.* Benefit of Dugere.

M. 18   *The Distrest Mother. Miss in her Teens.* Benefit of Miss Bellamy.

W. 20   *Romeo and Juliet. The Mad Lovers.* Benefit of Victor, Treasurer.[9]

F. 22   *Tamerlane.* "To celebrate the late Election of his Serene Highness the Prince of Orange to the Office and Dignity of Stadtholder."

M. 25   *Venice Preserved* (Third Subscription Play).[10]

W. 27   *Hamlet.* Benefit of Miss Jones and J. Elrington.

JUNE

M. 1   *The Conscious Lovers.* Farce. Benefit of Husband.

Tu. 2   *Much Ado About Nothing.* Entertainments. "By command of the Lords Justices. For the Entertainment of their Excellencies the Lord Chancellor, and the Chancellor of the Exchequer, the Right Hon. and Hon. the Judges, and the rest of the Hon. Society of King's-Inns." Benefit of the Widow of the late Mr. Francis Elrington.

Th. 4   *Othello.* Farce and singing. Benefit of Watson and Beamsley.

M. 15   *Richard III.* Entertainments of dancing by Mons. and Mlle. Mechel, "lately arrived from the Theatre-Royal in Drury-lane."

Th. 18 *King Lear* (Fourth Subscription Play).[11] Dancing.

M. 22   *Tancred and Sigismunda* (Fifth Subscription Play). Dancing. "No odd Money will be taken in any Part of the House during the whole Performance."

Th. 25 *Romeo and Juliet.* Dancing. No odd money.

M. 29   †*The Suspicious Husband.* "With several Entertainments of Dancing, viz. Act the 2d, the last new Dance called the Medley. At the End of the Play a new grand Comick Dance called

---

[9] Victor's benefit, originally scheduled for January 23, was rescheduled for May 11, deferred to May 15, and then to May 20. The May postponements were "occasioned by the fear of a Disappointment from a principal Performer." Sheridan did not arrive from England until May 15; he played Romeo in this benefit.

[10] This was to continue the Subscription Series begun in January and interrupted by the riot. *Aesop* had been the second play in the series.

[11] "Tickets delivered out for the same Play of the 28th and 29th of last Month, will be taken the above Night" (*Dublin Journal*, June 13–16, 1747).

Les Savoyardes by Monsieur and Mademoiselle Mechel, Monsieur Mechel sen. his Son and others." No odd money.

JULY

Th. 2   *The Suspicious Husband* (Last Subscription Play). New Entertainments of Dancing. *Miss in her Teens*. No odd money.

M. 13   *Macbeth*. Dancing. No odd money. Benefit of Sheridan.

Th. 16   *The Suspicious Husband*. Dancing. No odd money.

1747–1748

The Company: ACTORS: Beamsley, Dyer, Jo. Elrington, Ralph Elrington, Layfield, Morris (beginning May 11), Mynitt, Sheridan, Woodward. ACTRESSES: Miss Bellamy, Mrs. Dyer, Miss Jones, Miss Mason, Mrs. Mynitt, Miss Orfeur, Miss Pitt. DANCERS: Mons. Dumont, "Monsieur and Mademoiselle Mechel, Monsieur Mechel Senr. his Son," P. Morris. EQUILIBRIST: Guitar.

N.B. Although the benefits (see below) show a much larger company, these are the only persons who appear in the advertisements as performers.

Number of Performances: About 96.

Number of Command Performances: About 4.

Number of Benefit Performances: About 36. Miss Bellamy (2), Mlle. Mechel (2), Woodward (3), R. Elrington, Bardin, Victor (treasurer), a person in distress, Hospital for Incurables, Mechel, Vanderbank, Layfield, Mr. and Mrs. Dyer, Miss Jones and Miss Bourne, Mr. and Mrs. Mynitt, Mr. and Mrs. Layfield, Watson, Miss Pitt and the widow of the late F. Elrington, Beamsley, Neil (boxkeeper), Mr. and Miss Mason, Cushin (musician) and Guitar, sick and distressed Free-Masons, a distressed family, a surgeon's widow in distress, Mrs. Bayly (former actress) and Dumont, a family in distress, Signor Knerler (violinist), J. Elrington and Moreau, Giffard, Duval (former manager), Husband (former actor), a person in deep distress.

SEPTEMBER

M. 28   *The Busy Body. The Lying Valet*. Dancing by "Monsieur and Mademoiselle Mechel, Monsieur Mechel Senr. his Son, Monsieur Dumont, Mr. P. Morris and others, particularly a Dance called the German Camp."

OCTOBER

M. 5   *Love's Last Shift. The Schoolboy*. Dancing.

Th. 8   *The City Wives Confederacy. Miss in her Teens*. Dancing.

M. 12   *Love Makes a Man. Miss in her Teens.* Dancing. Anniversary performance by command of the Lord Lieutenant. Boxes free to the Ladies.

F. 16   †*Sir Courtly Nice.* †*Metamorphoses of Harlequin,* being the comick Part of the celebrated *Orpheus and Eurydice.*

M. 19   *Sir Courtly Nice. Metamorphoses of Harlequin.* Dancing.

W. 21   *The Busy Body. Metamorphoses of Harlequin.*

F. 23   †*The Little French Lawyer. Miss in her Teens.* Dancing.

M. 26   *The Revenge. Metamorphoses of Harlequin.* Dancing.

W. 28   *The Conscious Lovers. Miss in her Teens.* Dancing.

NOVEMBER

M. 2   *The Suspicious Husband.* "The Play to conclude with a new Country Dance, by the Performers in the Play." Dancing, "particularly at the end of the second Act, a Dance called the Savoyards; and after the Play a new Grand Comick Dance called, Les Chaffeurs."

W. 4   *Tamerlane.* "With a new Prologue on the Occasion, to be spoke by Mr. Sherridan [*sic*]." *Metamorphoses of Harlequin* (particularly desired). Anniversary performance.

F. 6   *The Suspicious Husband* (By particular Desire). *Miss in her Teens.* Dancing.

M. 9   *The Fair Penitent. The Necromancer,* or *Harlequin Doctor Faustus* (revived). "With the original Musick, Dances, and other Aecorations [*sic*]." Dancing.

W. 11   *The Relapse. The Necromancer,* or *Harlequin Doctor Faustus.*

M. 16   *Hamlet* (Shakespeare, First Night). "With several New Decorations." Dancing. "There will be also some select Pieces of Musick; particularly before the Curtain is drawn up a Grand Overture composed by Mr. Handel on the Suppression of the late Rebellion."

W. 18   *The Stratagem.*[1] *The Necromancer,* or *Harlequin Doctor Faustus.* Dancing.

F. 20   *All for Love* (revived). "With several new Scenes, Habits, Decorations and Dances."

M. 23   *Richard III* (Shakespeare, Second Night). "With the Distresses and Death of Henry VI, the artful Acquisition of the Crown by King Richard; the cruel Murder of King Edward V and his Brother in the Tower; the Landing of the Earl of Richmond, &c." Dancing.

---

[1] This play is sometimes advertised as *The Beaux Stratagem.* The present performance was at first intended for Friday the 13th but was deferred to the 18th.

W. 25   *All for Love.* "With Additional Decorations." Dancing. Wax. Curtain at half an Hour after Six.

M. 30   *Romeo and Juliet* (Shakespeare, Third Night). Dancing. Wax.

DECEMBER

W. 2   *Tancred and Sigismunda. The Intriguing Chambermaid.* Dancing. Wax. "N.B. There has been an extraordinary Demand for Places, there will be Boxes formed on the Stage for Ladies, but no Gentlemen will on any Account be admitted behind the Scenes." Benefit of Miss Bellamy.

F. 4   *Cato. The Metamorphoses of Harlequin.* Dancing. "Madem. Mechel will dance the Tambourine; Mons. and Madem. Mechel will dance a grand Switzer's Dance; they also will dance the grand Pierrot Dance, with its Entertainments, and other Dances not yet exhibited in this Kingdom. There will be Boxes made on the Stage for the Convenience of the Ladies." Benefit of Mademoiselle Mechel.

M. 7   *Othello* (Shakespeare, Fourth Night). Dancing. Wax.

W. 9   *Hamlet.* *New Pantomime Entertainment, *Trick Upon Trick.* "Harlequin to be performed by Mr. Woodward. In which (as an animated Statue) he will shew all the different Attitudes of that Character." Dancing. Benefit of Woodward.

F. 11   *All for Love. Intriguing Chambermaid.* Dancing, particularly the Tambourin. Wax.

M. 14   *Macbeth* (Shakespeare, Fifth Night). "N.B. Several Persons of Distinction having for some Time past desired to see the Play of K. Richard the Third, the Manager gives Notice that he will perform that Character on Wednesday next for the last Time this Season." Two grand comic dances, the Switzers and the Pierrots. Wax.

W. 16   *Richard III.*

W. 30   *The Royal Merchant.* "With the whole grand Procession of the Coronation of King Clause." *Metamorphoses of Harlequin.* Dancing.

JANUARY

F. 1   *A Bold Stroke for a Wife* (revived, not acted these 10 years). *The Intriguing Chambermaid.* Dancing.

F. 8   *The Squire of Alsatia* (revived, not acted these 7 years). *Trick Upon Trick.* Dancing. "N.B. Wednesday next being Twelfth Day, there will (on that Account) be no Play on that Night."

M. 11   *The Double Gallant* (revived, not acted these 7 years). *Miss in her Teens.* Dancing.

F. 15   *The Miser. The Emperor of the Moon,* "with all the Scenes, Machines and other necessary Decorations." Dancing.

M. 18   *All for Love.*

Tu. 19 *The Suspicious Husband. The Metamorphoses of Harlequin.*

W. 20   *The Double Gallant.* Anniversary performance by command of the Lord Lieutenant. Boxes free to ladies.

F. 22   *Romeo and Juliet* (Shakespeare, First Night). Wax.

M. 25   *Theodosius* (not acted these 2 years). *Miss in her Teens* (particularly desired).

Tu. 26 *The Stratagem.* "To conclude with a Country Dance by the Performers in the Play." *Trick Upon Trick.* Dancing.

W. 27   *The Recruiting Officer* (by particular Desire). *Duke and no Duke* (not acted these 10 years).

F. 29   *The Merchant of Venice. The Mock Doctor.* Dancing.

FEBRUARY

M. 1   *Macbeth* (Shakespeare, Third Night). *The Devil to Pay.*

Tu. 2   *The Recruiting Officer. Miss in her Teens.*

W. 3   *Theodosius. Duke and no Duke.* "Care shall be taken to have it more perfectly performed than it was last Time."

F. 5   *Much Ado About Nothing.* Dancing, by Monsieur Mechel, "who is now perfectly recovered from his Indisposition" and Mlle. Mechel.

M. 8   *The Distrest Mother.* With the original Epilogue. *Miss in her Teens.* Benefit of Miss Bellamy.

Tu. 9   *The Careless Husband* (revived). Dancing, "particularly at the End of the second Act the Minuet and Louvre. And at the End of the Play a new Grand Chacoon called the Masquerade, in which will be introduced a Variety of Grotesque Characters. . . . The whole Play will be entirely new drest in the Manufactures of our own Country, not even my Lord Foppington will have one Scrap of foreign Commodities about him in the whole Oeconomy of his Dress." *Miss in her Teens.*

W. 10   *The Busy Body.* Farce. Benefit of R. Elrington.

F. 12   *Venice Preserved.*

M. 15   *Venice Preserved.* *The new Pantomime Entertainment, composed by Mr. Woodward, called *Fairy Friendship,* or the *Triumph of Hibernia.* "To conclude with a new Scene painted by Mr. Tudor; and a grand Dance by Monsieur and Mademoiselle Mechel." [2]

---

[2] *Fairy Friendship,* originally advertised for Friday, February 12, is advertised for this Monday the 15th performance as "now first exhibited." Perhaps the whole February 12th bill was deferred to this date.

Tu. 16   *The Fair Penitent. Fairy Friendship.*

Th. 18   *Richard III* (by particular Desire).

F. 19   *As You Like It* (not acted these 6 years). Dancing. "N.B. The Play of K. John is postponed on Account of the Indisposition of a principal Performer." [3]

M. 22   *Love's Last Shift.* Farce. Dancing. By Special Command of his Excellency the Lord Lieutenant. Benefit of Bardin.

Th. 25   *Othello.* At end of 3d Act a Dance, the Switzers, and after the play a Grand Comic Dance, Les Savoyards. *The Little French Lawyer.* Benefit of Victor.

F. 26   *The Suspicious Husband.* Benfit of a Person in Distress.

S. 27   *The Provoked Husband.* "The principal Characters will be drest in the same Manner as those in the Careless Husband were." Dancing. *The Intriguing Chambermaid.* "As there has been an extraordinary Demand for Places, there will be commodious Boxes formed on the Stage for Ladies only, which will be illuminated with Wax." Benefit of The Hospital for Incurables.

M. 29   **The Loyal Subject*, "written originally by Mr. Beaumont and Fletcher, now first altered and adapted to the Stage by Mr. Sheridan." [4] Dancing, Les Savoyards and The Masquerade.

MARCH

Tu. 1   *All for Love. Fairy Friendship*, with Alterations.

W. 2   *The Loyal Subject.*

Th. 3   *King John* (Shakespeare, Sixth and Last Night).

F. 4   *Hamlet* (being the last time of Sheridan's appearing on the stage this season).

M. 7   *The Double Gallant.* Farce. Dancing "between every Act," the Minuet and Louvre, the Flying Peasant, La Foire de St. German, the Venetian Tambourine, a grand comic dance called Les Jardinies Swedois (?). Benefit of Mechel.

Tu. 8   *The Mourning Bride. The Mock Doctor.* Dancing. Benefit of Vanderbank.

Th. 10   *The Old Batchelor. Flora.* Dancing. Benefit of Layfield.

M. 14   *The Provoked Wife. Damon and Phillida.* Dancing. "N.B. Between the Play and Farce Mr. Woodward is to treat his Brother Atall with a Dish of his own Chocolate." Benefit of Mr. and Mrs. Dyer.

[3] The indisposition of a principal performer may well have been Miss Bellamy's grievance against Sheridan and Victor (see Ch. v).

[4] *Dublin Journal*, February 27–March 1, 1748: "Last Night the Play of the Loyal Subject, was performed at the Theatre-Royal in Smock-Alley, to a numerous and polite Audience, with Universal Applause, and we hear it is to be performed again there on Wednesday next."

W. 16   *She Would and She Would Not. The Intriguing Chambermaid.* Dancing. Benefit of Miss Jones and Miss Bourne.

F. 18   *The Miser. The Mock Doctor.* Dancing. Benefit of Mr. and Mrs. Mynitt.

M. 21   *The Double Dealer* (revived). *The What D'Ye Call It.* Dancing. "N.B. By particular Desire, Mr. Woodward will give Chocolate." Benefit of Mr. and Mrs. Layfield.

W. 23   *The City Wives Confederacy.* Dancing. "N.B. At the particular Request of several Persons of Quality, Mr. Woodward intends to Treat his Brother Atall, with a third Dish of his own Chocolate." Benefit of Watson.

F. 25   *The Way of the World. The What D'Ye Call It.* Dancing. Woodward's Chocolate, "being positively the last Time of his performing it in this Kingdom." Benefit of Miss Pitt, and the Widow of the late Mr. Francis Elrington.

M. 28   *Love Makes a Man. The Vintner Trick'd.* Dancing. "N.B. Being particularly desired. Mr. Woodward will drain out another Dish of Atall's Chocolate, after which he will give his Opinion of Mimickry in general, as a final Farewell to it." Benefit of Beamsley.

W. 30   *As You Like It* (Shakespeare, by Desire). *The What D'Ye Call It.* Dancing. "The Boxes will be laid open to the Pit, and two commodious Side Boxes formed on the Stage, for Ladies only, and Mr. Neill humbly requests that such Ladies as have taken Places in the Pitt will send their Servants early to prevent Mistakes." Benefit of Neil, Boxkeeper.

APRIL

F. 1   *The Relapse.* Dancing. Farce. Benefit of Mr. and Miss Mason.

M. 11   *The Royal Merchant.* "Containing the following Historical Relations. The Treachery of Hemskirk. The Trial of the three Boors. The fall of Welfort supposed Earl of Flanders. The Christening of Prince Hubert. With many other Remarkable Incidents. . . . With the whole Procession of the Coronation of King Clause." Dancing. Rope-dancing by Monsr. Guitar, with and without the Pole. "Particularly Mr. Guitar will tumble over a Man on Horseback, over twelve Men, and through a Hogshead ten Feet high, &c." Benefit of Cushin and Guitar.

W. 13   *The Busy Body. The What D'Ye Call It.* Dancing. By Command of the Right Worshipful Sir Marmaduke Wyvill, Bart., Grand Master of Ireland. For the Benefit of sick and distressed Free-Masons.

Th. 14 *The Squire of Alsatia. Miss in her Teens.* Dancing. "Mr.

Woodward intends giving Chocolate." For the Benefit of a distressed Family.

F. 15   *A Bold Stroke for a Wife. The Virgin Unmasked.* Dancing. At the Desire of Several Ladies of Quality. For the Benefit of a Surgeon's Widow, in Distress.

M. 18   *The Merry Wives of Windsor* (Shakespeare, by Desire). Dancing. Act 1, The Dutch Skipper; Act 2, Gondolier Venitian; Act 3, L'Allemande; Act 4, The Peasant Dance; Act 5, A Grand Comick Dance Samarquarade Devenise. Benefit of Mrs. Bayly and Mr. Dumont.

Tu. 19   *The Provoked Wife.* Dancing. Farce. At the request of several Persons of Quality. For the Benefit of a Family in Distress.

Th. 21   *The Beggar's Opera.* Dancing. "To which will be added a Grand New Dance called, The Hills Metamorphosed into Dwarfs; also another Dance by Madem. Mechel, in which she will perform all the Characters of Dancing." Benefit of Miss Mechel.

F. 22   *The Double Gallant.* "Between the Acts Signor Knerler will perform several Concertoes and a Solo on the Violin." *Flora.* Dancing. "And at the Request of several Persons of Quality Miss Talbot will sing . . . celebrated Songs, being the first Time of her appearing in this Kingdom." Benefit of Signor Knerler.

M. 25   *The Constant Couple.* Dancing. "After which Mr. Woodward will present the Audience with one Dish more of Atall's Chocolate; A second Dish of his own Imperial Tea; and lastly a Dish of fresh-rosted [*sic*] Strong Coffee, to settle the Head of Madam Pill-Kill-Tongue. . . ." Benefit of Woodward.

W. 27   *Sir Courtly Nice.* Dancing. Benefit of J. Elrington and Moreau.

Th. 28   †*The Foundling* (as it was lately acted in London, with universal Applause, written by Mr. Moore, Author of Fables for the Female Sex). Dancing. Farce. Benefit of Giffard.

F. 29   *Love for Love.* Dancing. Farce. Benefit of Duval.

MAY

M. 2   *Love's Last Shift.* Dancing. Benefit of Husband.

W. 4   *The Merry Wives of Windsor.* Farce. Dancing. For the Support of a Person in deep Distress.[5]

F. 6   *The Constant Couple.* Mr. Woodward will give Coffee. *Miss in her Teens.* "Mr. Woodward having many Tickets paid for which could not be admitted at his last Benefit (and in the

---

[5] In addition, "Charitable Contributions and Benefactions to be received for the Use of the distress'd Object, by Mr. Charles Lucas, at his House on Ormond-Quay" (*Dublin Journal*, April 30–May 3, 1748).

Hands of those who rather chuse to taste his Coffee than return them) has, he hopes without Offence, ventured upon this second Attempt." "At the Request of several Ladies, who were disappointed at his Last." For the Benefit of Mr. Woodward.

M. 9   *The Constant Couple. Miss in her Teens.*

W. 11   *The Twin Rivals. Trick Upon Trick.* "N.B. Mr. Woodward (by particular Desire) will once more give Coffee."

M. 16   *Richard III. Trick Upon Trick.*

F. 20   *The Beggar's Opera. Fairy Friendship.*

M. 23   *The Rehearsal. The Brave Irishman* (not acted these 2 years). Dancing. "Particularly a grand Comick Dance called, the Switzers; and at the End of the Play a Grand Ballet called, Les Pierots."

W. 25   *The Rehearsal,* with the usual Decorations.

F. 27   *The Loyal Subject* (the third night).

1748–1749

The Company: ACTORS: Barrington, Beamsley, Duncomb, Dyer, J. Elrington, R. Elrington, Gentleman, Kennedy, Macklin, Morris, Mozeen, Mynitt, Ross, Sheridan, Sparks, Storer, Vaughan, Watson, Williams (beginning May 8). ACTRESSES: Mrs. Bland, Miss Bourne, Miss Danvers, Mrs. Dyer, Miss Jones, Mrs. Macklin, Miss Minors, Mrs. Mynitt, Miss Orfeur (beginning May 5), Mrs. Vincent. SINGERS: Howard, Mrs. Lampe, Mrs. Mozeen, Miss Pocklington, Mrs. Storer, Sullivan (most of these also acted). MUSICIANS: Lampe (composer), Pasquali.

Number of Performances: About 111.

Number of Command Performances: About 5.

Number of Benefit Performances: About 33. Macklin, Mrs. Storer (2), Pasquali, R. Elrington, Mrs. Macklin, Mrs. Lampe, Sullivan, Mrs. Mozeen, Mrs. Vincent, Mr. and Mrs. Dyer, Mrs. Bland, Miss Jones, Neil (boxkeeper), Miss Bourne, Victor (treasurer), Miss Minors, Sparks, Mr. and Mrs. Mynitt, Harrington (prompter) and Bate (printer), Barrington, Beamsley, Jo. and Master Elrington, Morris, Kennedy and Dugere (limner), Ross and Cushin (musician), Watson, Husband (former actor), Vaughan and the widow of the late F. Elrington, the Lying-In Hospital, Layfield, Gentleman, decayed, distrest and superannuated players.

OCTOBER

M. 3   *As You Like It.* Singing. Several "new Pieces of Musick, particularly a grand Concerto for the Violin, Solo, by Sign. Pasquali."

F. 7   *The Beggar's Opera.* "With several Entertainments by Sign. Pasquali and others."

M. 10   *The Merchant of Venice. The Intriguing Chambermaid.* Music, particularly a song out of Handel's new Oratorio "Powerful Guardians." [1]

Tu. 11   Same bill as on October 10. Anniversary performance by command of the Lords Justices.

F. 14   *The Provoked Wife. The Contrivances.* Music and singing.

M. 17   *The Committee. Damon and Phillida.*

W. 19   *The Busy Body. The Devil to Pay.* Singing.

F. 21   *Love for Love.*

M. 24   *The Beggar's Opera.* "By particular Desire of some Ladies of Quality." Music. Overture begins at 6:30 and "no Musick will precede it."

W. 26   †*The Mistake. The Lottery* (not acted here for 5 years). Singing, particularly a favorite Cantata, Who'll buy a Heart; a Ballad, Advice to Husbands.

F. 28   *The Old Batchelor.*

M. 31   *As You Like It.* Anniversary performance by command of the Lords Justices. Boxes free to the ladies.

NOVEMBER

W. 2   *The Revenge.* "After the Play will be performed, The Birthday Ode, set to Musick by Mr. Lampe, as it was done last Night at the Grand Festino Room in Aungier-street."

F. 4   *Tamerlane.* **The Triumphs of Hibernia*, "set to Musick by Sgr. Pasquali." Anniversary performance.

M. 7   *The Suspicious Husband. The Triumphs of Hibernia.*

W. 9   *Love for Love. The Triumphs of Hibernia.*

F. 11   *Richard III* (Shakespeare, First Night).

M. 14   *The Mistake* (revived). *The Triumphs of Hibernia.* Entertainments.

W. 16   *The Stratagem. Flora.* Singing and music.

F. 18   *Richard III* (Shakespeare, Second Night). Wax.

S. 19   *Love for Love.* New prologue. Entertainments. Anniversary performance by command of the Lords Justices. Boxes free to ladies.

M. 21   *Hamlet* (Shakespeare, Third Night). "To which will be added,

[1] This performance was advertised in the *Dublin Courant* for Monday, October 10. It was played again the next night by command for His Majesty's Coronation, replacing *The Committee*, which had originally been planned for the occasion.

the second Part of Alexander's Feast. The Words by Mr. Dryden, the Musick by Mr. Handel."

W. 23   *The Double Dealer*. Singing, particularly "an old Scotch Song called the Highland Laddy." Music.

F. 25   *The Miser*.

M. 28   *Othello* (Shakespeare, Fourth Night). *The Triumphs of Hibernia*.

Tu. 29   *The Provoked Husband. The Dragon of Wantley*, composed by Mr. Lampe and to be conducted by him.

DECEMBER

Th. 1   *The Provoked Husband. The Dragon of Wantley*.

F. 2   *The Beggar's Opera*.

M. 5   *Much Ado About Nothing* (Shakespeare, Fifth Night). *The Dragon of Wantley*. Wax.

W. 7   †*The Refusal*. Singing and music.

F. 9   *The Old Batchelor*.[2]

M. 12   *Macbeth* (Shakespeare, Sixth and Last Night). "With the Original Songs and Musick." *The Triumphs of Hibernia*. Wax.

W. 14   *The Old Batchelor. The Dragon of Wantley*.

F. 16   *Comus*. "With the usual Decorations."

M. 19   *The City Wives Confederacy*. †*A Will and No Will*, written by Mr. Macklin, "as it was performed with universal Applause at the Theatre Royal in Drury Lane." Singing. Benefit of Macklin.

W. 21   *The Beggar's Opera. The Miller of Mansfield*. Benefit of Mrs. Storer.

F. 23   *The Provoked Wife. The Triumphs of Hibernia*. Wax. Being the last time of performing before the Holidays. Benefit of Sgr. Pasquali.

JANUARY

M. 2   *The Royal Merchant*. "With the whole Procession of the Coronation of Clause, King of the Beggars."

W. 4   *The Committee. Trick Upon Trick*. Entertainments.

F. 6   *The Miser*.

M. 9   *The Refusal. Flora*. Singing.

W. 11   *The Mistake. The Dragon of Wantley*. Singing.

F. 13   *The Tempest*.[3] "With the original Songs and Musick composed

---

[2] This performance of *The Old Batchelor* may have been deferred to December 14, when Sheridan is again advertised as playing Heartwell for the first time.

[3] A press item in the *Dublin Journal* (January 3–7, 1749) announces that this is *The Tempest* as altered by Dryden and Davenant.

by Mr. Purcell; the Scenes, Machines, and other Decorations proper to the Play being entirely new."

M. 16   *Richard III* (Shakespeare, First Night). Singing and music, "Particularly a Concerto for the Violin, Solo, after the Play."

W. 18   *Comus.* "With Decorations as before."

Th. 19   *The Tempest,* "being the second Time of its being performed in the present Manner in this Kingdom. Written originally by Shakespear, and altered for the Stage by Mr. Dryden. . . . The whole to conclude with a grand Masque of Neptune and Amphitrite. . . . Several new Scenes and Decorations."

F. 20   *The Refusal.* New prologue. *The Miller of Mansfield.* Anniversary performance by command of the Lords Justices. Boxes free to ladies.

M. 23   *Hamlet* (Shakespeare, Second Night). Singing and music. Wax.

W. 25   *The Tempest.* "With new Scenes, and an extraordinary Piece of Machinery representing the rising Sun, never but once exhibited in this Kingdom. . . . With the original Musick, composed by Purcel, Sinkings, Flyings, and other Decorations."

Th. 26   *The Suspicious Husband. Miss in her Teens.* Singing.

F. 27   *Cato.* †*Lady Moore, or the Dragoness,* being a Sequel to *The Dragon of Wantley.*

Tu. 31   *Othello* (Shakespeare, Third Night). Singing and music. Wax. "N.B. The above Play is postponed from Monday to Tuesday, as Monday is the Anniversary of K. Charles's Martyrdom."

FEBRUARY

W. 1   *Love for Love.* Singing. Benefit of R. Elrington.

Th. 2   *The Double Dealer. Lady Moore, or the Dragoness.*

F. 3   *The Conscious Lovers. Miss in her Teens.* Singing and music, particularly a new solo to be performed by Pasquali, "on the Stage in the Play."

M. 6   *Macbeth* (Shakespeare, Fourth Night). "With the original Songs and Musick by Purcel." *Lady Moore, or the Dragoness.* Wax.

Th. 9   *The Merchant of Venice.* **The Temple of Peace,* "on Occasion of the present happy Peace established over Europe." Includes several "favourite Songs of Mr. Handel, Boyce, Purcel and other eminent Masters. The rest of the Music composed by Signior Pasquali." New scenes and decorations, "particularly a grand View of the Temple of Peace."

M. 13   *Romeo and Juliet* (Shakespeare, Fifth Night). "With Additions and Alterations." *Lady Moore.*

W. 15   *The Relapse. The Temple of Peace.*

Th. 16   *Oroonoko* (not acted here these 4 years). "With Additions and new Decorations, particularly a Scene will be restored never exhibited here before, wherein Mrs. Lampe and Mrs. Storer will sing the two original Songs, new set to Musick by Mr. Lampe, in the Habits of American Slaves; and a Foreigner, lately arrived, will perform a Piece of Musick on a new invented Instrument, never heard in this Kingdom." [4] Entertainments.

F. 17   *The Tempest.*

M. 20   *Julius Caesar* (Shakespeare, Sixth Night). *The Temple of Peace.*

W. 22   *The Conscious Lovers.* Entertainments and Music. *The Temple of Peace.* "Between the Play and the Masque there will be a Piece of Musick performed on the Cymbalo, a new invented Instrument, by the Person who played on it before."

Th. 23   *The Beggar's Opera.* "To conclude with a Country Dance."

F. 24   *Romeo and Juliet.* "With Additions and Decorations as before."

M. 27   *First Part of King Henry IV* (Shakespeare, Seventh Night). Entertainments. Wax.

MARCH

W. 1   *The Rehearsal.* ". . . in which Mr. Bayes will exhibit a Set of new raised Troops never before seen on any Stage."

Th. 2   *Oroonoko.*[5] †*The Double Disappointment.*

F. 3   *The Way of the World.* Singing and music. Benefit of Mrs. Macklin.

M. 6   *The Tempest.* ". . . to conclude with a grand Masque, Neptune and Amphitrite." *Lady Moore, or the Dragoness.* Benefit of Mrs. Lampe.

W. 8   *Rule a Wife and Have a Wife* (not acted these 2 years). "With several new Cantatas and Songs by Mr. Sullivan; also a new Duet by Mr. Sullivan and Mrs. Lampe." *Lady Moore.* Benefit of Sullivan.

Th. 9   **The Orphan of Venice.* New prologue and epilogue.

F. 10   *The Foundling. The Virgin Unmasked.* Singing. Benefit of Mrs. Mozeen.

M. 13   *The City Wives Confederacy.* Benefit of Mrs. Vincent.

W. 15   *The Beggar's Opera.* To conclude with a Country Dance. *Miss in her Teens.* Music. Benefit of Mr. and Mrs. Dyer.

[4] The instrument was later revealed as the *cymballo*, or *cymbalo* (see February 22 entry).

[5] Announced as the second time of Sheridan's appearance in the title role, this performance of *Oroonoko* may have been canceled or the role may have been taken by another actor, since the April 4th production is also advertised as the second time for Sheridan in the part (*Dublin Journal*, March 28–April 1, 1749).

Th. 16 *The Recruiting Officer*. Singing. Benefit of Mrs. Bland.

M. 27 *Jack the Giant Queller*. New prologue and epilogue. Before the piece a new comic overture by Pasquali.

W. 29 *The Refusal. The Honest Yorkshireman*. Singing. Benefit of Miss Jones.

F. 31 *Love Makes a Man. The Lying Valet* (by particular Desire). Singing. "N.B. On Account of the extraordinary Demand for Places, at the Request of several Ladies, the Boxes will be laid open to the Pit." Benefit of Neil, Boxkeeper.

APRIL

Tu. 4 *Oroonoko*. Music on Cymballo. *The Devil to Pay.*

Th. 6 *The Foundling. The Miller of Mansfield*. Singing. Benefit of Miss Bourne.

S. 8 *King Henry V* (not acted these 5 years) (Shakespeare, Eighth and Last Night). *The Virgin Unmasked*. Wax.

M. 10 *The Tender Husband* (not acted these 7 years). Singing. At end of 4th Act, new medley solo by Pasquali; at end of play, "A new Epilogue, adapted to the Times, to be spoken by Mrs. Bland." *Lady Moore*. Benefit of Victor.

W. 12 *The Way of the World. The Mock Doctor*. Singing. Benefit of Miss Minors.

Th. 13 *The Orphan of Venice*. Prologue and epilogue.

F. 14 *King Henry V. *Apollo and Daphne*. With new decorations.

Tu. 18 [First Part of] *King Henry IV. The Vintner Tricked*. Singing. Benefit of Sparks.

W. 19 *The Drummer* (not acted these 10 years). *The Virgin Unmasked*. Singing. Benefit of Mr. and Mrs. Mynitt.

F. 21 *The Twin Rivals. Trick Upon Trick*. Singing. Benefit of Harrington, Prompter, and Mr. Edward Bate, Printer.

S. 22 *The Orphan* (First Subscription Night). *Apollo and Daphne*. With new Scenes, Habits, and other Decorations.

M. 24 *Rule a Wife and Have a Wife*. End of Act II, A Cantata, Sullivan; end of Act III, A Cantata set by Stanly, Mrs. Storer; end of Act IV, song by Mrs. Lampe; end of Act V, Ileen a Roon, Mrs. Storer. *The Double Disappointment*. After the farce, Mr. Barrington will sing the Roratorio. Benefit of Barrington.

W. 26 *The London Merchant* (not acted these 10 years). *The Mock Doctor*. Singing. Benefit of Mrs. Storer.

Th. 27 *The Provoked Husband* (by Desire of several Ladies of Quality). *The Temple of Peace* (by particular Desire). "The Pit will be laid open to the Boxes, and Servants allowed to keep Places there for Ladies."

F. 28   *The Merchant of Venice.* Singing. Farce. Benefit of Beamsley.
S. 29   *Theodosius* (Second Subscription Night). "Scenes, Habits, and
          other Decorations proper to the Play. With all the original Songs
          set to Musick by Mr. Lampe and now first performed." *The
          Miller of Mansfield.*

MAY

M. 1   *The Spanish Fryar. The Contrivances.* Singing. Benefit of J. El-
          rington and Master Elrington.
Tu. 2   *The Merry Wives of Windsor. A Will and No Will.* Singing.
          Benefit of Morris.[6]
W. 3   *The Stratagem. Miss in her Teens.* Singing. Benefit of Kennedy
          and Dugere,[7] Limner.
Th. 4   *The Fair Penitent* (Third Subscription Night). *Apollo and
          Daphne.* "N.B. The Curtain on the above Night will not be
          drawn up till seven o'Clock; and the Plays for the Future will
          not begin till that Hour."
F. 5   *The Recruiting Officer. The Lying Valet.* Singing. Benefit of
          Ross and Cushin.
M. 8   *The Miser.* Pantomime Entertainment, "in which will be repre-
          sented the Wonderful Escape of Harlequin, alias Don Jumpedo
          into a Quart Bottle, as it has been exhibited for Sixty Nights run-
          ning with universal Applause at the Theatre-Royal in Covent-
          Garden." Singing. By command of the Lords Justices. Benefit
          of Watson.
Tu. 9   *The Provoked Wife.* Prologue. *The Virgin Unmasked.* Benefit
          of Husband.
W. 10   *The Constant Couple.* Benefit of Vaughan and the widow of
          the late Francis Elrington.
Th. 11   *All for Love* (Fourth Subscription Night). "In the second Act
          will be introduced a short new Masque written by Henry Brooke,
          Esq; set to Musick by Sign. Pasquali." *Tom Thumb the Great.*
W. 17   *The Conscious Lovers.* Benefit of Lying-In Hospital in George's-
          Lane.

[6] Note added to Mr. Morris' advertisement in the *Dublin Journal* (April 8–
11, 1749): "Whereas some People have industriously spread a Report that this
Play is not for my Benefit; this is to assure the Publick that it really is, and I
therefore hope my Friends will think of it as such, which shall be gratefully
acknowledged among the many other Obligations conferred on their much
obliged, and very humble Servant. John Morris."
[7] Also spelled "Degeer" and "Dugar." An item in the April 25–29 *Journal*
reports that the famous Mr. Dugar, Miniature-Painter, is to perform the part of
Fribble "with some Alterations of his own."

Th. 18	*Tancred and Sigismunda* (Fifth Subscription Night). *Tom Thumb the Great.*
M. 22	*Theodosius. Apollo and Daphne.* "Interspersed with some Comick Scenes of the Entertainment called, Trick Upon Trick. Particularly the Escape of Harlequin into a Quart Bottle, and the Skeleton Scene."
Tu. 23	*The Drummer.* Singing. Benefit of Layfield.[8]
Th. 25	*The Spanish Fryar.* New Prologue and "a comic Epilogue to be spoken by Mr. Gentleman." Singing. Farce. Benefit of Gentleman.[9]
F. 26	*The Suspicious Husband. Apollo and Daphne* (as on May 22). Benefit of decayed, distrest, and superannuated Players.
M. 29	*Oroonoko*[10] (Sixth and Last Subscription Night). *Tom Thumb the Great.*

1749–1750

The Company: ACTORS: Bardin, Beamsley, Cibber, Digges, Dyer, J. Elrington, R. Elrington, Master Elrington, Gentleman, Hamilton, Kennedy, Macklin, Messink, Morgan, Mossop, Ross, Sheridan, Sparks, Vaughan. ACTRESSES: Mrs. Bland, Miss Bourne, Miss Copen, Miss Danvers, Miss Griffith, Mrs. Kennedy, Mrs. Lindley, Mrs. Macklin, Mrs. Mynitt, Miss Reynolds. SINGERS: Howard, Mrs. Lampe, Mrs. Mozeen, Mrs. Storer, Sullivan (most of these also acted). MUSICIANS: Lampe (composer), Pasquali. DANCERS: Mons. Granier, Mlle. Vandersluys.

Number of Performances: About 143.

Number of Command Performances: About 4.

Number of Benefits: About 36. Pasquali, Duval (former manager), Mrs. Storer, R. Elrington, Macklin, Digges (2), Mossop (3), Cibber (2),

[8] An N.B. in Mr. Layfield's notice: "As the Indisposition which Mr. Layfield has sometime languished under, deprives him of the Pleasure of waiting on his Friends, to solicit their Favour, on this Occasion; he most humbly hopes, from their known Humanity and Benevolence, that they will give him the honour of their Company at his approaching Benefit Play" (*Dublin Journal,* May 16–20, 1749).

[9] Note attached to Mr. Gentleman's notice: "Mr. Gentleman being informed that some Persons have insinuated the above Play is not for his Benefit, in Justice to himself, thinks it necessary to acquaint the Publick, that the Assertion is only devised to prejudice him, therefore hopes it will meet the Disregard such Calculations deserve" (*Dublin Journal,* May 20–23, 1749).

[10] *Oroonoko* was substituted rather suddenly for the new play Thomson's *Coriolanus,* which was postponed till next season because of "the Indisposition of a principal Performer." But it was not given then. (See Ch. v.)

Sullivan, Mrs. Lampe, Mrs. Bland, Miss Danvers, Bardin, Miss Griffith, Mrs. Mozeen, Victor (treasurer), Mr. and Mrs. Storer, Neil (boxkeeper), Miss Bourne and the widow of the late F. Elrington, a gentleman of the army and his family in distress, Watson, Ross, Layfield, Mr. and Mrs. Mynitt, Mlle. Vandersluys, Mr. and Mrs. Kennedy, Beamsley, J. and Master Elrington, Howard and Vaughan, Hamilton, Sparks, Husband (former actor).

SEPTEMBER

F. 22   *The Beggar's Opera.*

M. 25   *The Miser.*

W. 27   *Richard III.*

F. 29   *The Merchant of Venice.*

OCTOBER

M. 2   *Hamlet* (Shakespeare, Third Night). Dancing by Mons. Granier and Mademoiselle Vandersluys, from the Theatre-Royal in Covent Garden, the first time of their performing in this kingdom.

W. 4   *The Provoked Wife.* Dancing. Entertainments.

F. 6   *Othello.* Dancing.

M. 9   *Macbeth* (Shakespeare, Fifth Night). With the original music, songs, et cetera. Dancing.

W. 11   *The City Wives Confederacy.* Anniversary performance by command of the Lord Lieutenant.

F. 13   *Romeo and Juliet* (Shakespeare, Last Night). Entertainments.

M. 16   *The Conscious Lovers.* Singing and dancing. Solo by Pasquali.

W. 18   *The Stratagem.* Singing and dancing.

F. 20   *Romeo and Juliet.* Dancing.

M. 23   *Theodosius.* "With all the original Songs new set to Musick by Mr. Lampe." Dancing.

W. 25   *The Drummer.* Entertainments. "N.B. The Recruiting Officer is obliged to be deferred."

F. 27   *Oroonoko.* "With the original Songs set to Musick by Mr. Lampe." Dancing.

M. 30   *Love for Love.* Anniversary performance by command of the Lord Lieutenant. Boxes free to ladies.

NOVEMBER

W. 1   *The Recruiting Officer. Tom Thumb the Great.* Dancing.

F. 3   *The Provoked Husband. Chrononhotonthologos* (not performed here for 7 years).

338

S. 4   *Tamerlane.* Masque written in honour of the day and set to music by Pasquali.[1] Anniversary performance.

M. 6   *All for Love,* with the Brooke-Pasquali masque. A new dance by Mons. Granier, Mlle. Vandersluys and others.

W. 8   *The Drummer. Tom Thumb the Great.*

F. 10   *The Loyal Subject,* as altered by Sheridan. *The Triumphs of Hibernia.*

M. 13   *Love Makes a Man. The Honest Yorkshireman.* Dancing.

W. 15   *The Suspicious Husband.* Country dance by performers. *Tom Thumb the Great.*

F. 17   *The Refusal.* Farce. Dancing.

M. 20   *The Way of the World. The Stage Coach* (not acted here these 7 years). Anniversary performance by command of the Lord Lieutenant.

W. 22   *Richard III* (Shakespeare, First Night). *The Mock Doctor.* Singing and dancing. Wax.

F. 24   *The Double Dealer. Chrononhotonthologos.* Singing and dancing.

M. 27   *Hamlet* (Shakespeare, Second Night). Grand Concerto and Solo by Pasquali. Singing and dancing. Wax. "N.B. It is requested that the Ladies who have engaged Places in the Boxes will send their Servants at Half an Hour after four, to prevent Confusion."

W. 29   *Venice Preserved.*

Th. 30   *The Revenge.*

DECEMBER

F. 1   *Romeo and Juliet* (Shakespeare, Third Night). Entertainments.

M. 4   *Othello* (Shakespeare, Fourth Night). Singing, dancing, and music, particularly a solo by Pasquali. Wax.

W. 6   *Venice Preserved.*

Th. 7   *The Revenge.*

F. 8   *Macbeth* (Shakespeare, Fifth Night). *The What D'Ye Call It.* "Interposed with several new Songs set to Musick by Mr. Lampe, and now first performed in this Kingdom."

S. 9   *The Fair Penitent.*

M. 11   *As You Like It* (Shakespeare, Sixth Night). "Amiens with the Song of Blow, Blow, &c. by Mr. Sullivan; Celia, in which will be introduced the Song of the Cuckoo, by Mrs. Mozeen." After the 4th Act, Signior Pasquali will perform a Piano e Forte Con-

---

[1] This was apparently *The Triumphs of Hibernia,* the masque written for the same event the preceding year. (See *Dublin Journal,* October 28–31, 1749.)

certo, composed "in an intire new Taste." *The Mock Doctor.* Wax.

W. 13   *Othello.* Singing and dancing.

Th. 14   *The Fair Penitent* (by Desire). *The What D'Ye Call It.* No play on Friday, December 15, "on Account of Mr. Sheridan's Band being engaged to perform at the Messiah."

S. 16   *King Lear.* Dancing and Singing.

M. 18   *The Refusal.* With the following entertainments between the acts. Act I. The Medley Solo of Elen Aroon. Act II. A Cantata by Mrs. Mozeen. Act III. A Dance by Mons. Granier and Mlle. Vandersluys. Act IV. The Piano e Forte Concerto for the Violin Solo. "Between the Play and the Farce a new Medley Solo consisting of an Introduction and Variations upon Oroo Drimindoo and Daniel Cooper." *The Honest Yorkshireman.* Benefit of Pasquali.

Tu. 19   *Othello* (Shakespeare, Seventh Night). Entertainments and Concerto for Violin Solo by Pasquali. Wax.

W. 20   *The Mistake. The Mock Doctor.* Dancing and singing. Benefit of Duval.

Th. 21   *The Way of the World. The Anatomist.* Singing and dancing. Benefit of Mrs. Storer.

F. 22   *King Lear* (by Desire). Entertainments.

S. 23   *Julius Caesar* (Shakespeare, Last Night). Entertainments and music. Wax. "N.B. Mr. Mossop is prevented from appearing in the Character of Cassius by a sudden Indisposition."

W. 27   *The Beggar's Opera.* To conclude with a country dance by the performers.

Th. 28   *The Committee.* Farce.

JANUARY

M. 1   *Love Makes a Man. Trick Upon Trick.* "In which will be introduced the wonderful Scene of Harlequin's Escape into a Quart Bottle." Dancing.

W. 3   *The Mistake. The Miller of Mansfield.* Dancing.

Th. 4   *The Miser.* Farce. Dancing.

F. 5   *The Committee.* Farce. Dancing.

M. 8   *Julius Caesar.* Dancing.

W. 10   *The Careless Husband.* Concludes with a country dance by the performers. *The Anatomist.* Singing and dancing.

Th. 11   *Rule a Wife and Have a Wife. The Vintner Tricked.* Dancing.

F. 12   *Julius Caesar.*

M. 15   *Julius Caesar. The Dragon of Wantley.*

W. 17   *The Careless Husband.* "To conclude with a Country Dance by the Performers to a new Maggot." *The Brave Irishman* (not acted these 5 years).

Th. 18   *Jane Shore.*

F. 19   *The Merchant of Venice* (Shakespeare, First Night). *Pyramus and Thisbe,* in a new manner (revived). The words by Shakespeare, the music by Lampe. Wax.

S. 20   *The Way of the World. The Dragon of Wantley.* Dancing. Anniversary performance by command of the Lord Lieutenant. Boxes free to ladies.

Tu. 23   *Jane Shore. The Brave Irishman.* A new dance by Mons. Granier and Mlle. Vandersluys.

W. 24   *Othello* (Shakespeare, Second Night). *Pyramus and Thisbe,* a Mock Opera, performed in a new Manner. Concerto on the Violin Solo by Pasquali. Wax.

Th. 25   *The Fair Penitent.* Farce. Entertainments.

F. 26   *King Lear* (Shakespeare, Third Night). Piano e Forte Concerto by Pasquali. Wax.

S. 27   *The Tempest* (as altered by Dryden). To conclude with a grand Masque of Neptune and Amphitrite. "With all the original Musick and Decorations."

M. 29   *Richard III* (Shakespeare, Fourth Night). *Tom Thumb the Great.* Wax.

W. 31   *Jane Shore. The Brave Irishman.*

FEBRUARY

Th. 1   *The Tempest.*

S. 3   *The Orphan.*[2]

M. 5   *Hamlet* (Shakespeare, Fifth Night).[3] *The Brave Irishman.* Concerto for Violin Solo, Pasquali. Wax.

W. 7   *The Orphan.*

Th. 8   *Romeo and Juliet* (Shakespeare, Sixth Night). *The Mock Doctor.* Wax.

F. 9   *The Way of the World. The Match in Newgate.* By command of the Lord Lieutenant. For the entertainment of the Lord Chancellor, the Chancellor of the Exchequer, the Judges and

---

[2] A note in the January 30–February 3 *Dublin Journal* announces that "Mr. Sheridan is so well recovered from his Cold, as to be able to appear in the Character of Chamont [*The Orphan*] tonight." He had been too ill to do Romeo the night before.

[3] A performance of *Romeo and Juliet* (see footnote above), scheduled for February 2 and advertised as the Fifth Night in the Shakespeare series had had to be canceled and *Hamlet* is now called the Fifth Night. *Romeo and Juliet* was presented later in the week as the Sixth Night in the series.

the rest of the Society of King's Inns. Benefit of Ralph Elrington.

S. 10   *Comus*.[4] "N.B. The Upper Gallery is intirely removed; the
(A.S.)   Scenery and Decorations are intirely New."

M. 12   *First Part of King Henry IV* (Shakespeare, Seventh Night).
The Honest Yorkshireman. Music. Wax.

W. 14   *The Orphan. Tom Thumb the Great.*

Th. 15   *The Silent Woman* (revived). "Written by Ben Johnston."

F. 16   *The Provoked Husband* (by Desire). †*The Chaplet*, a new
musical entertainment, "as it was performed at the Theatre
Royal in Drury Lane forty Nights with universal Applause."

S. 17   *Comus.*
(A.S.)

M. 19   *King Henry V* (Shakespeare, Eighth Night). *Pyramus and
Thisbe*. Music. Wax.

Tu. 20   *The Strategem* (by Desire). *The Chaplet*. "N.B. The Chaplet
will be sold at the Theatre, Price Twopence."

F. 23   *Macbeth* (Shakespeare, Ninth and Last Night). *The Brave
Irishman*. Concerto for the Violin Solo by Pasquali. Wax.

S. 24   *Comus*. Concerto for the Violin Solo by Pasquali.
(A.S.)

M. 26   †*Edward the Black Prince*, "Attempted after the Manner of
Shakespear." Singing and dancing.

Tu. 27   *King Lear. The Dragon of Wantley.*

MARCH

Th. 1   *Edward the Black Prince. The Lottery.*

F. 2   *The Revenge. Lady Moore, or The Dragoness.*

S. 3   *The Orphan* (by Particular Desire). *The Brave Irishman.*

M. 5   *She Would and She Would Not. A Will and No Will* "translated
from the French by Mr. Macklin." Singing and dancing. Benefit of Macklin.

W. 7   *Hamlet. The Lottery*. Singing and dancing. Benefit of Digges.

Th. 8   †*The Alchymist* (never acted here).[5] *The Chaplet.*

F. 9   *The Distrest Mother*. Benefit of Mossop.

S. 10   *The Distrest Mother*.[6] *The Lottery*. Benefit of Mossop.

---

[4] In a news item in the January 23–27 *Dublin Journal* we hear that the
theater in Aungier-Street is now almost completed, and will soon be opened
with the masque of *Comus*. In this Calendar, Aungier-Street productions are
labeled A.S.

[5] *The Alchymist* seems to have been deferred from February 21, when it was
first advertised as "Never acted in this Kingdom."

[6] This second performance (and this second Mossop benefit) was given be-

M. 12   *The Recruiting Officer. Damon and Ananthe,* a new serenata, the words by Cibber, the music by Lampe. A Dramatic Satire of two Acts, Tea, Coffee, and Chocolate for Everybody, "in which will be introduced the Rehearsal of a Comedy called, The Humours of an Election; or, Who Bids for a Borough? Written by the Author of Tom Jones." Epilogue, "recommending the Cause of Liberty and Loyalty to the Beauties of this Kindom [*sic*]." To be spoken by Mr. Cibber. Benefit of Cibber.

W. 14   *The Careless Husband.*[7] With the following entertainments: End of Act I, A new Song by Mrs. Lampe. Act II, A favourite Song by Mrs. Storer. Act III, A new Song by Mr. Sullivan. Act IV, A Song by Mrs. Storer. At end of play, a Dance, called The Country Revels, by Mons. Granier and Mlle. Vandersluys. *The Virgin Unmasked.* Benefit of Sullivan.

F. 16   *Edward the Black Prince. Tom Thumb the Great.* Benefit of Mrs. Lampe.

S. 17   *King Arthur.* Words by Dryden, music by Purcel.
(A.S.)

M. 19   *She Would and She Would Not* (acted but once these 3 years). *The Honest Yorkshireman.* Singing and dancing. "N.B. At the particular Desire of several Ladies of Quality, Mrs. Bland changes the Play of the Refusal, or the Ladies Philosophy, to the abovementioned, and she hopes it will please much better. Tickets delivered out for the Refusal will be taken." Benefit of Mrs. Bland.

W. 21   *Jane Shore. The Lottery.* Singing and dancing. Benefit of Miss Danvers.

Th. 22   *The Suspicious Husband.* †*The Pleasures of the Town,* a satyrical Puppet Show. "In which will be . . . the whole Court of Dulness. Also the comical and diverting Humour Some Body and No Body, Punch and his wife Joan, performed by Living Figures, some of them six Feet high." [8] Benefit of Mr. Bardin.

F. 23   *The Fair Penitent.* Farce and entertainments. Benefit of Miss Griffith.

S. 24   *King Arthur.*
(A.S.)

---

cause of the number of people turned away on the preceding night. *Edward the Black Prince* and *Tom Thumb the Great* had been planned for this evening.

[7] This is the beginning of a series of replacements of plays featuring Macklin, who left the company about this time. Sheridan played in *The Careless Husband.*

[8] The similarity between this announcement and a passage in Henry Fielding's *Author's Farce* suggests that the entertainment offered here is related to the play within Fielding's play. Something called *The Pleasures of the Town* was also produced in Norwich, April 18, 1757 (Nicoll, III, 403).

M. 26 *The Tempest* (at the Particular Desire of several Gentlemen and Ladies). "With the original Musick, composed by Mr. Purcell, Sinkings, Flyings, and other Decorations, particularly the Grand Devil's Dance, by Mons. Granier." Farce. Benefit of Mrs. Mozeen.

Th. 29 *King Arthur*. New Scenes, Machines, and Decorations. Wax.
(A.S.)

F. 30 *Tancred and Sigismunda*. At end of Act I, Song by Mrs. Storer; Act III, Signior Pasquali will play his 2d Medley Solo with Variations upon Oroo Drimindoo and Daniel Cooper. Act v, dancing by Mons. Granier and Mlle. Vandersluys. *Lady Moore, or the Dragoness*. Benefit of Victor.

S. 31 *Othello. The Brave Irishman*.

APRIL

M. 2 *Theodosius*. With the original songs newly set to music by Lampe and sung by Sullivan, Mrs. Lampe, Mrs. Mozeen. Act III (by particular Desire) Ellin-a-Roon by Mrs. Storer. *The Devil to Pay*. Benefit of Mr. and Mrs. Storer.

Tu. 3 *Love's Last Shift* (not acted these 2 years). With an Epilogue on Some Body, in the Character of No Body to be spoken by Mr. Cibber. *Lady Moore*. Singing. At the request of several ladies, the boxes laid open to the pit. Benefit of Mr. Neil, Box-keeper.

W. 4 *King John* (revived). "At the End of each Act will be performed a new Chorus in the manner of the Ancients, set to Musick by Mr. Lampe." *The Honest Yorkshireman*.

Th. 5 *Love Makes a Man. The Lying Valet*. Singing and dancing. Benefit of Miss Bourne, and the Widow of the late Mr. Francis Elrington.

F. 6 *The Revenge. The Honest Yorkshireman*. At the particular Desire of several Ladies of Quality. For the Benefit of a Gentleman of the Army and his Family in Distress.

S. 7 *King Arthur* (Last time of performing before the Holidays).
(A.S.) Wax.

M. 16 *Tamerlane*. "Masque, wrote in Honour of the Birth-Day of K. William III of glorious Memory, with a new Prologue." [9] Anniversary performance.

Tu. 17 *The Distrest Mother*. With the original Epilogue to be spoken by Miss Griffith. *The Lottery*. Singing and dancing. Benefit of Watson.

W. 18 *Julius Caesar*, with the Death of Brutus and Cassius. Prologue

[9] Probably *The Triumphs of Hibernia*.

wrote by Dryden; "Concluding with Milton's Epitaph to the Memory of Shakespear, to be spoke by Mr. Digges, representing the Shade of Shakespear as figured on his Monument erected in Westminster Abbey." *Miss in her Teens.* Benefit of Ross.

Th. 19   *The Conscious Lovers.* Farce. Dancing. Benefit of Layfield.

F. 20   *The Provoked Husband. Chrononhotonthologos.* Singing and dancing. Benefit of Mr. and Mrs. Mynitt.

S. 21   *King Arthur.*
(A.S.)

M. 23   *The Beggar's Opera.* "With a new Prologue on the Occasion wrote by Dr. Clancy, and spoke by Mrs. Bland." Act I, a new Dance, the Drunken Tyroler, by Mons. Granier. Act II, The Lovure [*sic*] and Minuet by Mons. Granier and Mlle. Vandersluys. *The Vintner Tricked.* After the farce, a new harlequin dance never performed in this kingdom, by Mlle. Vandersluys. Benefit of Mlle. Vandersluys.

W. 25   *The Orphan. A Cure for a Scold,* a ballad opera (not acted these 3 years). "Taken from Shakespear's taming the Shrew [*sic*]." Benefit of Mr. and Mrs. Kennedy.

Th. 26   *The Merchant of Venice.*

F. 27   *Cato. The Honest Yorkshireman.* Benefit of Beamsley.

MAY

W. 2   *King John. The Virgin Unmasked.* Dancing. Benefit of J. Elrington and Master Elrington.

Th. 3   *The Recruiting Officer.*

F. 4   *As You Like It.* After Act II, Ellin-a-Roon, Mrs. Storer; Act III, Mirth admit me of thy Crew, Howard. Grand dance by Mons. Granier and Mlle. Vandersluys. *Nancy, or the Parting Lovers.* The Musick by Mr. Cary. Benefit of Howard and Vaughan.

S. 5   *King Arthur.*
(A.S.)

M. 7   **The Earl of Essex.* Written by Henry Brooke. With a new prologue, spoken by Sheridan; a new epilogue, spoken by Miss Danvers.

W. 9   *The Fair Penitent.* After Act I, A Favourite Song by Mrs. Lampe; Act II, A French Dance to an Irish Solo by Master Mahon; Act III, Daniel Cooper by Master Mahon. *The Honest Yorkshireman.* Dancing. Benefit of Hamilton.

Th. 10   *Venice Preserved. The Brave Irishman.* Singing. Benefit of Sparks.[10]

[10] An N.B. follows the notice for this performance: "For the Encouragement

M. 14   *Second Part of King Henry IV* (not acted these 7 years). Prologue by Dryden, and Milton's Epitaph on Shakespeare by Digges. New violin piece by Pasquali; new dance by Granier and Vandersluys; singing by Mrs. Storer and Mrs. Mozeen. Epilogue on Somebody in the Character of Nobody, by Cibber. *Mock Pamela* (new dramatic burlesque in two acts never performed before). With an epilogue on the modern Flashes and Fribbles to be spoken (in the character of a Beau) by Mrs. Bland, written by C. Cibber. Benefit of Cibber.

Tu. 15   *The Busy Body. Tom Thumb the Great.* Dancing.

W. 16   *The Beggar's Opera.* "With a new Prologue wrote for the Occasion to the Memory of Mr. Gay, to be spoke by Mr. Digges." Benefit of Digges.

Th. 17   *The Orphan. The Honest Yorkshireman.* Singing and dancing. Benefit of Husband.

F. 18   *The Earl of Essex.* The Play new dressed in the Habits of the Times. A new Prologue by Sheridan, Epilogue by Miss Danvers. *The Chaplet.* Concerto for the Violin Solo by Pasquali.

S. 19   *King Arthur.*[11]

Tu. 22   *King Lear. The Mock Doctor.* "Tickets delivered out for light guineas will be taken on this night, and Friday next."

W. 23   *Macbeth. The Chaplet.* Benefit of Mossop.

Th. 24   *The Earl of Essex.* After Act IV, a violin solo by Pasquali. *Lady Moore, or the Dragoness.* Dancing.

F. 25   *Comus.*
(A.S.)

S. 26   *King Arthur* (by Desire).
(A.S.)

1750–1751

The Company: ACTORS: Bardin, Beamsley, Cibber, Digges, J. Elrington, R. Elrington, Falkner, Hamilton, King, Maurice, Messink, Montgomery, Morris, Mossop, Mynitt, Master Mynitt, Packenham, Robertson, Ross, Sheridan, Sparks, Watson, Williams. ACTRESSES: Mrs. Bland, Miss Byrne (Bourne?), Miss Cole, Miss Copen, Miss Danvers, Miss Griffith, Mrs. Leslie, Mrs. Lindley, Mrs. Mynitt, Mrs. Packenham, Miss Reynolds, Mrs. Robertson, Mrs. Rowley. DANCERS: Miss Baker, Mons. Billioni,

---

of Purchasers, and the Conveniency of the Publick, Mr. Sparks will give, in Tickets, the full Value for Guineas in general" (*Dublin Journal,* May 5–8, 1750).

[11] Probably at Aungier-Street, though not so advertised.

Mlle. Granier, Mons. Granier, Master Mahon, Miss Mahon, Mlle. Pajot.
SINGERS: Mrs. Crump. MUSICIANS: Pasquali. EQUILIBRISTS: Mahomet
Caratta, Sign. Perghen. FIREWORKS: Sign. Gillio.

Number of Performances: About 157.

Number of Command Performances: About 6.

Number of Benefit Performances: About 38. Caratta, Mrs Bland (2),
Digges (2), Mossop, Victor (treasurer), Montgomery (2), Cibber (2),
Miss Griffith, King, Miss Cole, Billioni, Miss Danvers, Mlle. Pajot, Mons.
and Mlle. Granier, Miss Baker, Ross (2), Pasquali, Neil (boxkeeper), Mr.
and Mrs. Packenham, Mr. and Mrs. Mynitt, Brooke (author, 2), Sparks,
Cushin (musician), Beamsley, J. Elrington and Carmichael (prompter),
Husband (former actor), Miss Danvers and Miss Griffith, Hamilton and
Mahon, R. Elrington, Watson, Messink and Williams, Theatrical Fund
(for superannuated players).

SEPTEMBER

W. 19   *The Busy Body.* "With new Decorations." *The Virgin Unmasked.*

F. 21   *Love's Last Shift. The Devil to Pay.* Dancing by Granier and others, particularly Miss Baker from Drury Lane, "being the first Time of her Appearance on this Stage."

M. 24   *The Recruiting Officer. The Virgin Unmasked* (by Desire). Dancing.

W. 26   *Love Makes a Man. The Honest Yorkshireman.* Dancing.

F. 28   *The Suspicious Husband.* Entertainments.

OCTOBER

M. 1   *King Lear.* Written by Shakespeare, revised by Tate. *Flora.* A Grotesque Dance after the Chinese Manner by Mons. Granier and Miss Baker.

W. 3   *The Way of the World. The What D'Ye Call It.* Dancing.

F. 5   *The Old Batchelor* (by Desire). *The Lottery.*

M. 8   *The Double Gallant* (not acted these 3 years). "With the original Epilogue to be spoke by Mrs. Bland." *The Devil to Pay.* Dancing.

W. 10   *The Revenge* (by Desire). *Flora.* A new dance by Madem. Granier.

Th. 11   *Love's Last Shift.* "With a new Prologue on the Occasion to be spoke by Mr. Cibber." Anniversary performance by command of the Lords Justices.

F. 12   *The Suspicious Husband.*

M. 15   *The Orphan.* After Act III, a Concerto for Violin Solo by Pasquali. *The Mock Doctor.* Dancing.

W. 17   *The Merry Wives of Windsor. Damon and Phillida.* Dancing.
Th. 18   *The Stratagem.* Entertainments.
F. 19   *Venice Preserved. The Lying Valet.*
M. 22   *Richard III* (Shakespeare, First Night). Music by Pasquali.
W. 24   *Jane Shore. The Lying Valet.* Dancing.
Th. 25   *The Provoked Husband. The Honest Yorkshireman.* Dancing.
F. 26   *Hamlet* (Shakespeare, Second Night). Music by Pasquali. Wax.
M. 29   *Romeo and Juliet* (Shakespeare, Third Night). Music by Pasquali. Wax.
Tu. 30   *The Stratagem.* Farce and entertainments. Anniversary performance by command of the Lords Justices.
W. 31   *The Earl of Essex. The Lying Valet.*

NOVEMBER

Th. 1   *Much Ado About Nothing* (revived). Farce and entertainments.
F. 2   *Othello* (Shakespeare, Fourth Night). A new Solo, La Chasse Italienne, by Pasquali. Wax.
M. 5   *Tamerlane.* "With the usual Prologue on the Occasion to be spoke by Mr. Cibber." *The Mock Doctor.* Anniversary performance.
W. 7   *Julius Caesar* (Shakespeare, Fifth Night). Music by Pasquali. Wax.
Th. 8   *The Orphan.* †*Lethe.* With the last new Dance called the Fingallian Revels, by Granier, Baker, and others.
F. 9   *Macbeth* (Shakespeare, Sixth and Last Night). Music by Pasquali. Wax.
M. 12   *Theodosius* (revived). "With Musick, Songs, Choruses, &c., composed by Mr. Lampe." After Act III, Concerto for Violin Solo by Pasquali. At end of play, Fingallian Revels. *Lethe.* "The Principal Characters of the Play will be entirely New Dressed."
Tu. 13   *The Necromancer,* in a new Manner. "In which the Turk's
(A.S.)   Apprentice, Giacomo Perghen, will perform several surprizing Feats of Activity on the Tight Rope, which will be followed by the wonderful Equilibres on the Wire performed by the celebrated Turk Mahomet Caratta." [1] The Pit to be opened at 5 o'clock, the Gallery at four.
W. 14   *Othello* (by Desire). Entertainments.
Th. 15   *The Distrest Mother. The Lying Valet.* Dancing.
F. 16   *The Earl of Essex* (by Desire of several Persons of Quality). *Lethe.*

[1] A note in the November 10–13 *Dublin Journal* announcement reports that the entertainments will continue at Aungier-Street Theater on "every Saturday and Tuesday during the Season." Giacomo Perghen is called Giovanni Perghen, probably more correctly, in an order in Thomas Sheridan's own handwriting directing that money be paid to him.

S. 17   *The Necromancer.* With Mahomet Caratta and his apprentice.
(A.S.)

M. 19   *The Suspicious Husband. Lethe.* Dancing. Anniversary performance by command of the Lords Justices.

Tu. 20   *The Necromancer,* "in which the celebrated Mahomet Caratta
(A.S.)   will perform several new Equilibres on the Wire. There will
be also dancing on the tight Rope by his Apprentice."

W. 21   *Theodosius. Lethe.* Dancing.

Th. 22   *Richard III.* Dancing.

F. 23   *The Merchant of Venice* (Shakespeare, First Night). *Miss in
her Teens.* Music by Pasquali. Dancing. Wax.

M. 26   *Romeo and Juliet* (Shakespeare, Second Night). *Miss in her
Teens.* Music by Pasquali.

Tu. 27   *The Necromancer,* with several extraordinary and new Equili-
(A.S.)   bres by Mahomet Caratta: "particularly he will poize a naked
Sword upon the Brim of a Drinking Glass which he holds in
his Mouth. At the Conclusion he will be put in a Sack, after
having been blindfolded with an Handkerchief, the Mouth of
which Sack shall be tied over his Head, and in this Condition he
will perform his Exercise on the Wire. Then he will throw
away his Ballance Pole, charge a Gun, and shoot out several
Candles that shall be presented to him, this to be done upon the
Wire, and he blindfold." Also dancing on the tight rope by
his apprentice.

W. 28   *Othello* (by Desire). *Miss in her Teens.* Music by Pasquali.

Th. 29   *The Recruiting Officer. Lethe.* Dancing.

F. 30   †*Phaedra and Hippolitus.*

DECEMBER

S. 1   *The Necromancer.* "Particularly the Boy in the Wheelbarrow."
(A.S.)

M. 3   *The Earl of Essex* (by Desire). *Lethe.* Dancing.

Tu. 4   *The Necromancer.* Mahomet Caratta will stand on his Head on
(A.S.)   the slack Rope.

W. 5   *Phaedra and Hippolitus. The Mock Doctor.* Dancing.

Th. 6   **The Lovers Revels,* a new pantomime masque. With equilibres,
(A.S.)   new habits, scenes, machines, and other decorations. An Illumination Night.[2]

F. 7   *Hamlet* (Shakespeare, Third Night).

S. 8   *The Lovers Revels.* Mahomet Caratta.
(A.S.)

M. 10   *Richard III.* After Act IV, Concerto for Violin Solo by Pasquali.
After the play, a grand comic Ballet, Les Jardiniers Venetiens

---

[2] Probably illumination with wax candles.

by Mons. Billioni and Madem. Pajot,[3] being the first time of their appearing in this kingdom.

Tu. 11 (A.S.) *The Lovers Revels.*[4] "After which, amongst others, the cele-brated Mahomet Caratta will perform the following Equilibres, viz. He will ballance a Pipe upon a Glass, in the Mouth of which shall be three other Pipes, and a Pipe in the Mouth of each of them, in all seven Pipes. He will carry a Pyramid of nineteen Glasses upon his Chin. He will drink Coffee upon a Board placed on the Wire, with a Boy on the other End of the Board. He will also perform on the Wire blindfolded. . . ."

W. 12 *Phaedra and Hippolitus.* Dancing.

Th. 13 (A.S.) Mahomet Caratta will balance seven pipes upon a corner of his hat; a sword on the edge of a glass; a ladder with a number of glasses on the steps. "And, lastly, he will play with the Balls."

F. 14 *Cato.* Dancing

S. 15 (A.S.) *The Lovers Revels,* never performed here but once. With a new scene and alterations. Mahomet Caratta in new balancing tricks, also performing on the wire in wooden shoes.

M. 17 *The Earl of Essex* (by Desire). After Act II, a serious dance by Mlle. Pajot. After Act V, a Grand Pantomime Ballet, called the Cherry Tree.

Tu. 18 (A.S.) *The Lovers Revels,* In Three Interludes. Mahomet Caratta in new balancing tricks.

W. 19 *Cato.* Dancing.

F. 21 *She Would and She Would Not.* Dancing. The last time of playing before the holidays.

S. 22 (A.S.) *The Lovers Revels.* Mahomet Caratta.

W. 26 *She Would and She Would Not.* Equilibres by Mahomet Caratta, in his first appearance in Smock-Alley Theater. Dancing.

Th. 27 *The Stratagem.* Entertainments.

F. 28 *A Bold Stroke for a Wife.* Entertainments.

M. 31 *The Beggar's Opera.* A dance by the characters in the opera. Equilibres by Mahomet Caratta.

JANUARY

W. 2 *The Double Gallant.*[5] After Act II, a Chinese Dance. Equilibres by Mahomet Caratta.

[3] The names of these dancers from the Opera House in Paris, like the names of most foreigners and even many Englishmen and Irishmen, have several spellings, "Billiony" and "Pachos," for example.

[4] Only one among the December 6, 8, and 11 performances of *The Lovers Revels* may have been given. See the December 15 entry.

[5] "King Lear is oblig'd to be deferr'd on account of the Indisposition of a principal Performer" (*Dublin Journal,* December 29, 1750–January 1, 1751).

Th. 3   *The Suspicious Husband.* Entertainments.
F. 4   *The Distrest Mother* (by Desire). Entertainments.
M. 7   *The Recruiting Officer.* A Comic Ballet, Fingallian Revels. Equilibres by Mahomet Caratta.
W. 9   *She Would and She Would Not* (by Desire). *The Lovers Revels.* "With Alterations, new Scenes, Machines, Habits, Songs, Dances, and other Decorations." Equilibres by Mahomet Caratta.
Th. 10   *The Merry Wives of Windsor.* Entertainments.
F. 11   *First Part of King Henry IV* (by Desire). *The Lottery.* Dancing, the last new Pantomime Ballet, Le Ceresier.
M. 14   *Othello.* Dancing. Equilibres by Mahomet Caratta.
W. 16   *The Beggar's Opera. The Lovers Revels* (by Desire). Equilibres by Mahomet Caratta.
Th. 17   *King Lear.* Dancing.
F. 18   *The Amorous Widow* (not acted here these 20 years). Entertainments.
M. 21   *A Bold Stroke for a Wife.* "With a new Prologue (proper to the Occasion) to be spoke by Mr. Bardin." Dancing. Equilibres by Mahomet Caratta. Anniversary performance by command of the Lords Justices.
W. 23   *The Amorous Widow* (by Desire). *The Lovers Revels.* Equilibres by Mahomet Caratta.
Th. 24   *The Revenge.* Entertainments.
F. 25   *The Refusal.* Entertainments.
S. 26   *She Would and She Would Not. The Lottery.* Dancing. Equilibres. Benefit of Caratta.
M. 28   *The Refusal.* Equilibres by Mahomet Caratta. Dancing.
Th. 31   †*Lady Jane Grey.* Equilibres by Mahomet Caratta.

FEBRUARY

F. 1   *The Refusal.* Equilibres by Mahomet Caratta.
S. 2   *The Amorous Widow. The Lovers Revels.* Equilibres by Mahomet Caratta. "Last Night of the Turk's Performing."
W. 6   *Cato.* Dancing.
Th. 7   *Lady Jane Grey.* Dancing.
F. 8   *The Careless Husband. The Brave Irishman.* Dancing.
M. 11   *The Earl of Essex.* After the play the last new grand Pantomime Ballet, De Bucheuren en pas Deu trois Jalousie.
W. 13   *Phaedra and Hippolitus. The Brave Irishman.* Dancing.
Th. 14   *The Squire of Alsatia* (not acted here these 3 years). Dancing.
F. 15   *All for Love.* "With new Dresses and Decorations, particularly a new Grand Dance at the Beginning of the third Act, after the triumphant Entry of Anthony and Cleopatra."
M. 18   *Lady Jane Grey. Lethe.* Dancing.
Th. 21   *The Earl of Essex. The Anatomist.* Dancing.

F. 22   *All for Love. The Anatomist.* Dancing.

S. 23   †*The Roman Father.*

M. 25   *Oroonoko.* Dancing.

W. 27   *The Conscious Lovers. The Mock Doctor.* Entertainments.

Th. 28   *The Roman Father. The Anatomist.* Dancing.

MARCH

F. 1   *The Fair Penitent. The Brave Irishman.*

S. 2   *Phaedra and Hippolitus* (by Particular Desire). Entertainments.

M. 4   *The Roman Father. The Mock Doctor.* Dancing.

W. 6   *The Careless Husband. The Anatomist.*

Th. 7   *The Orphan. Miss in her Teens.* Entertainments.

F. 8   *The Spanish Fryar* (not acted these 2 years). *The Brave Irishman.* Entertainments. Benefit of Mrs. Bland.[6]

S. 9   *Theodosius* (by Particular Desire). *Lethe* (by Desire). Dancing.

M. 11   *The Tender Husband* (not acted these 3 years). *The Intriguing Chambermaid.* Dancing. "As there has been an extraordinary Demand for Places, the Boxes will be laid open and three [raised to five in later notices] Rows of the Pit railed in, in order to accommodate the Ladies." Benefit of Digges.

Tu. 12   *Theodosius* (by Particular Desire). *Lethe* (by Particular Desire).

W. 13   *Richard III.* Dancing. "By particular Desire, the Boxes will be laid open and four Rows of the Pit railed in." Benefit of Mossop.

Th. 14   *The Suspicious Husband.* Farce. Dancing. Benefit of Victor.

F. 15   *Venice Preserved. The Virgin Unmasked.* Dancing. Benefit of Montgomery.

S. 16   *Don Sebastian* (altered from Dryden).[7] Grand new Pantomime Ballet.

M. 18   *The Provoked Wife.* †*The Statue*, a dramatic Petit-Piece from La Comedie Italienne. Drinking Song from *The Chaplet*, sung by Mr. Ross. Benefit of Cibber.

Tu. 19   *Jane Shore.* Farce. Entertainments. Benefit of Miss Griffith.[8]

[6] "Mrs. Bland is very much concerned that it is not in her Power to wait on the Ladies in Person, her Time being wholly taken up in the Business of the Theatre" (*Dublin Journal*, March 2–5, 1751).

[7] *Don Sebastian*, with some omissions, had been given in 1745–46, but this time it has been so thoroughly altered that Sheridan advertises as "never acted before." (For explanation of the revision, see Ch. vi.)

[8] "N.B. As Miss Griffith has lost a Number of Box, Pit, and Gallery Tickets, she entreats every Gentleman to whom any of her Tickets may be offered at an under Price, to secure the Person who offers them, as she knows the Numbers; she gives this caution to prevent any Gentleman's being stopt at the Doors" (*Dublin Journal*, March 12–16, 1751).

W. 20   *The Rehearsal* (not acted these 2 years). "Interspersed with Chocolate, after the Manner of a very celebrated Actor." "And by particular Desire, Mr. Bayes will disband his Troops and give them an itinerant Profession, in Imitation of Mr. Foote." Farce. Dancing. Boxes to be laid open and three rows of the pit to be railed in. Benefit of King.

Th. 21   *The Conscious Lovers. The Brave Irishman.* Dancing. Benefit of Miss Cole.

F. 22   *King Lear.* After Act I, Minuet and Louvre by Billioni and Pajot; Act II, a new grand Ballet; Act III, a new Dance by the Graniers; Act IV, a new grand Ballet, the Savoyards, never danced before in this Kingdom; at the end, a new grand Pantomime Ballet, Le Fermier Vigilant. Benefit of Mons. Billioni.

S. 23   *The Roman Father.* The last new Grand Millers Dance. Equilibres by Mahomet Caratta.

M. 25   *Don Sebastian.* Equilibres by Mahomet Caratta.

Tu. 26   *The Orphan. The Anatomist.* Dancing. Benefit of Miss Danvers.

W. 27   *A Bold Stroke for a Wife.* Dancing between every act and at the end of play. Benefit of Mlle. Pajot.

Th. 28   *The Amorous Widow. Miss in her Teens.* Dancing between every act. Benefit of Mons. and Mlle. Granier.

F. 29   *Romeo and Juliet.* Farce. Dancing. Benefit of Miss Baker.

Theater closed in mourning for the Prince of Wales
from March 29 to April 15.

APRIL

M. 15   *The Recruiting Officer.* "An occasional prologue to be spoken by Mr. Montgomery." *The Lying Valet.* Dancing. Benefit of Ross.

W. 17   *The Tempest.* To conclude with a grand new Dance proper to the Play. After Act II, a new Concerto for Violin Solo, composed for the occasion. After Act IV, the second Medley Solo of Oroo Dremendoo and Variations on Daniel Cooper (by Desire). *The Virgin Unmasked.* Benefit of Pasquali.[9]

Th. 18   *She Would and She Would Not. The School Boy* (not acted these 3 years). Dancing. Benefit of Neil, Boxkeeper.

F. 19   *The Stratagem.* After Act III, dance of the Drunken Peasant

[9] "N.B. Whereas the Notice for opening the Theatre has been shorter by a full Week than was expected, Signor Pasquali hopes that many Gentlemen and Ladies that are disposed to favour him with their Company, will excuse his waiting on them regularly in Person, as he otherwise intended" (*Dublin Journal*, April 9–13, 1751).

by Mr. Messink. Farce. Benefit of Mr. and Mrs. Packenham.

S. 20 †*The Chances. The Lovers Revels.* Dancing, with the last new Miller's Dance.

M. 22 *The Way of the World. Chrononhotonthologos.* Singing and dancing. Benefit of Mr. and Mrs. Mynitt.

Tu. 23 *The Earl of Essex.* Dancing. Benefit of the author.

W. 24 *The Twin Rivals. The Cobler of Preston* (not acted those 10 years). Dancing. Benefit of Sparks.

Th. 25 *Oroonoko.* Farce. Dancing. Benefit of Cushin.

F. 26 *Venice Preserved.* Farce. Dancing. Benefit of Beamsley.[10]

S. 27 *The Merchant of Venice. The Virgin Unmasked.* Fireworks by Sign. Gillio (2nd time of his showing them in this kingdom).

M. 29 *As You Like It.* After Act I, a Dance by Miss Baker; Act II, A Minuet and Louvre by Mons. and Miss Moreau (1st appearance on any stage); Act III, a Hornpipe by Walsh; Act IV, a Dance by Miss Moreau; Act V, the Fingallian Revels. *The Brave Irishman.* Benefit of J. Elrington and Mr. Carmichael, Prompter.

Tu. 30 *The Spanish Fryar.* Dancing. Farce. "At the end of the Play, the High German Quack Doctor's Speech, which was never repeated on any Stage, will be spoken by a Gentleman from London." Benefit of Husband.

MAY

W. 1 *Don Sebastian.* Entertainments. Particularly fireworks by Gillio.

Th. 2 *The Conscious Lovers.* After Act II, violin solo by Pasquali. *Lethe.* Benefit of Miss Danvers and Miss Griffith.

F. 3 *The Provoked Wife.* After Act I, dance by Master Mahon; Act II, a new Song by Miss Rachel Baptist; Act III, a Dance by Master and Miss Mahon; Act IV, a new Song by Mrs. Crump. After the Play, a dance "in which (by particular Desire) will be introduced the Statue by Mr. Hamilton, as performed in Aungier-Street." *The Brave Irishman.* Benefit of Hamilton and Mahon.

M. 6 *The Roman Father. The Honest Yorkshireman.* Dancing. Benefit of Mrs. Bland.

W. 8 *The Stratagem. The Anatomist.* Dancing, by command of the Lords Justices. For the entertainment of the Lord Chancellor, the Chancellor of the Exchequer, the Judges, and the Society of King's Inns. Benefit of Ralph Elrington.

Th. 9 *Macbeth.* Dancing. Fireworks by Gillio.

[10] "As Mr. Beamsly's Indisposition prevents him making a personal Application, he humbly hopes for the Continuance of the Favour of his Friends and Acquaintance" (*Dublin Journal*, April 16–20, 1751).

F. 10   *The Double Gallant.* Farce. Dancing. By command of the Lords Justices. Benefit of Watson.

S. 11   †*Merope.*[11] After Act III, a dance, Les Grande Characters Francoise, by Mlle. Pajot. Fireworks.

M. 13   *The Funeral* (not acted these 8 years). Farce. Dancing. Benefit of Digges.

Tu. 14   *The Earl of Essex,* the original epilogue (by Desire) to be spoken by Miss Danvers in the character of Rutland. Benefit of Mr. Brooke, by the particular Desire of many of his Friends.

W. 15   *The Inconstant* (not acted these 10 years). "The Play to conclude with a Country Dance called Mirabel's Frolick by the Performers. An occasional Prologue to be spoken by Mr. Montgomery, on Himself; and an Epilogue by Miss Cole in Breeches." *The Devil to Pay.* Dancing. Benefit of Montgomery.

Th. 16   *Love for Love. Chrononhotonthologos.* Dancing. Benefit of Ross.[12]

F. 17   *The Double Dealer.* †*The Gentleman Gardener,* a Ballad Opera. "Concluding with a Dance proper to the Opera." Benefit of Cibber.

S. 18   *Merope.* Dancing. Fireworks by Gillio.
(A.S.)

M. 20   *Romeo and Juliet.* Dancing. Farce.

Tu. 21   *The Refusal.* Farce. Dancing. "Performances on the Wire by Mr. Messink (after the Manner of the celebrated Mahomet Caratta) being his first Attempt of that Kind in Publick." Benefit of Messink and Williams.

W. 22   *The Suspicious Husband.* Entertainments. Benefit for a Fund begun for the Support of maimed, reduced, and superannuated Players.

Th. 23   *The Twin Rivals.* Farce. Entertainments.

F. 24   *The Inconstant.* Dancing. Anniversary performance.

S. 25   *Lady Jane Grey.* A grand Peasant Dance by Billioni and Pajot.
(A.S.)   Equilibres by Messink, after the manner of the celebrated Mahomet Caratta. Fireworks by Gillio, for the last time.

[11] The plan had been to open *Merope* at Aungier-Street on May 4, but the opening had to be deferred to May 11, because of the indisposition of a principal performer; and then the theater had to be changed to Smock-Alley "because the other House could not be got ready in Time" (*Dublin Journal,* April 23–27, 1751). The next performance of the play (May 18) was given at Aungier-Street.

[12] "Mr. Ross would not have presumed to trouble the Town with a second Benefit, had he not been a considerable Loser by the former from the Alteration of his Play, and the Notice of opening the House being sooner by a Week than was expected, which prevented his waiting on his Friends, he therefore intreats the Favour of their Interest for this Play" (*Dublin Journal,* May 7–11, 1751).

1751–1752

The Company: ACTORS: Beamsley, Cibber, Conyers (beginning April 13), Davies, Digges, J. Elrington, Master Elrington, Falkner, Hamilton, Heaphy, Kennedy, King, Lee (beginning May 20), Longfield, Maurice, Messink, Montgomery, Mynitt, Master Mynitt, Packenham, Sheridan, Sparks, Stevens, Watson, Williams. ACTRESSES: Mrs. Bland, Miss Cole, Miss Comerford, Miss Danvers (not after November 29), Mrs. Davies, Mrs. Kennedy, Mrs. Lee, Mrs. Mynitt, Mrs. Packenham, Miss Reynolds, Mrs. Rowley, Mrs. Woffington. DANCERS: Miss Baker, McNeil, Mons. and Miss Moreau. SINGERS: Mrs. Crump.

Number of Performances: About 162.

Number of Command Performances: About 24.

Number of Benefit Performances: About 34. Clergymen's widows and children, Mrs. Woffington (2), Mrs. Bland (2), Digges, Cibber (2), King (2), Miss Cole, Victor (treasurer), Swift monument, Neil (box-keeper), Hamilton and Cushin, Messink, Husband (former actor), Mr. and Mrs. Kennedy, Mr. and Mrs. Mynitt and Master Mynitt, McNeil, Beamsley, Mr. and Mrs. Davies, Sparks, Miss Baker, Heaphy, Mrs. Rowley and Mrs. Crump, J. Elrington, Carmichael and Longfield, Watson, Williams, Mrs. Lee, Montgomery, Tracy (2).

SEPTEMBER

M. 23   *The Stratagem.* Dancing by Mr. McNeil "(from the Theatre Royal in Drury-Lane, being the first Time of his appearing on this Stage)," and Miss Baker.

W. 25   *She Would and She Would Not.* Dancing.

F. 27   *The Twin Rivals.* Dancing.

M. 30   *Romeo and Juliet.* With the Funeral Procession. *The Lying Valet.* Dancing.

OCTOBER

W. 2   *Lady Jane Grey. The Mock Doctor.* Comic Dance by McNeil and Baker.

Th. 3   *A Bold Stroke for a Wife.* Dancing, particularly a new Scotch Dance by McNeil and Baker.

F. 4   *The Busy Body. The Anatomist.* Dancing.

M. 7   *The Provoked Husband.* Scotch Dance.

W. 9   *The Distrest Mother.* Dancing.

Th. 10   *The Recruiting Officer.* Entertainments.

F. 11   "On Friday next [October 11] being the Anniversary of his

Majesty's Coronation will be presented a Comedy, of which Notice will be given in the Bills."

M. 14   *Jane Shore*. Scotch Dance.

W. 16   *The Distrest Mother*.

Th. 17   *The Provoked Husband*. Entertainments. By viceregal[1] command.

F. 18   *The Conscious Lovers*. Entertainments.

M. 21   *The Fair Penitent*. *The Mock Doctor*. Dancing.

W. 23   *The Constant Couple*.

Th. 24   *Lady Jane Grey*. *The Lying Valet*. A new Dance, the Hibernian Courier. By viceregal command.

F. 25   *King John*. Entertainments.

M. 28   *All for Love*. Dancing.

W. 30   *The Twin Rivals*. Anniversary performance by command of the Lord Lieutenant.

Th. 31   *The Careless Husband*. Farce. Entertainments. By viceregal command.

NOVEMBER

F. 1   *Rule a Wife and Have a Wife*.

M. 4   *Tamerlane*. *The Brave Irishman*. Anniversary performance.

W. 6   *Rule a Wife and Have a Wife* (revived, acted but once these 3 years).[2]

Th. 7   *Macbeth* (Shakespeare, First Night). "With the original Musick, Songs, Dances, &c." Wax. By viceregal command.

F. 8   *The Suspicious Husband*. To conclude with a Country Dance.

S. 9   *The Constant Couple*.

M. 11   *Venice Preserved*. *The Lying Valet*. Dancing.

W. 13   *The Provoked Husband*. Farce. Entertainments.

Th. 14   *The Merchant of Venice* (Shakespeare, Second Night). *The Virgin Unmasked*. Wax. By viceregal command.

F. 15   *The Earl of Essex*. Farce. Entertainments.

S. 16   *The Committee*. Farce. Entertainments.

M. 18   *The Constant Couple*.

Tu. 19   *The Busy Body*. Farce. Entertainments. Anniversary performance by command of the Lord Lieutenant.

W. 20   *The Non-Juror* (not acted these 8 years).

[1] "By viceregal command" signifies here the appearance of the Duke and Duchess of Dorset, newly arrived in Dublin and most generous in their patronage of the theater.

[2] Perhaps the November 1 performance was not given, since the January 11, 1750 performance may have been the "once in these 3 years." The showing before that had been almost three years before, on March 8, 1749.

Th. 21　*Hamlet* (Shakespeare, Third Night). Dancing. By viceregal command.

F. 22　*She Would and She Would Not.* Entertainments.

S. 23　*King John* (Shakespeare, Fourth Night).

M. 25　*Macbeth* (by Desire).

W. 27　*The Constant Couple.*

Th. 28　*The Non-Juror.* "After the Play, a Minuet by Mrs. Woffington, and a Country Dance by the Characters of the Comedy." By viceregal command.

F. 29　*The Amorous Widow.* Entertainments.

S. 30　*The Provoked Husband.* Farce. Entertainments.

DECEMBER

M. 2　*As You Like It* (Shakespeare, Fifth Night). *The Devil to Pay.*

W. 4　*Richard III* (Shakespeare, Sixth and Last Night). *The Brave Irishman.* Dancing. Wax.

Th. 5　*King John. Lethe.* Dancing. By viceregal command.

F. 6　*The Stratagem. *A Lass to be Let,* a Pantomime Entertainment. "With new Musick, Dances, and other Decorations."

S. 7　†*Zara.* Entertainments.

M. 9　*The Non-Juror.* With minuet and country dance.

W. 11　*Zara. A Lass to be Let.*

F. 13　*Cato.* For the benefit of "the Widows and Orphans of deceased Clergymen in the Diocese of Dublin." [3]

S. 14　*The Provoked Husband. The Lottery.* Entertainments.

M. 16　*King John. A Lass to be Let.*

W. 18　*The Stratagem.*

Th. 19　*The Man of Mode* (not acted these 8 years).[4] Dancing. By viceregal command.

F. 20　*The Beggar's Opera.*

---

[3] "N.B. The total Receipt at the Performance of this Play, will be applied to the Relief of distressed Widows and Children of Clergymen, in the Diocese of Dublin, under the Direction of the Society for that purpose. . . . The Society for the Relief of Clergymen's Widows and Children, was established in the Year 1749, and consists at present of about 220 Subscribers, many of whom are of the Laity of both Sexes. Their design is to provide a Subsistance for such Families . . . as are left destitute; and especially to put out their Children (as opportunity offers) to some useful Trade or Profession. They have within these 2 Years granted Pensions and Annuities to the Amount of 295 l., oos., 11d. and have Reason to expect farther Applications" (*Dublin Journal*, December 7–10, 1751).

[4] This performance had been planned for December 12, with *The Brave Irishman* and by viceregal command, but was apparently deferred until the 19th.

S. 21   *The Constant Couple*. Entertainments. "Being the last Time of performing before the Holydays."

Th. 26   *The Double Gallant* (by Desire). *The Necromancer*, "as lately revived with great Applause at the Theatre Royal in Covent Garden." Dancing. "Being the only Play this Week."

M. 30   *The Tempest*. Entertainments.

JANUARY

W. 1   *The Beggar's Opera*. *The Necromancer*. Dancing.

Th. 2   *Sir Courtly Nice* (not acted these 5 years). After the play a Scotch Dance. Entertainments.

F. 3   *The Inconstant*. Farce. Entertainments.

M. 6   *A Bold Stroke for a Wife*. *The Devil to Pay*. Dancing.

W. 8   *The Relapse* (not acted these 4 years). *The Lovers Revels*. "With new Scenes, Machines, and other Decorations, &c." Dancing.

Th. 9   *The Distrest Mother*. Dancing. By viceregal command.

F. 10   *The Man of Mode*. *The Necromancer*. Dancing.

S. 11   *The Provoked Husband*. Dancing.

M. 13   *The Non-Juror*. With minuet and country dance.

W. 15   *The Constant Couple*. By viceregal command.

Th. 16   *Jane Shore*. *Lethe*. Entertainments.

F. 17   *The Beggar's Opera*. *The Lovers Revels*.

S. 18   *The Provoked Wife*. *The Necromancer*. Entertainments.

M. 20   *Venice Preserved*. *The Vintner Tricked*.

W. 22   *The Old Batchelor* (Congreve, First Night). *The Necromancer*.

Th. 23   *The Fair Penitent* (by Desire of several Ladies of Quality). *The What D'Ye Call It*.

F. 24   *Love Makes a Man*. *The Lovers Revels*.

S. 25   *The Double Dealer* (Congreve, Second Night). *The Lovers Revels*.

M. 27   *Hamlet* (Shakespeare, First Night). *The Brave Irishman*. Wax.

Tu. 28   *The Provoked Wife*. *The Lovers Revels*. Dancing.

W. 29   *The Provoked Husband*.

Th. 30   "No Play on Thursday next [Jan. 30] on account of the Fast."

F. 31   *The Relapse*. Farce. Entertainments.

FEBRUARY

S. 1   *The Non-Juror*. "To conclude with a Minuet by Mrs. Woffington and Mr. McNeil and a Country Dance by the Characters in the Comedy."

M. 3   *The Distrest Mother*. *The Intriguing Chambermaid*.

W. 5   *The Way of the World* (Congreve, Third Night).

Th. 6   *The Constant Couple.* By viceregal command.

F. 7   *The Silent Woman* (not acted these 2 years). *The Lovers Revels.*

M. 10   *The Merry Wives of Windsor* (Shakespeare, Second Night). Wax.

Tu. 11   *Love for Love* (Congreve, Fourth Night).

Th. 13   *Richard III* (Shakespeare, Third Night). Entertainments. Wax. By viceregal command.

F. 14   *The Mourning Bride* (not acted these 8 years). (Congreve, Fifth Night.)

S. 15   *The Refusal. The Lovers Revels.*

M. 17   *The Non-Juror.* With minuet and dance.

W. 19   *Love for Love.* A Pastoral Dance by McNeil, Baker, et cetera.

Th. 20   *As You Like It* (Shakespeare, Fourth Night). *Tom Thumb the Great.* Wax.

F. 21   *The Old Batchelor.*

S. 22   *The Mourning Bride.* The dance, The Hibernian Courier.

M. 24   *King John. The Brave Irishman.* Wax.

W. 26   *The Careless Husband. Tom Thumb the Great.*

Th. 27   *The Double Dealer.* Wax. By viceregal command.

F. 28   *The Silent Woman.*

S. 29   **Coriolanus.*[5] With the original epilogue from Thomson. "With new Scenes, Dresses, and Decorations."

MARCH

M. 2   *The Constant Couple.* Entertainments.

W. 4   *Coriolanus.*

Th. 5   *The Distrest Mother.* By viceregal command.

F. 6   *The Alchymist* (not acted these 2 years). *Tom Thumb the Great.*

S. 7   *The Mourning Bride.*

M. 9   *The Provoked Husband.* Occasional Epilogue by Mrs. Woffington. **The Lawyer Outwitted.* By viceregal command. "N.B. On Account of the great Demand for Places, the Pit will be laid open to the Boxes for the Convenience of the Ladies." Benefit of Mrs. Woffington.

W. 11   *The Suspicious Husband.* With a Country Dance by the Performers. *The Intriguing Chambermaid.* Dancing. "N.B. The Pit will be laid open to Boxes, and Servants allowed to keep Places." Benefit of Mrs. Bland.

---

[5] This was the *Coriolanus* which Sheridan put together from Shakespeare and Thomson. (See Ch. VII for details and public reaction.) The epilogue was spoken by Mrs. Woffington.

Th. 12   *The Man of Mode. Tom Thumb the Great.* By viceregal command.

F. 13   *The Spanish Fryar.* Farce. Entertainments. "Pit and Boxes will be laid together." Wax. Benefit of Digges.

S. 14   *The Non-Juror.* With minuet and dance. *The Man of Taste,* an Interlude of two Acts. To conclude with a Comic Dance by McNeil, Baker, et cetera. "To prevent Mistakes, it is requested those who bespeak Places would take Tickets at the same Time." Benefit of Cibber.

M. 16   *The City Wives Confederacy.* With "a new Epilogue to be spoke by Mr. King." *The Lottery.* Dancing. Benefit of King.

W. 18   *The Merry Wives of Windsor.* Dancing. Benefit of Miss Cole.

Th. 19   *The Mourning Bride.* By viceregal command.

F. 20   *The Stratagem. The Lovers Revels* (by Desire). "With Alterations and Additions, particularly, there will be introduced the celebrated Skeleton Scene." A dance, The Hibernian Courier. Benefit of Victor.[6]

S. 21   *Coriolanus.* The Original Epilogue by Mrs. Woffington.

M. 23   *The Conscious Lovers.* "With a Prologue on the Occasion to be spoke by Mr. Sheridan." "The entire Receipt thereof will be appropriated to a Fund for erecting a Monument to that great and worthy Patriot Doctor Swift."

M. 30   *The Relapse.* After Act II, Minuet and Tamborine by Miss Baker; after the play, a Scotch Dance by McNeil and Baker. *The Stage Coach.* Benefit of Neil, Boxkeeper.

Tu. 31   *The Alchymist. The Lovers Revels,* with the Skeleton Scene. Dancing, especially The Hibernian Courier.

APRIL

Th. 2   *The Twin Rivals.* After Act II, by desire, the last new Song by Mrs. Crump, set by Mr. Cushin. Act III, The Minuet and Tamborine by Miss Baker. Act IV, a Concerto by Mr. Cushin. After the play, the Neapolitan Threshers by McNeil and Baker. *The Necromancer.* Grand Comic Dance. Benefit of Hamilton and Cushin.

F. 3   *She Would and She Would Not. The Necromancer,* in which will be introduced Equilibres on the Wire by Messink. "1st, He will balance a Straw on the Edge of a Glass. Next, He will balance a Feather on his Nose, and afterwards blow it from his

[6] "N.B. On Account of the great Number of Gallery Tickets Mr. Victor has disposed of, he is advised by his Friends to fix the Prices of both Galleries at 2s.2d., Pit 3s.3d., Boxes and Lattices 5s.5d." (*Dublin Journal,* March 14–17, 1752).

Nose on his Forehead. Next, He will wheel a Lapland Dog in a Wheel-Barrow. Next, He will play on the Pipe and doule [*sic*] Taber standing on the Wire. Next, He will toss the Balls. And lastly, He will balance a Horizontal Wheel of Fire Works." Benefit of Messink.

S. 4   *The Careless Husband. The Brave Irishman.* Benefit of Husband.

M. 6   *Rule a Wife and Have a Wife. The School Boy.* Dancing. Benefit of Mr. and Mrs. Kennedy.

W. 8   *The Double Gallant. Tom Thumb the Great.* "With an Epilogue to be spoke in the Character of Tom Thumb by Master Mynitt." Dancing. Benefit of Mr. and Mrs. Mynitt, and Master Mynitt.

Th. 9   *The Mourning Bride.*[7] **The Constant Captives.* "With new Dances, Musick, Habits, Scenes, Machines, and other Decorations."

F. 10   *The Provoked Wife.* After Act I, The Comic Millers; Act II, A new grand Fingallian Dance; Act III, The Comic Tiroler; Act IV, a Hornpipe by McNeil; Act V, a Minuet. *The Devil to Pay.* Benefit of McNeil.

S. 11   *Jane Shore. The Lovers Revels,* with the Skeleton Scene. Dancing. Benefit of Beamsley.

M. 13   *The Suspicious Husband.* "With an Epilogue on Some-body in the Character of No-body, by Mr. Cibber." *The Devil to Pay.* Dancing. Benefit of Mr. and Mrs. Davies.

W. 15   *The Refusal.* With a humorous Epilogue by Sparks, in the character of the Lord Chief Justice. *The Brave Irishman.* Benefit of Sparks.[8]

Th. 16   *The Man of Mode. The Constant Captives.*

F. 17   *She Would and She Would Not.* Farce. Dancing. Benefit of Miss Baker.

S. 18   *The Recruiting Officer. The Lying Valet.* Dancing. Benefit of Heaphy.

M. 20   *Phaedra and Hippolitus. The Brave Irishman.* By viceregal command. Benefit of Mrs. Woffington.

W. 22   *The City Wives Confederacy.* Singing between the Acts, by Mrs. Crump. *Damon and Phillida.* After Act II, by Desire, Where the Bee Sucks, by Mrs. Crump; Act III, by Desire, the

---

[7] *The Man of Mode,* planned for this evening, was put off, "by Desire," until further notice.

[8] "On Account of extraordinary Demand for Places in the Middle Gallery, Mr. Sparks is desired by his Friends, to make both Middle and Upper Gallery at 2s.2d." (*Dublin Journal,* April 4–7, 1752).

Early Horn, by Conyers; Act IV, If Love's a sweet Passion, Mrs. Crump. Dancing. Benefit of Mrs. Rowley and Mrs. Crump.

Th. 23   *The Constant Couple. The Constant Captives.*

F. 24   *The Merchant of Venice. The Virgin Unmasked.* Dancing. Benefit of J. Elrington.

S. 25   *The Beggar's Opera.* In the 3d Act, a Hornpipe by McNeil. *The Constant Captives.*

M. 27   *The Stratagem.* After Act II, a serious Dance by Mons. Moreau; Act III, a Hornpipe by McNeil; Act IV, a Shepherdess's Dance by Miss Moreau; Act V, the last new favourite Dance, the Fingallian Revels by McNeil, Baker, et cetera. *The Mock Lawyer* (not acted these 10 years). With a new humorous Epilogue by Sparks in the character of the Mock Lawyer. Benefit of Carmichael and Longfield.

W. 29   *Love for Love.* Dancing after 3d and 5th acts. *The Honest Yorkshireman.* Benefit of Mrs. Bland.

Th. 30   *The Conscious Lovers. The Constant Captives.* By viceregal command.

MAY

F. 1   *The Spanish Fryar* (by particular Desire of several Persons of Quality). Farce. Dancing. Benefit of Watson.

S. 2   *The Roman Father. The Constant Captives.*

M. 4   *The Merry Wives of Windsor.* After Act I, a Trumpet Concerto by Mr. Jacob; Act II, The Drunken Peasant by Messink; his Man by Williams; Act III, a Hornpipe by McNeil; Act IV, a Concert on the French Horn by Mr. Clarke and Mr. Forster; Act V, the Hibernian Courier. *The Lying Valet.* Benefit of Williams.

Th. 7   *Coriolanus.* By viceregal command. "N.B. By Command the Play will not begin 'till half an Hour after Seven, the first Musick at half an Hour after Six."

F. 8   †*The Rover. The Constant Captives.*

S. 9   *The Earl of Essex.*[9]

Tu. 12   *The Silent Woman. The Constant Captives.*

W. 13   *King Henry VIII* [10] (not acted these 18 years). "Containing, the Death of the Duke of Buckingham; the Fall and Death of Cardinal Wolsey; the Divorce and Death of Queen Catherine;

---

[9] "N.B. Tickets deliver'd out for Merope, (which was to have been Acted that Night) in the Names of the Widow Elrington, Mr. Fagan, and a Gentlewoman in Distress, will be taken that Night" (*Dublin Journal*, May 2–5, 1752).

[10] This is frequently advertised as *Harry the Eighth*, but entries have been regularized here for convenience.

the Coronation of Anna Bullen, and the Christening of Princess Elizabeth; with many other true Historical Passages. . . . With proper Habits, Scenes, and Decorations. With an Epilogue by Dryden, and an Epitaph by Milton, spoke by Mr. Digges, representing the Shade of Shakespear, as figured in Westminster Abbey." *The Constant Captives*. Benefit of Cibber.

Th. 14   *The Non-Juror*. With minuet and country dance. A new Epilogue spoken by Mrs. Woffington. By viceregal command.

F. 15   *The Relapse*. "At the End of the Play, Mr. King (by Desire) will speak Jo. Haynes's Epilogue, riding on an Ass." †*Harlequin Ranger*, a pantomime, "As performed at the Theatre Royal in Drury Lane, with great Applause." Dancing. Benefit of King.

S. 16   *Phaedra and Hippolitus*. Dance, The Hibernian Courier.

M. 18   *The Beggar's Opera. The Constant Captives*.

W. 20   *Romeo and Juliet*. "With Alterations, as performed at the Theatres in England. . . . In Act the first will be introduced, A Masquerade Scene." Dancing in character by McNeil and Baker. After Act iv, the Funeral Procession. Farce. Entertainments. Benefit of Mrs. Lee.

Th. 21   *King Henry VIII*.

S. 23   *The Mourning Bride. The Constant Captives*.

M. 25   *The Non-Juror*. Anniversary performance. Boxes free to ladies.

Tu. 26   *The Inconstant* (by particular Desire). With Occasional Prologue to be spoken by Montgomery, and an Epilogue by Miss Cole, "in Breeches." *Harlequin Ranger*, With Alterations and Additions. Dancing. Benefit of Montgomery.

Th. 28   *King Henry VIII*.

S. 30   †*The Fatal Marriage. The Constant Captives*.

JUNE

Tu. 2   *The Beggar's Opera*. New Equilibres by Messink. Hornpipe by McNeil, and a Tamberine by Miss Baker. A favourite Duet by Conyers and Mrs. Crump, to the Tune of Daniel Cooper. Benefit of Tracy.

Tu. 9   [First Part of] *King Henry IV*. After Act ii, Song of the True Blue by Conyers; Act v, Duet to the Tune of Daniel Cooper by Conyers and Mrs. Crump. Benefit of Tracy.

1752–1753

The Company: ACTORS: Beamsley, Costollo, Cunningham, Dexter (beginning May 30), Digges, J. Elrington, Green, Hamilton, Heaphy, Kennedy, King, Layfield, Longfield, Maurice, Messink, Montgomery, Mynitt,

Master Mynitt, Sheridan, Sowdon, Sparks, Stayley, Stevens, Watson, Williams. ACTRESSES: Mrs. Crofts, Miss Falkner (became Mrs. Donaldson), Mrs. Green, Miss Johnson, Mrs. Kennedy, Miss Mason, Mrs. Mynitt, Mrs. Packenham, Miss Reynolds, Mrs. Rowley, Mrs. Stevens, Mrs. Ward, Mrs. Woffington. DANCERS: Miss Baker, McNeil, Pitt. SINGERS: Mrs. Crump, Lee, Sullivan. Mrs. Donaldson (see Miss Falkner above) also sang. EQUILIBRIST: Maddox.

Number of Performances: About 132 (after a late start).

Number of Command Performances: About 4.

Number of Benefit Performances: About 29. Woffington (2), Sowdon, Mrs. Ward, Mrs. Green (2), Maddox, Digges, King, Mrs. Donaldson, Sullivan, Montgomery, Neil (boxkeeper), Victor (treasurer), Sparks, Miss Baker, McNeil, Knowles (assistant treasurer), Heaphy, Watson, Mr. and Mrs. Kennedy, Mr. and Mrs. Mynitt and Master Mynitt, Hamilton (?), Williams, Stevens, and Mrs. Crump, Elrington, gentlewoman in distress, Husband, Meath Hospital.

OCTOBER

M. 16   *The Beggar's Opera.* In Act III, a Hornpipe by Mr. Pitt.

W. 18   *Othello.* Dancing.

Th. 19   *The Provoked Husband.* Entertainments.

F. 20   *Love Makes a Man.* Dancing. "N.B. The Curtain will be drawn up precisely at Half an Hour past six o'Clock, after which no Money will be returned."

M. 23   *The Stratagem.* Anniversary performance by command of the Lords Justices. Boxes free to the ladies.

W. 25   *Venice Preserved. The Brave Irishman.* Singing and dancing.

Th. 26   *The Recruiting Officer.* Singing and dancing.

F. 27   *The Fatal Marriage.* Singing and dancing.

M. 30   *Phaedra and Hippolitus. The Brave Irishman.*

NOVEMBER

W. 1   *The Relapse. Lethe.*

Th. 2   *Tancred and Sigismunda* (not acted these 3 years).

S. 4   *Tamerlane.* "With the usual Prologue on the Occasion." Anniversary performance.

M. 6   *Hamlet* (Shakespeare, First Night). Entertainments. Singing. Wax.

W. 8   *The City Wives Confederacy. Lethe.*

Th. 9   *The Beggar's Opera.*

F. 10   *The Provoked Husband. The Lottery.* Anniversary performance.

M. 13   *Macbeth* (Shakespeare, Second Night). "With the original Musick and other Decorations." *The Lottery.* Dancing. Wax.

W. 15   *Phaedra and Hippolitus. The Devil to Pay.* Singing and dancing.

Th. 16   *The City Wives Confederacy. The Lottery.*

F. 17   *Tancred and Sigismunda. The Virgin Unmasked.*

M. 20   *King Henry VIII* (Shakespeare, Third Night). "In which will be introduced the Ceremony of the Coronation, with several Alterations and Additions."

W. 22   *The Stratagem. The Intriguing Chambermaid.*

Th. 23   *King Henry VIII.*[1]

F. 24   *The Orphan. The Virgin Unmasked.*

M. 27   *Romeo and Juliet* (Shakespeare, Fourth Night). "With the Funeral Procession and Solemn Dirge." Wax.

W. 29   *The Constant Couple.*

Th. 30   *The Conscious Lovers. The Mock Doctor.* Anniversary performance. "By Command, the Boxes will be free to the Ladies."

DECEMBER

F. 1   *King Henry VIII.*

S. 2   *The Distrest Mother.* "The Characters entirely new dressed."

M. 4   *Richard III* (Shakespeare, Sixth Night). *The Brave Irishman.* Wax.

W. 6   *The Provoked Husband. Miss in her Teens.*

Th. 7   *The Beggar's Opera.* "To conclude with a Country Dance by the Characters in the Opera."

F. 8   *The Mourning Bride* (Congreve, First Night).

M. 11   †*The Siege of Damascus.* "With new Dresses, and other Decorations."

W. 13   *The Merchant of Venice* (Shakespeare, Seventh Night). Wax.

Th. 14   *The Double Dealer* (Congreve, Second Night). *The Intriguing Chambermaid.*

F. 15   *King Henry VIII.*

S. 16   *Romeo and Juliet. The Virgin Unmasked.*

M. 18   *Julius Caesar* (Shakespeare, Eighth Night). Wax.

W. 20   *The Siege of Damascus. The Lying Valet.*

Th. 21   *The Constant Couple.*

F. 22   *The Funeral. The Honest Yorkshireman.*

JANUARY

M. 1   *The Committee.* "Several surprising Equilibres on the Wire, by the celebrated Mr. Maddox from the Theatre-Royal in Covent-Garden, being the first Time of his performing in this Kingdom."

W. 3   *Love Makes a Man.* Equilibres by Maddox.

---

[1] "N.B. The Play of the Fatal Marriage is deferred till further Notice" (*Dublin Journal*, November 18–21, 1752).

Th. 4   *The Twin Rivals.* Equilibres by Maddox.

F. 5   *The Suspicious Husband.* Equilibres by Maddox.

M. 8   *Love's Last Shift.* Equilibres by Maddox.

W. 10   *The Busy Body.* Equilibres by Maddox. "He will balance a Straw and play a Violin at the same Time."

Th. 11   *The Beggar's Opera.* With a Hornpipe by McNeil, and a Country Dance by the Characters in the Opera. Equilibres by Maddox.

F. 12   *The Rehearsal.* Equilibres by Maddox.

M. 15   *The Distrest Mother.* After Act IV, a song by Mrs. Donaldson. *The Virgin Unmasked.*

W. 17   *The Tempest.* Equilibres by Maddox.

Th. 18   *The Double Dealer. The Necromancer.*

F. 19   *The London Merchant* [2] (not acted for 4 years). Equilibres by Maddox.

M. 22   *The Tempest.*[3] "With all the original Musick, Songs, Dances, and other Decorations, and the Grand Dancing Devils by McNeil and Baker." Equilibres by Maddox. "Particularly, He will balance a Coach Wheel."

W. 24   *King Henry VIII.* With the Coronation of Ann Bullen.

Th. 25   *The Rehearsal.* Equilibres by Maddox.

F. 26   *Hamlet* (Shakespeare, First Night). Wax.

M. 29   *The Fair Penitent.*

W. 31   *Love for Love* (Congreve, Third Night). Singing and dancing.

FEBRUARY

Th. 1   *The Tempest.* Equilibres by Maddox.

F. 2   *Macbeth* (Shakespeare, Second Night). Wax.

S. 3   *The London Merchant.* Equilibres by Maddox.

M. 5   *The Fair Penitent.*

W. 7   *Phaedra and Hippolitus. The Devil to Pay.*

Th. 8   *The Tempest.* Equilibres by Maddox.

F. 9   *The Double Dealer.*[4] *The Necromancer.*

S. 10   *The Mistake* (not acted these 4 years). Equilibres by Maddox. "Particularly, He will turn several Times around the Wire,

[2] Sometimes advertised, as it was here, as *George Barnwell*.

[3] "The Tragedy of Phaedra and Hippolitus, which was to have been performed on the above Night, is obliged to be deferred till further Notice, on Account of the Indisposition of one who was to have performed a principal Character" (*Dublin Journal*, January 16–20, 1753). Perhaps this "one" was Digges, who was scheduled to play Hippolitus and who was ill off and on through most of this time.

[4] "N.B. The Play of Julius Caesar is deferred till further Notice" (*Dublin Journal*, February 3–6, 1753).

Head over Heels, without ever quitting it with his Feet, and will balance upon his Chin a Coach-Wheel."

W. 14   *The Mistake.* Equilibres by Maddox (for the last time).

Th. 15 *Love for Love.* Singing.

F. 16   *The Funeral. The Lottery.*

S. 17   *Comus* (revived). "With all the original Musick, Songs, Dances,
(A.S.) Scenery, Machinery, and other Decorations. . . . At the End of the 2d Act will be performed a Concerto on the Organ by a Boy of Ten Years Old."

M. 19   *Jane Shore.*[5]

W. 21   *The Old Batchelor* (Congreve, Fourth Night). *The Virgin Unmasked.* Singing.

Th. 22 *Comus.* With boy organist and equilibres by Maddox.
(A.S.)

F. 23   *The Merry Wives of Windsor* (Shakespeare, Third Night). *The Constant Captives.*

S. 24   *Comus.* Equilibres by Maddox.
(A.S.)

M. 26   *The Fair Penitent. The Brave Irishman.*

W. 28   *Jane Shore. The Lottery.*

MARCH

Th. 1   *Comus.* Equilibres by Maddox.
(A.S.)

F. 2   *The Way of the World* (Congreve, Fifth and Last Night). *The Constant Captives.*

S. 3   *Comus.* Equilibres by Maddox.
(A.S.)

M. 5   †*Ulysses.* "With a new Epilogue to be spoke by Mrs. Woffington."

Tu. 6   *The Mistake.* Equilibres by Maddox, "particularly, he will balance upon his Chin, a Pyramid with 20 Glasses full of Wine, in full Swing on the Wire. . . N.B. By Desire, Mr. Maddox will perform the few remaining Nights at Smock Alley."

Th. 8   *The Suspicious Husband.* With a country dance. Equilibres by Maddox.

F. 9   *The Provoked Wife. The Lovers Revels.* Singing.

S. 10   *The Committee.* Equilibres by Maddox.

M. 12   *Ulysses. The Devil to Pay.* "N.B. The Play [*Ulysses*] is much shortened, and considerable Alterations have been made in it since the last Performance."

[5] This had been planned for February 12, but postponed, perhaps because of Digges (see footnote 3 above).

W. 14　　*The Old Batchelor. The Lovers Revels.* Singing.

Th. 15　　*The Pilgrim* (not acted these 10 years). Equilibres by Maddox.

F. 16　　*Ulysses. The Devil to Pay.*

M. 19　　*The Non-Juror.* With minuet by Woffington and McNeil and a country dance by the characters. *The Lovers Revels.* "N.B. Four Rows of the Pit will be railed into the Boxes for Ladies, the rest of the Pit will be at the usual Price of 3s.3d." Benefit of Mrs. Woffington.

Tu. 20　　*King Arthur* (not acted these 4 years). "With all the original
(A.S.)　　Musick, Songs, Dances, Scenery, Machinery, and other Decorations." Equilibres by Maddox. Dancing.

W. 21　　*The Constant Couple. The Brave Irishman.* Benefit of Sowdon.

Th. 22　　*The Way of the World. Miss in her Teens.* Benefit of Mrs. Ward.

F. 23　　*The Refusal.* †*The Oracle* (by Desire). Benefit of Mrs. Green.

S. 24　　*Love's Last Shift.* After Act II, a Hornpipe by Maddox. New equilibres on the wire. Benefit of Maddox.

M. 26　　*The Fatal Marriage.* After Act I, a Solo by Mr. Lee; Act II, With Horns and with Hounds, to be sung by Mrs. Donaldson; Act v, a Grand Dance by McNeil and Baker. *Miss in her Teens* (by Desire). "Six Rows of the Pit will be laid into the Boxes, where Servants will be allowed to keep Places." Benefit of Digges.[6]

Tu. 27　　*King Arthur.*
(A.S.)

W. 28　　*Much Ado About Nothing.* After Act III, by particular Desire, a Hornpipe by Maddox. With a new Masquerade Scene, in which will be introduced a Dance by McNeil and Baker. After Act IV, a Song by Mrs. Donaldson; Act v, a Dance. *The Lovers Revels,* "With Alterations and Additions." Benefit of King.

Th. 29　　*The Merry Wives of Windsor.* After Act II (by Desire), a new Song called, the Oracle; Act III, an Italian Song by Mrs. Donaldson; Act IV, a favourite Song, Where the Bee sucks &c. out of the Tempest, by Mrs. Donaldson. *The Chaplet* (not acted these 4 years). Benefit of Mrs. Donaldson.

F. 30　　*As You Like It.* After Act II, by particular Desire, a favourite Song, Lango Lee, by Sullivan. Singing and dancing after other acts. *The Devil to Pay.* Benefit of Sullivan.

S. 31　　*Comus.* With the boy organist.
(A.S.)

[6] "N.B. As Mr. Digges's Indisposition prevents his waiting on his Friends, he hopes they will excuse a personal Application" (*Dublin Journal,* March 20–24, 1753).

APRIL

M. 2   *Hamlet.* "With a Eulogim on Shakespear, the Stage, and the Admirers of both, by way of Prologue, to be spoken by Mr. Montgomery." After Act II, Elin O'Roon by Mrs. Donaldson; singing and dancing after other acts. *The Honest Yorkshireman.* Benefit of Montgomery.[7]

W. 4   *The Double Dealer.* Singing and dancing between the acts. *The Lovers Revels.* "N.B. On Account of the extraordinary Demand for Places, the Boxes will be laid open to the Pit, and Servants admitted to keep Places." Benefit of Neil, Boxkeeper.[8]

M. 9   *The Double Gallant.* Singing and dancing between the acts. *The Constant Captives.* "The front Boxes will be laid open to the Pit, two Rows of which will be taken for the Accommodation of the Ladies. . . . Additional Lights and Attendance will be ordered to the Upper Gallery." Benefit of Victor.

W. 11   *The Provoked Husband.* A new Comic Epilogue to be spoken by Sparks and Stevens, in the characters of High Tragedy and Low Comedy. *The Brave Irishman.* Singing. Benefit of Sparks.[9]

Th. 12   *The Foundling* (not acted these 4 years). Singing between the acts. After the play a Minuet and Louvre by McNeil and Baker. *The Constant Captives.* Dancing. Benefit of Miss Baker.

F. 13   *Rule a Wife and Have a Wife.* "Act I, The comic Millers, Ralph and his Sue; Act II, A grand Scoth [*sic*] Ballet; Act III, The comic Irish Piper; Act IV, A Hornpipe by McNeil and a young Master, his Scholar, of 8 Years old. And after the Play, a Minuet." *The Honest Yorkshireman.* Benefit of McNeil.

S. 14   *King Arthur.*
(A.S.)

M. 23   *King Henry VIII. Lethe.* A dance, the Hibernian Courier, by McNeil and Baker. "The second Gallery will be cleaned, and properly illuminated, for the Reception of those who may not find Room in the first." Benefit of Knowles.

[7] Montgomery was so ill that he could not act in his benefit play. He died about a month later.

[8] "Mr. Neil humbly requests the Favour of the Ladies who have taken Places in the Pit, that they will order their Servants at Half an Hour after 3, and those for the Boxes at 4 o'Clock, to prevent Mistakes. The Galleries will be opened at 3, the Pit at Half an Hour after 5, and the Boxes at 6 o'Clock" (*Dublin Journal*, March 27–31, 1753).

[9] "On Account of the extraordinary Demands for Gallery Tickets, Mr. Sparks is desired by his Friends to have both Galleries at 2s.2d." (*Dublin Journal*, April 7–10, 1753). This benefit is reported by *Williamson's Universal Advertizer*, April 14, to have brought in over £165—a staggering sum.

W. 25   *Love for Love.* Singing and dancing between the acts. The Humorous Trial of Ananias Overdone Swadler, before the Lord Chief Joker Sparks, according to the Rules and Manner of the Court of Nassau (by particular Desire). Farce. The Pit will be laid open to the Boxes. Benefit of Heaphy.

Th. 26   *The Relapse.* Between the acts, singing and dancing; also a solo concerto by Mr. Lee. *The Honest Yorkshireman.* By command of the Lords Justices. Benefit of Watson.

F. 27   *Venice Preserved.* "An Epilogue addressed to the Town, to be spoke by Mrs. Kennedy." *The Constant Captives.* Singing and dancing. Benefit of Mr. and Mrs. Kennedy.

M. 30   *King John.* A humorous Epilogue by Master Mynitt. Singing and dancing between the acts. *The Intriguing Chambermaid.* Benefit of Mr. and Mrs. Mynitt and Master Mynitt.

MAY

W. 2   *Jane Shore.* After Act I, With Horns and with Hounds by Sullivan; Act IV, Elin O'Roon, Mrs. Donaldson. Dancing. Farce. Benefit of Hamilton.[10]

Th. 3   *The Provoked Wife.* Farce. Singing and dancing. Benefit of Williams.

F. 4   *Much Ado About Nothing.* With a new Masquerade Scene and Minuet. Singing between the acts. Farce.

S. 5   *The Spanish Fryar.* Singing between the acts. A dance, the Hibernian Courier. "After the Play, an Entertainment will be exhibited the Trial of Ananias Overdone, and the Examination of the Theatrical Disturbers . . . the Jury to be performed by the Pit." Benefit of Stevens and Mrs. Crump.

M. 7   *Coriolanus.*[11] The Savoyard Dance by McNeil and Baker.

F. 11   *The Non-Juror.* With the minuet and country dance.

M. 14   *The Earl of Essex.* Farce. Benefit of Mrs. Woffington.

Th. 17   *The Siege of Damascus.* "With new Dresses and other Decorations." Farce. Singing and dancing. Benefit of Elrington.

F. 18   *The Fair Penitent.* Farce. Entertainments. By particular Desire of several Ladies of Quality. Benefit of Mrs. Green.

M. 21   *Phaedra and Hippolitus.* Benefit of a Gentlewoman in Distress, and five small Children, the eldest but Six Years Old.

[10] This may not have been given. A note on the advertisement for *Ulysses* (scheduled for May 24) reports that "Tickets delivered out by the Widow Beamsly, Mr. Pit, Mr. Costollo, Mr. Maurice, and Tickets delivered out by Mr. Hamilton for Jane Shore, and all other Tickets for the above Play will be taken this Night" (*Dublin Journal,* May 19–22, 1753).

[11] "N.B. The Play of Oroonoko is obliged to be deferred 'till further Notice" (*Dublin Journal,* May 1–5, 1753).

Th. 24 *Ulysses.*
F. 25   *The Fatal Marriage.* After Act II, a Hornpipe by a Gentleman
        who never performed on any Stage; singing and dancing after
        other acts, especially the Hibernian Courier at the end of the
        play. *The Honest Yorkshireman.* Benefit of Husband.
M. 28   *The Stratagem.* Singing and dancing.
W. 30   *Oroonoko* (not acted these 2 years).

JUNE

F. 1   *The Mourning Bride.* Farce. Entertainments. "Towards the
        Encrease of a Fund for the Support of the Meath Hospital on
        the Coomb, a charitable Foundation lately Instituted." [12]
M. 4   *The Non-Juror.* With a Prologue on the Occasion. Dancing.
        The Lovers Revels. Anniversary performance by command of
        the Lords Justices. The boxes free to the ladies.
W. 6   *Jane Shore. The Lovers Revels.*

1753–1754
(through the *Mahomet* riot of March 2)

The Company: ACTORS: Cunningham, Dexter, Digges, J. Elrington,
Green, Hamilton, Heaphy, Hull, Kennedy, King, Layfield, Maurice, My-
nitt, Master Pye, Sheridan, Sowdon, Sparks, Stayley, Storer, Watson, Wil-
liams. ACTRESSES: Miss Comerford, Mrs. Cunningham, Mrs. Green, Mrs.
Kennedy, Mrs. Leslie, Miss Mason, Mrs. Mynitt, Mrs. Pye, Miss Reyn-
olds, Mrs. Roberts, Mrs. Ward, Mrs. Woffington. DANCERS: Miss Baker,
Master Blake, Harvey, McNeil, the Moor Abdalla. SINGERS: Butler, Mrs.
Storer. EQUILIBRIST: Stuart. FIRE-EATER: Powell.
  Number of Performances through March 2: About 93.
  Number of Command Performances through March 2: About 20.
  Number of Benefit Performances through March 2: None.

OCTOBER

M. 1   *Love's Last Shift. The Honest Yorkshireman.*
W. 3   *Oroonoko. The Virgin Unmasked.* Singing by Mrs. Storer.

[12] "N.B. The Fund, which depends only on private Subscriptions, has hitherto
been too small to admit of supporting more than two Beds; but since the opening of the House on the 2d of March last, no less than 1581 Out Patients have
been attended for various Complaints, and many had Medicines given them.
Hence appears the great Usefulness of a Charity of this Kind, in a Part of the
Town crouded with industrious Poor, and so remote from the City Hospitals,
that they are in a great Measure deprived of the Benefit of attending them. It
is therefore hoped, that the Publick will favour this Scheme, so as to enable the
Managers to enlarge it" (*Dublin Journal*, May 26–29, 1753).

Th. 4   *The Distrest Mother.*

F. 5   *The Stratagem.* To conclude with a Country Dance. Singing.

M. 8   *Phaedra and Hippolitus. The Lying Valet.* Singing.

W. 10   *The Double Dealer* (Congreve, First Night). In Act III, a Song by Mrs. Storer.

Th. 11   *Jane Shore. The Mock Doctor.*

F. 12   *Love for Love* (Congreve, Second Night). Singing.

M. 15   *Venice Preserved. The Devil to Pay.*

W. 17   *The Old Batchelor* (Congreve, Third Night).

Th. 18   *Ulysses.* "With an occasional Prologue to be spoke by Mrs. Woffington in the Character of the Tragick Muse, and the usual Epilogue." Wax. By viceregal command.

F. 19   *The Way of the World* (Congreve, Fourth Night). "With the following Entertainments of Dancing by the Moor Abdalla, lately arrived from Paris. At the End of the 3d Act, a serious Dance; and after the Play, a comick Dance."

M. 22   *The Suspicious Husband.* With the usual Prologue. Anniversary performance by viceregal command. "The Boxes will be free to the Ladies."

W. 24   *The Beggar's Opera.*

Th. 25   *The Provoked Husband.* By viceregal command.

F. 26   *Oedipus* (not acted these 10 years). With alterations and with "several new Decorations."

M. 29   †*The Comical Lovers.*

W. 31   *The City Wives Confederacy. The Lottery.*

NOVEMBER

Th. 1   *Oedipus. The Devil to Pay.* By viceregal command.

F. 2   *The Comical Lovers.* After Act III, "a Hornpipe by a Child of six Years old, Scholar to Mr. McNeil."

M. 5   *Tamerlane.* In Act IV, Oh Sleep! by Mrs. Storer. *The Mock Doctor.* Anniversary performance.

W. 7   *The Comical Lovers. The Lovers Revels.* Dancing by McNeil and Baker (their first performance of this season).

Th. 8   *The Committee.* Singing. By viceregal command.

F. 9   *Oedipus. The Anatomist.*

S. 10   *The Beggar's Opera.* In the last act, a Hornpipe by McNeil. Anniversary performance by viceregal command. "The Boxes free to the Ladies."

W. 14   *Hamlet* (Shakespeare, First Night). Dancing.

Th. 15   *The Fair Penitent.* Singing and dancing. By viceregal command.

F. 16   *The Double Dealer* (Congreve, First Night). *The Lovers Revels.*

S. 17   *The Merchant of Venice* (Shakespeare, Second Night). Singing between the acts, dancing at end of play. *The What D'Ye Call It.*

W. 21   *The Constant Couple. The Lovers Revels.* Dancing.

Th. 22   *The Old Batchelor* (Congreve, Second Night). A new Dance by McNeil, Harvey, and Miss Baker. By viceregal command.

F. 23   *The Stratagem.* Concluding with a country dance by the characters. *The What D'Ye Call It.* Dancing.

S. 24   *Macbeth* (Shakespeare, Third Night).[1] "With all the original Musick, Songs, Dances, Scenery, Machinery, and other Decorations." *The Lovers Revels.* Dancing.

M. 26   *The Pilgrim.* Dancing and singing between the acts. *The Necromancer,* with Mr. Powell, the celebrated Fire-Eater from London.

W. 28   *Much Ado About Nothing* (Shakespeare, Fourth Night). With a country dance by characters in the comedy. Farce. Singing and dancing.

Th. 29   *Phaedra and Hippolitus.* Dancing. By viceregal command.

F. 30   *The Committee.* Concluding with country dance by the characters. Equilibres on the wire by Mr. Stuart, "lately arrived from England, being the first Time of his performing here." Anniversary performance by viceregal command. Boxes free to the ladies.

DECEMBER

S. 1   *The Lady's Last Stake* (not acted here these 15 years). Singing and dancing.

M. 3   *The Mourning Bride* (Congreve, Third Night). *Lethe.*

W. 5   *The Provoked Husband.* Farce.

Th. 6   *The Provoked Wife.* At end of Act II, a Hornpipe by Master Blake. Singing and dancing. By viceregal command.

F. 7   *The Committee.* Equilibres by Stuart.

S. 8   *King Henry VIII.* With the Coronation of Anne Bullen. Dancing.

M. 10   *The Lady's Last Stake.* Singing and dancing.

W. 12   *The Pilgrim.* Equilibres by Stuart.

Th. 13   *Richard III.* Dancing. By viceregal command.

F. 14   *The Way of the World* (Congreve, Fourth Night). *Lethe.*

S. 15   *The Beggar's Opera.*[2] With hornpipe. Equilibres by Stuart.

M. 17   *The Non-Juror.* "To conclude with a Minuet by Heartly and

[1] A performance of *Richard III*, scheduled for Monday, November 19, was advertised as the third night in the Shakespeare series, but seems to have been canceled.

[2] "N.B. The Play of Romeo and Juliet is obliged to be deferred till Friday next" (*Dublin Journal*, December 11–15, 1753).

Maria, and a Country Dance by the Characters in the Comedy."

W. 19   *The Recruiting Officer.* With the last New Occasional Epilogue to be spoken by Mrs. Woffington. *Lethe.* Dancing.

Th. 20   *The Lady's Last Stake. The Brave Irishman.*

F. 21   *Romeo and Juliet.* "With Alterations." After Act IV, the Funeral Procession, accompanied with a solemn Dirge. *The School Boy.*

S. 22   *The Non-Juror.* With minuet and country dance.

M. 31   *The Rehearsal.* "With an Additional Reinforcement of Mr. Bays's new rais'd Troops." Equilibres by Stuart.

JANUARY

W. 2   *The Busy Body.* After Act IV, a Hornpipe by Master Blake. Dancing. Equilibres by Stuart.

Th. 3   *The London Merchant.* Singing and dancing. Equilibres by Stuart.

F. 4   *The Country Lasses* (not acted here these 16 years).

M. 7   *The Tempest.* "With all the original Musick, Songs, Dances, Scenery, Machinery, Sinkings, Flyings, and other Decorations." Dancing. Equilibres by Stuart. "Particularly, he will balance an Egg on the small End of a Tobacco Pipe, on his Nose."

W. 9   *The Tempest* (by particular Desire). *The Miller of Mansfield.* Dancing.

Th. 10   *The Pilgrim.* Dancing. Equilibres by Stuart. By viceregal command.

F. 11   *The Country Lasses. Flora.* Dancing.

M. 14   †*The Wonder, a Woman Keeps a Secret.* Equilibres by Stuart. "Particularly, He will balance a Pyramid of Fire-Works, which will be discharged while he is in full Swing."

W. 16   *The Merry Wives of Windsor.* Farce. Dancing.

Th. 17   *The Fatal Marriage.* A Grand Dutch Dance by McNeil and Baker. By viceregal command.

F. 18   *The Twin Rivals.* Entertainments. Equilibres by Stuart.

M. 21   *Oroonoko.* "In the second Act, will be revived the original Songs, set to Musick by the late celebrated Mr. Lampe, and sung by Mrs. Storer and Mr. Butler; and after the Play, the grand Fingallian Dance by Mr. McNeil, Mr. Harvey, and Miss Baker." *The School Boy.*

W. 23   *Phaedra and Hippolitus. The Brave Irishman.* Dancing.

Th. 24   *The Comical Lovers.* Dancing and singing. By viceregal command.

F. 25   *The Non-Juror.* With minuet and country dance. *The Constant Captives.*

S. 26   *The Wonder, a Woman Keeps a Secret.* Equilibres by Stuart.

". . . he will stand on his Head on the Wire, and entirely quit it with his Hands, in full Swing."

M. 28   *The Relapse. The Honest Yorkshireman.* Dancing and singing.

Tu. 29   *The Tempest.* Equilibres by Stuart.

W. 30   Anniversary of Martyrdom of King Charles. No play.

Th. 31   *The Fair Penitent.* In Act II, a Song by Mrs. Storer. Dancing. By viceregal command.

FEBRUARY

F. 1   *The Double Dealer* (by particular Desire). *The Constant Captives.*

S. 2   †*Mahomet. The School Boy.* Dancing.

M. 4   *King Henry VIII* (Shakespeare, First Night). Dancing.

W. 6   *The Old Batchelor. The Constant Captives.* Singing.

Th. 7   *The Non-Juror.* With minuet and country dance. By viceregal command.

F. 8   *Phaedra and Hippolitus. The Brave Irishman.* Dancing.

S. 9   *The Miser* (not acted these 5 years). *The Honest Yorkshireman.* Dancing.

M. 11   *Hamlet* (Shakespeare, Second Night). *The School Boy.*

W. 13   *The Provoked Husband.* †*Phoebe.* A Grand Dutch Dance by McNeil and Baker.

Th. 14   *Macbeth.* By viceregal command.

F. 15   *The Funeral. The Constant Captives.*

S. 16   *The Revenge. Phoebe.* "With the grand Dance of The Crutch by the Beggars in Character." Grand Dutch Dance.

M. 18   *Romeo and Juliet* (Shakespeare, Fourth Night [3]). "At the End of the 4th Act will be introduced, a New Grand Funeral Procession, to the Monument of the Capulets, according to the Custom of the Antients; accompanied with a Solemn Dirge, set to Musick by Sign. Pasquali; the Vocal Parts by Mrs. Storer, Mrs. Pye, Mr. Butler, and Others." *The Honest Yorkshireman.*

W. 20   *Oedipus. Phoebe.*

Th. 21   *The Careless Husband.* Singing and dancing. By viceregal command.

F. 22   *Coriolanus. The Devil to Pay.*

M. 25   *Julius Caesar* (Shakespeare, Fourth Night).

Th. 28   *Hamlet.* Dancing. By viceregal command.

[3] So advertised, but probably it was the third night in the Shakespeare series, since *Hamlet* on the 11th was the second night and *Julius Caesar* on the 25th was announced as the fourth night. *Macbeth* on the 14th was not advertised as part of the series.

MARCH

F. 1   *The Foundling. The Vintner Tricked.* Singing, and a hornpipe by Master Blake.

S. 2   *Mahomet.* (Sheridan left the company after the riot on this date.)

1754–1755; 1755–1756

Sheridan was in England during these seasons, having given up the management to Benjamin Victor and John Sowdon.

1756–1757

The Company: ACTORS: Aickin, Bate, Corry, Dexter, R. Elrington, Foote (beginning May 6), Glover, Hamilton, Heaphy, Hurst, Kennedy, Master Kennedy, King, Layfield, Lee, Messink, Mynitt, Sheridan, Sparks, Stayley, Watson, Wilder, Williams. ACTRESSES: Mrs. Butler, Miss Danvers, Mrs. Glen, Mrs. Kennedy, Miss Kennedy, Mrs. Lee, Miss Mason, Mrs. Mynitt, Mrs. Packenham, Miss G. Phillips, Miss (M.) Phillips, Mrs. Pye, Miss Rayner, Miss Wells, Mrs. Wilder, Miss Young. DANCERS: Miss Baker, Master Blake, Signora Bugiani, Garman, Mrs. Garman, Harvey, Miss Jones, Maranesi, Pike, Rayner, Steggeldolt. SINGERS: Mrs. Fagan, Miss Spencer, Mrs. Storer (beginning May 26), Miss Polly Young. Corry and Wilder (see under ACTORS) also sang solo pieces. MUSICIAN: Samuel Lee.

Number of Performances: About 130.

Number of Command Performances: About 6.

Number of Benefit Performances: About 32. Duval, the author of *Jack the Giant Queller*, Signora Bugiani, Lee, King, Dexter, Wilder, Miss Phillips, Maranesi, Miss Kennedy, Miss G. Phillips, Sparks, Mrs. Kennedy, Miss Danvers, Heaphy, Mr. and Mrs. Mynitt, Layfield and Corry, Knowles (assistant treasurer), Neil (boxkeeper), Samuel Lee, Miss Spencer, a family in distress, Meath Hospital, Mrs. Wilder, Watson, Pike, Miss Phillips and Miss G. Phillips, Foote, Hurst and Hamilton and Miss Wells, the author of *Douglas*, Ralph Elrington, Mrs. Storer.

Change in Admission Prices: The Upper Boxes at 2/8½ replaced the Upper Gallery seats at 1/1. Other prices remained the same: Boxes and Lattices, 5/5; Pit, 3/3; Middle Gallery, 2/2.

OCTOBER

M. 18   *The Busy Body. The Lying Valet.*

W. 20   *The Stratagem. The Virgin Unmasked.*

F. 22   *The Recruiting Officer.* Anniversary performance by command of the Lords Justices.

M. 25   *The Suspicious Husband. Catherine and Petruchio.*[1]

W. 27   *The Double Gallant. The Apprentice.* Dancing, particularly The Jocund Gardeners by Miss Baker, Mr. Harvey, et cetera.

F. 29   *Hamlet.*

NOVEMBER

M. 1   *Richard III. The Apprentice.* Entertainments.

W. 3   *King Lear.* Farce. Entertainments.

Th. 4   *Tamerlane* (with an occasional Prologue). Farce. Entertainments. Anniversary performance.

M. 8   *The Inconstant. The Miller of Mansfield.* Dancing. "N.B. On Account of some great Difficulties attending the Practice, and some Abuse arising from it, Servants will not hereafter be admitted to keep Places in the Upper Boxes."

W. 10   *The Committee.* Farce. Anniversary performance by command of the Lords Justices. Boxes free to ladies.

Th. 11   *The Stratagem.* Dancing by Maranesi and Bugiani: After Act II, a new Pantomime Ballad, La Niesa; after the Play, a comic Dance, The Country Revels.

F. 12   *Romeo and Juliet.*

M. 15   *The Suspicious Husband. Flora.* Dancing.

W. 17   *The Miser.* Farce.

Th. 18   *Romeo and Juliet.* "With a Grand Funeral Procession, and a Solemn Dirge." *The Devil to Pay.*

F. 19   [First Part of] *King Henry IV.* Dancing, particularly a new Pantomime Dance, The English Taylor.

M. 22   *The Merchant of Venice.* Dancing: After Act II, The Country Revels; Act V, The English Taylor.

W. 24   *Jane Shore. The Apprentice.* A new song by Miss Spencer.

Th. 25   *The Provoked Husband.* Dancing: After Act II, The Country Revels; Act V, The English Taylor.

F. 26   *The Old Batchelor.* A new Wooden Shoe Dance. Also the English Taylor Dance.

M. 29   *Jane Shore. The Lottery.* The Wooden Shoe Dance.

Tu. 30   *The Miser.* With an Occasional Prologue. Dancing: The Coun-

---

[1] It was at this performance that Sheridan made his apology (see Ch. IX). His first acting was in *Hamlet* on the 29th.

try Revels, The English Taylor. Anniversary performance by command of the Lords Justices. Boxes free to ladies.

DECEMBER

W. 1   *Hamlet.* Dancing: La Niesa; Wooden Shoe Dance.

Th. 2   *The Rehearsal* (not acted these 4 years). Dancing.

F. 3   *The Orphan. The Devil to Pay.*

M. 6   *Much Ado About Nothing* (not acted these 3 years). In Act II, a Grand Masquerade Scene with a New Masquerade Dance by Maranesi, Bugiani et cetera. After Act V, a Dance, The English Taylor.

W. 8   *The Conscious Lovers. The Lottery.*

Th. 9   *The Orphan. The Lying Valet.* Dancing, The Wood Cutters.

F. 10   *First Part of King Henry IV.* Dancing, La Niesa, The Country Revels. *Catherine and Petruchio.* By Lords Justices' Command. Benefit of Duval.

S. 11   *The Fair Penitent. The Brave Irishman.* Dancing, The Wood Cutters.

M. 13   *The Rehearsal.* Dancing, The Wood Cutters.

W. 15   *The Conscious Lovers.* In Act II, a Solo by Mr. Lee. *Catherine and Petruchio.* Dancing, The Wood Cutters.

Th. 16   *Much Ado About Nothing.*

F. 17   *The Beggar's Opera.*

S. 18   *Cato* (not acted these 5 years). "With the Original Epilogue, written by Sir Samuel Garth, to be spoken by Miss G. Phillips." By Desire, *The Brave Irishman.* Dancing, The Wood Cutters. (Being the last Time of the Company performing until after the Holidays.)

W. 29   *The Beggar's Opera.* In Act III, a Hornpipe by Master Blake.

Th. 30   *Romeo and Juliet.* With the new Masquerade Scene and Dance. *The Virgin Unmasked.*

F. 31   *The Stratagem.* A new dance, Les Pasteurs.

JANUARY

S. 1   *Love for Love.* Dancing, La Niesa, The Wood Cutters. *Damon and Phillida.* "N.B. The Door to the Upper Boxes will, for the Future, be opened at the same Time as that to the middle Gallery, precisely at four o'Clock; and at the same Price of two Shillings."

M. 3   *The Orphan. Lethe.* Dancing, La Niesa.

W. 5   *The Conscious Lovers. A Duke and No Duke.* A Solo on the Violin, by Mr. Lee. After Act IV, a Song by Miss Spencer. A Dance, Les Pasteurs.

379

Th. 6	*Love Makes a Man.* Farce. Dancing.
F. 7	*The Tempest.* "With all the original Musick and Dances, with new Scenes and other Decorations."
M. 10	*The Beggar's Opera.* Hornpipe by Master Blake. Dancing, Les Pasteurs.
W. 12	*Cato. Lethe.* A new Dance, Blind Man's Buff.
Th. 13	*The Tempest.* "With several new Pieces of Scenery and Machinery, particularly, a Representation of a Ship in a Storm at Sea, and of a Shipwreck. With all the original Musick, Dances, Sinkings, Flyings, &c. The Vocal Parts by Mr. Corry, Mr. Layfield, Miss Spencer, and others. Lilliputian Dancers . . . The Whole to conclude with a Grand Masque of Neptune and Amphitrite."
F. 14	*Venice Preserved. Florizel and Perdita.* Dancing.
M. 17	*Othello* (Shakespeare, First Night). After Act v, Blind Man's Buff. *The Oracle.* Wax.
W. 19	*The Beggar's Opera.* Dancing, Les Pasteurs.
Th. 20	*The Tempest.* A new Dance, The Venetian Gondoliers.
F. 21	*The Way of the World.* After Act II, Blind Man's Buff; after Act v, Country Revels. *The Devil to Pay.*
M. 24	*Macbeth* (Shakespeare, Second Night). *Florizel and Perdita.* Dancing, Les Pasteurs. Wax.
W. 26	*The Mourning Bride* (by particular Desire). *Miss in her Teens.* Dancing, including a new dance, The Colliers.
Th. 27	*The Beggar's Opera.* Dancing.
F. 28	*The Tempest.* Dancing, The Venetian Gondoliers.
M. 31	*Hamlet* (Shakespeare, Third Night). *Miss in her Teens.* Dancing, The Colliers. Wax.

FEBRUARY

W. 2	*The Beggar's Opera.* Dancing, The Colliers.
Th. 3	*The Double Dealer. Lethe.* Dancing, Les Pasteurs.
S. 5	*Coriolanus,* as altered from Shakespeare and Thomson (not acted these 3 years). "In the first Act will be a Grand Military Procession after the Manner of a Roman Ovation." "N.B. As the Ovation is to be at the Beginning of the Play, by Desire, the Curtain will not be drawn by till seven o'Clock."
M. 7	*Richard III* (Shakespeare, Fourth Night). *Lethe.* Dancing, The Colliers. Wax.
W. 9	*The Beggar's Opera.* Dancing, The Colliers.
Th. 10	*The Tempest.* Dancing, The Venetian Gondoliers. "By Desire, the Curtain will not be drawn up till seven o'Clock, on Account of the Shipwreck beginning the Play."
M. 14	*The Merchant of Venice* (Shakespeare, Fifth Night). *The Oracle.* "With new Scenery and Songs." Dancing. Wax.

W. 16	*The Beggar's Opera.* Dancing, The Country Revels.
Th. 17	*Coriolanus.* Dancing, Les Pasteurs.
F. 18	*The Recruiting Officer. The Oracle.* "In which will be introduced a new Serious Dance."
S. 19	*Tancred and Sigismunda* (not acted these 4 years). *The Oracle,* with a new Serious Dance. Dancing, The Colliers.
M. 21	*Julius Caesar* (Shakespeare, Sixth and Last Night).
Th. 24	*Coriolanus. The Oracle.*
F. 25	*The Beggar's Opera.* Dancing, Les Pasteurs.
S. 26	*Comus.* Dancing.
M. 28	*The Stratagem.* After Act I, a Song by Miss Spencer; after Act IV, The Country Revels. *The Oracle,* with a new Serious Dance.

MARCH

W. 2	*The Beggar's Opera.* Dancing, Les Pasteurs.
Th. 3	*Jack the Giant Queller.*
F. 4	*Comus.*
M. 7	*Jack the Giant Queller.* Benefit of the author.
W. 9	*Jack the Giant Queller.* Dancing, The Colliers.
Th. 10	*The Stratagem.* With a Song by Miss Spencer and The Country Revels. *The Oracle* (being particularly Desired), with a new Serious Dance.
F. 11	*The Tempest* (by Desire). Dancing, The Venetian Gondoliers.
S. 12	*Hamlet.* After Act IV, The Country Revels. *The Oracle,* with a new Serious Dance. By command of the Earl of Kildare.
M. 14	*The Loyal Subject,* "as altered from Beaumont and Fletcher" (not acted these 7 years). **The Emperor of the Moon.* "With a Variety of new Scenery and Decorations done by Mr. Lewis."
W. 16	*Macbeth. The Emperor of the Moon.* "N.B. In Order to shew the Scenery in the Entertainment the better, the House will be illuminated with Wax."
F. 18	*The Conscious Lovers.* A Solo on the Violin by Mr. Lee. Dancing.
S. 19	*The Loyal Subject. The Emperor of the Moon.*
M. 21	*The Suspicious Husband.* Dancing and singing between the acts: an Italian song by Miss Spencer, a new dance by Maranesi and Bugiani, a comic dance by Bugiani in "Men's Cloaths" and Maranesi in "Woman's Cloaths." *The Oracle.* "By Desire, the whole Pit will be laid into the Boxes." Benefit of Signora Bugiani.
Tu. 22	*The Provoked Wife* (not acted these 2 years). †*The Author.* Prologue by Lee, Epilogue by Miss G. Phillips. Benefit of Lee.
W. 23	*She Would and She Would Not* (not acted these 5 years).

Singing by Mr. Wilder and Miss Spencer. "At the End of the Play (by Desire) Mr. King will speak Bucks Have At Ye All, with considerable Alterations and Additions." *Lethe.* Benefit of King.

Th. 24   *Barbarossa.* After Act ii, a new Song by Corry; after Act iii, a favorite Cantata by Wilder; after Act iv, Ellin-a-Roon by Miss Spencer. *Phoebe.* Benefit of Dexter.

F. 25   *The Beggar's Opera.* Farce. Dancing. "N.B. Part of the Pit will be railed into the Boxes." Benefit of Wilder.

S. 26   *The Provoked Husband. Florizel and Perdita.* "A Song by Miss Polly Young, in the Character of the Genius of England." Benefit of Miss Phillips.

M. 28   *Oroonoko.* Dances between the acts, none of which were ever performed here: Love and Jealousy, The Neapolitan Peasants, a comic Minuet. Farce. Benefit of Maranesi.

Tu. 29   *The Merry Wives of Windsor. The Honest Yorkshireman.* Singing by Wilder and Miss Spencer. Benefit of Miss Kennedy.

W. 30   *The Careless Husband.* After Act iv, a Song by Mr. Wilder. Dancing. *Miss in her Teens.* Benefit of Miss G. Phillips.

Th. 31   *The Twin Rivals. Lethe.* Singing by Wilder and Miss Spencer. Benefit of Sparks.

APRIL

F. 1   *Rule a Wife and Have a Wife.* After Act i, a Song by Wilder; Act ii, a Song by Miss Spencer; Act iii, a Song by Mr. Corry; Act iv, a Hornpipe by Master Blake. *Tom Thumb the Great,* with an Epilogue in Character by Master Kennedy. Benefit of Mrs. Kennedy.

S. 2   *The City Wives Confederacy.* After Act i, a Song by Mr. Corry; Act ii, The Lark's Shrill Note by Miss Spencer; Act iii, Les Louvres by Maranesi and Bugiani; Act iv, a Song by Mr. Wilder; Act v, Country Revels. *Phoebe.* Benefit of Miss Danvers.

M. 11   *Love's Last Shift. The Apprentice.* Singing by Corry, Wilder, Miss Spencer. (By particular Desire.) Bucks Have At Ye All by Mr. King. Benefit of Heaphy.[2]

Tu. 12   *The Fair Quaker of Deal* (not acted these 8 years). *The Emperor of the Moon.* Singing and dancing.[3]

[2] For this Heaphy benefit, prices went back to the old rate of 1/1 for the Upper Gallery.

[3] This may have been a kind of make-up benefit for disappointed actors, since the notice carries the announcement that "Tickets delivered out by Mr. Goodfellow, Mrs. Pye, and Mr. Harvey, and Mr. Cushin will be taken the above Night" (*Dublin Journal,* April 9–12, 1757). Such make-up notices have oc-

W. 13   *Romeo and Juliet.* A Humorous Epilogue by Mrs. Mynitt. *The Lying Valet.* Singing. Benefit of Mr. and Mrs. Mynitt.

Th. 14   *Othello.* Farce. Singing. Benefit of Layfield and Corry.

F. 15   *The Rehearsal.* After Act IV, a new Song by Miss Spencer. *The Devil to Pay.* By desire, Mr. King in Bucks Have At Ye All. Benefit of Knowles.

M. 18   *The Fatal Marriage* (not acted these 4 years). *Florizel and Perdita.* Mr. King in "Bucks Have At Ye All, with considerable Alterations and Additions." Dancing and singing. "N.B. The Boxes will be opened to the Pit." Galleries 2/2. Benefit of Neil, Boxkeeper.

Tu. 19   *Jack the Giant Queller. Lethe.* Epilogue of Bucks Have At Ye All, by Mr. King. Dancing.

W. 20   *The Conscious Lovers.* After Act I, The Lark's Shrill Note by Miss Spencer; in Act II, a Solo on the Violin by Mr. Lee; after Act II, The Country Revels; Act III, The Song of a Cock and a Bull by Mr. Wilder (by Desire); Act IV, Les Pasteurs. Bucks Have At Ye All by Mr. King. *Lethe.* Benefit of Mr. Samuel Lee.

F. 22   *The Suspicious Husband. Catherine and Petruchio.* Singing by Miss Spencer. Dancing. Benefit of Miss Spencer.

S. 23   *The Recruiting Officer. The Lying Valet.* Dancing. Benefit of a Family in Distress.

M. 25   *The Merchant of Venice. Lethe.* Dancing. Benefit of Meath Hospital.

W. 27   *The Beggar's Opera. The Oracle* (by Desire). With new Scenery and Songs, and a new Serious Dance. Original Epilogue by Mrs. Wilder. Dancing. Benefit of Mrs. Wilder.

F. 29   *The Tempest.*

MAY

M. 2   *The Spanish Fryar.* Farce. Singing by Wilder, Corry, Miss Spencer. Dancing. Benefit of Watson.

Tu. 3   *The Country Lasses.* With the original Sheep-Shearing Song by Mr. Wilder. †New Pantomime Entertainment, *Harlequin Captive in Spain.* N.B. The Machinery will be entirely new. Dancing, and singing by Miss Spencer. Mr. King in Bucks Have At Ye All. Boxes opened into part of the Pit. Benefit of Pike.

---

curred occasionally through the years but have not usually been noted because they are not advertised as benefits. This performance, however, is especially interesting: Mrs. Pye and Mr. Goodfellow had an overflow representation at this performance, and disappointed friends were asked to submit their tickets at a May 7 performance of the same play (*Dublin Journal*, May 3–7, 1757).

F. 6   *The Orphan. The Englishman returned from Paris*, with an occasional Prologue by Mr. Foote.

S. 7   *The Fair Quaker of Deal. The Emperor of the Moon.* Dancing and singing.

M. 9   *The Loyal Subject. The Knights.* Dancing.

Tu. 10 *Jane Shore. Lethe.* Singing. Benefit of Miss Phillips and Miss G. Phillips.

Th. 12 †*Douglas. Harlequin Captive in Spain.* Dancing.

F. 13   *The Double Dealer. The Author.* Dancing.

S. 14   *The Beggar's Opera. Harlequin Captive in Spain.* Dancing.

M. 16   *The Rehearsal. The Knights* (by Desire). Dancing. Benefit of Foote.

Tu. 17 *The Wonder* (not acted these 3 years). *The Emperor of the Moon.* Mr. King in Bucks Have At Ye All. Dancing and singing. Benefit of Hurst,[4] Hamilton, and Miss Wells.

W. 18   *Douglas. The Oracle.* Benefit of the Author.

Th. 19 *She Would and She Would Not.* Farce. Singing. Benefit of Ralph Elrington.

S. 21   *The Fair Quaker of Deal. The Emperor of the Moon.* Singing and dancing.

M. 23   *The Old Batchelor. The Author.* "With an occasional Prologue to be spoken by Mr. Foote." Dancing.

Tu. 24 *The Twin Rivals. The Emperor of the Moon.* Singing and dancing. Upper Gallery 1/1.

W. 25   *The Wonder. The Mock Doctor.* Dancing. Gallery 1/1.

Th. 26 *The Beggar's Opera. Miss in her Teens.* Dancing. Benefit of Mrs. Storer.

F. 27   *Hamlet* (by Particular Desire). *Harlequin Captive in Spain.* Dancing.

JUNE

S. 4   *The Recruiting Officer. The Virgin Unmasked.* Singing by Mrs. Storer and Corry. Anniversary performance by command of the Lords Justices.

1757–1758

The Company: ACTORS: Aickin, Bate, Corry, Davenport, Dexter, R. Elrington, Foote, Glover, Hamilton, Heaphy, Hurst, Kennedy, King,

[4] "N.B. Some Box Tickets of Mr. Hurst's having been dropped, from No. 96 to 104, this Notice is given that none of the above Numbers will be admitted this Night" (*Dublin Journal*, May 14–17, 1757).

Lewis, M' Mahon, Messink, Oliver, Packenham, Preston, Ryder, Sheridan, Sparks, Stayley, Storer, Wall, Watson, Wilder, Wilkinson, Williams. ACTRESSES: Miss Danvers, Mrs. Farrell, Mrs. Fitzhenry (formerly Mrs. Gregory), Mrs. Godwin, Mrs. Hopkins, Miss Jackson, Mrs. Kennedy, Miss Kennedy, Miss Mason, Mrs. Packenham, Miss G. Phillips, Miss (M.) Phillips, Mrs. Pye, Miss A. Storer, Miss E. Storer, Miss Taylor, Miss Wells, Mrs. Wilder. DANCERS: Miss Baker (also acted), Garman, Mrs. Garman, Harvey (also acted), Maranesi, Masset, Mrs. Masset, Signora Provencale, Rayner, Signora Ricci, Tioli, Welch. SINGERS: Corry (see under ACTORS), Mrs. Fagan, Mrs. Storer (also acted). MUSICIAN: Bianchi. EQUILIBRIST: a Laplander. HOUSEKEEPER: Keegan.

Number of Performances: About 149.

Number of Command Performances: About 26.

Number of Benefit Performances: About 40. Duval, Foote, Jones (author of *The Earl of Essex*), Pike, family in distress, Mr. Grey Townsend, Mrs. Beauclerk, Wilkinson, Dexter (2), Tioli, King, Knowles, Mr. and Mrs. Kennedy, Wilder, Mrs. Storer, Miss G. Phillips, Miss Danvers, Miss Kennedy, Heaphy, Neil (boxkeeper), Sparks, Miss Phillips, Hurst and Mrs. Pye, Miss Taylor, Signora Ricci, Corry and Cushin, Mrs. Storer's children, Mrs. Wilder, Stayley and Signor Bianchi, Miss Baker, distressed Free and Accepted Masons, Meath Hospital, Mrs. Fitzhenry, Maranesi, Hospital for Incurables, Watson, R. Elrington, Signora Provencale, a family in distress.

OCTOBER

M. 10   *The Fair Quaker of Deal. The Mock Doctor.*[1]

W. 12   *The Fair Quaker of Deal. The Lottery.*

Th. 13   *The Busy Body. The Devil to Pay.*

F. 14   *The Country Lasses. The Lying Valet.*

M. 17   *The Beggar's Opera.* In Act III, a Hornpipe by Mr. Harvey.

W. 19   *Oroonoko.* In Act II, a Song by Mrs. Storer. *The Virgin Unmasked.* New Grand Dance, The Tartars, by Signor Tioli, Miss Baker, et cetera.

Th. 20   *The Miser. The Miller of Mansfield.* Dancing.

F. 21   *The Recruiting Officer.* Farce. Dancing.

---

[1] This performance may not have materialized, since it was given (the main part of it, at least) two days later, on the 12th, replacing an advertised performance of *The Suspicious Husband*. Perhaps the artificers mentioned in an October 1 notice had found even more "Works" than they had estimated: "We hear that the Theatre Royal will not be opened till Monday se'nnight, as the several Artificers employed in the various new Decorations of the House, cannot possibly complete their Works sooner" (*Dublin Journal*, September 27–October 1, 1757).

S. 22   *Love for Love.* With an occasional Prologue to be spoken by Mr. Hurst. *The Mock Doctor.* Anniversary performance.

M. 24   *Hamlet. Miss in her Teens.* Wax. By viceregal command.

W. 26   *The Beggar's Opera.* Dancing.

Th. 27   *The Fair Penitent. The Vintner Tricked.*

F. 28   *The Committee.* Farce. Dancing.

M. 31   *Macbeth. The Stage Coach.* Wax. By viceregal command.

NOVEMBER

W. 2   *The Rehearsal.* A new Dance, The Bedlamites, by Tioli, Miss Baker, and Signora Ricci.

Th. 3   *The Stratagem. The Contrivances.*

F. 4   *Tamerlane.* Occasional prologue by Stayley. Farce. Anniversary performance.

M. 7   *Richard III. The Brave Irishman.*

W. 9   *Jane Shore. Florizel and Perdita.* Dancing.

Th. 10   *The Suspicious Husband.* Farce. Singing by Mrs. Storer. Dancing. Anniversary performance. "N.B. By Command the Boxes free to the Ladies."

F. 11   *The Distrest Mother.* Farce.

M. 14   *Coriolanus.* In Act I "will be a Grand Military Procession, after the Manner of a Roman Ovation." *The Honest Yorkshireman.*

W. 16   *The Beggar's Opera.* Grand Pantomime Dance, The Bedlamites.

Th. 17   *Hamlet. The Oracle.* New serious dance by Tioli and Baker.

F. 18   *Double Dealer. The Author.* New Grand Pantomime Dance, The Negroes.

M. 21   *Richard III.* Dancing.

W. 23   *The Conscious Lovers. The Devil to Pay.* Wax. By viceregal command. Benefit of Duval.

Th. 24   *Love for Love. The Knights.* With a new Prologue to be spoken by Mr. Foote.

F. 25   *The Fair Penitent.* In Act II, a Song by Mrs. Storer. *Florizel and Perdita.*

S. 26   *The Old Batchelor. The Author,* with the usual Prologue.

M. 28   *The Mourning Bride. The Brave Irishman.* Singing. By viceregal command.

W. 30   *The Fair Quaker of Deal. The Honest Yorkshireman.* Anniversary performance by viceregal command. Boxes free to Ladies.

DECEMBER

Th. 1   *The Spanish Fryar. The Englishman in Paris.*

F. 2   *The Mourning Bride. The Mock Doctor.* Entertainments.

M. 5	*The Double Dealer. The Englishman return'd from Paris.*
W. 7	*The Recruiting Officer. The Author.*
Th. 8	*Romeo and Juliet.* "With the Funeral Procession to the Family of the Capulets." *The Devil to Pay.*
F. 9	*The Rehearsal.*
S. 10	*The Earl of Essex* (not acted these 5 years). "The Characters drest in the Habits of the Times." *The Virgin Unmasked.* Singing.
M. 12	*The Relapse. The Author.*
W. 14	*Oroonoko.* "After which Mr. Foote will give Tea. In which will be introduced a Character of Mr. Puzzle's first Pupil, to be performed by a Young Gentleman,[2] being his first Appearance on the Stage."
Th. 15	†*The Gamester. The Oracle.*
F. 16	*The Rehearsal.*
S. 17	*The Distrest Mother. Duke and No Duke.* By viceregal command.
M. 19	*The Beggar's Opera.* "After which Mr. Foote will give Tea."
W. 21	*Sir Courtly Nice.* "Mr. Foote will give Tea." By viceregal command. Benefit of Foote.
Th. 22	*The Spanish Fryar. The Author* (by particular Desire).
F. 23	*The Old Batchelor.* In Act III, A Song by Mr. Corry. *The Englishman in Paris.* Being the last time before the holidays.
M. 26	*The Double Dealer. The Englishman in Paris.* Benefit of Mr. Jones, author of *The Earl of Essex.*

JANUARY

M. 2	*Romeo and Juliet.* "With a Masquerade Scene, and a Funeral Procession to the Monument of the Capulets." *Lethe.* By viceregal command. Benefit of Mr. Pike.
W. 4	*The Twin Rivals. The Lying Valet.* By special viceregal command. Benefit of a family in distress.[3]
Th. 5	*The Suspicious Husband. The Brave Irishman.* Singing.
F. 6	[The First Part of] *King Henry IV*, With the Humours of Sir

[2] The young gentleman was Tate Wilkinson, who had not appeared on the preceding Monday in *The Rehearsal*, as had been expected. He did, however, take part in the December 16 performance of *The Rehearsal*. The notice for that performance includes this N.B.: "The young Gentleman who was to have performed in it [*The Rehearsal*] before, was so weak after a dangerous Indisposition, that he found himself unable to attempt it, but hopes by that Time to be perfectly recovered" (*Dublin Journal*, December 10–13, 1757).

[3] The notice for this benefit carries the unusual information that tickets were to be had at Mr. Sheridan's in College Green (*Dublin Journal*, December 31–January 3, 1758).

John Falstaff. Farce and other entertainments. By viceregal command. Benefit of Mr. Grey Townsend.

M. 9   *The Way of the World.* A Dance, The Bedlamites, in which "will be introduced several surprising Performances on the Wire, by a Laplander; particularly, he puts on Jack Boots, with the Bottoms of Quart Bottles fastened to the Soles, and stands on the Wire in full Swing on the Mouths of the Bottles."

W. 11   *The Tempest.* "With a Variety of new Scenes, Machines, Dresses, and other Decorations. The Play will open with a Scene of a Ship at Sea in a Storm, and an exact Representation of a Shipwreck." In Act IV, a grand comic Dance of Lilliputians. "With all the original Songs, Chorusses, &c." The whole to conclude with a grand Masque of Neptune and Amphitrite. At the end, a grand Dance, The Negroes.

Th. 12   *The Gamester. The Author.*

F. 13   *The Beggar's Opera. The Emperor of the Moon.* "With a Variety of new Scenery and Decorations by Mr. Lewis." A new dance by Tioli, Baker, etc.

M. 16   *Barbarossa. The Emperor of the Moon.* Dancing.

W. 18   *She Would and She Would Not.* A Pantomime Dance, The Bedlamites. "In which will be introduced several surprizing Performances on the Wire, by a Laplander; particularly, he will stand on his Head on the Wire in full swing, and discharge a Case of Pistols at the same Time."

Th. 19   *Othello. The Emperor of the Moon.* Dancing.

F. 20   *The Tempest.* Masque of Neptune and Amphitrite. Dancing, The Negroes. "In which will be introduced several surprising Performances on the Wire, by a Laplander."

M. 23   *King John* (not acted these 3 years). By command, *The Vintner Tricked.* By viceregal command.

W. 25   *The Merry Wives of Windsor. The Chaplet.* A Grand Pastoral Dance.

Th. 26   *The Mourning Bride. The Emperor of the Moon.* Dancing.

F. 27   *The Wonder.* Farce. Dancing. Performances on the wire by the Laplander, "for the last Time."

S. 28   *The Earl of Essex.* A new Dance, The Painters, with Tioli, Baker, Harvey, &c., and with a Comic Solo by Signora Ricci. *The Virgin Unmasked.*

Tu. 31   *The Distrest Mother. The Chaplet.* Dancing.

FEBRUARY

W. 1   *The Tempest,* with Shipwreck, Dance of the Lilliputians, and Masque of Neptune and Amphitrite. *The Lying Valet.*

Th. 2   *Venice Preserved. The Emperor of the Moon.* Dancing.

F. 3   *The Beggar's Opera.* *A New Pantomime, *The Whim, or Harlequin Villager.* Dancing.

S. 4   *The Provoked Husband.* A grand Dance, The Negroes. *The Mock Doctor.* Wax. By viceregal command.

M. 6   *Hamlet.* Dancing, The Bedlamites. *Florizel and Perdita.* Wax.

Th. 9   *The Earl of Essex. The Whim.* A new Dance, The Cries of London.

F. 10   †*Amphitryon,* as altered from Dryden. In Act IV, a Grand Dance. "With New Machinery, Dresses and other Decorations." *Flora.*

S. 11   *Phaedra and Hippolitus* (not acted these 5 years). *The Whim.* Dancing.

M. 13   *The Merchant of Venice* (Shakespeare, Second Night). Dancing, The Negroes. *The Apprentice.* "With the Prologue to the Author to be spoken after the Manner of the Original by Mr. Wilkinson." Wax.

W. 15   *Amphitryon.* Dancing, The Bedlamites. *The Honest Yorkshireman.*

Th. 16   *Comus. The Whim.* Dancing.

S. 18   *The Stratagem.* Singing between the acts by Mrs. Storer. *The Emperor of the Moon.* Dancing. Wax. By viceregal command.

M. 20   *Macbeth* (Shakespeare, Third Night). New Grand Pantomime Dance, The Chinese Festival. Wax.

W. 22   *Amphitryon. The Emperor of the Moon.* Dancing. Wax.

Th. 23   *The Fair Penitent.* After Act III, Mad Bess, set by Mr. Henry Purcell, sung by Mrs. Storer in character. After the Play, Mr. King will speak Bucks Have At Ye All. *Florizel and Perdita.* Dancing. "N.B. By particular Desire of several Ladies of Quality, the Play to begin at Half an Hour after six o'Clock precisely." Benefit of Mrs. Beauclerk.

F. 24   *The Beggar's Opera.* Dancing, The Chinese Festival. *The Whim.*

S. 25   *Jane Shore. Tom Thumb the Great.* "N.B. Part of the Pit will be rail'd in to the Boxes." Benefit of Wilkinson.

M. 27   *Richard III* (Shakespeare, Fourth Night). *The Lying Valet.* Dancing, The Negroes. Wax.

MARCH

W. 1   *The Committee. The Oracle.* Dancing, The Chinese Festival. Wax. By viceregal command.

Th. 2   *Amphitryon. The Whim.*

F. 3   *Tancred and Sigismunda. The Apprentice.* Dancing.

S. 4   *The Merchant of Venice. Flora.* Dancing, The Bedlamites. Wax. By viceregal command.

M. 6   *Coriolanus*, with Grand Military Procession (Shakespeare, Fifth Night). Dancing, The Chinese Festival. Wax.

W. 8   *The Fair Quaker of Deal. The Emperor of the Moon*. Dancing.

Th. 9   *Phaedra and Hippolitus. The Brave Irishman*. Dancing, The Chinese Festival.

F. 10   *Douglas. The Vintner Tricked*. Dancing, The Negroes.

S. 11   *Richard III*. After Act IV, a Cantata by Mrs. Storer. Dancing, The Chinese Festival. "End of the Dance, A Dialogue between Pallas and Cupid, called, The Drum." Wax. By viceregal command.

M. 13   *Romeo and Juliet* (Shakespeare, Sixth and Last Night). "In Act 2d, a Grand Masquerade Scene. With a Minuet by Juliet. And a Grand Funeral Procession to the Monument of the Capulets, and a Solemn Dirge." *Florizel and Perdita*. With a new Dance by Tioli, Baker, et cetera. Wax.

W. 15   *Tancred and Sigismunda. The What D'Ye Call It* (not acted these five years). Dancing.

Th. 16   *Douglas. The Whim*. Dancing, The Bedlamites.

F. 17   *Amphitryon*. "To which will be added a new Dance, called, The Inchanted Peasant, by Signor Tioli and Miss Baker, in which they will change their Characters several Times. The Scenery and Habits entirely new." *The Brave Irishman*.

S. 18   *Measure for Measure* (not acted these 2 years). *Catherine and Petruchio*. Dancing. Wax. Last time of performing till the holidays. "N.B. Part of the Pit will be railed into the Boxes." By viceregal command. Benefit of Mrs. Fitzhenry.

M. 27   *Isabella*, "As lately altered by Mr. Garrick from the Fatal Marriage or Innocent Adultery, and now acting with great Applause at the Theatre Royal in Drury-lane." In Act III, "a new Epithalamium, with the original Musick." *Florizel and Perdita*. Dancing. "N.B. Part of the Pit will be laid into the Boxes." Benefit of Dexter.

W. 29   *Barbarossa*. After Act I, a favourite Song by Mrs. Storer; after Act II, "A genteel Dance by Signor Tioli in Petticoats, and Miss Baker in Man's Cloaths." By Desire, Mr. King will speak Bucks Have At Ye All. A new Dance, The Inchanted Peasant. "The Whole to be new dressed in the Italian Manner." Farce. A Grand Pantomime Dance. Benefit of Tioli.

Th. 30   *Every Man in his Humour*. By particular Desire, *The Author*, in which Mr. King "will speak the original Prologue, and treat the Writer with a Dish of his own Tea." Benefit of King.

F. 31   *The Mourning Bride. The Cheats of Scapin* (not acted these 2 years). Dancing. Benefit of Knowles.

APRIL

M. 3   *The Double Dealer. Catherine and Petruchio.* "Before which will be spoke Mr. Foote's Prologue to the Author, with Alterations, by way of Chocolate, by Master Kennedy, being the first and only Time of his appearing this Season." Dancing. Benefit of Mr. and Mrs. Kennedy.

Tu. 4   *The Beggar's Opera.* "To which will be added a new Entertainment in Grotesque Characters, called, The Formation of Harlequin. (The Music all Irish Tunes) interspersed with a grand pantomime Dance, called, Bacchus and Ariadne. . . . The Scenes, Machines, Dresses, and all other Decorations, entirely new." Benefit of Wilder.

W. 5   *Jane Shore. The Oracle.* "All the Character's [*sic*] to be performed by Mrs. Storer's Children." Original Epilogue by Miss Storer, in the character of Cynthia. Singing and dancing. Benefit of Mrs. Storer.

F. 7   *Theodosius. The Brave Irishman.* Entertainments. Wax. By viceregal command. Benefit of Miss Gr. Phillips.

S. 8   *King Henry VIII* (Shakespeare, First Night). "With the Coronation of Anna Bullen, and the Ceremony of the Champion in Westminster Hall." Dancing, The Inchanted Peasants. Wax. By viceregal command.

M. 10   *Isabella.* By particular Desire, *Catherine and Petruchio.* Dancing and singing. Benefit of Miss Danvers.

Tu. 11   *Cato.* Dancing, The Chinese Festival.

W. 12   *As You Like It* (not acted these 6 years). Farce. Dancing. Wax. By viceregal command. Benefit of Miss Kennedy.

Th. 13   *All for Love* (not acted these 3 years). By particular Desire, Mr. King will speak the Epilogue of Bucks Have At Ye All. *The Emperor of the Moon.* Dancing and singing. "N.B. Part of the Pit will be railed into the Boxes." Benefit of Heaphy.

F. 14   *The Conscious Lovers. The Whim.* "With new Scenes, Musick, and Decorations." Dancing and singing. By viceregal command. "By Desire of several Ladies, the Boxes will be opened to the Pit, and some Rows railed in, where Servants will be allowed to keep Places." Benefit of Neil, Boxkeeper.

S. 15   *Othello* (Shakespeare, Second Night). Dancing, Les Characteres des Dances by Mrs. Masset. *The Honest Yorkshireman.*

M. 17   *Love and a Bottle* (not acted these 18 years). Epilogue to the Fair Ladies by Mrs. Trudge (played by I. Sparks). *Catherine and Petruchio.* Dancing. Benefit of Sparks.

Tu. 18   *The Distrest Mother.* By particular Desire, *Damon and Phillida.*

Singing and dancing. Wax. By command of the Duke and Duchess of Bedford and Lady Caroline Russell. Benefit of Miss Phillips.[4]

W. 19   *The Suspicious Husband. Miss in her Teens.* Singing and dancing. Benefit of Hurst and Mrs. Pye.

Th. 20   *The Fair Penitent. Lethe.* Dancing and singing. Wax. By viceregal command. Benefit of Miss Taylor.

F. 21   *King John.* Farce. Dancing, and singing by Mrs. Storer. Benefit of Signora Ricci.

S. 22   *The Merchant of Venice. The Whim.* Dancing, The Negroes.

M. 24   *The Stratagem.* Singing between the acts by Mrs. Storer and Mr. Corry. Dancing. *The Devil to Pay.* Benefit of Corry and Cushin.

Tu. 25   *Love Makes a Man.* Singing between the acts by Mrs. Storer. Dancing. *The Oracle* (by Desire). "All the Characters to be performed by Mrs. Storer's Children. With the original Epilogue to be spoke by Miss Storer, in the character of Cynthia." By Desire of several Ladies. Benefit of Mrs. Storer's Children.

W. 26   *The Revenge* (revived). After Act III, a Dance, The Irish Revels; after the play, The Chinese Festival. *Damon and Phillida.*

Th. 27   *Romeo and Juliet,* as altered by David Garrick, Esq. "In Act 2nd, a Grand Masquerade Scene. And a Grand Funeral Procession to the Monument of the Capulets, and a Solemn Dirge." *The Upholsterer, or What News?* (Written by Mr. Murphy. Author of The Apprentice, &c.) Dancing. By viceregal command. Benefit of Mrs. Wilder.

F. 28   *Measure for Measure.* After Act III, a new Concerto Solo on the Violin, by Bianchi. Singing between the acts by Mrs. Storer. Dancing. After the play, "Mr. Stayley will give a new Dish of Something or Other, called the Chocolate Makers." Principal parts by Mr. Stayley, Master Kennedy, and the Prompter.

> "Ye Takers-off, stand all aloof
>   Unless ye're sure, ye're Pepper-Proof."

The Apprentice. Benefit of Stayley and Bianchi.

S. 29   *King Lear.* Singing by Corry and Mrs. Storer. *The Apprentice.* Dancing, The Chinese Festival.

MAY

M. 1   *Tunbridge Walks* (not acted these 18 years). Singing by Mrs. Storer. Dancing, The Inchanted Peasant, and a new Dance (to

---

[4] "N.B. On Account of the charitable Performance of L'Endimione, Miss Philipps hath put off her Benefit to the above Day, when Tickets delivered out for the 6th will be taken" (*Dublin Journal,* April 11–15, 1758).

Irish Airs), May Day. *The Author,* in which Mr. King "(by particular Desire) will speak the original Prologue, and for the last Time this Season treat the Writer with a Dish of his own Tea." Benefit of Miss Baker.

Tu. 2   *King Henry VIII.* "With the Coronation of Anna Bullen." Dancing, The Ribbon Merchants. After the Play, The Prussian Bearkeeper by Maranesi and Signora Provencale, her first appearance in this kingdom.

W. 3   *Love for Love. The Brave Irishman.* Dancing. Command of the Duke and Duchess of Bedford and Lord Newton, Grand Master. "N.B. The Grand Master, attended by his Deputy the Hon. Lord Moore, the Grand Wardens, the other Grand Officers and the Members of the Grand Master's Lodge &c. will appear on the Stage with their proper Cloathing and Jewels, agreeable to antient Custom." Benefit of distressed Free and Accepted Masons.

Th. 4   *Julius Caesar* (not acted these 4 years). By particular Desire, the last new Dance, The Inchanted Peasant. *The Oracle,* with Mrs. Storer's children (by Desire). Benefit of the Meath Hospital.[5]

F. 5   *Love and a Bottle.* Farce. Dancing.

M. 8   *Douglas. Lethe.* Dancing. Benefit of Mrs. Fitzhenry.

Tu. 9   *Love's Last Shift.* (By particular Desire) *Miss in her Teens.* Singing by Mrs. Storer. Dancing, particularly a Minuet and Louvre, and May Day (to Irish tunes).

W. 10   *The Distrest Mother.* Dancing by Maranesi and Provencale: After Act I, The Prussian Bearkeeper. After Act III, The Ribbon Merchants. After the Play, a new Dance, The Cossack, "being the first of the Kind ever performed in Dublin." (By particular Desire) *The Upholsterer.* "By particular Desire, the Boxes will be opened into Part of the Pit." Benefit of Maranesi.

Th. 11   *The Double Dealer.* Singing and dancing. Benefit of the Hospital for Incurables.

F. 12   *The Twin Rivals.* Farce. Singing and dancing. Benefit of Ralph Elrington.

S. 13   *The Revenge.* After Act II, The Prussian Bearkeeper. After the Play, The Ribbon Merchants. *The Cheats of Scapin.*

M. 15   *Isabella.* In Act III, a new Epithalamium, "with the original Musick." After the Play, a grand Dance. Farce.

Th. 18   *Tunbridge Walks.* After the Play, Mr. Stayley "will introduce,

---

[5] "N.B. The Governors of the above Charity did not intend troubling the Publick with a Play this Season, but the Assembly which they substituted in its Place having failed, has laid them under a Necessity of this second Application" (*Dublin Journal,* April 29–May 2, 1758).

Something or Other, called, The Chocolate-Makers." Farce. Dancing.

F. 19   *Venice Preserved.* Farce. Dancing. Benefit of Watson.

M. 22   *The Roman Father,* with considerable Alterations (not acted these 8 years). (First Subscription Night.) In Act v, a Grand Procession. After Act i, The Bedlamites; Act ii, The Prussian Bearkeeper; Act iii, The Chinese Festival; Act v, The Ribbon Merchants. Wax. Pit 3/3; First Gallery 2/2; Upper Gallery 1/1.[6]

W. 24   *King Lear.*

F. 26   *Douglas.*

M. 29   *Richard III* (Fourth and Last Subscription Night).[7] After Act iii, The Ribbon Merchants. After the Play, The Lamp-lighter. Wax. By desire, to begin exactly at eight o'Clock.

W. 31   *The Stratagem.* After Act i, The Ribbon Weavers;[8] Act ii, The Cossacks; Act iv, An Entire New Dance; Act v, a Minuet by Maranesi and Provencale. Benefit of Signora Provencale.

JUNE

Th. 1   *The Fair Penitent.* Singing between the acts by Mrs. Storer. *The Whim.* Dancing. Benefit of Dexter.

S. 3   *Hamlet.* After Act ii, The Ribbon Merchants; Act iv, a New Serio Comic Dance; Act v, The Cossack. "To begin exactly at Seven o'Clock."

M. 5   *The Beggar's Opera.* In Act iii, a Hornpipe by Mr. Harvey. *The Lying Valet.* Anniversary performance. By command of the Lords Justices.

Tu. 6   *Barbarossa. The Mock Doctor.* Benefit of a family in distress.[9]

[6] "Besides the additional Ventilators, there will be a large AIR LOUVRE fixt over the Centre of the Stage, and several other Passages opened behind the Scenes, in order to render the House quite cool" (*Dublin Journal,* May 16–20, 1758).

[7] *King Lear* (May 24) and *Douglas* (May 26) were obviously the other two subscription nights although not advertised as such.

[8] So advertised in *Dublin Journal,* May 27–30, 1758, but probably intended to be the dance elsewhere called The Ribbon Merchants.

[9] "Mr. Sheridan has given the House Wardrobe and whole Company gratis" (*Williamson's Universal Advertizer,* June 3, 1758).

PART II

An Alphabetical List of Plays and Their Casts Given Under Sheridan's Management 1745-March 2, 1754; 1756-1758

THIS PART of the Smock-Alley Calendar gives alphabetically under their titles the plays listed chronologically in Part I, and includes the casts, when known, for each performance of the play. The sources for roles and players are the same as for Part I. Because of the complications for the reader, no attempt has been made to distinguish sources in the entries. As in Part I, titles of plays and names of characters and players have been regularized, as have been spellings, capitalizations, and punctuation elsewhere, except in quotations. Plays with more than one title (like *George Barnwell* and *The London Merchant*) have been entered under one title, with cross references supplied. When the same character appears under a different name in different notices (like Carlos and Charles in *Love Makes a Man*), the identity has been indicated in parentheses within the entry. The names of authors, composers, et cetera, when given in the notices, are quoted directly after the title; otherwise they have been supplied, if available in the usual source books. For afterplays, because they may be less familiar, the type of entertainment—farce, burlesque opera, et cetera—has been indicated where possible.

When giving the casts, I have followed in general the method used by Professor Dougald MacMillan because here, as in his *Drury Lane Calendar*, only one theatrical company is involved. The principle used *for each season* is cumulative. After each season's first date the full cast for that date is given. Thereafter:

If only a date follows, the cast is the same as on the preceding date.

If a date is followed by "but," a substitution in one or more of the characters or some change in wording is indicated, with the rest of the cast the same as on the preceding date.

If a date is followed by "only . . . listed," the characters named appear with the same actors (unless otherwise noted) as on the preceding date, but the rest of the cast has been omitted from the notice.

If a date is followed by "without," the cast is the same as on the preceding date except that the names following "without" have been dropped from the notice.

If a date is followed by "plus," the cast is the same as on the preceding date, but with the additional characters following the "plus."

If, in the middle of the season, none of the restrictive expressions given above appears after a date and, instead, the date is followed directly by a character's name, the entire cast for that date follows, either because the changes are too numerous or because the cumulative method has become too complicated for the reader to follow comfortably.

If both comfort and economy could be served, a date in the middle of a season is sometimes followed by "as on (an earlier date)" when the casts of both dates were the same.

The order of players in the eighteenth-century newspaper notice, as well as the style of naming players, is noteworthy. The men are grouped together first, and arranged roughly in order of descending importance; women follow, arranged in order of ascending importance. Thus the principal actor usually appears first and the principal actress last in the listing. Players' names are always preceded by the titles "Mr.," "Mrs.," and "Miss." Given names, unhappily for theater historians, appear only when needed for distinguishing brothers, sisters, et cetera. In the entries below, "Mr." has been omitted to save space, with some loss—it must be understood—to the formal tone of the notice and the dignity of the actors.

Aesop, by Sir John Vanbrugh
1746–47: Jan. 15, *Aesop,* Sheridan (first time); *Doris,* Miss Bellamy (first time); Jan. 19.

The Alchymist, by Ben Jonson
1749–50: Mar. 8, *Face,* Macklin; *Subtle,* Beamsley; *Doll Common,* Mrs. Macklin; *Drugger,* Cibber.
1751–52: Mar. 6, *Drugger,* Cibber; *Kastril,* King; *Face,* Stevens; *Subtle,* Beamsley; *Sir Epicure,* Sparks; *Tribulation,* Davies; *Ananias,* Mynitt; *Lovewit,* Heaphy; *Surley,* J. Elrington; *Dame Plyant,* Mrs. Rowley; *Doll Common,* Mrs. Bland; Mar. 31, plus *Dapper,* Hamilton; *Neighbours,* Longfield, Maurice, and Messink; and *Officer,* Williams.

All for Love, by John Dryden
1745–46: Nov. 28, *Antony,* Barry; *Cleopatra,* Miss Bellamy; *Octavia,* Mrs. Furnival; *Ventidius,* Sheridan; Dec. 5; Feb. 13, only *Antony* and *Cleopatra* listed.

1747–48: Nov. 20, *Antony*, Sheridan (first time); *Cleopatra*, Miss Bellamy; Nov. 25; Dec. 11, no cast; Jan. 18, only *Antony*
listed; Mar. 1, as on Nov. 20.

1748–49: May 11, *Antony*, Sheridan; *Cleopatra*, Mrs. Bland.

1749–50: Nov. 6, *Antony*, Sheridan; *Cleopatra*, Mrs. Bland.

1750–51: Feb. 15, *Antony*, Digges; *Dollabella*, King; *Alexas*, Ross;
Octavia, Miss Danvers; *Cleopatra*, Mrs. Bland; *Ventidius*,
Sheridan; Feb. 22, plus *Serapion*, R. Elrington; *Priest*, Myn-
itt; *Charmion*, Miss Cole; and *Iras*, Mrs. Lindley.

1751–52: Oct. 28, *Ventidius*, Sheridan; *Antony*, Digges; *Octavia*, Mrs.
Bland; *Cleopatra*, Mrs. Woffington.

1757–58: Apr. 13, *Antony*, Dexter; *Dollabella*, Kennedy; *Alexas*, Ryder; *Ventidius*, Heaphy; *Octavia*, Miss Danvers; *Cleopatra*,
Mrs. Fitzhenry.

The Amorous Widow, or *The Wanton Wife.* "Taken from Moliere,
and Dancourt, by Mr. [Thomas] Betterton, and has since been revised by Colley Cibber, Esq; Poet Laureate"

1750–51: Jan. 18, *Barnaby Brittle*, Cibber; *Lovemore*, King; *Cunning-
ham*, Ross; *Merryman*, Sparks; *Sir Peter Pride*, Beamsley;
Clodpole, Mynitt; *Jeffery*, Watson; *Jeremy*, Hamilton; *Phil-
adelphia*, Miss Cole; *Lady Laycock*, Mrs. Mynitt; *Damaris*,
Mrs. Lindley; *Lady Pride*, Miss Copen; *Prudence*, Mrs. Row-
ley; *Wanton Wife*, Mrs. Bland; Jan. 23, without *Sir Peter,
Clodpole, Jeffery,* and *Jeremy;* Feb. 2; Mar. 28, without
Damaris, Lady Pride, and *Prudence*.

1751–52: Nov. 29, *Barnaby Brittle*, Cibber; *Lovemore*, King; *Merryman*, Sparks; *Philadelphia*, Miss Danvers; *Damaris*, Miss
Cole; *Mrs. Brittle* (*Wanton Wife*), Mrs. Bland.

Amphitryon, or *The Two Sosias.* "A Comedy as altered from Dryden"

1757–58: Feb. 10, *Jupiter*, Dexter; *Mercury*, Stayley; *Phoebus*, Davenport; *Amphitryon*, Wilder; *Polidas*, Preston; *Tranio*, Oliver;
Sosia, King; *Judge Gripus*, Glover; *Alcmena*, Miss Kennedy;
Bromia, Mrs. Farrell; *Night*, Mrs. Pye; *Phaedra*, Mrs. Kennedy; Feb. 15; Feb. 22; Mar. 2; Mar. 17.

The Anatomist, or *The Sham Doctor,* by Edward Ravenscroft.
(Farce)

1745–56: Feb. 17, *M. LeMedicin*, Bardin.

1749–50: Dec. 21, no cast; Jan. 10.

1750–51: Feb. 21, *M. LeMedicin*, King (first time); *Crispin*, Sparks;
Feb. 22, plus *Beatrice*, Mrs. Mynitt; Feb. 28; Mar. 6; Mar.
26; May 8.

1751–52: Oct. 4, *M. LeMedicin*, King; *Crispin*, Sparks.

1753–54: Nov. 9, *M. LeMedicin*, King; *Crispin*, Sparks; *Beatrice*, Mrs. Mynitt.

Apollo and Daphne. "The Words by the celebrated Mr. [John] Hughes, Author of the Siege of Damascus. The Musick by Signor Pasquali" (Musical Entertainment)

1748–49: Apr. 14, *Apollo*, Mrs. Storer; *Daphne*, Mrs. Mozeen; *Peneus*, Sullivan; Apr. 22; May 4, plus *Doris*, Mynitt; May 22, no cast, but "Interspersed with some Comick Scenes of the Entertainment called, Trick upon Trick. Particularly the Escape of Harlequin into a Quart Bottle, and the Skeleton Scene," with *Pierot*, Morris; May 26.

The Apprentice, by Arthur Murphy. (Farce)

1756–57: Oct. 27, *Dick*, King; Nov. 1; Nov. 24; Apr. 11, plus *O'Bralaghan*, Sparks.

1757–58: Feb. 13, *Dick*, King; *O'Bralaghan*, Sparks; *Principal Spouter*, Wilkinson; Mar. 3, only the *Apprentice* (*Dick*) listed; Apr. 28, plus *Irish Actor* (*O'Bralaghan*), Sparks, and *Scotchman*, "with a new Song in Character," Corry; Apr. 29, only *Dick* listed.

As You Like It, by William Shakespeare

1747–48: Feb. 19, *Jaques*, Sheridan; *Lancelot*, [error for *Touchstone?*], Woodward; *Rosalind*, Miss Jones; Mar. 30, only "*Touchstone the Clown*, Woodward," listed.

1748–49: Oct. 3, *Rosalind*, Mrs. Vincent, "from the Theatre Royal in Covent-Garden"; *Celia*, Mrs. Mozeen, "from the Theatre Royal in Drury-Lane"; Oct. 31, no cast.

1749–50: Dec. 11, *Jaques*, Sheridan; *Celia*, "in which will be introduced the Song of the Cuckoo," Mrs. Mozeen; *Rosalind*, Mrs. Bland; *Touchstone*, Macklin; *Amiens*, "with the Song of Blow, Blow, &c.," Sullivan; May 4, but *Touchstone*, Vaughan; plus *Orlando*, Ross; and *Phoebe*, Miss Bourne.

1750–51: Apr. 29, *Jaques*, Digges; *Touchstone*, King; *Orlando*, Ross; *Duke Senior*, J. Elrington; *Adam*, R. Elrington; *Phoebe*, by a young Lady who never appeared on any Stage; *Celia*, Miss Cole; *Rosalind*, with the Song of the Cuckoo and a humorous Epilogue, Mrs. Bland.

1751–52: Dec. 2, *Jaques*, Sheridan; *Touchstone*, King; *Celia*, Miss Cole; *Rosalind*, Mrs. Woffington; Feb. 20, plus *Adam*, Heaphy.

1752–53: Mar. 30, *Jaques*, Sowdon; *Orlando*, Digges; *Touchstone*,

King; *Amiens*, with Songs in Character, Sullivan; *Celia*, with the Song of the Cuckoo, Mrs. Green; *Rosalind*, Mrs. Woffington.

1757–58: Apr. 12, *Jaques*, Dexter (first time); *Orlando*, Hurst; *Adam*, Heaphy; *Duke Senior*, Storer; *Duke Frederick*, Lewis; *Amiens*, with Songs in Character, Corry; *Oliver*, Kennedy; *Corin*, Oliver; *Sylvius*, Preston; *Charles*, Sparks; *Touchstone*, King; *Phoebe*, Mrs. Pye; *Audrey*, Mrs. Farrell; *Celia*, with Songs in Character, Mrs. Storer; *Rosalind*, Miss Kennedy.

The Author, "written by Samuel Foote" (Farce)

1756–57: Mar. 22, *Cadwallader*, King; *Young Cape*, Glover; *Mrs. Cadwallader*, Miss G. Phillips; May 13, but *Mrs. Cadwallader*, Mrs. Kennedy; and plus *Governor Cape*, Heaphy; *Sprightly*, Kennedy; and *Arabella*, Miss Kennedy; May 23, only *Cadwallader*, Foote, listed.

1757–58: Nov. 18, *Cadwallader*, Foote; Nov. 26, plus *Mrs. Cadwallader*, Mrs. Kennedy; Dec. 7; Dec. 12; Dec. 22; Jan. 12, but *Cadwallader*, "after the Manner of the Original," Wilkinson; Mar. 30, but *Cadwallader*, King, "who will speak the original Prologue, and treat the Writer with a Dish of his own Tea"; May 1, without *Mrs. Cadwallader*.

Barbarossa, by John Brown

1756–57: Mar. 24, *Achmet*, Dexter; *Barbarossa*, Heaphy; *Sadi*, Layfield; *Othman*, Hurst; *Aladin*, Stayley; *Officer*, Watson; *Irene*, Miss Kennedy; *Zaphira*, Mrs. Kennedy.

1757–58: Jan. 16, *Achmet*, Dexter; *Othman*, Hurst; *Aladin*, Stayley; *Sadi*, Glover; *Barbarossa*, Heaphy; *Slave*, Watson; *Officer*, Davenport; *Irene*, Miss Kennedy; *Zaphira*, Mrs. Fitzhenry; Mar. 29, only *Achmet* and *Zaphira* listed; June 6, as on Jan. 16, but without *Officer*.

The Beaux Stratagem (see *The Stratagem*)

The Beggar's Opera, by John Gay

1745–46: Apr. 25, *Macheath*, Sullivan (first time); *Polly*, Mrs. Storer; *Lucy*, Miss Davis; *Peachum*, Morris; *Lockit*, Beamsley; *Filch*, Dyer; *Diana Trapes*, Layfield. "The rest of the Parts to the best Advantage."

1746–47: Dec. 29, no cast; Mar. 23, *Macheath*, Layfield.

1747–48: Apr. 21, *Polly*, Miss Mechel (first time); *Macheath*, Dyer; May 20, only *Polly* listed.

1748–49: Oct. 7, *Polly*, Mrs. Mozeen; *Lucy*, Mrs. Vincent; *Macheath*, Dyer; Oct. 24; Dec. 2 but *Polly*, Mrs. Storer; plus *Peachum*, Macklin, and *Mrs. Peachum*, Mrs. Macklin; Dec. 21, plus *Lockit*, Beamsley, and *Diana Trapes*, Mrs. Macklin; Feb. 23, only *Macheath*, *Mrs. Peachum*, and *Polly*, Mrs. Mozeen, listed; Mar. 15, *Macheath*, Dyer; *Polly*, Mrs. Mozeen; *Lucy*, Mrs. Lampe (first time); *Mrs. Peachum* and *Diana Trapes*, Mrs. Macklin.

1749–50: Sept. 22, *Macheath*, Dyer; *Polly*, Mrs. Storer; *Lucy*, Mrs. Lampe; Dec. 27, but *Macheath* "to be attempted by Mr. Ross," and *Polly*, Mrs. Mozeen; plus *Mrs. Peachum* and *Diana Trapes*, Mrs. Macklin; Apr. 23, *Polly*, Mademoiselle Vandersluys "being the first Time of her acting any Part on the Stage"; *Macheath*, Ross; *Lucy*, Mrs. Lampe; May 16, *Macheath*, Digges by particular Desire; *Diana Trapes*, Cibber, by Desire; *Mat o'th' Mint*, Ross; *Lucy*, Mrs. Lampe; *Polly*, Mrs. Mozeen.

1750–51: Dec. 31, *Macheath*, Ross; *Peachum*, Sparks; *Lockit*, Beamsley; *Lucy*, Mrs. Lindley; *Mrs. Peachum*, Mrs. Mynitt; *Polly*, Miss Cole (first time); Jan. 16.

1751–52: Dec. 20, *Macheath*, Digges; *Lucy*, Miss Cole; *Polly*, Mrs. Davies; Jan. 1, plus *Peachum*, Sparks; and *Lockit*, Beamsley; Jan. 17; Apr. 25, *Macheath*, Conyers; *Peachum*, Sparks; *Lockit*, Beamsley; *Lucy*, Miss Cole; *Mrs. Peachum*, Mrs. Mynitt; *Polly*, Mrs. Davies; May 18; June 2, but *Peachum*, Mynitt; *Lucy*, Mrs. Mynitt; *Diana Trapes* and *Mrs. Peachum*, Mrs. Rowley.

1752–53: Oct. 16, *Macheath*, Digges; *Peachum*, Sparks; *Lockit*, Beamsley; *Mat o'th' Mint*, Layfield; *Filch*, Williams; *Ben Budge*, Stevens; *Crookfinger Jack*, Hamilton; *Beggar*, Maurice; *Wat Dreary*, J. Elrington; *Nimming Ned*, Longfield; *Harry Paddington*, Mynitt; *Player*, Watson; *Lucy*, a young Gentlewoman, being the first Time of her Appearance on any Stage; *Mrs. Peachum* and *Diana Trapes*, Mrs. Mynitt; *Jenny Diver*, Mrs. Crump; *Mrs. Slammekin*, Mrs. Kennedy; *Molly Brazen*, Mrs. Packenham; *Mrs. Vixen*, Mrs. Stevens; *Sukey Tawdry*, Mrs. Rowley; *Mrs. Coaxer*, Miss Johnson; *Polly*, Miss Falkner, "from the Theatre Royal in Covent Garden, being the first Time of her Appearance on this Stage"; Nov. 9, *Macheath*, Digges; *Peachum*, Sparks; *Lucy*, Mrs. Green; *Polly*, Mrs. Donaldson; Dec. 7, plus *Lockit*, Beamsley; *Mrs. Peachum*, Mrs. Mynitt; Jan. 11, plus *Diana Trapes*, Mrs. Mynitt.

1753–54: Oct. 24, *Macheath*, Digges; *Peachum*, Sparks; *Lockit*, Layfield; *Mat o'th' Mint*, Kennedy; *Lucy*, Mrs. Green; *Mrs. Peachum*, Mrs. Mynitt; *Jenny Diver*, Mrs. Pye; *Mrs. Slammekin*, Mrs. Kennedy; *Mrs. Coaxer*, Mrs. Roberts; *Polly*, Mrs. Storer; Nov. 10, without *Mat o'th' Mint*; Dec. 15, without *Mrs. Coaxer*.

1756–57: Dec. 17, *Macheath*, Wilder, from Drury Lane; *Polly*, Mrs. Wilder, "being their first Appearance on this Stage"; Dec. 29, plus *Lockit*, Layfield; *Mat o'th' Mint*, Kennedy; *Peachum*, Sparks; *Mrs. Slammekin*, Mrs. Kennedy; *Jenny Diver*, Miss Wells; *Lucy*, Mrs. Pye; and *Diana Trapes*, Mrs. Mynitt; Jan. 10, only *Peachum*, *Polly*, and *Macheath*, "in which Character (by Desire)" Wilder "will introduce the Song of a Cock and a Bull"; Jan. 19; Feb. 2; Feb. 9; Feb. 16; Feb. 25; Mar. 2; Mar. 25; Apr. 27, *Macheath*, Wilder; *Lockit*, Layfield; *Mat o'th' Mint*, Kennedy; *Peachum*, Sparks; *Mrs. Slammekin*, Mrs. Kennedy; *Jenny Diver*, Miss Wells; *Lucy*, Mrs. Pye; *Diana Trapes*, Mrs. Mynitt; *Polly*, Mrs. Wilder; May 14; May 26, but *Polly*, Mrs. Storer.

1757–58: Oct. 17, *Macheath*, Wilder, "in which Character he will introduce the Cock and the Bull"; *Peachum*, Sparks; *Lockit*, Heaphy; *Mat o'th' Mint*, Kennedy; *Filch*, Williams; *Ben Budge*, Hamilton; *Harry Paddington*, R. Elrington; *Wat Dreary*, Lewis; *Jemmy Twitcher*, Wall; *Crookfinger Jack*, M'Mahon; *Robin o' Bagshot*, Hurst; *Nimming Ned*, Bate; *Beggar*, Stayley; *Player*, Watson; *Drawer*, Messink; *Mrs. Slammekin*, Mrs. Kennedy; *Mrs. Peachum*, Miss Mason; *Jenny Diver*, Miss Wells; *Mrs. Vixen*, Mrs. Packenham; *Mrs. Coaxer*, Mrs. Godwin; *Dolly Trull*, Miss Jackson; *Lucy*, Mrs. Pye; *Polly*, Mrs. Wilder; Oct 26, without *Crookfinger Jack*, *Robin o' Bagshot*, *Nimming Ned*, and *Player*; Nov. 16; Dec. 19, only *Macheath*, *Peachum*, *Lockit*, *Lucy*, and *Polly* listed.

A Bold Stroke for a Wife, by Susannah Centlivre

1747–48: Jan. 1, *Fainwell*, Woodward; Apr. 15.

1750–51: Dec. 28, *Fainwell*, King; *Anne Lovely*, Mrs. Bland; Jan. 21, plus *Periwinkle*, Sparks; *Obadiah Prim*, Mynitt; *Mrs. Prim*, Mrs. Mynitt; *Sackbut*, Beamsley; *Sir Philip Modelove*, Watson; and *Freeman*, Falkner; Mar. 27, without *Mrs. Prim* and *Sir Philip Modelove*.

1751–52: Oct. 3, *Fainwell*, King; *Periwinkle*, Sparks; *Anne Lovely*,

Mrs. Bland; Jan. 6, plus *Obadiah Prim*, Mynitt; *Sir Philip Modelove*, Watson; *Freeman*, Falkner; *Sackbut*, Beamsley; *Tradelove*, Maurice; *Mrs. Prim*, Mrs. Rowley; and *Betty*, Mrs. Kennedy.

The Brave Irishman, by Thomas Sheridan. (Farce)

1745–46: Mar. 10, *O'Blunder*, Morris; Mar. 14.

1747–48: May 23, *O'Blunder*, Morris.

1749–50: Jan. 17, *O'Blunder*, Sparks; *Lucinda*, Mrs. Mozeen; Jan. 23, no cast; Feb. 5, *O'Blunder*, Sparks; Feb. 23; Mar. 3; Mar. 31; May 10.

1750–51: Feb. 8, *O'Blunder*, Sparks; Feb. 13; Mar. 1; Mar. 8; Mar. 21; Apr. 29, plus *Lucinda*, Miss Cole; May 3, plus *Scheme-well*, Hamilton.

1751–52: Nov. 4, *O'Blunder*, Sparks; Dec. 4, plus *Lucinda*, Miss Cole; Jan. 27, without *Lucinda*; Feb. 24; Apr. 4, plus *Lucinda*; Apr. 15; Apr. 20.

1752–53: Oct. 25, *O'Blunder*, Sparks; Oct. 30; Dec. 4; Feb. 26; Mar. 21; Apr. 11, plus *Lucinda*, Miss Mason.

1753–54: Dec. 20, *O'Blunder*, Sparks; Jan. 23; Feb. 8.

1756–57: Dec. 11, *O'Blunder*, Sparks; Dec. 18.

1757–58: Nov. 7, *O'Blunder*, Sparks; Nov. 28; Jan. 5; Mar. 9; Mar. 17; Apr. 7; May 3.

The Busy Body, by Susannah Centlivre

1747–48: Sept. 28, *Marplot*, Woodward, "from the Theatre-royal in Covent Garden"; Oct. 21, no cast; Feb. 10, *Busy Body* (*Marplot*), Woodward; *Sir George Airy*, R. Elrington; Apr. 13, no cast.

1748–49: Oct. 19, *Marplot*, Macklin.

1749–50: May 15, *Marplot*, Cibber; *Miranda*, Mrs. Bland.

1750–51: Sept. 19, *Marplot*, Cibber; *Miranda*, Mrs. Bland; *Isabinda*, Miss Cole, "from the Theatre Royal in Drury-lane."

1751–52: Oct. 4, *Marplot*, King; *Sir George Airy*, Kennedy; *Sir Jealous Traffick*, Sparks; *Charles*, Heaphy; *Isabinda*, Miss Cole; *Miranda*, Mrs. Bland; Nov. 19, without *Charles*; and plus *Patch*, Mrs. Mynitt.

1752–53: Jan. 10, *Marplot*, King; *Sir George Airy*, Kennedy; *Charles*, Heaphy; *Sir Jealous Traffick*, Sparks; *Sir Francis Gripe*, Mynitt; *Whisper*, Cunningham; *Patch*, Mrs. Green; *Miranda*, Mrs. Ward.

1753–54: Jan. 2, *Marplot*, King; *Sir George Airy*, Dexter; *Charles*, Heaphy; *Sir Jealous Traffick*, Sparks; *Sir Francis Gripe*,

Mynitt; *Whisper*, Green; *Patch*, Mrs. Green; *Scentwell*, Mrs. Cunningham; *Isabinda*, Miss Mason; *Miranda*, Mrs. Ward.

1756–57: Oct. 18, *Marplot*, King; *Charles*, Stayley; *Whisper*, Hurst; *Sir George Airy*, Dexter; *Sir Francis Gripe*, Mynitt; *Sir Jealous Traffick*, Sparks; *Isabinda*, Mrs. Pye; *Patch*, Mrs. Mynitt; *Scentwell*, Mrs. Packenham; *Miranda*, Miss Kennedy.

1757–58: Oct. 13, *Busy Body (Marplot)*, King; *Sir George Airy*, Dexter; *Charles*, Stayley; *Sir Francis Gripe*, Glover; *Whisper*, Hamilton; *Sir Jealous Traffick*, Sparks; *Patch*, Mrs. Kennedy; *Isabinda*, Mrs. Pye; *Scentwell*, Mrs. Packenham; *Miranda*, Miss Kennedy.

The Careless Husband, by Colley Cibber

1745–46: May 10, *Lord Foppington*, Bardin.

1746–47: Apr. 27, *Lord Foppington*, Dyer; *Lord Morelove*, J. Elrington; *Edging*, Mrs. Dyer; *Lady Betty Modish*, Miss Bellamy (first time).

1747–48: Feb. 9, *Sir Charles Easy*, Sheridan (first time); *Lady Betty Modish*, Miss Bellamy; *Edging*, Miss Pitt; *Lord Foppington*, Woodward.

1749–50: Jan. 10, *Sir Charles Easy*, Sheridan; *Lady Graveairs*, Mrs. Macklin; *Lady Easy*, Miss Danvers; *Lady Betty Modish*, Mrs. Bland; *Lord Foppington*, Cibber; Jan. 17; Mar. 14, but *Lady Graveairs*, Mrs. Lindley.

1750–51: Feb. 8, *Sir Charles Easy*, Sheridan; *Lord Foppington*, Cibber; *Lord Morelove*, Ross; *Lady Easy*, Miss Danvers; *Lady Graveairs*, Mrs. Lindley; *Edging*, Miss Cole; *Lady Betty Modish*, Mrs. Bland; Mar. 6.

1751–52: Oct. 31, *Sir Charles Easy*, Sheridan; *Lord Foppington*, Cibber; *Lord Morelove*, Heaphy; *Lady Easy*, Mrs. Davies; *Lady Graveairs*, Mrs. Lee; *Edging*, Miss Cole; *Lady Betty Modish*, Mrs. Woffington; Feb. 26; April 4.

1753–54: Feb. 21, *Sir Charles Easy*, Sheridan; *Lord Foppington*, King; *Lord Morelove*, Heaphy; *Lady Easy*, Mrs. Ward; *Lady Graveairs*, Mrs. Kennedy; *Edging*, Mrs. Green; *Lady Betty Modish*, Mrs. Woffington.

1756–57: Mar. 30, *Lord Foppington*, King; *Sir Charles Easy*, Dexter; *Lord Morelove*, Heaphy; *Lady Graveairs*, Mrs. Lee; *Edging*, Mrs. Kennedy; *Lady Easy*, Miss Phillips; *Lady Betty Modish*, Miss G. Phillips (first time).

Catherine and Petruchio, altered from Shakespeare by David Garrick. (Comedy of Three Acts)

1756–57: Oct. 25, *Petruchio*, King; *Grumio*, Sparks; *Catherine*, Mrs. Kennedy; Dec. 10, no cast; Dec. 15, *Petruchio*, King; *Catherine*, Mrs. Kennedy; Apr. 22, *Catherine*, with Songs in Character, Miss Spencer (first time "of her attempting a Character on the Stage"); *Petruchio*, King.

1757–58: Mar. 18, *Petruchio*, King; *Catherine*, Mrs. Fitzhenry; Apr. 3; Apr. 10; Apr. 17.

Cato, by Joseph Addison

1745–46: Apr. 21, *Cato*, Sheridan; *Juba*, Barry (first time); *Marcia*, Miss Bellamy (first time); May 9, plus *Syphax*, F. Elrington; *Lucia*, Miss Jones.

1746–47: Jan. 12, *Cato*, Sheridan; *Marcia*, Miss Bellamy; Mar. 30, only *Cato*, by Desire, Sheridan, listed.

1747–48: Dec. 4, *Cato*, Sheridan.

1748–49: Jan. 27, *Cato*, Sheridan.

1749–50: Apr. 27, *Cato*, Sheridan; *Lucius*, Beamsley; *Sempronius*, J. Elrington; *Juba*, Ross; *Syphax*, Cibber; *Marcia*, Miss Griffith; *Lucia*, Miss Danvers.

1750–51: Dec. 14, *Cato*, Sheridan; *Juba*, Digges; *Sempronius*, Mossop; *Syphax*, Montgomery; *Portius*, Ross; *Marcus*, King; *Lucius*, Beamsley; *Lucia*, Miss Danvers; *Marcia*, Mrs. Bland; Dec. 19, without *Lucius*; Feb. 6, plus *Lucius*.

1751–52: Dec. 13, *Cato*, Sheridan; *Juba*, Digges; *Syphax*, Cibber; *Lucia*, Miss Cole; *Marcia*, Mrs. Bland.

1756–57: Dec. 18, *Cato*, Sheridan; *Juba*, Dexter; *Syphax*, Glover; *Lucia*, Miss G. Phillips; *Marcia*, Miss Phillips; Jan. 12, but *Syphax*, King.

1757–58: Apr. 11, *Cato*, Sheridan; *Syphax*, King; *Juba*, Dexter; *Sempronius*, Heaphy; *Portius*, Stayley; *Lucius*, Hurst; *Decius*, Storer; *Lucia*, Miss G. Phillips; *Marcia*, Miss Taylor (first time).

The Chances, "altered from Beaumont and Fletcher, by the Duke of Buckingham"

1750–51: Apr. 20, *Don John*, King; *Frederick*, Ross; *Antonio*, Sparks; *First Constantia*, Miss Cole; *Landlady*, Mrs. Mynitt; *Aunt*, Mrs. Rowley; *Second Constantia*, Mrs. Bland.

The Chaplet, by Moses Mendez. "Set to Music by Mr. Boyce." (Musical Entertainment)

1749–50: Feb. 16, vocal parts by Sullivan, Mrs. Storer, Mrs. Lampe,

Mrs. Mozeen; Feb. 20; Mar. 8, *Damon*, Sullivan; *Palaemon*, Mrs. Lampe; *Pastora*, Mrs. Storer; *Laura*, Mrs. Mozeen; May 18, as on Feb. 16; May 23, no cast.

1752–53: Mar. 29, *Damon* and *Palaemon*, Sullivan; *Pastora*, Mrs. Green; *Laura*, Mrs. Donaldson.

1757–58: Jan. 25, *Damon*, Wilder; *Palaemon*, Corry; *Pastora*, Mrs. Wilder; *Laura*, Mrs. Storer; Jan. 31.

The Cheats of Scapin, adapted from Thomas Otway

1757–58: Mar. 31, *Scapin*, King; *Thrifty*, Lewis; *Shift*, Stayley; *Sly*, Hamilton; *Leander*, Hurst; *Octavian*, Preston; *Gripe*, Glover; May 13, only *Scapin* listed.

Chrononhotonthologos, by Henry Carey. "The Most Tragical Tragedy that ever was Tragedized"

1746–47: Mar. 16, no cast.

1749–50: Nov. 3, *Chrononhotonthologos*, Bardin; *Tatlanthe*, Mrs. Lampe; *Venus*, Mrs. Mozeen; *The Queen*, Mrs. Storer; Nov. 24, plus *Bombardinion*, Sparks; and *Cupid*, Miss Reynolds; Apr. 20, no cast.

1750–51: Apr. 22, *Cupid*, Master Mynitt; May 16.

The City Wives Confederacy, by Sir John Vanbrugh

1747–48: Oct. 8, *Brass*, Woodward; *Flippanta*, Miss Bellamy; Mar. 23, plus *Dick Amlet*, Dyer.

1748–49: Dec. 19, *Brass*, Macklin; *Mrs. Amlet*, Mrs. Macklin; Mar. 13, plus *Clarissa*, Mrs. Vincent; *Corinna*, Mrs. Mozeen; and *Flippanta*, Mrs. Bland.

1749–50: Oct. 11, *Brass*, Macklin; *Clarissa*, Miss Copen; *Flippanta*, Mrs. Bland; *Mrs. Amlet*, Mrs. Macklin.

1751–52: Mar. 16, *Brass*, King; *Dick Amlet*, Digges; *Gripe*, Sparks; *Moneytrap*, Cibber; *Flippanta*, Mrs. Bland; *Araminta*, Mrs. Davies; *Corinna*, Miss Cole; *Mrs. Amlet*, Mrs. Mynitt; *Clarissa*, Mrs. Woffington; Apr. 22, but *Araminta*, Mrs. Rowley.

1752–53: Nov. 8, *Clarissa*, Mrs. Woffington; *Brass*, King; *Gripe*, Sparks; *Moneytrap*, Costollo, "from the Theatre Royal in Drury-lane (being the first Time of his appearing on this Stage)"; *Flippanta*, Mrs. Green; Nov. 16.

1753–54: Oct. 31, *Brass*, King; *Gripe*, Sparks; *Dick Amlet*, Kennedy; *Flippanta*, Mrs. Green; *Araminta*, Mrs. Pye; *Mrs. Amlet*, Mrs. Mynitt; *Corinna*, Mrs. Kennedy; *Clarissa*, Mrs. Woffington.

1756–57: Apr. 2, *Dick Amlet*, Dexter; *Gripe*, Sparks; *Moneytrap*,

Glover; *Jessamin*, Hamilton; *Clip*, Watson; *Brass*, King; *Clarissa*, Miss Phillips; *Corinna*, Mrs. Wilder; *Mrs. Amlet*, Mrs. Mynitt; *Araminta*, Miss Danvers; *Flippanta*, Miss G. Phillips.

The Cobler of Preston, by Christopher Bullock
1750–51: Apr. 4, *Toby Guzzle*, Sparks.

The Comical Lovers, "altered from Dryden by [Colley] Cibber"
1753–54: Oct. 29, *Celadon*, Sheridan; *Rhodophil*, Sowdon; *Palamede*, King; *Florimel*, Mrs. Ward; *Doralice*, Mrs. Kennedy; *Philotas*, Mrs. Pye; *Flavia*, Mrs. Roberts; *Melissa*, Mrs. Mynitt; *Olinda*, Miss Mason; *Beleza*, with Songs in Character, Mrs. Storer; *Melantha*, Mrs. Woffington; Nov. 2, without *Melissa*, *Olinda*, and *Beleza*; Nov. 7; Jan. 24, but *Palamede*, Sheridan (first time), and *Celadon*, King; plus *Sabrina*, Miss Reynolds.

The Committee, or *The Faithful Irishman*, by Sir Robert Howard
1745–46: Jan. 20, *Careless*, Bardin; *Teague*, Morris.
1748–49: Oct. 17, *Teague*, Barrington, "in which he will introduce his celebrated Roratorio"; Jan. 4, plus *Day*, Mynitt; *Careless*, Kennedy; *Blunt*, J. Elrington; *Abel*, Storer; *Obadiah*, Vaughan; *Mrs. Day*, Mrs. Mynitt; *Ruth*, Miss Jones; and *Arabella*, Mrs. Dyer.
1749–50: Dec. 28, no cast; Jan. 5, *Teague*, Macklin; *Ruth*, Mrs. Bland; *Arabella*, Miss Copen; *Mrs. Day*, Mrs. Macklin.
1751–52: Nov. 16, *Teague*, Sparks; *Abel*, King; *Obadiah*, Stevens; *Mrs. Day*, Mrs. Mynitt; *Arabella*, Miss Cole; *Ruth*, Mrs. Bland.
1752–53: Jan. 1, *Teague*, Sparks; *Ruth*, Mrs. Green; Mar. 10, plus *Careless*, Kennedy; *Blunt*, Heaphy; *Day*, Mynitt; *Abel*, Green; *Mrs. Day*, Mrs. Mynitt; and *Arabella*, Mrs. Kennedy.
1753–54: Nov. 8, *Blunt*, Sowdon; *Careless*, Dexter; *Teague*, Sparks; *Day*, Cunningham; *Abel*, Green; *Obadiah*, Storer; *Story*, Maurice; *Nathaniel Catch*, Watson; *Bookseller*, Williams; *Ruth*, Mrs. Green; *Arabella*, Mrs. Kennedy; *Mrs. Day*, Mrs. Woffington (first time); Nov. 30, but *Mrs. Day*, Mrs. Mynitt; and without *Obadiah*, *Story*, *Nathaniel Catch*, and *Bookseller*; Dec. 7, but *Day*, Mynitt.
1756–57: Nov. 10, *Careless*, Dexter; *Abel*, King; *Teague*, Sparks; *Ruth*, Miss Kennedy.
1757–58: Oct. 28, *Careless*, Dexter; *Blunt*, Heaphy; *Story*, Stayley; *Day*, Storer; *Abel*, King; *Obadiah*, Glover; *Committeeman*,

Watson; *Porter*, Messink; *Bookseller*, Williams; *Teague*, Sparks; *Arabella*, Mrs. Kennedy; *Mrs. Day*, Mrs. Farrell; *Ruth*, Miss Kennedy; Mar. 1, plus *Second Committeeman*, Lewis; *Bailiff*, Davenport; and *Mrs. Chat*, Mrs. Packenham; and without *Porter*.

Comus, "written by Milton, and set to Musick by Mr. Arne"

1745–46: Apr. 22, *Comus*, Sheridan (first time); *Elder Brother*, by a Gentleman; *Lady*, Mrs. Elmy; *Bacchanal* and *Attendant Spirit*, Sullivan; *Sabrina*, Mrs. Storer (first time).

1748–49: Dec. 16, *Comus*, Sheridan; *Sabrina*, Mrs. Storer; *Second Spirit*, Mrs. Mozeen; *First Bacchanal*, Sullivan; *Euphrosine*, Mrs. Lampe; *Lady*, Mrs. Vincent; Jan. 18.

1749–50: Feb. 10, *Comus*, Sheridan; *First Spirit*, Digges; *Lady*, Miss Griffith; *First Bacchanal*, Sullivan; *Second Bacchanal*, Howard; *Euphrosine*, Mrs. Lampe; *Sabrina*, Mrs. Storer; *Second Spirit*, Mrs. Mozeen; Feb. 17; Feb. 24; May 25, but *Comus*, Mossop, and *First Spirit*, Mrs. Bland.

1752–53: Feb. 17, *Comus*, Sowdon; *First Bacchanal*, Sullivan; *First Spirit*, Heaphy; *Lady*, Mrs. Kennedy; *Euphrosine*, Mrs. Crump; *Sabrina*, Mrs. Donaldson; Feb. 22; Feb. 24; Mar. 1; Mar. 3; Mar. 31.

1756–57: Feb. 26, *Comus*, Sheridan; *Elder Brother*, Dexter; *First Bacchanal*, Wilder; *Pastoral Nymph*, Mrs. Wilder; *Euphrosine*, Miss Spencer; the other vocal parts by Corry, Miss Wells, Mrs. Pye, &c.; *Lady*, Mrs. Kennedy; Mar. 4.

1757–58: Feb. 16, *Comus*, Sheridan; *Elder Brother*, Dexter; *Younger Brother*, Ryder; *First Spirit*, Heaphy; *Second Spirit*, Miss Mason; *First Bacchanal*, Wilder; *Second Bacchanal*, Corry; *Euphrosine*, Mrs. Wilder; *Sabrina*, Mrs. Storer; the other vocal parts by Mrs. Pye, Miss Wells, Hamilton, Oliver, Messink, &c.; *Lady*, Mrs. Fitzhenry.

The Confederacy (see *The City Wives Confederacy*)

The Conscious Lovers, by Sir Richard Steele

1745–46: Nov. 19, no cast.

1746–47: Nov. 10, *Bevil Junior*, Sheridan (first time); *Indiana*, Miss Bellamy (first time); Nov. 19; Mar. 5, no cast; Apr. 3, *Tom*, Dyer; *Indiana*, Miss Bellamy; June 1, *Bevil Junior*, Sheridan; *Indiana*, Miss Bellamy.

1747–48: Oct. 28, *Bevil Junior*, Sheridan; *Indiana*, Miss Bellamy; *Tom*, Woodward.

1748–49: Feb. 3, *Bevil Junior*, Sheridan; *Tom*, Macklin; *Myrtle*, Dyer;

Phillis, Mrs. Vincent; *Indiana*, "by a young Lady, who never appeared on any Stage"; Feb. 22, but *Indiana*, "by the young Lady who performed it before"; May 17, but *Indiana*, Miss Danvers.

1749–50: Oct. 16, *Bevil Junior*, Sheridan; *Tom*, Macklin; *Phillis*, Mrs. Bland; *Indiana*, Miss Danvers; Apr. 19, but *Tom*, Cibber; and plus *Lucinda*, Mrs. Mozeen; *Mrs. Sealand*, Mrs. Mynitt; and *Isabella*, Miss Copen.

1750–51: Feb. 27, *Bevil Junior*, Sheridan; *Tom*, Cibber; *Myrtle*, Ross; *Indiana*, Miss Danvers; *Phillis*, Mrs. Bland; Mar. 21, but *Bevil Junior*, Digges (first time); *Phillis*, Miss Cole; and *Indiana*, Mrs. Bland; and plus *Sealand*, Montgomery; *Sir John Bevil*, Beamsley (Sparks in *Dublin Courant*); *Lucinda*, Mrs. Lindley; May 2, *Bevil Junior*, Sheridan; *Tom*, Cibber; *Sealand*, Montgomery; *Myrtle*, Ross; *Indiana*, Miss Danvers; *Mrs. Sealand*, Mrs. Mynitt; *Isabella*, Miss Copen; *Lucinda*, Miss Griffith; *Phillis*, Mrs. Bland.

1751–52: Oct. 18, *Bevil Junior*, Sheridan; *Myrtle*, Digges; *Tom*, King; *Cimberton*, Cibber; *Indiana*, Mrs. Davies, "being her first Appearance on this Stage"; *Phillis*, Mrs. Woffington; Mar. 23, but *Cimberton*, Davies; Apr. 30, plus *Sir John Bevil*, J. Elrington; *Sealand*, Heaphy; *Lucinda*, Miss Cole; and *Mrs. Sealand*, Mrs. Mynitt.

1752–53: Nov. 30, *Bevil Junior*, Sheridan; *Myrtle*, Digges; *Cimberton*, Costollo; *Sealand*, Heaphy; *Tom*, King; *Indiana*, Mrs. Ward; *Phillis*, Mrs. Green.

1756–57: Dec. 8, *Bevil Junior*, Sheridan; *Myrtle*, Lee; *Tom*, King; *Cimberton*, Glover; *Phillis*, Miss G. Phillips; *Indiana*, Miss Phillips; Dec. 15; Jan. 5; Mar. 18, but *Indiana*, Mrs. Glen (first time); Apr. 20, but *Bevil Junior*, Dexter; and *Indiana*, Miss Phillips; and plus *Lucinda*, Mrs. Pye.

1757–58: Nov. 23, *Bevil Junior*, Dexter; *Myrtle*, Heaphy; *Sir John Bevil*, Lewis; *Sealand*, Storer; *Cimberton*, Glover; *Humphrey*, Stayley; *Daniel*, Hamilton; *Tom*, King; *Phillis*, Miss G. Phillips; *Mrs. Sealand*, Mrs. Farrell; *Lucinda*, Mrs. Pye; *Isabella*, Miss Mason; *Indiana*, Miss Phillips; Apr. 14, but *Sealand*, Hurst; and *Indiana*, Mrs. Fitzhenry (first time).

The Constant Captives. (Pantomime Entertainment)

1751–52: Apr. 9, *Harlequin*, Stevens; *Columbine*, Miss Cole; *Bashaw*, Falkner; *Cupid*, Miss Reynolds; *Bashaw's Man*, Sparks; *Capt. of Corsairs*, McNeil; *Capt.'s Lady*, Miss Baker; *Corsairs*, Williams, Messink, Hamilton, and others; *Captives*, Mrs. Rowley, Mrs. Packenham, Miss Comerford, &c.; Apr. 16, but Mrs. Kennedy replaces Mrs. Packenham; Apr. 23, no cast; Apr. 25, as on Apr. 16; Apr. 30; May 2, no cast; May 8; May 12; May 13; May 18; May 23; May 30.

1752–53: Feb. 23, *Harlequin*, King; *Bashaw*, Stevens; *Bashaw's Man*, Sparks; *Columbine*, Mrs. Kennedy; *Capt. of Corsairs*, McNeil; *his Lady*, Miss Baker; Mar. 2; Apr. 9, only *Harlequin* and *Bashaw's Man* listed; Apr. 12, plus *Bashaw*, *Capt. of Corsairs* and *his Lady*, "with a proper Dance," and *Columbine*; Apr. 27, without *Bashaw*, *Capt. of Corsairs*, and *his Lady*.

1753–54: Jan. 25, *Harlequin*, King; *Bashaw's Man*, Sparks; *Capt. of Corsairs*, McNeil; *his Lady*, Miss Baker; Feb. 1, plus *Bashaw*, Layfield; Feb. 6, but *Bashaw*, Stayley; Feb. 15, plus *Columbine*, Miss Mason.

The Constant Couple, or *A Trip to the Jubilee*, by George Farquhar

1745–46: Oct. 30, no cast; Nov. 21, *Sir Harry Wildair*, Sheridan (first time); Mar. 19, but *Sir Harry Wildair*, Garrick.

1746–47: Dec. 17, *Sir Harry Wildair*, Bardin; Mar. 3, plus *Angelica*, Mrs. Storer.

1747–48: Apr. 25, *Sir Harry Wildair*, Woodward; May 6; May 9.

1748–49: May 10, *Sir Harry Wildair*, Mrs. Bland (first time); *Lady Lurewell*, Mrs. Vincent.

1751–52: Oct. 23, *Sir Harry Wildair*, Mrs. Woffington; *Beau Clincher*, Cibber; *Lady Lurewell*, Mrs. Bland (first time); Nov. 9, plus *Alderman Smuggler*, Sparks, and *Angelica*, Miss Cole; Nov. 18; Nov. 27, plus *Standard*, Kennedy; Dec. 21; Jan. 15; Feb. 6; Mar. 2 without *Standard*; Apr. 23.

1752–53: Nov. 29, *Sir Harry Wildair*, Mrs. Woffington; *Beau Clincher*, King; *Standard*, Kennedy; *Alderman Smuggler*, Sparks; *Young Clincher*, Hamilton; *Vizard*, Stevens; *Angelica*, Miss Mason; *Lady Darling*, Mrs. Mynitt; *Parley*, Mrs. Kennedy; *Lady Lurewell*, Mrs. Ward; Dec. 21, *Sir Harry Wildair*, Mrs. Woffington; *Beau Clincher*, King; *Alderman Smuggler*, Sparks; *Young Clincher*, Green; *Lady Lurewell*, Mrs. Ward; Mar. 21, plus *Standard*, Sowdon.

1753–54: Nov. 21, *Sir Harry Wildair*, Mrs. Woffington; *Standard*, Sowdon; *Beau Clincher*, King; *Young Clincher*, Green; *Alderman Smuggler*, Sparks; *Lady Lurewell*, Mrs. Ward.

The Contrivances, or *More Ways Than One*, by Henry Carey. (Farce)

1745–46: Apr. 28, *Arethusa*, Mrs. Storer; *Rovewell*, Dyer; *Argus*, Morris.

1748–49: Oct. 14, *Arethusa*, Mrs. Storer, "being her first Appearance since her Return from England"; May 1, no cast.

1757–58: Nov. 3, *Rovewell*, Wilder; *Arethusa*, Mrs. Storer.

Coriolanus, "taken partly from Shakespear and partly from Thompson," by Thomas Sheridan

1751–52: Feb. 29, *Coriolanus*, Sheridan; *Aufidius*, Digges; *Menenius*, Sparks; *Cominius*, Davies; *Minucius*, Beamsley; *Volusius*, Stevens; *Galesus*, Heaphy; *Volumnia*, Mrs. Davies; *Veturia*, Mrs. Woffington, "who will speak in that Character the original Epilogue to Thompson's Play"; Mar. 4; Mar. 21, plus *Brutus*, Kennedy, and *Sicinius*, J. Elrington; May 7, without *Brutus* and *Sicinius*.

1752–53: May 7, *Coriolanus*, Sheridan; *Aufidius*, Digges; *Volumnia*, Mrs. Ward; *Veturia*, Mrs. Woffington.

1753–54: Feb. 22, *Coriolanus*, Sheridan; *Aufidius*, Digges; *Cominius*, Layfield; *Menenius*, Sparks; *Minucius*, Storer; *Galesus*, Heaphy; *Volusius*, Stayley; *Sicinius*, Kennedy; *Brutus*, J. Elrington; *Plebeians*, Mynitt, Cunningham, &c.; *Volumnia*, Mrs. Ward; *Veturia*, Mrs. Woffington.

1756–57: Feb. 5, *Coriolanus*, Sheridan; *Aufidius*, Dexter; *Menenius*, Sparks; *First Plebeian*, Glover; *Volumnia*, Miss Phillips; *Veturia*, Mrs. Kennedy (first time); Feb. 17; Feb. 24.

1757–58: Nov. 14, *Coriolanus*, Sheridan; *Cominius*, Storer; *Minucius*, Hurst; *Volusius*, Stayley; *Galesus*, Heaphy; *Aufidius*, Dexter; *Brutus*, Kennedy; *Sicinius*, Lewis; *Aedile*, Watson; *First Plebeian*, Glover; *Second Plebeian*, Messink; *Menenius*, Sparks; *First Senator*, Corry; *Second Senator*, R. Elrington; *Herald*, Bate; *Lady*, Miss Mason; *Volumnia*, Miss Kennedy; *Veturia*, Mrs. Fitzhenry; Mar. 6, but *Herald*, Preston; and plus *Third Citizen*, Williams, and *Conspirator*, Davenport.

The Country Lasses, or *The Custom of the Manor*, by Charles Johnson

1753–54: Jan. 4, *Modely*, King; *Heartwell*, Dexter; *Freehold*, Sparks; *Sir John English*, Layfield; *Lurcher*, Kennedy; *Shacklefigure*, Mynitt; *Doublejugg*, Cunningham; *Carbuncle*, Maurice; *Vulture*, Hamilton; *Longbottom*, Hull; *Sneak*, Williams; *Flora*, Mrs. Kennedy; *Aura*, Mrs. Green; Jan. 11, without *Doublejugg*, *Carbuncle*, *Vulture*, and *Sneak*.

1756–57: May 3, *Modely*, King; *Sir John English*, Layfield; *Lurcher*, Kennedy; *Heartwell*, Dexter; *Carbuncle*, Aickin; *Shacklefigure*, Mynitt; *Doublejugg*, Hurst; *Freehold*, Sparks; *Vul-*

ture, Hamilton; *Longbottom,* Messink; *Sneak,* Glover; *Flora,* Mrs. Kennedy; *Aura,* Miss Kennedy.

1757–58: Oct. 14, *Modely,* King; *Heartwell,* Dexter; *Freehold,* Sparks; *Sir John English,* Storer; *Lurcher,* Kennedy; *Sneak,* Williams; *Vulture,* Hamilton; *Longbottom,* Messink; *Flora,* Mrs. Kennedy; *Aura,* Miss Kennedy.

The Country Wake (see *Flora*)

A Cure for a Scold, by James Worsdale, "taken from Shakespear's taming the Shrew [*sic*]." (Ballad Opera)

1749–50: Apr. 25, *Manly,* Kennedy; *Peg,* Mrs. Lampe.

Damon and Phillida, by Colley Cibber. (Ballad Opera)

1746–47: Dec. 1, *Damon,* Dyer; *Phillida,* Mrs. Storer; Jan. 2; Jan. 12, no cast; Mar. 10.

1747–48: Mar. 14, no cast.

1748–49: Oct. 17, *Damon,* Dyer; *Phillida,* Mrs. Storer.

1750–51: Oct. 17, *Damon,* Ross; *Phillida,* Miss Cole.

1751–52: Apr. 22, *Damon,* Conyers; *Phillida,* Miss Cole.

1756–57: Jan. 1, *Damon,* Wilder; *Cimon,* Sparks; *Phillida,* Mrs. Wilder.

1757–58: Apr. 18, *Damon,* Ryder (first time); *Lord Arcas,* Stayley; *Mopsus,* Lewis; *Cimon,* Hamilton; *Phillida,* Miss Phillips (first time); Apr. 26, *Damon,* Wilder; *Phillida,* Mrs. Storer.

The Devil to Pay, or *The Wives Metamorphosed,* by Charles Coffey. (Ballad Farce)

1745–46: Feb. 10, no cast; Apr. 30, *Nell,* Mrs. Storer; *Jobson,* Layfield.

1747–48: Feb. 1, no cast.

1748–49: Oct. 19, *Nell,* Mrs. Vincent; Apr. 4, plus *Jobson,* Barrington, and *Sir John Loverule,* Dyer.

1749–50: Apr. 2, *Sir John Loverule,* Ross; *Jobson,* Sparks; *Nell,* Mrs. Storer.

1750–51: Sept. 21, *Sir John Loverule,* Ross; *Jobson,* Sparks; *Nell,* Miss Cole; Oct. 8, without *Sir John;* May 15, plus *Sir John.*

1751–52: Dec. 2, *Jobson,* Sparks; *Sir John Loverule,* Kennedy; *Lady Loverule,* Mrs. Rowley; *Nell,* Miss Cole; Jan. 6, without *Lady Loverule;* Apr. 10, without *Sir John;* Apr. 13, plus *Sir John,* Conyers.

1752–53: Nov. 15, *Jobson,* Sparks; *Nell,* Mrs. Green; Feb. 7, plus *Sir John Loverule,* Sullivan; Mar. 12; Mar. 16; Mar. 30, but *Sir John Loverule,* "with the Early Horn"; and without *Jobson.*

1753–54: Oct. 15, *Jobson*, Sparks; *Nell*, Mrs. Green; Nov. 1, without *Jobson*; Feb. 22, plus *Jobson*, Sparks; and *Sir John Loverule*, Layfield.

1756–57: Nov. 18, no cast; Dec. 3, *Nell*, Miss Wells (first Appearance on this Stage); Jan. 21, *Sir John Loverule*, Wilder; *Jobson*, Sparks; *Lady Loverule*, Mrs. Kennedy; *Nell*, Mrs. Wilder; Apr. 15, but *Sir John Loverule*, "in which Character he [Wilder] will introduce the Early Horn."

1757–58: Oct. 13, *Sir John Loverule*, Wilder, "in which Character he will introduce the Early Horn"; *Jobson*, Sparks; *Lady Loverule*, Mrs. Kennedy; *Nell*, Mrs. Storer; Nov. 23; Dec. 8, without *Lady Loverule*; Apr. 24, but *Sir John Loverule*, Corry, "in which he will introduce the Early Horn."

The Distrest Mother, by Ambrose Philips

1745–46: Feb. 3, *Orestes*, Barry; *Pyrrhus*, R. Elrington; *Andromache*, Miss Bellamy; *Hermione*, Mrs. Furnival; Mar. 6, but *Orestes*, Garrick (first time), and *Pyrrhus*, Barry (first time); Mar. 21, but *Orestes*, Sheridan (first time); Apr. 15.

1746–47: May 18, *Orestes*, Sheridan; *Andromache*, Miss Bellamy.

1747–48: Feb. 8, *Orestes*, Sheridan; *Andromache*, Miss Bellamy.

1749–50: Mar. 9, *Orestes*, Mossop; *Pyrrhus*, Digges; *Andromache*, Miss Griffith; *Hermione*, Mrs. Bland; Mar. 10; Apr. 17.

1750–51: Nov. 15, *Orestes*, Mossop; *Andromache*, Miss Griffith; *Hermione*, Mrs. Bland; *Pyrrhus*, Digges; Jan. 4, plus *Phoenix*, Beamsley; *Pylades*, Watson; *Cephisa*, Mrs. Leslie; and *Cleone*, Mrs. Rowley.

1751–52: Oct. 9, *Orestes*, Sheridan; *Pyrrhus*, Digges; *Hermione*, Mrs. Bland; *Andromache*, Mrs. Woffington; Oct. 16, but *Andromache*, Mrs. Bland; and *Hermione*, by Desire, Mrs. Woffington; Jan. 9, but *Hermione*, Mrs. Bland; and *Andromache*, Mrs. Woffington; Feb. 3, but *Andromache*, Mrs. Bland; and *Hermione*, Mrs. Woffington; Mar. 5.

1752–53: Dec. 2, *Orestes*, Sheridan; *Pyrrhus*, Sowdon; *Andromache*, Mrs. Ward; *Hermione*, Mrs. Woffington; Jan. 15.

1753–54: Oct. 4, *Orestes*, Sheridan; *Pyrrhus*, Sowdon; *Andromache*, Mrs. Ward; *Hermione*, Mrs. Woffington.

1757–58: Nov. 11, *Orestes*, Dexter; *Pylades*, Stayley; *Pyrrhus*, Heaphy; *Phoenix*, Hurst; *Andromache*, by a young Lady "who never appeared on any Stage"; *Cleone*, Mrs. Pye; *Cephisa*, Miss Mason; *Hermione*, Mrs. Fitzhenry; Dec. 17, *Orestes*, Sheridan; *Pyrrhus*, Dexter; *Andromache*, Miss Taylor; *Hermione*, Mrs. Fitzhenry; Jan. 31; Apr. 18, *Orestes*, Dexter; *Pyrrhus*, Heaphy; *Phoenix*, Hurst; *Andromache*, Miss Phillips (first time); *Cephisa,* Miss Mason; *Cleone,* Mrs. Pye; *Hermione,* Mrs. Kennedy; May 10, only *Orestes* and *Hermione,* Mrs. Fitzhenry, listed.

Doctor Faustus (see *The Necromancer*)

Don Sebastian, by John Dryden. In the 1745–46 performance "the Comic Part of the Play, on account of the great Length of the Performance," was "by particular Desire omitted." This revision was apparently by Sheridan. The 1750–51 (March 16) performance is advertised as "altered from Dryden" and "never acted before." Here the alterations were not by Sheridan. (See Chs. III and VI.)

1745–46: Mar. 10, *Dorax,* Sheridan (first time); *Almeyda,* Miss Bellamy.
1750–51: Mar. 16, *Dorax,* Sheridan; *Don Sebastian,* Digges; *Muley Moluch,* Montgomery; *The Mufti,* Cibber; *Mustapha,* Sparks; *Morayma,* Miss Cole; *Johayma,* Mrs. Mynitt; *Almeyda,* Mrs. Bland; Mar. 25; May 1, plus *Antonio,* King.

The Double Dealer, by William Congreve
1747–48: Mar. 21, *Brisk,* Woodward; *Lady Froth,* Miss Bellamy (first time).
1748–49: Nov. 23, *Sir Paul Pliant,* Macklin; *Lady Touchwood,* Mrs. Bland; *Lady Froth,* Mrs. Vincent; *Lady Pliant,* Mrs. Macklin, "from the Theatre-Royal in Drury-Lane, being the first Time of her appearing on this Stage." Feb. 2, plus *Maskwell,* by Desire, Sheridan (first time).
1749–50: Nov. 24, *Maskwell,* Sheridan; *Sir Paul Pliant,* Macklin; *Brisk,* Cibber; *Lady Touchwood,* Mrs. Bland; *Lady Pliant,* Mrs. Macklin.
1750–51: May 17, *Maskwell,* Sheridan; *Careless,* Digges; *Lord Touchwood,* Montgomery; *Mellefont,* Falkner; *Brisk,* King; *Sir Paul Pliant,* Cibber (first time); *Lord Froth,* Watson; *Saygrace,* Mynitt; *Tim,* Messink; *Lady Pliant,* Mrs. Mynitt; *Lady Froth,* Mrs. Lindley; *Cynthia,* Miss Cole; *Lady Touchwood,* Mrs. Bland.
1751–52: Jan. 25, *Maskwell,* Sheridan; *Careless,* Digges; *Sir Paul Pliant,* Cibber; *Brisk,* King; *Lady Touchwood,* Mrs. Bland; *Lady Froth,* Miss Cole; *Cynthia,* Mrs. Davies; *Lady Pliant,* Mrs. Woffington (first time); Feb. 27.
1752–53: Dec. 14, *Maskwell,* Sheridan; *Careless,* Digges; *Brisk,* King; *Sir Paul Pliant,* Costollo; *Lady Touchwood,* Mrs. Ward; *Lady Froth,* Mrs. Green; *Lady Pliant,* Mrs. Woffington; Jan.

18, plus *Lord Froth,* Green; Feb. 9; Apr. 4, but *Maskwell,* Layfield; and plus *Mellefont,* J. Elrington.

1753–54: Oct. 10, *Maskwell,* Sheridan; *Careless,* Digges; *Brisk,* King; *Lord Froth,* Green; *Sir Paul Pliant,* Storer; *Lady Touchwood,* Mrs. Kennedy; *Lady Froth,* Mrs. Green; *Lady Pliant,* Mrs. Woffington; Nov. 16; Feb. 1, plus *Lord Touchwood,* Stayley; *Mellefont,* J. Elrington; and *Cynthia,* Miss Mason.

1756–57: Feb. 3, *Maskwell,* Sheridan; *Brisk,* King; *Careless,* Dexter; *Lord Froth,* Glover; *Sir Paul Pliant,* Lee (first time); *Lady Touchwood,* Mrs. Kennedy; *Lady Froth,* Mrs. Lee; *Lady Pliant,* Miss. G. Phillips (first time); May 13, but *Sir Paul Pliant,* Foote.

1757–58: Nov. 18, *Sir Paul Pliant,* Foote; *Maskwell,* Heaphy; *Lord Touchwood,* Stayley; *Mellefont,* Kennedy; *Careless,* Dexter; *Brisk,* King; *Saygrace,* Lewis; *Lord Froth,* Glover; *Lady Froth,* Mrs. Kennedy; *Cynthia,* Mrs. Pye; *Lady Pliant,* Miss G. Phillips; *Lady Touchwood,* Mrs. Fitzhenry; Dec. 5, only *Sir Paul, Maskwell, Lord Froth, Lady Pliant,* and *Lady Touchwood,* but played by Mrs. Kennedy, listed; Dec. 26; Apr. 3, *Sir Paul Pliant,* to be performed by a Gentleman; *Careless,* Dexter; *Brisk,* King; *Lord Froth,* Glover; *Maskwell,* Kennedy; *Lady Pliant,* Mrs. Kennedy (first time); *Lady Froth,* with a Song in Character, Mrs. Storer; *Lady Touchwood,* Mrs. Fitzhenry; May 11, *Maskwell,* Sheridan; *Lady Touchwood,* Mrs. Fitzhenry.

The Double Disappointment, by Moses Mendez. (Farce)

1748–49: Mar. 2, *Phelim O'Blunder,* Barrington; *Marquis de Fanfaron,* Sparks; Apr. 24, plus *Loveless,* Dyer; and *Isabella,* Mrs. Mozeen.

The Double Gallant, or *The Sick Lady's Cure,* by Colley Cibber

1747–48: Jan. 11, *Atall (the Double Gallant),* Woodward (first time); *Lady Sadlife,* Miss Bellamy (first time); Jan. 20; Mar. 7; Apr. 22, only *Atall* listed.

1750–51: Oct. 8, *Atall,* Cibber; *Careless,* J. Elrington; *Sir Solomon,* Mynitt; *Clerimont,* Ross; *Old Willful,* Sparks; *Strut,* Watson; *Finder,* Robertson; *Supple,* Hamilton; *Dr. Bolus,* Messink; *Rhubarb,* Maurice; *Wishwell,* Mrs. Rowley; *Lady Sadlife,* Mrs. Bland; *Lady Dainty,* Mrs. Lindley; *Sylvia,* Miss Griffith, first Appearance in Comedy; *Clarinda,* Miss Cole, "being the first Time of her Appearance in Boy's Cloaths"; Jan. 2, but *Careless,* Falkner, and *Finder,* Hamilton; and without *Strut, Supple, Dr. Bolus,* and *Rhubarb;* but plus *Situp,*

Mrs. Leslie; May 10, *Atall*, Cibber; *Sir Solomon*, Mynitt; *Clerimont*, Ross; *Careless*, J. Elrington; *Old Willful*, Sparks; *Strut*, Watson; *Lady Dainty*, Mrs. Lindley; *Sylvia*, Miss Griffith; *Wishwell*, Mrs. Rowley; *Clarinda*, Miss Cole; *Lady Sadlife*, Mrs. Bland.

1751–52: Dec. 26, *Atall*, Cibber; *Old Willful*, Sparks; *Sir Solomon*, Mynitt; *Clerimont*, Heaphy; *Careless*, Falkner; *Lady Dainty*, Mrs. Lee; *Sylvia*, Mrs. Rowley; *Wishwell*, Mrs. Kennedy; *Lady Sadlife*, Mrs. Bland; Apr. 8, but *Careless*, J. Elrington; *Wishwell*, Mrs. Mynitt; and *Lady Sadlife*, Mrs. Woffington.

1752–53: Apr. 9, *Atall*, King; *Old Willful*, Sparks; *Sir Solomon*, Mynitt; *Careless*, Kennedy; *Clerimont*, Heaphy; *Lady Dainty*, Mrs. Ward; *Sylvia*, Mrs. Green; *Clarinda*, Mrs. Kennedy; *Wishwell*, Mrs. Mynitt; *Lady Sadlife*, Mrs. Woffington.

1756–57: Oct. 27, *Atall*, King; *Sir Solomon*, Mynitt; *Careless*, Kennedy; *Clerimont*, Heaphy; *Dr. Bolus*, Hurst; *Rhubarb*, Aickin; *Finder*, Williams; *Supple*, Messink; *Old Willful*, Sparks; *Strut*, Watson; *Sylvia*, Mrs. Pye; *Situp*, Mrs. Packenham; *Lady Dainty*, Miss Danvers; *Clarinda*, Mrs. Kennedy; *Wishwell*, Mrs. Mynitt; *Lady Sadlife*, Miss Kennedy.

Douglas, by John Home

1756–57: May 12, *Douglas* (*Young Norval*), Sheridan; *Old Norval*, Lee; *Lord Randolph*, Dexter; *Glenalvon*, Stayley; *Anna*, Miss G. Phillips; *Lady Randolph*, Mrs. Kennedy; May 18.

1757–58: Mar. 10, *Douglas*, Sheridan; *Lord Randolph*, Dexter; *Old Norval*, Heaphy; *Glenalvon*, Stayley; *Anna*, Mrs. Kennedy; *Lady Randolph*, Mrs. Fitzhenry (first time); Mar. 16; May 8, only *Douglas* and *Lady Randolph* listed; May 26, plus *Lord Randolph*, *Old Norval*, *Glenalvon*, and *Anna*.

The Dragon of Wantley, by Henry Carey. "Musick by John Frederick Lampe." (Burlesque Opera)

1745–46: Mar. 13, *Moor*, "at the Request of several Persons of Quality," Sullivan, first time "in any Character on this Stage"; *Gubbins*, Morris; Mar. 17.

1748–49: Nov. 29, *Moor*, Sullivan; *Gubbins*, Morris; *Dragon*, Howard; *Mauxalinda*, Mrs. Mozeen; *Margery*, Mrs. Lampe; Dec. 1; Dec. 5; Dec. 14, but only "Vocal Parts by" Sullivan, Morris, Mrs. Lampe, Mrs. Mozeen, "and others"; Jan. 11, no cast.

1749–50: Jan. 15, *Moor*, Sullivan; *Dragon*, Howard; *Mauxalinda*, Mrs. Mozeen; *Margery*, Mrs. Lampe; Jan. 20; Feb. 27.

The Drum. A Dialogue between Pallas and Cupid

1757–58: Mar. 11, *Pallas*, Mrs. Kennedy; *Cupid*, Miss Storer.

The Drummer, or *The Haunted House*, by Joseph Addison

1748–49: Apr. 19, *Vellum*, Macklin; *Lady Trueman*, Mrs. Vincent; *Abigail*, Mrs. Macklin; May 23.

1749–50: Oct. 25, *Vellum*, Macklin; *Abigail*, Mrs. Macklin; Nov. 8.

A Duke and No Duke, by Nahum Tate. (Farce)

1747–48: Jan. 27, *Trappolin*, Woodward; Feb. 3, no cast.

1756–57: Jan. 5, *Trappolin*, King.

1757–58: Dec. 17, *Trappolin*, King.

The Earl of Essex, "written by Henry Brooke." The 1757–58 version may have been by Henry Jones (see Calendar Part I, p. 387).

1749–50: May 7, characters by Sheridan, Digges, Beamsley, J. Elrington, Mrs. Bland, Miss Danvers, Miss Griffith; May 18, *Essex*, Sheridan; *Southampton*, Digges; *Queen Elizabeth*, Mrs. Bland; *Rutland*, Miss Danvers; *Nottingham*, Miss Griffith; May 24.

1750–51: Oct. 31, *Essex*, Sheridan; *Southampton*, Digges; *Rutland*, Miss Danvers; *Nottingham*, Miss Griffith; *Queen Elizabeth*, Mrs. Bland; Nov. 16; Dec 3; Dec. 17; Feb. 11; Feb. 21; Apr. 23, plus *Cecil*, Beamsley; *Raleigh*, Falkner; and *Lieutenant of the Tower*, Watson; May 14.

1751–52: Nov. 15, *Essex*, Sheridan; *Southampton*, Digges; *Rutland*, Mrs. Davies; *Nottingham*, Mrs. Lee; *Queen Elizabeth*, Mrs. Bland; May 9, plus *Cecil*, Beamsley.

1752–53: May 14, *Essex*, Sheridan; *Southampton*, Digges; *Rutland*, Mrs. Ward; *Queen Elizabeth*, Mrs. Woffington (first time).

1757–58: Dec. 10, *Essex*, Sheridan; *Southampton*, Dexter; *Burleigh*, Hurst; *Nottingham*, Mrs. Kennedy; *Rutland*, Miss Kennedy; *Queen Elizabeth*, Mrs. Fitzhenry (first time); Jan. 28, but *Southampton*, Mrs. Kennedy; and plus *Raleigh*, Storer; and without *Nottingham*; Feb. 9, but *Southampton*, Dexter, and *Nottingham*, Mrs. Kennedy.

Edward the Black Prince, or *The Battle of Poictiers*, by William Shirley

1749–50: Feb. 26, *Edward* (*the Black Prince*), Sheridan; *Ribemont*, Mossop; *Arnold*, Ross; *Mariana*, Mrs. Bland; Mar. 1; Mar. 16.

The Emperor of the Moon, by Aphra Behn. The 1747–48 performance is advertised as a farce of one act; the 1756–58 performances were considered a *new* entertainment, advertised as such and as having three acts.

1747–48: Jan. 15, *Harlequin*, Woodward.

1756–57: Mar. 14, principal characters by King, Sparks, Glover, Miss Kennedy, Mrs. Kennedy; Mar. 16, *Harlequin*, King; *Scaramouch*, Sparks; *Dr. Balliardo*, Glover; *Cinthio*, Aickin; *Charmante*, Stayley; *Clerk*, Mynitt; *Officer*, Hamilton; *Elaria*, Miss Mason; *Bellemante*, Miss Kennedy; *Mopsophil*, Mrs. Kennedy; Mar. 19; Apr. 12, only *Harlequin*, *Balliardo*, *Scaramouch*, and *Bellemante* listed; May 7, plus *Cinthio*, Aickin; *Charmante*, Stayley; *Clerk*, Mynitt; *Officer*, Hamilton; *Elaria*, Miss Mason; and *Mopsophil*, Mrs. Kennedy; May 17; May 21; May 24.

1757–58: Jan. 13, *Harlequin*, King; *Scaramouch*, Sparks; *Balliardo*, Glover; *Bellemante*, Miss Kennedy; *Mopsophil*, Mrs. Kennedy; Jan. 16, plus *Charmante*, Stayley; *Cinthio*, Preston; *Officer*, Hamilton; and *Clerk*, Lewis; Jan. 19; Jan. 26; Feb. 2; Feb. 18, without *Cinthio*; Feb. 22; Mar. 8, plus *Cinthio*; Apr. 13, no cast.

The Englishman in Paris, by Samuel Foote. (Farce)

1757–58: Dec. 1, *Buck*, Foote; *Lucinda*, Miss Baker; Dec. 23, only *Buck* listed; Dec. 26, plus *Lucinda*.

The Englishman Returned from Paris, by Samuel Foote. (Farce)

1756–57: May 6, *Sir Charles Buck*, Foote; *Crab*, Heaphy; *Lord John*, Stayley; *McRuthen*, Sparks; *Tallyhoe*, Glover; *Racket*, Hamilton; *Lucinda*, Miss Kennedy; Dec. 5, only *Buck*, *Crab*, and *Lucinda* listed.

Every Man in his Humour, by Ben Jonson

1757–58: Mar. 30, *Captain Bobadil*, King (first time).

The Fair Penitent, by Nicholas Rowe

1745–46: Jan. 2, *Lothario*, Garrick; *Horatio*, Sheridan; *Sciolto*, F. Elrington; *Altamont*, Lacy; *Lavinia*, Mrs. Walter; *Calista*, Miss Bellamy; Feb. 7, *Horatio*, Sheridan; *Lothario*, Garrick; *Altamont*, Barry (who may not have performed; see next performance); Feb. 14, but *Altamont*, Barry, "being the first Time of his appearing in that Character"; Feb. 27, plus *Calista*, Miss Bellamy.

1746–47: Jan. 21, *Horatio*, Sheridan; *Calista*, Miss Bellamy; Feb. 11; Mar. 19.

1747–48: Nov. 9, *Horatio*, Sheridan; *Calista*, Miss Bellamy; Feb. 16.

1748–49: May 4, *Horatio*, Sheridan; *Sciolto*, Macklin; *Lothario*, Dyer; *Calista*, Mrs. Bland.

1749–50: Dec. 9, *Horatio*, Sheridan; *Calista*, Mrs. Bland; *Lothario*, Digges; Dec. 14; Jan. 25; Mar. 23, but *Calista*, Miss Griffith (first time); May 9, but *Calista*, Mrs. Bland; plus *Sciolto*, Beamsley; and *Altamont*, Ross.

1750–51: Mar. 1, *Horatio*, Sheridan; *Lothario*, Digges; *Sciolto*, Montgomery; *Altamont*, Ross; *Lavinia*, Miss Danvers; *Lucilla*, Miss Cole; *Calista*, Mrs. Bland.

1751–52: Oct. 21, *Horatio*, Sheridan; *Lothario*, Digges; *Sciolto*, Davies, "first Time of his appearing on this Stage"; *Lavinia*, Mrs. Davies; *Calista*, Mrs. Woffington; Jan. 23, but *Sciolto*, Beamsley; plus *Altamont*, Heaphy.

1752–53: Jan. 29, *Lothario*, by Desire, Mrs. Woffington (first time); *Horatio*, Sheridan; *Altamont*, Sowdon; *Sciolto*, Digges; *Lavinia*, Mrs. Crofts, "being the first Time of her Appearance on this Stage"; *Calista*, Mrs. Ward; Feb. 5, but *Lavinia*, Miss Mason; Feb. 26, but *Sciolto*, Layfield; May 18, but *Sciolto*, Digges; and without *Lavinia*.

1753–54: Nov. 15, *Lothario*, Mrs. Woffington; *Horatio*, Sheridan; *Sciolto*, Digges; *Altamont*, Dexter; *Lavinia*, Mrs. Pye; *Lucilla*, Mrs. Kennedy; *Calista*, Mrs. Ward; Jan. 31, plus *Rossano*, Stayley.

1756–57: Dec. 11, *Horatio*, Sheridan; *Lothario*, Lee; *Altamont*, Dexter; *Lavinia*, Miss G. Phillips; *Calista*, Miss Phillips.

1757–58: Oct. 27, *Horatio*, Sheridan; *Sciolto*, Heaphy; *Altamont*, Stayley; *Rossano*, Hurst; *Lothario*, Dexter; *Lavinia*, Miss G. Phillips; *Lucilla*, Mrs. Pye; *Calista*, Mrs. Fitzhenry; Nov. 25, but *Lavinia*, Mrs. Kennedy; Feb. 23, but *Horatio*, Hurst; *Lavinia*, Miss G. Phillips; and *Calista*, Mrs. Beauclerk; Apr. 20, but *Calista*, Miss Taylor (first time); June 1, *Horatio*, Sheridan; *Sciolto*, Heaphy; *Altamont*, Stayley; *Rossano*, Preston; *Lothario*, Dexter; *Lavinia*, Miss Kennedy; *Lucilla*, Mrs. Pye; *Calista*, Mrs. Fitzhenry.

The Fair Quaker of Deal, by Charles Shadwell

1756–57: Apr. 12, *Beau Mizen*, King; *Worthy*, Stayley; *Sir Charles Pleasant*, Glover; *Rovewell*, with Songs, Wilder; *Flip*, Sparks; *Coxen*, Layfield; *Arabella Zeal*, Mrs. Kennedy; *Jenny Private*, Mrs. Pye; *Belinda*, Miss G. Phillips; *Fair Quaker*, Mrs. Wilder; May 7, but *Belinda*, Miss Mason; and plus *Easy*, Aickin; *Indent*, Watson; *Scruple*, Mynitt; *1st sailor*, Hamilton; *2nd sailor*, Messink; *3d sailor*, Bate; *4th sailor*, Williams;

Jiltup, Miss Wells; *Advocate*, Mrs. Packenham; and *Barmaid*, Mrs. Butler; May 21, plus *Cribbage*, Hurst.

1757–58: Oct. 10, *Beau Mizen*, King; *Worthy*, Stayley; *Sir Charles Pleasant*, Kennedy; *Cribbage*, Hurst; *Rovewell*, with Songs, Wilder; *Indent*, Watson; *Flip*, Sparks; *Coxen*, Glover; *1st sailor*, Hamilton; *2nd sailor*, Messink; *3d sailor*, Bate; *4th sailor*, Williams; *Arabella Zeal*, Mrs. Kennedy; *Advocate*, Mrs. Packenham; *Fair Quaker*, Mrs. Wilder; Oct. 12; Nov. 30, plus *Jenny Private*, Mrs. Pye; *Belinda*, Miss Kennedy; Mar. 8, but *3d sailor*, Oliver; and without *Advocate*.

Fairy Friendship, or *The Triumph of Hibernia*, by Henry Woodward. (Pantomime Entertainment)

1747–48: Feb. 15, no cast; Feb. 16; Mar. 1; May 20.

The Fatal Marriage, or *The Innocent Adultery*, by Thomas Southerne. (See also *Isabella*.)

1751–52: May 30, *Biron*, Digges; *Carlos*, Cibber; *Frederick*, King; *Villeroy*, Heaphy; *Count Baldwin*, Beamsley; *Fernando*, Mynitt; *Fabian*, Falkner; *Jaqueline*, Stevens; *Sampson*, Sparks; *Victoria*, Mrs. Bland; *Julia*, Mrs. Davies; *Nurse*, Mrs. Mynitt; *Isabella*, Mrs. Woffington; *Young Biron*, Master Mynitt.

1752–53: Oct. 27, *Villeroy*, Sowdon; *Biron*, Digges; *Isabella*, Mrs. Woffington; Mar. 26, plus *Carlos*, King, and *Count Baldwin*, Layfield; May 25, plus *Frederick*, Stayley; *Fernando*, Mynitt; *Sampson*, Sparks; *Young Biron*, Master Mynitt; *Victoria*, Mrs. Kennedy; *Julia*, Miss Mason; and *Nurse*, Mrs. Mynitt.

1753–54: Jan. 17, *Villeroy*, Sowdon; *Biron*, Digges; *Carlos*, King; *Count Baldwin*, Layfield; *Frederick*, Stayley; *Fernando*, Mynitt; *Sampson*, Sparks; *Fabian*, Hull; *Belford*, Watson; *Officer*, Williams; *Pedro*, Maurice; *Jaqueline*, Green; *Young Biron*, Master Pye; *Victoria*, Mrs. Kennedy; *Julia*, Miss Mason; *Nurse*, Mrs. Mynitt; *Isabella*, Mrs. Woffington.

1756–57: Apr. 18, *Biron*, Dexter; *Count Baldwin*, Layfield; *Villeroy*, Heaphy; *Carlos*, King; *Frederick*, Stayley; *Fabian*, Hurst; *Jaqueline*, Glover; *Belford*, Watson; *Officer*, Hamilton; *Sampson*, Sparks; *Victoria*, Miss Kennedy; *Julia*, Miss Mason; *Nurse*, Mrs. Mynitt; *Isabella*, Mrs. Kennedy.

Flora, or *The Country Wake*, or *Hob in the Well*, from Colley Cibber's *Hob*, or *The Country Wake*. (Ballad Farce)

1747–48: Mar. 10, *Hob*, Layfield, "as he originally performed it in this Kingdom"; Apr. 22, but *Hob*, Woodward.

1748–49: Nov. 16, no cast; Jan. 9.
1750–51: Oct. 1, *Flora,* Miss Cole; *Friendly,* Ross; *Hob,* Sparks; *Sir Thomas Testy,* Mynitt; *Old Hob,* Beamsley; *Dick,* Robertson; *Hob's Mother,* Mrs. Mynitt; Oct. 10, only *Flora, Friendly,* and *Hob* listed.
1753–54: Jan. 11, *Hob,* Sparks; *Friendly,* Kennedy; *Old Hob,* Layfield; *Hob's Mother,* Mrs. Mynitt; *Flora,* Mrs. Pye [on the playbill "Mrs. Pye" is crossed out and "Mrs. Storer" written in by hand].
1756–57: Nov. 15, *Hobby,* Sparks.
1757–58: Feb. 10, no cast; Mar. 4, *Hob,* Sparks; *Friendly,* Corry; *Flora,* Mrs. Storer.

Florizel and Perdita, by David Garrick. (Dramatic Pastoral)
1756–57: Jan. 14, *Florizel,* Dexter; *Autolicus* (*the Ballad Singing Pedlar*), King; *Perdita,* Mrs. Kennedy; Jan. 24; Mar. 26, but *Perdita,* Miss Phillips, "in which she will attempt a Song sung by Mrs. Cibber in that Character"; Apr. 18, but *Perdita,* Mrs. Kennedy.
1757–58: Nov. 9, *Florizel,* Dexter; *Autolicus* (*the Ballad Singing Pedlar*), King; *Perdita,* Miss Kennedy; Nov. 25; Feb. 6; Feb. 23; Mar. 13, no cast; Mar. 27.

The Formation of Harlequin. (An Entertainment in Grotesque Characters. The Music all Irish Tunes)
1757–58: Apr. 4, *Harlequin,* King; *Hecate,* Wilder; *Clown,* Sparks; *Witches,* Hamilton, Storer, Messink, Mrs. Pye, Miss Wells, &c.; *Columbine,* with a Variety of Songs, Mrs. Wilder; *Bacchus,* Tioli; *Theseus,* Harvey; *Savages,* Garman, Rayner, Welch, Masset; *Phaedra,* Signora Ricci; *Ariadne,* Miss Baker.

The Foundling, "written by Mr. [Edward] Moore, Author of Fables for the Female Sex"
1747–48: Apr. 28, *Faddle,* Woodward.
1748–49: Mar. 10, *Faddle,* Macklin; *Rosetta,* Mrs. Bland; *Fidelia,* "with the Original Song in Character," Mrs. Mozeen; Apr. 6, but *Fidelia,* by Desire, to be attempted by Miss Bourne.
1752–53: Apr. 12, *Sir Charles Raymond,* Sowdon; *Faddle,* King; *Belmont,* Heaphy; *Col. Raymond,* Kennedy; *Villiard,* Layfield; *Fidelia,* Miss Baker; *Rosetta,* Mrs. Woffington.
1753–54: Mar. 1, *Sir Charles Raymond,* Sowdon; *Faddle,* King; *Belmont,* Heaphy; *Sir Roger Belmont,* Sparks; *Col. Raymond,* Kennedy; *Villiard,* Layfield; *Fidelia,* Miss Baker; *Rosetta,* Mrs. Woffington.

The Funeral, or *Grief-a-la-Mode,* by Sir Richard Steele

1745–46: Feb. 6, *Lady Brumpton,* Mrs. Furnival.
1750–51: May 13, *Lord Hardy,* Digges; *Lord Brumpton,* Montgomery; *Campley,* King; *Trim,* Cibber; *Cabinet,* Ross; *Sable,* Sparks; *Puzzle,* Bardin; *Tom,* Hamilton; *Trusty,* Sheridan; *Lady Charlotte,* Miss Cole; *Lady Harriet,* Mrs. Lindley; *Madem. D'Epingle,* Mrs. Rowley; *Kate Matchlock,* Mr. Mynitt; *Tattleaid,* Mrs. Mynitt; *Lady Brumpton,* Mrs. Bland.
1752–53: Dec. 22, *Lord Hardy,* Digges; *Trim,* King; *Sable,* Sparks; *Lord Brumpton,* Heaphy; *Trusty,* Layfield; *Lady Charlotte,* Mrs. Ward; *Lady Harriet,* Mrs. Green; *Lady Brumpton,* Mrs. Woffington; Feb. 16, plus *Campley,* Kennedy.
1753–54: Feb. 15, *Lord Hardy,* Sowdon; *Trim,* King; *Campley,* Dexter; *Lord Brumpton,* Heaphy; *Trusty,* Layfield; *Sable,* Sparks; *Lord Hardy,* Digges; *Puzzle,* Green; *Fardingale,* Mrs. Kennedy [Mrs. Cunningham in the playbill]; *Lady Charlotte,* Mrs. Ward; *Lady Harriet,* Mrs. Green; *Tattleaid,* Mrs. Mynitt; *Madem. D'Epingle,* Mrs. Pye; *Lady Brumpton,* Mrs. Woffington.

The Gamester, by Susannah Centlivre

1757–58: Dec. 15, principal characters by Dexter, King, Sparks, Mrs. Kennedy, Miss Kennedy; Jan. 12.

The Gentleman Gardener, "taken from the French of Dancourt by the late C. Johnson Esq." (Ballad Opera)

1750–51: May 17, *Colin,* Ross; *Sir Jefferey Addlehead,* Sparks; *Sir Jasper Freeman,* Mynitt; *Evergreen,* Messink; *Frisk,* Bardin; *Sham,* Hamilton; *Harriet,* Mrs. Crump; *Kitty,* Miss Cole.

Hamlet, by William Shakespeare

1745–46: Nov. 7, *Hamlet,* Sheridan; *Polonius,* Morris, "being the first Time of his appearing these two Years"; *Laertes,* Lacy [?]; *Ophelia,* Mrs. Storer; *Queen,* Mrs. Furnival; Dec. 9, but *Hamlet,* Garrick, and *Laertes,* Lacy; and plus *Gravediggers,* Layfield and Morgan; Mar. 13, only *Hamlet,* Sheridan, listed; Apr. 3, *Hamlet,* Garrick; *Ghost* to be performed by a Gentleman.
1746–47: Nov. 20, *Hamlet,* Sheridan; Apr. 6; May 27.
1747–48: Nov. 16, *Hamlet,* Sheridan; Dec. 9, plus *Polonius,* Woodward; Mar. 4, without *Polonius.*

1748–49: Nov. 21, *Hamlet*, Sheridan; *Queen*, Mrs. Bland; *Ophelia*, Mrs. Vincent; *Gravedigger*, Macklin; Jan. 23, only *Hamlet* and *Gravedigger* listed.

1749–50: Oct. 2, *Hamlet*, Sheridan; *Gravedigger*, Macklin; Nov. 27, plus *Queen*, Mrs. Bland, and *Ophelia*, Mrs. Mozeen; Feb 5; Mar. 7, but *Hamlet*, Digges (first time).

1750–51: Oct. 26, *Hamlet*, Sheridan; *Osrick*, King; *Gravedigger*, Sparks; *Laertes*, Ross; *Queen*, Mrs. Bland; *Ophelia*, Miss Cole; *Ghost*, Digges (first time); Dec. 7, plus *Polonius*, Cibber; and without *Gravedigger* and *Laertes*.

1751–52: Nov. 21, *Hamlet*, Sheridan; *Ghost*, Digges; *Polonius*, Cibber; *Osrick*, King; *Gravedigger*, Sparks; *Ophelia*, Miss Cole; *Queen*, Mrs. Bland; Jan. 27.

1752–53: Nov. 6, *Hamlet*, Sheridan; *Ghost*, Digges; *Osrick*, King; *Gravedigger*, Sparks; *Ophelia*, Mrs. Donaldson (first time); *Queen*, Mrs. Woffington; Jan. 26, plus *King*, Layfield; and *Laertes*, Heaphy; Apr. 2, but *Hamlet*, Digges; and *Ghost*, Heaphy; and without *Laertes*.

1753–54: Nov. 14, *Hamlet*, Sheridan; *Ghost*, Digges; *Osrick*, King; *King*, Layfield; *Laertes*, Heaphy; *Ophelia*, Mrs. Storer; *Queen*, Mrs. Woffington; Feb. 11, plus *Polonius*, Mynitt; *Gravedigger*, Sparks; and *Horatio*, J. Elrington; Feb. 28.

1756–57: Oct. 29, *Hamlet*, Sheridan; Dec. 1, plus *Osrick*, Glover; *First Gravedigger*, Sparks; *Ophelia*, Miss Kennedy; *Queen*, Mrs. Kennedy; Jan. 31, but *Osrick*, King; and *Ophelia*, Mrs. Wilder; and plus *Polonius*, Glover; Mar. 12; May 27, only *Hamlet* listed.

1757–58: Oct. 24, *Hamlet*, Sheridan; *Ghost*, Heaphy; *King*, Hurst; *Horatio*, Kennedy; *Laertes*, Stayley; *Rosincrans*, Watson; *Guildenstern*, Davenport; *Polonius*, Glover; *Francisco*, Williams; *Marcellus*, Wall; *Player King*, Lewis; *Osrick*, King; *Priest*, R. Elrington; *Sailor*, Messink; *First Gravedigger*, Sparks; *Second Gravedigger*, Hamilton; *Bernardo*, Corry; *Ophelia*, Miss Kennedy; *Player Queen*, Mrs. Pye; *Queen*, Mrs. Kennedy; Nov. 17, but *Queen*, Mrs. Fitzhenry; and without *Marcellus*; Feb. 6, *Hamlet*, Sheridan; *Ghost*, Heaphy; *Polonius*, Glover; *Osrick*, King; *Gravedigger*, Sparks; *Ophelia*, Miss Kennedy; *Queen*, Mrs. Fitzhenry; June 3, plus *King*, Hurst; *Horatio*, Ryder; *Laertes*, Stayley; *Second Gravedigger*, Hamilton; *Bernardo*, Corry; and *Player Queen*, Mrs. Pye.

Harlequin Captive in Spain (Pantomime Entertainment)
1756–57: May 3, *Harlequin*, Maranesi; *Colombine*, Mrs. Kennedy;

Sancho, Glover; May 12, but *Colombine,* by particular Desire, Signora Bugiani; and without *Sancho;* May 14, plus *Clown [Sancho?],* Glover; May 27, *Harlequin,* Maranesi; *Colombine,* Signora Bugiani.

Harlequin Dr. Faustus (see *The Necromancer*)

Harlequin Ranger, by Henry Woodward. (Pantomime)
1751–52: May 15, *Harlequin Ranger,* King; *Mr. Strictland,* Falkner; *Constable,* Longfield; *Lawyer,* Maurice; *Lamp-lighter,* Messink; *Sharper,* Stevens; *Taylor,* Packenham; *Taylor's Man,* Hamilton; *Tester,* Williams; *Ranger's servant,* Sparks; *Miller,* with a Song in Character, Conyers; *Savoyards* by McNeil and Miss Baker; *Lucetta,* Mrs. Kennedy; *Milliner,* Mrs. Crump; *Mrs. Strictland,* Miss Cole; May 26, only *Harlequin Ranger* listed.

Harlequin Skeleton (see *Trick Upon Trick*)

Hob in the Well (see *Flora*)

The Honest Yorkshireman, by Henry Carey. (Farce)
1748–49: Mar. 29, no cast.
1749–50: Nov. 13, *Gaylove,* Ross; *Arabella,* Mrs. Storer; *Combrush,* Mrs. Bland; Dec. 18, without *Gaylove;* Feb. 12, only *Combrush* listed; Mar. 19, plus *Arabella;* Apr. 4; Apr. 6; Apr. 27; May 9, plus *Sapscull,* Hamilton; May 17, without *Sapscull.*
1750–51: Sept. 26, *Arabella,* Miss Cole; *Combrush,* Mrs. Bland; Oct. 25, plus *Gaylove,* Ross; May 6, plus *Blunder,* Sparks.
1751–52: Apr. 29, no cast.
1752–53: Dec. 22, *Gaylove,* Sullivan; *Arabella,* Mrs. Donaldson; *Combrush,* Mrs. Green; Apr. 2, only *Combrush* listed; Apr. 13; Apr. 26, plus *Arabella,* Mrs. Crump; May 25, plus *Blunder,* Sparks.
1753–54: Oct. 1, *Combrush,* Mrs. Green; *Arabella,* Mrs. Storer; Jan. 28; Feb. 9; Feb. 18.
1756–57: Mar. 29, *Gaylove,* Wilder; *Arabella,* Mrs. Wilder; *Combrush,* Miss Kennedy (first time).
1757–58: Nov. 14, *Gaylove,* Wilder; *Sapscull,* Hamilton; *Blunder,* Glover; *Slango,* Williams; *Muckworm,* Lewis; *Combrush,* Miss Kennedy; *Arabella,* Mrs. Storer; Nov. 30, no cast; Feb. 15, *Gaylove,* Wilder; *Sapscull,* Hamilton; *Blunder,* Glover; *Combrush,* Miss Kennedy; *Arabella,* Mrs. Storer; Apr. 15, no cast.

The Humorous Trial of Ananias Overdone, Swadler. The second and last performance, May 5, was advertised as "The Trial of Ananias Overdone, and the Examination of the Theatrical Disturbers."

1752–53: Apr. 25, *Ananias*, Stevens; May 5, *Ananias*, Stevens; *Attorney General*, Heaphy; *Counsel*, pro and con, Costollo; *Lady Loudlaugh*, Mrs. Kennedy; *Tom Tipple*, Pitt; *the Jury* to be performed by the Pit; *Lord Chief Joker*, Sparks.

The Humours of an Election, or *Who Bids for a Borough?* "Written by the Author of Tom Jones"

1749–50: Mar. 12, *Trapwit*, Cibber.

The Hussar

1745–46: May 26, *Pierrot*, Morris.

The Inconstant, or *The Way to Win Him*, "by [George] Farquhar"

1750–51: May 15, *Young Mirabel*, Montgomery, "his first Attempt in Comedy"; *Old Mirabel*, Sparks; *Dugard*, Falkner; *Petit*, Hamilton; *Duretete*, Cibber; *Oriana*, Miss Cole; *Lamorce*, Mrs. Lindley; *Bisarre*, Mrs. Bland; May 24, plus *Bravoes*, Maurice, Messink, Williams, and Packenham.

1751–52: Jan. 3, *Young Mirabel*, King; *Duretete*, Cibber; *Old Mirabel*, Sparks; *Dugard*, Falkner; *Petit*, Hamilton; *Bisarre*, Mrs. Lee; *Lamorce*, Mrs. Rowley; *Oriana*, Miss Cole; May 26, but *Young Mirabel*, Montgomery; and *Bisarre*, Mrs. Bland.

1756–57: Nov. 8, *Young Mirabel*, Dexter; *Duretete*, King; *Old Mirabel*, Sparks; *Oriana*, Mrs. Kennedy; *Bisarre*, Miss Kennedy.

The Intriguing Chambermaid, by Henry Fielding. (Comedy of Two Acts)

1747–48: Dec. 2, *Drunken Bully* (*Colonel*), Woodward; *Chambermaid* (*Lettice*), Miss Pitt; Dec. 11; Jan. 1; Feb. 27; Mar. 16, no cast.

1748–49: Oct. 10, *Drunken Colonel*, Macklin; Oct. 11.

1750–51: Mar. 11, *Drunken Colonel*, King; *Oldcastle*, Sparks; *Lettice*, Miss Cole.

1751–52: Feb. 3, *Drunken Colonel*, King; *Oldcastle*, Sparks; *Lettice*, Miss Cole; Mar. 11, only *Drunken Colonel* listed.

1752–53: Nov. 22, *Drunken Colonel*, King; *Lettice*, Mrs. Green; Dec. 14, plus *Oldcastle*, Sparks; Apr. 30, plus *Old Goodall*, Mynitt.

Isabella, "as Lately altered by Mr. Garrick from the Fatal Marriage or Innocent Adultery" (see *The Fatal Marriage*)

1757–58: Mar. 27, *Biron*, Dexter; *Isabella*, Mrs. Fitzhenry (first time); Apr. 10; May 15, plus *Villeroy*, Heaphy; *Count Baldwin*, Hurst; *Carlos*, King; *Sampson*, Sparks; and *Nurse*, Mrs. Farrell.

Jack the Giant Queller, "written by Henry Brooke, Esq." (Operatical Play of Five Acts)

1748–49: Mar. 27, *Jack*, Mrs. Lampe; *Galligantes (or Power)*, the first Giant, Morris; *Rumbo (or Violence)*, the second Giant, Sparks; *Blunderbore (or Wrong)*, the third Giant, Barrington; *Plutus* and *the Prince*, Dyer; *Dorothy Good, Mother to Jack*, Mrs. Vincent; *Gracey Good, sister to Jack*, Mrs. Mozeen; *Gillyflower the Princess*, Mrs. Storer. With *Beggars, Courtiers, Ladies, &c.*

1756–57: Mar. 3, principal characters by Wilder, King, Sparks, Glover, Layfield, Mrs. Pye, Miss Wells, Mrs. Wilder; Mar. 7; Mar. 9; Apr. 19.

Jane Shore, by Nicholas Rowe.

1745–46: Apr. 7, *Jane Shore*, Miss Bellamy; *Dumont*, Sheridan (first time); Apr. 26, *Hastings*, Garrick; *Dumont*, Barry (first time); *Gloster*, Beamsley; *Alicia*, Mrs. Furnival; *Jane Shore*, Miss Bellamy.

1746–47: Nov. 13, *Dumont*, Sheridan; *Jane Shore*, Miss Bellamy; Jan. 2.

1749–50: Jan. 18, *Dumont*, Sheridan; *Hastings*, Digges; *Gloster*, Mossop; *Jane Shore*, Miss Danvers; *Alicia*, Mrs. Bland; Jan. 23; Jan. 31; Mar. 21.

1750–51: Oct. 24, *Dumont*, Sheridan; *Hastings*, Digges; *Gloster*, Mossop; *Jane Shore*, Miss Danvers; *Alicia*, Mrs. Bland; Mar. 19, *Hastings*, Digges; *Gloster*, Beamsley; *Dumont*, Ross; *Jane Shore*, Miss Griffith; *Alicia*, Mrs. Bland.

1751–52: Oct. 14, *Dumont*, Sheridan; *Hastings*, Digges; *Alicia*, Mrs. Bland; *Jane Shore*, Mrs. Woffington; Jan. 16; Apr. 11, but *Dumont*, Heaphy; and plus *Gloster*, Beamsley, and *Bellmour*, J. Elrington.

1752–53: Feb. 19, *Hastings*, Sheridan (first time); *Gloster*, Sowdon; *Shore (Dumont)*, Digges; *Jane Shore*, Mrs. Ward; *Alicia*, Mrs. Woffington (first time); Feb. 28, but *Shore (Dumont)*, Heaphy; and plus *Bellmour*, J. Elrington; May 2, but *Hastings*, Digges; June 6, *Hastings*, Sheridan; *Gloster*, Sowdon; *Dumont*, Digges; *Jane Shore*, Mrs. Ward; *Alicia*, Mrs. Woffington.

1753–54: Oct. 11, *Hastings*, Sheridan; *Gloster*, Sowdon; *Dumont*, Digges; *Jane Shore*, Mrs. Ward; *Alicia*, Mrs. Woffington.

1756–57: Nov. 24, *Dumont*, Sheridan; *Hastings*, Lee (first time); *Alicia*, Mrs. Kennedy; *Jane Shore*, a young Lady; Nov. 29; May 10, *Hastings*, Lee; *Gloster*, Layfield; *Bellmour*, Heaphy; *Catesby*, Stayley; *Ratcliffe*, Watson; *Dumont*, Dexter; *Alicia*, Miss G. Phillips (first time); *Jane Shore*, Miss Phillips.

1757–58: Nov. 9, *Shore* (*Dumont*), Sheridan; *Gloster*, Stayley; *Catesby*, Hurst; *Ratcliffe*, Watson; *Bellmour*, Heaphy; *Earl of Derby*, Davenport; *Hastings*, Dexter; *Jane Shore*, Miss Phillips; *Alicia*, Mrs. Fitzhenry; Feb. 25, *Hastings*, Wilkinson; *Bellmour*, Heaphy; *Gloster*, Stayley; *Shore*, Dexter; *Jane Shore*, Miss Phillips; *Alicia*, Mrs. Fitzhenry; Apr. 5, *Hastings*, Dexter; *Gloster*, Stayley; *Bellmour*, Hurst; *Shore*, Heaphy; *Alicia*, Mrs. Kennedy; *Jane Shore*, Mrs. Fitzhenry.

Julius Caesar, by William Shakespeare.

1745–46: Nov. 25, *Brutus*, Sheridan; *Calphurnia*, Mrs. Elmy; *Portia*, Mrs. Furnival; *Cassius*, R. Elrington; *Antony*, Barry; Apr. 17, but *Brutus*, Sheridan, "being particularly desired."

1748–49: Feb 20, *Brutus*, Sheridan.

1749–50: Dec. 23, *Brutus*, Sheridan; *Cassius*, Mossop [but N.B. "Mr. Mossop is prevented from appearing in the Character of Cassius by a sudden Indisposition"]; *Antony*, Digges; Jan. 8, plus *Cassius*, Mossop, and *Portia*, Mrs. Bland; Jan. 12; Jan. 15; Apr. 18, but *Cassius*, Ross; and without *Portia*.

1750–51: Nov. 7, *Brutus*, Sheridan; *Antony*, Digges; *Portia*, Mrs. Bland.

1752–53: Dec. 18, *Brutus*, Sheridan; *Cassius*, Sowdon; *Antony*, Digges; *Portia*, Mrs. Woffington.

1753–54: Feb. 25, *Brutus*, Sheridan; *Cassius*, Sowdon; *Antony*, Digges; *Caesar*, J. Elrington; *Casca*, Layfield; *Octavius Caesar*, Heaphy; *Decius Brutus*, Kennedy; *Citizens*, Sparks, Cunningham, Mynitt, and others; *Calphurnia*, Miss Mason; *Portia*, Mrs. Woffington.

1756–57: Feb. 21, *Brutus*, Sheridan; *Cassius*, Lee; *Antony*, Dexter; *1st citizen*, Sparks; *2d citizen*, Glover; *Calphurnia*, Miss Kennedy; *Portia*, Miss Phillips.

1757–58: May 4, *Brutus*, Sheridan; *Cassius*, Hurst; *Caesar*, Heaphy; *Antony*, Dexter; *Portia*, Mrs. Fitzhenry.

The King and the Miller of Mansfield (see *The Miller of Mansfield*)

King Arthur. "The Words by Dryden. The Musick by Purcel." (Dramatic Opera)

1749–50: Mar. 17, no cast; Mar. 24; Mar. 29; Apr. 7; Apr. 21;
May 5; May 19; May 26.

1752–53: Mar. 20, *King Arthur*, Heaphy; *Osmond*, Sparks; *Philidel*,
with Songs, Mrs. Donaldson; *Shepherd*, Sullivan; *Venus*, Mrs.
Crump; *Emmeline*, Mrs. Ward. Vocal Parts, Mrs. Donaldson, Sullivan, Mrs. Crump, Layfield, and others; Mar. 27;
Apr. 14.

King Henry IV (Part 1), by William Shakespeare

1745–46: Feb. 17, *Falstaff*, "at the particular Desire of several Gentle-
men and Ladies," Pinchbeck; *Hotspur*, Barry; *Lady Percy*,
Miss Bellamy; Apr. 30, but *Falstaff*, Morris; and without
Lady Percy.

1746–47: Nov. 24, *Falstaff*, Sheridan (first time); Jan. 5, "By the
Desire of several Ladies and Gentlemen who were not present
at the last Representation of the first Part of Henry the 4th,
Mr. Sheridan intends once more to play the Character of
Falstaff. . . ."

1748–49: Feb. 27, *Falstaff*, Sheridan; *Hostess*, Mrs. Macklin; Apr. 18,
Falstaff, Sparks; *King Henry*, J. Elrington; *Prince of Wales*,
Dyer; *Hotspur*, R. Elrington; *Worcester*, Beamsley; *Carriers*,
Barrington and Mynitt; *Lady Percy*, Mrs. Mozeen.

1749–50: Feb. 12, *Falstaff*, Sheridan; *Hostess*, Mrs. Macklin.

1750–51: Jan. 11, *Hotspur*, Mossop; *Prince of Wales*, King; *Falstaff*,
Sparks; *Hostess*, Mrs. Mynitt; *Lady Percy*, Miss Cole.

1751–52: June 9, *Falstaff*, "to be attempted by Mr. Tracy"; *Hotspur*,
Davies; *King Henry*, J. Elrington; *Prince of Wales*, Kennedy;
Worcester, Beamsley; *Lancaster*, Master Elrington; *Vernon*,
Longfield; *Douglas*, Hamilton; *Carrier*, Mynitt; *Blunt*, Falk-
ner; *Westmoreland*, Watson; *Francis*, Williams; *Lady Percy*,
Mrs. Rowley; *Hostess*, Mrs. Mynitt.

1756–57: Nov. 19, *Hotspur*, Lee; *Prince of Wales*, Dexter; *Falstaff*,
Sparks; *Lady Percy*, Miss Kennedy; Dec. 10.

1757–58: Jan. 6, *Falstaff*, Mr. Grey Townsend.

King Henry IV (Part 2), by William Shakespeare

1749–50: May 14, *Pistol*, Cibber; *King Henry*, Sheridan; *Prince of
Wales*, Digges; *Falstaff*, Sparks.

King Henry V, by William Shakespeare

1748–49: Apr. 8, *King Henry*, Sheridan; *Hostess*, Mrs. Macklin; *Fluellen*, Macklin; *French Queen*, Mrs. Bland; *Pistol*, Dyer; *Macmorris*, Barrington; *Jamy*, Sparks; Apr. 14, without *French
Queen* and *Jamy*.

1749–50: Feb. 19, *King Henry*, Sheridan; *Fluellen*, Macklin; *Pistol*,

Cibber; *Princess Catherine*, Mrs. Mozeen; *Macmorris*, Sparks; *Hostess*, Mrs. Macklin.

King Henry VIII, by William Shakespeare

1751–52: May 13, *Wolsey*, Cibber; *Buckingham*, Digges; *Surrey*, King; *Lord Sands*, Sparks; *Cromwell*, Heaphy; *King Henry*, Stevens; *Anna Bullen*, Mrs. Davies; *Queen Catherine*, Mrs. Woffington; May 21; May 28.

1752–53: Nov. 20, *Wolsey*, Sheridan; *King Henry*, Sowdon; *Buckingham*, Digges; *Queen Catherine*, Mrs. Woffington; Nov. 23; Dec. 1; Dec. 15; Jan. 24, plus *Anna Bullen*, by a young lady who never yet made her appearance on any stage; *Surrey*, King; and *Lord Sands*, Sparks. Apr. 23, *King Henry*, Sowdon; *Wolsey*, Digges (first time); *Surrey*, King; *Buckingham*, Kennedy; *Cranmer*, Layfield; *Cromwell*, Heaphy; *Lord Chamberlain*, Green; *Lord Chancellor*, J. Elrington; *Norfolk*, Stayley; *Lord Sands*, Sparks; *Marchioness of Dorset*, Mrs. Mynitt; *Anna Bullen*, Mrs. Ward (first time); *Patience*, with a Song in Character, Mrs. Donaldson; *Queen Catherine*, Mrs. Woffington.

1753–54: Dec. 8, *Wolsey*, Sheridan; *King Henry*, Sowdon; *Buckingham*, Digges; *Surrey*, King; *Lord Sands*, Sparks; *Cromwell*, Heaphy; *Cranmer*, Layfield; *Patience*, with a Song, Mrs. Storer; *Queen Catherine*, Mrs. Woffington; Feb. 4, plus *Norfolk*, Stayley; and *Anna Bullen*, Mrs. Ward.

1757–58: Apr. 8, *Wolsey*, Sheridan; *Norfolk*, Stayley; *Suffolk*, Watson; *Abergavenny*, R. Elrington; *King Henry*, Sparks; *Surrey*, King; *Lord Sands*, Wilder; *Cromwell*, Heaphy; *Lord Chamberlain*, Kennedy; *Surveyor*, Hurst; *Guildford*, Corry; *Buckingham*, Dexter; *Lovell*, Hamilton; *Winchester*, Storer; *Dr. Butts*, Lewis; *Cranmer*, Glover; *Patience*, with a Song in Character, Mrs. Storer; *Anna Bullen*, Miss Kennedy; *Queen Catherine*, Mrs. Fitzhenry; May 2, but *Surrey*, Wilder; and *Lord Sands*, King.

King John, "as written originally by Shakespear"

1745–46: Feb. 5, *King John*, Garrick; *Bastard*, Sheridan (first time); *Constance*, Mrs. Furnival.

1747–48: Mar. 3, *Bastard*, Sheridan; *Constance*, Miss Bellamy.

1749–50: Apr. 4, *King John*, Mossop; *Constance*, Mrs. Bland; *Bastard*, Sheridan; May 2, plus *Hubert*, Beamsley; *Prince Arthur*, Master Elrington; *Blanch*, Mrs. Mozeen; and *Lady Faulconbridge*, Mrs. Mynitt.

1751–52: Oct. 25, *Bastard*, Sheridan; *King John*, Davies; *Hubert*, Heaphy; *Prince Arthur*, Miss Reynolds; *Constance*, Mrs.

Woffington; Nov. 23, but *King John,* Digges; Dec. 5; Dec. 16; Feb. 24, only *Bastard, King John,* and *Constance* listed.

1752–53: Apr. 30, *Bastard,* Sowdon; *King John,* Digges; *Prince Arthur,* Master Mynitt; *Lady Faulconbridge,* Mrs. Mynitt; *Constance,* Mrs. Woffington.

1757–58: Jan. 23, *King John,* Dexter; *Prince Henry,* Hamilton; *Hubert,* Hurst; *Salisbury,* Stayley; *Pembroke,* R. Elrington; *Faulconbridge,* Williams; *Bastard,* Heaphy; *Austria,* Preston; *Melun,* Watson; *King of France,* Wilder; *Dauphin,* Kennedy; *Citizen of Angiers,* Storer; *Cardinal Pandulph,* Glover; *Prince Arthur,* Miss Storer; *Blanch,* Miss Mason; *Lady Faulconbridge,* Mrs. Pye; *Constance,* Mrs. Fitzhenry; Apr. 21, but *Lady Faulconbridge,* Mrs. Godwin.

King Lear, "written by Shakespear, revised by Tate"

1745–46: Jan. 13, *Lear,* Garrick; *Edgar,* Barry (first time); *Goneril,* Mrs. Furnival; *Cordelia,* Miss Bellamy; Jan. 31, no cast; Mar. 14, *Lear,* Garrick; *Edgar,* Barry; *Cordelia,* Miss Bellamy; Apr. 23, plus *Goneril,* Mrs. Furnival; and *Regan,* Mrs. Storer.

1746–47: June 18, *Lear,* Sheridan; *Cordelia,* Miss Bellamy.

1749–50: Dec. 16, *Lear,* Digges; *Cordelia,* Miss Griffith; Dec. 22; Jan. 26; Feb. 27; May 22.

1750–51: Oct. 1, *Lear,* Digges; *Cordelia,* Miss Griffith; *Gentleman Usher,* Cibber; *Gloster,* Bardin; *Edgar,* R. Elrington; *Bastard,* Ross; *Kent,* Beamsley; *Goneril,* Mrs. Mynitt; *Regan,* Mrs. Rowley; Jan. 17; Mar. 22, without *Kent.*

1756–57: Nov. 3, *Lear,* Lee.

1757–58: Apr. 29, *Lear,* Sheridan; *Edgar,* Dexter; *Kent,* Sparks; *Gloster,* Stayley; *Cornwall,* Hurst; *Albany,* Watson; *Burgundy,* R. Elrington; *Old Man,* Lewis; *Bastard,* Heaphy; *Gentleman Usher,* King; *Goneril,* Mrs. Kennedy; *Regan,* Mrs. Pye; *Aranthe,* Miss Mason; *Cordelia,* Mrs. Fitzhenry (first time); May 24.

King Richard III (see *Richard III*)

The Knights, by Samuel Foote. (Farce)
1756–57: May 9, *Hartop,* Foote; May 16.
1757–58: Nov. 24, *Hartop,* Foote.

Lady Jane Grey, by Nicholas Rowe
1750–51: Jan. 31, *Lord Guilford Dudley,* Digges; *Pembroke,* Mossop; *Northumberland,* Montgomery; *Gardiner,* Cibber; *Lady Jane*

Grey, Mrs. Bland; Feb. 7; Feb. 18; May 25, but *Pembroke*, Sheridan (first time).

1751–52: Oct. 2, *Pembroke*, Sheridan; *Lord Guilford Dudley*, Digges; *Bishop of Winchester (Gardiner)*, Cibber; *Lady Jane Grey*, Mrs. Bland; Oct. 24, but *Lady Jane*, Mrs. Woffington.

Lady Moore, or *The Dragoness of Wantley*, "being the Sequel to the Dragon of Wantley by the same Author [Henry Carey], and set to Musick by Mr. Lampe"

1748–49: Jan. 27, *Moore*, Sullivan; *Gubbins*, Morris; *Mauxalinda*, Mrs. Mozeen; *Lady Moore*, Mrs. Lampe; Feb. 2; Feb. 6; Feb. 13; Mar. 6; Mar. 8; Apr. 10, no cast.

1749–50: Mar. 2, no cast; Mar. 30, *Moore*, Sullivan; *Gubbins*, Messink; *Mauxalinda*, Mrs. Mozeen; *Lady Moore*, Mrs. Lampe; Apr. 3; May 24, without *Gubbins*.

The Lady's Last Stake, by Colley Cibber

1753–54: Dec. 1, *Lord George Brilliant*, Sheridan; *Lord Wronglove*, Sowdon; *Sir Friendly Moral*, Heaphy; *Brush*, Green; *Lady Gentle*, Mrs. Ward; *Miss Notable*, Mrs. Green; *Lady Wronglove*, Mrs. Kennedy; *Hartshorn*, Mrs. Pye; *Mrs. Conquest*, Mrs. Woffington; Dec. 10; Dec. 20.

A Lass to be Let, or *The Grotesque Rivals*. (Pantomime Entertainment)

1751–52: Dec. 6, no cast; Dec. 11; Dec. 16.

The Lawyer Outwitted, "taken from Beaumont and Fletcher." (Farce)

1751–52: Mar. 9, principal parts, King, Sparks, Mynitt, Kennedy, Miss Cole.

Lethe, or *Aesop in the Shades*, by David Garrick. (Dramatic Satire)

1750–51: Nov. 8, *Fine Gentleman* and *Frenchman*, King; *Aesop*, Beamsley; *Old Man*, Mynitt; *Mercury*, Ross; *Drunken Man*, Sparks; *Mrs. Tattoo*, Miss Cole; *Mrs. Riot (Fine Lady)*, Mrs. Bland; Nov. 12, without *Old Man* and *Mercury*; Nov. 16; Nov. 19; Nov. 21, but *Mrs. Riot*, Miss Cole [since *Fine Lady*, usually another name for *Mrs. Riot*, is still listed for Mrs. Bland, there is some confusion here and in the notice for the next performance]; Nov. 29, *Fine Gentleman* and *Frenchman*, King; *Mrs. Riot*, Miss Cole [see note above]; *Fine Lady*, Mrs. Bland; *Drunken Man*, Sparks; *Aesop*, Beamsley; *Miser (Old Man)*, Mynitt; Dec. 3, without *Fine*

Lady and *Miser;* Feb. 18, only *Fine Gentleman* and *French-man, Drunken Man, Aesop,* and *Mrs. Riot* (played by Miss Cole) listed; Mar. 9, no cast; Mar. 12, *Fine Gentleman* and *Frenchman,* King; *Drunken Man,* Sparks; *Aesop,* Beamsley; *Fine Lady,* Miss Cole; May 2, but *Aesop,* Maurice; and plus *Mercury,* Ross.

1751–52: Dec. 5, *Fine Gentleman* and *Frenchman,* King; *Drunken Man,* Sparks; *Aesop,* Beamsley; *Fine Lady,* Miss Cole; Jan. 16.

1752–53: Nov. 1, *Fine Gentleman* and *Frenchman,* King; *Drunken Man,* Sparks; *Fine Lady,* Mrs. Green, "in which Character will be introduced a Song, called, The Life of a Belle"; Nov. 8; Apr. 23, without *Drunken Man.*

1753–54: Dec. 3, *Fine Gentleman* and *Frenchman,* King; *Drunken Man,* Sparks; *Mrs. Riot (Fine Lady),* Mrs. Green, with "The Life of a Belle"; *Aesop,* Stayley; *Old Man,* Mynitt; *Charon,* Storer; *Mercury,* Kennedy; Dec. 14, without *Aesop, Old Man,* and *Charon;* Dec. 19, but *Mercury,* Butler.

1756–57: Jan. 3, *Fine Gentleman,* King; *Mercury,* Wilder; *Drunken Man,* Sparks; *Old Man,* Glover; *Fine Lady,* Miss G. Phillips; Jan. 12, plus *Frenchman,* Lee; Feb. 3, no cast; Feb. 7, as on Jan. 12; Mar. 23, *Fine Gentleman,* King, "who will add a new Character, called, Lord Chalkstone as lately performed by the author, Mr. Garrick"; *Frenchman,* Lee; *Mercury,* Wilder; *Fine Lady,* Miss G. Phillips; Mar. 31; Apr. 19; Apr. 20; Apr. 25; May 10, plus *Drunken Man,* Sparks, and *Old Man,* Glover.

1757–58: Jan. 2, no cast, merely "*Lethe,* in which Mr. King will introduce the Character of Lord Chalkstone"; Apr. 20, plus *Mercury,* Wilder; *Old Man,* Glover; *Drunken Man,* Sparks; *Fine Lady,* Miss G. Phillips; May 8, but *Fine Lady,* Miss Kennedy.

The Little French Lawyer, "taken from the Comedy of Beaumont and Fletcher." (Farce)

1747–48: Oct. 23, *Monsieur Le Writ (The French Lawyer),* Woodward; *Lamira,* Miss Bellamy; Feb. 25, without *Lamira.*

The London Merchant, or *The Tragical History of George Barnwell,* by George Lillo

1748–49: Apr. 26, *George Barnwell,* Mrs. Storer (first time); *Uncle,* R. Elrington; *Maria,* Mrs. Mozeen; *Thorowgood,* Storer; *Lucy,* Mrs. Vincent; *Blunt,* Duncomb; *Trueman,* Dyer; *Millwood,* Mrs. Bland.

1752–53: *Barnwell,* Digges; *Trueman,* Heaphy; *Lucy,* Mrs. Green; *Millwood,* Mrs. Ward; Feb. 3.

1753–54: Jan. 3, *Barnwell,* Digges; *Thorowgood,* Layfield; *Trueman,* Heaphy; *Uncle,* J. Elrington; *Blunt,* Stayley; *Lucy,* Mrs. Green; *Maria,* Miss Mason; *Millwood,* Mrs. Ward.

The Lottery, by Henry Fielding. (Ballad Farce)

1748–49: Oct. 26, *Jack Stocks (alias Lord Lace),* Macklin; *Chloe (alias Lady Lace),* Mrs. Storer.

1749–50: Mar. 1, *Jack Stocks,* Cibber; *Chloe,* Mrs. Storer; Mar. 7; Mar. 10, no cast; Mar. 21, as on Mar. 1; Apr. 17, only *Jack Stocks* listed.

1750–51: Oct. 5, *Jack Stocks,* Cibber; *Chloe,* Miss Cole; Jan. 11, plus *Lovemore,* Ross; Jan. 26, plus *Mr. Stocks,* Maurice; *Whisk,* Hamilton; *Coachman,* Mynitt; *Mac O'Brogue,* Sparks; *Jenny,* Mrs. Rowley; and *Mrs. Stocks,* Miss Copen.

1751–52: Dec. 14, *Jack Stocks,* Cibber; *Chloe,* Miss Cole; Mar. 16, but *Jack Stocks,* King (first time); and plus *Mac O'Brogue,* Sparks.

1752–53: Nov. 10, *Jack Stocks,* King; *Chloe,* Mrs. Green; Nov. 13; Nov. 16; Feb. 16; Feb. 28.

1753–54: Oct. 31, *Jack Stocks,* King; *Chloe,* Mrs. Green.

1756–57: Nov. 29, *Jack Stocks,* King; *Chloe,* Miss Kennedy; Dec. 8.

1757–58: Oct. 12, *Jack Stocks,* King; *Chloe,* Miss Kennedy.

Love and a Bottle, by George Farquhar

1757–58: Apr. 17, *Roebuck,* King; *Lyrick,* Stayley; *Pamphlet,* Davenport; *Rigadoon,* Harvey; *Lovewell,* Dexter; *Nimble Wrist,* Hamilton; *Brush,* Ryder; *Club,* Lewis; *Mockmode,* Glover; *Trudge (an Irish Gentlewoman),* Sparks; *Leanthe,* Mrs. Kennedy; *Mrs. Bullfinch,* Mrs. Farrell; *Pindress,* Mrs. Pye; *Lucinda,* Miss Kennedy; May 5, without *Brush* and *Club.*

Love for Love, by William Congreve

1745–46: Mar. 5, *Ben,* Morris; *Miss Prue,* at the Desire of several Ladies, Miss Bellamy.

1746–47: Oct. 30, no cast.

1747–48: Apr. 29, *Ben,* Woodward.

1748–49: Oct. 21, *Ben,* Macklin; Nov. 9, plus *Angelica,* Mrs. Vincent; *Miss Prue,* Miss Minors; *Mrs. Frail,* Mrs. Bland; Nov. 19; Feb. 1, plus *Valentine,* R. Elrington.

1749–50: Oct. 30, *Valentine,* Macklin; *Angelica,* Mrs. Bland.

1750–51: May 16, *Valentine,* Ross; *Tattle,* Cibber; *Ben,* King; *Sir Sampson,* Sparks; *Scandal,* J. Elrington; *Foresight,* Mynitt;

Jeremy, Hamilton; *Mrs. Foresight*, Mrs. Rowley; *Mrs. Frail*, Mrs. Lindley; *Miss Prue*, Miss Cole; *Angelica*, Mrs. Bland.

1751–52: Feb. 11, *Valentine*, Sheridan (first time); *Scandal*, Digges; *Tattle*, Cibber; *Jeremy*, King; *Sir Sampson*, Sparks; *Ben*, Stevens; *Foresight*, Mynitt; *Angelica*, Mrs. Bland; *Miss Prue*, Miss Cole; *Mrs. Foresight*, Mrs. Lee; *Nurse*, Mrs. Mynitt; *Mrs. Frail*, Mrs. Woffington; Feb. 19; Apr. 29, but *Valentine*, Digges; and *Scandal*, Heaphy.

1752–53: Jan. 31, *Valentine*, Sheridan; *Scandal*, Digges; *Tattle*, King; *Sir Sampson*, Sparks; *Foresight*, Costollo; *Jeremy*, Green; *Ben*, Stevens; *Angelica*, Mrs. Ward; *Miss Prue*, Mrs. Green; *Nurse*, Mrs. Mynitt; *Mrs. Frail*, Mrs. Woffington; Feb. 15, plus *Scandal*, J. Elrington; and without *Nurse*; Apr. 25, but *Valentine*, Digges, and *Scandal*, Heaphy; and plus *Mrs. Foresight*, Mrs. Kennedy, and *Nurse*, Mrs. Mynitt.

1753–54: Oct. 12, *Valentine*, Dexter; *Scandal*, Digges; *Tattle*, King; *Sir Sampson*, Sparks; *Jeremy*, Green; *Ben*, Cunningham; *Foresight*, Mynitt; *Trapland*, Storer; *Angelica*, Mrs. Ward; *Miss Prue*, Mrs. Green; *Mrs. Foresight*, Mrs. Kennedy; *Nurse*, Mrs. Mynitt; *Mrs. Frail*, Mrs. Woffington.

1756–57: Jan. 1, *Valentine*, Dexter; *Scandal*, Wilder; *Sir Sampson*, Sparks; *Tattle*, King; *Foresight*, Glover; *Angelica*, Miss Kennedy; *Miss Prue*, Mrs. Wilder; *Mrs. Frail*, Mrs. Kennedy.

1757–58: Oct. 22, *Valentine*, Dexter; *Scandal*, Heaphy; *Sir Sampson*, Sparks; *Trapland*, Storer; *Jeremy*, Hamilton; *Tattle*, King; *Buckram*, Williams; *Snap*, Messink; *Ben*, with a Song in Character, Wilder; *Foresight*, Glover; *Angelica*, Miss Kennedy; *Nurse*, Mrs. Farrell; *Mrs. Foresight*, Mrs. Pye; *Miss Prue*, Mrs. Wilder; *Mrs. Frail*, Mrs. Kennedy; Nov. 24, but *Ben*, Foote, and *Trapland*, Lewis; and without *Buckram* and *Snap*; May 3, no cast.

Love Makes a Man, or *The Fop's Fortune*, by Colley Cibber

1745–46: Feb. 25, *Carlos*, by a Gentleman "who never appeared on any Stage in this Kingdom"; *Don Lewis*, Morris; *Clodio*, Bardin; *Louisa*, Mrs. Furnival; *Angelina*, Mrs. Elmy.

1747–48: Oct. 12, *Clodio*, Woodward; Mar. 28, *Clodio*, *alias Dondismallo-Thick-Scullo-de-half-Witto*, Woodward; *Charles (Carlos)*, Dyer; *Don Lewis*, *alias Don Cholerick-Snap-Shorto-de-Testy*, Beamsley.

1748–49: Mar. 31, *Don Cholerick* (*Don Lewis*), Macklin; *Antonio*, Sparks; *Charino*, Mynitt; *Charles*, R. Elrington; *Sancho*, Barrington; *Don Duart*, J. Elrington; *Monsieur*, Watson;

Clodio, Dyer; *Angelina*, Mrs. Mozeen; *Elvira*, Mrs. Dyer; *Louisa*, Mrs. Vincent.

1749–50: Nov. 13, *Clodio*, Cibber; *Louisa*, Mrs. Bland; *Angelina*, Mrs. Mozeen; *Don Cholerick*, Macklin; Jan. 1; Apr. 5, but *Don Cholerick*, Morgan; and plus *Elvira*, Miss Bourne; and *Honoria*, Mrs. Kennedy.

1750–51: Sept. 26, *Clodio*, Cibber; *Don Cholerick*, Beamsley; *Antonio*, Sparks; *Charino*, Mynitt; *Sancho*, Robertson; *Don Duart*, J. Elrington; *Carlos*, R. Elrington; *Angelina*, Miss Cole; *Elvira*, Mrs. Lindley; *Louisa*, Mrs. Bland.

1751–52: Jan. 24, *Clody* (*Clodio*), Cibber; *Don Cholerick*, Sparks; *Charles* (*Carlos*), Heaphy; *Angelina*, Miss Cole; *Louisa*, Mrs. Bland.

1752–53: Oct. 20, *Charles*, Sowdon; *Don Cholerick*, Sparks; *Clody*, King; Jan. 3.

1756–57: Jan. 6, *Don Cholerick*, Lee; *Clodio*, King; *Charles*, Dexter; *Sancho*, Glover; *Angelina*, Miss Kennedy; *Elvira*, Miss Danvers; *Louisa*, Mrs. Kennedy.

1757–58: Apr. 25, *Carlos*, Dexter; *Clody*, King; *Don Duart*, Stayley; *Sancho*, Glover; *Don Lewis* (*Don Cholerick*), Sparks; *Angelina*, Miss Kennedy; *Elvira*, Miss Danvers; *Louisa*, Mrs. Kennedy.

The Lover's Opera, by William Chetwood
1746–47: Dec. 8, *Lucy*, Mrs. Storer.

The Lovers Revels, or *A Trip to Vaux-Hall*, or *A Jubilee Ball at Vaux-Hall Gardens* (Pantomime Masque)

1750–51: Dec. 6, no cast; Dec. 8; Dec. 11 [but see footnote 4 under this date in Part 1]; Dec. 15; Dec. 18; Dec. 22; Jan. 9; Jan. 16; Jan. 23; Feb. 2; Apr. 20.

1751–52: Jan. 8, no cast; Jan. 17; Jan. 24; Jan. 25; Jan. 28; Feb. 7; Feb. 15; Mar. 20, *Colombine*, Miss Cole; *Harlequin*, Messink; *Clown*, Sparks; Mar. 31; Apr. 11.

1752–53: Mar. 9, *Harlequin*, King; *Pantaloon*, Hamilton; *Squire Gawky*, Stevens; *Colombine*, Mrs. Kennedy; *Squire's Man* [*Clown?*], Sparks; Mar. 14; Mar. 19; Mar. 28, only *Harlequin* and *Clown* (played by Sparks) listed; Apr. 4, no cast; June 4, *Harlequin*, Pitt; *Pierot*, Layfield; June 6.

1753–54: Nov. 7, *Harlequin*, King; *Colombine*, Mrs. Kennedy; *Clown*, Sparks; Nov. 16; Nov. 21; Nov. 24.

Love's Last Shift, or *The Fool in Fashion*, by Colley Cibber
1747–48: Oct. 5, *Sir Novelty Fashion*, Woodward; *Amanda*, Miss Bellamy; Feb. 22; May 2, without *Amanda*.

1749–50: Apr. 3, *Sir Novelty Fashion*, Cibber; *Amanda*, Miss Danvers; *Hillaria*, Mrs. Mozeen; *Flareit*, Mrs. Mynitt; *Narcissa*, Mrs. Bland.

1750–51: Sept. 21, *Sir Novelty Fashion*, Cibber; *Amanda*, Miss Danvers; *Hillaria*, Miss Cole; *Narcissa*, Mrs. Bland; *Snap*, Robertson "being the first Time of his Appearance on this Stage"; Oct. 11, no cast.

1752–53: Jan. 8, *Loveless*, Sowdon; *Sir Novelty Fashion*, King; *Sir William Wisewou'd*, Sparks; *Snap*, Costollo; *Flareit*, Mrs. Green; *Amanda*, Mrs. Ward; Mar. 24, without *Sir William* and *Snap*.

1753–54: Oct. 1, *Loveless*, Sowdon; *Sir Novelty Fashion*, King; *Flareit*, Mrs. Green; *Amanda*, Mrs. Ward.

1756–57: Apr. 11, *Sir Novelty Fashion*, King; *Elder Worthy*, Stayley; *Snap*, Glover; *Young Worthy*, Heaphy; *Sir William Wisewou'd*, Sparks; *Sly*, Hamilton; *Loveless*, Dexter; *Amanda*, Miss Kennedy; *Hillaria*, Miss Mason; *Flareit*, Mrs. Kennedy; *Narcissa*, Miss G. Phillips.

1757–58: May 9, *Sir Novelty Fashion*, King; *Sir William Wisewou'd*, Sparks; *Elder Worthy*, Stayley; *Younger Worthy*, Kennedy; *Sly*, Hamilton; *Snap*, Glover; *Loveless*, Dexter; *Amanda*, Miss Kennedy; *Narcissa*, Mrs. Wilder; *Hillaria*, Miss Mason; *Maid*, Mrs. Packenham; *Flareit*, Mrs. Kennedy.

The Loyal Subject, "written originally by Mr. Beaumont and Fletcher, now first altered and adapted to the Stage by Mr. Sheridan"

1747–48: Feb. 29, *Archas*, Sheridan; *Ancient*, Woodward; *Alinda*, Miss Bellamy; Mar. 2, without *Ancient*; May 27, no cast.

1749–50: Nov. 10, *Archas*, Sheridan; *Alinda*, Miss Griffith.

1756–57: Mar. 14, *Archas*, Sheridan; *Theodore*, King; *Ancient*, Sparks; *Olympia*, Miss Kennedy; *Alinda*, Mrs. Kennedy; Mar. 19; May 9, plus *Burris*, Glover.

The Lying Valet, by David Garrick. (Farce)

1745–46: Apr. 26, *Lying Valet*, Garrick.

1747–48: Sept. 28, *Lying Valet*, Woodward.

1748–49: Mar. 31, *Sharp* (*Lying Valet*), Dyer (first time); May 5, *Sharp*, by the Gentleman who played *Aboan* [probably Mr. Gentleman]; *Kitty Pry*, Miss Minors.

1749–50: Apr. 5, *Lying Valet*, Kennedy; *Kitty Pry*, Miss Bourne.

1750–51: Oct. 19, *Sharp* (*Lying Valet*), King; *Kitty Pry*, Miss Cole; Oct. 24; Oct. 31; Nov. 15; Apr. 15, no cast.

1751–52: Sept. 30, *Sharp*, King; *Kitty Pry*, Miss Cole; Oct. 24; Nov. 11; Apr. 18; May 4.

1752–53: Dec. 20, *Lying Valet*, King.

1753–54: Oct. 8, *Lying Valet*, King; *Kitty Pry*, Mrs. Kennedy.

1756–57: Oct. 18, *Sharp* (*Lying Valet*), King; Dec. 9; Apr. 13, plus *Justice Guttle*, Mynitt; and *Kitty Pry*, Mrs. Kennedy; Apr. 23, without *Justice Guttle*.

1757–58: Oct. 14, *Sharp*, King; *Kitty Pry*, Mrs. Kennedy; Jan. 4, only *Sharp* listed; Feb. 1, no cast; Feb. 27, *Sharp*, King; *Kitty Pry*, Mrs. Kennedy; June 5.

Macbeth, "as written originally by Shakespear"

1745–46: Jan. 7, *Macbeth*, Garrick; *Lady Macbeth*, Mrs. Furnival; *Lady Macduff*, Mrs. Elmy; *Hecate*, Layfield; *three Witches*, F. Elrington, Vanderbank, and Watson; *first Singing Witch*, Mrs. Storer.

1746–47: July 13, *Macbeth*, Sheridan; *Lady Macbeth*, Miss Bellamy (first time).

1747–48: Dec. 14, *Macbeth*, Sheridan; *Lady Macbeth*, Miss Bellamy; Feb. 1.

1748–49: Dec. 12, *Macbeth*, Sheridan; *Lady Macbeth*, Mrs. Bland. "The vocal Parts by Mr. Sullivan, Mr. Howard, Mrs. Lampe, Mrs. Storer, Mrs. Mozeen, and others"; Feb. 6.

1749–50: Oct. 9, *Macbeth*, Sheridan; *Lady Macbeth*, Mrs. Bland. "The Vocal Parts by Mr. Sullivan, Mrs. Lampe, Mrs. Storer, and Mrs. Mozeen"; Dec. 8; Feb. 23, plus *Macduff*, Digges; May 23, *Macbeth*, Mossop; *Macduff*, Digges.

1750–51: Nov. 9, *Macbeth*, Sheridan; *Macduff*, Digges; *Lenox*, King; *Lady Macduff*, Miss Griffith; *Lady Macbeth*, Mrs. Bland; May 9, only *Macbeth*, *Macduff*, and *Lady Macbeth* listed.

1751–52: Nov. 7, *Macbeth*, Sheridan; *Macduff*, Digges; *Lady Macbeth*, Mrs. Woffington; Nov. 25

1752–53: Nov. 13, *Macbeth*, Sheridan; *Banquo*, Sowdon; *Macduff*, Digges; *Lady Macbeth*, Mrs. Woffington. "The Vocal Parts by Mrs. Donaldson, Mr. Sullivan, and others"; Feb. 2, plus *King*, J. Elrington; *Lenox*, Heaphy; *Hecate*, Layfield; and *Singing Witches*, Mrs. Donaldson, Mrs. Crump, and Sullivan.

1753–54: Nov. 24, *Macbeth*, Sheridan; *Banquo*, Sowdon; *Macduff*, Digges; *Lenox*, Heaphy; *Hecate*, Layfield; *first Singing Witch*, Mrs. Storer; *Dancing Witches*, McNeil, Harvey, and Miss Baker; *Lady Macbeth*, Mrs. Woffington; Feb. 14, plus *King*, J. Elrington; *Lady Macduff*, Miss Mason; and *additional Singing Witches*, Mrs. Pye, Butler, and others.

1756–57: Jan. 24, *Macbeth*, Sheridan; *Macduff*, Dexter; *Banquo*,

Glover; *Hecate,* with Songs in Character, Wilder; *Lady Mac-beth,* Mrs. Kennedy; *Singing Witches,* Corry, Mrs. Pye, Miss Wells, Miss Spencer, Mrs. Fagan, &c.; *Dancing Witches,* Harvey, Garman, Pike, Rayner, Steggeldolt, Mrs. Packenham, Mrs. Garman, &c.; Mar. 16.

1757–58: Oct. 31, *Macbeth,* Sheridan; *King,* Hurst; *Malcolm,* Kennedy; *Donalbain,* Wall; *Lenox,* Heaphy; *Macduff,* Dexter; *Seyton,* Watson; *Seward,* Stayley; *Physician,* R. Elrington; *Captain,* Williams; *Banquo,* Glover; *1st Witch,* Messink; *2d Witch,* Lewis; *3d Witch,* Hamilton; *Hecate,* with Songs in Character, Wilder; *First Singing Witch,* Mrs. Storer; *other Singing Witches,* Corry, Storer, Mrs. Pye, Miss Wells, &c.; *Dancing Witches,* Harvey, Garman, Rayner, Masset, Walsh, Mrs. Masset, Mrs. Garman, Mrs. Godwin, Mrs. Packenham, Miss Jackson, &c.; *Lady Macduff,* Miss Kennedy; *Lady Mac-beth,* Mrs. Fitzhenry; Feb. 20, but *Donalbain,* Preston.

The Mad Lovers, "taken from Beaumont and Fletcher"
1746–47: May 20, no cast.

Mahomet, taken from Voltaire by James Miller and John Hoadly
1753–54: Feb. 2, *Zaphna,* Sheridan; *Mahomet,* Sowdon; *Alcanor,* Digges; *Mirvan,* Layfield; *Pharon,* Heaphy; *Ali,* Stayley; *Palmira,* Mrs. Woffington; Mar. 2.

The Man of Mode, or *Sir Fopling Flutter,* by George Etherege
1751–52: Dec. 19, *Dorimant,* Sheridan; *Sir Fopling,* Cibber; *Medley,* Heaphy; *Old Bellair,* Sparks; *Young Bellair,* Kennedy; *Shoemaker,* Stevens; *Harriet,* Mrs. Bland; *Belinda,* Miss Cole; *Emilia,* Mrs. Davies; *Lady Woodvil,* Mrs. Mynitt; *Pert,* Mrs. Kennedy; *Lady Townly,* Mrs. Rowley; *Mrs. Loveit,* Mrs. Woffington; Jan. 10, but *Lady Townly,* Mrs. Lee, and *Lady Woodvil,* Mrs. Rowley; and plus *Busy,* with the proper Songs, Mrs. Crump; Mar. 12, without *Shoemaker* and *Busy;* Apr. 16, plus *Busy,* Mrs. Crump.

The Man of Taste, "An Interlude of two Acts, taken from Moliere," by James Miller
1751–52: Mar. 14, *Martin,* Cibber; *Reynard,* King; *Harcourt,* Kennedy; *Horatio,* Falkner; *Dorothea,* Mrs. Kennedy; *Margaretta,* Miss Cole.

The Match in Newgate, by Christopher Bullock [?] (Farce)
1749–50: Feb. 9, no cast.

Measure for Measure, by William Shakespeare

1757–58: Mar. 18, *Duke,* Dexter (first time); *Angelo,* Hurst; *Escalus,* Heaphy; *Lucio,* King; *Claudio,* Ryder; *Provost,* Stayley; *Clown,* Sparks; *Mariana,* Miss Mason; *Juliet,* Mrs. Pye; *Isabella,* Mrs. Fitzhenry; Apr. 28, but *Angelo,* Stayley; and plus *Bawd,* Mrs. Farrell; and without *Provost, Mariana,* and *Juliet.*

The Merchant of Venice, by William Shakespeare

1745–46: May 8, *Shylock,* Sheridan (first time); *Lorenzo,* "with the Songs proper to the Part," Sullivan.

1746–47: Dec. 1, *Jew (Shylock),* Sheridan; *Portia,* Miss Bellamy (first time).

1747–48: Jan. 29, *Shylock,* Sheridan; *Launcelot,* Woodward; *Portia,* Miss Bellamy.

1748–49: Oct. 10, *Jew (Shylock),* Macklin; *Portia,* Mrs. Vincent; *Jessica,* "with the Songs proper to the Character," Mrs. Mozeen; *Lorenzo,* "with the usual Songs," Sullivan; Oct. 11; Feb. 9, plus *Nerissa,* Miss Minors; and *Launcelot,* Barrington; and without *Jessica* and *Lorenzo;* Apr. 28, plus *Antonio,* Beamsley; *Lorenzo,* "with the Songs in Character," Sullivan; and *Jessica,* "with the Songs in Character," Mrs. Mozeen.

1749–50: Sept. 29, *Shylock,* Macklin; *Portia,* Mrs. Bland; *Jessica,* Mrs. Mozeen; *Lorenzo,* Sullivan; Jan. 19; Apr. 26, but *Jew (Shylock),* Sheridan; and plus *Merchant (Antonio),* Digges; and *Gratiano,* Cibber.

1750–51: Nov. 23, *Shylock the Jew,* Sheridan; *Merchant,* Digges; *Gratiano,* Cibber; *Bassanio,* King; *Lorenzo,* "with the usual Songs," Ross; *Launcelot,* Sparks; *Old Gobbo,* Mynitt; *Nerissa,* Miss Cole; *Jessica,* Mrs. Crump, "first Time of her attempting a Character"; *Portia,* Mrs. Bland; Apr. 27, but *Nerissa,* Mrs. Rowley; and without *Launcelot* and *Old Gobbo.*

1751–52: Nov. 14, *Shylock,* Sheridan; *Antonio,* Digges; *Gratiano,* Cibber; *Bassanio,* King; *Launcelot,* Sparks; *Jessica,* "with the Songs in Character," Mrs. Crump; *Nerissa,* Miss Cole; *Portia,* Mrs. Woffington; Apr. 24, but *Antonio,* J. Elrington; and plus *Lorenzo,* "with the usual Songs," Kennedy.

1752–53: Dec. 13, *Shylock,* Sheridan; *Antonio,* Digges; *Gratiano,* King; *Lorenzo,* "with the Songs in Character," Sullivan; *Bassanio,* Heaphy; *Tubal,* Costollo; *Launcelot,* Sparks; *Nerissa,* Mrs. Green; *Jessica,* "with the Songs," Mrs. Donaldson; *Portia,* Mrs. Woffington.

1753–54: Nov. 17, *Shylock,* Sheridan; *Antonio,* Digges; *Gratiano,*

King; *Bassanio,* Heaphy; *Launcelot,* Green; *Nerissa,* Mrs.
Green; *Jessica,* Mrs. Pye; *Portia,* Mrs. Woffington.

1756–57: Nov. 22, *Shylock,* Sheridan; *Launcelot,* Glover; *Nerissa,* Mrs.
Kennedy; *Portia,* Miss Kennedy; Feb. 14, plus *Gratiano,*
King; and *Lorenzo,* "with Songs," Wilder; Apr. 25.

1757–58: Feb. 13, *Shylock,* Sheridan; *Antonio,* Hurst; *Bassanio,* Heaphy;
Gratiano, King; *Salanio,* Davenport; *Salarino,* Watson; *Lorenzo,* "with Songs," Wilder; *Duke,* Storer; *Tubal,* Stayley;
Launcelot, Glover; *Old Gobbo,* Lewis; *Nerissa,* Mrs. Kennedy; *Jessica,* Mrs. Pye; *Portia,* Miss Kennedy; Mar. 4, without *Salanio* and *Salarino;* Apr. 22, but *Jessica,* Miss Mason;
and without *Duke* and *Old Gobbo.*

Merope, by Aaron Hill

1750–51: May 11, *Eumenes,* Sheridan; *Poliphontes,* Digges; *Narbas,*
Montgomery; *Euricles,* Ross; *Ismene,* Miss Griffith; *Merope,*
Mrs. Bland; May 18.

The Merry Wives of Windsor, by William Shakespeare

1747–48: Apr. 18, *Slender,* Woodward; May 4, no cast.

1748–49: May 2, *Falstaff,* Morris; *Mrs. Ford,* Mrs. Bland; *Mrs. Page,*
Miss Jones; *Anne Page,* Mrs. Mozeen; *Mrs. Quickly,* Mrs.
Macklin; *Sir Hugh Evans,* Macklin.

1750–51: Oct. 17, *Dr. Caius,* Cibber (first time); *Falstaff,* Sparks; *Mrs.
Ford,* Mrs. Bland; Jan. 10, plus *Mrs. Quickly,* Mrs. Mynitt;
Anne Page, Miss Cole; *Mrs. Page,* Mrs. Lindley; *Ford,* R. Elrington; *Justice Shallow,* Watson; *Slender,* Hamilton; and *Sir
Hugh Evans,* Mynitt.

1751–52: Feb. 10, *Falstaff,* Sparks; *Dr. Caius,* Cibber; *Ford,* Heaphy;
Slender, King; *Sir Hugh Evans,* Mynitt; *Mrs. Page,* Mrs.
Lee; *Anne Page,* Miss Cole; *Mrs. Ford,* Mrs. Woffington;
Mar. 18, but *Mrs. Page,* Miss Cole, and *Anne Page,* Mrs.
Davies; and plus *Page,* J. Elrington; *Host,* Beamsley; and
Justice Shallow, Longfield; May 4, plus *Fenton,* Kennedy;
Bardolf, Packenham; *Pistol,* Maurice; *Nym,* Williams; *Simple,* Hamilton; *Rugby,* Messink; *Robin,* Miss Reynolds; and
Mrs. Quickly, Mrs. Mynitt.

1752–53: Feb. 23, *Falstaff,* Sparks; *Dr. Caius,* King; *Ford,* Heaphy;
Justice Shallow, Layfield; *Sir Hugh Evans,* Costollo; *Slender,*
Green; *Mrs. Page,* Mrs. Ward; *Mrs. Quickly,* Mrs. Mynitt;
Mrs. Ford, Mrs. Woffington; Mar. 29, plus *Page,* J. Elrington; *Host,* Stevens; *Fenton,* Kennedy; *Robin,* Miss Reynolds;
and *Anne Page,* Miss Mason.

1753–54: Jan. 16, *Falstaff,* Sparks; *Dr. Caius,* King; *Ford,* Heaphy;

Page, J. Elrington; *Justice Shallow*, Mynitt; *Sir Hugh Evans*, Cunningham; *Slender*, Green; *Host*, Layfield; *Mrs. Page*, Mrs. Ward; *Anne Page*, Miss Mason; *Mrs. Quickly*, Mrs. Mynitt; *Mrs. Ford*, Mrs. Woffington.

1756–57: Mar. 29, *Ford*, Heaphy; *Page*, Stayley; *Justice Shallow*, Watson; *Slender*, Glover; *Falstaff*, Sparks; *Host*, Layfield; *Fenton*, Hurst; *Bardolph*, Aickin; *Dr. Caius*, King; *Sir Hugh Evans*, Mynitt; *Pistol*, Hamilton; *Simple*, Williams; *Rugby*, Messink; *Mrs. Page*, Mrs. Kennedy; *Mrs. Quickly*, Mrs. Mynitt; *Anne Page*, Mrs. Pye; *Mrs. Ford*, Miss Kennedy.

1757–58: Jan. 25, *Ford*, Heaphy; *Page*, Stayley; *Justice Shallow*, Storer; *Falstaff*, Sparks; *Nym*, R. Elrington; *Simple*, Hamilton; *Dr. Caius*, King; *Host*, Preston; *Fenton*, Hurst; *Rugby*, Messink; *Slender*, Glover; *Sir Hugh Evans*, Lewis; *Pistol*, Davenport; *Mrs. Page*, Mrs. Kennedy; *Anne Page*, Mrs. Pye; *Mrs. Quickly*, Mrs. Farrell; *Mrs. Ford*, Miss Kennedy.

The Metamorphoses of Harlequin, "being the Comick Part of the celebrated Orpheus and Eurydice." (Pantomime Entertainment)

1747–48: Oct. 16, *Harlequin*, Woodward; *Columbine*, Miss Mechel (first time); Oct. 19, no cast; Oct. 21; Oct. 26, as on Oct. 16; Nov. 4; Dec. 4, no cast; Dec. 30, as on Oct. 16; Jan. 19.

The Miller of Mansfield, by Robert Dodsley. (Dramatic Tale)

1748–49: Dec. 21, *Miller*, Sparks; Jan. 20, plus *Kate*, "with a Song in Character," Mrs. Mozeen; Apr. 6, only *Kate* listed; Apr. 29, no cast.

1749–50: Jan. 3, *Miller*, Morgan; *Peggy*, Mrs. Mozeen.

1753–54: Jan. 9, *Miller*, Sparks.

1756–57: Nov. 8, no cast.

1757–58: Oct. 20, *Miller*, Sparks.

The Miser, by Henry Fielding

1745–46: Apr. 29, *Lovegold*, F. Elrington; *Lappet*, Mrs. Furnival.

1747–48: Jan. 15, *Miser* (*Lovegold*), Mynitt; *Lappet*, Mrs. Mynitt; Mar. 18, plus *Starved Cook*, Woodward

1748–49: Nov. 25, *Miser*, Macklin; *Lappet*, Mrs. Macklin; Jan. 6, plus *Mariana*, Mrs. Bland; and *Harriet*, Mrs. Vincent; May 8, plus *Frederick*, J. Elrington; *Ramelie*, Barrington; *Decoy*, Beamsley; *James*, Storer; *Mrs. Wisely*, Miss Jones; *Wheedle*, Miss Orfeur; *Clerimont*, Ross; *Furnish*, Duncomb; *Sparkle*, Watson; *Sattin*, Williams; and *List*, Vaughan. (From a playbill cited by Hitchcock, I, 198–199.)

1749–50: Sept. 25, *Miser*, Macklin; *Mariana*, Mrs. Bland; *Lappet*, Mrs. Macklin; Jan. 4, plus *Harriet*, Mrs. Mozeen.

1753–54: Feb. 9, *Lovegold*, Green; *Ramilie*, King; *Frederick*, Kennedy; *Clerimont*, Stayley; *Decoy*, Cunningham; *James*, Layfield; *Mariana*, Mrs. Ward; *Harriet*, Mrs. Pye; *Mrs. Wisely*, Mrs. Mynitt; *Lappet*, "with a Song called the Life of a Beau," Mrs. Green.

1756–57: Nov. 17, *Miser*, King (first time); Nov. 30, plus *Mariana*, Miss Kennedy; and *Lappet*, Mrs. Kennedy.

1757–58: Oct. 20, *Miser*, King; *Frederick*, Stayley; *Ramilie*, Kennedy; *Clerimont*, Heaphy; *Decoy*, Lewis; *Furnish*, Messink; *Sparkle*, Watson; *Sattin*, Williams; *List*, Hamilton; *Starved Cook*, Glover; *Lappet*, Mrs. Kennedy; *Harriet*, Mrs. Pye; *Mrs. Wisely*, Miss Mason; *Wheedle*, Miss Wells; *Mariana*, Miss Kennedy.

Miss in her Teens, "written by Mr. Garrick." (Farce)

1746–47: Mar. 9, *Miss Biddy*, Miss Bellamy; Mar. 23, no cast; Mar. 30, *Miss Biddy*, Miss Bellamy; *Fribble*, Dyer; Apr. 3, only *Miss Biddy* listed; Apr. 6, no cast; Apr. 8; Apr. 27, *Fribble*, Dyer; *Miss Biddy*, Miss Bellamy; Apr. 30, only *Miss Biddy* listed; May 18; July 2, plus *Fribble*, Giffard, and *Flash*, Dyer.

1747–48: Oct. 8, *Flash*, Woodward; *Miss Biddy*, Miss Bellamy; Oct. 12; Oct. 23; Oct. 28; Nov. 6; Jan. 11; Jan. 25, but *Miss Biddy*, "to be attempted by" Miss Orfeur; Feb. 2; Feb. 8, only *Flash* listed; Feb. 9, no cast; Apr. 14, *Flash*, Woodward; *Fribble*, Dyer; *Miss Biddy*, Miss Orfeur; May 6, only *Fribble*, "by particular Desire," Woodward (alamode Garrick); May 9, plus *Flash*, Dyer.

1748–49: Jan. 26, *Flash*, Macklin; *Fribble*, Dyer; *Miss Biddy*, Miss Minors (first time); Feb. 3; Mar. 15, *Miss Biddy*, Miss Minors; *Fribble*, "to be attempted by Mrs. Storer"; *Flash*, "a la mode de — by Mr. Dyer"; May 3, *Fribble*, "(by particular Desire) to be attempted by Mr. Degeer. With some Alterations of his own"; *Tagg*, Miss Orfeur; *Miss Biddy*, Miss Minors; *Flash*, by Desire, Layfield.

1749–50: Apr. 18, *Flash*, by Desire, Cibber; *Miss Biddy*, Mrs. Mozeen; *Fribble*, Ross.

1750–51: Nov. 23, *Fribble*, King; *Flash*, Ross; *Puff*, Sparks; *Tag*, Mrs. Lindley; *Miss Biddy*, Miss Cole; Nov. 26, but *Flash*, King, and *Fribble*, Ross; and without *Puff* and *Tag*; Nov. 28, but *Fribble*, King, and *Flash*, Ross; Mar. 7; Mar. 28, *Miss Biddy* "(by particular Desire) to be attempted by Madem. Granier"; *Fribble*, King; *Flash*, Ross.

1752–53: Dec. 6, *Fribble*, King; *Flash*, Green; *Puff*, Sparks; *Miss Biddy*, Mrs. Green; Mar. 22, only *Fribble*, Mrs. Ward, "being the first Time of her appearing in Boy's Cloaths"; Mar. 26, plus *Flash*, King, and *Miss Biddy*, Mrs. Green.

1756–57: Jan. 26, *Flash*, Lee; *Fribble*, King; *Puff*, Sparks; *Tag*, Mrs. Mynitt; *Miss Biddy*, Mrs. Wilder; Jan. 31; Mar. 30, but *Tag*, Miss G. Phillips (first time); May 26, but *Tag*, Mrs. Mynitt; and *Miss Biddy*, Mrs. Storer.

1757–58: Oct. 24, *Fribble*, King; *Flash*, Glover; *Miss Biddy*, Miss Storer; Apr. 19, plus *Puff*, Sparks; May 9, but *Miss Biddy*, Mrs. Wilder.

The Mistake, "written by Sir John Vanbrugh"

1748–49: Oct. 26, *Lopez*, Macklin; Nov. 14; Jan. 11.

1749–50: Dec. 20, *Lopez*, Macklin; *Sancho*, Bardin; *Leonora*, Mrs. Bland; *Camilla*, Miss Copen; *Jacintha*, Mrs. Macklin; Jan. 3, without *Sancho* and *Camilla*.

1752–53: Feb. 10, *Carlos*, Sowdon; *Lopez*, King; *Don Alvarez*, Layfield; *Don Felix*, Costollo; *Lorenzo*, J. Elrington; *Sancho*, Sparks; *Metaphrastus*, Mynitt; *Jacintha*, Mrs. Green; *Camilla*, Mrs. Kennedy; *Leonora*, Mrs. Ward; Feb. 14; Mar. 6.

The Mock Doctor, by Henry Fielding

1747–48: Jan. 29, *Mock Doctor*, Woodward; Mar. 8, no cast; Mar. 18, *Mock Doctor*, Woodward.

1748–49: Apr. 12, *Mock Doctor*, Macklin; *Leander*, Dyer; *Charlotte*, Miss Minors; *Dorcas*, Mrs. Macklin; Apr. 26, without *Charlotte*.

1749–50: Nov. 22, *Mock Doctor*, Cibber; *Dorcas*, Mrs. Storer; Dec. 11; Dec. 20, without *Dorcas*; Feb. 8, plus *Dorcas*; May 22.

1750–51: Oct. 15, *Mock Doctor*, Cibber; *Dorcas*, Miss Cole; Nov. 5; Dec. 5; Feb. 27; Mar. 4.

1751–52: Oct. 2, *Mock Doctor*, Cibber; *Dorcas*, Miss Cole; Oct. 21.

1752–53: Nov. 30, *Mock Doctor*, King; *Dorcas*, Mrs. Green.

1753–54: Oct. 11, *Mock Doctor*, King; *Dorcas*, Mrs. Storer; Nov. 5.

1756–57: May 25, *Mock Doctor*, King.

1757–58: Oct. 10, *Mock Doctor*, King; *Dorcas*, Mrs. Storer; Oct. 22, without *Dorcas*; Dec. 2, plus *Dorcas*; Feb. 4; June 6.

The Mock Lawyer, by Edward Phillips

1751–52: Apr. 27, *Mock Lawyer*, Sparks; *Justice Lovelaw*, Mynitt; *Valentine*, "with the proper Songs," Conyers; *Dash*, Longfield; *Cheatly*, Hamilton; *Betty*, Mrs. Kennedy; *Laetitia*, Miss Cole.

Mock Pamela, or *a Kind Caution to Country Coxcombs.* (Dramatic Burlesque in Two Acts)

1749–50: May 14, *Squire Gudgeon,* Cibber; *Sir John Whip,* with Songs, Sullivan; *Biddy Blossom,* with Songs, Mrs. Lampe.

The Mourning Bride, by William Congreve

1747–48: Mar. 8, *King,* J. Elrington; *Osmyn,* R. Elrington; *Almeria,* Miss Bellamy (first time).

1751–52: Feb. 14, *Osmyn,* Sheridan (first time); *Zara,* Mrs. Bland (first time); *Almeria,* Mrs. Woffington (first time); Feb. 22; Mar. 7; Mar. 19; Apr. 9; May 23.

1752–53: Dec. 8, *Osmyn,* Sheridan; *King,* Sowdon; *Zara,* Mrs. Ward; *Almeria,* Mrs. Woffington; June 1, only *Osmyn* and *Almeria* listed.

1753–54: Dec. 3, *Osmyn,* Sheridan; *King,* Sowdon; *Gonsalez,* Layfield; *Garcia,* Kennedy; *Alonzo,* Stayley; *Heli,* J. Elrington; *Perez,* Hull; *Selim,* Maurice; *Leonora,* Miss Mason; *Zara,* Mrs. Kennedy; *Almeria,* Mrs. Woffington.

1756–57: Jan. 26, *Osmyn,* Sheridan; *Zara,* Mrs. Kennedy; *Almeria,* Miss Phillips.

1757–58: Nov. 28, *Osmyn,* Sheridan; *Zara,* Mrs. Fitzhenry; *Almeria,* "a Gentlewoman who never appeared on any Stage"; Dec. 2, but *Almeria,* Miss Taylor, "being the second Time of her appearing on the Stage"; Jan. 26, *Osmyn,* Dexter; *King,* Heaphy; *Gonsalez,* Stayley; *Garcia,* Kennedy; *Heli,* Hurst; *Selim,* Davenport; *Alonzo,* Watson; *Perez,* Preston; *Almeria,* Miss Phillips; *Leonora,* Miss Mason; *Zara,* Mrs. Beauclerk; Mar. 31, but *Almeria,* Miss Taylor; and *Zara,* Mrs. Fitzhenry; and without *Selim.*

Much Ado About Nothing, by William Shakespeare

1746–47: Nov. 27, *Benedict,* Sheridan; *Beatrice,* Miss Bellamy; Dec. 8, plus *Prince of Arragon,* J. Elrington; *Governor of Messina,* Beamsley; *Don John,* Watson; *Claudio,* MacLean; *Borachio,* Layfield; *Fryar,* R. Elrington; *Conrade,* Gemea; *Sexton,* Vanderbank; *Dogberry,* Dyer; *Verges,* Storer; *Hero,* Mrs. Dyer; *Margaret,* Mrs. Walter; and *Ursula,* Miss Jones; June 2, *Benedict,* Sheridan; *Beatrice,* Miss Bellamy; "and all other Parts to the best Advantage."

1747–48: Feb. 5, *Benedict,* Sheridan; *Beatrice,* Miss Bellamy.

1748–49: Dec. 5, *Benedict,* Sheridan; *Beatrice,* Mrs. Bland.

1750–51: Nov. 1, *Benedict,* King; *Hero,* Miss Cole; *Beatrice,* Mrs. Bland.

1752–53: Mar. 28, *Benedict,* King; *Leonato (Governor of Messina),*

Layfield; *Dogberry*, Sparks; *Balthazar*, with a Song, Sullivan; *Hero*, Mrs. Ward; *Beatrice*, Mrs. Woffington (first time); May 4, plus *Claudio*, Heaphy; *Don Pedro* (*Prince of Arragon*), J. Elrington; *Don John*, Stayley; and *Antonio*, Costollo.

1753–54: Nov. 28, *Benedict*, Sheridan; *Claudio*, Heaphy; *Leonato*, Layfield; *Dogberry*, Sparks; *Verges*, Cunningham; *Hero*, Mrs. Pye; *Beatrice*, Mrs. Woffington.

1756–57: Dec. 6, *Benedict*, Lee; *Dogberry*, Sparks; *Hero*, Miss Kennedy; *Beatrice*, Mrs. Lee; Dec. 16.

Nancy, or *The Parting Lovers*. "The Musick by Mr. Cary." (Musical Entertainment)

1749–50: May 4, *True Blue*, Sullivan; *Nancy*, Mrs. Storer; *Lieutenant and Father to Nancy*, Howard.

The Necromancer, or *Harlequin Dr. Faustus*, or *Doctor Faustus* (Pantomime Entertainment)

1745–46: May 8, *Faustus*, Morris (first time); *Leander*, Sullivan; *Helen*, Mrs. Storer.

1747–48: Nov. 9, *Faustus*, Woodward; *Miller's Wife*, Madem. Mechel; *First Fury*, Mons. Mechel; Nov. 11, only *Columbine*, played by Madem. Mechel, listed; Nov. 18, plus *Harlequin* (*Faustus*), Woodward.

1750–51: During this season this pantomime became a main play; it was given at Aungier-Street Theater and advertised as "Dr. Faustus, in a new Manner," with Mahomet Caratta's equilibres incorporated. No casts were listed. Performances on Nov. 13; Nov. 17; Nov. 20; Nov. 27; Dec. 1; Dec. 4.

1751–52: Dec. 26, *Harlequin*, Stevens; *Doctor's Man*, Sparks; other characters by Kennedy, Mynitt, Watson, Messink, Hamilton, Falkner, Williams, Mrs. Crump, Mrs. Kennedy, Mrs. Rowley, and others; Jan. 1, only *Harlequin* and *his Man* listed; Jan. 10; Jan. 18; Jan. 22, no cast; Apr. 2, *Harlequin*, Stevens; *Harlequin's Man*, Sparks; *Statue*, Hamilton; Apr. 3, without *Statue*.

1752–53: Jan. 18, no cast; Feb. 9.

1753–54: Nov. 26, *Faustus*, King; *Faustus' Man*, Sparks; *Pluto*, Powell, "the celebrated Fire-Eater from London; in which Character he will exhibit several of his surprizing Performances."

The Non-Juror, "written by Colley Cibber, Esq."

1751–52: Nov. 20, *Doctor Wolf*, Cibber; *Charles*, Digges; *Colonel*

[*Woodvil*], King; *Sir John Woodvil*, Heaphy; *Heartly*, Kennedy; *Lady Woodvil*, Mrs. Davies; *Maria*, Mrs. Woffington; Nov. 28; Dec. 9, without *Heartly* and *Lady Woodvil*; Jan. 13, only *Doctor Wolf*, *Charles*, *Colonel Woodvil*, and *Maria* listed; Feb. 1, plus *Heartly*, Kennedy; *Sir John Woodvil*, Heaphy; and *Lady Woodvil*, Mrs. Davies; Feb. 17; Mar. 14; May 14; May 25.

1752–53: Mar. 19, *Colonel Woodvil*, King; *Doctor Wolf*, Layfield; *Sir John Woodvil*, Heaphy; *Heartly*, Kennedy; *Charles*, a Young Gentleman "who never yet appeared on any Stage"; *Lady Woodvil*, Mrs. Kennedy; *Maria*, Mrs. Woffington; May 11, but *Charles*, Digges; June 4, but *Colonel Woodvil*, Dexter.

1753–54: Dec. 17, *Heartly*, Sheridan; *Charles*, Digges; *Colonel Woodvil*, Dexter; *Doctor Wolf*, Layfield; *Sir John Woodvil*, Heaphy; *Lady Woodvil*, Mrs. Ward; *Maria*, Mrs. Woffington; Dec. 22; Jan. 25; Feb. 7.

Oedipus, by John Dryden and Nathaniel Lee. "With Alterations"

1753–54: Oct. 26, *Oedipus*, Sheridan; *Creon*, Sowdon; *Tiresias*, Digges; *Adrastus*, Dexter; *Haemon*, Stayley; *Ghost of Laius*, Heaphy; *Alcander*, Kennedy; *Phorbas*, Layfield; *Aegeon*, J. Elrington; *Dymas*, Maurice; *Diocles*, Hull; *Pyracmon*, Watson; *Priests*, Storer and Mynitt; *Citizens*, Sparks, Cunningham, and Hamilton; *Eurydice*, Mrs. Ward; *Manto*, "with a Song in Character," Mrs. Storer; *Jocasta*, Mrs. Woffington; Nov. 1, without *Dymas*, *Diocles*, *Pyracmon*, and *Priests*; Nov. 9; Feb. 20, without *Haemon*, *Alcander*, *Aegeon*, *Citizens*.

The Old Batchelor, "written by [William] Congreve"

1747–48: Mar. 10, *Sir Joseph*, Woodward; *Laetitia*, Miss Bellamy (first time).

1748–49: Oct. 28, *Fondlewife*, Macklin; Dec. 9, plus *Heartwell*, Sheridan (first time) [but Sheridan may not have appeared until later—see next entry—or the whole performance may have been postponed]; *Laetitia*, Mrs. Bland; *Sylvia*, Mrs. Vincent; Dec. 14, but *Heartwell*, Sheridan (first time).

1750–51: Oct. 5, *Fondlewife (alias Nykin)*, Cibber; *Sir Joseph Wittol*, Robertson; *Bluff*, Sparks; *Heartwell*, Beamsley; *Bellmour*, Bardin; *Vainlove*, Ross; *Sharper*, J. Elrington; *Setter*, Watson; *Araminta*, Mrs. Rowley; *Lucy*, Mrs. Mynitt; *Laetitia*, Mrs. Bland; *Belinda*, Mrs. Robertson, "being the first Time of her appearing on this Stage"; *Sylvia*, Miss Cole.

1751–52: Jan. 22, *Old Batchelor* (*Heartwell*), Sheridan; *Bellmour*, Digges; *Fondlewife*, Cibber; *Sir Joseph Wittol*, King; *Vain-love*, Heaphy; *Sharper*, Kennedy; *Setter*, Stevens; *Belinda*, Mrs. Bland; *Araminta*, Mrs. Lee; *Sylvia*, Miss Cole; *Lucy*, Mrs. Kennedy; *Laetitia*, Mrs. Woffington; Feb. 21, but *Fondlewife*, Sheridan (first time); *Heartwell*, Beamsley; and *Lucy*, Mrs. Mynitt; and plus *Bluff*, Sparks.

1752–53: Feb. 21, *Fondlewife*, Sheridan; *Heartwell*, Sowdon; *Sir Joseph Wittol*, King; *Bellmour*, Kennedy; *Vainlove*, Heaphy; *Sharper*, J. Elrington; *Sylvia*, Mrs. Green; *Lucy*, a young Gentle-woman "who never appeared on any Stage"; *Laetitia*, Mrs. Woffington; Mar. 14, but *Lucy*, young Gentlewoman (second appearance); and plus *Bluff*, Sparks; *Araminta*, Mrs. Kennedy; and *Belinda*, Miss Mason; and without *Sharper*.

1753–54: Oct. 17, *Fondlewife*, Sheridan; *Heartwell*, Sowdon; *Bellmour*, Digges; *Sir Joseph Wittol*, King; *Bluff*, Sparks; *Sharper*, J. Elrington; *Vainlove*, Heaphy; *Setter*, Green; *Belinda*, Mrs. Ward; *Sylvia*, Mrs. Green; *Araminta*, Mrs. Kennedy; *Lucy*, Mrs. Mynitt; *Laetitia*, Mrs. Woffington; Nov. 22; Feb. 6.

1756–57: Nov. 26, *Fondlewife*, Sheridan; May 23, *Old Batchelor*, Sheridan; *Bellmour*, Dexter; *Sir Joseph Wittol*, King; *Bluff*, Sparks; *Araminta*, Miss Danvers; *Sylvia*, Mrs. Pye; *Belinda*, Mrs. Kennedy; *Laetitia*, Miss Kennedy; *Fondlewife*, Foote.

1757–58: Nov. 26, *Fondlewife*, Foote; *Heartwell*, Heaphy; *Bellmour*, Dexter; *Sir Joseph Wittol*, King; *Bluff*, Sparks; *Araminta*, Miss Danvers; *Belinda*, Mrs. Kennedy; *Laetitia*, Miss Kennedy; Dec. 23.

The Oracle, "written by Mrs. [Susannah Maria] Cibber." (A Comedy of One Act)

1752–53: Mar. 23, *Cynthia*, Mrs. Green; *Queen of the Fairies*, Mrs. Mynitt; *Oberon*, King.

1756–57: Jan. 17, *Oberon*, Wilder; *Cynthia*, Mrs. Wilder; Feb. 14; Feb. 18; Feb. 19; Feb. 24; Feb. 28; Mar. 10; Mar. 12; Mar. 21; Apr. 27; May 18.

1757–58: Nov. 17, *Oberon*, Wilder; *Queen of the Fairies*, Miss Mason; *Cynthia*, Mrs. Wilder; Dec. 15, without *Queen*; Mar. 1, plus *Queen*; Apr. 5, "All the Character's [*sic*] to be performed by Mrs. Storer's Children"; Apr. 25, characters by Mrs. Storer's Children, "by Desire"; May 4.

Oroonoko, "by Mr. [Thomas] Southern"

1745–46: Feb. 24, *Oroonoko*, Barry; *Imoinda*, Miss Bellamy; "all other Parts performed to the best Advantage"; May 26, without *Imoinda*.

1746–47: Mar. 10, *Oroonoko*, R. Elrington.

1748–49: Feb. 16, *Oroonoko*, Sheridan (first time); *Aboan*, "by a Gentleman who never yet appeared on any Stage"; *Imoinda*, Mrs. Vincent; *Charlotte Welldon*, Mrs. Bland; *Lucy*, Miss Minors; *Widow Lackit*, Mrs. Macklin; *Daniel*, Macklin; Apr. 4, but *Aboan*, "by the Gentleman who performed it before"; May 29, but *Aboan*, Mr. [Francis] Gentleman; and plus *Blandford*, J. Elrington; *Governor*, Kennedy; *Stanmore*, Ross; *Younger Stanmore*, Watson; *Capt. Driver*, Morris; *Hotman*, Beamsley; *First Planter*, Vaughan; and *Second Planter*, Duncomb.

1749–50: Oct. 27, *Oroonoko*, Sheridan; *Aboan*, Gentleman; *Imoinda*, Miss Danvers (first time); *Widow Lackit*, Mrs. Macklin; *Charlotte Welldon*, Mrs. Bland; *Daniel*, Macklin.

1750–51: Feb. 25, *Oroonoko*, Sheridan; *Aboan*, Mossop; *Daniel*, King; *Imoinda*, Miss Danvers; *Widow Lackit*, Mrs. Mynitt; *Charlotte Welldon*, Mrs. Bland; Apr. 25, but *Oroonoko*, Montgomery (first time), and *Aboan*, Ross; and plus *Lucy*, Mrs. Lindley.

1752–53: May 30, *Oroonoko*, Dexter, "from the Theatre Royal in Drury-lane, being the first Time of his appearing on this Stage"; *Daniel*, Cunningham; *Imoinda*, Mrs. Ward; *Charlotte Welldon*, Mrs. Kennedy; *Widow Lackit*, Mrs. Woffington (first time).

1753–54: Oct. 3, *Oroonoko*, Dexter; *Imoinda*, Mrs. Ward; Jan. 21, but *Oroonoko*, Sheridan; and plus *Aboan*, Sowdon; *Capt. Driver*, Sparks; *Daniel*, Cunningham; *Charlotte Welldon*, Mrs. Kennedy; and *Widow Lackit*, Mrs. Woffington.

1756–57: Mar. 28, *Oroonoko*, Dexter; *Aboan*, Heaphy; *Governor*, Stayley; *Capt. Driver*, Sparks; *Blandford*, Kennedy; *Stanmore*, Hurst; *Younger Stanmore*, Aickin; *Hotman*, Layfield; *Daniel*, King; *Widow Lackit*, Mrs. Mynitt; *Charlotte Welldon*, Mrs. Kennedy; *Lucy*, Mrs. Pye; *Imoinda*, Miss Kennedy.

1757–58: Oct. 19, *Oroonoko*, Dexter; *Aboan*, Heaphy; *Blandford*, Kennedy; *Governor*, Stayley; *Stanmore*, Hurst; *Younger Stanmore*, Wall; *Daniel*, Glover; *Hotman*, Lewis; *Planters*, Watson, R. Elrington, Williams, M'Mahon, &c.; *Capt. Driver*, Sparks; *Charlotte Welldon*, Mrs. Kennedy; *Lucy*, Mrs. Pye; *Widow Lackit*, Mrs. Farrell; *Imoinda*, Miss Kennedy; Dec. 14, only *Oroonoko*, *Aboan*, and *Imoinda* listed.

The Orphan, or *The Unhappy Marriage,* by Thomas Otway

1745–46: Nov. 11, *Monimia,* Miss Bellamy, "being the first Time of her appearing on this Stage"; *Castalio,* Barry; *Polydore,* Lacy; *Chamont,* Sheridan; Jan. 9, but *Polydore,* "by particular Desire," Sheridan (first time), and *Chamont,* Garrick; Jan. 22, without *Monimia;* Feb. 11.

1746–47: Dec. 11, *Chamont,* Sheridan, "by particular Desire"; *Monimia,* Miss Bellamy; Mar. 9, only *the Orphan (Monimia)* listed.

1748–49: Apr. 22, *Chamont,* Sheridan; *Monimia,* Miss Danvers.

1749–50: Feb. 3, *Chamont,* Sheridan; *Castalio,* Digges; *Polydore,* Mossop; *Monimia,* Miss Danvers; *Chaplain,* Cibber; Feb. 7; Feb. 14; Mar. 3, without *Chaplain;* Apr. 25, plus *Serina,* Mrs. Mozeen; May 17, plus *Chaplain.*

1750–51: Oct. 15, *Chamont,* Sheridan; *Castalio,* Digges; *Polydore,* Mossop; *Chaplain,* Cibber; *Serina,* Miss Cole; *Monimia,* Mrs. Bland (first time); Nov. 8; Mar. 7, but *Polydore,* Montgomery; and plus *Acasto,* Beamsley; Mar. 26, *Chamont,* Digges (first time); *Polydore,* Montgomery; *Castalio,* Ross; *Page,* Miss Reynolds; *Chaplain,* Cibber; *Serina;* Miss Cole; *Monimia,* Miss Danvers.

1752–53: Nov. 24, *Chamont,* Sheridan; *Polydore,* Sowdon; *Castalio,* Digges; *Page,* Master Mynitt; *Monimia,* Mrs. Ward, "from the Theatre Royal in Drury-lane, being the first Time of her appearing in this Kingdom."

1756–57: Dec. 3, *Chamont,* Sheridan; *Polydore,* Lee; *Castalio,* Dexter; *Monimia,* Miss G. Phillips; Dec. 9; Jan. 3; May 6.

The Orphan of Venice, by James Darcy

1748–49: Mar. 9, principal characters by Sheridan, Macklin, Beamsley, Dyer, Kennedy, Mrs. Vincent, Mrs. Bland, Mrs. Dyer; Apr. 13.

Othello, by William Shakespeare

1745–46: Nov. 18, *Othello,* Sheridan; *Emilia,* Mrs. Furnival; *Desdemona,* Miss Bellamy; Feb. 26, but *Othello,* Garrick; and plus *Iago,* Sheridan; Feb. 28, but only *Othello,* Sheridan, and *Iago,* Garrick, listed.

1746–47: Apr. 8, no cast; June 4, *Othello,* Sheridan; *Desdemona,* Miss Bellamy.

1747–48: Dec. 7, *Othello,* Sheridan; *Roderigo,* Woodward; *Desdemona,* Miss Bellamy; Feb. 25.

1748–49: Nov. 28, *Othello,* Sheridan; *Iago,* Macklin; *Desdemona,* Mrs. Vincent; *Emilia,* Mrs. Macklin; Jan. 31, plus *Cassio,* J. Elrington; *Montano*, Mozeen; *Roderigo*, Dyer; *Lodovico*, Kennedy; *Brabantio*, Beamsley; and *Duke*, Sparks.

1749–50: Oct. 6, *Othello*, Sheridan; *Iago*, Macklin; *Emilia*, Mrs. Macklin; Dec. 4, plus *Desdemona*, Mrs. Mozeen; Dec. 13, but *Othello*, Mossop; Dec. 19; Jan. 24; Mar. 31, only *Othello*, Mossop, and *Iago*, Sheridan, listed.

1750–51: Nov. 2, *Othello*, "by a Gentleman, who never appeared on any Stage"; *Desdemona*, Miss Cole; *Emilia*, Mrs. Bland; *Roderigo*, King; *Iago*, Sheridan; Nov. 14, but *Othello*, Montgomery, and *Iago*, Sheridan, "by particular Desire"; Nov. 28, but *Othello*, Sheridan; and *Iago*, Montgomery; Jan. 14, but *Othello*, Mossop; and plus *Cassio*, Ross.

1752–53: Oct. 18, *Othello*, Sowdon, "from the Theatre Royal in Drury-Lane, being the first Time of his appearing on this Stage"; *Roderigo*, King; *Iago*, Montgomery.

1756–57: Jan. 17, *Othello*, Sheridan; *Iago*, Lee; *Roderigo*, King; *Emilia*, Mrs. Kennedy; *Desdemona*, Miss G. Phillips; Apr. 14, but *Othello*, Dexter, and *Iago*, Layfield; and plus *Brabantio*, Heaphy; *Montano*, Hurst; *Lodovico*, Stayley; *Gratiano*, Watson; and *Duke*, Aickin.

1757–58: Jan. 19, *Othello*, Wilkinson (first time); *Cassio*, Kennedy; *Roderigo*, Oliver; *Lodovico*, Stayley; *Brabantio*, Heaphy; *Gratiano*, Watson; *Montano*, Hurst; *Iago*, King; *Duke*, Lewis; *Officer*, Williams; *Emilia*, Mrs. Kennedy; *Desdemona*, Miss G. Phillips; Apr. 15, but *Othello*, Sheridan; and *Roderigo*, Ryder.

Phaedra and Hippolitus, by Edmund Smith

1750–51: Nov. 30, *Theseus*, Sheridan; *Hippolitus*, Digges; *Lycon*, Mossop; *Ismena*, Miss Griffith; *Phaedra*, Mrs. Bland; Dec. 5; Dec. 12; Feb. 13; Mar. 2.

1751–52: Apr. 20, *Theseus*, Sheridan; *Hippolitus*, Digges; *Phaedra*, Mrs. Woffington (first time); May 16, plus *Lycon*, Beamsley; and *Ismena*, Mrs. Davies.

1752–53: Oct. 30, *Theseus*, Sheridan; *Hippolitus*, Digges; *Phaedra*, Mrs. Woffington; Nov. 15; Feb. 7, plus *Lycon*, Layfield; and *Ismena*, Mrs. Ward; May 21.

1753–54: Oct. 8, *Theseus*, Sheridan; *Lycon*, Sowdon; *Hippolitus*, Dexter; *Cratander*, Watson; *Attendant*, Mrs. Leslie; *Ismena*, Mrs. Ward; *Phaedra*, Mrs. Woffington; Nov. 29, without *Cratander* and *Attendant*; Jan. 23; Feb. 8.

1757–58: Feb. 11, *Theseus*, Sheridan; *Lycon*, Heaphy; *Hippolitus*, Dex ter; *Ismena*, Miss Phillips; *Phaedra*, Mrs. Fitzhenry; Mar. 9, plus *Cratander*, Watson; and *Officer*, Storer.

Phoebe, or *The Beggar's Wedding*, by Charles Coffey. (Opera)

1753–54: Feb. 13, *Chaunter*, Sparks; *Hunter*, Layfield; *Tib Tatter*, "with the Dust Man's Cantata, in Character," Mrs. Storer; *Tippet*, Mrs. Pye; *Phoebe*, Mrs. Green; Feb. 16; Feb. 20.

1756–57: Mar. 24, *Hunter*, Wilder; *Grig*, King; *Chaunter*, Sparks; *Justice*, Mynitt; *Cant*, Glover; *Gage*, Stayley; *Tippet*, Miss Spencer; *Phoebe*, Mrs. Wilder; Apr. 2, but *Tippit*, Mrs. Pye; and without *Justice*.

The Pilgrim, by John Fletcher, as altered by Sir John Vanbrugh

1752–53: Mar. 15, *Alphonso*, Sparks; *Pedro*, Heaphy; *Roderigo*, Stevens; *Mad Englishman*, Layfield; *Mad Parson*, Green; *Mad Welshman*, Cunningham; *Mad Scholar*, Kennedy; *Juletta*, Mrs. Green.

1753–54: Nov. 26, *Mad Scholar*, Sowdon; *Roderigo*, Dexter; *Alphonso*, Sparks; *Pedro*, Heaphy; *Mad Englishman*, Layfield; *Mad Welshman*, Cunningham; *Stuttering Cook*, Green; *Alinda*, Mrs. Kennedy; *Juletta*, Mrs. Green; Dec. 12; Jan. 10, plus *Mad Taylor*, Williams; and *Mad Bess*, Mrs. Storer.

The Pleasures of the Town, or *Punch turn'd Swadler*, by Henry Fielding [?]. [See Part 1, March 22, 1750, and note.] ("A satyrical Puppet Show")

1749–50: Mar. 22, no cast.

The Provoked Husband, or *The Journey to London*, by Colley Cibber

1745–46: Dec. 4, no cast; Mar. 17, *Lord Townly*, Sheridan; *Lady Grace*, Miss Jones, "from England, being the first Time of her Appearing in this Kingdom"; *Lady Wronghead*, Mrs. Furnival; *Miss Jenny*, "with the Original Songs," Mrs. Storer; *Lady Townly*, Mrs. Elmy.

1746–47: Jan. 20, *Lord Townly*, Sheridan; *Lady Townly*, Miss Bellamy (first time); Mar. 12, only *Lady Townly* listed.

1747–48: Feb. 27, *Lord Townly*, Sheridan; *Lady Townly*, Miss Bellamy.

1748–49: Nov. 29, *Lord Townly*, Sheridan; *Sir Francis Wronghead*, Macklin; *Lady Townly*, Mrs. Bland; *Lady Wronghead*, Mrs. Macklin; *Miss Jenny*, Miss Minors; Dec. 1; Apr. 27, plus *Squire Richard*, Dyer.

1749–50: Nov. 3, *Lord Townly*, Sheridan; *Lady Townly*, Mrs. Bland;

Sir Francis Wronghead, Macklin; *Lady Wronghead*, Mrs. Macklin; *Miss Jenny*, Mrs. Mozeen; *Lady Grace*, Miss Danvers (first time); Feb. 16, without *Miss Jenny* and *Lady Grace*; Apr. 20, but *Sir Francis Wronghead*, Morgan; and *Lady Wronghead*, Mrs. Mynitt; and plus *Lady Grace* and *Manly*, Cibber.

1750–51: Oct. 25, *Lord Townly*, Sheridan; *Manly*, Cibber; *John Moody*, Sparks; *Lady Townly*, Mrs. Bland; *Lady Grace*, Miss Danvers; *Miss Jenny*, Miss Cole.

1751–52: Oct. 7, *Lord Townly*, Sheridan; *Sir Francis Wronghead*, Cibber; *John Moody*, Sparks; *Manly*, Heaphy, "being his first Attempt on this Stage"; *Lady Grace*, Miss Cole; *Lady Townly*, Mrs. Woffington, "from the Theatre Royal in Covent-garden"; Oct. 17, plus *Lady Wronghead*, Mrs. Mynitt; and without *Manly*; Nov. 13, without *Lady Wronghead*; Nov. 30, plus *Manly*; and without *John Moody*; Dec. 14, plus *Lady Wronghead*; Jan. 11, but *Lady Wronghead*, Mrs. Lee; and plus *John Moody*, Sparks; *Count Basset*, Kennedy; and *Miss Jenny*, Mrs. Kennedy; Jan. 29, plus *Squire Richard*, Stevens; and without *John Moody*; Mar. 9, but *Lady Wronghead*, Mrs. Mynitt; and plus *John Moody*.

1752–53: Oct. 19, *Lord Townly*, Sheridan; *Manly*, Stayley; *Lady Townly*, Mrs. Woffington; Nov. 10, plus *Miss Jenny*, Mrs. Green; and without *Manly*; Dec. 6, plus *Manly*, Heaphy; *Sir Francis Wronghead*, Layfield; and *John Moody*, Sparks; Apr. 11, but *Lord Townly*, Digges; and plus *Count Basset*, Kennedy; *Squire Richard*, Pitt; *Lady Grace*, Miss Mason; and *Lady Wronghead*, Mrs. Mynitt.

1753–54: Oct. 25, *Lord Townly*, Sheridan; *Manly*, Heaphy; *Sir Francis Wronghead*, Layfield; *John Moody*, Sparks; *Lady Grace*, Mrs. Ward; *Miss Jenny*, Mrs. Green; *Lady Wronghead*, Mrs. Mynitt; *Lady Townly*, Mrs. Woffington; Dec. 5; Feb. 13, plus *Count Basset*, Kennedy; and *Squire Richard*, Cunningham.

1756–57: Nov. 25, *Lord Townly*, Sheridan; *Lady Townly*, Mrs. Glen; Mar. 26, *Lord Townly*, Dexter; *Manly*, Heaphy; *Sir Francis Wronghead*, Layfield; *Squire Richard*, Glover; *John Moody*, Sparks; *Count Basset*, Kennedy; *Lady Wronghead*, Mrs. Mynitt; *Trusty*, Mrs. Pye; *Miss Jenny*, Miss G. Phillips; *Myrtilla*, Miss Mason; *Lady Townly*, Miss Phillips.

1757–58: Feb. 4, *Lord Townly*, Sheridan; *Manly*, Heaphy; *Count Basset*, Kennedy; *Squire Richard*, Hamilton; *Sir Francis Wronghead*, Glover; *John Moody*, Sparks; *Lady Wronghead*,

Mrs. Kennedy; *Lady Grace,* Miss Danvers; *Miss Jenny,* Mrs. Wilder; *Myrtilla,* Miss Mason; *Trusty,* Mrs. Pye; *Lady Townly,* Mrs. Fitzhenry.

The Provoked Wife, "wrote (and revised with Alterations) by the late Sir John Vanbrugh"

1745–46: Jan. 27, *Sir John Brute,* Garrick; Apr. 14, plus *Lady Brute,* Mrs. Furnival.

1747–48: Mar. 14, *Sir John Brute,* Woodward (first time); Apr. 19.

1748–49: Oct. 14, *Sir John Brute,* Macklin; Dec. 23, plus *Lady Brute,* Mrs. Bland; *Lady Fanciful,* Mrs. Vincent; and *Mademoiselle,* Mrs. Macklin; May 9, plus *Belinda,* Mrs. Mozeen.

1749–50: Oct. 4, *Sir John Brute,* Macklin; *Mademoiselle,* Mrs. Macklin; *Lady Brute,* Mrs. Bland; *Lady Fanciful,* Miss Copen, "from the Theatre-Royal in Drury-lane, being the first Time of her appearing on the Stage in this Kingdom."

1750–51: Mar. 18, *Sir John Brute,* "attempted after the Manner of the celebrated Colley Cibber, Esq.," Cibber (first time); *Col. Bully,* Sparks; *Constant,* Ross; *Lord Rake,* Falkner; *Taylor,* Mynitt; *Heartfree,* King; *Justice,* Watson; *Razor,* Bardin; *Page,* Miss Reynolds; *Constable,* Packenham; *Porter,* Messink; *Watchman,* Williams; *Cornet,* Mrs. Leslie; *Lovewill,* Miss Copen; *Lady Fanciful,* Mrs. Lindley; *Belinda,* Miss Cole; *Mademoiselle,* Mrs. Rowley; *Lady Brute,* Mrs. Bland; May 3, *Sir John Brute,* Digges (first time); *Col. Bully,* Sparks; *Constant,* Ross; *Lord Rake,* Hamilton; *Heartfree,* King; *Lady Fanciful,* Mrs. Lindley; *Belinda,* Miss Cole; *Lady Brute,* Mrs. Bland.

1751–52: Jan. 18, *Sir John Brute,* Sheridan (first time); *Heartfree,* King; *Constant,* Heaphy; *Belinda,* Miss Cole; *Mademoiselle,* Mrs. Rowley; *Lady Brute,* Mrs. Bland; *Lady Fanciful,* Mrs. Woffington; Jan. 28, plus *Lord Rake,* Kennedy, and *Razor,* Stevens; Apr. 10, but *Sir John Brute,* Digges; and plus *Col. Bully,* Stevens; and without *Razor.*

1752–53: Mar. 9, *Sir John Brute,* Sheridan; *Heartfree,* King; *Constant,* Heaphy; *Col. Bully,* Sparks; *Lady Fanciful,* Mrs. Green; *Lady Brute,* Mrs. Woffington; May 3, *Sir John Brute,* Digges; *Heartfree,* King; *Constant,* Heaphy; *Lord Rake,* Kennedy; *Col. Bully,* Sparks; *Razor,* Green; *Taylor,* Mynitt; *Lady Brute,* Mrs. Ward; *Belinda,* Mrs. Kennedy; *Mademoiselle,* Mrs. Green; *Lady Fanciful,* Mrs. Woffington.

1753–54: Dec. 6, *Sir John Brute,* Sheridan; *Heartfree,* King; *Constant,* Dexter; *Col. Bully,* Sparks; *Razor,* Green; *Lord Rake,* Kennedy; *Justice,* Watson; *Taylor,* Mynitt; *Constable,* Maurice;

Watchman, Williams; *Lady Brute,* Mrs. Ward; *Mademoiselle,* Mrs. Green; *Belinda,* Mrs. Kennedy; *Lady Fanciful,* Mrs. Woffington.

1756–57: Mar. 22, *Sir John Brute,* Lee; *Constant,* Dexter; *Heartfree,* King; *Lord Rake,* "with a Song in Character," Wilder; *Col. Bully,* Sparks; *Razor,* Glover; *Lady Fanciful,* Mrs. Lee; *Belinda,* Miss G. Phillips; *Mademoiselle,* Mrs. Pye; *Lady Brute,* Miss Phillips.

Pyramus and Thisbe. "The Words are to be found in Shakespear's Midsummer's Night's Dream. The Musick by Mr. [John Frederick] Lampe." (Burlesque Opera)

1746–47: Dec. 19, *Pyramus,* Dyer; *Thisbe,* Mrs. Storer; *Wall* and *Lion,* Layfield.

1749–50: Jan. 19, *Pyramus,* Mrs. Lampe; *Thisbe,* Mrs. Mozeen; *Wall* and *Moonshine,* Sullivan; *Lion,* Howard; *Mons. Papilot,* Cibber; Jan. 24; Feb. 19.

The Recruiting Officer, by George Farquhar

1745–46: Jan. 16, *Plume,* Garrick; *Kite,* Morris; *Brazen,* Bardin; *Sylvia,* Mrs. Elmy; *Melinda,* Mrs. Walter.

1747–48: Jan. 27, *Plume,* Sheridan; *Brazen,* Woodward; Feb. 2.

1748–49: Mar. 16, *Brazen,* Macklin; *Sylvia,* Mrs. Bland; May 5, plus *Rose,* Mrs. Mozeen; and *Lucy,* Miss Orfeur.

1749–50: Nov. 1, *Plume,* Sheridan; *Brazen,* Macklin; *Melinda,* Miss Copen; *Sylvia,* Mrs. Bland; Mar. 12, *Brazen,* Cibber; *Plume,* Digges, "being his first Attempt in Comedy"; May 3, plus *Sylvia,* Mrs. Bland.

1750–51: Sept. 24, *Plume,* Digges; *Brazen,* Cibber; *Kite,* Sparks; *Justice Ballance,* Beamsley; *Worthy,* Ross; *Recruits,* Mynitt, Robertson, Hamilton, and Williams; *Melinda,* Mrs. Lindley; *Lucy,* Mrs. Mynitt; *Sylvia,* Mrs. Bland; *Rose,* Miss Cole; Nov. 29, only *Plume, Brazen,* and *Sylvia* listed; Jan. 7, plus *Justice Ballance, Worthy, Kite, Melinda, Lucy, Rose,* and *Bullock,* Mynitt; *Appletree,* Williams; *Peniman,* Hamilton; *Constable,* Maurice; and *Welsh Collier,* Packenham; Apr. 15, without *Justice Ballance, Bullock, Appletree, Peniman, Constable, Welsh Collier,* and *Lucy.*

1751–52: Oct. 10, *Plume,* Digges; *Brazen,* Cibber; *Kite,* Sparks; *Melinda,* Mrs. Lee; *Rose,* Miss Cole; *Sylvia,* Mrs. Woffington; Apr. 18, but *Plume,* Heaphy; and plus *Justice Ballance,* Beamsley; *Worthy,* Kennedy; *Bullock,* Mynitt; and *Lucy,* Mrs. Kennedy.

1752–53: Oct. 26, *Plume*, Sheridan; *Brazen*, King; *Kite*, Sparks; *Sylvia*, Mrs. Woffington.

1753–54: Dec. 19, *Plume*, Dexter; *Brazen*, King; *Justice Ballance*, Layfield; *Kite*, Sparks; *Worthy*, Stayley; *Bullock*, Mynitt; *Recruits*, Green and Hamilton; *Scruple*, Watson; *Scale*, Hull; *Welsh Collier*, Cunningham; *Constable*, Maurice; *Servant*, Williams; *Melinda*, Miss Mason; *Lucy*, Mrs. Mynitt; *Rose*, Mrs. Kennedy; *Sylvia*, Mrs. Woffington.

1756–57: Oct. 22, *Plume*, Dexter; *Worthy*, Stayley; *Justice Ballance*, Layfield; *Bullock*, Mynitt; *Brazen*, King; *Recruits*, Williams and Messink; *Constable*, Hurst; *Scale*, R. Elrington; *Scruple*, Watson; *Kite*, Sparks; *Melinda*, Miss Mason; *Rose*, Mrs. Kennedy; *Lucy*, Mrs. Pye; *Sylvia*, Miss Kennedy; Feb. 18, *Plume*, Dexter; *Brazen*, King; *Kite*, Sparks; *Bullock*, Glover; *Rose*, Mrs. Kennedy; *Sylvia*, Mrs. Glen (first time); Apr. 23, but *Sylvia*, Miss Kennedy; and plus *Worthy, Justice Ballance, Scale, Scruple, Constable*; *Welsh Collier*, Mynitt; and *Recruits*, Hamilton and Williams; June 4, without *Recruits, Scale, Scruple, Constable*, and *Welsh Collier*.

1757–58: Oct. 21, *Plume*, Dexter; *Justice Ballance*, Heaphy; *Worthy*, Stayley; *Bullock*, Glover; *Brazen*, King; *Recruits*, Williams and Hamilton; *Welsh Collier*, Lewis; *Kite*, Sparks; *Scale*, R. Elrington; *Scruple*, Watson; *Melinda*, Miss Mason; *Lucy*, Mrs. Pye; *Rose*, Mrs. Kennedy; *Sylvia*, Miss Kennedy; Dec. 7, *Brazen*, Foote; *Sylvia*, Miss Kennedy; *Plume*, Ryder, "being his first Appearance on this Stage."

The Refusal, or *The Ladies Philosophy*, "by Colley Cibber"

1748–49: Dec. 7, *Wrangle*, Macklin; *Sophronia*, Mrs. Vincent; *Charlotte*, Mrs. Bland; *Lady Wrangle*, Mrs. Macklin; *Granger*, Mozeen; *Frankly*, Dyer; *Witling*, Kennedy; Jan. 9, only *Wrangle* and *Lady Wrangle* listed; Jan. 20; Mar. 29, plus *Sophronia*, Mrs. Vincent; and *Charlotte*, Mrs. Bland.

1749–50: Nov. 17, *Wrangle*, Macklin; *Sophronia*, Miss Copen; *Charlotte*, Mrs. Bland; *Lady Wrangle*, Mrs. Macklin; *Witling*, Cibber; Dec. 18.

1750–51: Jan. 25, *Witling*, Cibber; *Frankly*, King; *Granger*, Ross; *Wrangle*, Sparks; *Lady Wrangle*, Mrs. Mynitt; *Sophronia*, Mrs. Lindley; *Charlotte*, Mrs. Bland; Jan. 28; Feb. 1; May 21, plus *Cook*, Williams; and *Maid*, Mrs. Rowley.

1751–52: Feb. 15, *Witling*, Cibber; *Wrangle*, Sparks; *Frankly*, King; *Granger*, Heaphy; *Lady Wrangle*, Mrs. Mynitt; *Sophronia*, Miss Cole; *Charlotte*, Mrs. Woffington; Apr. 15, plus *Cook*, Mynitt; and *Maid*, Mrs. Kennedy.

1752–53: Mar. 23, *Wrangle*, Sparks; *Witling*, King; *Frankly*, Kennedy; *Granger*, Heaphy; *Cook*, Mynitt; *Sophronia*, Mrs. Green; *Lady Wrangle*, Mrs. Mynitt; *Maid*, Mrs. Kennedy; *Charlotte*, Mrs. Woffington.

The Rehearsal, "wrote by the Duke of Buckingham"

1745–46: Dec. 20, *Bayes*, Garrick; Dec. 30.

1747–48: May 23, *Bayes*, Woodward; May 25.

1748–49: Mar. 1, *Bayes*, Macklin.

1750–51: Mar. 20, *Bayes*, King, "interspersed with Chocolate, after the Manner of a very celebrated Actor"; *Amarillis*, Miss Cole; *Smith*, Ross; *Johnson*, Digges.

1752–53: Jan. 12, *Bayes*, King; *Johnson*, Stayley; *Smith*, Beamsley; *Prince Prettyman*, J. Elrington; *Prince Volscius*, Kennedy; *Physician*, Green; *Thunder*, Sparks; Jan. 25.

1753–54: Dec. 31, *Bayes*, King; *Gentleman Usher*, Green; *Thunder*, Sparks; *Johnson*, Stayley; *Smith*, Hull; *Prince Prettyman*, J. Elrington; *Prince Volscius*, Kennedy; *Physician*, Mynitt; *Amarillis*, Mrs. Pye; *Chloris*, Miss Mason.

1756–57: Dec. 2, *Bayes*, King; Dec. 13; Apr. 15, plus *Johnson*, Dexter; *Smith*, Heaphy; and other characters by Sparks, Glover, Layfield, Kennedy, Stayley, Corry, Hurst, Watson, Hamilton, Williams, Aickin, Bate, R. Elrington, Messink, Mrs. Pye, Miss Mason, Mrs. Packenham, Miss Rayner, &c.; May 16, only *Bayes*, Foote, listed.

1757–58: Nov. 2, *Bayes*, King; *Johnson*, Dexter; *Smith*, Heaphy; rest of characters by Sparks, Stayley, Kennedy, Hurst, Storer, Watson, Hamilton, Corry, Lewis, Williams, Messink, R. Elrington, Davenport, Wall, Bate, Mrs. Packenham, Miss Mason, Mrs. Pye, &c; Dec. 9, only *Bayes*, Foote; and "with an additional Character as an Assistant to Mr. Bays to be performed by a Gentleman, being his first Appearance on any Stage" [but see next entry]; Dec. 16, "N.B. The young Gentleman who was to have performed in it [The Rehearsal] before was so weak after a dangerous Indisposition, that he found himself unable to attempt it, but hopes by that Time [Dec. 16] to be perfectly recovered." [The "young Gentleman" was Wilkinson.]

The Relapse, or *Virtue in Danger*, "by Sir John Vanbrugh"

1747–48: Nov. 11, *Lord Foppington*, Woodward; Apr. 1, plus *Miss Hoyden*, Miss Mason.

1748–49: Feb. 15, *Lord Foppington*, Macklin; *Amanda*, Mrs. Vincent; *Berinthia*, Mrs. Bland; *Miss Hoyden*, Miss Minors.

1751–52: Jan. 8, *Lord Foppington*, Cibber; *Loveless*, Digges; *Young Fashion*, King; *Sir Tunbelly Clumsy*, Sparks; *Worthy*, Kennedy; *Lory*, Stevens; *Coupler*, Mynitt; *Bull*, Longfield; *Seringe*, Beamsley; *Verole*, Watson; *Constable*, Williams; *Page*, Miss Reynolds; *Amanda*, Mrs. Davies; *Miss Hoyden*, Miss Cole; *Nurse*, Mrs. Rowley; *Amanda's Maid*, Mrs. Kennedy; *Berinthia*, Mrs. Woffington; Jan. 31, without *Bull, Seringe, Verole, Constable, Page*, and *Amanda's Maid*; Mar. 30, but *Nurse*, Mrs. Mynitt; May 15, without *Lory* and *Coupler*.

1752–53: Nov. 1, *Loveless*, Digges; *Lord Foppington*, King; *Sir Tunbelly Clumsy*, Sparks; *Miss Hoyden*, Mrs. Green, "from the Theatre Royal in Drury-lane, being the first Time of her appearing on this Stage"; *Berinthia*, Mrs. Woffington; Apr. 26, plus *Worthy*, Kennedy; *Young Fashion*, Stayley; *Amanda*, Mrs. Ward; and *Nurse*, Mrs. Mynitt.

1753–54: Jan. 28, *Lord Foppington*, King; *Loveless*, Dexter; *Sir Tunbelly Clumsy*, Sparks; *Worthy*, Kennedy; *Young Fashion*, Stayley; *Lory*, Green; *Coupler*, Mynitt; *Nurse*, Mrs. Mynitt; *Miss Hoyden*, Mrs. Green; *Amanda*, Mrs. Ward; *Berinthia*, Mrs. Woffington.

1757–58: Dec. 12, *Lord Foppington*, Foote; *Loveless*, Dexter; *Worthy*, Kennedy; *Lory*, Glover; *Friendly*, Watson; *Coupler*, Lewis; *Seringe*, Hamilton; *Bull*, Storer; *Amanda*, Miss Mason; *Berinthia*, Mrs. Kennedy; *Miss Hoyden*, Mrs. Wilder; *Nurse*, Mrs. Farrell.

The Revenge, "written by Dr. [Edward] Young"

1745–46: Apr. 28, *Zanga*, Sheridan; *Leonora*, Miss Bellamy.

1746–47: Nov. 17, *Zanga*, Sheridan; *Leonora*, Miss Bellamy; May 4, plus *Don Carlos*, Dugere, "by particular Desire"; and without *Zanga*.

1747–48: Oct. 26, *Zanga*, Sheridan; *Leonora*, Miss Bellamy.

1748–49: Nov. 2, *Zanga*, Sheridan.

1749–50: Nov. 30, *Zanga*, Mossop, "a Gentleman of this Country, who never yet appeared on any Stage"; *Leonora*, Mrs. Bland; Dec. 7; Mar. 2; Apr. 6.

1750–51: Oct. 10, *Zanga*, Mossop; *Leonora*, Mrs. Bland; Jan. 24, plus *Carlos*, Ross; *Alvarez*, Beamsley; *Alonzo*, Montgomery; and *Isabella*, Mrs. Rowley.

1753–54: Feb. 16, *Zanga*, Sheridan; *Alonzo*, Sowdon; *Carlos*, Dexter; *Alvarez*, Heaphy; *Manuel*, Stayley; *Isabella*, Mrs. Kennnedy [in playbill, Mrs. Pye]; *Leonora*, Mrs. Ward.

1757–58: Apr. 26, *Zanga*, Sheridan; *Carlos*, Stayley; *Alvarez*, Heaphy;

Manuel, Aickin; *Alonzo*, Dexter; *Isabella*, Mrs. Kennedy; *Leonora*, Mrs. Fitzhenry; May 13.

Richard III, by William Shakespeare, as altered by Colley Cibber

1745–46: Nov. 14, *Richard*, Sheridan; *Lady Anne*, Mrs. Elmy; *Queen*, Mrs. Furnival; Dec. 12, but *Richard*, Garrick.

1746–47: Dec. 4, *Richard*, Sheridan; *Queen*, Miss Bellamy; Feb. 9; June 15.

1747–48: Nov. 23, *Richard*, Sheridan; *Queen*, Miss Bellamy; Dec. 16, only *Richard* listed; Feb. 18; May 16.

1748–49: Nov. 11, *Richard*, Sheridan; Nov. 18; Jan. 16.

1749–50: Sept. 27, *Richard*, Sheridan; Nov. 22, plus *Queen*, Mrs. Bland; Jan. 29, only *Richard* listed.

1750–51: Oct. 22, *Richard*, Sheridan; *Tressel*, King; *Richmond*, Ross; *Lady Anne*, Miss Cole; *Queen*, Mrs. Bland; Nov. 22, but *Richard*, Montgomery; Dec. 10, but *Richard*, Sheridan; and without *Richmond* and *Lady Anne*; Mar. 13, but *Richard*, Mossop (first time); and plus *Richmond* and *Lady Anne*; *King Henry*, Montgomery; *Buckingham*, Bardin; and *Lord Stanley*, Beamsley.

1751–52: Dec. 4, *Richard*, Sheridan; *King Henry*, Davies; *Lady Anne*, Mrs. Davies; *Queen*, Mrs. Bland; Feb. 13, but *Queen*, by Desire, Mrs. Woffington; and without *King Henry* and *Lady Anne*.

1752–53: Dec. 4, *Richard*, Sheridan; *King Henry*, Montgomery; *Queen*, Mrs. Woffington.

1753–54: Dec. 13, *Richard*, Sheridan; *Buckingham*, Sowdon; *King Henry*, Digges; *Richmond*, Dexter; *Tressel*, King; *Lord Stanley*, Heaphy; *Lady Anne*, Mrs. Pye; *Queen*, Mrs. Ward.

1756–57: Nov. 1, *Richard*, Sheridan; Feb. 7, plus *Tressel*, King; *Richmond*, Dexter; *Lady Anne*, Miss Kennedy; and *Queen*, Mrs. Kennedy.

1757–58: Nov. 7, *Richard*, Sheridan; *King Henry*, Heaphy; *Buckingham*, Kennedy; *Stanley*, Lewis; *Norfolk*, Storer; *Tressel*, King; *Catesby*, Stayley; *Ratcliff*, Watson; *Lord Mayor*, Sparks; *Lieutenant*, Hurst; *Tirrele*, Williams; *Forrest*, Messink; *Oxford*, Hamilton; *Blunt*, R. Elrington; *Prince Edward*, Miss E. Storer; *Duke of York*, Miss A. Storer; *Richmond*, Dexter; *Lady Anne*, Miss Kennedy; *Duchess of York*, Mrs. Farrell; *Queen*, Mrs. Fitzhenry; Nov. 21, but *Lord Mayor*, Packenham; Feb. 27, but *Lord Mayor*, Storer; and *Duchess of York*, Miss Mason; and without *Lieutenant*, *Tirrell*, *Forrest*, *Oxford*, and *Blunt*; Mar. 11; May 29, as on

Nov. 7, but *Buckingham,* Aickin; and *Norfolk,* Davenport; and without *Lord Mayor.*

The Roman Father, "written by William Whitehead, Esq; Poet Laureat"

1750–51: Feb. 23, *Roman Father,* Sheridan; *Publius,* Digges; *Valerius,* King; *Tullus Hostilius,* Beamsley; *Valeria,* Miss Danvers; *Horatia,* Mrs. Bland; Feb. 28; Mar. 4; Mar. 23, without *Tullus Hostilius;* May 6, plus *Tullus Hostilius.*

1751–52: May 2, *Roman Father,* Sheridan; *Publius,* Digges; *Valerius,* Heaphy; *Tullus Hostilius,* Stevens; *Valeria,* Miss Cole; *Horatia,* Mrs. Bland.

1757–58: May 22, *Roman Father,* Sheridan; *Publius,* Dexter; *Tullus Hostilius,* Heaphy; *Valerius,* Ryder; *Valeria,* Mrs. Kennedy; *Horatia,* Mrs. Fitzhenry.

Romeo and Juliet, "written by Shakespear, with Alterations"

1746–47: Dec. 15, *Romeo,* Sheridan; *Juliet,* Miss Bellamy; Dec. 19; Jan. 8; Apr. 10, no cast; May 20, *Romeo,* Sheridan; *Juliet,* Miss Bellamy; June 25.

1747–48: Nov. 30, *Romeo,* Sheridan; *Juliet,* Miss Bellamy; Jan. 22.

1748–49: Feb. 13, *Romeo,* Sheridan; *Nurse,* Mrs. Macklin; *Juliet,* "with a Song in Character set by Signior Pasquali," Mrs. Mozeen, "being the first Time of her attempting a Character in Tragedy"; Feb. 24.

1749–50: Oct. 13, *Romeo,* Sheridan; *Nurse,* Mrs. Macklin; *Juliet,* "by a young Lady who never appeared yet on any Stage"; Oct. 20, but *Juliet,* Miss Griffith, "being the second Time of her appearing on any Stage"; Dec. 1; Feb. 8.

1750–51: Oct. 29, *Romeo,* Sheridan; *Mercutio,* King; *Juliet,* Miss Griffith; Nov. 26; Mar. 29, but *Romeo,* Digges, and *Juliet,* Miss Baker, "it being the first Time of her appearing in a Character on any Stage"; May 20, but *Romeo,* Sheridan; and plus *Nurse,* Mrs. Mynitt.

1751–52: Sept. 30, *Romeo,* Digges; *Mercutio,* King; *Juliet,* Mrs. Lee, "first Time of her appearing on the Stage"; May 20, but *Romeo,* Lee, "from the Theatre Royal in Drury-lane, being his first Appearance on this Stage"; and plus *Fryar Lawrence,* Beamsley; *Tybalt,* J. Elrington; *Prince,* Kennedy; *Paris,* Falkner; *Capulet,* Mynitt; *Montague,* Longfield; *Sampson,* Sparks; *Apothecary,* Maurice; *Gregory,* Packenham; *Lady Capulet,* Mrs. Rowley; and *Nurse,* Mrs. Mynitt.

1752–53: Nov. 27, *Romeo,* Sheridan; *Mercutio,* King; *Nurse,* Mrs. Mynitt; *Juliet,* Mrs. Ward; Dec. 16, without *Nurse.*

1753–54: Dec. 21, *Romeo*, Sheridan; *Mercutio*, King; *Fryar Lawrence*, Heaphy; *Capulet*, Layfield; *Lady Capulet*, Mrs. Kennedy; *Nurse*, Mrs. Mynitt; *Juliet*, Miss Baker; Vocal Parts, Mrs. Storer, Mrs. Pye, Mr. Butler, and others; Feb. 18, without *Lady Capulet*.

1756–57: Nov. 12, *Romeo*, Sheridan; *Juliet*, a Young Lady "who never appeared on any Stage"; Nov. 18; Dec. 30, but *Juliet*, Miss G. Phillips; and plus *Mercutio*, King; Apr. 13, but *Romeo*, Dexter; and plus *Capulet*, Layfield; *Montague*, R. Elrington; *Tybalt*, Hurst; *Fryar*, Heaphy; *Benvolio*, Stayley; *Escalus (Prince)*, Watson; *Lady Capulet*, Miss Mason; and *Nurse*, Mrs. Mynitt.

1757–58: Dec. 8, *Romeo*, Ryder; *Juliet*, Mrs. Hopkins, "being her first Appearance on this Stage"; Jan. 2, *Romeo*, Dexter; *Mercutio*, King; *Juliet*, Mrs. Wilder; Mar. 13, *Romeo*, Sheridan; *Escalus*, Watson; *Benvolio*, Stayley; *Tybalt*, Hurst; *Mercutio*, King; *Fryar Lawrence*, Heaphy; *Capulet*, Storer; *Montague*, R. Elrington; *Lady Capulet*, Miss Mason; *Nurse*, Mrs. Farrell; *Juliet*, Miss Baker; Apr. 27, but *Romeo*, Dexter; and plus *Gregory*, Lewis; and *Abraham*, Hamilton; and without *Escalus* and *Montague*.

The Rover, or The Banish'd Cavaliers, by Aphra Behn

1751–52: May 8, *Blunt*, Cibber; *Willmore*, King; *Belvil*, Heaphy; *Don Pedro*, Stevens; *Frederick*, Kennedy; *Don Antonio*, Falkner; *Stephano*, Watson; *Philippo*, Longfield; *Sancho*, Williams; *Florinda*, Mrs. Davies; *Angelica*, Miss Cole; *Valeria*, Mrs Rowley; *Moretta*, Mrs. Mynitt; *Lucetta*, Mrs. Kennedy; *Hellena*, Mrs. Bland.

The Royal Merchant, or The Beggars Bush, by Henry Norris

1746–47: Apr. 30, *Royal Merchant*, "Mr. Elrington"; *Clause*, Beamsley; *Jaculine*, Mrs. Gemea; *Bertha*, Mrs. Dyer.

1747–48: Dec. 30, *Orator Higgin*, Woodward; Apr. 11.

1748–49: Jan. 2, *Clause*, Morris; *Orator Higgin*, Barrington; *Prince Prig*, Dyer; *Florez*, R. Elrington; *Woolfort*, Beamsley; *Hemskirk*, Watson; *Hubert*, J. Elrington; *Vandunk*, Sparks; *Bertha*, Mrs. Dyer; *Jaculine*, Miss Jones.

Rule a Wife and Have a Wife, by John Fletcher

1746–47: Mar. 16, *Leon*, J. Elrington; *Copper Captain*, R. Elrington; *Margaretta*, Mrs. Storer; *Estifania*, Miss Bellamy (first time).

1748–49: Mar. 8, *Copper Captain*, R. Elrington; *Margaretta*, Mrs. Bland; *Estifania*, Mrs. Macklin; Apr. 24, but *Copper Captain*, Macklin; and plus *Cacafogo*, Barrington.

1749–50: Jan. 11, *Copper Captain*, Macklin; *Leon*, J. Elrington; *Margaretta*, Mrs. Bland; *Estifania*, Mrs. Macklin.

1751–52: Nov. 1, *Leon*, Sheridan; *Copper Captain*, King; *Margaretta*, Mrs. Bland; *Estifania*, Mrs. Woffington; Nov. 6; Apr. 6, but *Leon*, Kennedy; and plus *Cacafogo*, Sparks; and *Altea*, Miss Cole.

1752–53: Apr. 13, *Copper Captain*, King; *Leon*, Kennedy; *Cacafogo*, Sparks; *Duke*, Stevens; *Margaretta*, Mrs. Kennedy; *Clara*, Mrs. Mynitt; *Estifania*, Mrs. Woffington.

1756–57: Apr. 1, *Copper Captain*, King; *Duke*, Hurst; *Don Juan*, Stayley; *Cacafogo*, Sparks; *Alonzo*, Watson; *Sancho*, Aickin; *Old Woman*, Mynitt; *Leon*, Kennedy; *Margaretta*, Miss Kennedy; *Altea*, Mrs. Mynitt; *Clara*, Mrs. Pye; *Estifania*, Mrs. Kennedy.

The School Boy, by Colley Cibber. (Farce of Two Acts)

1745–46: Jan. 27, *Master Johnny*, Garrick.

1747–48: Oct. 5, *Schoolboy* (*Master Johnny*), Woodward.

1750–51: Apr. 18, *Master Johnny*, King; *Major Rakish*, Sparks; *Young Rakish*, Falkner; *Friendly*, Watson; *Lettice*, Miss Cole; *Lady Manlove*, Mrs. Mynitt.

1751–52: Apr. 6, *Master Johnny*, Mrs. Kennedy; *Major Rakish*, Sparks; *Young Rakish*, Kennedy; *Lettice*, Miss Cole.

1753–54: Dec. 21, *Schoolboy* (*Master Johnny*), Mrs. Green; *Major Rakish*, Sparks; Jan. 21; Feb. 2; Feb. 11.

She Would and She Would Not, or *The Kind Imposter*, "by Colley Cibber, Esq."

1747–48: Mar. 16, *Trapanti*, Woodward; *Hypolita*, Miss Jones.

1749–50: Mar. 5, *Don Manuel*, Macklin; *Trapanti*, Cibber; *Viletta*, Mrs. Macklin; *Rosara*, Mrs. Mozeen; *Hypolita*, Mrs. Bland; Mar. 19, *Trapanti*, Cibber; *Rosara*, Mrs. Lindley; *Flora*, Mrs. Kennedy; *Hypolita*, Mrs. Bland.

1750–51: Dec. 21, *Don Manuel*, Cibber (first time); *Don Philip*, Ross; *Trapanti*, King (first time); *Soto*, Sparks; *Don Lewis*, Watson; *Octavio*, Falkner; *Corrigidor*, Morris; *Flora*, Miss Cole; *Rosara*, Mrs. Lindley; *Viletta*, Mrs. Rowley; *Hypolita*, Mrs. Bland; Dec. 26, plus *Diego*, Mynitt; and without *Don Lewis* and *Corrigidor*; Jan. 9, but *Viletta*, Mrs. Mynitt; and plus *Don Lewis*; Jan. 26; Apr. 18, without *Don Lewis*.

1751–52: Sept. 25, *Don Manuel*, Cibber; *Trapanti*, King; *Flora*, Miss Cole; *Hypolita*, Mrs. Bland; Nov. 22; Apr. 3, plus *Don Philip*, Kennedy; *Octavio*, Falkner; *Soto*, Sparks; *Host*

(*Diego*), Mynitt; *Rosara*, Mrs. Kennedy; and *Viletta*, Mrs. Mynitt; Apr. 17, but *Flora*, Miss Baker, "being the first Time of her appearing in Boys Cloaths," and *Hypolita*, Mrs. Woffington; and plus *Don Lewis*, Watson; and without *Host*.

1756–57: Mar. 23, *Trapanti*, King; *Octavio*, Dexter; *Soto*, Glover; *Don Manuel*, Sparks; *Flora*, Mrs. Kennedy; *Hypolita*, Miss Kennedy; May 19, plus *Don Philip*, Kennedy; *Host*, Mynitt; *Don Lewis*, Watson; *Corrigidor*, Hurst; *Rosara*, Miss Mason; and *Viletta*, Mrs. Mynitt.

1757–58: Jan 18, *Trapanti*, King; *Don Philip*, Kennedy; *Octavio*, Hurst; *Host*, Lewis; *Don Manuel*, Sparks; *Corrigidor*, Preston; *Alguazile*, Oliver; *Don Lewis*, Watson; *Soto*, Glover; *Flora*, Mrs. Kennedy; *Rosara*, Miss Mason; *Viletta*, Mrs. Pye; *Hypolita*, Miss Kennedy.

The Siege of Damascus, by John Hughes

1752–53: Dec. 11, *Phocyas*, Sheridan; *Caled*, Sowdon; *Eumenes*, Digges; *Abudah*, Montgomery; *Herbis*, Beamsley; *Daran*, Layfield; *Artamon*, Heaphy; *Eudocia*, Mrs. Woffington; Dec. 20; May 17, but *Abudah*, J. Elrington; and *Herbis*, Longfield.

The Silent Woman, "written by Ben Johnston"

1749–50: Feb. 15, *Morose*, Macklin; *Sir John Daw*, Cibber; *Epicoene*, Mrs. Bland; *Mrs. Otter*, Mrs. Macklin.

1751–52: Feb. 7, *Sir John Daw*, Cibber; *Sir Amorous LaFool*, King; *Morose*, Beamsley; *Truewit*, J. Elrington; *Tom Otter*, Sparks; *Clerimont*, Kennedy; *Cutbeard*, Mynitt; *Dauphine Eugene*, Falkner; *Lady Haughty*, Miss Cole; *Centaur*, Mrs. Lee; *Doll Mavis*, Mrs. Davies; *Mrs. Otter*, Mrs. Mynitt; *Epicoene*, Mrs. Bland; Feb. 28, only *Sir John, Sir Amorous, Otter, Morose, Truewit*, and *Silent Woman* (*Epicoene*) listed; May 12, plus *Clerimont, Dauphine, Lady Haughty, Centaur, Doll Mavis*, and *Mrs. Otter*.

Sir Courtly Nice, or It Cannot Be, by John Crowne

1747–48: Oct. 16, no cast; Oct. 19, *Sir Courtly Nice*, Woodward; Apr. 27.

1751–52: Jan. 2, *Sir Courtly Nice*, Cibber; *Lord Belguard*, Heaphy; *Farewell*, Kennedy; *Surly*, Sparks; *Hothead*, Stevens; *Testimony*, Mynitt; *Crack*, King; *Violante*, Miss Cole; *Aunt*, Mrs. Kennedy; *Leonora*, Mrs. Bland.

1757–58: Dec. 21, *Sir Courtly Nice*, Foote; *Crack*, King; *Leonora*, Mrs. Kennedy.

The Spanish Fryar, "written by [John] Dryden"

1745–46: Dec. 2, *Torrismond,* Barry (first time); *Queen,* Miss Bellamy (first time); *Elvira,* Mrs. Walter, "from the Theatre Royal in Covent Garden"; *Bertran,* Lacy; *Gomez,* Morgan; *Fryar,* Morris.

1748–49: May 1, *Gomez,* Macklin; *Fryar,* Morris; *Torrismond,* R. Elrington; *Lorenzo,* J. Elrington; *Queen,* Mrs. Vincent; *Elvira,* Mrs. Bland; May 25, but *Torrismond,* Gentleman; and without *Fryar* and *Lorenzo.*

1750–51: Mar. 8, *Torrismond,* Mossop (first time); *Raymond,* Montgomery; *Lorenzo,* King; *Bertran,* Ross; *Gomez,* Cibber; *Teresa,* Mrs. Lindley; *Leonora* (*Queen*), Miss Griffith; *Fryar,* Sparks; *Elvira,* Mrs. Bland; Apr. 30, but *Torrismond,* R. Elrington, and *Raymond,* Falkner.

1751–52: Mar. 13, *Torrismond,* Digges (first time); *Colonel* (*Lorenzo*), King; *Gomez,* Cibber; *Fryar,* Sparks; *Raymond,* Heaphy; *Queen,* Mrs. Davies; *Elvira,* Mrs. Woffington; May 1, plus *Bertran,* Kennedy; *Alphonzo,* Beamsley; and *Pedro,* Watson.

1752–53: May 5, *Torrismond,* Digges; *Lorenzo,* King; *Fryar,* Sparks; *Gomez,* Green; *Bertran,* Kennedy; *Raymond,* Heaphy; *Alphonzo,* Layfield; *Queen,* Mrs. Ward; *Teresa,* Mrs. Kennedy; *Elvira,* Mrs. Woffington.

1756–57: May 2, *Torrismond,* Dexter (first time); *Bertran,* Stayley; *Alphonzo,* R. Elrington; *Pedro,* Watson; *Lorenzo,* King; *Raymond,* Heaphy; *Gomez,* Layfield; *Captain,* Williams; *Fryar,* Sparks; *Queen,* Miss Kennedy; *Teresa,* Mrs. Pye; *Elvira,* Miss Grace Phillips.

1757–58: Dec. 1, *Gomez,* Foote; *Fryar,* Sparks; *Torrismond,* Dexter; *Colonel,* King; *Elvira,* Mrs. Kennedy; *Leonora,* Miss Kennedy; Dec. 22, plus *Raymond,* Heaphy; *Bertran,* Stayley; and *Pedro,* Preston.

The Squire of Alsatia, by Thomas Shadwell

1747–48: Jan. 8, *Squire,* Woodward; Apr. 14, plus *Mrs. Termagant,* Miss Pitt.

1750–51: Feb. 14, *Squire,* King; *Sir William Belfond,* Sparks; *Sir Edward Belfond,* Beamsley; *Mrs. Termagant,* Miss Cole.

The Stage Coach, by George Farquhar. (Farce)

1749–50: Nov. 20, *Macahone,* Sparks.

1751–52: Mar. 30, *Macahone,* Sparks; *Squire Somebody,* King; *Capt. Basil,* Kennedy; *Micher,* Mynitt; *Fetch,* Hamilton; *Jolt,* Longfield; *Constable,* Williams; *Dolly,* Mrs. Kennedy; *Isabella,* Miss Cole.

1757–58: Oct. 31, *Squire Somebody*, King; *Macahone*, Sparks.

The Statue, or *The Devil in the Wine Cellar,* "written by the late Aaron Hill, Esq., and revived with Alterations"

1750–51: Mar. 18, *Corporal Cuttum*, Cibber, "in which Character will be represented the Clock-Work Statue, in the Manner it was originally performed by him . . . in . . . the Pantomime called Doctor Faustus, at the Theatre Royal in Drury-lane"; *Mademoiselle Fripperie* (*alias Intriguing Toby*), Sparks; *Leonora*, Miss Cole; *Sir Timothy Tough*, Mynitt; *Sprightly*, Falkner; *Servants*, Williams, Hamilton, Messink, Morris, and others.

The Stratagem, by George Farquhar

1745–46: Dec. 16, *Archer,* Garrick; *Foigard,* Morris; *Scrub,* Bardin; *Cherry,* Miss Bellamy; *Mrs. Sullen,* Mrs. Walter; Jan. 24, only *Archer* listed; Jan. 29, plus *Foigard, Cherry,* and *Mrs. Sullen.*

1747–48: Nov. 18, *Archer,* Sheridan (first time); *Mrs. Sullen,* Miss Bellamy (first time); *Scrub,* Woodward (first time); Jan. 26.

1748–49: Nov. 16, *Archer,* Sheridan; *Scrub,* Macklin; May 3, but *Archer,* Kennedy; and plus *Foigard,* Barrington; *Dorinda,* Mrs. Bland; *Cherry,* Mrs. Mozeen; and *Mrs. Sullen,* Mrs. Vincent.

1749–50: Oct. 18, *Archer,* Sheridan; *Scrub,* Macklin; *Dorinda,* Miss Copen; *Mrs. Sullen,* Mrs. Bland; Feb. 20, but *Dorinda,* Mrs. Lindley; and plus *Foigard,* Sparks, and *Cherry,* Mrs. Mozeen.

1750–51: Oct. 18, *Archer,* King; *Mrs. Sullen,* Mrs. Bland; *Cherry,* Miss Cole; *Scrub,* Cibber; Oct. 30; Dec. 27, plus *Aimwell,* Ross; *Foigard,* Sparks; *Boniface,* Mynitt; *Sir Charles Freeman,* Falkner; *Sullen,* Beamsley; *Gibbet,* Bardin; *Dorinda,* Mrs. Lindley; *Lady Bountiful,* Miss Copen; and *Gipsy,* Mrs. Leslie; Apr. 19, but *Sullen,* Watson; and *Gibbet,* Packenham; May 8, without *Sir Charles, Gibbet,* and *Boniface.*

1751–52: Sept. 23, *Archer,* King; *Scrub,* Cibber; *Aimwell,* Kennedy; *Foigard,* Sparks; *Sullen,* Beamsley; *Sir Charles Freeman,* Falkner; *Boniface,* Mynitt; *Gibbet,* Hamilton; *Cherry,* Miss Cole; *Dorinda,* Mrs. Kennedy; *Lady Bountiful,* Mrs. Mynitt; *Mrs. Sullen,* Mrs. Bland; Dec. 6, *Archer,* Sheridan; *Scrub,* Cibber; *Foigard,* Sparks; *Cherry,* Miss Cole; *Dorinda,* Mrs. Davies; *Mrs. Sullen,* Mrs. Woffington; Dec. 18, plus *Aimwell,* Kennedy; and without *Foigard;* Mar. 20, *Archer,* King; *Aimwell,* Kennedy; *Foigard,* Sparks; *Scrub,* Cibber; *Sullen,*

Beamsley; *Sir Charles Freeman*, Falkner; *Boniface*, Mynitt; *Gibbet*, Hamilton; *Lady Bountiful*, Mrs. Rowley; *Gypsy*, Mrs. Kennedy; *Cherry*, Miss Cole; *Dorinda*, Mrs. Davies; *Mrs. Sullen*, Mrs. Woffington; Apr. 27, but *Boniface*, Mynitt, and *Gibbet*, Stevens; and without *Sullen*, *Lady Bountiful*, and *Gypsy*.

1752–53: Oct. 23, *Archer*, Sheridan; *Scrub*, King; *Foigard*, Sparks; *Mrs. Sullen*, Mrs. Woffington; Nov. 22, plus *Aimwell*, Kennedy; May 28, plus *Sullen*, Layfield; *Gibbet*, Green; *Dorinda*, Miss Mason; and *Cherry*, Miss Johnson.

1753–54: Oct. 5, *Archer*, Sheridan; *Scrub*, King; *Foigard*, Sparks; *Aimwell*, Kennedy; *Sullen*, Layfield; *Gibbet*, Storer; *Sir Charles Freeman*, Stayley; *Boniface*, Mynitt; *Bagshot*, Williams; *Hounslow*, Maurice; *Cherry*, a young Gentlewoman, "first Appearance on any Stage"; *Lady Bountiful*, Mrs. Mynitt; *Gipsy*, Mrs. Leslie; *Dorinda*, young Gentlewoman, "first Time of her appearing on this Stage"; *Mrs. Sullen*, Mrs. Woffington; Nov. 23, but *Cherry*, Mrs. Roberts; and *Dorinda*, Mrs. Pye; and only *Archer*, *Scrub*, *Foigard*, and *Sullen* listed besides.

1756–57: Oct. 20, *Archer*, Dexter; *Aimwell*, Heaphy; *Sullen*, Layfield; *Sir Charles Freeman*, Watson; *Scrub*, King; *Boniface*, Mynitt; *Gibbet*, Stayley; *Hounslow*, Messink; *Bagshot*, Williams; *Foigard*, Sparks; *Dorinda*, Miss Danvers; *Lady Bountiful*, Mrs. Mynitt; *Cherry*, Mrs. Kennedy; *Gipsy*, Mrs. Packenham; *Mrs. Sullen*, Miss Kennedy; Nov. 11, but *Archer*, Lee, and *Mrs. Sullen*, Mrs. Kennedy; and only *Scrub* and *Foigard* listed besides; Dec. 31, only *Archer*, Sheridan, and *Mrs. Sullen*, Miss G. Phillips, listed; Feb. 28, plus *Scrub* and *Foigard*; Mar. 10.

1757–58: Nov. 3, *Archer*, Sheridan; *Aimwell*, Heaphy; *Sullen*, Hurst; *Sir Charles Freeman*, Stayley; *Foigard*, Sparks; *Gibbet*, Hamilton; *Boniface*, Lewis; *Hounslow*, Williams; *Bagshot*, Messink; *Scrub*, King; *Dorinda*, Miss Kennedy; *Cherry*, Mrs. Wilder; *Gipsy*, Miss Wells; *Lady Bountiful*, Mrs. Farrell; *Mrs. Sullen*, Mrs. Fitzhenry; Feb. 18; Apr. 24, but *Archer*, Dexter; May 31, without *Gibbet*, *Boniface*, *Hounslow*, *Bagshot*, and *Gipsy*.

The Suspicious Husband, by Benjamin Hoadly

1746–47: June 29, *Ranger*, Sheridan; *Clarinda*, Miss Bellamy; July 2; July 16.

1747–48: Nov. 2, *Ranger*, Sheridan; *Clarinda*, Miss Bellamy; Nov. 6, plus *Jack Maggot,* by Desire, Woodward; Jan. 19; Feb. 26.

1748–49: Nov. 7, *Ranger,* Sheridan; *Strictland,* Macklin; *Jacintha,* Mrs. Vincent; *Clarinda,* Mrs. Bland, "from the Theatre Royal in Covent-Garden, being the first Time of her appearing on this Stage"; Jan. 26, plus *Jack Maggot,* Dyer; and *Lucetta,* Miss Minors; May 26, without *Jack Maggot.*

1749–50: Nov. 15, *Ranger,* Sheridan; *Strictland,* Macklin; *Jack Maggot,* Bardin; *Mrs. Strictland,* Mrs. Mozeen; *Jacintha,* Miss Copen; *Clarinda,* Mrs. Bland; Mar. 22, but *Jacintha,* Mrs. Lindley; and without *Strictland* and *Jack Maggot.*

1750–51: Sept. 28, *Ranger,* King, "from the Theatre Royal in Drury-lane, being the first Time of his appearing on this Stage"; *Clarinda,* Mrs. Bland; Oct. 12, plus *Jacintha,* Miss Danvers; Nov. 19; Jan. 3, plus *Frankly,* Ross; *Strictland,* Beamsley; *Bellamy,* Falkner; *Jack Maggot,* Bardin; *Lucetta,* Mrs. Rowley; and *Mrs. Strictland,* Mrs. Lindley; Mar. 14, but *Lucetta,* Mrs. Mynitt; and plus *Buckle,* Messink; *Tester,* Williams; *Landlady,* Miss Copen; and *Milliner,* Mrs. Leslie; May 22, *Strictland,* Sheridan; *Frankly,* Digges; *Jack Maggot,* Cibber; *Bellamy,* Ross; *Clarinda,* Mrs. Bland; *Jacintha,* Miss Cole; *Ranger,* King.

1751–52: Nov. 8, *Strictland,* Sheridan; *Frankly,* Digges; *Bellamy,* Heaphy; *Jack Maggot,* Kennedy; *Ranger,* King; *Mrs. Strictland,* Miss Cole; *Lucetta,* Mrs. Kennedy; *Clarinda,* Mrs. Bland; *Jacintha,* Mrs. Woffington; Mar. 11, but *Strictland,* Beamsley; *Jacintha,* Miss Cole; and *Mrs. Strictland,* Mrs. Lee; and without *Lucetta;* Apr. 13, *Ranger,* King; *Frankly,* Digges; *Strictland,* Davies; *Bellamy,* Heaphy; *Jack Maggot,* Conyers, "first Time of his appearing on this Stage"; *Tester,* Williams; *Jacintha,* Mrs. Davies, "first Time of her appearing in Boys Cloaths"; *Mrs. Strictland,* Mrs. Lee; *Lucetta,* Mrs. Kennedy; *Landlady,* Mrs. Mynitt; *Milliner,* Mrs. Crump; *Clarinda,* Mrs. Woffington.

1752–53: Jan. 5, *Ranger,* King; *Frankly,* Digges; *Jacintha,* Mrs. Green; *Clarinda,* Mrs. Ward; Mar. 8, but *Frankly,* Kennedy.

1753–54: Oct. 22, *Ranger,* King; *Frankly,* Digges; *Strictland,* Layfield; *Bellamy,* Heaphy; *Jack Maggot,* Green; *Jacintha,* Mrs. Green; *Mrs. Strictland,* Mrs. Kennedy; *Clarinda,* Mrs. Ward.

1756–57: Oct. 25, *Ranger,* King; *Bellamy,* Heaphy; *Jack Maggot,* Kennedy; *Frankly,* Dexter; *Buckle,* Messink; *Simon,* Hurst; *Tester,* Williams; *Ranger's Servant,* Watson; *Strictland,* Layfield; *Mrs. Strictland,* Miss Danvers; *Jacintha,* Mrs. Kennedy; *Landlady,* Mrs. Butler; *Milliner,* Mrs. Packenham;

Lucetta, Mrs. Mynitt; *Clarinda*, Miss Kennedy; Nov. 15, without *Bellamy, Jack Maggot, Buckle, Simon, Tester, Ranger's Servant, Landlady*, and *Milliner*; Mar. 21, plus *Bellamy* and *Jack Maggot*; and without *Lucetta* and *Clarinda*; Apr. 22 with *Lucetta* and *Clarinda*.

1757–58: Nov. 10, *Ranger*, King; *Frankly*, Dexter; *Bellamy*, Stayley; *Strictland*, Heaphy; *Jack Maggot*, Kennedy; *Tester*, Glover; *Simon*, Watson; *Ranger's Servant*, Hamilton; *Buckle*, Messink; *Landlady*, Mrs. Packenham; *Mrs. Strictland*, Miss Danvers; *Jacintha*, Mrs. Kennedy; *Lucetta*, Mrs. Pye; *Milliner*, Miss Jackson; *Clarinda*, Miss Kennedy; Nov. 10; Apr. 19, but *Bellamy*, Preston; and *Strictland*, Hurst; and without *Jack Maggot, Simon, Ranger's Servant, Buckle*, and *Landlady*.

Tamerlane, by Nicholas Rowe

1745–46: Nov. 4, *Tamerlane*, Sheridan; *Bajazet*, Barry; *Arpasia*, Mrs. Furnival; *Selima*, Mrs. Elmy; *Moneses*, "a Gentleman, being the first Time of his appearing on the Stage."

1746–47: Nov. 4, *Tamerlane*, Sheridan; *Arpasia*, Miss Bellamy (first time); May 22.

1747–48: Nov. 4, *Tamerlane*, Sheridan; *Arpasia*, Miss Bellamy.

1748–49: Nov. 4, *Tamerlane*, Sheridan.

1749–50: Nov. 4, *Tamerlane*, Sheridan; *Selima*, Mrs. Mozeen; *Arpasia*, Mrs. Bland; Apr. 16, *Tamerlane*, Sheridan; *Bajazet*, Mossop.

1750–51: Nov. 5, *Tamerlane*, Sheridan; *Bajazet*, Mossop; *Moneses*, King; *Axalla*, Ross; *Selima*, Miss Cole; *Arpasia*, Mrs. Bland.

1751–52: Nov. 4, *Tamerlane*, Sheridan; *Arpasia*, Mrs. Bland.

1752–53: Nov. 4, *Tamerlane*, Sheridan; *Bajazet*, Sowdon; *Arpasia*, Mrs. Woffington.

1753–54: Nov. 5, *Tamerlane*, Sheridan; *Bajazet*, Sowdon; *Moneses*, Dexter; *Selima*, Mrs. Ward; *Arpasia*, Mrs. Woffington.

1756–57: Nov. 4, *Tamerlane*, Sheridan.

1757–58: Nov. 4, *Tamerlane*, Sheridan; *Axalla*, Kennedy; *Omar*, Hurst; *Dervise*, Stayley; *Moneses*, Dexter; *Prince of Tanais*, Watson; *Mirvan*, R. Elrington; *Zama*, Williams; *Haly*, Hamilton; *Stratocles*, Bate; *Bajazet*, Heaphy; *Selima*, Miss Kennedy; *Arpasia*, Mrs. Fitzhenry.

Tancred and Sigismunda, "by Mr. [James] Thomson"

1745–46: Feb. 19, *Tancred*, Garrick; *Siffredi*, Sheridan; *Osmond*, Barry; *Sigismunda*, Miss Bellamy.

1746–47: June 22, *Tancred*, Sheridan; *Osmond*, Giffard, "the first

Time on this Stage"; *Sigismunda*, Miss Bellamy; *Laura*, Mrs. Giffard, "the first Time on this Stage."

1747–48: Dec. 2, *Tancred*, Sheridan; *Sigismunda*, Miss Bellamy.

1748–49: May 18, *Tancred*, Sheridan; *Sigismunda*, Miss Danvers.

1749–50: Mar. 30, *Tancred*, Sheridan; *Siffredi*, Beamsley; *Osmond*, J. Elrington; *Rodolpho*, Ross; *Sigismunda*, Miss Danvers; *Laura*, Miss Griffith.

1752–53: Nov. 2, *Tancred*, Sheridan; *Siffredi*, Montgomery; *Osmond*, Sowdon; *Sigismunda*, Mrs. Woffington; Nov. 17.

1756–57: Feb. 19, *Tancred*, Sheridan; *Osmond*, Dexter; *Siffredi*, Stayley; *Laura*, Mrs. Kennedy; *Sigismunda*, Miss G. Phillips.

1757–58: Mar. 3, *Tancred*, Sheridan; *Osmond*, Dexter; *Siffredi*, Stayley; *Rodolpho*, Heaphy; *Laura*, Mrs. Kennedy; *Sigismunda*, Mrs. Fitzhenry; Mar. 15.

The Tempest, or *The Enchanted Isle*, "written originally by Shakespear, and altered for the Stage by Mr. Dryden." A *Dublin Journal* press item (January 3–7, 1749) adds the name of Davenant. Most of the performances are advertised as concluding with a Grand Masque of Neptune and Amphitrite.

1748–49: Jan. 13, *Trincolo*, Macklin; Jan. 19, plus *Monster*, Sparks; *Ariel*, "with the Songs in Character," Mrs. Storer; *Dorinda*, "who never saw a Man, with the Song of Dear pretty Youth," Mrs. Mozeen; *Hippolito*, "who never saw a Woman," Mrs. Bland; *Neptune*, Sullivan; *Amphitrite*, Mrs. Lampe; Jan. 25; Feb. 17; Mar. 6, without *Monster*.

1749–50: Jan. 27, *Trincolo*, Macklin; *Hippolito*, Mrs. Bland; *Caliban* (*Monster*), Sparks; *Ariel*, Mrs. Storer; *Dorinda*, "with the Song of Dear pretty Youth," Mrs. Mozeen; *Neptune*, Sullivan; *Amphitrite*, Mrs. Lampe; Feb. 1; Mar. 26, but *Trincolo*, Cibber.

1750–51: Apr. 17, *Trincolo*, Cibber; *Dorinda*, Miss Cole, "with the Song of Dear pretty Youth"; *Miranda*, Mrs. Lindley; *Ariel*, "with Songs in Character," Mrs. Crump; *Caliban*, Sparks; *Ferdinand*, Ross; *Hippolito*, Mrs. Bland.

1751–52: Dec. 30, *Prospero*, Beamsley; *Ferdinand*, Kennedy; *Trincolo*, Stevens; *Caliban*, Sparks; *Dorinda*, "with the Song of Dear pretty Youth," Miss Cole; *Miranda*, Mrs. Davies; *Ariel*, "with the Songs in Character," Mrs. Crump; *Hippolito*, Mrs. Bland.

1752–53: Jan. 17, *Trincolo*, King; *Prospero*, Beamsley; *Caliban*, Sparks; *Neptune*, Sullivan; *Amphitrite*, Mrs. Crump; *Dorinda*, Mrs. Green; *Ariel*, "with the Songs in Character," Mrs. Donaldson; Jan. 22, plus the *Grand Dancing Devils*, McNeil and Miss Baker; Feb. 1, but *Prospero*, Maurice; Feb. 8.

1753–54: Jan. 7, *Trincolo*, King; *Prospero*, Heaphy; *Caliban*, Sparks; *Ariel*, "with the Songs," Mrs. Storer; *Hippolito*, Mrs. Kennedy; *Dorinda*, Mrs. Green; Jan. 9; Jan. 29, plus *Stephano*, Layfield; *Neptune*, Butler; *Miranda*, Miss Mason; *Amphitrite*, Mrs. Pye; and *Grand Dancing Devils*, McNeil and Miss Baker.

1756–57: Jan. 7, *Trincolo*, King; *Prospero*, Heaphy; *Stephano*, Glover; *Caliban*, Layfield; *Hippolito*, Miss Kennedy; *Dorinda*, "with the Song of Dear pretty Youth," Mrs. Wilder; *Ariel*, Miss Young; *Neptune*, Corry; *Amphitrite*, Miss Spencer; Jan. 13, plus Vocal Parts by Corry, Layfield, Miss Spencer, and others; *Lilliputian Dancers*, Master Blake, Garman, Pike, Rayner, Steggeldolt, Mrs. Garman, Mrs. Packenham, Miss Jones; and *Singing Triton*, Wilder; Jan. 20; Jan. 28; Feb. 10; Mar. 11; Apr. 29, principal characters by King, Heaphy, Glover, Sparks, Miss Kennedy, Mrs. Wilder, Miss Wells.

1757–58: Jan. 11, principal characters by King, Sparks, Heaphy, Glover, Miss Kennedy, Mrs. Wilder, Miss Storer; *Lilliputian Dancers*, Harvey, Garman, Rayner, Masset, Mrs. Masset, Mrs. Packenham, Mrs. Godwin, and Mrs. Garman; Vocal Parts by Corry, Mrs. Storer, Mrs. Wilder, Mrs. Pye, Miss Wells, and others; *Neptune*, Corry; *Amphitrite*, Mrs. Storer; Jan. 20, plus principal parts by Kennedy, Hamilton, and Mrs. Pye; Feb. 1.

The Temple of Peace (Masque)

1748–49: Feb. 9, *Mars*, Howard; *Venus*, Mrs. Storer, "in which Character she will introduce the Song of O Peace by Mr. Arne"; *Cupid*, Miss Pocklington; *Peace*, Mrs. Mozeen, "with the Song of Rosey Chaplets" by Pasquali; *Ceres*, Mrs. Mynitt; *First Attendant on Ceres*, Dyer, "with the Song of Harvest Home; the Words by Mr. Dryden, the Musick by Mr. Purcel"; *Silenus*, Morris; *Pan*, Sparks; *Bacchus*, Sullivan, "with the Song, Let the deep Bowl, by Mr. Handel"; *Diana*, Mrs. Lampe, "with the Song, with Hounds and with Horns"; Feb. 15; Feb. 20; Feb. 22; Apr. 27, no cast.

The Tender Husband, or *The Accomplish'd Fools*, "by the late Sir Richard Steele"

1748–49: Apr. 10, *Humphry Gubbin*, Macklin; *Capt. Clerimont*, Dyer; *Mr. Clerimont*, Beamsley; *Sir Harry Gubbin*, Sparks; *Tipkin*,

Mynitt; *Pounce*, Morris; *Jenny*, Miss Minors; *Mrs. Clerimont*, Mrs. Bland; *Mrs. Fainlove*, Miss Jones; *Niece*, Mrs. Vincent; *Aunt*, Mrs. Macklin.

1750–51: Mar. 11, *Capt. Clerimont*, Digges (first time); *Mr. Clerimont*, Ross; *Sir Harry Gubbin*, Sparks; *Tipkin*, Mynitt; *Pounce*, Beamsley; *Numps*, King (first time); *Fainlove*, Miss Cole; *Biddy Tipkin* (*Niece*), Mrs. Lindley; *Aunt*, Mrs. Mynitt; *Mrs. Clerimont*, Mrs. Bland.

Theodosius, or *The Force of Love*, by Nathaniel Lee

1745–46: Feb. 10, *Varanes*, Barry "who is recovered from his late Illness"; *Athenais*, Miss Bellamy.

1747–48: Jan. 25, *Varanes*, Sheridan (first time); *Athenais*, Miss Bellamy; Feb. 3.

1748–49: Apr. 29, *Varanes*, Sheridan; *Theodosius*, Dyer; *Pulcheria*, Mrs. Bland; *Athenais*, Miss Danvers; May 22.

1749–50: Oct. 23, *Varanes*, Sheridan; *Pulcheria*, Mrs. Bland; *Athenais*, Miss Danvers; Apr. 2, plus *Theodosius*, Ross.

1750–51: Nov. 12, *Varanes*, Sheridan; *Theodosius*, Digges; *Athenais*, Mrs. Bland; *Marcian*, Mossop; Nov. 21; Mar. 9, plus *Leontine*, Beamsley; and *Pulcheria*, Miss Griffith; Mar. 12, without *Leontine*.

1757–58: Apr. 7, *Theodosius*, Dexter; *Marcian*, Stayley; *Leontine*, Heaphy; *Varanes*, Ryder; *Pulcheria*, Mrs. Kennedy; *Athenais*, Miss G. Phillips (first time).

Tom Thumb the Great, by Henry Fielding. "Set to Musick by Mr. Lampe." (Mock Opera)

1748–49: May 11, *Tom Thumb*, Mrs. Lampe; *King*, Sullivan; *Queen*, Mrs. Storer; *Huncamunca*, Mrs. Mozeen; May 18, principal characters by Mrs. Lampe, Mrs. Storer, Mrs. Mozeen, Sullivan, Dyer, Sparks, Mynitt, Howard; May 29, only *Tom Thumb*, Mrs. Lampe, listed.

1749–50: Nov. 1, *Tom Thumb*, Mrs. Lampe; *King*, Sullivan; *Queen*, Mrs. Storer; *Queen of the Giants* (*Glumdalca*), Sparks; *Huncamunca*, Mrs. Mozeen; Nov. 8; Nov. 15; Jan. 29, no cast; Feb. 14, as on Nov. 1; Mar. 16; May 15, no cast.

1751–52: Feb. 20, *Tom Thumb*, Master Mynitt; *Queen of the Giants*, Sparks; Feb. 26; Mar. 6; Mar. 12, no cast; Apr. 8, as on Feb. 20.

1756–57: Apr. 1, *Tom Thumb*, Master Kennedy.

1757–58: Feb. 25, *Queen Dollalolla*, Wilkinson.

Trick Upon Trick, or *The Adventures of Three Quarters of an Hour,* or *Harlequin Skeleton*

1747–48: Dec. 9, *Harlequin,* Woodward; *Columbine,* Madem. Mechel; Jan. 8, only *Harlequin* listed; Jan. 26, plus *Columbine;* May 11, plus *Pierrot,* Morris; and without *Columbine;* May 16.

1748–49: Jan. 4, no cast; Apr. 21.

1749–50: Jan. 1, *Columbine,* Madem. Vandersluys; *Pierrot,* Sparks.

The Triumphs of Hibernia (Masque)

1748–49: Nov. 4, no cast; Nov. 7, principal performers, Sullivan, Howard, Mrs. Storer, Mrs. Lampe, Mrs. Mozeen; Nov. 9; Nov. 14; Nov. 28, no cast; Dec. 12; Dec. 23.

1749–50: Nov. 4, principal performers, Sullivan, Howard, Mrs. Lampe, Mrs. Storer, Mrs. Mozeen; Nov. 10; Apr. 16 [see Part 1].

Tunbridge Walks, or *The Yeoman of Kent,* by Thomas Baker

1757–58: May 1, principal parts by King, Sparks, Glover, Ryder, Stayley, Mrs. Kennedy; May 18, *Reynard,* King; *Squib,* Glover; *Maiden,* Ryder; *Loveworth,* Stayley; *Woodcock, the Yeoman,* Sparks; *Mrs. Goodfellow,* Mrs. Farrell; *Hillaria,* Mrs. Kennedy.

The Twin Rivals, by George Farquhar

1747–48: May 11, *Young Wouldbe,* Woodward; *Teague,* Morris, "from the Theatre Royal in London."

1748–49: Apr. 21, *Young Wouldbe,* Dyer; *Teague,* Barrington; *Constance,* Mrs. Vincent; *Aurelia,* Mrs. Bland.

1750–51: Apr. 24, *Elder Wouldbe,* Digges; *Young Wouldbe,* Cibber; *Trueman,* King; *Richmore,* Ross; *Teague,* Sparks, "in which Character he will introduce an humorous Epilogue"; *Subtleman,* Watson; *Balderdash,* Mynitt; *Constable,* Williams; *Midnight,* Miss Copen; *Steward's Wife,* Mrs. Leslie; *Constance,* Mrs. Lindley; *Aurelia,* Mrs. Bland; May 23, plus *Fairbank,* Falkner; and *Steward,* Morris.

1751–52: Sept. 27, *Elder Wouldbe,* Digges; *Young Wouldbe,* Cibber; *Trueman,* King; *Richmore,* Stevens, "being the first Time of appearing on this Stage"; *Teague,* Sparks; *Constance,* Miss Cole; *Aurelia,* Mrs. Bland; Oct. 30, without *Richmore;* Apr. 2, plus *Richmore.*

1752–53: Jan. 4, *Elder Wouldbe,* Digges; *Young Wouldbe,* King; *Teague,* Sparks; *Aurelia,* Mrs. Ward.

1753–54: Jan. 18, *Elder Wouldbe,* Digges; *Young Wouldbe,* King; *Teague,* Sparks; *Trueman,* Heaphy; *Richmore,* Stayley; *Subtleman,* Green; *Fairbank,* Layfield; *Constance,* Miss Mason; *Mrs. Midnight,* Mrs. Mynitt; *Aurelia,* Mrs. Ward.

1756–57: Mar. 31, *Elder Wouldbe*, Dexter; *Richmore*, Stayley; *Trueman*, Heaphy; *Young Wouldbe*, King; *Balderdash*, Mynitt; *Steward*, Hurst; *Alderman*, Glover; *Fairbank*, Layfield; *Teague*, "with a new Song in Character," Sparks; *Constance*, Mrs. Kennedy; *Mrs. Midnight*, Mrs. Mynitt; *Aurelia*, Miss G. Phillips (first time); May 24, plus *Subtleman*, Kennedy.

1757–58: Jan. 4, *Young Wouldbe*, King; *Richmore*, Stayley; *Trueman*, Heaphy; *Fairbank*, Hurst; *Elder Wouldbe*, Dexter; *Balderdash*, Lewis; *Steward*, Preston; *Subtleman*, Storer; *Alderman*, Glover; *Teague*, Sparks; *Constance*, Mrs. Kennedy; *Steward's Wife*, Mrs. Packenham; *Mrs. Midnight*, Mrs. Farrell; *Aurelia*, Miss G. Phillips; May 12, without *Balderdash*, *Steward*, and *Steward's Wife*.

Ulysses, by Nicholas Rowe

1752–53: Mar. 5, *Ulysses*, Sheridan; *Eurymachus*, Sowdon; *Telemachus*, Heaphy; *Mentor*, Layfield; *Semanthe*, Mrs. Ward; *Penelope*, Mrs. Woffington; Mar. 12; Mar. 16; May 24, but *Telemachus*, Digges.

1753–54: Oct. 18, *Ulysses*, Sheridan; *Eurymachus*, Sowdon; *Telemachus*, Digges; *Semanthe*, Mrs. Ward; *Penelope*, Mrs. Woffington.

The Upholsterer, or *What News?* "written by Mr. [Arthur] Murphy, Author of the Apprentice, etc." (Farce)

1757–58: Apr. 27, no cast; May 10, principal parts by King, Sparks, Glover, Mrs. Kennedy.

Venice Preserved, or *The Plot Discover'd*, by Thomas Otway

1745–46: June 2, *Pierre*, Barry; *Belvidera*, Mrs. Furnival.

1746–47: May 25, *Pierre*, Sheridan; *Belvidera*, Miss Bellamy (first time).

1747–48: Feb. 12, *Pierre*, Sheridan; *Belvidera*, Miss Bellamy; Feb. 15.

1749–50: Nov. 29, *Pierre*, Sheridan; *Renault*, Cibber; *Belvidera*, Miss Danvers; *Jaffier*, Digges, "a Gentleman lately arrived from England, who never yet appeared on any Stage"; Dec. 6, without *Renault* and *Belvidera*; May 10, plus *Renault* and *Belvidera*.

1750–51: Oct. 19, *Pierre*, Sheridan; *Jaffier*, Digges; *Renault*, Cibber; *Belvidera*, Mrs. Bland (first time); Mar. 15, but *Pierre*, Montgomery; Apr. 26, but *Pierre*, Sheridan; and plus *Priuli*, Watson; *Duke*, Sparks; *Spinosa*, R. Elrington; *Bedamar*, Falkner; *Theodore*, Hamilton; and *Eliot*, Maurice.

471

1751–52: Nov. 11, *Pierre*, Sheridan; *Jaffier*, Digges; *Renault*, Cibber; *Belvidera*, Mrs. Woffington (first time); Jan. 20.

1752–53: Oct. 25, *Pierre*, Sheridan; *Jaffier*, Digges; *Belvidera*, Mrs. Woffington; Apr. 27, but *Pierre*, Sowdon; and plus *Renault*, Kennedy; and *Priuli*, Layfield.

1753–54: Oct. 15, *Pierre*, Sheridan; *Jaffier*, Digges; *Belvidera*, Mrs. Woffington.

1756–57: Jan. 14, *Pierre*, Sheridan; *Jaffier*, Dexter; *Belvidera*, Mrs. Glen.

1757–58: Feb. 2, *Pierre*, Sheridan; *Priuli*, Heaphy; *Renault*, Stayley; *Bedamar*, Kennedy; *Jaffier*, Dexter; *Duke*, Lewis; *Spinosa*, Watson; *Elliot*, Preston; *Durand*, R. Elrington; *Officer*, Williams; *Belvidera*, Mrs. Fitzhenry; May 19, only *Pierre*, *Jaffier*, and *Belvidera* listed.

The Vintner Tricked, or *The White Fox Chac'd*, by Henry Ward. (Farce)

1745–46: Apr. 17, no cast.

1747–48: Mar. 28, no cast.

1748–49: Apr. 18, *Vizard*, Dyer; *Vintner*, Sparks.

1749–50: Jan. 11, no cast; Apr. 23.

1751–52: Jan. 20, *Mixum* (*Vintner*), Sparks; *Vizard*, Stevens; *Mrs. Mixum*, Mrs. Kennedy.

1753–54: Mar. 1, *Vizard*, King; *Mixum*, Sparks; *Padwell*, Layfield; *Mrs. Mixum*, Mrs. Mynitt.

1757–58: Oct. 27, *Vizard*, King; *Mixum*, Sparks; *Mrs. Mixum*, Mrs. Farrell; Jan. 23, no cast; Mar. 10, as on Oct. 27.

The Virgin Unmasked, by Henry Fielding. (Farce)

1745–46: Dec. 4, *Lucy*, Mrs. Storer; June 2.

1747–48: Apr. 15, *Coupee*, Woodward.

1748–49: Mar. 10, *Lucy*, Mrs. Mozeen; Apr. 8; Apr. 19; May 9.

1749–50: Mar. 14, *Quaver*, Sullivan; *Lucy*, Mrs. Mozeen; May 2.

1750–51: Sept. 19, *Lucy*, Miss Cole; Sept. 24; Mar. 15, plus *Coupee*, King; *Blister*, Sparks; *Quaver*, Ross; Apr. 17; Apr. 27.

1751–52: Nov. 14, *Lucy*, Miss Cole; *Blister*, Sparks; *Quaver*, Kennedy; *Coupee*, King; Apr. 24, only *Coupee* and *Lucy* listed.

1752–53: Nov. 17, *Coupee*, King; *Lucy*, Mrs. Green; Nov. 24; Dec. 16; Jan. 15, plus *Quaver*, Sullivan; and *Blister*, Sparks; Feb. 21.

1753–54: Oct. 3, *Coupee*, King; *Lucy*, Mrs. Green.

1756–57: Oct. 20, *Coupee*, King; *Quaver*, Corry; *Goodwill*, Mynitt; *Blister*, Sparks; *Wormwood*, Stayley; *Thomas*, Williams;

Lucy, Mrs. Pye; Dec. 30, *Coupee,* King; *Lucy,* Mrs. Wilder; *Quaver,* Wilder; June 4, plus *Blister.*

1757–58: Oct. 19, *Coupee,* King; *Quaver,* Wilder; *Blister,* Sparks; *Goodwill,* Lewis; *Wormwood,* Stayley; *Thomas,* Williams; *Lucy,* Mrs. Wilder; Dec. 10, without *Goodwill, Wormwood,* and *Thomas;* Jan. 28.

The Way of the World, "written by [William] Congreve"

1747–48: Mar. 25, *Witwould,* Woodward; *Millamant,* Miss Bellamy; *Lady Wishfor't,* Miss Pitt.

1748–49: Mar. 3, *Lady Wishfor't,* Mrs. Macklin; *Sir Willfull Witwould,* Macklin; Apr. 12, plus *Witwould,* Dyer; *Mrs. Marwood,* Mrs. Bland; *Millamant,* Mrs. Vincent; and *Foible,* Miss Minors.

1749–50: Nov. 20, *Sir Willfull Witwould,* Macklin; *Witwould,* Cibber; *Millamant,* Mrs. Bland; *Lady Wishfor't,* Mrs. Macklin; Dec. 21; Jan. 20; Feb. 9, plus *Fainall,* R. Elrington; *Mrs. Marwood,* Mrs. Mynitt; and *Mrs. Fainall,* Mrs. Mozeen.

1750–51: Oct. 3, *Witwould,* Cibber; *Millamant,* Mrs. Bland; *Marwood,* Miss Cole; *Fainall,* R. Elrington; *Mirabel,* J. Elrington; *Sir Willfull,* Sparks; *Petulant,* Watson; *Waitwell,* Bardin; *Lady Wishfor't,* Mrs. Mynitt; *Mrs. Fainall,* Mrs. Lindley; *Foible,* Mrs. Rowley; *Mincing,* Miss Byrne; *Peg,* Mrs. Packenham; Apr. 22, but *Mirabel,* King; *Fainall,* Ross; *Sir Willfull,* Mynitt; *Waitwell,* Sparks; *Mincing,* Mrs. Leslie; and without *Peg.*

1751–52: Feb. 5, *Mirabel,* Digges; *Witwould,* Cibber; *Petulant,* King; *Sir Willfull,* Sparks; *Fainall,* Davies; *Waitwell,* Stevens; *Marwood,* Mrs. Bland; *Mrs. Fainall,* Mrs. Lee; *Lady Wishfor't,* Mrs. Mynitt; *Foible,* Miss Cole; *Mincing,* Mrs. Kennedy; *Millamant,* Mrs. Woffington.

1752–53: Mar. 2, *Fainall,* Sowdon; *Witwould,* King; *Sir Willfull,* Sparks; *Petulant,* Costollo; *Mirabel,* J. Elrington; *Waitwell,* Stevens; *Marwood,* Mrs. Ward; *Foible,* Mrs. Green; *Lady Wishfor't,* Mrs. Mynitt; *Mrs. Fainall,* Mrs. Kennedy; *Millamant,* Mrs. Woffington; Mar. 22, but *Mirabel,* Digges.

1753–54: Oct. 19, *Fainall,* Sowdon; *Mirabel,* Dexter; *Witwould,* King; *Sir Willfull,* Sparks; *Petulant,* Green; *Marwood,* Mrs. Ward; *Lady Wishfor't,* Mrs. Mynitt; *Mrs. Fainall,* Mrs. Kennedy; *Foible,* Mrs. Green; *Millamant,* Mrs. Woffington; *Mincing,* Mrs. Leslie; *Peg,* Miss Comerford; *Waitwell,* Layfield; Dec. 14, without *Mincing* and *Peg.*

1756–57: Jan. 21, *Mirabel,* Dexter; *Fainall,* Wilder; *Witwould,* King; *Sir Willfull,* Sparks; *Petulant,* Glover; *Lady Wishfor't,* Mrs.

Mynitt; *Mrs. Marwood*, Mrs. Kennedy; *Millamant*, Mrs. Glen.

1757–58: Jan. 9, *Mirabel*, Dexter; *Fainall*, Wilder; *Witwould*, King; *Petulant*, Stayley; *Sir Willful*, Sparks; *Waitwell*, Glover; *Millamant*, Miss Kennedy; *Mrs. Fainall*, Mrs. Pye; *Foible*, Miss Mason; *Mincing*, Mrs. Kennedy.

The What D'Ye Call It, "wrote by Mess. Pope, Gay and Arbuthnot." (A Tragi-Comi-Pastoral Farce)

1747–48: Mar. 21, *Timothy Peascod*, Woodward; Mar. 25; Mar. 30; Apr. 13, no cast.

1749–50: Dec. 8, Vocal Parts by Sullivan, Mrs. Storer, Mrs. Lampe, Howard, and others; Dec. 14, no cast.

1750–51: Oct. 3, *Kitty Carrot*, Miss Cole.

1751–52: Jan. 23, no cast.

1753–54: Nov. 17, *Timothy Peascod*, Sparks; *Filbert*, Green; *Dorcas*, Mrs. Storer; *Kitty Carrot*, Mrs. Green; Nov. 23.

1757–58: Mar. 15, *Timothy Peascod*, Sparks; *Filbert*, Glover; *Corporal*, Hamilton; *Kitty Carrot*, Mrs. Pye; *Dorcas*, "with the Songs in Character," Mrs. Storer.

The Whim, or *Harlequin Villager* (Pantomime Entertainment)

1757–58: Feb. 3, *Harlequin*, King; *Clown*, Sparks; *Squire Gawky*, Glover; *Colombine*, Mrs. Kennedy; Feb. 9, plus *Pantaloon*, Hamilton; *Drawer*, Messink; and *Venus*, Miss Mason; Feb. 11, as on Feb. 3; Feb. 16, as on Feb. 9; Feb. 24, as on Feb. 3; Mar. 2; Mar. 16; Apr. 14, as on Feb. 9; Apr. 22, as on Feb. 3; June 1.

A Will and No Will, or *A New Case for the Lawyers*, "translated from the French by Mr. [Charles] Macklin." (Farce)

1748–49: Dec. 19, no cast; May 2.

1749–50: Mar. 5, *Shark*, Macklin.

The Wonder, a Woman Keeps a Secret, by Susannah Centlivre

1753–54: Jan. 14, *Don Felix*, Sowdon; *Col. Briton*, Dexter; *Lissardo*, King; *Gibby*, Sparks; *Don Lopez*, Layfield; *Frederick*, Kennedy; *Don Pedro*, Green; *Isabella*, Mrs. Pye; *Flora*, Mrs. Mynitt; *Inis*, Mrs. Kennedy; *Violante*, Mrs. Ward; Jan. 26.

1756–57: May 17, *Col. Briton*, Dexter; *Don Lopez*, Layfield; *Frederick*, Kennedy; *Lissardo*, King; *Don Pedro*, Glover; *Gibby*, Sparks; *Vasquez*, Messink; *Alguazile*, Mynitt; *Don Felix*, Hurst; *Flora*, Miss Wells; *Inis*, Miss Mason; *Isabella*, Mrs. Pye; *Violante*, Miss Kennedy; May 25.

1757–58: Jan. 27, *Lissardo*, King; *Don Felix*, Hurst; *Vasquez*, Messink; *Don Lopez*, Storer; *Don Pedro*, Glover; *Alguazile*, Lewis; *Frederick*, Kennedy; *Col. Briton*, Dexter; *Gibby*, Sparks; *Inis*, Miss Mason; *Flora*, Miss Wells; *Violante*, Miss Kennedy.

Zara, "taken from the French of Voltaire by the late Aaron Hill, Esq."

1751–52: Dec. 7, *Osman*, Sheridan; *Nerestan*, Digges; *Lusignan*, Heaphy; *Chatilion*, Beamsley; *Orasmin*, Stevens; *Selima*, Miss Cole; *Zara*, Mrs. Woffington; Dec. 11.

Bibliography and Index

Selected Bibliography

The notation, often an abbreviation, at the end of some entries is for the name of the library in which the work, usually rare, may be found.

B. M.	British Museum, London
Bodleian Library	Bodleian Library, Oxford
Cambridge U.	Cambridge University Library, Cambridge, England
Col. U.	Columbia University Library, New York
Cork Lib.	Cork Library, Cork
Folger	Folger Shakespeare Library, Washington, D.C.
Harvard	Library of Harvard University
N.L.I.	National Library of Ireland, Dublin
N.Y.P.L.	New York Public Library, New York
Pearse St. Lib.	Pearse Street Library, Dublin
R.I.A.	Royal Irish Academy, Dublin
T.C.D.	Trinity College Library, Dublin

Address to the Town, Mr. Sheridan's. (*In Cibber and Sheridan . . . ,* q.v., pp. 26–35.)

A. F. (pseudonym for Charles Lucas). (See *A Second Letter to the Free Citizens . . . , A Third Letter to the Free-Citizens. . . .*)

a Freeman (pseudonym for Charles Lucas). (See *A Letter to the Free-Citizens. . . .*)

Angelo, Henry. *Reminiscences of Henry Angelo, with the Memoirs of his Late Father and Friends. . . .* 2 vols. London, 1828–30.

Annual Register. London.

An Answer In Behalf of Spranger Barry, the Proprietor of the New Theatre in Crow-Street, to the Case and Petition of Thomas Sheridan . . . and also to the Petition of two of the Proprietors of said united Theatres. . . . 4pp. [1758.] B. M.

An Apology for the Conduct of Mr. Charles Macklin. British Museum Pamphlet Collection.

An Appeal to the Public, Against Mr. Sheridan's Intended Scheme for a Monopoly of the Stage. 27pp. Dublin, 1772. R.I.A.

Appleton, William W. *Charles Macklin.* Cambridge, Mass., 1960.

The Art of Speaking. (See [Burgh, James].)

B—n, B—t. *The Stage: or Coronation of King Tom. A Satyr.* Dublin, 1753. Pearse St. Lib.

Bacon, Wallace A. *The Elocutionary Career of Thomas Sheridan (1719–1788).* Speech Monographs, xxxi, No. 1 (March 1964).

Baker, David Erskine. *Biographia Dramatica, or, A Companion to the Playhouse.* 2 vols. London, 1782.

Barrington, Jonah. *Personal Sketches of his Own Times.* 2 vols. Philadelphia, 1827.

Bath Chronicle and Weekly Gazette. Bath.

Bays in Council. Dublin, 1751. R.I.A.

Beauclerk, Mrs. D. J. *Mrs. Beauclerk's Letters to Mr. Sheridan and Mr. Victor, with their Answers.* . . . Dublin, 1758. B. M

Bellamy, George Anne. *An Apology for the Life of George Anne Bellamy.* 2d. edn. 2 vols. Dublin, 1785.

Bernard, John. *Retrospections of the Stage.* 2 vols. Boston, 1832.

Betsy Sheridan's Journal. (See Sheridan, Betsy.)

Boswell, James. *The Life of Samuel Johnson.* (See Hill, George B., ed.)
————. *Boswell's London Journal 1762–1763,* Frederick A. Pottle, ed. New York, 1950.

The British Theatre, containing the lives of the English Dramatic Poets. . . . Together with the Lives of most of the Principal Actors. Dublin, 1750. R.I.A.

Brown, Stephen J. *A Guide to Books on Ireland.* Dublin, 1912.

Brown, W. C. *Charles Churchill.* Lawrence, Kansas, 1953.

Brutus's Letter to the Town. [By William Dennis.] 8pp. 1747. R.I.A.

[Burgh, James.] *The Art of Speaking.* 2d edn. Dublin, printed for S[amuel] W[hyte], 1763.

Burke, Edmund. *The Early Life, Correspondence and Writings of the Rt. Hon. Edmund Burke . . . With an introduction and supplementary chapters on Burke's contributions to the Reformer.* Arthur P. I. Samuels, ed. Cambridge, England, 1923.

Burtchaell, George D., and Sadleir, T. U. *Alumni Dublinensis. A Register of the students, graduates, professors, and provosts of Trinity College, in the University of Dublin (1593–1860).* Dublin, 1935.

Bush, J. (See *Hibernia Curiosa.* . . .)

The Buskin and Sock; being Controversial Letters between Mr. Thomas Sheridan, Tragedian, and Mr. Theophilus Cibber, Comedian; Just Published in Dublin. Dublin Printed; London Reprinted. . . . 1743. B. M.

By Peter Shee, Painter. . . . *By Thomas Sheridan, Orator.* 1p. [1758?] B. M.

The Cambridge Journal. Cambridge, England.

The Case of the Stage in Ireland; containing the Reasons for and against a Bill for limiting the Number of Theatres in the City of Dublin; wherein the Qualifications, Duty, and Importance of a Manager are carefully considered and explained, and the Conduct and Abilities of Mr. Sheridan, the present Manager of the Theatre in Smock-Alley, are particularly reviewed and examined. The Whole occasionally interspersed with critical Observations on Mr. Sheridan's Oration. . . . Dublin, [December 1757 or early in 1758]. Col. U.

Bibliography

The Case of Thomas Sheridan. (See Sheridan, Thomas.)

The Censor. By Frank Somebody, Esq. Dublin, June 3, 1749.

Chalmers, Alexander. *The Works of the English Poets, from Chaucer to Cowper.* XVII. London, 1810.

Chetwood, William R. *A General History of the Stage . . . with the Memoirs of most of the principal Performers that have appeared on the English and Irish Stage for these last Fifty Years.* London, 1749. N.Y.P.L.

Churchill, Charles. *The Rosciad.* London, 1761. N.Y.P.L.

Cibber, Theophilus. *Theophilus Cibber, to David Garrick, Esq; with Dissertations on Theatrical Subjects.* London, 1759. Col. U.

Cibber and Sheridan: or, the Dublin Miscellany. Containing All the Advertisements, Letters, Addresses, Replys, Apologys, Verses, &c., &c., &c. Lately publish'd on Account of the Theatric Squabble. . . . Dublin, 1743. Col. U.

The City of Dublin. (See *A Description of the City of Dublin. . . .*)

Clark, William S. *The Early Irish Stage, The Beginnings to 1720.* Oxford, 1955.

Clippings relating to Sheridan's performances, Attic Evenings, readings, Rhetorical Prelections, etc. B. M. Mss. Coll.

Congreve, William. (See Summers, Montague, ed.)

Cooke, William. *The Elements of Dramatic Criticism.* London, 1775.

————. *Memoirs of Charles Macklin.* 2d edn. London, 1806.

————. *Memoirs of Samuel Foote, Esq.* 2 vols. New York, 1806.

Coriolanus: or, the Roman Matron. (See Sheridan, Thomas.)

Cork Chronicle. Cork.

Cork Remembrancer. Cork.

The Cornish Squire. A Comedy. As it is Acted at the Theatre-Royal in Drury-Lane, By His Majesty's Servants. [Preface by J. Ralph.] London, 1734. N.Y.P.L.

Crone, John S. *A Concise Dictionary of Irish Biography.* Dublin, 1937.

Cove, Joseph W. (See Gibbs, Lewis.)

The Curtain Lecture: or, The Manager Run Mad. A Dialogue between a Stage Manager & his Wife. London, 1758. Folger

Davies, Thomas. *Dramatic Miscellanies.* 3 vols. London, 1784.

————. *Memoirs of the Life of David Garrick, Esq. . . .* 2 vols. London, 1780.

Deeds. Irish deeds available at the Office of the Registry of Deeds in Dublin.

Delany, Mary Granville. *The Autobiography and Correspondence of Mary Granville, Mrs. Delany.* Lady Llanover, ed. 3 vols. London, 1861.

Dennis, William. (See *Brutus's Letter to the Town.*)

Derrick, Samuel. (See Wilkes, Thomas.)

A Description of the City of Dublin in Ireland. By a Citizen of London, who liv'd twenty Years in Ireland. . . . and is lately returned from Dublin. London, 1732. N.L.I.

Dibden, James C. *The Annals of the Edinburgh Stage.* Edinburgh, 1888.

The Dramatic Censor. (See [Gentleman, Francis].)

Drury Lane Calendar. (See MacMillan, Dougald.)

Drury Lane Nightly Accounts (1776–1779). Folger.

The Dublin Courant. Dublin.

The Dublin Gazette. Dublin.

Dublin in an Uproar: or, The Ladies robb'd of their Pleasure. Being a Full and Impartial Relation of the Remarkable Tumult that lately happen'd at the Dublin Theatre. With the Genuine Letters that pass'd on both Sides. Dublin Printed; London Reprinted. . . . [1746–47.] B. M.

The Dublin Journal, George Faulkner, ed. Dublin.

The Dublin Spy, II, No. xxx. December 6, 1753. Pearse St. Lib.

Duggan, George C. *The Stage Irishman.* London, [1937].

Eldredge, H. J., comp. *"The Stage" Cyclopaedia; a bibliography of plays.* London, 1909.

Ellis, W. P. *Extracts from Jackson's Oxford Journal illustrating Oxford History, 1753–1850.* Bodleian.

An Enquiry into the Plan and Pretensions of Mr. Sheridan. Dublin, 1758. Col. U.

Enthofen Collection of Playbills. Victoria and Albert Museum, London.

An Epistle from Th—s Sh—n, Esq; to the Universal Advertiser. 7pp. [1754.] R.I.A.

Esdall's News-Letter. Dublin.

European Magazine and London Review. London.

A Faithful Narrative. (See Sheridan, Thomas.)

The Farmer's Yard; a New Fable for Aesop. 1747. R.I.A.

Faulkner, George. (See *The Dublin Journal.*)

Fitzgerald, Percy H. *The Lives of the Sheridans.* 2 vols. London, 1886.

———. *A New History of the English Stage, from the Restoration to the Liberty of the Theatres, in Connection with the Patent Houses.* 2 vols. London, 1882.

Flynn, J. W. *Random Recollections of an Old Play-Goer.* Cork, 1890. Cork Lib.

Forshall, Frederic H. *Westminster School, Past and Present.* London, 1884.

Foss, Kenelm. *Here Lies Richard Brinsley Sheridan.* New York, 1940.

Foster, Joseph. *Alumni Oxonienses (1715–1886)*. Bodleian.

Frank Somebody (pseudonym). (See *The Censor*.)

Freeman, a. (pseudonym for Charles Lucas). (See *A Letter to the Free-Citizens*. . . .)

The Freeman's Journal. Dublin.

A Full and True Account of the Woefull and Wonderfull Apparition of Hurloe Harrington, Late Prompter to the Theatre-Royal in Dublin: Who, by the Instigation of some evil Spirits, threw himself down a considerable Precipice, by which great, violent and sudden Fall, he first destroyed his Intellectuals, and soon after departed this mortal Life, to the great Grief of his Majesty's company of Commedians [sic] of Ireland, as well, Male as Female. In a Letter From the Reverend Parson Fitz-Henery to his G—e the A.B. of C—y. London, 1750. Folger.

A Full Vindication. (See Sheridan, Thomas.)

Garrick, David. *The Letters of David Garrick*, David M. Little and George M. Kahrl, eds. Cambridge, Mass., 1963.

———. *Some Unpublished Correspondence of David Garrick*, George P. Baker, ed. Boston, 1907.

———. *The Private Correspondence of David Garrick*. 2 vols. London, 1831–32.

Garrick's Looking Glass. Dublin, 1776. R.I.A.

Genest, John. *Some Account of the English Stage, from the Restoration in 1660 to 1830*. 10 vols. Bath, 1832.

[Gentleman, Francis.] *The Dramatic Censor; or, Critical Companion*. 2 vols. London, 1770.

The Gentleman. An Heroic Poem. [1747.] Pearse St. Lib.

The Gentleman's Magazine and Historical Chronicle. London.

Gibbs, Lewis (pseudonym for Joseph W. Cove). *Sheridan, His Life and His Theatre*. New York, 1948.

Gilbert, John Thomas. *A History of the City of Dublin*. 3 vols. Dublin, 1861.

A Grand Debate between Court and Country, at the Theatre-Royal, in Smock-Alley, Lately in a Letter to the C—t Party with Mr. Sh—n's Apology to the C—ry Party. [1754.] N.L.I.

Heron, Denis. *The Constitutional History of the University of Dublin*. Dublin, 1847.

Hibernia Curiosa. A Letter from a Gentleman in Dublin to his Friend at Dover in Kent. Giving a general View of the Manners, Customs, Dispositions, &c. of the Inhabitants of Ireland. . . . Collected in a Tour through the Kingdom in the Year 1764. [Dedication signed by J. Bush.] London, n.d. N.Y.P.L.

Hibernian Chronicle. Cork.

Hibernian Journal. Dublin.

Hibernian Magazine. (See *Walker's Hibernian Magazine*.)

[Hiffernan, Paul.] *The Tickler*. Nos. I, II, III, IV, V, VI, and VII. *The Second Edition, Review'd, Corrected, and Augmented, with Notes humorous and serious; and an Epistle dedicatory to Ch-rl-s L-c-s, Freeman*. Dublin, 1748. R.I.A.

Hill, George B., ed. *Boswell's Life of Johnson*. Oxford, 1887.

Hitchcock, Robert. *An Historical View of the Irish Stage; from the earliest period down to the close of the season 1788. . . . *2 vols. Dublin, 1788–94. (Actually goes only to 1774.)

Hogan, Charles B. *Shakespeare in the Theatre 1701–1800*. 2 vols. Oxford, 1952–57.

Hughes, Leo, and Scouten, A. H. *Ten English Farces*. Austin, Texas, 1948.

An Humble Address to the Ladies of the City of Dublin. By a Plebeian. 20pp. Dublin, 1747. R.I.A.

An Humble Address to the Publick. (See Sheridan, Thomas.)

An Humble Appeal. (See Sheridan, Thomas.)

The Humble Petition of Thomas Punch. (See *To the Honourable K—s, . . .*)

Irish Newspapers Prior to 1750 in Dublin Libraries. In Positive Microfilm. University of Michigan, 1950.

The Irishman in London. 1755. From MS. Larpent Coll. #120 in Microprint Edition of *Three Centuries of English and American Plays*.

Jackson's Oxford Journal. Oxford.

Johnson's England, Arthur S. Turberville ed. 2 vols. Oxford, 1933.

Joseph, Bertram. *The Tragic Actor*. London, 1959.

Journal Drury Lane Theatre. Messrs. Sheridan, Linley & Ford Proprietors, beginning 18th Sept. 1779 and ending May 31st, 1780. Folger.

K—, S—. *The Hibernian Rosciad*. Dublin, 1765. Pearse St. Lib.

Kavanagh, Peter. *The Irish Theatre*. Tralee, 1946.

Kemble, John Philip. *Manuscript Diary Record of the Theatre-Royal from The Dublin Journal 1730–1751*. Shaw Collection, Widener Library, Harvard University. (This Kemble MSS has been used in the foregoing book only when issues of the *Dublin Journal* are missing in the National Library of Ireland.)

Kirkman, James Thomas. *Memoirs of the Life of Charles Macklin*. 2 vols. London, 1799.

Knight, Joseph. *David Garrick*. London, 1894.

Latocnaye, M. de. *Rambles through Ireland; by a French Emigrant.* Cork, 1798. Cork. Lib.

Lawrence, William J. *The Drama and the Theatre.* (See *Johnson's England*, II.)

————. "Trinity and the Theatre." *Irish Times,* September 2, 1922. From newspaper cuttings, N.L.I.

Lee, John. (See *A Letter from Mr. Lee.*)

Lefanu, Alicia. *Memoirs of the Life and Writings of Mrs. Frances Sheridan . . . and Biographical Anecdotes of her Family and Contemporaries. By her grand-daughter, Alicia Lefanu.* London, 1824.

Lefanu MSS. Various Manuscripts in the Possession of William LeFanu. Microfilmed at the Royal College of Surgeons and available through the courtesy of William R. LeFanu.

Lenihan, Maurice. *Limerick, Its History and Antiquities.* Dublin, 1866. Cork Lib.

A Letter from Mr. Lee to Mr. Sheridan. Dublin, 1757. B. M.

A Letter from Tom the First, King of Ireland, to John the Second, King of Scotland, with the King of Scotland's Answer thereto. Dublin, 1757. R.I.A.

A Letter of Thanks to the Barber, for his Indefatigable Pains To Suppress the Horrid and Unnatural Rebellion, Lately broke out in this City; But by His Means, now happily almost Extinguished. By Mr. Francis Liberty, A Freeman and Citizen of Dublin. 15pp. Dublin, 1747. R.I.A.

A Letter to Messieurs Victor and Sowdon, Managers of the Theatre-Royal. Dublin, 1755. B. M.

A Letter to Mr. W—dw—rd, Comedian. 1p. [1748.] B. M.

A Letter to the Admirers of Mr. S—n. 2pp. 1748. B. M.

A Letter to the Free-Citizens of Dublin. By a Freeman, Barber and Citizen (pseudonym for Charles Lucas). Dublin, February 12th, 1746/7. B. M.

Libertus. *Remarks on Two Letters signed Theatricus and Hibernicus, and Published in the Dublin Journal of the 12th and 23d of February, 1754.* Dublin, 1754. B. M.

Liberty, Mr. Francis (pseudonym). (See *A Letter of Thanks to the Barber.*)

The Life of Mr. James Quin comedian, with the history of the stage from his commencing actor to his retreat to Bath. London, 1766, 1887.

The Life of Mrs. Abington . . . Celebrated Comic Actress . . . Including also interesting notes upon the history of the Irish Stage. By the Editor of the "Life of Quin." London, 1888.

The Limerick Chronicle. Limerick. N.L.I.

Loewenberg, Alfred. *The Theatre of the British Isles excluding London. A Bibliography.* London, 1950.

The London Chronicle. London.

The London Stage 1660–1800. Pts. 3 and 4. Carbondale, Illinois, 1961–62.

Lucas, Charles (writing under pseudonyms A. F. and a Freeman). (See *A Letter to the Free-Citizens of Dublin, A Second Letter . . .* , and *A Third Letter. . . .*)

Macklin, Charles. (See *An Apology for the Conduct of Mr. Charles Macklin.*)

MacMillan, Dougald. *Catalogue of the Larpent Plays in the Huntington Library*. San Marino, 1939.

———. *Drury Lane Calendar 1747–1776*. Oxford, 1938.

Macqueen-Pope, W. J. *Theatre-Royal, Drury Lane*. London, 1945.

Madden, Richard R. *A History of Irish Periodical Literature . . . 17th-19th century*. 2 vols. London, 1867.

Mallam, Duncan, ed. *Letters of William Shenstone*. Minneapolis, 1939.

Man of Honour; but Not of his Word. Inscribed to Mr. Sheridan. 16pp. Dublin, 1750. B. M.

Maxwell, Constantia E. *Dublin Under the Georges*. London, [1936].

Mitchell, John. *The History of Ireland, from the Treaty of Limerick to the Present Time*. 2d edn. 2 vols. Dublin, 1869.

Molloy, J. Fitzgerald. *The Romance of the Irish Stage*. 2 vols. New York, 1897.

Moore, Thomas. *Memoirs of the Life of the Right Honourable Richard Brinsley Sheridan*. 5th edn. 2 vols. London, 1827.

The Morning Chronicle. London.

The Morning Post. London.

Mr. Orde's Plan of an improved System of Education in Ireland. 1787. R.I.A.

Mr. Sh—n's Apology to the Town; with the Reasons which unfortunately induced him to his late Misconduct. Written by himself. And published by his very good Friend H—y S—r. Dublin, 2754 [*sic*]. B. M.

Mr. Sheridan's Address to the Town. (In *Cibber and Sheridan . . .* , *q.v.*, pp. 26–35.)

Mrs. Beauclerk's Letters. . . . (See Beauclerk.)

The Nettle. No. 1. October 24, 1751. 2pp. Dublin. B. M.

Nicoll, Allardyce. *A History of English Drama 1660–1900*. 6 vols. Cambridge, England, 1952–59.

No-Body, Nicholas. *A Critical Examination of the Sense, Style, and Grammar, of Mr. Sheridan's Printed Oration. Humbly submitted to all Noblemen, Gentlemen, and Others, who sincerely wish to see a*

Well-Planned Publick School and Academy established in this Kingdom, under the Conduct of able Instructors; and whose Attachment is not to the Man, but to the Thing. Dublin, 1758. B. M.

O'Donoghue, D. J. *The Geographical Distribution of Irish Ability.* Dublin, 1906.

O'Keeffe, John. *Recollections of the Life of John O'Keeffe, Written by himself.* 2 vols. London, 1826.

O'Mahony, Charles. *The Viceroys of Ireland.* London, 1912.

Oulton, Walley C. *A History of the Theatres of London from 1771 to 1795,* 2 vols. London, 1796.

Parish Register, St. Mary's Church, Dublin.

Parry, Edward A. *Charles Macklin.* London, 1891.

Pedicord, Harry W. *The Theatrical Public in the Time of Garrick.* New York, 1954.

Pilkington, Letitia. *Memoirs of Mrs. Letitia Pilkington 1712–1750. Written by Herself.* New York, 1928 (1st edn., 1748–54).

The Play-House Journal. No. 1. January 18, 1749–50. 2pp. Dublin. B. M.

The Play-House prorogued: or, a Vindication of the Conduct of the Manager. Addressed to the Town. Dublin, 1754. T.C.D. Lib.

A Poem on Mr. Sheridan and Mr. Barry. Dublin, 1746. R.I.A.

The Political Manager: or, the Invasion of the Music-Hall, set forth. No. 1. October 2, 1749. 2pp. Dublin, 1749. B. M.

The Present State of the Stage in Great-Britain and Ireland. And the Theatrical Characters of the Principal Performers, In both Kingdoms, Impartially Considered. London, 1753. B. M.

The Proceedings of the Hibernian Society, drawn up by their Order, By a Committee, Composed of the following Members. . . . Dublin, 1758. B. M.

A Prologue to Julius Caesar As it was Acted at Madam Violante's Booth December the 15th, 1732, by some of the young Gentlemen in Dr. Sheridan's School. Folger.

The Prophecies of the Book of the Prophet Lucas. Reprinted in Samuels' edition of Burke, *q.v.,* p. 120.

The Public Advertiser. London.

Pue's Occurrences. Dublin.

Punch's Petition to Mr. S——n, to be admitted into the Theatre Royal. 1p. Dublin, [1747 or 1748]. B. M.

Quin, James. (See *The Life of Mr. James Quin. . . .*)

Bibliography

Rae, W. Fraser. *Sheridan, A Biography*. 2 vols. London, 1896.

——. "Sheridan's Sons," *Temple Bar*, CXVI (January-April, 1899), 407–426.

Ralph, J. (See *The Cornish Squire*.)

The Record of Old Westminsters (*A Biographical List of all who are known to have been educated at Westminster School from the Earliest Time to 1927*). Compiled by G. F. Russell Barker and A. H. Stenning. 2 vols. London, 1928.

Reflections of a Gentleman in the Country on the present Theatrical Disturbances, in a Letter to the Printer of the Dublin-Courant. 1p. Incomplete. [1747.]

The Reformer. (See Burke, Edmund.)

Remarks on Mr. Lee's Letter to Mr. Sheridan. 1757. R.I.A.

Richardson, Samuel. *The Correspondence of Samuel Richardson*, Anna L. Barbauld, ed. 6 vols. London, 1804.

Rosenfeld, Sybil. *Strolling Players & Drama in the Provinces 1660–1765*. Cambridge, England, 1939.

Rules of Accommodation As Drawn up by a Select Committee of Gentlemen, Appointed for that Purpose, in order to establish a right Understanding between the Town and the Manager of Smock-Alley Theatre. . . . Dublin, 1754. T.C.D. Lib.

Samuels, Arthur P. I. (See Burke, Edmund.)

Sargeaunt, John. *Annals of Westminster School*. London, 1898.

Scurr, Helen M. *Henry Brooke*. University of Minnesota thesis, 1922.

A Second Letter to the Free Citizens of Dublin. By A. F. Barber and Citizen (pseudonym for Charles Lucas). 16pp. March 3, 1746/7. R.I.A.

A Serious Enquiry into the Causes of the Present Disorders [*in the City, humbly offered to the Consideration of the Inhabitants*. 1747.] (Title page missing. Material in brackets is from Loewenberg.) 16pp. R.I.A.

Shadwell, Charles. *The Plotting Lovers, or The Dismal Squire As it was acted, At the Theater-Royal in Smock-Alley*. In *The Works of Mr. Charles Shadwell*, I. Dublin, 1720.

Shea, P. *A Full Vindication of Thomas Sheridan, Esq; being an Answer To a Scurrilous Pamphlet*. Dublin, 1758. R.I.A.

Sheridan, Betsy. *Betsy Sheridan's Journal, Letters from* [Richard] *Sheridan's Sister 1784–1786 and 1788–1790*, William LeFanu, ed. London, 1960.

[Sheridan, Frances.] *The Discovery*. In *English Comedy*, IV. London, 1810.

[——.] *Frances C. Sheridan's Journey to Bath* (first three acts). British Museum Mss. Coll.

[————.] *Memoirs of Miss Sidney Bidulph extracted from her own Journal.* 4th edn. 3 vols. London, 1772.

Sheridan, Thomas. (See separate list of works, p. 492.)

Sichel, Walter S. *Sheridan, from new and original Material.* 2 vols. Boston, 1909.

The Sighs and Groans of Mr. Sh—n, with A full Account of a Comical Farce that was acted last Saturday Night at the Theatre in Smock-Alley, and the Occasion thereof. Also, An Account of the Manager's rude Behaviour to the Audience at the Play of Mahomet. Dublin, 1754. Cambridge U.

Snagg, Thomas. *Recollection of Occurrences, The Memoirs of Thomas Snagg (or Snagge) with an introduction by Harold Hobson.* . . . Dropmore Press (privately printed), 1951.

Somebody, Frank (pseudonym). (See *The Censor.*)

The Stage: or Coronation of King Tom. A Satyr. (See B—n, B—t.)

A State of Mr. Sheridan's Case. (See Sheridan, Thomas.)

A State of the Case In Regard to the Point in Dispute between Mr. Mosse and Mr. Sheridan. (See Sheridan, Thomas.)

Stayley, George. *Mr. Stayley's Reference to the Public.* 1760.

————. *The Life and Opinions of an Actor.* I. Dublin, 1767.

Stephenson, P. J. *Dublin Theatre Notes.* Ms read before the Old Dublin Society, 1949. Pearse St. Lib.

Stockwell, La Tourette. *Dublin Theatres and Theatre Customs, 1637–1820.* Kingsport, Tenn., 1938.

Summers, Montague, ed. *The Complete Works of William Congreve.* III. London, 1923.

Swift, Jonathan. *The Correspondence of Jonathan Swift, D.D.,* F. E. Ball, ed. 6 vols. London, 1910–14.

————. *The Drapier's Letters to the People of Ireland against receiving Wood's Halfpence,* Herbert Davis, ed. Oxford, 1935.

————. *Letters of Jonathan Swift to Charles Ford,* David Nichol Smith, ed. Oxford, 1935.

————. *The Poems of Jonathan Swift,* Harold Williams, ed. Oxford, 1937.

————. *The Prose Works of Jonathan Swift,* Temple Scott, ed. 12 vols. London, 1897–1922.

Tanner, Lawrence E. *Westminster School; its Buildings and their Associations.* London, [1923].

Theatrical Monopoly; Being An Address to the Public on the Present Alarming Coalition of the Managers of the Winter Theatres. London, 1779. B. M.

The Thespian Dictionary; or, Dramatic Biography of the Eighteenth

Century; Containing Sketches of the Lives, Productions, &c. of all the Principal Managers, Dramatists, Composers, Commentators, Actors, and Actresses, of the United Kingdom. . . . London, 1802.

A Third Letter to the Free-Citizens of Dublin. By A. F. Barber and Citizen (pseudonym for Charles Lucas). 22pp. Dublin, 1747. R.I.A.

Three Centuries of English and American Plays: A Checklist, G. W. Bergquist, ed. New York, 1963.

Tickell, Richard Eustace, comp. *Thomas Tickell and the Eighteenth Century Poets (1685–1740)*. London, 1931.

The Tickler. (See Hiffernan, Paul.)

The Tickler Tickled. (Included in *The Tickler,* though not by Hiffernan, but a criticism of him.)

Tom's Stage. A Satyr. Dublin, 1758. Pearse St. Lib. (Same as B—n, B—t, *The Stage,* except for a final notice: "Speedily will be publish'd by the same Author, a new Picture of Tom and his Cat's Paw.")

To the Honourable K—s, C—s and B—s in P—t assembled. The humble petition of Thomas Punch, Esq., Principal Performer and sole Manager of the Still-Life-Theatre in Caple-Street. 2pp. [1758.] B. M.

To the Honourable the Knights, Citizens, and Burgesses, in Parliament assembled: the Humble Petition of John Putland, Esquire, and Captain Theophilus Desbrisay. 2pp. [1758.] B. M.

To the Honourable the Knights . . . the humble Petition of Thomas Sheridan. (See Sheridan, Thomas.)

To the Ladies and Gentlemen. . . . (In *Cibber and Sheridan . . . , q.v.,* pp. 7–10.)

To the Publick. (Contains affidavits signed on the "19th Day of March 1749/50.") 3pp. [1750.] R.I.A.

The Trial of John Magee for printing and publishing a slanderous and defamatory libel against Richard Daly, Esq. . . . Dublin, 1790.

The Tricks of the Town laid open: or, a Companion for Country Gentlemen: Being the Substance of Sixteen Letters from a Gentleman in Dublin to his Friend in the Country, To dissuade him from coming to Town. . . . Dublin, n.d. (Dated *ca.* 1748 by Stockwell.) Pearse St. Lib.

Victor, Benjamin. *The History of the Theatres of London and Dublin, From the Year 1730 to the present Time. To which is added, an Annual Register of all the Plays, &c. performed at the Theatres-Royal in London, from the year 1712. With Occasional Notes and Anecdotes.* 2 vols. London, 1761.

———. *Original Letters, Dramatic Pieces, and Poems.* 3 vols. London, 1776.

A Vindication. (See Sheridan, Thomas.)

Walker's *Hibernian Magazine*. Dublin.

Watkins, John. *Memoirs of the Public and Private Life of the Right Honorable Richard Brinsley Sheridan, with a Particular Account of his Family and Connexions*. London, 1817.

Webb, Alfred. *A Compendium of Irish Biography*. Dublin, 1878.

Weeks, James Eyre. *A Rhapsody on the Stage, or the Art of Playing.* . . . Dublin, 1746. R.I.A.

Whyte, S[amuel] and his son, Whyte, E. A. *Miscellanea Nova; containing amidst a variety of other matters curious and interesting, remarks on Boswell's Johnson.* . . . Dublin, 1800.

Wilkes, Thomas (pseudonym). *A General View of the Stage*. London, 1759.

Wilkinson, Tate. *Memoirs of his own life by Tate Wilkinson*. 4 vols. York, 1790.

Wilks (pseudonym). (See Snagg, Thomas.)

Williams, Marjorie, ed. *The Letters of William Shenstone*. Oxford, 1939.

Williamson's Universal Advertizer. Dublin. (For information from this paper, I am indebted to Mrs. William S. Clark.)

Winston's Manuscript Diaries of Performances, Covent Garden, 1754–1755. Folger.

A list of those writings still extant, not including letters or announcements in the newspapers. A † preceding an entry means that the work appeared anonymously, i.e., without Sheridan's name as author on the title page or at the end of the work. For abbreviations of libraries at the ends of entries, see Bibliography.

An Appeal to the Public: containing an account of the rise, progress, and establishment of the first regular theatre, in Dublin: with the causes of it's decline and ruin. By Thomas Sheridan, formerly manager of the Theatre-Royal. First Published in the year 1758 [as *An Humble Appeal . . . q.v.*]. Dublin, 1771. (The sixth edition, also Dublin, 1771, and printed by J. Hoey, at the Mercury, in Parliament-Street, is available at N.Y.P.L.)

†*The Brave Irishman* (in Thomas Sheridan's handwriting in the *Lefanu MSS*, 57pp.).

†*The Brave Irishman: or, Captain O'Blunder. A Farce. As it is acted at the Theatre-Royal in Smock-alley: with the genuine songs, Not in any other Edition. Supposed to be Written by T—s S—n, Esq; And Revised with Several Corrections and Additions by J—n P—st—n.* Dublin: Printed, and Sold by R. Watts, Bookseller, at the Bible in Skinner-row. MDCCLIV. (Item K-D284 in Kemble-Devonshire Collection of Plays at the Huntington Library.)

British Education: or, the Source of the Disorders of Great Britain. Being an Essay toward proving, that the Immorality, Ignorance, and false Taste, which so generally prevail, are the natural and necessary Consequences of the present defective System of Education. With an Attempt to shew, that a Revival of the Art of Speaking, and the Study of our own Language, might contribute in a great measure, to the Cure of those Evils. In Three Parts. London, R. & J. Dodsley, 1756.

Captain O'Blunder. (See *The Brave Irishman.*)

†*The Case of Thomas Sheridan, Lessee and Manager of the united Theatres of Aungier-Street and Smock-Ally.* 2pp. [Dublin, 1758.] B. M.

A Complete Dictionary of the English Language, Both with regard to Sound and Meaning. One main Object of which is, to establish a plain and permanent Standard of Pronunciation. To which is prefixed A Prosodial Grammar. By Thomas Sheridan, A.M. . . . The Second Edition, Revised, Corrected, and Enlarged by the Author. London, Charles Dilly, MDCCLXXXIX. (The first edition was published as a *General Dictionary of the English Language, q.v.*)

†*Coriolanus: or, the Roman Matron. A Tragedy Taken from Shake-*

spear and Thomson. As it is Acted at the Theatre-Royal in Covent-Garden: To which is added, the Order of the Ovation. London, A. Millar, 1755.

A Course of Lectures on Elocution: Together with Two Dissertations on Language; and some other Tracts relative to those Subjects. By Thomas Sheridan, A.M. London: Printed by W. Strahan, for A. Millar, R. and J. Dodsley, T. Davies, C. Henderson, J. Wilkie, and E. Dilly. MDCCLXII.

A Discourse Delivered in the Theatre at Oxford, in the Senate-House at Cambridge, and at Spring-Garden in London. By Thomas Sheridan, M.A. Being Introductory to His Course of Lectures on Elocution and the English Language. . . . The Second Edition. London: Printed for A. Millar, J. Rivington and J. Fletcher, J. Dodsley, and sold by J. Wilkie. MDCCLIX.

A Dissertation on the Causes of the Difficulties which occur, in learning the English Tongue. With a scheme for publishing an English Grammar and Dictionary, Upon a Plan entirely New. The Object of which shall be, to facilitate the Attainment of the English Tongue, and establish a Perpetual Standard of Pronunciation. Addressed to a certain Noble Lord. By Thomas Sheridan, A.M. London, MDCCLXII. (Also appears as the last item in *A Course of Lectures on Elocution.*)

The Elements of English: Being a New Method of Teaching the Whole Art of Reading, Both with regard to Pronunciation and Spelling. Part the First. By Thomas Sheridan, A.M. London, C. Dilly, 1786. Edinburgh Library.

†*A Faithful Narrative Of what happen'd at the Theatre On Monday the 19th Instant, which gave Rise to the following Disturbance there, with some Observations upon it, humbly submitted to the Consideration of the Publick.* 14pp. Dublin, MDCCXLVII. Harvard.

A Full Vindication of the Conduct of the Manager of the Theatre-Royal. Written by Himself. Dublin, Printed by S. Powell in Crane-lane, 1747. (Dated "March 4, 1746–7.") B. M.

A General Dictionary of the English Language. One main Object of which, is, to establish a plain and permanent Standard of Pronunciation. To which is prefixed A Rhetorical Grammar. By Thomas Sheridan, A.M. London: Printed for J. Dodsley, Pall-Mall; C. Dilly, in the Poultry; and J. Wilkie, St. Paul's Church-Yard. MDCCLXXX.

The Rhetorical Grammar prefacing this dictionary was, with a few changes necessary to its new role, published separately along with some seventy pages, without acknowledgement, from [Burgh]'s *The Art of Speaking.* The title page for the earliest edition I have seen reads: *A Rhetorical Grammar of the English Language. Calculated solely for the Purposes of Teaching Propriety of Pronunciation, and Justness of Delivery, in that Tongue, by the Organs of Speech. By Thomas Sheridan, A.M. Dublin,* MDCCLXXXI. (N.L.I.) The compiler may have been Samuel Whyte, who had brought out an edition of *The Art of Speaking* years before. (See Bibliography under Burgh.)

An Humble Address to the Publick, from Mr. Sheridan, In Consequence of his Appeal. 3pp. (Dated "Dublin, May 6th, 1758.") B. M.

An humble Appeal to the Publick, Together with some Considerations on the Present critical and dangerous State of the Stage in Ireland. By Thomas Sheridan, Deputy Master of the Revels, and Manager of the Theatre-Royal. Dublin: Printed for G. Faulkner. MDCCLVIII. (Contains a reprinting of Sheridan's *Vindication, q.v.*) Col. U.

Last Will and Testament, 1785. Probate Registry, Somerset House, London.

Lectures on the Art of Reading; First Part: Containing the Art of Reading Prose. By Thomas Sheridan, A.M. London: Printed for J. Dodsley, Pall-Mall; J. Wilkie, St. Paul's Church-Yard; E. and C. Dilly, in the Poultry; and T. Davies, Russel-Street, Covent-Garden. MDCCLXXV.

Lectures on the Art of Reading; Second Part: Containing The Art of Reading Verse. By Thomas Sheridan, A.M. London: [as in preceding entry]. MDCCLXXV.

The Life of the Rev. Dr. Jonathan Swift, Dean of St. Patrick's Dublin. London, MDCCLXXXIV.

Mr. Sheridan's Address to the Town. In *Cibber and Sheridan . . .* , pp. 26–35. (See Bibliography.)

Mr. Sheridan's Plan for Acting with the Managers of Drury-lane. In Garrick's *Private Correspondence*, II, 250. (See Bibliography.)

Mr. Sheridan's Speech addressed to a Number of Gentlemen Assembled with a View of considering the best Means to establish one good Theatre in this city. Dublin: Printed by and for George Faulkner, in Parliament-Street. MDCCLXXII. Col. U.

An Oration, Pronounced before a Numerous Body of the Nobility and Gentry, Assembled at the Musick-Hall in Fishamble-street, On Tuesday the 6th of this instant December, And now first Published at their unanimous Desire. By Thomas Sheridan, A.M. The Second Edition. Dublin: Printed for M. Williamson. MDCCLVII. B.M.

A Plan of Education for the Young Nobility and Gentry of Great Britain. Most humbly addressed to the Father of his People. By Thomas Sheridan, A.M. London: Printed for E. and C. Dilly, in the Poultry. MDCCLXIX.

†*Prologue, designed to be spoken before a Play, the profits of which are to be applied towards the Expence of a Monument for Dr. Swift.* (Spoken March 23, 1752.) B. M. MSS Collection.

A Rhetorical Grammar. (See under *A General Dictionary.*)

A Short Address to the Public, upon A Subject of the utmost Importance to the future Safety and Welfare of the British Dominions. By Thomas Sheridan, A.M. London: Printed for J. Dodsley, C. Dilly, and T. Evans. MDCCLXXXIII.

A Short Sketch of a Plan for the Improvement of Education in this Country. Most humbly submitted to the consideration of Parliament. By Thomas Sheridan, A.M. Dublin: Printed by M. Mills, No. 36 Dorset-street. MDCCLXXXVIII.

†*A State of Mr. Sheridan's Case, Humbly submitted to the Consideration of the Publick.* 1p. Dublin, 1747. Marsh's Library, Dublin.

†*A State of the Case In Regard to the Point in Dispute between Mr. Mosse and Mr. Sheridan.* 26pp. Appendix i–xix. Dublin, 1750. B. M.

To the Honourable the Knights, Citizens, and Burgesses, in Parliament assembled: the humble Petition of Thomas Sheridan. 1p. [Dublin, 1758.] B. M.

To the Ladies and Gentlemen who were Present at the Play of Cato last Thursday. In *Cibber and Sheridan . . .* , pp. 7-10. (See Bibliography.)

A View of the State of School-Education in Ireland: wherein the numerous errors and defects of the present system, are fully exposed; and the necessity of adopting a new one, clearly demonstrated. With a sketch of a plan for that purpose. Dublin, MDCCLXXXVII. R.I.A.

A Vindication of the Conduct of the late Manager of the Theatre-Royal Humbly address'd to the Publick. The Third Edition. Dublin, MDCCLIV. Col. U. (1st edn., same year.)

Will. (See *Last Will and Testament.*)

Because Part II of the Smock-Alley Calendar, with its alphabetically arranged play-titles, serves as an index to Part I, titles of plays in the index below have been kept to a minimum, the names of their authors often sufficing instead. After most performers' entries, the pages from Part II of the Calendar giving their roles in various casts have been indexed, but not for Sheridan, Sparks, and King, whose names, from their long stay at Smock-Alley, appear on almost every page. For the elusive first names of many of these performers I must again thank my generous friend, Mrs. William S. Clark.

15; death, 10, 17; last will, 19n; as author, 7, 8, 17n, 18; his classical seminary, 6, 8n, 10; as composer, 159n; his finances, 10, 13; his interest in drama and theater, 6–8; his politics, 68; and son Thomas, 8, 11–12, 31, 246; and Swift, *see* Swift, Jonathan; on Ireland, 10n–11n; on John Brown of the Neale, 100n; on John Sheen, 19

SHERIDAN, THOMAS

PERSONAL LIFE AND EXTRA-THEATRI-CAL INTERESTS; birth and family background, 4, 5n, 6, 20n, 27; early home and education, 6; at Westminster School, 8, 10, 100n; at Trinity College Dublin, 4, 14, 16–17, 17n, 19, 82; academic degrees, 17, 97n, 256; marriage, 44–45; his home, 198n; in England (1758–62), 248, 255–68; government pension, 256, 261n; exile in Blois, 269, 270n; after final retirement from theater, 257, 301–307; death and burial, 302, 306–307; last will, 301, 307; as author (*see* list of works on p. 492, then under titles in index); character, 31, 38–39, 45–46, 45n, 107, 185, 187, 221 (contemporary estimates of, 11, 13, 17n, 43, 59, 61, 67n, 72, 75, 121, 126n, 136, 226, 257n, 288–89, 290–91, 294); educational interests, 5–6, 16–17, 27, 181, 212, 215, 216, 217, 230, 234, 236–39, 242, 244, 248, 255, 272, 279, 301, 301n, 302, 306, 306n; elocutionary interests, 6, 27, 216–17, 230, 237, 249, 255, 272, 279, 303n, 306; finances, 191, 193–94, 211, 216, 243, 250, 253, 257, 260, 269–70, 271, 278, 280, 282, 286, 300, 301; health and physical qualities, 5, 5n, 11, 37, 42, 47, 118, 121, 135–36, 179n, 207, 221, 223, 264–65, 266, 280, 282, 300, 302n, 305, 341n; literary style, 97, 122, 171, 216;

politics, 68, 144, 197, 202, 245; readings and lectures, 17, 212n, 217, 230, 255, 256, 259, 263, 267, 269, 270, 270n, 301; tutoring, 257, 270. *See also* names of relatives and other people associated with him

THEATRICAL CAREER AND INTERESTS: in the audience, 11, 14, 20, 29, 71; debut, 3, 30–31, 36, 70; as would-be manager, 13, 25, 36; as manager of "scratched" company, 48–50; as manager of Smock-Alley and Aungier-Street, 55, 107, 306, Chs. III–VIII; and the theater proprietors, 55, 77, 118, 118n–19n, 123, 129; resumes management, 378n, Ch. IX; proposals for saving theater, 242–43; gives up management permanently, 249; acting at Drury Lane under Garrick (1760–61, 1763), 260–68; acting in Dublin intermittently (1763–77), 268–83; on provincial stage, 278–80; at Covent Garden (1775–76), 280–82, 284; helping Richard manage Drury Lane, 258, 284–301; as actor: 13, 40–42, 49, 50, 56, 84, 108, 109, 124, 155, 233, 252, 255, 258, Ch. X, 285 (contemporary estimates of: adverse, 62n, 79, 118, 121–22, 128, 143–44, 180, 216, 228, 282, 304, 305; favorable, 8, 30, 36, 53, 63n, 75, 76n, 153n, 156, 164n, 175, 178, 197, 261, 262, 263, 264–65, 274, 303–306), and *see also* roles, below; on acting, 251, 258, 303, 305–306; acting on shares, 52, 61, 215, 258–59, 260, 263, 269; and his actors, 63–67, 77, 124, 152, 168, 185–87, 202, 212, 232, 235n, 243n, 251–52, 286, 292, 299n; as adapter, 4n, 17–18, 69, 79, 111, 122, 160, 177, 236n, 262–63, 282, 288, 327, 339, 360n, 410, 413, 435; attitude toward stage, 5–6, 27, 31, 49–50, 127, 182, 203, 229–30, 296; as author, *see* list of works (p. 492),